RELIGIONS OF THE UNITED STATES IN PRACTICE

PRINCETON READINGS IN RELIGIONS

———

Donald S. Lopez, Jr., Editor

TITLES IN THE SERIES

———

RELIGIONS OF THE

UNITED STATES

IN PRACTICE · *Volume One*

Colleen McDannell, Editor

PRINCETON READINGS IN RELIGIONS

PRINCETON UNIVERSITY PRESS

PRINCETON AND OXFORD

Copyright © 2001 by Princeton University Press
Published by Princeton University Press, 41 William Street,
Princeton, New Jersey 08540
In the United Kingdom: Princeton University Press, 3 Market Place, Woodstock,
Oxfordshire OX20 1SY

All Rights Reserved
Library of Congress Cataloging-in-Publication Data
Religions of the United States in practice / Colleen McDannell, editor.
p.cm. — (Princeton readings in religions)
Includes bibliographical references and index.
ISBN 0-691-00998-8 (vol. 1) — ISBN 0-691-00999-6 (vol. 1 : pbk.) — ISBN
0-691-01000-5 (vol. 2) — ISBN 0-691-01001-3 (vol. 2 : pbk.)
1. United States—Religious life and customs. I. McDannell, Colleen. II. Series.
BL2525 .R4688 2002
200.973—dc21
2001036269
British Library Cataloging-in-Publication Data is available
This book has been composed in Berkeley

Printed on acid-free paper. ∞

www.pup.princeton.edu

Printed in the United States of America

1 3 5 7 9 10 8 6 4 2
1 3 5 7 9 10 8 6 4 2
(Pbk.)

PRINCETON READINGS
IN RELIGIONS

———

Princeton Readings in Religions is a new series of anthologies on the religions of the world, representing the significant advances that have been made in the study of religions over the last thirty years. The sourcebooks used by previous generations of students, whether for Judaism and Christianity or for the religions of Asia and the Middle East, placed a heavy emphasis on "canonical works." Princeton Readings in Religions provides a different configuration of texts in an attempt to better represent the range of religious practices, placing particular emphasis on the ways in which texts have been used in diverse contexts. The volumes in the series therefore include ritual manuals, hagiographical and autobiographical works, popular commentaries, and folktales, as well as some ethnographic material. Many works are drawn from vernacular sources. The readings in the series are new in two senses. First, very few of the works contained in the volumes have ever been made available in an anthology before; in the case of the volumes on Asia, few have even been translated into a Western language. Second, the readings are new in the sense that each volume provides new ways to read and understand the religions of the world, breaking down the sometimes misleading stereotypes inherited from the past in an effort to provide both more expansive and more focused perspectives on the richness and diversity of religious expressions. The series is designed for use by a wide range of readers, with key terms translated and technical notes omitted. Each volume also contains a substantial introduction by a distinguished scholar in which the histories of the traditions are outlined and the significance of each of the works is explored.

Religions of the United States in Practice is the tenth title in the series. The forty-two contributors include many of the leading scholars of American religions. Each scholar has provided one or more selections of key works, some of which are published here for the first time. These works include prayers and songs from Christian, Jewish, and Native American traditions, accounts of visions and trances, instructions on healing and health, and rites of passage. Each chapter begins with a substantial introduction that discusses the history and influence of the work, identifying points of particular difficulty or interest. Colleen McDannell, the editor of these groundbreaking volumes, opens the book with a masterful introduction to the multiple worlds of the religions of United States.

Donald S. Lopez, Jr.
Series Editor

CONTENTS

Healing: Health, Happiness, and the Miraculous

Imagining: The Unseen World

Persuading: Witnessing, Controversies, and Polemics

CONTRIBUTORS

Dianne Ashton teaches in the Department of Philosophy and Religion at Rowan University.

Julia Boss is a doctoral candidate at Yale University.

Ann Braude is the director of the Women's Studies in Religion Program and teaches at Harvard University.

Paul Jerome Croce teaches in the Department of American Studies at Stetson University.

Matthew Dennis teaches in the Department of History at the University of Oregon.

Peter Gardella teaches in the Department of World Religions at Manhattanville College.

Carolyn DeSwarte Gifford is a research associate in gender studies at Northwestern University.

Robert R. Grimes, S. J. teaches in the Department of Theology at Fordham University.

Paul Harvey teaches in the Department of History at the University of Colorado.

Liz Szabo Hernadi is an independent scholar living in Norfolk, Virginia.

Patricia O'Connell Killen teaches in the Department of Religion at Pacific Lutheran University.

Joel W. Martin teaches in the Department of Religious Studies at the University of California, Riverside.

Michael J. McClymond teaches in the Department of Theological Studies at St. Louis University.

Michael D. McNally teaches in the Department of Religion at Carleton College.

Timothy J. Meagher is the Director of Archives, Manuscripts, and Museum Collections and teaches at the Catholic University of America.

Daniel James Meeter is pastor of the Central Reformed Church in Grand Rapids, Michigan.

Kenneth P. Minkema is the editor of *The Works of Jonathan Edwards* and teaches at Yale University.

Robert Bruce Mullin is Sub-Dean for Academic Affairs and teaches at the General Theological Seminary.

Janet C. Olson is Assistant University Archivist at Northwestern University.

Craig R. Prentiss teaches in the Department of Theology and Religious Studies at Rockhurst University.

Stephen Prothero teaches in the Department of Religion at Boston University.

Elizabeth Reis teaches in the Department of History at the University of Oregon.

A. Gregory Schneider teaches in the Department of Behavioral Science at Pacific Union College.

Grant Underwood is director of the Smith Institute for Latter-day Saint History and teaches at Brigham Young University.

RELIGIONS OF THE UNITED STATES IN PRACTICE

INTRODUCTION

_____

Colleen McDannell

This anthology presents the contours of religious practices in the United States by examining a selection of primary documents. There are many virtues to this varied collection. It offers readers a series of texts, in the broadest sense of that term, that impart a sense of the remarkable diversity and range of practices that have existed throughout American religious history. Each text is preceded by an essay that sets the document in context. The primary documents and essays bring readers into contact with people of the past by introducing voices that have recently caught the attention of scholars. These voices urge us to broaden the range of what we consider religious and to consider the many significant ways that religious practice shapes American life. The documents also provide examples of the kinds of source materials scholars use when trying to understand religious impulses at specific moments in American history.

By constructing an anthology based on primary documents, the contributors to this volume introduce a fresh perspective into the discussion of American religious history. The two volumes present religion as a dynamic process of borrowing, conflict, and interaction between and within religious traditions. The volumes focus on religious _behaviors_ rather than on historical movements, church-state issues, or theological developments. Religious thought and ethics are approached from the perspective of the lived experiences of average people. An introductory essay accompanying each primary text clarifies the practice described in the document. The essay sets the historical scene and explains difficult ideas contained in the primary text. Rather than assemble the documents chronologically or by faith communities, I have thematically grouped the texts around the common activities of religious people: praying, singing, healing, teaching, imagining, and persuading. These aspects of religious life are shared by many people. I have deliberately juxtaposed materials from different religious traditions, time periods, geographical areas, and modes of expression in order to encourage readers to reflect on the relationship between religious practices often regarded as separate and distinct. Too often we take traditional periodization as a type of natural ordering of the messiness of human affairs. Fortunately, religious people behave in ways that scholars cannot predict. Religious events happen at times when we least expect them. Rather than present a neatly ordered system of thought and action, the volume offers a multiplicity of religious expressions. Like the overarching themes and categories, the documents and their introductions should be considered starting points for discussion and reflection. If the anthology accomplishes its purpose, it will encourage readers to challenge my way of dividing the "American pie" and to discover other ways of handling the complexity of religion in the United States.

The documents and essays should also raise—but not unequivocally answer— the question of whether or not an "American religion" is apparent in these diverse practices. What, if any, are the common elements in praying at a Methodist holiness meeting, singing at an Ojibwe funeral, or cooking without using seasonings? Most of the texts included in this volume come from recognizable religious communities, while a few, such as the lecture by William James, are of a more general character. These documents, especially those from Native American communities, illustrate the difficulty of separating "religion" from culture and society. I hope that the anthology will challenge readers to find evidence within these texts of what might be called the religion of American nationalism (Robert Bellah's "civil religion") or the religion of pop culture (Catherine Albanese's "cultural Religion") and then to evaluate these concepts.

The anthology is indebted to the recent movement in the study of American religions that places religious practice at the center of religious life. Religious practice and behavior range from formal, communal rituals with long histories to spontaneous actions that an individual may understand as religious. Regardless of their history, all religious practices convey knowledge through action. In a very obvious way, information is contained in the words of a ritual, the lyrics of a hymn, or the instructions of a vision. When colonial New Englanders sing, "Ah guilty sinner ruined by transgression," the meaning is clear. Every text in this anthology is made up of words, and those words have meanings. Meanings, of course, are multiple, and words are notoriously slippery. Sometimes people say and sing things they wish were the case rather than articulating what is the case. Meanings are created by religious practices, but they can also be challenged and remade. The introductory essays are designed to make sense of the information contained in the words of the practices. Knowledge and meaning, however, are conveyed in many ways: the movements of liturgical gestures, the design of vestments, the poetics of place, the emotion of music, and so on. Religious practices are visceral and sensual. They involve the body in action. We must be prepared not only to analyze religious practices but to feel their poetic expression. If we are to understand how religious individuals, as well as religious communities, create, re-create, and sustain themselves through their practices, we must be sensitive to the many different ways practices can be interpreted.

Recent scholarship not only stresses the importance of religious practice in the United States but also recognizes a wide range of religious actors. This volume extends the trend by presenting texts that reveal the everyday thinking and doing of lay men and women. The essays and documents illustrate how people become engaged with their religious traditions. This engagement can occur in a variety of places: in churches and synagogues, of course, but also in parlors and fields, beside rivers, on lecture platforms, and in the streets. Women and children engage in religion perhaps even more than adult men. Plenty-coups was only nine years old when he had the vision that foretold his success as a Crow leader. Penina Moise is not a familiar name in American religious history, but her hymns shaped reformed Jewish worship. The texts produced by average people, even people who have had extraordinary religious experiences, may be more straightforward, basic, or even aggressive than texts produced by an educated elite. These documents reveal the ways that religion may contribute to pain and suffering, social chaos, domestic discord, uncertainty, and intolerance. Consequently, we need to acknowledge that religion as it is lived out has rough edges and may not always be as subtle—or as virtuous—as we would like.

The texts in this volume, though, do not merely describe *lived* religion. Religious practice certainly is lived out in the family circle, in religious communities, and in the marketplace. People pray, sing, dance, shout, and sit quietly. They struggle to raise their children, fend off bad influences, and adapt to changing social environments, all using guidelines set by their religious communities. And, being an inventive people, Americans creatively adapt and improvise. They create living, as well as lived, religion. Religious practice, however, is more than merely lived. Religious practice is also *imagined*. In dreams, visions, and fictional accounts, people participate in worlds that are not a part of everyday life. These special worlds can eventually become as real as everyday life or they can remain speculative fantasies. Just as through rituals people learn and construct religious worldviews, so they build religious environments through vision and imagination. In both lived and imagined religion, people use the cultural forms of their society. They may stretch and modify those forms, but they cannot entirely escape the givens of their culture.

In the introductions to the texts the "givens of culture" are laid out for the reader. At times the primary documents read as if religious practices are free from historical contingency. Religious people often assert that their beliefs and behaviors are absolutely natural and have rarely changed. However, as a historian I cannot understand a text apart from the society that produced it, uses it, and modifies it. Even though a ritual may have a set of words and movements that everyone performs in the same way, people bring to the ritual the world in which they live. People participate in religion at a particular time and in a particular place. The exorcism conducted in Puritan Massachusetts in 1671 was experienced in ways that differ sharply from experiences of the exorcism conducted by the Mormon prophet Joseph Smith in 1830. Religious practices are not stable but are constantly in process. Consequently, the authors of the introductory essays place religious practices in their historical and social contexts. At times the authors reach far back into history to show the development of a particular practice. At other times they connect religious behavior with the economic, sociological, scientific, or artistic forces of a given time period.

When we see how religious practices are intimately connected to society and culture, we notice that people "use" religion in many different ways. Religious practices can reflect social harmony and consensus just as they can inspire dissent and subversion. People can feel empowered or restricted, unified or divided by the religions they live and imagine. There are no simple formulas, and thus one goal of the student of religious practices is to make sense of what people *do* with their texts, visions, rituals, sermons, tracts, songs, or letters. To accomplish this, we must read critically. Who wrote (or dreamed or sang or danced) the text? Was the text addressed to a small coterie of fellow believers or to an entire nation? Was the text intended to slander, uplift, inform, or transform? When was a particular practice recorded, by whom, and for what purpose? In reading an anthology of religious texts we need to do the impossible—to be sympathetic to practices while at the same time being aware of their limits.

Religious practices are "multimedia events," where speech, vision, gesture, touch, and sound combine. Unfortunately, in an anthology we can never do justice to the ways the senses converge in religious practices. The book form sets severe limits on understanding. It forces us to rely on the descriptive power of scholars and then on our own imaginations to conjure what it might have been like to see a young woman in trance on a stage, hear a choir sing a hymn to St. Patrick, or dance long into the night. The anthology's limits, however, should motivate readers to find supplemental texts that more directly engage our ears and eyes, our senses of touch, smell, and taste. Readers can bring into the discussion various forms of material culture that cannot be collapsed into a book. The documents have been chosen because they are rich, stimulating, or controversial. They should provoke conversation and reflection, as well as further research. This anthology is a starting point for raising questions, pointing out continuities, examining juxtapositions, and contemplating about what it means to be religious.

Like the other volumes in The Princeton Readings series, this anthology presents its documents in thematic sections. The section categories seek to illustrate some of the common ways that people participate in their religions. Putting the documents and essays in categories helps us see how religious beliefs and values are created and maintained. Within the categories are long-established, formal rites and ceremonies as well as more spontaneous practices. Some of the categories are familiar—most of us understand prayer to be a religious practice—but others ask us to expand our notion of what constitutes a religious practice.

Religious practices of "imagining" or "persuading" are equally important in the makeup of religious life in the United States. These categories ask us to consider such activities as reading an anti-Catholic novel or dreaming about heaven as religious practices. All of the categories are elastic, and texts that appear in one category might easily fit into another. When a man and woman marry in the Dutch Reformed Church, they not only learn about their duties as husband and wife; they also offer their prayers to God. The visions of African American slaves not only articulate and maintain a supernatural world; they also give the newly made Christians a vivid image of how they should lead their lives. While the introductory essays stress a particular theme, the clever reader will be able to construct his or her own essays based on other themes embedded within the primary documents.

Within each category the texts and introductory essays are arranged in approximate chronological order. Some texts, however, do not have precise dates of composition. No one knows when, for example, the Muskogee Indians began their Green Corn Ceremony. Other practices have existed for centuries, but the essays pin the practices to a specific time. The hymns of Issac Watts, for instance, are still sung in churches across the country, but here we depict how they were sung in early America. The essays in this volume focus on the time period prior to the twentieth century, although some texts—like some of the letters sent to *St. Anthony's Messenger*—span the year 1900. Religious practices do not easily fall into chronological boxes. One of their distinctive features is the practitioners' effort to transcend time boundaries, to claim that, within a ritual or while singing a hymn, time no longer is important. Rituals can transport the individual to another time and place. How do we date, for instance, the African American spiritual "Go Down Moses," which has been sung by slaves in Southern fields, freedmen in concert halls, and marching civil rights protesters? Religious practices collapse time in addition to being bound by it.

The problem of establishing the dates of religious practices is similar to the problem of fixing the borders of the United States. Most of the documents included here were produced within the current U.S. national boundaries. The religious practices of Canada and Mexico have their own stories. On the other hand, national borders are continuously crossed in the anthology. The Ojibwe moved between what is now Canada and the United States. Mother Marie de Saint Joseph lived in the New World but probably never thought of herself as an "American." Mary Ann Sadlier's novels were read in both Ireland and the United States. Clarifying the practices of colonial Jews brings us in contact with the Middle East, Spain, Brazil, Holland, and England. Transnationalism in the twenty-first century has made us sensitive to the transnationalism of previous generations of "Americans." So, while the United States is the locus of the volume, the borders of both the nation and the anthology are porous.

The anthology begins with the section *Praying: Individual and Communal Worship*. The texts in this section include formal liturgies as well as more spontaneous expressions of praise. The Jewish and Christian texts recount God's deeds and virtues, express wonder and awe, and celebrate the human/divine relationship. At times the texts call for repentance after recognition of sin. In testimonials such as the Puritan conversion narratives, individuals praise God in story form. Their autobiographical accounts articulate their personal relationships with God, which may include episodes of trouble, distress, and deliverance. Although there is an informal quality to the testimonials, the narratives reflect specific theological and cultural frameworks. In the Green Corn Ceremony, praise is directed not toward a supernatural deity, but toward nature. Here ritual is a collective renewal of the cosmic and social order. In all the texts we see the creation and re-creation of the transcendental as a permanent reality.

For many people, the most positive memories they have of religion are connected with music. In the section *Singing: Songs of Devotion, Praise, and Protest*, sound and text combine to praise, teach, and express the human situation. The spaces of singing are varied—churches, synagogues, community halls, homes, even the outsides of saloons. In the cases of Penina Moise's hymns and the songs of antebellum Catholics, new styles of music appear, reflecting cultural, theological, and geographical change. Songs may be tightly connected to traditional scriptures, as with the *Bay Psalm Book,* or written for specific purposes, as with temperance songs. Like all communal rituals, singing connects people with each other and links the living with those who have sung the same songs in the past. People adapt music, as they do all behaviors, to their own needs. The text of the songs might stay the same, but where the songs are sung, how they are sung, and who sings them changes.

The section *Teaching: Learning How to Live Correctly* explores the practices that socialize people into a particular religious culture. Through religious practices we learn appropriate behavior. We learn right and wrong. We gain information about our gender roles and sexuality. And, of course, we are partial learners not passive learners. Religious and social ethics are created and sustained in relationship to wider social realities. People respond in many different ways to how they are told to act. In the case of Plenty-coups, his visions helped him not only to understand his own path within his community but also to find the proper attitude that the Crow people should take toward the "white men." Not all religious practices, however, are embedded within specific rituals or ceremonies. Religions also have "intellectual rituals" that center on the reading and study of texts. People learn about what they should do in life by reading novels, letters, and pious tracts. The creation, distribution, and consumption of written materials is an important part of religious practice in the United States. The Protestant minister Charles Sheldon not only gave sermons but put his ideas on paper. Eventually his book, *In His Steps,* reached millions of readers. *In His Steps* illustrates how religious practices are not always discrete ritual units but frequently come in complicated, nested layers. Sheldon created fictional characters that modeled Christian behavior. He then presented those characters in a sermon, a traditional Christian practice. Then he transformed the sermons into serial form, and still later he made them into a book. Religious practices come in many forms. Teaching as a religious practice inculcates morality, passes on knowledge, provokes emotional responses, and shapes notions of ethnicity, sexuality, gender, class, place, and time.

A major function of religion is transformation. In the section *Healing: Health, Happiness, and the Miraculous*, we examine practices that move people from states of ill health (broadly defined) to health. For many religious people, physical health is a sign of blessing, a part of the empowerment that comes through close contact with what is sacred. Some people see close contact—sometimes even a shared nature—between the physical and spiritual worlds. Healing may come from an outside, supernatural power as described in Latter-day Saints' accounts and the letters from Catholics cured by the intervention of St. Anthony of Padua. In these texts, God's help is not confined to a past age but reaches down to our own generation and will continue into the future. For other religious people, healing power is within everyone. The writings of Mary Baker Eddy and the health advice of William Alcott suggest how people can, using their own faith and intelligence, make themselves whole and happy. Healing practices form a central part of the religious lives of many Americans.

In the section *Imagining: The Unseen World,* we explore realms of experience considered not the normal way things are. I use *unseen* to mean *typically* unseen, *usually* unseen. This is the uncanny world, the ideal world, the hoped-for world. The texts included here explore the supernatural. They discuss places outside of the natural world, and they describe people who are intimately in contact with these other worlds. An important task of religious practice is to define this "seen unseen" world and to set the boundaries between the commonplace and the extraordinary. Through religious practices one can cross these boundaries and bring together various ways of experiencing reality. For some people these boundaries are crossed in dreams and visions. For others they are crossed via literary fiction. The unseen world can be experienced through imagining. *Imagining* means forming a mental image of something not typically present to the senses. The documents in this section illustrate how people form ideas and pictures of things that are not typically part of the everyday world but may become intimately connected to people's lives. These mental images help construct an ongoing relationship with supernatural characters, beings that range from saints to devils. By imagining, people experience places like heaven or a renewed earth. The dreams, visions, possessions, and miracles reported in these texts do not merely provide evidence of the supernatural. The practice of imagining prompts changes in other religious practices. Handsome Lake's vision contained instructions from the Creator on how native people should live their lives. Puritan imaginings of the devil moved them to execute members of their own church. Experiencing the unseen world is intense and dramatic. Imagining stimulates the senses and motivates action.

In the final section, *Persuading: Witnessing, Controversies, and Polemics,* texts illustrate the exchange, often tense and unpredictable, between different religious communities in the United States. To a certain extent, these documents illustrate the competitive spirit that religious communities developed in the pluralistic religious marketplace of the United States. Through their sermons, jokes, visions, lectures, and writings, people try to overturn old ways and establish new viewpoints. Or, they try to restate the old ways in hopes of fending off competing ideas. Protestants, who promoted the tales of Maria Monk, thought they were countering the pernicious spread of undemocratic Catholicism. At the same time, the very popularity of Monk's book leads us to suspect there was something enviable (as well as despicable) in Catholic sensuality and clerical authority. In other texts, pleas are addressed to people who may already be sympathetic "fellow travelers." Sermons in defense of slavery, such as the one by James Henley Thornwell, were rituals of self-defense in the antebellum South. Likewise, the audience at Lizzie Doten's trance lecture may already have been friendly to the claims of spiritualism and women's rights. In persuading, people convince themselves as well as others. The language of persuading, in contrast to that of teaching, is often polemical, inflammatory, and even macabre. Lies may be spread and careful reasoning rejected in favor of rhetorical flare. The practices of persuasion are often fueled by hatred.

Taken together, the contents of this volume and the second, twentieth-century volume should dispel the old views of American religion that stressed institutional development and disembodied theology or focused on religion in a narrowly construed public context. This collection, among other things, asks us to rethink the division between public and private in religious experience and practice. By offering a sampling of perspectives rather than an authoritative canon, the anthology more closely approximates the living texture of religious thought and practice in the United States. Readers should place the texts and practices in conversation with one another, and listen in on their discussion of mutual concerns and fears.

Further Reading

Sydney E. Ahlstrom, *A Religious History of the American People* (New Haven and London: Yale University Press, 1972); Catherine L. Albanese, *America: Religions and Religion* (Belmont, Calif: Wadsworth, 1999); David Hall, ed., *Lived Religion in America: Toward a History of Practice* (Princeton: Princeton University Press, 1997); Bernhard Lang, *Sacred Games: A History of Christian Worship* (New Haven and London: Yale University Press, 1997); Colleen McDannell, *Material Christianity: Religion and Popular Culture in America* (New Haven and London: Yale University Press, 1995); Robert A. Orsi, *Thank You, St. Jude: Women's Devotion to the Saint of Hopeless Causes* (New Haven and London: Yale University Press, 1996); Thomas A. Tweed, ed., *Retelling U.S. Religious History* (Berkeley and Los Angeles: University of California Press, 1997).

Praying: Individual and Communal Worship

—1—

The Amidah in Colonial American Synagogues

Dianne Ashton

In 1654 a handful of Jewish families totaling twenty-three individuals booked passage on a ship leaving Brazil and ultimately landed in New Amsterdam, in what would become New York City. By resettling in Dutch territory, they left behind the Inquisition that threatened to return as Portugal reclaimed Brazil from Holland. They were the first Jews to settle in North America, but other Caribbean Jews soon followed as the eastern seaports of North America came under British rule. As Protestant colonies, Dutch territories were relatively safe havens for Jews because the Catholic Inquisition could not reach them there. By the late seventeenth century, Jewish communities also flourished in Newport, Savannah, Charleston, and Philadelphia.

These small but vibrant groups traced their heritage and religious customs to the traditions of those Jews who had lived for hundreds of years in Spain, first under Muslim and then under Catholic kings. As a Muslim country with a robust economy, Spain welcomed Jews and accorded them a respected second-class status as "people of the book" who shared some religious customs in common with Muslims. After the Catholic reconquest, Spain feared its minorities and drove Muslims and Jews underground with forced conversions before expelling them in 1492. These two historical experiences combined to create a tradition in which Spanish Jews participated in the surrounding culture while maintaining their religious rituals and practices unchanged. They were called Sephardim, or Spanish Jews, and their customs and traditions set the standard for Judaism in North America throughout the colonial period.

Although they carefully maintained Judaism's religious practices, these North American communities were too small to support religious specialists such as rabbis. In fact, no properly ordained rabbi settled in North America until the mid nineteenth century. Thus for almost one hundred years, colonial American Jews performed religious functions among themselves, looking to those members of their communities who were best able to serve when occasions arose requiring religious teachers, prayer leaders, kosher butchers, or circumcisers. Jews in colonial America also looked to larger congregations of Sephardim in London and Amsterdam for ritual items such as prayer books, Torah scrolls, and other items.

When Britain's David Levi published his prayer books following the customs of Spanish Jews in 1790, they were adopted quickly by congregations in America. An excerpt from this prayer book is examined in this essay. A respected Hebraist, Levi soon published defenses of Judaism that answered the famous Christian and Deist writers Dr. Joseph Priestly and Thomas Paine. Levi's volumes were republished often in New York and Philadelphia and made their way into the libraries and synagogues of Jews in British North America.

Just as their ancestors embraced Iberian culture, so colonial Jews embraced American culture. Their painted portraits depict stylish people, coifed and clothed in the fashions of their day. Because they were primarily city dwellers, often merchant families linked through marriages, such individual portraits were sometimes shipped to distant relatives and placed on parlor walls. Women were far more likely to attend religious services in the synagogue than were Jewish women in Europe at that time, and their commitment set the pattern followed by later female Jewish immigrants.

Colonial and early American Jews enjoyed a degree of religious freedom unknown to Jews in Europe. Not only were they allowed to worship as they pleased, they were allowed to live and work as they chose, as well. Although colonial Jews could not hold public office, they relished their freedom. They joined their non-Jewish neighbors in building local charitable, educational, financial, and cultural institutions, participated in political debates, and joined in public affairs and parades. Sending their children to American schools and lacking the expertise to train their children in Hebrew texts and lore, many eighteenth-century Jews relied on the English translations of prayers that Levi provided. The quiet nature of the Amidah prayer provided them treasured moments for personal devotions.

Levi's and other prayer books were most likely to be used during Sabbath worship in synagogues on Saturday morning. The core of that service is the Torah reading and the Amidah prayer that precedes it. During the Torah portion of the service, the scroll is ceremonially chanted in its original Hebrew by several members of the congregation while the rest of the congregation follows along in their Bibles. Although observant Jews pray together on Sabbaths, festivals, and three times daily, it is the Sabbath morning communal worship that provides the main focus of weekly prayer.

The Amidah, or prayer said while standing, serves in various forms as the foundation of all Jewish worship. On weekdays it consists of nineteen paragraphs, each of which is a benediction. Divided into three sections, the first part of the Amidah praises God, the middle part petitions God, and the last section thanks God. On Sabbaths the middle part is omitted to better support the day's purpose of joy and spiritual awakening, and an additional blessing is inserted instead, totaling seven benedictions in all for the Sabbath Amidah.

The first forms of Jewish worship date back to early biblical times. David's psalms especially became the foundation for later activities. Jewish liturgy as a whole is based upon the Hebrew Bible, both in its spirit and text, and draws on more than the psalms. Other portions of the Bible can be found incorporated into prayer books, and many new creations were written in a manner that drew on biblical phrases and images. Some of the Amidah's benedictions were recited by the High Priest in the Temple in Jerusalem (ca. 600 B.C.E.) and sung by others who served in the second Temple (ca. 480 B.C.E.–70 C.E.).

The general content of the Amidah seems to date back to the Babylonian exile, which began with the destruction of the Temple in Jerusalem and was followed by the Persian conquest of Judea (587–332 B.C.E.). In those days, people gathered for worship and religious instruction outside of Temple activities and traditions. Perhaps the trauma of exile, which broke Jews' immediate tie to their land and their communities, made the bond with ancestors so important to Jewish spirituality. Later, when the synagogue emerged as a place for religious study and worship, people continued to recite the prayer that had, by then, taken on traditional significance. Its exact wording, however, remained fluid until the first century C.E., when leading rabbis shaped the order of the synagogue worship service and gave the Amidah's benedictions an official order. These rabbis also inaugurated daily prayer, teaching that each person should understand himself or herself as speaking directly to God without any intermediary.

After the destruction of the second Temple in Jerusalem (70 C.E.), men of the synagogue taught that prayer is more pleasing to God than sacrifices are, assuring Jews that even without the Temple, where sacrifices had been conducted, they could continue their relationship with God. In that way, the synagogue permanently assumed the central role in Jewish communal worship. As rabbis fixed a pattern of prayers, the Amidah prayer itself stayed quite flexible for many centuries.

The first prayer book, printed in 875 C.E., was the result of more than nine hundred years of growth and change. Although the general structure and specific elements of Jewish liturgy were established by the second century, Jews ever since have added prayers and songs they found meaningful. In the Amidah, only the first and last portions were ordered—the middle was left fluid. Liturgy grew through improvisation as the fruits of private inspirations became popular and were accepted by larger communities. Before Jews arrived in America, changes to the liturgy usually meant additions, not deletions. By the late Middle Ages, when the first printed prayer books appeared in the Iberian peninsula, they reflected a blend of Jewish religious practices from small communities all around the Iberian peninsula, Turkey, and Italy. The Sephardim of colonial America continued those traditions.

For the first hundred years of Jewish life in colonial North America, all prayer books were imported from Amsterdam, which meant there was usually a shortage of books. By the end of the eighteenth century, American Jews needed prayer books that offered an English translation alongside the Hebrew prayers. Unfortunately, they lacked a scholar who could produce the volume they needed. In 1761 American Jews made their first effort at composing a Jewish prayer book— a slim fifty-two–page work. The prayer book was all in English, intended to help those worshipers who understood none of the languages of the Amsterdam books. A similar holiday prayer book appeared five years later, but neither book was widely distributed. Ten years later a Hebrew-English prayer book was published in London, but again only a few were printed. By the time David Levi published his books near the close of the century, demand had grown on both sides of the ocean, and his books remained in use in American synagogues and homes for the next forty years.

Unfortunately, there never were enough of Levi's books. Sephardi congregations, especially the largest in New York, soon felt the need for a new prayer book. In 1826 another was produced in New York, but few copies were printed. By then, however, the landscape of American Jewry was changing dramatically, as immigrants from northern and central Europe came west. Their worship customs differed from those of the Sephardim in several ways, including the pronunciation of Hebrew, the extrabiblical religious poetry sung at worship, the melodies used, and the names for ritual items. Although these differences may seem slight, they were treasured by their practitioners and began to split apart congregations. New congregations following the customs of northern European Jews, the Ashkenazim, formed in Charleston and Philadelphia by 1800. By 1848 at least seventy-five synagogues and religious gatherings practiced the Ashkenazi rite in the United States. Yet because these newcomers were often poor, new congregations sometimes began by using prayer books of the Sephardim, which supplemented the privately owned volumes many immigrants had brought with them. In 1836, in an attempt to unify the growing diversity of Jewish practices, Isaac Leeser, religious leader of Philadelphia's Sephardi congregation, published a Hebrew-English translation of the Sephardi prayers. He hoped that the Sephardi rite would continue to be the standard in America and unite American Jews of differing backgrounds who came to the United States. By the time of the Civil War, American Jews numbered 150,000. By then most of the original colonial Sephardi congregations had passed bylaws to their constitutions declaring that their rites would remain in accord with the Sephardi custom. Apart from those few groups, American Jewish practice in dozens of small and large towns around the country followed the Ashkenazi rites of the more recent immigrants. The era of religious unity in Sephardi practice that had characterized colonial American Jewry was over.

Mystical traditions taught that Jewish worship and ceremonies should be observed only while concentrating one's mind upon the act. To help promote the inwardness, humility, and devotion appropriate to worship, Sephardi synagogues often inscribed—and continue to inscribe—the Hebrew words "Know Before Whom You Stand" above the cabinet holding the Torah scroll on the east wall of the sanctuary. The Amidah, also known simply as the tefillah, or prayer, is seen as the "service of the heart" commanded in the book of Exodus. The standard opening line of Jewish blessings, "Blessed art Thou, O Lord, our God, King of the universe . . . ," also expresses the attitudes of humility and gratitude toward God that are seen to be essential in Jewish worship.

Although the goal of inner devotion remains uppermost, the rabbis who first established the prayers believed that devotion was more likely to be felt if prayers were recited regularly, rather than by waiting for religious feeling to occur. They believed that the whole of life could be sanctified through regular prayer by a continuous act of sanctification. Rabbis felt that individuals who prayed privately trod a spiritually lonely road and that congregational prayer better lifted the spirit. The architecture of most Sephardi synagogues, today as yesterday, enhances the communal experience. These structures continue the traditional Jewish style that places seating around the walls so that congregants face each other during worship.

The prayer leader in Sephardi congregations hopes to elicit appropriate prayerful responses from the congregation, not to perform as in a concert. Silent portions in the Amidah leave room for spontaneity, and the introductory prayers said before the Amidah help the individual make a mental transition from the workaday world to religious devotion. The well-being of the individual is seen as intricately entwined with that of the community, and so most Jewish prayers are written in plural form. The Amidah begins in first person with "Open thou my lips and my mouth shall declare thy praise," but it soon turns to plural forms, as in "Remember us unto life, O God." The prayers for health, peace, and life are requested for all of Israel, not for "me."

Like most Jewish prayers, the Amidah connects the time of the worshiper with the past history of all Jews who worshiped God. These prayers serve first to construct a memory of the Jewish past that participates in the merit of the ancients— Abraham, Isaac, Jacob (whose name was changed to 'Israel'), and Moses—all of whom established a relationship with God for their descendants. Second, the worshiper is linked imaginatively to these ancestors by the intervening generations of Jews who have worshiped similarly, and thus Jewish prayer regenerates the past. Finally, Jewish prayer connects the worshiper with the eternal timelessness of the Holy itself. In the Amidah, the reference to Moses, "Let Moses rejoice," is deliberately structured to speak simultaneously to the eternal, the past, and the present. Is Moses rejoicing in Heaven, in eternal time? Or is the prayer a reminder of the past, in which he lived? Or is it a suggestion that Jews who carry on his teachings ought to rejoice? It is all three, because Moses' past actions continue to shape the lives of Jews today.

Sephardi congregations recite the Amidah in a soft voice, understandable to the individual but not audible to those standing alongside. The biblical figure Hannah provides the ideal for how to pray. She prayed standing, moving her lips but speaking so softly that the priest Eli did not understand what she was doing. So congregants stand still without body movement when reciting the Amidah. The congregation's religious leader, whether a rabbi or cantor (chanter/reader), begins reciting the prayer aloud immediately after the quiet prayer. The reader's goal is to conduct worship correctly and to help congregants pronounce Hebrew properly rather than to display personal creativity. (So carefully did Sephardi congregations maintain correct Hebrew pronunciation that, when the current state of Israel was formed, the Sephardi pronunciation became the national standard.) The reader repeats the prayer aloud so that people who do not know Hebrew can participate without embarrassment. After the Amidah comes a ceremonial public reading of the Torah, a means through which those who cannot spend time in Torah study during the week can gain instruction. Torah study is felt to be a kind of worship incumbent on all Jewish men. The Jewish worship service as a whole aims at providing religious education for congregants while offering them a vehicle for religious expression and the fulfillment of religious obligations. The process of prayer creates a relationship between the worshiper and the divine whereby worshipers can praise God, thank God, make requests of God, and seek forgiveness for their sins.

The Amidah is recited three times during Sabbath worship, and the congregation stands each time. The third recitation follows the Torah reading and is framed by a statement describing God's glory called the Kaddish. The Kaddish, too, is said first silently by each worshiper and then aloud by the reader. The third time the Amidah is recited, the congregation and reader together begin it aloud, then move to a soft voice. Toward the end, the reader resumes speaking aloud. By then the entire congregation is expected to have completed the prayer in soft voice. Anyone who has not finished must do so before rejoining the congregation in unison.

The Amidah's complex arrangement of private and communal prayer provides a centerpiece to the worship service. Its importance is signaled as the congregation rises to its feet and remains standing together throughout the prayer. Softly whispered, it provides expression for personal relationships to the divine. Loudly sung, it connects the individual to the religious meaning and purpose of both the local congregation and Israel as a people. Inserted statements that link the Amidah to various holidays and seasons of the year shape and fit it to a variety of religious and temporal concerns. Its content proclaims Judaism's core ideas and beliefs, and its repetitions provide opportunities for individuals to meditate on and ponder the importance of these ideas and beliefs. The congregation's experience of the Amidah, then, is a profound affirmation of belief as the members praise and thank God for their life as a people. For the Sephardim of colonial North America, for whom the local congregation served and united all Jews residing in their vicinity, the Amidah's powerful message about the glory of God was a weekly reminder of their own dedication and purpose as Jews.

Formal congregational prayer speaks to two audiences. It both addresses God and instructs those who read the text aloud. Beginning with a request for God to "open my lips" so that "my mouth shall declare thy praise," the prayer quickly establishes the devotion essential to true worship of God. The Sabbath Amidah also provides spiritual awakening throughout its seven-part structure. The first blessing is a paragraph reminding the congregants of both God's greatness and their utter dependence on the Holy since the days of their ancestors Abraham, Isaac, and Jacob. At the same time, the prayer speaks to God, requesting an immediate connection to the divine.

In the second blessing, God is praised for serving as the shield of Abraham— for sustaining the living, healing the sick, freeing slaves, and granting eternal life to the dead. Special insertions tailor the prayer to different seasons of the year. In summer and winter, praises note God's control of the life-giving elements of nature, specifically dew and rain. Insertions for the ten penitential days, which are framed by Rosh Hashanah (the New Year of the Jewish calendar) and Yom

Kippur (the Day of Atonement, marked by a twenty-four-hour fast), are scattered throughout the prayer. The first of these insertions draws on the image of the Heavenly Book, in which God writes his plan for the coming year. So prevalent is that image in Rosh Hashanah and Yom Kippur liturgy that a common new year greeting among Jews is "May you be inscribed for a good year in the Book of Life," meaning "May God keep you alive and well for the next year."

The third blessing praises God's holiness, which surpasses that of all other heavenly beings, that is, the angels. So awesome is God's greatness that the angels sing his praises three times daily, corresponding to the Jewish custom. According to Judaism, through worship of God and maintaining God's law, Jews can participate in the holiness of the divine. Divinity is eternal and unchanging.

After these first three blessings, Exodus 31:16–17, in which the children of Israel are instructed to keep the Sabbath, is recited. The phrase "children of Israel" refers to the descendants of Jacob, meaning Jews. The excerpt is introduced by a few sentences that point out that Moses, through whom God instructed all Israelites about the Sabbath and the holy law, ought to rejoice at his good fortune to be chosen by God for the task. Through Moses all Jews assumed the responsibility of keeping God's commandments, including the commandment to remember the Sabbath and keep it holy. Thus, while the prayer speaks of Moses, the biblical figure most admired by Jews, it indirectly instructs all Jews to rejoice in their good fortune in receiving and living by God's laws.

The Sabbath Amidah's three concluding blessings ask God to accept the congregation's prayer and thank him for divine protection, mercy, and salvation throughout the generations. These blessings mention Abraham, Isaac, and Jacob, as well as their descendants, many times. One of the insertions for the penitential days reminds God of his covenant with Israel, that is, with the community of Jews who claim Abraham, Isaac, and Jacob as their ancestors.

The Amidah also reminds the worshipers of their covenant with God. A covenantal relationship is a two-way street, requiring both parties to honor the terms of their agreement. By remaining faithful to God, Jews can claim God's protection and blessing. This core idea of Judaism is reiterated on Rosh Hashanah, Yom Kippur, and the penitential days. Finally, the closing blessing includes the priestly blessing for peace and mercy, as it was recited in the Temple in Jerusalem.

The text below is taken from David Levi, *Seder Tefilot; Order of Prayers in Hebrew and English According to the Custom of the Spanish and Portuguese Jews as read in their Synagogues and used in their Families* (London, 1790). From the 1810 edition, pp. 91–94.

Further Reading

Stanley Feldstein, *The Land That I Show You* (New York: Doubleday, 1979); Lawrence A. Hoffman, *The Canonization of the Synagogue Service* (Notre Dame: University of Notre Dame Press, 1979); A. Z. Idelsohn, *Jewish Liturgy and Its*

Development (New York: Schocken, 1960); Jacob Rader Marcus, *The Colonial American Jew*, 3 vols. (Detroit: Wayne State University Press, 1970); Jacob Rader Marcus, *United States Jewry 1776–1985* (Detroit: Wayne State University Press, 1989); Abraham E. Milgram, *Jewish Worship* (Philadelphia: Jewish Publication Society, 1971); David and Tamar De Sola Pool, *An Old Faith in the New World: Portrait of Shearith Israel, 1654–1954* (New York: Columbia University Press, 1955); Vera Shwarcz, *Bridge across Broken Time: Chinese and Jewish Cultural Memory* (New Haven: Yale University Press, 1998); Lance Sussman, *Isaac Leeser and the Making of American Judaism* (Detroit: Wayne State University Press, 1995).

Amidah

O Lord! Open thou my lips and my mouth shall declare thy praise.

Blessed art thou, O Lord, our God! And the God of our fathers, the God of Abraham, the God of Isaac, and the God of Jacob: the great God, mighty and tremendous: the most high God, who bestoweth gracious favors, possessor of all things: who remembereth the piety of the patriarchs, and will in love send a Redeemer to their children, for the sake of his name.

During the 10 Penitential Days, they say this

(Remember us unto life, O God, the King! Who delighteth in life: O write us in the book of life, for thine own sake, O God of life; who art the living God.)

Till here

O King, Supporter, Saviour, and Shield. Blessed art Thou, O Lord! Shield of Abraham. Thou, O Lord, *art* mighty forever; it is thou who revivest the dead, *and art* mighty to save.

In summer say

Causing the dew to descend.

And in winter say

Causing the wind to blow, and the rain to descend.

Who sustainest the living with beneficence, *and* with great mercy quickenest the dead; supportest the fallen, and healest the sick; thou loosenest those who are in bonds, *and* wilt accomplish thy faith unto those who sleep in the dust. Who *is* like unto thee, O Lord of mighty acts? Or who can be compared unto thee, who art the King, who killest and restorest to life, and causest salvation to spring forth?

During the 10 Penitential Days, they say this

(Who is like unto thee, O merciful Father; who in mercy remembereth his creatures to life?)

Till here.

Thou art also faithful to revive the dead. Blessed art thou, O Lord! Who reviveth the dead.

In the Readers' Repetition of this prayer, he says the Kadish.

We will sanctify and reverence thee with harmonious speech, as used in the assembly of the holy seraphim, who thrice rehearse an holy praise to thee: for thus it is written by the hand of thy prophet: and one cried to another, and said,

> *Cong.* Holy, Holy, Holy is the Lord of Hosts! The whole earth is full of his glory.
>
> *Reader. While* those *angels* who are over against them, continue praising, saying,
>
> *Cong.* Blessed is the glory of the Lord, from the place of his residence.
>
> *Reader.* And in thy holy word it is written, saying,
>
> *Cong.* The Lord shall reign forever: *even* thy God, O Zion, unto all generations: Hallelujah! Thou art Holy, and thy name is holy, and the saints praise thee daily. Selah. Blessed art Thou, O Lord! The Holy God.

On the Penitential Days, say, the Holy King!

Let Moses rejoice at the lot assigned him, for thou didst call him a faithful servant, and set a glorious crown on his head, when he stood before thee on Mt. Sinai. The two tables of stone he brought down in his own hand, on which was written the commandment for the observance of the Sabbath: and thus it is written in thy law. And the children of Israel shall keep the Sabbath, observing the Sabbath throughout their generations, for a perpetual covenant. It is a sign between me and the children of Israel forever: for in *six* days the Lord made heaven and earth, and on the seventh day he rested, and was refreshed. But thou, O Lord, our God! Didst not bestow it on the other nations of the earth; neither didst thou, O our King! Make it the heritage of those who worship idols. The uncircumcised also shall not inhabit its repose; because in love thou hast bestowed it upon thy people Israel; *even* the seed of Jacob, whom thou hast chosen. They who observe the Sabbath and call it a delight: the people who sanctify the seventh day, shall rejoice in thy kingdom; they shall all be satisfied, and delighted with thy goodness; for thou wast pleased with, and didst sanctify the seventh day; the most desirable of days, didst thou call it.

Our God, and the God of our fathers, we beseech thee to accept our day of rest. O sanctify us with Thy goodness, rejoice our souls with thy salvation, and purify our hearts to serve thee in truth; and cause us, O Lord, Our God! To inherit thy holy Sabbath with love and delight: and grant that all Israel, who sanctify thy name, may have rest thereon. Blessed art thou, O Lord! Who sanctifiest the Sabbath.

O Lord, our God! Let thy people Israel be acceptable to thee, and have regard unto their prayers. Restore the service to the oracle of thine house: so that burnt offerings of Israel, and their prayers, may be speedily accepted by thee with love and favor, and the worship of thy people Israel be ever pleasing unto thee.

And through thy abundant mercy *deign* thou to regard us kindly, and be favorable unto us, that our eyes may behold *Thee* at thy return to Zion with mercy. Blessed art thou, O Lord! Who restoreth his divine presence unto Zion.

We gratefully acknowledge that thou art the Lord, our God! And the rock of our fathers, for evermore. Thou art our Rock, the Rock of our life, and Shield of our salvation; to all generations we render thanks unto thee, and recount thy praise, for our life, which is delivered into thine hand; and for our souls, which are *ever* deposited with thee: and for thy miraculous *providence*, which we daily experience; and for thy wonder, and thy kindness, *which are* at all times *exercised towards us*, at morn, noon, and even. *Thou alone* art good, for thy mercies never fail: *thou alone* art merciful, for thy kindness never ceases; for from ever have we put our faith in thee.

And for all these mercies, may thy name, O our King! Be continually praised, and highly exalted for ever and ever: and all the living shall give thanks to thee. Selah.

During the Penitential Days say

(And vouchsafe to inscribe all the children of thy covenant for an happy life.)
   Till here.

And may they ever in truth, praise and adore thy great name, for it is good. The God of our salvation and our help, for ever, the beneficent God. Blessed art thou, O Lord! For goodness is *thy name*, and unto thee it is proper *continually* to give thanks.

In the Readers' Repetition of the Amidah he says the following:

Our God, and the God of our fathers, bless us with that threefold blessing mentioned in the law, written by the hands of thy servant Moses, and solemnly pronounced by Aaron and his sons, the priests, on thy sanctified people: as it is said, "The Lord bless and preserve thee: the Lord make his face shine upon thee, and be gracious unto thee: the Lord lift up his countenance upon thee, and give thee peace." And they shall put my name upon the children of Israel and I shall bless them.

   O grant us peace, happiness, and blessing, with life, grace, favor, charity, and mercy unto us, and all thy people Israel: and bless us, even all of us together, O our Father! With the light of thy countenance, for by the light of thy countenance, hast thou given us, O Lord, our God! The Law and with it, Life, love, benevolence; righteousness, and mercy, blessing, and peace: and may it please thee to bless thy people Israel, with abundant fortitude and peace.

During the Penitential Days say

(And in the book of life, blessing, peace, and prosperity, salvation, comfort, and good decrees, may we, and all thy people Israel, be remembered, and written before thee to a good and peaceable life.)

Blessed art thou, O Lord! Who blesseth his people Israel with peace. Amen.

2

Seventeenth-Century Puritan Conversion Narratives

Elizabeth Reis

Although weekly church attendance was required in Puritan New England's Congregational churches, becoming a full church member was not as easy as one might imagine. Nonetheless, church membership was among the most important matters in the lives of colonial New Englanders; indeed, controversies over the constitution of churches were among the factors that prodded emigration from England in the seventeenth century. Potential church members had to deliver conversion narratives—oral testimonies—to prove themselves worthy to the minister and church elders before they were allowed to become full members and participate in the Lord's Supper and vote in church meetings. The rationale for this test was not to limit membership per se but to ensure that all those admitted were of the elect; in other words, that all members were among the saved. Calvinist theology taught that all people, not only the obvious sinners, were essentially depraved but even the worst of sinners could receive God's free grace if they turned from their evil ways to Christ. No one could earn God's love, but everyone could accept the free gift of grace. Conversion narratives, or "relations," were expressions of hopefulness, as prospective saints reported and sought to authenticate their experiences of saving grace and thereby join a church.

Puritans believed in predestination. Salvation and damnation were foreordained by God, not chosen or earned by individuals. Only God knew who would end up in heaven or in hell. Nonetheless, women and men did not simply wait for God to reveal their fates to them on Judgment Day. Laity and clergy alike constantly searched for clues about their destinies, alternating in their feelings between strongly felt hope and deeply dreaded fear. Though Puritans knew that the visible churches to which they belonged could never perfectly mirror the invisible church of God's elect, they struggled nonetheless to gather together only the godly.

Several steps were prescribed to ensure that Puritan churches comprised only worthy members. Conversion relations represented the last measures taken before individuals were allowed to join a church. First, a potential congregant would arrange a meeting with the minister and two elders of the church to determine fitness for membership. Did the applicant know the tenets of the faith? Was his or her character admirable? At this point, the minister and elders sometimes outright denied prospects, advising them to rethink the states of their souls and perhaps return in several months. If this small group approved the candidate, then the minister would announce a proposed member's candidacy to the entire congregation, allowing two or three weeks for congregant comments concerning the public or private life of the applicant. Finally, if everything went smoothly, and if the candidate had no outstanding obligations to show repentance for any number of sins, he or she would appear before the entire meeting for that final test, the public conversion relation.

The ritual of conversion took place in the community's only public building, the meetinghouse church that stood at the center of town. Architecturally and aesthetically rustic and austere, the meetinghouse symbolized the basic centrality of religion and one's ultimate submission before God. The building's plainness could be a virtue because it emblemized the purity of primitive Christianity; the grandeur of the church did not reside in structures but instead rested with individuals' and the community's relationship with God and with each other. Puritans struggled to differentiate their divine experiment from what they saw as corrupt churches in England, especially with regard to church membership and church discipline. Unlike the Church of England, Puritan churches in America would be constituted only when a group of faithful decided to come together to worship, not because a distant hierarchy of church elders decided to form a church.

It was to ensure that all church members were truly committed to God and to each other that seventeenth-century Congregational churches began to require that congregants offer public conversion narratives. Church membership, then, represented a commitment to the sacred covenant formed among the faithful gathered together, as well as an individual covenant between a believer and God. Despite the uncertainty of knowing who was truly among the saved, potential congregants were to show God's work in their souls by professing their faith through narrations, which were approximately fifteen minutes long. Conversion represented a turning point for sinners. The ritual marked a passage from sin to salvation, though always within the bounds of Puritan theology, which stressed ultimate unknowability about God's salvation of an individual soul. By offering their conversion relations, potential church members demonstrated both their knowledge of Christian doctrine and their introspective yearnings to cast off sin and turn to Christ in the hope that he would save them.

The conversion narratives followed a pattern. Sinners first expressed contrition, guilt, fear, and hopelessness. Then they described the emotional relief of saving grace, God's free gift to them despite their human failings. Conversion narratives offered potential church members, most of whom were between twenty-five and thirty-five years of age when they gave their relations, the opportunity to reflect on their spiritual lives. People chose to testify at particular times in their lives for particular reasons. Some may have been awakened by the loss of family and friends; others became influenced by the conversion of those close to them. Women and men recounted stories of God's work in their lives, recalling a series of encounters with God that had convinced them that it was time to receive their calling. Many aspirants mentioned notable sermons that had persuaded them to mend the error of their ways before it was too late. All spoke of their own spiritual journeys that brought them to a greater understanding of the states of their souls. In the world of New England Puritans, conversion narratives expressed thoughts, feelings, and experiences that moved even beyond the realm of institutionalized religion. The relations became scripts of personal identity as congregants reviewed their past histories and created for themselves—and the broader congregation—a religious sense of self. Moreover, these relations, and church membership itself, identified saints to others as people of consequence in the social or political community.

In many churches, both women and men spoke these narratives publicly. In some communities, controversy over female public speech precluded women's oral testimony. In 1 Corinthians 14:34–35, Paul advised: "Let your women keep silence in the churches: for it is not permitted unto them to speak; but they are commanded to be under obedience, as also saith the law. And if they will learn anything, let them ask their husbands at home: for it is a shame for women to speak in the church." Some ministers took the Apostle's words literally and held that church elders must examine women privately and then read aloud their confessions to the congregation. Other clergymen took a more liberal approach, explaining that a conversion relation was submissive in nature and therefore permissible. In this context, they argued, a woman's words were to be judged by others and so would be considered admissible.

Women and men both participated in the conversion ritual, and Puritan conversion narratives have generally been seen as androgynous. According to historian Charles L. Cohen, for example, "The experience of grace submerges the peculiarities of gender; women and men spoke with 'one tongue'." If the Spirit worked equally in Puritan women and men, their narratives nonetheless reflect disparity between them with regard to a sense of self. Women heeded their ministers' words that unregenerate sinners were completely reprobate in the strictest sense.

In her 1648 conversion narrative, Elizabeth Oakes, a member of the Reverend Thomas Shepard's congregation in Cambridge, Massachusetts, described herself as "so unfit and unworthy that I was unfit." She admitted, "I saw I was dead and darkness, and Christ was peace and life and light." She mentioned she had "denied the Lord often" but did not list any more specific sins for which she now repented; instead, she recounted only a debased sense of her soul—the very essence of her being—as completely unworthy of Christ's advances. Neither did another female parishioner, Goodwife Jackson, speak of particular sins, other than mentioning deceit in a generic way. Calling herself a "poor silly creature," she sadly admitted, "I thought I was a rebellious wretch against God, and so I continued long."

By contrast, their male coreligionist Abram Arrington did not mention the depravity of his soul in his conversion narrative. Instead, Arrington admitted that he "minded nothing but sin and my own pleasure and lusts." His compatriot Robert Browne confessed to the "evil of company keeping" as well as the "evil of Sabbath breaking and of not praying." Oakes, Arrington, Browne, and Jackson all qualified for admission to Thomas Shepard's church, but their notions of sin, and of their soul's relationship to themselves and Satan, differed in subtle but significant ways. Women, like Oakes and Jackson, tended to identify themselves with their debauched souls, which were seen as completely under the devil's dominion in their natural state. In contrast, men, like Arrington and Browne, focused on particular sins, separating their natures from the sins they committed.

In the context of the meetinghouse, men seemed to differentiate their *identity* from their *actions*. They concerned themselves with the various sins they had committed, and they dutifully repented. Only rarely, however, did they take the further step of internalizing their ministers' words: sinful is as sinful does. The conversion narratives suggest that Puritan men could distinguish between their innate selves (their souls) and the rest of themselves (their minds and bodies) and thus could repent for particular sins without perceiving themselves as worthless. Women, in contrast, more often conceived of a darker wholeness, equating their transgressive behavior with a perceived basic depravity. Their repentance of particular sins was insufficient to redeem their souls because a woman's sinfulness encompassed her entire being.

Both women and men shared a vocabulary for every stage of their spiritual experiences, a vocabulary inculcated through years of Bible study and gospel preaching. They described first their humiliation, then their saving faith, and finally their obedience. As the seventeenth century progressed, though, fewer and fewer people underwent this experience of saving grace. In 1662, in an effort to maintain church membership without diluting the significance of a cadre of visible saints, ministers instituted the "Half-Way Covenant." Under the new rules, the children of "outward" church members, those who had never formally converted, could still be baptized but would not be granted full membership unless they themselves became confessing members. They would still be subject to church discipline, but they could not participate in the Lord's Supper or vote in church meetings. These privileges would extend only to full members. The Half-Way Covenant successfully ensured that New England churches did not become mere sects, that they remained central within their communities. People continued to join the churches, and many halfway members ultimately converted and became full members.

Conversion narratives were meant to mark one's entrance into the cadre of visible saints, but doubt pervaded the relations. This was fitting for Puritans because their theology dictated a cycle of anxiety and assurance regarding hopes for one's salvation. Church members could never be completely sure that they were truly among the saved. In fact, the faithful believed that overconfidence, ironically, might signal damnation rather than salvation. It is not surprising, therefore, that the formal relations of converts would betray uncertainty mixed with conviction that they had received God's grace. If we imagine Puritanism as a roller coaster ride, with the faithful experiencing highs and lows with respect to the states of their souls, the conversion narratives presented to fellow congregants represented the "up" side of the ride. Confession had affirmative meanings for women no less than men. If church members knew that their spiritual work was just beginning, they had confidence that they were moving in the right direction toward communion with God. Through this ritual individual sinners, no less than the community itself, could confirm their identities and sense of purpose.

The selections given here are from Mary Rhinelander McCarl, ed., "Thomas Shepard's Record of Relations of Religious Experience, 1648–1649," *William and Mary Quarterly,* 3rd Ser., 48 (July 1991): 432–66.

Further Reading

Charles Lloyd Cohen, *God's Caress: The Psychology of Puritan Religious Experience* (New York: Oxford University Press, 1986); Charles E. Hambrick-Stowe, *The Practice of Piety: Puritan Devotional Disciplines in Seventeenth-Century New England* (Chapel Hill: University of North Carolina Press, 1982); ed. Michael McGiffert, *God's Plot: Puritan Spirituality in Thomas Shepard's Cambridge*. (Amherst: University of Massachusetts Press, 1994); Edmund S. Morgan, *Visible Saints: The History of a Puritan Idea* (Ithaca: Cornell University Press, 1963); Harry Stout, *The New England Soul: Preaching and Religious Culture in Colonial New England* (New York: Oxford University Press, 1986).

Elizabeth Oakes

After the Lord brought me to this country, my father being taken away, Mr. S[hepard] told me that he had laid up many prayers, and after that, thinking of those words, I thought I had no father to take care for me nor pray for me. But I read, God would be a father to fatherless, after which, the Lord laying affliction and sickness on me, and thinking it was for my sin, I was little affected, yet sought God in private duties, yet thought God would not hear because all wicked prayers are abomination to God. After which the Lord left me to neglect seeking him, and then I thought God would never give me a heart to seek again. Yet the Lord visiting me with his hand, yet I not sensible. And hearing out of catechise (1) the Lord make me see, (2) to be sensible, I thought I fell short. Yet reading catechise, (3) the Lord set upon me upon question, what [were the] beginnings of second death[?] (1) terror of conscience; (2) Satan's power; (3) curse on all blessings. And I thought I was troubled in conscience yet under power of Satan, and I a curse. After this I saw my sin but thought I was not humbled. I was troubled but spake to none and could [not] desire to speak. And Mr. S[hepard], coming to my father, said now was acceptable day, if now God gave me a heart to seek him. And he told me God would make the self sensible of it as the greatest evil, and hence I thought whether the Lord ever intended any mercy to me—Hosea 6, They that follow on to know me shall know me—and the Lord gave me a heart to seek him in some measure. And after this, being afflicted and examining myself what would become of me if I was taken away, yet hearing that place,

They that come to him, he would not cast away, I having little hope, yet seeing promise not only to faithful but to their seed, I had some hope. After that, hearing out of John 13 that when Peter denied Christ he went out and wept, and I thought on those words, and I thought I had denied the Lord often, convincing me by his word yet unhumbled, and out of those words, Out of me ye can do nothing, he [Shepard] showed that the soul could do nothing without Christ, and I saw it then, that of myself I could do nothing good. Mr. S[hepard] preaching out of John 14 of humiliation after soul saw his sin, I thought the Lord now let me see my sin as greatest evil on [ ] of consolation, if God let soul saw [sic] sin though not humbled in that measure, but I thought I was not as others were. Hearing Mr. Symmes, he preach[ed] upon Oft as they denied Christ's offer, they had trod under foot Christ's blood, and I thought I had done so. And Mr. S[hepard] preaching in John, All that were called not elected, and how shall I know whether I was elected, and I heard if the Lord gave the soul a heart to choose Christ, Christ had chose[n] Christ [sic] before. And I thought the Lord gave me a heart to choose him above all things here in this world. After the Lord giving me a heart to seek him to enjoy him in all his ordinances, I thought I was so unfit and unworthy that I was unfit, and I heard that some might not find God because they did not seek him in all his ordinances, and that the Sacrament was a means wherein the Lord would coming [sic] more.

Upon question what she saw in Christ to make her prize Christ. Answer: peace, life, light, all things; for I saw I was dead and darkness, and Christ was peace and life and light.

Goodwife Jackson

In ministry out of Isaiah, Hear, Oh child, I have brought up rebellious child, and I thought I was a rebellious wretch against God, and so I continued long. I was in a sad condition long together, and I heard, They that seek the Lord shall find him, and hearing, Fatherless find mercy in me.

Isaiah the 1:2: Hear, oh heavens, and give ear, oh earth, for the Lord hath spoken, I have nourished and brought [up] my children, and they have rebelled against me. A minister preaching out of those words and showing the rebellion of the heart against the Lord, she thought the Lord did convince her that she had a heart as all others had which did rebel against the Lord, which did much affect her.

So out of the 2 of Corinthians 4:3–4 For if our gospel be hid, it is hid to them that are lost, in whom the God of this world hath blinded the minds of them that believe not, which was made known unto me to be hid from me, and that I was lost, which did affect my heart a long time, till one did preach out of 42 Isaiah and 3, A bruised reed will [he] not break and the smoking flax will not be quench[ed], from which scripture the Lord did let her have some hope that though she was weak, yet he would not break the bruised reed, and by some godly minister's instruction she was somewhat help[ed]. And a godly minister preaching out of the whole prophecy of Malachi, I thought I did receive much good, although I cannot remember and was but a poor silly creature as I am still, which she saith is a great trouble to her that she is so bad that hath had so much means to make her better but she is not.

Again the minister preaching out of the 23 of Jeremiah 29, Is not my word like a fire, saith the Lord, and like a hammer that breaketh the rock in pieces[?] Where, saith he, If thy heart be as hard as a stone, this hammer, if it come at it, it will break it. And I, finding my heart hard as a stone, did pray to the Lord that he would break it, and the Lord did affect her heart.

So out of 17 Jeremiah 9, The heart is deceitful above all things, where the deceit of the heart being opened, I did not think there had been so much deceit in my heart till then that the minister did discover the same. And though she said, My memory is weak, and [she] cannot remember what was said, yet this she did desire, that the Lord would humble her heart for that deceit, and that she had spent her time and got no more good.

And after this Mr. Shepard [preached] out of the 38 Isaiah wherein it said, I am oppressed, for I thought I was oppressed: but, said the minister, though thou can but sigh and breathe or chatter after the Lord. That did refresh that there should be any hope for such a poor creature as I am. And when I was come to New England, I did look on myself as cast in the open field, and so saw myself in a sad condition, and though[t] others thought ill and meanly of me, and I thought worst of myself, and I was in a sad condition, and my sleep did depart away from [me], so that I did not know what to do. Then that in 14 Hosea was brought to me: In thee the fatherless find mercy. That place did much refresh me, that the Lord should look on so poor miserable sinner as I was. I might have been better, but I thought the Lord saw I would be lifted up; therefore the Lord did leave me so much. More comfort and refreshment I might have had if I had made use of what I did enjoy.

1 Question: What need have you observed of Christ and coming to him[?]

Answer: A great deal of need of him, for there is nothing to be had without coming to him.

2 Question: By what means did you see need of Christ, and by what scripture were you helped[?]

From that place out of 42 Isaiah 3 of the bruised reed, where it was showed that what the Lord did for a poor creature, it was out of free mercy, and though it were but a little that the Lord had wrought in the soul, the Lord would not quench it.

But had you not prayed to the Lord Jesus that he for free grace and mercy sake would pity you[?]

Answer: Yes, for I thought there was no free grace without him, nor no free mercy without him, and I thought it great mercy that the Lord should stoop down so low, to such a distressed one that was nothing but sin and corruption, and that he would look on such a poor creature.

Question: What did oppress [her] and what kind of undertaking did she desire[?]

Answer: My sins was great and many, and I did desire that the Lord would pity and pardon her of all.

Question: Whether it was the guilt or power of sin that did oppress her.

Answer: Was both.

Upon an occasion of some words that did fall out between her and one other, I saying to that party, Why did you not speak to myself? The party answered that I was without. The word "without" did much trouble me, not knowing what the party meant, whether I was without Christ or out of the church. But I put me upon examining of my estate, and being thereupon in a very sad condition, not knowing what to make of myself, then that place again in [scripture], The fatherless find mercy. The beginning of this trouble was before that party [spoke to me], only that did further evil to my trouble. But my trouble was chiefly for my sin, and misery by reason of my sin.

Having been asked, because she did much complain of ignorance and rebellion, if she did find any help or healing of them.

Answer: She had in some measure, though much did still remain which she did apprehend did so unfit her that it did keep her back, and complained of the proneness that was in her heart to evil, which was so much as no man did know how much was in her heart.

Question: When the Lord do let you see the sin and misery that is in your heart daily, what then is your refuge[?]

Answer: By going to the Lord by prayer to humble her soul. She went to the Lord, she said, for her prayer was sinful.

Question: But do you find the Lord a refuge to support her soul[?]

Answer: Sometime I do, and if the Lord will not support me, still I think with Job to stick to him and mourn and wait till he help me.

At what gate or promise do you stay for help[?]

Answer: 61 Isaiah 1: To bind up the brokenhearted, to proclaim liberty to the captives, and the opening of the prison to them that are bound. For I have sometime looked on myself as a prisoner shut up in sin and corruption. Yet that place being once opened, I was much helped by it, and though I do not feel help from it daily, yet sometime I do. Once being in discourse with a godly minister, he bade me take that as my own and not let it go, but she told him she could not. Then, said he, You will lose the benefit of it by your unbelief. And inward[ly] I had not the benefit of it till she was come here, being in very great trouble. Yet that word came in, that he doth open the prison to them that are bound, and God did give me great comfort. I thought myself unworthy of any such mercy and did much fear my falling away.

And the question being what other scriptures was there that did afford her any comfort[?]

Answer: Galatians 5:6, For in Jesus Christ neither circumcision now availeth anything nor uncircumcision but faith that worketh by love. The chief thing she noted there was her love to the saints.

So out of the 18 of Matthew where it is said, Except you become as little children, you cannot inherit the kingdom of God, which did help her when she had troubles upon her, both inward and outward, and her heart did not so quietly lie under them as she thought it should. Then that scripture coming in made her heart glory when she thought she might become as a little child.

So Isaiah 11, The wolf shall dwell with the lamb and the leopard shall lie down with the kid, and the calf and the young lion and the fatling together, and a young child shall lead them. All which did show her of what a meek spirit she should be of, that was naturally like to leopard and lion.

She did also express much how she was afraid of her falling away, having known and been well acquainted with some that had been eminent in profession yet falling away to the great dishonor of the Lord and scandal to religion, and they being strong and tall cedars and she but weak and a low shrub. This did much affect her heart.

Question: But do you not fear deceit in your own heart[?]

Yes. And she did pray to the Lord to direct her heart in the right way, and so to cast low weight that hung so fast on, and the sin that be [i.e., do] so easily beset, and to run with patience the race that was set before her. And [she] also did desire to set the Lord always before her and to seek him in the first place.

Question: What is the evil in sin that you have seen[?]

Answer: [It] is because it is a dishonor to the Lord, how as Adam did dishonor the Lord by breaking of the Commandments.

Abram Arrington

The first time Lord did me any good was what [sic] a friend, a godly man, brother [John] Isaac, being at work together, he spake to me how it stood with me about my estate and asked me (1) whether God gave me a heart to seek him. So I told him I had little mind or heart that way. And he then said it was high time to look to it, for now was a fair season. And his words affected me, and he took much pains in his family. Ecclesiastes 12: Remember Creator. He pressed it upon me as my duty now in my youth to seek after God. And coming to hearing word [of the] Lord out of John 14, penultimate, The Prince of the world comes, [which] showed that Satan did assault Christ at time of his departure, when [he] found no sin [in Christ], and hence terror to all wicked men, the Lord will find something in them. And I was affected with this sermon, and he let me see that there was that sin in my heart for which the Lord might justly condemn and cast me out of sight. But going on in use of [m]eans, another man, Mr. [Samuel] Newman, [preached on] If gospel be hid, 'tis to them that be lost, and I saw I was lost and under wrath. And going on, Look to things which are eternal, and I saw I minded nothing but sin and my own pleasure and lusts. And hearing another [preach on] God be merciful to me a sinner, he saw nothing but sin and misery and hence cried out to God for mercy but yet thought mercy did not belong to me, had not made it such a misery yet 6 Hosea, If [ye] follow on to know the Lord, ye shall know him. And thus the Lord spake by Mr. Shepard concerning sight and sense of sin, that it must be an intolerable burden to make it restless to seek after Christ. And hence I thought I wanting this, I was not fit for mercy. But that scripture, Lord came to seek that which is lost, which did somewhat encourage me to seek after God still. And so by Mr. [Richard] Mather [preaching on] John 6:37, All given shall come to him, use of exhortation to come to Christ unless prove yourselves reprobates, Lord's desire was. And hence I was encouraged to seek after himself. Lord let me see my desires were after him and to seek him.

Robert Browne

The Lord in England showed me the evil of sin by a godly man who showed miserable estate of wicked men, that they were without God in world and without hope. And I thought I must be one of those which were so. And so I saw evil of Sabbath breaking and of not praying, for people of God do not [sic] pray. And then Psalm 8 [of] David, [God] makes man master of all, and hence I thought God requires something of me to live as I list that [received] so much mercy from God. And I saw evil of company keeping, and if I went on, there was no hope of mercy for me. And so I thought I would reform myself and endeavored to pray and to keep Sabbath, and so I thought it would be better with me than others who had no regard. Yet seeing others sport, I was tempted to break off all but was struck with such a fear and trembling that I must go back again. And I lived under a bad master, and I thought I would go hear one 3 miles off [preaching on] As new born babes, and how precious he was to believers. And hence he showed the miserable condition of them out of Christ, and I saw myself such a one, for I was ignorant if Christ knew me, what Christ was, and without knowledge heart cannot be good. And then the Lord brought innumerable sins I could not tell them, and I thought there was no hope of mercy for me. Yet I thought I would use means. I could read a little, and that place, Matthew 11 came to me, Come to me, and I was glad of that scripture as of anything in my life. And I desired Lord to rid me of sin and that burden. And [I remembered] Isaiah 1, Though sins of crimson [they shall be] whiter than snow. And so in seeking God I found some refreshing and ease and strength against it, and love to God's people. And then I could go by my companions and loathe them. And I found delight in Sabbath word [and] ordinances, and then the word was not tedious, but [I was] sorry [it was] done so soon, and I loved to keep their company that would speak of it. And so the times being bad, and good people departing, I thought to come to New England. And here God hath endeared my heart more to himself, hath showed me more of my vileness and wretchedness, and needing all his love to look upon such a wretch to show me evil of sin and love me. John 6, I'll not forsake you: draw near to me, and I'll draw nigh to you; Seek and find. Consideration of Christ's excellency made me love him.

3

The Book of Common Prayer
and Eighteenth-Century Episcopalians

Robert Bruce Mullin

The Book of Common Prayer has been the foundational book for the life and worship of Anglicans. Anglicans are members of the Church of England or of the many churches (mostly in former English colonies) that accept Anglican liturgy, doctrine, and disciplines. For instance, after the American colonies separated from England they called their church the Protestant Episcopal Church (now simply the Episcopal Church), but they still accepted the theology and liturgy of the Church of England. As the great product of the English Reformation of the sixteenth century, the Book of Common Prayer has shaped the life of Anglicans throughout the world for over 450 years. It also made colonial Anglicans (Episcopalians) in America unique, because they alone, of English-speaking Protestants, used a set liturgy or form of prayers as the regular basis of their worship.

The Prayer Book reflected a number of the particular aspects of the Reformation in England. The first was an attempt to combine both Protestant and Catholic elements. The Prayer Book included many of the theological ideas of the Reformation, such as the doctrine of justification by faith and the centrality of the Bible, but it also contained many traditional practices. One example is the use of special vestments or apparel for the clergy performing the service. A second element was the continuation of the idea of three distinct levels of ministry: bishop, priest, and deacon. The Prayer Book instructed not only what was to be done at church but also who should do it. Certain services and parts of services were restricted to particular levels of clergy. The ordination of clergy was reserved for bishops, and only bishops or priests could celebrate Holy Communion or pronounce the absolution for the remission of sin.

It is important to emphasize that the Prayer Book was not simply a book of devotion. It contained not only the services of public prayer but also the services of baptism, confirmation, marriage ordination, and burial of the dead, as well as a catechism for the instruction of children. It was the principle book for the ordering of religious life. Furthermore, it was a national book. The Church of England and its liturgy received their authority by a series of legal acts of the English Parliament. As the prayer book of the established church, the book contained services and prayers that to a modern individual sound much more political than religious, such as the services of national thanksgiving, but in the British context this is a false distinction. Well into the early nineteenth century, church and state remained closely connected, and one of the church's important roles was to pray for the monarch. The legal status of the Book of Common Prayer gave to it one other peculiarity. Clergy were required by both law and oath to follow the services precisely as they were written—to omit any part subjected a cleric to both civil and ecclesiastical punishment.

The Prayer Book used by late-eighteenth-century Americans had changed over the years. Earlier editions, in 1549, 1552, 1559, and 1662, had each reflected different theological concerns. The 1549 edition provided the first English language liturgy but kept most of the ceremonies and rituals of the medieval church. The book of 1552 was far more radical in excising medieval Catholic practices and reformulating the liturgy to be more in keeping with the continental Protestant Reformation. While keeping a Protestant theological emphasis, the Prayer Book of 1559, issued under the reign of Queen Elizabeth, restored some of the older practices. It was intended as a book that could be used by both Catholics and Protestants. In many ways the distinctive Anglican self-understanding—as being both Protestant and a Catholic—stemmed from this "Elizabethan compromise." The compromise, however, provoked opposition from persons who wanted a Church of England closer to the model of the more thorough Protestantism of the continental churches. Beginning in the 1570s, critics complained about the inclusion of traditional but unscriptural practices such as clerical vestments and the use of a ring in the marriage ceremony. These persons were known as "Puritans" because they desired to purify the Church of England (and particularly its Prayer Book) by removing all lingering Catholic forms and practices. They succeeded in the 1640s during the English Civil Wars in abolishing the Prayer Book, but it returned when Anglicanism was reestablished in 1660. A revised version of the Prayer Book (1662) remained the official liturgy of American Anglicans until 1789.

Members of the Church of England brought the Prayer Book with them to the New World and used it throughout the colonial period. The first Prayer Book service in what is now the United States probably took place in 1579 in California under the auspices of Francis Drake during his circumnavigation of the world. Regular worship began with the establishment of the Virginia colony in 1607. The Church of England became the official church in the colonies of Virginia, Maryland, North and South Carolina, and Georgia. By the eighteenth century, Anglicanism had also taken root in the northern colonies. The work of the English missionary society, the Society for the Propagation of the Gospel in Foreign Parts (established in 1701), was influential in planting Anglican churches in these colonies. Anglicanism often found favor from the royal governors as well as from those who desired a closer connection between the colonies and England. By mid century it had also attracted a number of converts in New England, who found Anglican worship an attractive alternative to the religious excitement that affected the region as a result of the religious revival of the 1740s. The Revolutionary era, however, would be a difficult period for colonial Anglicans. The dispute between England and the colonies put colonial Anglicans in a difficult position. During the war many clergy decided to close their churches rather than modify the liturgy by removing prayers for the British monarch. From their perspective the clergy were duty bound to say the service exactly as it was prescribed.

With the coming of American independence, Anglicans had to reconstitute themselves as a church independent from England (thus becoming the Protestant Episcopal Church). They also had to revise their liturgy to more closely match the new political reality. The extensive prayers for the crown and the royal family were removed and replaced by prayers for American civil authorities. Other changes reflected the American environment, such as allowing for more of the services to be read by laypersons in areas where clergymen were scarce. Some smaller changes were also incorporated that reflected theological trends of the period, but because of the importance of the Book of Common Prayer for Anglicans the number of changes were minimal. As the preface to the 1789 book stated, "It will also appear that this church is not intending to depart from the Church of England in any essential point of doctrine, discipline, or worship."

The service of Morning Prayer was perhaps the most common religious service for eighteenth-century Episcopalians. Medieval in origin, it had been a part of the daily Catholic monastic offices of prayer. The compiler of the Prayer Book combined elements of the services of Mattins and prime into a more simplified service suitable for general use. According to the preface of the Book of Common Prayer, clergy were required to say the Morning Prayer service daily, although this was almost always done privately rather than in the church itself. On Sundays it made up a key part of the public liturgy. The Morning Prayer was regularly combined with two other services: the Litany, which was a long series of prayers and responses and the first part of the service of Holy Communion, known as the ante-communion. These three services were used in combination until the middle of the nineteenth century.

The service of Morning Prayer reflects many of the key themes of Prayer Book worship. The service begins with a set of instructions for both ministers and worshippers, known as rubrics. These instructions explain who should be doing what—that is, whether an action was to be done simply by a "minister" or had to be done by a priest—and also what bodily positions clergy and laity should assume. The Prayer Book's vision of appropriate worship involved both uniformity in response and uniformity in action.

The service can be divided into five parts. After a call to worship, the people are called to ask forgiveness for their sins and to participate in a prayer of repentance. This prayer contains the famous phrase of lamentation, "We have erred and strayed from thy ways like lost sheep." It is immediately followed by a declaration of absolution, to be said by the priest while the people continue to kneel. Immediately afterward the people stand while the triune God is praised. The Prayer Book not only called for common action but also distinctive bodily positions for different aspects of worship. Each of the three bodily positions of worship—kneeling, sitting, and standing—reflected different focuses. A worshiper knelt to pray, sat to be instructed, and stood to offer praise.

The second part of the service involved the regular reading of the Bible. The reading of scripture was as organized as the reading of the prayers. Included in the Prayer Book was a calendar of appointed readings for every day of the year, taken from the Psalms, the Old Testament, and the New Testament. For example, the Psalms were to be read sequentially through once each month. The readings from the Old Testament were organized so that the complete text would be read almost in its entirety over the course of each year; the New Testament would be read through twice each year. Scriptural readings came from the King James Bible, but American Episcopalians used the 1538 translation of the Psalter by Miles Coverdale.

A third part of the Morning Prayer Service included the recitation of set hymns of praise. "O Lord, open thou our lips," the minister would call out, and the congregation would respond, "And our mouth shall show forth thy praise." These set hymns were known as canticles (from the Latin for "song"). Before the reading of the Psalter or section of the Psalms, the Venite, which was a modification of the Ninety-fifth Psalm, would be said or sung. Its first line, "O come let us sing unto the Lord," set the tone for the rest of the service. Following the reading of the Old Testament section, the "Te Deum Laudamus" ("We Praise Thee O God"), an ancient hymn addressed to the triune nature of God, was usually recited. After the New Testament lesson, still another canticle was recited, most typically a hymn found in the first chapter of the Gospel of Luke and known as the Benedictus ("Blessed be the Lord God of Israel"), which celebrates the coming of Jesus into the world.

After the scriptures and canticles, the people stood to recite a summary of the faith, usually through a text known as the Apostles' Creed. Laws of the Church of England required persons to bow their heads when the name of Jesus was mentioned, and although this law was not reproduced in the organization of the American church, the custom probably continued in the eighteenth century.

The final part of the liturgy concerned the prayers. The section beginning "O Lord show thy mercy upon us" exemplifies one of the distinctive aspects of Prayer Book worship among American Protestants. There would be a scripted dialogue of prayer (known technically as versicles and responses) between the minister and the congregation. (Since the Prayer Book tradition was a "common" prayer tradition, a great emphasis was placed on the active participation of all.) Next followed a series of special prayers known as collects: One for the particular day (a special prayer), one for peace, and one for grace. The prayer for peace stated, "O God who art the author of peace and lover of concord, in knowledge of whom standeth our eternal life, whose service is perfect freedom." In the English Prayer

Book these collects were followed by a number of prayers for the monarch and the royal family. In America these were replaced with a prayer for the president and civil authorities. The presence of this prayer *before* any prayers for the church reflects the fact that the American service was modeled on the order of the Church of England, in which the monarch was the supreme governor of the church and was thus prayed for first. The service continued with more prayers, including "A General Thanksgiving," which is often considered one of the most beautiful prayers in the entire book and includes the phrase, "We bless thee for our creation, preservation, and all the blessings of this life, but above all for thine inestimable love in the redemption of the world by our Lord Jesus Christ; for the means of grace and for the hope of glory." The service ends with still another invocation of the Holy Trinity.

An important part of this liturgical act was its physical setting. Although the Prayer Book was designed for use in many different locations, its meaning was highlighted by a distinctive architectural setting. Colonial churches were required to be built facing east. Against the east wall of the church not only would be the altar (technically the "holy table"), but behind the altar would be painted the Ten Commandments, often flanked by the Lord's Prayer and the Apostles' Creed. These three texts summarized for Anglicans the essence of prayer, doctrine, and morality. Perhaps the most dominant architectural part of the early American Episcopalian church was the pulpit. The pulpit often consisted of three levels. On the uppermost level the minister delivered his sermon. On the second level he conducted the reading of the prayers. On the lowest level the "clerk," a lay reader, led the congregation in its responses and in the singing. Sometimes the clerk "lined out" the responses, calling them out line by line, and the lines were in turn repeated by the congregation. This procedure became necessary when the congregation lacked a sufficient number of Prayer Books (which were supplied by individuals, not the church) or there were a large number of illiterate persons in the congregation. When the minister performed the service he generally wore a long flowing white garment known as a surplice. At the time of the sermon the surplice would be removed, and the minister would reappear in a black gown to deliver the sermon.

Another distinctive aspect of early American Episcopalian worship was the use of music. Most of the English-speaking Protestant world had rejected the music of the medieval church and held that congregational singing should be limited to the Psalms. Anglicans, however, continued to sing medieval canticles. Furthermore, Anglicans continued the use of choirs and organs, both of which were largely rejected by other English Protestants. Indeed, throughout the eighteenth century the Anglican tradition of choral music greatly developed. Grand choral services were particularly the rule in the cathedral churches of England, where choir schools were attached to the church. There, vested in special garb, professional choristers, both men and boys, sang the liturgy to elaborate settings. Until the middle of the nineteenth century the musical life of American Episcopalians was but a shadow of their English cousins. Because of the absence of choir schools the few choirs in American churches were of a modest character. They were referred to as "cock and hen" choirs and comprised untrained local men and women. Episcopal churches that could afford to, however, did regularly make use of organs to enhance the musical beauty of their services. Especially during the colonial period, organ use distinguished Episcopalians from their English-speaking Protestant neighbors.

The use of the Book of Common Prayer allowed American Episcopalians, despite their social situations, to worship in unity. The service could as easily be said in a wealthy and formal worship setting such as Christ Church in Philadelphia as by a lay reader in a rented schoolroom. It also provided a sense of social and linguistic continuity between American congregations and the rest of the Anglican world. And, as in the words of the General Thanksgiving, the book constantly placed before worshipers "the means of grace and the hope of glory."

The text printed here is from William McGarvey, *Liturgiae Americanae: or the Book of Common Prayer as Used in the United States of America Compared with the Proposed Book of 1786 and with the Prayer Book of the Church of England, and an Historical Account and Documents* (Philadelphia: Philadelphia Church Publishing Company, 1907).

Further Reading

Marion J. Hatchett, *The Making of the First American Book of Common Prayer, 1776–1789* (New York: Seabury, 1982); David L. Holmes, *A Brief History of the Episcopal Church* (Valley Forge, Pa.: Trinity Press International, 1993); William W. Manross, *The Episcopal Church in the United States, 1800–1840* (New York: Columbia University Press, 1938); Arthur Pierce Middleton, *New Wine in Old Wine Skins: Liturgical Change and the Setting of Worship* (Wilton, Conn.: Morehose Barlow, 1988); Francis Proctor and Walter Howard Frere, *A New History of the Book of Common Prayer: With a Rationale of Its Offices* (London: Macmillan, 1932); Massey H. Shepherd, Jr., *At All Times and at All Places* (New York: Seabury, 1985); William Sydnor, *The Story of the Real Prayer Book, 1549–1979* (Wilton, Conn.: Morehouse, 1979); Dell Upton, *Holy Things and Profane: Anglican Parish Churches in Colonial Virginia* (Cambridge: Harvard University Press, 1986).

The Order for Daily Morning Prayer

The Minister shall begin the MORNING PRAYER, by reading one or more of the following Sentences of Scripture.

THE LORD is in his holy temple; let all the earth keep silence before him. Hab. ii. 20.

From the rising of the sun even unto the going down of the same, my Name shall be great among the Gentiles; and in every place incense shall be offered unto my Name, and a pure offering: for my Name shall be great among the heathen, saith the LORD of hosts. Mal. i. 11.

Let the words of my mouth, and the meditation of my heart, be alway acceptable in thy sight, O LORD, my strength and my redeemer. Psalm xix. 14, 15.

When the wicked man turneth away from his wickedness that he hath committed, and doeth that which is lawful and right, he shall save his soul alive. Ezek. xviii. 27.

I acknowledge my transgressions; and my sin is ever before me. Psalm li. 3.
Hide thy face from my sins and blot out all mine iniquities. Psalm li. 9.
The sacrifices of God are a broken spirit a broken and a contrite heart O God thou wilt not despise. Psalm ii. 17.

Rend your heart and not your garments and turn unto the LORD your God for he is gracious and merciful slow to anger and of great kindness and repenteth him of the evil. Joel ii. 13.

To the Lord our God belong mercies and forgivenesses, though we have rebelled against him, neither have we obeyed the voice of the LORD our God to walk in his laws which he set before us. Dan ix. 9, 10.

O LORD, correct me, but with judgment; not in thine anger, lest thou bring me to nothing. Jer. x. 24, Psalm vi. 1.

Repent ye; for the Kingdom of heaven is at hand. St. Matt. iii. 2.

I will arise, and go to my father, and will say unto him, Father, I have sinned against heaven, and before thee, and am no more worthy to be called thy son. St. Luke xv. 18, 19.

Enter not into judgment with thy servant, O LORD; for in thy sight shall no man living be justified. Psalm cxliii. 2.

If we say that we have no sin, we deceive ourselves, and the truth is not in us; but if we confess our sins, God is faithful and just to forgive us our sins, and to cleanse us from all unrighteousness. 1 John i. 8, 9.

Then the Minister shall say,

DEARLY beloved brethren, the Scripture moveth us, in sundry places, to acknowledge and confess our manifold sins and wickedness; and that we should not dissemble nor cloak them before the face of Almighty God our heavenly Father; but confess them with an humble, lowly, penitent, and obedient heart; to the end that we may obtain forgiveness of the same, by his infinite goodness and mercy. And although we ought, at all times, humbly to acknowledge our sins before God; yet ought we chiefly so to do, when we assemble and meet together to render thanks for the great benefits that we have received at his hands, to set forth his most worthy praise, to hear his most holy Word, and to ask those things which are requisite and necessary, as well for the body as the soul. Wherefore I pray and beseech you, as many as are here present, to accompany me with a pure heart, and humble voice, unto the throne of the heavenly grace, saying—

A GENERAL CONFESSION

To be said by the whole congregation, after the Minister, all kneeling.

ALMIGHTY and most merciful Father; We have erred, and strayed from thy ways like lost sheep. We have followed too much the devices and desires of our own hearts. We have offended against thy holy laws. We have left undone those things which we ought to have done; And we have done those things which we ought not to have done; And there is no health in us. But thou O Lord have mercy upon us, miserable offenders. Spare thou those, O God, who confess their faults. Restore thou those who are penitent; According to thy promises declared unto mankind in Christ Jesus our Lord. And grant, O most merciful Father, for his sake; That we may hereafter live a godly, righteous, and sober life, To the glory of thy holy Name. Amen.

THE DECLARATION OF ABSOLUTION, OR REMISSION OF SINS

To be said by the Priest alone, standing; the People still kneeling.

ALMIGHTY God, the Father of our Lord Jesus Christ, who desireth not the death of a sinner, but rather that he may turn from his wickedness and live hath given power, and commandment, to his Ministers, to declare and pronounce to his people, being penitent, the Absolution and Remission of their sins. He pardoneth and absolveth all those who truly repent and unfeignedly believe his holy Gospel. Wherefore let us beseech him to grant us true repentance, and his Holy Spirit, that those things may please him which we do at this present; and that the rest of our life hereafter may be pure and holy; so that at the last we may come to his eternal joy; through Jesus Christ our Lord.

The People shall answer here, and at the end of every Prayer, Amen.

Or this.

ALMIGHTY God, our heavenly Father, who of his great mercy hath promised forgiveness of sins to all those who, with hearty repentance and true faith, turn unto him; Have mercy upon you; pardon and deliver you from all your sins; confirm and strengthen you in all goodness; and bring you to everlasting life; through Jesus Christ our Lord. Amen.

Then the Minister shall kneel, and say the Lord's Prayer; the people still kneeling and repeating it with him, both here, and wheresoever else it is used in divine service.

OUR Father, who art in heaven, Hallowed be thy Name. Thy kingdom come. Thy will be done on earth, As it is in heaven. Give us this day our daily bread. And forgive us our trespasses, As we forgive those who trespass against us. And lead us not into temptation; But deliver us from evil: For thine is the kingdom, and the power, and the glory, for ever and ever. Amen.

Then likewise he shall say,

O Lord, open thou our lips.
Answer. And our mouth shall show forth thy praise

Here, all standing up, the Minister shall say,

Glory be to the Father, and to the Son, and to the Holy Ghost;
Answer. As it was in the beginning, is now, and ever shall be, world without end.
Minister. Praise ye the Lord.
Answer. The Lord's Name be praised.

Then shall be said or sang the following Anthem; except on those days for which other Anthems are appointed; and except also, when it is used in the course of the Psalms, on the nineteenth day of the month.

VENITE, EXULTEMUS DOMINO

> O COME, let us sing unto the LORD; let us heartily rejoice in the strength of our salvation.
> Let us come before his presence with thanksgiving; and show ourselves glad in him with psalms.
> For the LORD is a great God; a great King above all gods.
> In his hand are all the corners of the earth, and the strength of the hills is his also.
> The sea is his, and he made it, and his hands prepared the dry land.
> O come let us worship and fall down, and kneel before the LORD our Maker.
> For he is the Lord our God and we are the people his pasture and the sheep of his hand.
> O worship the LORD in the beauty of holiness; let the whole earth stand in awe of him.
> For he cometh, for he cometh to judge the earth; and with righteousness to judge the world and the people with his truth.

Then shall follow a Portion of the Psalms, as they are appointed, or one of the Selections of the Psalms set forth by this Church. And at the end of every Psalm, and likewise at the end of the Venite, Benedicite, Jubilate Benedictus, Cantate Domino, Bonum est confiteri, Deus miseratur, Benedic Anima mea MAY be said or sung the

*Gloria Patri; and at the end of the whole Portion, or Selection of Psalms for the day
SHALL be said or sung the Gloria Patri, or else the Gloria in excelsis, which followeth.*

GLORIA IN EXCELSIS

GLORY be to God on high and on earth peace, good will towards men. We
praise thee, we bless thee, we worship thee we glorify thee, we give thanks to
thee for thy great glory, O Lord God heavenly King, God the Father Almighty.

O Lord, the only-begotten Son Jesus Christ; O Lord God, Lamb of God, Son
of the Father, that takest away the sins of the world, have mercy upon us.
Thou that takest away the sins of the world, have mercy upon us. Thou that
takest away the sins of the world, receive our prayer. Thou that sittest at the
right hand of God the Father, have mercy upon us.

For thou only art holy; thou only art the Lord; thou only, O Christ, with the
Holy Ghost, art most high in the glory of God the Father. Amen.

Then shall be read the first Lesson, according to the Table or Calendar.

After which shall be said or sung the following hymn.
*Note, That before every Lesson, the Minister shall say Here beginneth such a Chap-
ter, or verse of such a Chapter, of such a Book: and after every Lesson, Here endeth
the first, or the second Lesson.*

TE DEUM LAUDAMUS

WE praise thee, O God; we acknowledge thee to be the Lord.
All the earth doth worship thee, the Father everlasting.
To thee, all Angels cry aloud; the Heavens, and all the Powers therein.
To thee, Cherubim and Seraphim continually do cry,
Holy, Holy, Holy, Lord God of Sabaoth;
Heaven and earth are full of the Majesty of thy Glory.
The glorious company of the Apostles praise thee.
The goodly fellowship of the Prophets praise thee.
The noble army of Martyrs praise thee.
The holy Church throughout all the world doth acknowledge thee;
The Father, of an infinite Majesty;
Thine adorable, true, and only Son;
Also the Holy Ghost, the Comforter.
Thou art the King of Glory, O Christ.
Thou art the everlasting Son of the Father.
When thou tookest upon thee to deliver man, thou didst humble thyself
    to be born of a Virgin.
When thou hadst overcome the sharpness of death, thou didst open the
    Kingdom of Heaven to all believers.
Thou sittest at the right hand of God, in the Glory of the Father.

We believe that thou shalt come to be our Judge.

We therefore pray thee, help thy servants, whom thou hast redeemed with thy precious blood.

Make them to be numbered with thy Saints, in glory everlasting.

O Lord save thy people and bless thine heritage.

Govern them and lift them up for ever.

Day by day we magnify thee;

And we worship thy Name ever world without end.

Vouchsafe, O Lord, to keep us this day without sin.

O Lord, have mercy upon us, have mercy upon us.

O Lord let thy mercy be upon us as our trust is in thee.

O Lord in thee have I trusted let me never be confounded.

Or this Canticle.

BENEDICITE OMNIA OPERA DOMINE

O ALL ye Works of the Lord bless ye the Lord; praise him and magnify him for ever.

O ye Angels of the Lord, bless ye the Lord; praise him and magnify him for ever.

O ye Heavens, bless ye the Lord; praise him, and magnify him for ever.

O ye Waters that be above the firmament bless ye the Lord; praise him, and magnify him for ever.

O all ye Powers of the Lord bless ye the Lord; praise him and magnify him for ever.

O ye Sun and Moon bless ye the Lord; praise him and magnify him for ever.

O ye Stars of Heaven, bless ye the Lord; praise him and magnify him for ever.

O ye Showers and Dew bless ye the Lord; praise him and magnify him for ever.

O ye Winds of God, bless ye the Lord; praise him, and magnify him for ever.

O ye Fire and Heat, bless ye the Lord; praise him, and magnify him for ever.

O ye Winter and Summer, bless ye the Lord; praise him, and magnify him for ever.

O ye Dews and Frosts, bless ye the Lord; praise him, and magnify him for ever.

O ye Frost and Cold, bless ye the Lord; praise him, and magnify him for ever.

O ye Ice and Snow, bless ye the Lord; praise him, and magnify him for ever.

O ye Nights and Days, bless ye the Lord; praise him, and magnify him for ever.

O ye Light and Darkness, bless ye the Lord; praise him, and magnify him for ever.

O ye Lightnings and Clouds, bless ye the Lord; praise him, and magnify him for ever.

O let the Earth bless the Lord; yea, let it praise him, and magnify him for ever.

O ye Mountains and Hills, bless ye the Lord; praise him, and magnify him for ever.

O all ye Green Things upon the earth, bless ye the Lord; praise him, and magnify him for ever.

O ye Wells, bless ye the Lord; praise him, and magnify him for ever.

O ye Seas and Floods, bless ye the Lord; praise him, and magnify him for ever.

O ye Whales, and all that move in the waters, bless ye the Lord; praise him, and magnify him for ever.

O all ye Fowls of the Air, bless ye the Lord; praise him, and magnify him for ever.

O all ye Beasts and Cattle, bless ye the Lord; praise him, and magnify him for ever.

O ye Children of Men, bless ye the Lord; praise him, and magnify him for ever.

O let Israel bless the Lord; praise him, and magnify him for ever.

O ye Priests of the Lord, bless ye the Lord; praise him, and magnify him for ever.

O ye Servants of the Lord, bless ye the Lord; praise him, and magnify him for ever.

O ye Spirits and Souls of the Righteous, bless ye the Lord; praise him, and magnify him for ever.

O ye holy and humble Men of Heart, bless ye the Lord; praise him, and magnify him for ever.

Then shall be read, in like manner, the second Lesson, taken out of the New Testament according to the Table or Calendar.

And after that, the following Psalm.

JUBILATE DEO. PSALM C

O BE joyful in the LORD, all ye lands; serve the LORD with gladness, and come before his presence with a song.

Be ye sure that the LORD he is God; it is he that hath made us, and not we ourselves; we are his people, and the sheep of his pasture.

O go your way into his gates with thanksgiving and into his courts with praise; be thankful unto him and speak good of his Name.

For the LORD is gracious, his mercy is everlasting, and his truth endureth from generation to generation.

Or this Hymn.

BENEDICTUS. ST. LUKE I. 68

BLESSED be the Lord God of Israel for he hath visited and redeemed his
   people;
And hath raised up a mighty salvation for us, in the house of his servant
   David;
As he spake by the mouth of his holy Prophets which have been since
   the world began;
That we should be saved from our enemies and from the hand of all that
   hate us.

*Then shall be said the Apostles' Creed by the Minister and the People, standing.
And any Churches may omit the words, He descended into hell, or may, instead of
them, use the words, He went into the place of departed spirits, which are considered as words of the same meaning in the Creed.*

I BELIEVE in God the Father Almighty, Maker of heaven and earth:
   And in Jesus Christ his only Son our Lord; Who was conceived by the
Holy Ghost, Born of the Virgin Mary; Suffered under Pontius Pilate, Was cru-
cified, dead, and buried; He descended into hell, The third day he rose from
the dead; He ascended into heaven, And sitteth on the right hand of God the
Father Almighty; From thence he shall come to judge the quick and the
dead.
   I believe in the Holy Ghost; The holy Catholic Church; The Communion of
Saints; The Forgiveness of sins; The Resurrection of the body; And the Life
everlasting. Amen.

Or this.

I BELIEVE in one God the Father Almighty, Maker of heaven and earth, And
of all things visible and invisible:
   And in one Lord Jesus Christ, the only-begotten Son of God, Begotten of His
Father before all worlds, God of God, Light of Light, Very God of very God;
Begotten, not made; Being of one substance with the Father; By Whom all
things were made: Who for us men, and for our salvation came down from
heaven, And was incarnate by the Holy Ghost of the Virgin Mary, And was
made man: And was crucified also for us under Pontius Pilate; He suffered and
was buried: And on the third day He rose again according to the Scriptures:
And ascended into Heaven, And sitteth on the right hand of the Father. And
He shall come again with glory to judge both the quick and the dead; Whose
kingdom shall have no end.
   And I believe in the Holy Ghost, The Lord, and Giver of Life Who
proceedeth from the Father and the Son Who with the Father and the Son
together is worshipped and glorified, Who spake by the Prophets. And I
believe in one Catholick and Apostolick Church. I acknowledge one Baptism

for the remission of sins: And I look for the Resurrection of the dead: And the Life of the world to come. Amen.

And after that, these Prayers following, all devoutly kneeling; the Minister first pronouncing,

The Lord be with you.
Answer. And with thy spirit.
Minister. Let us pray.

O Lord show thy mercy upon us.
Answer. And grant us thy salvation.
Minister. O God make clean our hearts within us.
Answer. And take not thy holy Spirit from us.

Then shall follow the Collect for the day except when the Communion Service is read; and then the Collect for the day shall be omitted here.

A COLLECT FOR PEACE

O GOD who art the author of peace and lover of concord, in knowledge of whom standeth our eternal life, whose service is perfect freedom; Defend us thy humble servants in all assaults of our enemies that we, surely trusting in thy defence may not fear the power of any adversaries, through the might of Jesus Christ our Lord. Amen.

A COLLECT FOR GRACE

O LORD our heavenly Father Almighty and everlasting God who hast safely brought us to the beginning of this day; Defend us in the same with thy mighty power and grant that this day we fall into no sin, neither run into any kind of danger; but that all our doings being ordered by thy governance may be righteous in thy sight; through Jesus Christ our Lord. Amen.

A PRAYER FOR THE PRESIDENT OF THE UNITED STATES, AND ALL IN CIVIL AUTHORITY

O LORD, our heavenly Father, the high and mighty Ruler of the universe, who dost from thy throne behold all the dwellers upon earth; Most heartily we beseech thee, with thy favour to behold and bless thy servant The President of the United States, and all others in authority; and so replenish them with the grace of thy Holy Spirit, that they may always incline to thy will, and walk in thy way. Endue them plenteously with heavenly gifts; grant them in health and prosperity long to live; and finally, after this life, to attain everlasting joy and felicity; through Jesus Christ our Lord. Amen.

The following Prayers are to be omitted here when the Litany is read.

A PRAYER FOR THE CLERGY AND PEOPLE

ALMIGHTY and everlasting God, from whom cometh every good and perfect gift; Send down upon our Bishops, and other Clergy, and upon the Congregations committed to their charge, the healthful Spirit of thy grace; and, that they may truly please thee, pour upon them the continual dew of thy blessing. Grant this, O Lord, for the honour of our Advocate and Mediator, Jesus Christ. Amen.

A PRAYER FOR ALL CONDITIONS OF MEN

O GOD, the Creator and Preserver of all mankind, we humbly beseech thee for all sorts and conditions of men; that thou wouldest be pleased to make thy ways known unto them, thy saving health unto all nations. More especially we pray for thy holy Church universal; that it may be so guided and governed by thy good Spirit that all who profess and call themselves Christians may be led into the way of truth, and hold the faith in unity of spirit in the bond of peace and in righteousness of life. Finally we commend to thy fatherly goodness all those who are any ways afflicted or distressed in mind body or estate; that it may please thee to comfort and relieve them according to their several necessities giving them patience under their sufferings and a happy issue out of all their afflictions. And this we beg for Jesus Christ's sake. Amen.

A GENERAL THANKSGIVING

ALMIGHTY God Father of all mercies, we, thine unworthy servants do give thee most humble and hearty thanks for all thy goodness and loving kindness to us and to all men. We bless thee for our creation, preservation, and all the blessings of this life, but above all for thine inestimable love in the redemption of the world by our Lord Jesus Christ; for the means of grace and for the hope of glory. And we beseech thee give us that due sense of all thy mercies that our hearts may be unfeignedly thankful and that we may show forth thy praise not only with our lips but in our lives; by giving up ourselves to thy service, and by walking before thee in holiness and righteousness all our days; through Jesus Christ our Lord to whom with thee and the Holy Ghost be all honour and glory, world without end. Amen.

A PRAYER OF ST. CHRYSOSTOM

ALMIGHTY God, who hast given us grace at this time with one accord to make our common supplications unto thee; and dost promise that when two or three are gathered together in thy Name thou wilt grant their requests;

Fulfil now, O Lord, the desires and petitions of thy servants, as may be most expedient for them; granting us in this world knowledge of thy truth, and in the world to come life everlasting. Amen.

2 Cor. xiii. 14.

THE grace of our Lord Jesus Christ, and the love of God, and the fellowship of the Holy Ghost, be with us all evermore. Amen.

Here endeth the Order of Morning Prayer.

—4—

The Green Corn Ceremony of the Muskogees

Joel W. Martin

In the seventeenth and eighteenth centuries, no Native Americans of the Southeast identified themselves as Creeks. Rather, the name Creeks was originally applied by English traders to a certain group of native people living near an English post on a large creek. These people had moved eastward from the Chattahoochee River towns of Coweta and Kashita for the purpose of trading with Carolinians. They called themselves Ochese (ò ci sì), and the English knew them as the people living on Ochese Creek. With time, the traders started calling them the Ochese Creek or, more simply, the Creeks. In 1715 these Creeks returned to their former homelands on the Chattahoochee River. English traders began applying the name Creeks generically to the whole montage of peoples living along the Chattahoochee. By the mid eighteenth century, Creeks had become the name that the English applied to most native peoples living in what is now central Georgia and Alabama, an area of roughly ten thousand square miles. However, from before European contact up until today, many Creeks have used the name *mosko:kalki* (Muskogee or Muscogee) to designate their cultural identity or tribal affiliation.

Muskogees did not experience time as homogeneous, words as totally mundane, or space as uniform. Rather, some times, narratives, and spaces stood out as special, incongruous, or symbolically charged. These times, narratives, and spaces were carefully marked and anticipated. In approaching or telling them, villagers altered their behaviors, thoughts, and practices, intentionally preparing themselves for a qualitatively different kind of experience, perception, and expression. Once the time arrived, or the storyteller began, or the space was entered, villagers abandoned key aspects of ordinary life and thought. Depending on the occasion, they might alter their vocabulary or temporarily cease consuming salt, eating food, or relating to the opposite sex. They might wear special clothing, use esoteric speech, seek visions, and perform holy dances. In these and many other ways, southeastern Native Americans symbolized that ordinary time, speech, and space had been transcended and something extraordinary encountered.

The awareness of sacred times was especially keen and gave rise to a considerable richness of symbolic action and display. For the Muskogees, the most important and serious communal rite was the *póskita*. The póskita is also called by its Anglicized name, the Busk. In the eighteenth and nineteenth centuries, Anglo-American travelers referred to it as the "Green Corn Ceremony." A ceremony requiring considerable preparation, involving the entire community, and carrying tremendous social and spiritual significance, the Busk was the Muskogee's greatest rite. One scholar has stated that, to match its meaning, Europeans or Anglo-Americans would have had to combine Thanksgiving, New Year's festivities, Yom Kippur, Lent, and Mardi Gras. The Busk emphasized collective renewal. Its intent was to rekindle a sense of the sacredness of life. Its effect was to strengthen Muskogee cultural traditions during a period of intensive cultural contact.

An annual ceremony, the Busk lasted four days in smaller towns and eight days in important ones such as Cussetuh or Tuckabatchee. It almost always occurred in July or August. Linked to the ripening of the second, or late, crop of corn, the ceremony was the most important of twelve monthly feasts dedicated to the first fruits of horticulture and hunting. Other feasts celebrated the gathering of chestnuts, mulberries, and blackberries. In the Muskogees' lunar calendar, the Busk took place at the time of "the big ripening moon," and its celebration marked the turning of the seasons from summer (primarily devoted to horticulture and harvest) to winter (primarily devoted to gathering and hunting). The Busk was the time that the Muskogees set aside to appreciate the plant on which they depended for more than fifty percent of their caloric needs. Despite their sophisticated knowledge of cultivating maize, the Muskogees did not consider themselves masters of the plant. As a celebration of the primordial origins of maize, the Busk challenged the Muskogees to remember that maize was rooted not just in little hills of earth but in a mystery.

The plant, as sacred myths related, was originally given to the Muskogees by a woman. More precisely, corn came from the body of a primordial woman, an earth goddess. In one myth, "She washed her feet in water and rubbed them, whereupon what came from her feet was corn." In another, she scratched "the front of one of her thighs, whereupon corn poured down into the riddle [sieve]." In both these stories, ungrateful males would rather not consume food thus produced. Always giving, the goddess ultimately sacrificed herself by telling these men to burn her body or drag her bloody corpse across the ground, so that they might have future crops of corn. Thus the story symbolized the way life came from death, the unlimited power of female fertility, and the important but circumscribed power of males to impose order on that fertility. The myth reminded listeners that, no matter how successfully they controlled the production of corn, maize was ultimately a gift given to the Muskogee by a primordial mother. The myth may not have been formally recited during the Busk, but its profound message was communicated. Just as the myth of the Corn Mother used words, symbols, and narratives to remind listeners of the sacred origins of corn, the Busk ritual resacralized corn by carefully orchestrating human energy and action in time and space.

Before the ritual began, the square ground was cleansed and refurbished; fresh white sand was spread in the plaza to sanctify the area. No footprints were allowed to press the new earth until the consecration was complete. New pottery vessels were crafted to be employed in the ceremony. Warriors painted the posts and beams of their cabin with red clay, shamans coated the white-drink shed with white clay, and men refurbished all cabins with new cane seating mats. But cleansing was not restricted to the square ground. While adult men renovated the public space, fasted, and drank an emetic beverage (button snakeroot), women swept the domestic structures, extinguished the individual den fires burning on domestic hearths, repaired those hearths, decorated their houses with green boughs, and cared for the children. In some towns, the effort to cleanse the community was radical and involved the wholesale destruction of old things. The people of Autossee made new clothes and household utensils and burned all of their old worn-out possessions. In Autossee, as in all Muskogee towns, fire purified and was sacred.

Each town square had a hearth with a burning fire that represented the entire community and the people's connection to their ancestors and the Maker of Breath. This particular fire was most sacred, but it could become polluted. Acts of violence, misuse of spiritual power, mistreatment of game, violations of sexual taboos, and the unsanctioned consumption of newly ripened or green corn symbolically polluted the fire. A pure fire enabled the people to communicate their wants to the Maker of Breath, the purifying power that rebalanced the cosmos. In contrast, a polluted fire could not connect people to the Maker of Breath. Over the course of a year, as the people's fire became tainted, its power eroded and needed renewal. Proper context for this vital renewal was provided by the Busk.

One of the crucial ritual acts of the Busk was the kindling of a new, pure fire. In the Busk ceremony of Autossee, the making of new fire occurred on the fourth morning. In some square grounds it occurred on the third morning. In Little Tallassie the fire was ignited on the first day. On the morning of the first day, the priest, dressed in white leather moccasins and stockings with a white dressed deerskin over his shoulders, came alone into the square. He made a new fire through the friction of two sticks. After the fire was produced, four young men entered at the openings of the four corners of the square, each holding a stick of wood for the new fire. They approached the fire with reverence and placed the logs on the fire so that they pointed to the four cardinal directions, thus invoking the symbolism of the entire world.

Once ignited and sufficiently kindled, the new fire, understood to be supremely pure, was an extraordinarily powerful embodiment of the sacred. It was used for cooking meat or warming hominy, but it also possessed the power to sanctify things, relationships, and the entire community anew. During the Busk, the Muskogees tapped this power in a series of carefully performed rites, the first and perhaps most important being the sacrifice of corn. After the fire was kindled, four other young men each carried an ear of new corn to the priest, who then placed the corn into the fire where it was consumed. By allowing holy fire to burn and destroy the first ears of new corn, the Muskogees expressed their profound awareness that corn had once belonged entirely to the sacred realm.

Although their ancestors had subjugated and domesticated this plant, and living men and women now cleared fields and cultivated it, the Muskogees knew that the plant must periodically be returned to the sacred. By ritually removing corn from ordinary patterns of human consumption and giving it instead to the new and powerful sacred fire, this rite of sacrifice sanctified corn anew. Similar sacrifices often followed. White-drink tea leaves were "given to the new fire." Also consumed by the fire were portions of bear oil, freshly killed deer meat, and button snakeroot medicine. The most important medicines and foods known to the Muskogees were temporarily removed from ordinary life and once again immersed in the sacred.

Broken human relationships were also healed. Because the Busk marked a critical threshold in time, the end of the previous year and the beginning of the new, it enabled the Muskogees to put personal grievances and animosities behind them and grant amnesty to all criminals, except murderers. But if the major social import of the ceremony was to bring people back together and strengthen their ties to each other and to the square ground, one very important effect of the Busk was to reinforce differences based on gender. During most of the ceremony, the sexes were not only segregated but were also required to perform gender-coded activities. It was common for townsmen to perform war dances and engage in a mock battle and a ritual hunt. Meanwhile, women were expected to cleanse the domestic space, harvest and prepare food, and care for children. During the Busk both men and women sought purity, but they achieved it through different means and by respecting different taboos. Men in the square ground could not directly refer to or even touch women. For their part, women were ritually excluded from the square ground for most of the Busk ceremony. Such physical restriction had profound symbolic and social meaning.

Because men fasted and slept in the square ground during the Busk, they enjoyed a closer, much more intimate relationship to the sacred fire. The men kindled the new fire and made the key sacrifices to it. They were its first beneficiaries. Only after the men had witnessed its flame were the women allowed to enjoy its purifying power. Eventually, some of the new fire would be placed on the outside of the square for public use, and the women were allowed to come and take it to their houses. This symbolism was powerful and clearly patriarchal. Placing males first and at the center and females second and on the periphery, the ritual claimed for males superior access to the sacred. Thus, during the ritual, men were aligned with the sacred, women with the profane.

This carefully framed elevation of men and subordination of women stands out when contrasted with the spiritual statuses of men and women in everyday life, in which the relationship between the genders was modeled not on dominance but on complementarity. Moreover, in everyday life women could hardly be considered profane. Women had access to sacred powers that men poorly understood. Because they knew the secrets of plants and fertility, women made better herbalists or medicine people and monopolized midwifery. To explain why women were spiritually subordinated during the Busk ritual, interpretative energy should focus not just on the relationship between genders but also on the relationship between two kinds of space. When the new fire was carried out of the square ground to supply every habitation in the town, it was not just moving from men to women but also moving from communal space to clan space. This movement from square ground to periphery, and from men to women, symbolized the tension between the common collective identity and the multiplicity of clan identities. The political tension was ritually resolved in favor of the collective identity.

In any town, several clans were present, and conflicts were endemic among them. If a woman discovered that her husband had committed adultery, her clan pursued and beat the man, even at the risk of offending his clan. If a man from the Bear clan killed a Fox, the latter's clan felt justified in killing a member of the Bear clan. In turn, if the members of the Bear clan felt the retaliation unwarranted, they might seek vengeance, and a spiral of violence would result. Such conflicts, and some less dramatic ones, seriously threatened to tear a town apart and make impossible the communal efforts of clearing fields and defending territory. In sum, clan loyalties centrifugally pulled villagers away from a common identity.

Opposing this fragmentation were those rites, spaces, and symbols that transcended clan diversity. Public ceremonies, particularly the white-drink ceremony and the Busk, assembled and unified men from all clans. Public spaces—the rotunda and the square ground—provided space for a common discourse and set of communal symbols to emerge, and for men to define and display their achieved status. Public symbols such as the sacred fire gave men, women, and children a common point of orientation beyond the clan. Together, these communal rites, spaces, and symbols forged diverse clans into a unified *i:tálwa* (town). Thus, when the new sacred fire was transmitted from center to periphery, its movement symbolized the supremacy, not just of men over women, but of the public over the domestic, of "fire" over "blood," and of the power of male order over the power of female fertility. This symbolism was powerful, but it would require repetition. The ritual could never finally banish or resolve the fundamental oppositions and tensions that constituted and energized Muskogee society. Nor could its patriarchal construction of gender relations establish in any final way the sacredness of men or the profanity of women. Because clan identities and women's access to the sacred always remained strong in everyday life, the symbolic rites would have to be repeated. In another year, a new fire would be needed.

With the conclusion of the Busk, the ritual restrictions and symbolic boundaries, which had been so carefully constructed and enforced, were decisively abandoned. Symbolic boundaries that had kept men and women separate (and unequal), taboos that had imposed a fast on men, and rules that had prevented the access of women and children to the square ground no longer held force. On the last day of the ceremony, the whole town assembled in the square. Women cooked new corn over the new fire, and men, women, and children mixed freely and devoted themselves to feasting, dancing, and other amusements. With joy and relief, villagers ended the ceremony. Before this moment of collective celebration, the Busk, with its extraordinarily strict boundaries, taboos, and restrictions, had forced villagers to inhabit an uncanny and oddly imbalanced world. The ritual had constructed an impossible world of maximum difference between men and women, town council and clan, public and domestic, center and periphery, and sacred and profane. The Busk had placed villagers in a world of stark polarities and abnormal patriarchy. Feasting together, villagers returned to ordinary life with new zeal, and new appreciation of their complex community and its sacred foundations. By generating a tremendous desire for renewal of purity, balance, and wholeness, by placing the Muskogees in vigorous contact with what was most sacred to their collective identity, the Busk gave villagers the energy to resume social life as if the world were once again fresh and balanced, integrated and complimentary.

Because the ceremony enabled the Muskogees to deal with some of the fundamental tensions inherent in their social order, to celebrate the harvest of corn, and to renew their collective life and public spaces, its performance remained very important throughout the period of colonial contact. The ceremony changed in only minor ways. For instance, new rules had to be created governing the consumption of alcohol and the use of manufactured goods during the Busk. In some towns, both were banned. In the account reprinted here, Muskogees were not to touch non-Muskogees until after the purification ceremony. This was the case in 1833, but it could have been true much earlier as well. Since rituals are dynamic expressions of a people's evolving relation to the sacred, rituals can and must change to fit new contexts. In the history of religions in North America, there are probably few examples of rituals that have succeeded as well in surviving through change and crisis as the Busk. In Oklahoma, the Busk, or Green Corn Ceremony, remains to this day a vital ceremony performed by the Muskogee people. The symbolism of the square ground, the sacred fire, and the fasting remains powerful despite five centuries of intense contact with non-Native peoples.

During the colonial period, Muskogee tradition proved itself to be very resilient, capable of linking an ancestral past to ever changing contexts. As they passed this tradition down through the generations, Muskogee elders communicated to their children some important symbols and values that were hundreds, and even thousands, of years old. Nevertheless, even as they carefully communicated this and other traditions, the Muskogees actively and continually modified their culture of the sacred. For example, eighteenth- and nineteenth-century Muskogees supplemented and reworked their lore by importing fresh ideas, materials, and techniques from other peoples. Significant "imports," which demonstrated an unconscious pan-Native Americanism, included songs from the Choctaws, a dance from the Shawnees, and a sacred stone from the Yamasees. The Muskogees also borrowed from non-Native Americans, taking, among other things, folktales from Africans and the symbolically powerful idea of the Book from Europeans.

Moreover, a small number of specialists—medicine men and women, knowers, and shamans—were specially charged with preserving, disseminating, and applying the most important inherited traditions. These specialists modified sacred tradition to respond to specific needs and events. In interpreting the ceremony, then, it is important to examine multiple accounts of it. The account excerpted here gives a good view of the ceremony as it unfolded in a single village in 1833. Tied to that particular ceremony, the account also reflects the perspective of its author, John Howard Payne. Born in New York in 1792, Payne led a very interesting life, working as a dramatist, actor, journalist, composer, and diplomat. Most remembered for writing the song "Home, Sweet Home," he traveled widely and sought the "exotic," anticipating ethnographers, orientalists, and tourists. He felt strongly attracted to native peoples and befriended Cherokee Chief John Ross. At a time when U.S. leaders and ordinary settlers sought the forced removal of southeastern Indians, Payne was an advocate on the Indians' behalf. In November 1835 he and Ross were arrested by the Georgia Guard, a force dedicated to undermining Cherokee sovereignty.

Two years prior to this event, Payne had visited a Muskogee village, observed its Green Corn Ceremony, and written a long letter to a friend describing it. As the letter reveals, Payne appreciated the ceremony's solemnity, complexity, color, symbolism, and drama, but he could not understand much of what he witnessed. Moreover, his account reflects and enacts colonialist power relations, with white tourists consuming the Muskogees' ceremony as entertainment. In his description of the female participants' dance, he perpetuated the stereotype of the Indian Princess, a beautiful, naturally aristocratic native woman who seems romantically interested in the visiting European male. Indulging his own fantasies, Payne also does not analyze how the paying white audience affected the ritualization. Finally, Payne incorrectly concluded that he was witnessing the last performance of the Green Corn Ceremony in Alabama. While his conclusion reflected the grim realities of that moment in Muskogee history—almost all Muskogees were stripped of their land and forced to relocate westwards to Oklahoma within a few years—Payne could not anticipate or imagine their resurgence in Alabama. About one hundred and fifty years later, the Poarch Band of Creek Indians became the only federally recognized tribe in Alabama. They have strengthened their ties to their cousins in Oklahoma and talked of restoring the Green Corn Ceremony to the land of its origins. The Muskogees, like the Busk, have not disappeared, but colonialism's days may be numbered.

The text given here is from John Howard Payne, "The Green-Corn Dance," *Continental Monthly* 1 (1862): [17-29].

Further Reading

Joel W. Martin, "Indians, Contact, and Colonialism In the Deep South: Themes for a Postcolonial History of American Religion," in *Retelling U.S. Religious History* edited by Thomas A. Tweed (Berkeley: University of California Press, 1997), pp. 149–180. Joel W. Martin, *Sacred Revolt: The Muskogees' Struggle for a New World* (Boston: Beacon, 1991); J. Leitch Wright, Jr., *Creeks and Seminoles: The Destruction and Regeneration of the Muscogulge People* (Lincoln: University of Nebraska Press, 1986); Peter Wood, Gregory A. Waselkov, and M. Thomas Hatley, eds., *Powhatan's Mantle:*

Indians in the Colonial Southeast (Lincoln: University of Nebraska Press, 1989); and Patricia Galloway, ed., *The Southeastern Ceremonial Complex: Artifacts and Analysis* (Lincoln: University of Nebraska Press, 1989).

The Green-Corn Dance

Macon, Georgia—1833

My Dear,

I have been among the Indians for a few days lately. Shall I tell you about them? You make no answer, and silence gives consent;—so I will tell you about the Indians.

The State of Alabama, you may remember, has been famous as the abode of the Creek Indians, always regarded as the most warlike of the southern tribes. If you will look over the map of Alabama, you will find, on the west side of it, nearly parallel with the State of Mississippi, two rivers,—one the Coosa and the other the Talapoosa,—which, descending, unite in the Alabama. Nearly opposite to these, about one hundred miles across, you will find another river,—the Chatahoochie, which also descends to form, with certain tributaries, the Apalachicola. It is within the space bounded by these rivers, and especially at the upper part of it, that the Creeks now retain a sort of sovereignty. [. . .]

The festival in question is called the Green-Corn Festival. All the nation assemble for its celebration at a place set apart for its celebration at a place set apart for the purpose, as the Temple at Jerusalem was for the religions assemblages of all the Jewish tribes. It has been kept by the Creeks, and many other Indian nations,—indeed, perhaps, by the entire race,—from time immemorial. It is prepared for, as well as fulfilled with, great form and solemnity.

When the green corn is ripe, the Creeks seem to begin their year. Until after the religious rites of the festival with which their New Year is ushered in, it is considered as an infamy to taste the corn. On the approach of the season, there is meeting of the chiefs of all the towns forming any particular clan. First an order is given out for the manufacture of certain articles of pottery to be employed in the ceremonies. A second meeting gives out a second order. New matting is to be prepared for the seats of the assembly. There is a third meeting. A vast number of sticks are broken into parts, and then put up in packages, each containing as many sticks as there are days intervening previous to the one appointed for the gathering of the clans. Runners are sent with these. One is flung aside every day by each receiver. Punctually, on the last day, all, with their respective families, are at the well-known rendezvous. [. . .]

The chosen spot is remote from any habitations, and consists of an ample square, with four large log houses, each one forming a side of the square, at every angle of which there is a broad opening into the area. The houses are of logs and clay, and a sort of wicker-work, with sharp-topped, sloping roofs, like those of our log houses, but more thoroughly finished. The part of the houses fronting the square is entirely open. Their interior consists of a broad platform from end to end, raised a little more than knee-high, and so curved and inclined as to form a most comfortable place for either sitting or lying. It is covered with the specially-prepared cane matting, which descends in front of it to the ground. A space is left open along the entire back of each house, to afford a free circulation of air. It starts from about the height of my chin, so that I could peep in from the outside through the whole of each structure, and obtain a clear view of all that was going on. Attached to every house towers a thick, notched mast. Behind the angle of one of the four broad entrances to the square, rises a high, cone-roofed building, circular and dark, with an entrance down an inclined plane, through a low door. Its interior was so obscured that I could not make out what it contained; but some one said it was a council-house. I occupied one corner of an outer square, next to the one I have already described, two sides of which outer square were formed by thick cornfields, a third by a raised embankment apparently for spectators, and a fourth by the back of one of the buildings before mentioned. In the center of this outer square was a very high circular mound. This, it seems, was formed from the earth accumulated yearly by removing the surface of the sacred square thither. At every Green-Corn Festival, the sacred square is strewn with soil yet untrodden; the soil of the year preceding being taken away, but preserved as explained. No stranger's foot is allowed to press the new earth of the sacred square until its consecration is complete. A gentleman told me that he and a friend chanced once to stroll along through the edge, just after the new soil had been laid. A friendly chief saw him and remonstrated, and seemed greatly incensed. He explained that it was done in ignorance. The chief was pacified, but nevertheless caused every spot which had been polluted by their unhallowed steps to be uptorn, and a fresh covering substituted.

The sacred square being ready, every fire in the towns under the jurisdiction of the head chief is, at the same moment, extinguished. Every house must also at that moment have been newly swept and washed. Enmities are forgotten. If a person under sentence for a crime can steal in unobserved and appear among the worshippers when their exercises begin, his crime is no more remembered. The first ceremonial is to light the new fire of the year. A square board is brought, with a small circular hollow in the center. It receives the dust of a forest tree, or of dry leaves. Five chiefs take turns to whirl the stick, until the friction produces a flame. From this sticks are lighted and conveyed to every house throughout the tribe. The original flame is taken to the center of the sacred square. Wood is heaped there, and a strong fire lighted. Over this fire the holy vessels of new-made pottery are placed. Drinking-gourds, with long handles, are set around on a bench. Appointed officers keep up an untiring surveillance over the whole, never moving from the spot; and here what they call the black drink is brewed, with many forms and with intense solemnity.

Now, then, having rendered you, by these numerous prefaces, much better informed about the Creek Jerusalem and its paraphernalia than I was when I got there, I will proceed with my travel story, just as if I had not enabled you to ponder all that I saw so much more understandingly than I myself did.

I cannot describe to you my feelings when I first found myself in the Indian country. We rode miles after miles in the native forest, seeing neither habitation nor an inhabitant to disturb the solitude and majesty of the wilderness. At length we met a native in his native land. He was galloping on horseback. His air was oriental;—he had a turban, a robe of fringed and gaudily-figured calico, scarlet leggings, and beaded belts and garters and pouch. We asked how far it was to the Square. He held up a finger; and we understood him to mean one mile. Next we met two Indian women on horseback, laden with watermelons. In answer to our question of the road, they half covered a finger to express that it was half a mile further . . . We passed groups of Indian horses tied in the shade, with cords long enough to let them graze freely. We then saw the American flag—a gift from the government—floating over one of the hut-tops in the square. We next passed numbers of visitors' horses and carriages, and servants, and under the heels of one horse a drunken vagabond Indian, or half-Indian, asleep. And, finally, we found ourselves at the corner of the sacred square, where the aborigines were in the midst of their devotions.

As soon as I left the carriage, seeing an elevation just outside of one of the open corners of the sacred square, whence a clear view could be obtained of what was going on within, I took my station there. I was afterwards told that this mound was composed of ashes which had been produced during many proceding years by such fires as were now blazing in the center; and that ashes of the sort are never permitted to be scattered, but must thus be gathered up, and carefully and religiously preserved.

Before the solemnities begin,—and, some one said, though I am not sure it was on good authority, ere new earth is placed,—the women dance in the sacred square, and entirely by themselves. I missed seeing this. They then separate from the men, and remain apart from them until after the fasting and other religious forms are gone through, when they have ceremonies of their own, of which I shall speak in due course.

As I gazed from my stand upon the corner mound, the sacred square presented a most striking scene. Upon each of the notched masts, of which I have already spoken as attached to each of the structures within, was a stack of tall canes, hung all over with feathers, black and white. There were rude paint-daubs about the posts and roof-beams of the open house-fronts, and here and there they were festooned with gourd vines. Chiefs were standing around the sides and corners, alone, and opposite to each other, their eyes riveted on the earth, and motionless as statues. Every building was filled with crowds of silent Indians,—those on the back rows seated in the Turkish fashion, but those in front with their feet to the ground. All were turbaned, all fantastically painted, all in dresses varying in ornament but alike in wildness. One chief wore a tall black hat, with a broad massive silver band around it, and a pea-cock's feather; another had a silver scull-cap, with a deep silver bullion fringe down to his eyebrows, and plates of silver from his breast to his knee, descending his tunic. Most of them had the eagle plume, which only those may wear who have slain a foe; numbers sported military plumes in various positions about their turbans; and one had a tremendous tuft of black feathers declining from the back of his head over his back; while another's head was all shaven smooth, excepting a tuft across the center from the back to the front, like the crest of a helmet.

I never saw an assembly more absorbed with what they regarded as the solemnities of the occasion.

The first sounds I heard were a strange low, deep wail,—a sound of many voices drawn out in perfect unison, and only dying away with the breath itself, which indeed was longer sustained than could be done by any singer I ever yet heard. This was followed by a second wail, in the same style, but shrill, like the sound of musical glasses, and giving a similar shiver to the nerves. And after a third wail in another key, the statue-like figures moved and formed two diagonal lines opposite to each other, their backs to opposite angles of the square. One by one, they then approached the huge bowls in which the black drink was boiling, and, in rotation, dipped a gourd, and took, with a most rev-erential expression, a long, deep draught each. The next part of the ceremony with them was somewhat curious; but the rapt expression of the worshippers took away the effect which such an evolution would be apt to produce on a fastidious stomach if connected with an uninterested head. In short, these dig-nitaries, without moving a muscle of the face, or a joint of the body, after a few seconds, and with great solemnity, ejected what had been swallowed upon the ground. It seemed as if given forth in the spirit of a libation among the ancients. The chiefs having afterwards tasted, each replacing the gourd, and returning to his stand before the next came forward, they all went to their seats, and two old men approached and handed round gourds full to the other parties present who had remained stationary. The looks on each side were as full of solemn awe as I have ever seen at any Christian ceremony; and certainly the awe was more universal than usually pervades our churches.

This done, a chief made a speech, but without rising. It was listened to with profound attention, and in one place, at a pause, called forth a very unanimous and emphatic shout of approbation,—a long sound, seemingly of two sylla-bles, but uttered by all in the same breath. I asked a professed *linkister* [inter-preter] what the speech was about; but he was either indifferent or ignorant, for he only replied that it was an appeal to them not to forsake their ancient ceremonies, but to remain faithful in their fulfillment to the last, and that it wound up with a sort of explanatory dissertation upon the forms which were to follow.

One chief then walked round, and, in short, abrupt sentences, seemed to give directions; whereupon some whitened, entire gourds, with long handles, and apparently filled with pebbles, were produced; and men took their stations with them on mats, while those who had been seated all arose, and formed in circles around the fire, led by a chief, and always beginning their movement towards the left. The gourds were shaken;—there arose a sort of low sustained chant as the procession went on; and it was musical enough, but every few seconds, at regular intervals, a sound was thrown in by all the dancers, in chorus, like the sharp, quick, shrill yelp of a dog. The dance seemed to bear reference to the fires in the center. Every time they came to a particular part of the square, first the head chief turned and uplifted his hands over the flame, as if invoking a benediction, and all the people followed his example in rotation. The dance was very unlike anything I ever saw before. The dancers never crossed their feet, but first gave two raps each with the hell and toe of one foot, then of the other, making a step forward as each foot was tapped on the earth; their bodies all the while stately and erect, and each, with a feather fan,—their universal and indispensable companion,—fanning himself, and keeping time with his fan as he went on. The dance was quickened, at a signal, till it became nearly a measured run, and the cries of the dancers were varied to suit the motion, when, suddenly, all together uttered a long, shrill whoop, and stopped short, some few remaining as guards about the sacred square, but most of the throng forthwith rushing down a steep, narrow ravine, canopied with foliage, to the river, into which they plunged; and the stream was black on every side with their heads as they swam about, playing all sorts of antics; the younger ones diving to fetch up pieces of silver money which the visitors flung into the water, to put their dexterity to the test.

Returning to the sacred square, they went through other dances around the fire, varying in figure and accompaniment. All were generally led by some aged chief, who uttered a low, broken sound, to which the others responded in chorus. Sometimes the leader, as he went around, would ejaculate a feeble, tremulous exclamation, like alleluliah, alleluliah, laying the stress upon the last syllable, to which all would respond in perfect accord and with a deep, sonorous bass, 'alleluliah,' and the same alternation continued to the close, which was invariably sudden, and after a long general whoop.

Each dance seemed to have a special form and significance;—one in particular, where the dancers unstaked the tall canes with feathers suspended from them, each taking one from the mast sustaining it; and this one, I was told meant to immortalize triumphs won at ball-plays. The feathered canes are seized as markers of points gained by the bearers in the ball-play, which is the main trial of strength and skill among rival clans of the same tribe, in friendship, and even between tribe and tribe, when in harmony. The effect of these canes and feathers, as they glanced around, with an exulting chorus, was very inspiring, and the celebrants became almost wild with their delight as it drew near its climax, ending their closing whoop with a general laugh of triumphant recollection.

Other dances were represented as alluding to conquests over bears and panthers, and even the buffalo, which last memorial is remarkable enough, having among them survived all traces of the buffalo itself. But expecting these vague hints, I could not find any bystander capable of giving me a further explanation of any point on which I inquired, than that it was 'an old custom;' or, if they wished to be more explicit, with a self-satisfied air, they would gravely remark that it was 'the green-corn dance,'—which I knew as well as they. Could I have been instructed even in their phrases and speeches, I might have made valuable conjectures. But even their language, on these occasions, seems, by their own admission, beyond the learning of the 'linkisters.' It is a poetical, mystical idiom, varying essentially from that of trading and of familiar intercommunication, and utterly incomprehensible to the literal minds of mere trafficking explainers. Even were it otherwise, the persons hovering upon the frontier most ingenuously own, when pressed for interpretations of Indian customs, that they care nothing for the Indians excepting to get their lands, and that they really consider all study concerning them as egregious folly, save only that of finding out how much cotton their grounds will yield, and in what way the greatest speculations can be accomplished with the smallest capital.

The last of the ceremonies of the day consisted of a sort of trial of fortitude upon the young.

Old chiefs were seated at the back of the council-house, and of the four houses of the square. They had sharp instruments,—sail-needles, awls and flints. Children of from four to twelve, and youths, and young men, presented their limbs and the instrument was plunged into the thighs and the calves of the legs, and drawn down in long, straight lines. As the blood streamed, the wounded would scoop it up with bark or sticks, and dash it against the back of the building; and all the building thus became clotted with gore. The glory of the exercise seemed to be to submit without flinching, without even consciousness. The youngest children would sometimes show the most extraordinary self-control. All offered themselves to the experiment voluntarily. If a shudder were detected, the old chiefs gashed deeper. But where they saw entire firmness, an involuntary glow of admiration would flit over their stony faces. [. . .]

I sat to look at the evening dances till very late. The blazing fire through the darkness gave a new aspect and still more striking wildness to the fantastic scene. Some ceremonies yet unattempted seemed to be going on over the drinks in the deep cauldrons; and the figures around them, with those of the dancers, reminded me of the witch scenes in Macbeth, as conceived by Shakspeare, not by the actors of them upon the stage. Four grim figures were stirring the cauldrons incessantly, with a sort of humming incantation, the others dancing around. In one of their dances they used a sort of small kettle-drum, with a guitar-like handle to it. But after a while, the evening dances seemed to vary from the devotional to the complimentary and to the diverting; but the daylight ones were altogether devotional. Apotheola led one of the less lofty order, and he is one of the most popular and respected of their chiefs. Its music seemed to consist of an exclamation from him of Yo, ho, ho! yo, ho, ho!—to which the response appeared as if complimentary, and to contain only the animated and measured repetition of Apotheola! Apotheola! Another dance, which excited most boisterous mirth, was led by a chief who is called by the borderers Peter the Gambler. He is a great humorist, and famous for his love of play,—famous even among the Indians, who are all gamblers. Once throwing dice with a chief, he staked himself against a negro slave, and won the negro. I never saw a party more diverted than were the looker-on at this dance. It was all monkey capers, but all with a meaning to the Indians beyond the perception of the whites. The Indian spectators made their remarks from their couches as the solemn mockeries proceeded, and the object of the remarks seemed to be to provoke the dancers to laugh by making fun, and the object of the dancers to provoke the fun-makers to laugh by performing extravagant caricatures with imperturbable gravity. [. . .]

I have not mentioned, I believe, that no one is allowed in the sacred square who tastes food during the devotional part of the ceremonies; but to get drunk on this occasion is a specially great offence. It is also considered as a desecration for an Indian to allow himself to be touched by even the dress of a white man, until the ceremony of purification is complete. There was a finely, though slightly, built Indian,—more French than Tartar in his look and manner.— a *linkister*, too,—the whites called him Charley,—and Charley had got very drunk. He was, of course, compelled to keep among the crowd outside. During the evening dance, a chief censured those who stayed from the ceremony, and those who dishonored it by appearing in this unworthy state. Charley was by that time very drunk indeed, but very good humored. He came nearly naked to listen. He heard the lecture and, as he reeled around, pretending to cover his face for shame, it was amusing to see his tricks to evade tumbling against any of the bystanders, lifting his hands with an air of dandified disdain as he staggered to one side, and repeating the mock contemptuousness when rolling towards the same peril on the other. Next morning I heard members of the natives, sitting all along the outside of the sacred square, laughing very loud, and very good-naturedly quizzing poor Charley, who had slept off somewhat of his exhilaration, but none of his good humor. Charley laughed, too, and looked foolish and laughed again.

So, to go back and resume my story. [. . .]

I found them preparing for the ceremonies which close the fast. Many were standing about, and all intent on the preparations for the morning forms. They went through the taking of the black drink, repeating all they had done the day previous. But on this occasion I more particularly observed two circular plates of brass and steel, which appeared the remains of very antique shields. They were borne with great reverence by two chiefs. The natives do not pretend to explain whence they came. They keep them apart, as something sacred. They are only produced on great occasions. I was told, too, that ears of green corn were brought in at a part of the ceremony to-day, which I missed, and that they were presented to a chief. He took them, and, after an invocation that the corn might continue plentiful among them the year through, handed them back.

This seemed the termination of the peace-offering, and the religious part of the affair was now to wind up with emblems of war. These were expressed in what they call a Gun-Dance. When the dispositions were making for it, some persons in carriages were desired by a white *linkister* to fall back and to remove their horses to a distance. Some ladies, especially, were warned. "Keep out of their way, ma'am," said the *linkister* to a lady, "for when they come racing about here with their guns, they gits powerful scary." I saw them dressing for the ceremony, if it may be called dressing to throw off nearly every part of a scanty covering. But the Indians are especially devoted to dress, in their way. Some of them went aside to vary their costume with nearly every dance.

Now appeared a procession of some forty or fifty women. They entered the square, and took their seats together in one of the open houses. Two men sat in front of them, holding gourds filled with pebbles. The gourds were shaken so as to keep time, and the women began a long chant, with which, at regular intervals, was given a sharp, short whoop from male voices. The women's song was said to be intended for the wail of mothers, wives, and daughters at the departure of the warriors for the fight; the response conveyed the resolution of the warriors not to be withheld, but to fight and conquer. And now were seen two hideous-looking old warriors, with tomahawks and scalping-knives, painted most ferociously. Each went half round the circle, exchanged exclamations, kept up a sort of growl all the while, and at length stopped with a war-whoop.

At this juncture, we were told to hurry to the outer square. The females and their male leaders left their places inside, and went to the mound in the centre of the outer square. The mound became entirely covered with their forms, and the effect was very imposing. Here they resumed their chant. The spectators mounted on the embankment. I got on a pile of wood,—holy wood, I believe, and heaped there to keep up the sacred fires. There were numbers of Indian women in the crowd. Four stuffed figures were placed, one in each of the four corners of the square.

We now heard firing and whooping on all sides. At length in the high corn on one side we saw crouching savages, some with guns of every sort, some, especially the boys, with corn-stalks to represent guns. A naked chief with a long sabre, the blade painted blood color, came before them, flourishing his weapon and haranguing vehemently. In another corn-field appeared another party. The two savages already mentioned as having given the war dance in the sacred square, now hove in sight on the third side, cowering. . . . Both these warriors crept slyly towards the outer square. One darted upon one of the puppets, caught him from behind, and stole him off; another grasped another puppet by the waist, flung him in the air, tumbled on him as he fell, ripped him with his knife, tore off the scalp, and broke away in triumph. A third puppet was tomahawked, and a fourth shot. These were the emblems of the various forms of warfare.

After the first shot, the two parties whooped, and began to fire indiscriminately, and every shot was answered by a whoop. One shot his arrow into the square, but falling short of the enemy, he covered himself with corn and crept thither to regain the arrow, and bore it back in safety, honored with a triumphant yell as he returned. After much of this bush skirmishing, both parties burst into the square. There was unremitted firing and war-whooping, the music of chanting and of the pebbled gourd going all the while. At length the fighters joined in procession, dancing a triumphal dance around the mound, plunging thence headlong into the sacred square and all around it, and then scampering around the outside, and pouring back to the battle square; and the closing whoop being given, the entire multitude from the battle square rushed, helter-skelter, yelping, some firing as they went, and others pelting down the spectators from their high places with the cornstalks that had served for guns, and which gave blows so powerful that those who laughed at them as weapons before, rubbed their shoulders and walked away ashamed.

We resumed our conveyances homeward, and heard the splashing and shouting, as we departed, of the warriors in the water.

Leave was now given to taste the corn, and all ate their fill, and, I suppose, did not much refrain from drinking; for I heard that every pathway and field around was in the morning strewed with sleeping Indians.

We passed the day following in visits to the picturesque scenery of the neighborhood. We saw the fine falls of the Talapoosa, where the broken river tumbles over wild and fantastic precipices, varying from forty to eighty or a hundred feet in hight; and when wandering among the slippery rocks, we passed an old Indian with his wife and child and bow and arrows. They had been shooting fishes in the stream, from a point against which the fishes were brought to them by the current. The scenery and the natives would have formed a fine picture. An artist of the neighborhood made me a present of a view of these falls, which I will show you when we meet.

The next part of the festival among the red folks—and which I did not see, being that day on my 'tour in search of the picturesque'—consisted, I was told, in the display of wives urging out their husbands to hunt deer. When, from our travels among fine scenery, we went down to the sacred square, towards night, we met Indians with deer slung over their horses. The skin of the first that is shot is presented to a priest, who flings it back to the slayer to be retained by him as a trophy, and at the same time asks from the Great Spirit that this may prove only harbinger of deer in abundance whenever wanted. There was some slight dancing that evening in the sacred square, but not of significance enough to make it an object with me to remain for it, and as so many were reserving themselves for the winding-up assembly of the ladies, on Sunday morning, I thought I would do the same. Some of our party stayed, however, for the night. . . .

The assemblage of the females I was rather solicitous to see, and so I was at my post betimes. I had long to wait. I heard the gathering cry from the men on all sides, in the corn-fields and bushes; it was like the neighing to each other of wild horses. After a while the ladies began to arrive. The spectators crowded in.

The Indian men went to their places, and among them a party to sing while the women danced, two of the men rattling the gourds. The cauldrons had disappeared from the centre of the sacred square.

And now entered a long train of females, all dressed in long gowns, like our ladies, but all with gay colors, and bright shawls of various hues, and beads innumerable upon their necks, and tortoise-shell combs in their hair, and ears bored all around the rim, from top to bottom, and from every bore a massive ear-drop, very long, and generally of silver. A selected number of the dancers wore under their robes, and girded upon their calves, large squares of thick leather, covered all over with terrapin-shells closed together and perforated and filled with pebbles, which rattled like so many sleigh-bells. These they have the knack of keeping silent until their accompaniment is required for the music of the dance. The dresses of all the women were so long as nearly to conceal the feet, but I saw that some had neither shoes nor stockings on, while others were sandalled. The shawls were principally worn like mantles. Broad ribbons, in great profusion and of every variety of hue, hung from the back of each head to the ground, and, as they moved, these, and the innumerable spar-kling beads of glass and coral and gold, gave the wearers an air of graceful and gorgeous, and, at the same time, unique wildness.

The procession entered slowly, and wound around the central fire, which still blazed gently there, although the cauldrons had been removed; and the train continued to stretch itself out, till it extended to three circles and a half. The shorter side then became stationary, and stood facing the men, who were seated in that building which contained the changers. This last rank of dancers seemed to include the principle wearers of the terrapin leg-bands, which they continued to rattle, keeping time with the chant, without shifting their posi-tion. At each end of their line was a leader, one an old woman and the other not young, both bearing a little notched stick, with two feathers floating from it. At a particular turn of the general figure of the dance, these two broke off from their fixed rank and made a circuit outside of all the rest, and more briskly, while the main body of the dancers, the three circles before mentioned, which had never ceased to move, still proceeded slowly round and round, only turning at a given signal to face the men, as the men had turned to face the emblem of the Deity, the central fire. Every eye among the women was planted on the ground. I never beheld such an air of universal modesty. It seemed a part of the old men's privilege to make comments aloud, in order to surprise the women into a laugh. These must often have been very droll, and always personal, I understand, and not always the most delicate. I saw a few instances among the young girls where they were obliged to smother a smile by putting up their handkerchiefs. But it was conquered on the instant. The young men said nothing; but the Indian men, whether old or young, seemed all to take as much interest in the show as we. The chief, Apotheola, had two daughters there. Both are very elegant girls, but the eldest delighted me exceedingly. She seemed about seventeen or eighteen. She is tall, a fine figure; her carriage graceful and *distinguished*, and quite European. She had a white muslin gown; a black scarf, wrought all over with flowers in brilliant colors; an embroidered white *collarette*, I believe you call it; gold chains, coral beads, gold and jeweled ear-rings,—single ones, not in the usual Indian superabundance,—her hair beautifully dressed in the Parisian style; a splendid tortoise-shell comb, gemmed; and from one large tuft of hair upon one temple to that upon the other there passed a beautiful gold ornament. Her sister's head-dress was nearly the same. The aforesaid elder Princess Apotheola, I am happy to say, looked only at me. Some one must have told her that I meant to run away with her, for I had said so before I saw her to many of her friends. There was a very frolicksome, quizzical expression in her eye; and now and then it seemed to say, 'No doubt you think all these things wonderfully droll. It diverts me to see you so puzzled by them.' But, excepting the look at me, which only proved her excellent taste, her eye dwelt on the ground, and nothing could have been more interestingly reserved than her whole deportment.

The dance over, all the ladies went from the square in the same order that they entered it.

In about an hour, the same dance was repeated. When it ended, signal was made for what they call The Dance of the Olden Time,—the breaking up of the ceremonial, when the men and women are again allowed to intermingle.

This was done in a quick movement around and around and around again, all the men yelping wildly and merrily, as struck their fancy, and generally in tones intended to set the women laughing, which they did, and heartily. The sounds most resembled the yelpings of delighted dogs. Finally came the concluding whoop, and all the parties separated.

Between these last two dances, I sent for a chief, and desired him to take charge of some slight gifts of tobacco and beads which I had brought for them. The chief took them. I saw the others cut the tobacco, and share it. Ere long my ambassador returned, saying, 'The chiefs are mighty glad, and count it from you as a very great friendship.' I had been too bashful about my present, and kept it back too long, through over-shyness. If I had sent it before, I might have seen the show to more advantage. As it was, I was immediately invited to sit inside the square, and witness the last dance from one of the places of honor.

But I was now obliged to depart, and to give up all hopes of ever again seeing my beautiful Princess Apotheola. My only chance of a guide through the wilderness would have been lost had I delayed. So I reluctantly mounted my pony; and I left the Indians of Tuckabatchio and their Green-Corn Festival, and their beautiful Princess Apotheola.

It was a great gratification to me to have seen this festival; with my own eyes to have witnessed the Indians in their own nation, with my own ears to have heard them in their own language. Nor was it any diminution of the interest of the spectacle to reflect that this ceremony, so precious to them, was now probably performing in the land of their forefathers for the last, last time. I never beheld more intense devotion; and the spirit of the forms was a right and a religious one. It was beginning the year with fasting, with humility, with purification, with prayer, with gratitude. It was burying animosities, while it was strengthening courage. It was pausing to give thanks to Heaven, before daring to partake its beneficence. It was strange to see this, too, in the midst of my own land; to travel, in the course of a regular journey in the New World, among the living evidences of one, it may be, older than what we call the Old World;—the religion, and the people, and the associations of the untraceable past, in the very heart of the most recent portion of the most recent people upon earth. And it was a melancholy reflection for ourselves, that comparing the majority of the white and red assemblage there, the barbarian should be so infinitely the more civilized and the more interesting of the two.

$$5$$

The Way of Holiness: The Friday Meeting

A. Gregory Schneider

The Friday meeting for the promotion of holiness at Philadelphia's Arch Street Methodist Episcopal Chapel was a ritual rooted deeply in the experience, practice, and publications of Phoebe Worall Palmer (1807–1874). Palmer was a best-selling author of eighteen books, some still in print today. She owned and edited one of the nation's most successful religious periodicals, *Guide to Holiness*. She was an internationally known evangelist and a prominent activist in humanitarian causes. She is also one of the more neglected figures in the historiography of religion in America. Palmer was a second-generation Methodist who grew up in an upper-middle-class family in New York City while the church of her youth was growing from a small and disreputable sect into the largest religious body in the nation. As Methodists vied for social eminence and cultural influence with the likes of the Presbyterians and Episcopalians, devout children of the church, including Phoebe Palmer, struggled with a dilemma: how to retain and renew the flame of Methodist revival piety in the face of new and pervasive temptations to worldliness. Methodism had always defined itself in opposition to "the world," but the new worldliness that challenged Palmer and her followers involved the confusions of the market, the divisions of social class, the constraints and demands of middle-class respectability, and, especially, the division of private domestic life from public business life.

In answer to these forces of fragmentation and constriction, Palmer formulated her famous "altar phraseology," a theological rhetoric that called the believer to lay all of herself—time, talents, family, possessions, hopes, fears, and so on—upon "the altar." The altar in Palmer's biblical exegesis was Jesus Christ, and "laying all upon the altar" was understood as an act of "entire consecration" to God. Palmer claimed that the altar "sanctified the gift," hence the believer should accept by faith the assurance that she was entirely sanctified once she had so committed herself. Religious experience would be felt only after the believer's choice to surrender herself totally to God.

Such emotional experiences did indeed come to Palmer and her many followers, and these emotions were understood to be tangible evidence of the believers' entire sanctification. Alternative names for the experience were "holiness," "perfect love," or the "second blessing." The blessing was understood to be a "definite" one, subsequent to conversion, and thus capable of being clearly and concretely testified to. Such testimony was not optional. Believers who did not testify to their attainment of holiness were liable to lose the blessing. Hence the practice of weekly meetings for the promotion of holiness. In these meetings, testimony about religious experience generated a community of feeling and encouraged and confirmed believers in their quest to become holy. The archetype of such meetings was Palmer's own "Tuesday Meeting for the Promotion of Holiness," which spawned hundreds of similar meetings across North America and as far away as India and New Zealand.

Just as the offering of one's whole being on the altar was a kind of ritual incantation to heal the divisions of the self, so the weekly meeting for the promotion of holiness was a ritual that bridged the strong, gendered division between public and private. American cities in the middle decades of the nineteenth century firmly divided social life between male-dominated public places and private domestic places occupied by women. Palmer's Tuesday Meeting, on the other hand, pointedly mixed the genders on an equal footing. It cultivated a community of feeling through the sharing of inner states of mind and heart, an intimacy usually reserved by convention for private life. At the same time, it moved its participants into the world to reform the world—a public function, or at least one with public implications. Palmer herself heavily participated in reform, missionary, and other benevolent work, including the founding of what may have been the first settlement house in the United States.

The spiritual ethos Palmer and her followers left behind was one of religious enthusiasm, the ethos of the old "shouting Methodist," who valued strenuous, even frenzied demonstrations of divine visitation upon believers' bodies and minds. It was also an ethos in which people readily gave themselves to charismatic authorities who became fathers and mothers to their spiritual children. In her best-known book, *The Way of Holiness,* Palmer used the example of her own religious quest to urge her fellow believers to heed one another's emotional demonstrations less and practice a more simple appropriation of biblical promises. She seemed to invest the Bible with the powers of spiritual direction that Methodists had been giving to their class leaders and pastors. Her more decorous religious practice and more abstract sense of religious authority matched well with the Methodist rise into middle-class social status, which both blessed and vexed her newly arrived generation. On the other hand, her reformulations of piety facilitated a continued sense of direct conscious encounter with God and a continued motivation to bring others into this experience of the divine. Thus Palmer's reordering of the self allowed her and her followers to feel that in arriving they had not left home.

In the document included here, a weekly newspaper column, "The Way of Holiness," reporting on a "Friday Meeting," the writer evokes self-conscious echoes of Palmer's ritual and theological innovations. So, too, does Miss Laura Boydon's testimony, a testimony that led to the emotional high point of the meeting. Boydon is so effective because her story so aptly reflects the altar formula pioneered by Palmer. "She presented herself a living sacrifice" is a kindred phrase to "laying all upon the altar" and means the same thing. The phrases "rested on the promises" and "then believed" refer to Palmer's insistence that believers not wait to feel the inner stirrings of God within them before they claim to have been sanctified. Rather, they should exercise simple or "naked" faith in the "naked" word of God given in the Bible. The Bible says it is God's will to sanctify His people wholly and that He will do it. A Bible-loving Christian, therefore, dares not disbelieve the word of God. Only after the deliberately willed act of belief is Boydon blessed with the inner feeling of power and cleansing that signifies entire sanctification. Worries over whether such experience is really on par with the emotional demonstrations of an earlier era are identified as temptations to doubt and are attributed to Satan. Satan's temptation is answered definitively with yet another appeal to scripture, an allusion to 1 John 1:7, which declares that the blood of Jesus Christ cleanses all from sin.

Boydon's experience and the fervent group response it elicited would seem to be evidence of how Phoebe Palmer's altar formula allowed believers to be confident in their religious experience without having to produce an emotional and bodily performance that no longer felt right, or even possible, for many. Similar concerns over the role of feeling are evident in the remarks of Brother Thompson and the sister whose remarks follow his. The reader should also note that throughout the report, especially in the poetry of the hymns that are sung, there are the claims and yearnings for cleansing, perfect love, and salvation from all sin. All these are part of the characteristic language of the nineteenth-century Protestant quest for holiness.

The meeting reported on here, however, took place some thirty years after Phoebe Palmer began leading the famous Tuesday Meeting, and its context is significantly different from that of the early meeting. By 1869 the holiness movement within the Methodist Episcopal Church had begun to develop separate institutions of its own. Just two years earlier, a group of rank-and-file preachers in the Methodist Episcopal Church had founded the National Camp-Meeting Association for the Promotion of Holiness and called John S. Inskip to serve as its president. This fact accounts for the special pleasure and attentiveness accorded Inskip when he showed up at this weekly meeting and shared both his report on the holiness work and his testimony. The National Camp-Meeting Association was formed with the idea that the promotion of holiness required an encampment designed for a national audience, rather than just the local and regional venues that were common at the time. In addition to the higher visibility such meetings would bring to the holiness movement, the founders aimed to improve the spiritual tone of camp meeting practice, feeling that many camps had lost their religious focus and become too much like sites for family vacations and carnival amusements. The organization that published the *Methodist Home Journal,* furthermore, would soon grow into the National Publishing Association for the Promotion of Holiness.

The Arch Street Methodist Episcopal Church, where this meeting took place, was a center of agitation for holiness as a test of true Methodist religion. The stage was being set, albeit unintentionally, for the many holiness schisms that occurred at the end of the century and that led to several new denominations, the largest of which became what is now known as the Church of the Nazarene. The National Camp-meeting Association eventually became the Christian Holiness Association, an umbrella organization that fostered cooperation among the many holiness denominations and various individual supporters within larger communities such as the United Methodist Church.

"The Way of Holiness" was a regular column in the weekly periodical *Methodist Home Journal,* which was published in Philadelphia beginning in 1867. "The Friday Meeting" was regularly reported in that column along with meetings in other cities. This report of the November 19, 1869, Friday meeting appeared in the November 27 issue, p. 382.

Further Reading

Melvin E. Dieter, *The Holiness Revival of the Nineteenth Century,* 2nd ed. (Lanham, Md.: Scarecrow, 1996); George Hughes, *Fragrant Memories of the Tuesday Meeting and the Guide to Holiness and Their Fifty Years' Work for Jesus* (New York: Palmer and Hughes, 1886); Timothy L. Smith, *Revivalism and Social Reform: American Protestantism on the Eve of the Civil War* (Nashville, Tenn.: Abingdon Press, 1957).

The Way of Holiness

It was an agreeable surprise to the congregation assembled at Arch Street M. E. Chapel, on Friday 19th inst, when at three o'clock, p.m. Rev J. S. Inskip, accompanied by Bro. Thompson, entered and took his place on the platform. He had been spending Thanksgiving day at Frankford, and tarried to visit the meeting.

The opening services devolved upon him, which consisted of reading the fifteenth chapter of the gospel by St. John, singing the hymn;

"O for a heart to praise my God, &c." and prayer. At his request, when the people knelt down, all joined in the supplicatory stanza:

"Refining fire go through my heart." &c.

Mr. Inskip then referred to the spread of this work—Scriptural Holiness, that it was extending to all branches of the Church. Although there might be difference in phraseology, there was agreement with regard to the thing itself, and this is the great matter after all. In Baltimore the cause was advancing. Where, a few months since, there were but two meetings held for the promotion of holiness—one on Sabbath afternoon, and the other on Wednesday evening, and both but poorly attended—there were at present *thirteen,* and some of these were very largely attended, and quite powerful in their influence. He was surprised to see such a large gathering on the present occasion, and was highly gratified to be present.

He then related his own experience, saying that he entered into this blessed state of grace about five years since. While preaching the doctrine to others, the Spirit distinctly directed him to seek full salvation. He found it, and the Lord had kept him in its enjoyment ever since. He was saved through the blood of the Lamb. He felt that self had been dethroned. He was nothing; but, giving glory to Christ, his testimony was, that he was fully saved. He was very happy. If there was anything better in reserve, in that heaven to which he was bound, he would be glad to know it; but here he was as happy as he could be. (Glory to God!)

A brother, after the hymn had been sung which refers to "dark clouds" in the sky, said "Blessed be God, there are no dark clouds in *my* horizon, all is clear; for I feel that I am saved from all sin. Everything looks new, and radiant with the glory of God."

Brother Thompson, said his heart overflowed with gratitude. The Lord had brought him into a land of rest; not a state of inactivity, or freedom from toil; but entire freedom from all conflict between his soul and God.

He used to tell the people in preaching, of rest, but referred to heaven, as the place where it was found; but he, had found it here. He enjoyed great happiness although he did not pray much for it. He was careful mainly to abide in the will of God. In this state no duty is toilsome—all is rest. "O, I praise God for *rest!*"

Then was sung:

> "I have entered the valley of blessing so sweet,
>   And Jesus abides with me there;
> And his spirit and blood make my cleansing complete;
>   And his perfect love casteth out fear."

A sister, referring to Brother Thompson, said she was not in the habit of asking God to make her happy. It was enough to have God dwelling in the heart, and working "to will and to do of his own good pleasure." She sought this grace of sanctification because the living Word presented it as a duty. She could not incur the responsibility of those whom the Saviour said they neither enter themselves, nor allow others to go in.

Her mind had been brought into subjection to the written word, and God had honored her greatly in unfolding its precious meaning to her apprehension.

Here, a ragged looking brother, who from his *tout ensemble* we should have supposed, was a country farmer, arose and started the verse:

"Take my poor heart and let it be" &c. after the singing of which, he alluded to the different kind of vessels formed by the hand of the potter; some were chaste and beautiful for parlor ornaments &c. —but as for himself he was satisfied to be merely a *spittoon*. He had traveled from Western New York, and was bound for a place in Chester County Pa., where he expected to encounter the devil, and get some sinners converted. (We immediately formed the idea that this was Brother Purdy.) He told some incidents of the wonderful meeting he attended at Havre De Grace, last Winter, where the gospel triumphed through the means employed to awaken and save souls. His remarks were of thrilling interest.

A Brother followed saying:

At a camp meeting in one of the valleys of Maine, he frequently heard the sweet voice of a minister exhorting the people in their meetings—"keep your faith steady." He had been led from wandering, back to his Father's house. He found this doctrine of sanctification in the Bible, and rested not until he possessed it in his heart. He was resting in Jesus. Singing

"O how I love Jesus" &c.

A Sister thought that clouds and occasional dark hours were necessary to us, to destroy all confidence in self and lead us to lean entirely on God, she could truly say: "Forever here, my rest shall be: &c." As the shades of evening began to steal over the scene, Miss Laura Boydon, of New York, who has been efficiently laboring for the Master, at Hestonville, Frankford, and Central Church, gave in her peculiarly impressive style of voice and manner, an account circumstantially of her conversion, and entire consecration. She received this grace two weeks after God had first spoken peace to her soul. She sought it for seven days, pleading on her knees, reading the Bible and otherwise intent on the evidence of her purity. Her interest in this question became so absorbing and intense that it amounted to agony. She determined to prevail, rested on the promises, presented herself a living sacrifice, then believed, and the power came down, with light as clear as the noonday sun, that she was cleansed from all sin. Satan came with a temptation in this form: "When you were converted, you were very joyful and shouted aloud the praise of God; now you are professing to have entered the higher life; but you are not making as much noise as when you were converted." To this she replied, "Whether I shout or no, Mr. Satan, I know the blood of Jesus cleanseth." She said, in all subsequent trials she found safety in holding on to Christ, and through his Name she hoped to "overcome." The emotion of the audience, at this point broke forth in various exclamations which however, speedily took form in singing

"Glory to the Lamb!" Two verses were sung, and now, while the room was almost dark all bowed again, and sung on, repeating:

"my sins are washed away,
In the blood of the Lamb.
The world is overcome,
Through the blood of the Lamb.

Glory to the Lamb!" A verse implying consecration was next sung, after which, Mr. Inskip directing the exercises, the congregation united in the strain

"'Tis done, the great transaction's done;

I am my Lord's and he is mine." Closing with the doxology, which, in the fervor of the occasion was several times repeated. This was an extraordinary meeting.

6

Reception of Novices into the Order
of the Sisters of St. Benedict

Patricia O'Connell Killen

Commonly called the clothing ritual, the reception of novices into the Sisters of St. Benedict is a very old rite of passage in the history of Roman Catholic women religious. Women formed themselves into Benedictine monastic communities as early as the sixth century. Today's Benedictine communities continue the oldest form of vowed, cenobitic (communal) religious life for women in the history of Christianity.

Benedictine women arrived in the United States from various European locations beginning in the early nineteenth century. Some followed immigrants from the towns and villages in Europe where their monasteries were located. Others arrived in the United States at the request of Roman Catholic bishops to help provide education, health care, and other services to the stream of Catholic immigrants who spread across the continent during the nineteenth century. Save for cloistered Benedictine communities, most Benedictine women in the nineteenth century moved away from their monastic roots into a more apostolic or active life. In the twentieth century, beginning with the early initiatives of the liturgical renewal and accelerated by the instruction of Vatican Council II (1962–65) to religious communities to rediscover their charisms (original inspiration and purpose), Benedictine women have moved back to organizing their lives around monastic life, choosing ministries that are congruent with a life rooted in participation in the Divine Office, the constant prayer of the church.

Reception of novices is a rite of passage. Rites of passage mark and effect a person's transformation from one state of life or being to another. The rite exists within the larger context of vowed religious life in the history of Christianity and the tradition of Benedictine monasticism. During the first three Christian centuries, no formal rules existed that governed public expression of entering a religious community. There is evidence of persons who were particularly dedicated to God—widows, deacons, elders, and virgins—but the exact structure and form of their dedication and lives is not fully known. Sometimes individuals would make private or public vows of poverty, chastity, and obedience. At other times they would simply behave in ways that the larger Christian community recognized as those of persons specially dedicated, and their behavior was accepted as tacit profession—proclamation (though not necessarily verbal) of commitment to this state of life.

Monasticism emerged in Christianity during the second and third centuries and developed more fully in the fourth through the sixth centuries. When Christianity became the preferred, and later the official and majority, religion of the Roman Empire, the persecution of Christians ended. Without the danger of being killed for their witness to Jesus the Christ, the social costs of being a Christian disappeared and membership in the Church became a social asset. This changed state of affairs disturbed some Christians who became concerned about the quality and depth of commitment on the part of those joining the Church.

Monasticism counterbalanced the expansion of the Church and the perceived dilution of baptismal fervor. Many Christians saw monastic life as a spiritual martyrdom that substituted for the physical martyrdom of early Christianity. By the mid-fourth century, this understanding of monastic life was widely accepted. The spiritual martyrdom of monasticism also was interpreted as a second baptism, and so entering a monastic community carried the same power of sanctifying grace as baptism. This meant that on the day of formal acceptance in the religious community or "profession," the Christian woman's soul was cleansed from sin, just as it had been at baptism.

Some early Christian thinkers, such as Pseudo-Dionysius, considered religious profession a sacrament and put it in the category of baptism and eucharist. St. Thomas Aquinas did not consider it a sacrament but saw it as having the power of satisfying for sins; in other words, the power to make up for the punishment justly due for sins even after they had been forgiven by God. However it was explained, most Christian thinkers viewed monastic life as intensifying God's presence in space and time. Life in a monastic community should prefigure the perfect community of love that would occur when God reigned at the end of time. Christians lived out the baptismal calling to discipleship in monastic life. By the end of the medieval period, monasticism was universally accepted as a superior form of Christian life. Martin Luther and the other Protestant Reformers rejected this position.

With the development of the Rule of St. Benedict (480–543), the clothing worn by the monastic became a sign of the ascetic, sacramental, and penitential life of monasticism. Putting on the habit signified renunciation of the world and rebirth into new life with Christ. The renunciation dimension of donning the habit was accented as Christianity became increasingly world-denying.

The symbolic significance of the habit developed for the next seven hundred years as the elaborate institutional and sacramental structures of Christianity were molded. By 1100, rituals for reception of novices involved the blessing of the habit. Reception rituals became increasingly and distinctively ritualized, drawing especially on the imagery of death to the world and rebirth via baptism.

Putting on the habit each day of a monastic's life required special prayers and constituted a renewal of the dying to self and the putting on of Christ that was enacted most powerfully at a nun's profession. "Putting on the habit" referred to dressing in each item of clothing, including wimple, veil, scapular, belt, and crucifix. For example, the nun would kiss the crucifix (cross with an image of the body of the crucified Jesus on it) that she had received as part of her profession, and hang it around her neck. She would pray while putting on her wimple and veil, also symbols of her union with Christ and death to self. Dressing in the habit each morning renewed the death to self and her putting on of Christ that was the entire purpose of monastic life. Putting on the habit located a sister again in her role as disciple of Jesus and as a sacramental person. The habit also reminded the sister of her nature as an ascetic, one willing to discipline all desires of the flesh separating her from God.

As the impulse toward rejecting the material world eclipsed impulses toward a creative new Christian life rooted in the resurrection of Jesus, religious life came to be identified with this rejection. As a consequence, by the late Middle Ages the habit of monks and nuns signified rejection of the body and sexuality. For women this meant covering their female identity. Women's habits hid any hint of the female body, particularly hair and physical form.

Benedictine women in the United States used the rite featured in the following excerpt beginning in 1875. The women who participated in the clothing ritual, their monastic sisters, and their families viewed monasticism, part of the Roman Catholicism of this time, as a "higher" form of Christian life than marriage and family. Some of the women who took on this calling removed themselves entirely from "the world" and spent their lives in secluded prayer. Other Benedictines engaged in education, health care, and other activities that aided the quickly growing immigrant Catholic community. Catholics viewed a woman's embrace of this higher calling as a serious commitment, and so the institutional church regulated the entire process of entering monastic life. The clothing ceremony reprinted here conveys the understanding of religious life as a higher state.

The bishop's elaborate role in the ritual exemplifies the extent and significance of the church's control over religious life. Church control over monastic life should not be understood as simple and straightforward. Precisely because monastic life constituted a special life in Christ, the women who participated in it experienced—and periodically even claimed—a spiritual power equal, if not superior, to that of bishops. In short, their special status legitimated thought and action that subverted clerical control. From at least the twelfth century onward, the history of institutionalized religious life demonstrates the conflict for control over spiritual power. This conflict continued unabated into the nineteenth century in Europe and the United States. Frequently the conflict was expressed in language regarding the appropriate and legitimate forms of vowed religious life, especially the kind of vows religious initiates might make, their rule of life, and the extent of their activity in the world.

Women who entered Benedictine communities in the United States in 1875 would not have articulated the conflict noted above, even as their choice of monastic life rendered them participants in it. Women entered the Benedictines and other communities for many reasons. For some the choice flowed from an almost mystical experience, at Mass, during private prayer, or surrounding the death of a loved one. For many the decision came early in their lives, a small inner voice uttering the invitation. Many attributed their decision to the inspiration of a sister who taught them or whom they encountered in their parish. Some women were drawn to monastic life by their inclination to study and learning. Others were attracted by the idea of a community of friendship among women. Above all else, however, women who entered the convent described a desire to serve God.

The women who entered religious life, their families, and the larger Catholic community in the United States during the nineteenth century considered celibate, vowed religious life a higher or better choice on the path to God. The women took on the challenge of a life of intense spirituality. The larger community acknowledged them for it. These women, besides providing needed educational, nursing, and social services to the Catholic community, stood between the laity and an often harsh and demanding God. In the eyes of many Catholics these women lived perpetually in a liminal or transitional state between this world and the world after death.

Some women's families supported their choice to enter the monastery. Mothers and fathers experienced having a daughter in religious life as a sign of status, an indication that one had done well as a Catholic parent. Giving a child to the Church meant something in the accounting of eternal salvation. More than one mother perceived her daughter to be fulfilling a vocation that she for some reason had not. Records from different religious communities show a regular pattern of two, three, or four biological sisters entering.

Not all families saw a daughter's choice for the convent positively, even as they acknowledged religious life as a higher state. God's choosing a dearly loved daughter could be a cruel blessing. Depending upon the religious community, the parents might never see their daughter again. In no women's communities during the late nineteenth century were family visitations frequent. For some parents the sense of real and potential loss was more pragmatic. A daughter's choice could mean the loss of an able-bodied worker, especially a woman who might care for her parents in old-age. Of course, it also meant the loss, potentially, of a son-in-law and grandchildren. Objections from family kept some women from following their call to enter the convent. Significant numbers of women, however, entered despite objections, often without telling their families. For many of these women the choice to follow their religious vocation severed family ties completely and irrevocably.

Most of the women who entered Benedictine communities in 1875 were first- or second-generation Americans, mainly from German or Irish ethnic communities. Most came from agrarian or blue-collar, working class settings. Others came from wealthier, more socially elite backgrounds. For all, however, religious life provided opportunities for meaningful work, the exercise of creativity and imagination, administrative positions where they could wield power and influence, freedom from the responsibilities of marriage and motherhood, and opportunities to live in communities of egalitarian friendship. Devoting their lives to God gave women who entered the convent expanded spheres of influence. Sisters could make decisions that other women enmeshed in family life never would have to consider.

The opportunities that religious life offered women should not be allowed to obscure the genuinely spiritual motivation underlying the choice women made to enter the convent. To become a sister meant dying to the world, accepting a life-long process of conforming oneself to the rule of the community, embracing self-sacrifice, hard work, and depending upon the community and its mission, poverty, and deprivation. For many, deeply felt spiritual experiences and motivations transformed these sacrifices into valued activities but they remained sacrifices nonetheless. Dying to the world, putting on Christ, was a life-long process, the full meaning of which a woman would know only after death. Often a religious woman's comfort lay in knowing that her community shared with her a desire for God that transcended all else.

A woman entering religious life in 1875 progressed through a process that involved postulancy, novitiate, temporary profession, and final profession. The postulancy period provided an introduction to a religious community. At the end of postulancy, successful candidates were received into the novitiate. The novitiate, a probationary period lasting at least a year and often two, involved a time of formation, study and evaluation by senior sisters. The Mistress of Postulants and the Mistress of Novices were fully professed sisters who oversaw the candidates under their care. Women who continued to desire religious life after postulancy and were accepted into the novitiate received a habit in the ceremony described below. As part of this ceremony a woman received a new name to signify her new identity. This would be the name of a saint or some dimension of the life of Jesus or Mary. The new name symbolized the renewal of identity or new baptism that monastic life was understood to be. Following the novitiate, a sister made simple vows (promises to live the monastic life for a set period) and usually received a different veil, generally black, to replace the white veil she had worn as a novice. At final profession a sister made her last, often solemn (perpetual, for life), vows, in a ritual that incorporated elements of the funeral service to signify fully her dying to the world. Toward the end of the ceremony the candidate making her final profession lay prostrate on the floor of the sanctuary and her sister nuns covered her with a funeral pall. At the final profession the sister also received a blessed ring as a sign of her commitment to Christ, the Church, and her specific community.

Over the course of her religious life, the habit symbolized for a woman the choice she had made to answer God's call. Putting on the habit each day constituted the re-enactment of the consecration of a sister's life that the clothing ceremony began. Members of one Benedictine community described what the habit meant to them. It symbolized the changes taking place within them, the operative presence of God; their consecration and dedication; their separation from the world; religious poverty and simplicity of life; being part of the community and the Benedictine Order; a link to community traditions; the unity of the community. It also was a form of sacrifice, of self-denial, an incentive to behave properly, a way to combat vanity, a way to combat individualism, and a form of public witness. The habit symbolized for these women the life-long transformation that was their lives in religion. Receiving the habit as novices transposed the women in time and space, linking them to Benedictines from the sixth century to their own time. The ritual situated the women diffferently in their world and they knew it. The ritual transformed their identity, and the women knew this as well, even if they did not fully comprehend it until they underwent the ritual and lived their entire lives in religion.

Immediate family members were allowed to attend the ritual for the reception of novices in Benedictine and other women's religious communities. On occasion, even those who objected to a daughter's vocation would do so. Sitting in the church, they watched their daughters process up the aisle, attired as brides in wedding gowns and veils. At the end of the ritual they watched their daughters process out, dressed in the habit of Benedictine sisters, with crucifix and white novice's veil. As with any ritual marking a rite of passage, the reception of novices evoked a range of reaction in those attending: joy, pride, sadness, grief, even anger. Even parents glad to give a daughter to God experienced some grief as the ritual confronted them with the definitive separation from family that a woman's choice of religious life entailed.

The Rule of St. Benedict, from which this ritual is taken, prescribes three scrutinies (examinations) held at regular intervals before final admission into the community. The questioning in the rite below is one scrutiny. Originally religious profession took place in the oratory (chapel for praying the Divine Office) of the monastery. By the seventh century, however, the ceremony often took place within the Mass, an indication of increasing hierarchical control over monastic life. In the rite below the Benediction of the Blessed Sacrament would be omitted, if the reception of novices were held as part of a Mass.

Monasticism continues today as a living form of religious life. Monastics embrace an entire way of life and understand the particular Benedictine vows—obedience to the rule, stability (commitment to their particular monastic community), and conversion of life (ongoing conversion and development of spirit)—as supports for this life. This distinguishes monastic vows from those of more active (apostolic) communities where vows of poverty, chastity, and obedience are understood as freeing a sister for her particular active ministry in the world.

The rite included here contains prayers and images that convey the understandings of monastic life as spiritual martyrdom, penance, baptism, and the monastic as a living sacrament. The rite addresses the dying to self, especially death to desires not oriented toward union with God, that constitutes spiritual martyrdom. The sacrifices of monastic life are presented as penance which involves sorrow for sin and the desire to amend one's life. Baptismal imagery in the rite conveys the new life in Christ that the nun enters. Finally, the rite conveys vividly how the monastic becomes to herself and to those around her a living sacrament, a person whose whole being is oriented toward being an intensification of divine presence and grace in the world. The "Veni Creator" (Come Creator) beseeches the Holy Spirit to enkindle the women. As the new novices put on their habits the Bishop intones Psalm 50, a penitential psalm.

This rite transformed a woman into a novice in 1875, in its contemporary form it does the same in 2001. The constituent elements of transformation in this 1875 ritual are receiving the blessed habit, the cutting of hair, dressing and publicly appearing in the habit, and receiving a new name for one's life in religion. These combine with the prayers and petitions of bishop, other clergy, candidates, monastic community, families, and the entire church to effect the transformation of a woman from postulant to novice. Through the physical enactments of the candidates, monastic community, and clergy, combined with the prayers of an entire community, the women set aside their old selves and are born new selves in Christ. This is how postulants are transformed into novices.

The text printed here is from *Reception of Novices, According to the Rite Used by the Sisters of Saint Benedict*. Adapted from the "Caeremoniale Monasticum" (First edition, 1875) of the American Cassinese Congregation of the Order of Saint Benedict, English translation (1938). The author acknowledges the assistance of Sr. Ruth Boedigheimer, O.S.B., St. Benedict's Monastery, St. Joseph, Minn.; Sr. Marie Louise Krenner, O.S.B., Mount St. Scholastica Convent, Atchison, Kansas; Sr. Lucy Wynkoop, O.S.B., Sr. Placidia Haehn, O.S.B., Sr. Rosemarie Terwey, O.S.B., St. Placid Priory, Lacey, Washington; Sr. Rosemary Rader, O.S.B., St. Paul Priory, St. Paul, Minn..

Further Reading

Joan Chittister, O.S.B., Stephanie Campbell, O.S.B., Mary Collins, O.S.B., Ernestine Johann, O.S.B., and Johnette Putnam, O.S.B., *Climb Along the Cutting Edge: An Analysis of Change in Religious Life* (New York: Paulist Press, 1977); Terence Kardong, *The Benedictines* (Wilmington, Del.: M. Glazier, 1988); Timothy Fry, O.S.B., ed., *The Rule of St. Benedict in English* (Collegeville, Minn.: Liturgical Press, 1982); Peter Brown, *The Body and Society: Men, Women and Sexual Renunciation in Early Christianity* (New York: Columbia University Press, 1988); Carol K. Coburn and Martha Smith, *Spirited Lives: How Nuns Shaped Catholic Culture and American Life, 1836–1920,* (Chapel Hill, N.C.: University of North Carolina Press, 1999).

Reception of Novices (1875)

OUTLINE OF CEREMONIES

I. PROCESSION TO CHURCH.
II. CEREMONY OF RECEPTION:

1. Questioning of Candidates.
2. Invocation of Holy Ghost.
3. Religious Tonsure and Blessing of Habits and Veils.
4. Conferring of Religious Dress.

5. Sermon.

6. Entrance of Newly Invested Novices.

III. BENEDICTION WITH BLESSED SACRAMENT.

IV. PROCESSION FROM CHURCH

I. PROCESSION TO CHURCH

The members of the reception class dressed in bridal attire, assemble with their Mistress in the Sisters' community room shortly before the time appointed for the ceremony.

At a given signal, the procession is formed in the adjoining corridor near the Bishop's room, and all proceed to the church in the following order: The Master of Ceremonies accompanied by two acolytes [ministers who assist the presider]—*Mother Prioress* [superior of the priory] *and Mistress of Postulants—the reception class in double (or single) file, the youngest first,—Sister Subprioress* [assistant superior] *and Mistress of Novices—the Clergy—the Bishop with the two boy pages and his Ministers in their proper rank. The four attending Sisters wear their choir cloaks.*

If the officiant is a Bishop, the "Ecce Sacerdos" is sung as a processional, and all present kneel and make the sign of the cross as the Bishop imparts his blessing in passing. The candidates and the four Sisters in attendance occupy the choir stalls reserved for them in the transept.

II. CEREMONY OF RECEPTION

1. Questioning of Candidates

After vesting [putting on special liturgical garb] *at the throne* [chair of honor reserved for a bishop], *the Bishop goes to the altar accompanied by the ministers, and having received the miter* [special head dress of a bishop signifying his authority] *and crozier* [a crooked staff carried by a bishop to signify pastoral authority and responsibility], *sits on the faldstool* [low stool with no back] *in the middle of the altar platform. The postulants rise promptly with the four attending Sisters, and enter the sanctuary* [portion of the church around the altar and separated from the rest of the church by an altar rail] *preceded by Mother Prioress and the Mistress of Postulants, and followed by the Sister Subprioress and the Mistress of Novices. The candidates arrange themselves in rows across the sanctuary, and, at a signal from the Master of Ceremonies, all genuflect* [lower themselves momentarily on their right knee as an acknowledgment of divine presence], *rise, bow, and kneel together. The Bishop questions the class as follows:*

Dearest daughters, despising the world with its deceits and vanities do you still desire to embrace the Rule of Saint Benedict?

The candidates reply in unison:

Most Reverend Father, I desire it most earnestly and ask for it most humbly.

Thereupon the Bishop answers:

Thanks be to God.

2. Invocation of Holy Ghost

The Bishop comes down to the foot of the altar, and after the miter has been removed and the staff given up, he kneels with his ministers and intones the "Veni Creator." All kneel and sing the entire hymn to the end, in alternate choirs, using the following monastic text:

> Come, Creator Spirit, visit the souls of thy children, and with heavenly grace fill the hearts which thou has created.
> Thou art called the Paraclete [Holy Spirit], the gift of God Most High, the living fountain, fire, love, and spiritual unction.
> Thou art sevenfold in thy gifts, the finger of the right hand of the Father; Thou art the spoken promise of the Father, endowing tongues with speech.
> Enkindle thy light within our minds, infuse thy love into our hearts; strengthen the weakness of our flesh by thy neverfailing power.
> Drive our enemy far away, and forthwith grant us peace; so that while thou leadest the way as our guide, we may avoid everything harmful.
> Grant that through thee we may know the Father, and through thee know the Son; and may we ever believe in thee, the Spirit of them both.

The following conclusion never varies:

Glory be to the Father, Lord; and to the Son, who arose from the dead, and to the Paraclete, for ever and ever. Amen.

    V. Send forth thy spirit and they shall be created.

    R. And thou shalt renew the face of the earth.

After this response, only the Bishop rises, and still facing the altar, recites or sings the following orations:

Let us pray

    Inflame, O Lord, our veins and our hearts with the fire of the Holy Spirit, that we may serve thee with a chaste body and please thee with a clean heart.

    May the Paraclete, who proceedeth from thee, O Lord, we beseech thee, enlighten our minds, and lead us unto all truth as thy Son hath promised. Through the same Christ our Lord.

    R. Amen.

3. Religious Tonsure and Blessing of Habits and Veils

Turning toward the candidates who remain kneeling, the Bishop continues with folded hands, and says while standing:

Let us pray

We beseech thee, O almighty God, pour out thy Holy Spirit upon these thy handmaids, who for love of Christ thy Son, are about to receive the religious tonsure [cutting of a portion of the candidate's hair on the crown of the head]; and may the same Holy Spirit always preserve them in holy religion, and keep their hearts far from every worldly occasion and desire, that, as they are now outwardly changed, so also may thy right hand grant them an inward growth in virtue, take away human blindness from their eyes, and grant them the light of eternal glory. Through the same Christ our Lord.

R. Amen.

The Bishop then turns toward the Epistle side of the altar, and blesses the religious habits, saying:

V. The Lord be with you.

R. And with thy spirit.

Let us pray

O Lord God, the Author of all goodness, and the bountiful Dispenser of all blessings, we humbly beseech thee, that thou wouldst deign to bless and sanctify these garments [the bishop makes the sign of the cross over the habits], with which thy handmaids desire to be clothed as a sign of their religious profession; so that, being thus specially consecrated to thee, they may be recognized as women dedicated to thy service. Through Christ our Lord.

R. Amen.

Having sprinkled the habits with holy water, the Bishop blesses the white veils, saying:

Let us pray

We humbly beseech thee, O Lord, may thy merciful blessing [the bishop makes the sign of the cross over the veils] descend upon these veils which are about to be placed upon the heads of thy handmaids; and may these veils be blessed, consecrated, spotless, and holy. Through Christ our Lord.

R. Amen.

Having sprinkled the veils with holy water, the Bishop returns to the faldstool, and wearing the miter, bestows the religious tonsure on each candidate. This is a deeply significant religious observance which has been preserved throughout the centuries as a special ceremony of admission, or initiation, into the order of Saint Benedict. It is administered by the Bishop, and consists in the cutting of the hair in four places in the form of a cross.

When the Bishop is seated, each of the candidates comes up singly and kneels on the highest step of the altar platform, with the Mistress of Postulants standing at her left, and the Mother Prioress at her right. The former removes the bridal veil which she hands to the Mistress of Novices, and the latter holds the strands of hair which the Bishop clips off with a scissors, and deposits in a basket.

4. Conferring of Religious Dress

The Bishop receives the religious garb, neatly folded, from the Master of Ceremonies, and gives it to the candidate, saying at the same time:

May the Lord remove from you the old man with all his deeds, and clothe you with the new man who has been created according to God in justness and holiness of truth.

Having received the religious habit, the candidate rises, goes down from the altar, genuflects with the candidate who is to succeed the one already kneeling before the Bishop, and retires to the lower sacristy [preparation or vesting room located to one side of the sanctuary] *on the Gospel side. Here she is met by several Sisters who complete the cutting of the hair, and help her to exchange her secular dress for the religious garb. When the last candidate has received the religious tonsure and the holy habit, the four Sisters in attendance genuflect together, and go to the lower sacristy. After each candidate has been invested, she kneels at the side of the Mother Prioress, and receives from her a crucifix, and the name by which she is henceforth to be known in religion.*

During the vesting of the candidates, the Bishop comes down to the foot of the altar, and after the miter has been removed, he intones Psalm 50, which he recites in alternate verses with his ministers as follows:

[Bishop:] Have mercy on me, O God: [Attending priests:]* according to thy great mercy.

And according to the multitude of thy tender mercies * blot out my iniquity.

Wash me yet more from my iniquity, * and cleanse me from my sin.

For I know my iniquity, * and my sin is always before me.

To thee only have I sinned, and have done evil before thee, * that thou mayest be justified in thy words, and mayest overcome when thou art judged.

For behold I was conceived in iniquities: * and in sins did my mother conceive me.

For behold thou hast loved truth: * the uncertain and hidden things of thy wisdom thou hast made manifest in me.

Thou shalt sprinkle me with hyssop, and I shall be cleansed, * thou shalt wash me, and I shall be made whiter than snow.

To my hearing thou shalt give joy and gladness: * and the bones that have been humbled shall rejoice.

Turn away thy face from my sin: * and blot out all my iniquities.

Create a clean heart in me, O God: * and renew a right spirit within me.

Cast me not from thy face: * and take not thy Holy Spirit from me.

Restore unto me the joy of thy salvation: * and strengthen me with a perfect spirit.

I will teach the unjust thy ways: * and the wicked shall be converted to thee.

Deliver me from blood, O God, thou God of my salvation: * and my tongue shall extol thy justice.

O Lord, thou wilt open my lips: * and my mouth shall declare thy praise.

For if thou hadst desired sacrifice, I would indeed have given it: * with burnt-offerings thou wilt not be delighted.

A sacrifice to God is an afflicted spirit: * a contrite and humble heart, O God, thou wilt not despise.

Deal favorably, O Lord, in thy good will with Sion: * that the walls of Jerusalem may be built up.

Then shalt thou accept the sacrifice of justice, oblation and whole-burnt offerings: * then shall they lay calves upon thy altar.

Glory be to the Father, etc.

As it was in the beginning, etc.

5. Sermon

The recitation of the psalm is followed by a sermon; if this is preached by the offici-ating Bishop, he goes to the middle of the sanctuary with his miter and crozier, and is accompanied by the assisting ministers. After the sermon the Bishop returns to the altar and sits on the faldstool as before.

6. Entrance of Newly Invested Novices

The reception class returns to the sanctuary from the sacristy immediately after the sermon. The new novices enter in single file, preceded by the Mother Prioress and the Mistress of Postulants, and followed by the other two Sisters in attendance. Having arranged themselves in rows across the sanctuary, they genuflect together at a sign from the Master of Ceremonies, bow and kneel. The bishop, facing the Sis-ters, and without the miter, says, while standing with hands folded:

Let us pray

Raise up, O Lord, in thy Church, the Spirit wherewith our Holy Father Bene-dict, Abbot, was animated, that, filled with the same holy Spirit, we may strive to love what he loved, and to practice what he taught. Through Christ our Lord.

R. Amen.

After the conclusion of this prayer, he sprinkles the novices with holy water [water that has been blessed], sits on the faldstool and receives the miter. Beginning with the senior in rank each novice with her partner approaches the Bishop for the kissing of the ring [sign of respect and submission to the bishop as the ecclesiastical authority] in the following manner. Four novices having genuflected together, the inner two go up and kneel before the Bishop who says to each as she kisses the ring:

May God strengthen you in your holy resolution.

As soon as they have kissed the Bishop's ring, they rise promptly, separate to give place to the two who follow after them, descend the steps, and stand in line with the two who are to follow next. After the four have genuflected, the inner two

*ascend the steps as described above, whilst the outer two return to their places in
the transept* [extended north and south side of the area between the nave, the
part of the church for laity, and the choir, the space between the sanctuary and
the nave] *through the side gates at the opposite ends of the communion railing.
The remaining novices follow in the order described, until all have returned to their
appointed places in choir.*

*When the last of the group is leaving the sanctuary, the Sisters in attendance
genuflect, bow, and walking down the middle aisle, return to their places in the
transept.*

III. BENEDICTION WITH THE BLESSED SACRAMENT

*The ceremony of reception into the novitiate being ended, the Bishop officiates at
Benediction with the Blessed Sacrament.*

IV. PROCESSION FROM CHURCH

*Having unvested at the throne after Benediction, the Bishop walks out through the
church with his ministers, preceded by the acolytes and the clergy, and followed by
the reception class, and the four attending Sisters. All present kneel and make the
sign of the cross as the Bishop blesses them in passing.*

Singing: Songs of Devotion, Praise, and Protest

— 7 —

English Hymnody in Early America

Michael J. McClymond

The metrical psalms of the Pilgrims at Plymouth and the Puritans in Massachusetts Bay were not the first Christian songs to be sung in the Americas. In 1539 a printing press was established in Mexico City, and in 1556 it printed an edition of the *Ordinary of the Mass,* the first printed American book with music. The first Protestant music came in 1562–65 with the French Huguenots, immigrants to the coasts of South Carolina and Florida. They brought with them French metrical psalms and psalm tunes. It is said that the Native Americans who befriended these settlers learned these tunes and continued to sing them long after the Spanish drove the French from their settlements. English psalm tunes reached America through the visit of Sir Francis Drake to the coast of northern California in 1579 and through the Jamestown settlers, who arrived in Virginia in 1607. These settlers brought with them a version of the psalms set to the tunes in Estes's 1592 Psalter.

Yet despite these early episodes of hymn singing, it was colonial New England that played a predominant role in the shaping of a North American tradition of sacred music. At the time of the Protestant Reformation, John Calvin (unlike Luther) largely rejected the Catholic heritage of contrapuntal settings for choirs and the use of musical instruments in worship. Following Calvin's lead, the churches of colonial New England allowed only rhymed versions of the psalms to be sung in unison, without any instruments or choral music separate from the congregation's own singing. The churches of the Reformed tradition therefore were characterized by their liturgical use of metrical psalms. Harmonized or polyphonic psalm settings were intended for use at home and not in church services.

Among colonial New Englanders there was a preoccupation with finding an English translation of the psalms that was as literal as possible. The first complete English metrical Psalter, published in England in 1562 and typically known as "Sternhold and Hopkins" for its chief authors, did not closely enough preserve the original meanings of the psalms for the Pilgrims who were to land at Plymouth Rock. After fleeing England and while still residing in Holland, Henry Ainsworth, one of the Pilgrims' leaders, published in 1612 in Amsterdam an English translation of the Psalter. Despite its cumbersome literalism, Ainsworth's Psalter found use in worship at Plymouth and later in Salem, Massachusetts. The settlers at Massachusetts Bay also judged "Sternhold and Hopkins" to be an insufficiently literal translation, and in 1636 they appointed thirty ministers to translate and versify the psalms. Four years later this led to the publication of *The Whole Book of Psalmes* (1640), better known as *The Bay Psalm Book*. It was the first book printed in North America for the English-speaking colonies. Like Ainsworth's Psalter, this translation was very literalistic, and the "Preface" to the *The Bay Psalm Book* makes it clear that beauty was less important to the translators than fidelity: "If therefore the verses are not always so smooth and elegant as some may desire or expect; let them consider that Gods Altar needs not our pollishings."

Throughout the seventeenth century the phrasing of the English Psalter continued to be debated on both sides of the Atlantic, and even small changes in wording provoked opposition. A London minister reported the response of his brother's maidservant when the 1562 Sternhold and Hopkins Psalter was replaced with the 1696 Tate and Brady version: "If you must know the plain truth, sir, as long as you sung Jesus Christ's psalms I sung along with ye; but now that you sing psalms of your own invention, ye may sing by yourselves." The texts below include four versions of the First Psalm, from the *Authorized Version* (1611), Ainsworth's *Book of Psalmes* (1612), *The Bay Psalm Book* (1640), and the *New England Psalm Book* (1651)—the last a revision of *The Bay Psalm Book*. Ainsworth's version of the First Psalm demonstrates the literal, cumbersome quality of his translation: "For, of the just, Iehovah he / acknowledgeth the way: / and way of the ungracious / shall utterly-decay." The New Englanders knew this was bad poetry but believed that it was what God wanted them to sing! The differences between *The Bay Psalm Book* and the *New England Psalm Book* are slight: "longing delight" becomes "whole delight," while "leaf never withers" is changed to "leaf shall never fall." Yet such was the stuff of controversy during the early colonial period.

The earlier editions of *The Bay Psalm Book* contained no music, presumably because no one in the colony was capable of engraving it for the printers. The first book printed in the English colonies that is known to have contained music as well as words was the ninth edition of *The Bay Psalm Book* (1698). It contained thirteen tunes inserted at the back of the book, along with "some few directions for ordering the Voice—without *Squeaking* above, or *Grumbling* below." It may seem odd that words and music were printed in separate portions of a book or even in separate books. Throughout the seventeenth century, and even into the eighteenth, a real distinction was made between the words of a psalm (or hymn) and its tune. Theoretically, any psalm could be sung to any tune, so long as the meters matched. The 1640 edition of *The Bay Psalm Book* contains an "Admonition" stating that the psalms fall into six different kinds of meters and noting that differing tunes fit each respective meter. The same text also refers to the 1621 English Psalter of Thomas Ravenscroft, which offered the best selection of tunes of any seventeenth-century Psalter—some ninety-seven in total. Some seventeenth-century colonists would learn the psalm tunes by hearing them in worship, while the musically literate could consult Ravenscroft or other Psalters that had printed notes as well as words.

The development of American hymnody in the eighteenth and early nineteenth centuries involved a gradual loosening of the musical and lyrical constraints imposed by the metrical psalmody of the Calvinist tradition. As new communities sprang up in the American colonies, it was often difficult for many of the congregations to gain or to maintain the musical know-how necessary for the performance of the Psalter tunes. The hardships of pioneer life did not leave much time or energy for the cultivation of the fine arts. The early Pilgrims and Puritans sang their psalms straight through and at a surprisingly vigorous pace. Later New Englanders developed a different mode of singing. They adopted the custom of "lining out," in which one person sang or read a psalm line by line, with the rest of the congregation repeating the sung line. Some scholars suggest that each line was repeated three times: once read aloud by the worship leader, then sung by the leader, and finally sung by the congregation. When one imagines a congregation doing this with every line in a hymn, without the aid of musical instruments, it is easy to see why difficulties arose. Though lining out began as a practical expedient wherever hymnals were not available or congregants were unacquainted with the tunes, the practice caught on and spread throughout England, Scotland, and New England, and even among German immigrants in America.

Despite these practical measures to maintain metrical psalmody, by the early eighteenth century sacred music in the American churches had become increasingly undisciplined. People forgot many of the tunes, the number of tunes in common use diminished, and the pace of singing slowed. To fill up the vacuum created by a slow tempo and unknown tunes, congregants started to improvise and add their own turns and flourishes to the music. A cacophony resulted, with everyone sounding out a different version of the melody and no two persons singing the same thing at the same time. Thomas Walter, a musician from the period, complained that hymn singing sounded like "five hundred tunes roared out at the same time," producing "an horrid medley of confused and disorderly sounds." In 1721 he published *The Grounds and Rules of Music Explained,* where he argued for a return to singing "according to the rules of music." His was only one of a number of publications during this period that sought to reform congregational singing.

The ministers who argued for "regular singing" or "singing by note" correctly perceived that they were attempting to revive the practice of the earlier New Englanders, but this fact did not convince parishioners to amend their ways. The disorderly practice of "singing by rote" had been established as a kind of folk tradition, and the reforming ministers were regarded as innovators. Their suggestions thus met with resistance. The gradual refinement of musical standards and taste in New England that accompanied the decline of lining out and singing by rote was a process that occurred over decades. Some urban congregations, such as the progressive Brattle Street Church in Boston, had opted for "singing by note" as early as 1700. At the same time that city churches were abandoning lining out, the practice was spreading to rural regions in New England. Lining out then moved south and west, following the frontier to places like Blackey, Kentucky, where Old Regular Baptists have continued the practice up to the present time.

One of the long-term results of the "regular singing" reformers was the establishment of singing schools. By the mid eighteenth century these schools had become important cultural institutions in the northeast, and their influence lasted well into the nineteenth century. Organized by ministers or laypersons, who found patrons to underwrite costs and music teachers to conduct lessons, singing schools met in church rooms or basements, private homes, or even local taverns. The teacher instructed the pupils in the rudiments of musical notation and singing so that they could sing the psalms. Students typically paid a fee for the lessons and were expected to bring along a candle, an instruction book, and a board to hold these items. While some singing schools were held on an ongoing basis, it was more common for churches to conduct them for a limited number of sessions.

Singing schools made important contributions to the development of Protestant church music in America. The schools generated hundreds of instructional texts, or "tunebooks," which by the late 1700s were printed in a characteristic oblong shape. The books almost always contained an introduction to musical notation and performance, followed by an anthology of examples that usually included metrical psalms, hymns, fuguing tunes, and anthems. Such books helped in the development of church choirs, which often came into existence as a result of the musical instruction received in the school. In urban centers, larger choral societies that were no longer tied to any one parish emerged. The Handel and Haydn Society of Boston, for example, was founded in 1815 and devoted itself to high art music from the other side of the Atlantic.

Teachers in the singing schools commonly used a pitch pipe and bass viol to keep their singers in pitch. While using these instruments for practice was acceptable, controversy erupted when singing teachers attempted to bring these instruments into worship services. Congregations that used bass viols in services were unfavorably termed "catgut churches." The new practice weakened the Calvinist stricture against instruments in worship, and yet the subsequent introduction of organs into Congregational churches was slow. As New England became a more affluent colony, some wealthy merchants imported organs to be used in their homes. When Bostonian Thomas Brattle died in 1713, he bequeathed his household's organ to his church. Although the congregation comprised many forward-looking Puritans, even it could not be so bold as to accept the instrument. The church members rejected the gift. Brattle, anticipating their action, had stated in his will that if his church refused the organ it was to be offered to the Episcopalians worshiping at King's Chapel. Since the Episcopalians did not share the Puritans' scruples against instrumental music in church, they accepted the organ. Aside from an organ that may have been used in 1703 by the Wissahickon Pietists in Pennsylvania, Brattle's organ was the first used in a North American church.

Some congrgations held out in their opposition to the organ as late as the mid 1800s, although a Boston observer claimed in 1846 that every church in the city was in possession of an organ, with the exception of three or four churches of small size. Because the piano could substitute for the organ in accompanying singing, it was often used in churches too poor or remote to have an organ. When the Mormons made their trek to Utah in the 1840s, they went to great effort to bring a piano with them. The piano was not, however, a functional equivalent for the organ, despite the many similarities between the two instruments. While the piano could be played in the same fashion as the organ, it also facilitated a more percussive, energetic, and forceful style of accompaniment. The ecstatic style of singing that one associates with revivalist religion and with much of African American worship is based on piano rather than organ accompaniment. Another important use of the piano was in the domestic sphere, where communal hymn-singing was a frequent practice in devout families on Sundays and other occasions.

Singing schools helped to provide Americans with the musical abilities to sing the more complicated hymns being written in Europe and the colonies. One of the pivotal figures in the development of English-language hymnody, revered on both sides of the Altantic, was the English Independent minister Isaac Watts (1674–1748). Watts argued in favor of freely composed hymns that expressed the singer's own thoughts. Not wishing entirely to abandon Old Testament psalmody, however, Watts sought to Christianize and contemporize the psalms in addition to writing new hymns. He stated that he had "brought down the royal author [that is, David, to whom most of the psalms are ascribed] into the common affairs of the Christian life, and led the Psalmist of Israel into the Church of Christ." Watts's publications included *Hymns and Spiritual Songs* (1707) and *Psalms of David Imitated in the Language of the New Testament* (1719). Many of his hymns are still in common use, such as "Joy to the World," "O God Our Help in Ages Past," and "When I Survey the Wondrous Cross." Watts's hymns and psalms were warmly welcomed in New England as devotional literature to be sung or read outside of church, but only gradually were they introduced into worship. In 1729 Benjamin Franklin reprinted Watts's *Psalms* in Philadelphia, yet the book did not sell well and was not reprinted until 1741.

The brothers John Wesley (1703–1791) and Charles Wesley (1707–1788) also played a role in the development of trans-Atlantic hymnody. When the two came as missionaries of the Church of England to Georgia, they brought with them Watts's psalms and hymns. John Wesley, however, soon compiled his own hymnbook, published in Charlestown, South Carolina, as *A Collection of Psalms and Hymns* (1737). This was the first hymnbook, as distinct from a psalmbook or Psalter, to be published in America. It included many of Watts's hymns and John Wesley's translations of German hymns, yet ironically it lacked hymns by John's brother, Charles, who was eventually to write nearly 6500 hymns as compared with Watts's 700 hymns and psalms. Charles Wesley's best hymns exhibit a compact felicity of expression virtually unsurpassed among English-language hymnodists, and a large number of his hymns remain in common use today.

A comparison of Watts's hymns with those of Charles Wesley reveals differences as well as similarities. Both hymnodists concentrate on the person and deeds of Jesus, and their words attempt to capture the devout soul's responses to God. Yet of the two, Watts adheres more closely to the psalter tradition. Although his hymns paraphrase and rework scriptural ideas and images, they usually remain anchored to particular biblical texts, which are specified in the early editions of his work. The hymn "Crucifixion to the World by the Cross of Christ," better known by its first line as "When I Survey the Wondrous Cross," is based on Galatians 6:14, and "Salvation by Grace in Christ" on 2 Timothy 1:9–10. Watts's approach is doctrinal and didactic, as shown for instance in the Calvinism implied in the "Salvation by Grace" hymn: "'Twas his own Purpose that begun / To rescue Rebels doom'd to die; / He gave us Grace in Christ his Son / Before he spread the Starry Sky." Charles Wesley's hymns are saturated with scriptural phrases and images, and yet the ideas and words are drawn from many different passages and then woven into a new pattern. "Oh, for a Thousand Tongues to Sing" expresses the hymnodist's urge to evangelize, while "Love Divine All Loves Excelling" is a song of spiritual aspiration and longing. Wesley's hymns are songs of evangelical experience, while Watts's are meditations on the meaning and application of biblical texts. The former generally start from experience, the latter from text and doctrine—a subtle but significant difference. The "I" of individual experience was to play a steadily increasing role in the American hymns of the nineteenth and twentieth centuries.

The religious awakenings in the middle of the eighteenth century and at the beginning of the nineteenth fomented enthusiasm for the adoption of the new hymns. When George Whitefield came over to America to preach in what became known as the Great Awakening (1740–1741), he brought with him John and Charles Wesley's 1739 edition of *Hymns and Sacred Poems*. In 1740 the book was reprinted in Philadelphia. John Wesley and Whitefield fell into contention over Calvinism and Arminianism, leading Whitefield to discourage the use of Wesley's hymns. Moreover, Watts's doctrinal positions were not entirely agreeable to many in the prorevival party. Yet in the long run such theological squabbles did little to hinder the adoption of hymns composed by the Wesleys and Isaac Watts. Their hymns became staples in Protestant church worship from the late eighteenth century onward.

English-speaking Baptists, who originally had objected to congregational singing because it required "set forms," began to adopt hymn singing following the Great Awakening. In the decade prior to the Revolution, American Baptists began to publish their first hymnals, which included songs by Watts as well as the English Congregationalist Philip Doddridge and the English Baptist Anne Steele. Methodists in America, who began to form their own societies by 1766, used hymnals produced by the Wesleys. John Wesley, acting through the American Methodist bishops, sought to uphold aesthetic and liturgical standards on the American frontier. He insisted that preachers sing no hymns of their own composing, although his followers did not always follow his advice in this matter.

During the latter half of the eighteenth century, the compositions of native-born American composers also became an important part of Protestant religious music.

William Billings (1746–1800) was an unlikely individual to become a leader in the field of music. Born in Boston, he was a tanner by trade and entirely untutored in music. Billings had only a limited knowledge of reading notes, which he may have acquired in one of the singing schools of his period. When writing his first tunes he sometimes lacked paper, so he chalked them on the walls of the tannery where he worked or even carved them onto leather. Billings's physical appearance might also have limited his role as an early American musician since he was physically disfigured, with one leg shorter than the other, one arm withered, and one eye blind. He also had a loud, rasping voice, and contemporaries mentioned his slovenly appearance. Yet his creativity, earnestness, and enthusiasm attracted the respect and attention of many. Governor Samuel Adams and Rev. Dr. Pierce of Brookline, both music lovers, encouraged Billings's efforts and sang beside him in the choir. After abandoning his tanning trade, he devoted himself to musical instruction and trained choirs in some of the most important congregations in Boston, including the Brattle Street Church and the Old South Church. One of Billings's best-known publications was his first book, *The New England Psalm-Singer* (1770). William Billings's influence was deep and far-reaching. He improved the rhythmic singing of the choirs and insisted on exact pitch. Since instruments were not in common use in church, it was difficult for all singers to agree on the same note. The striking up of a song often spelled musical disaster. Billings popularized the use of the pitch pipe and the bass viol to help choirs find and maintain a proper pitch.

Like Billings, Daniel Read (1757–1836) did more than write music. He spent most of his life in New Haven, Connecticut, and was a comb manufacturer as well as a composer and musical publisher and advocate. His first musical book was *The American Singing Book* (1785), which contained forty-seven tunes of his own composition. He also had the distinction of publishing, albeit briefly, *The American Musical Magazine*, which was the first periodical of its kind published in the United States.

Many of the hymns of Billings and Read were printed in the popular hymn collection *The American Vocalist*. Published in Boston by W. J. Reynolds in 1848, and then in a more widely distributed revised edition in 1849, the book contains a broad selection of tunes, anthems, and hymns. The title page states that the songs in *The American Vocalist* are appropriate for use inside or outside of church. It encourages people to sing the songs at home in their parlors or in the church vestry—a meeting place where discussions are held and church decisions made. The same page boasts that the book contains songs "adapted to every variety of metre in common use, and appropriate to every occasion where God is worshipped and men are blessed . . . embracing a greater variety of music for congregations, societies, singing schools, and choirs than any other collection extant." *The American Vocalist* was divided into three parts: the first containing church music; the second, more serious vestry music; and the third, a lighter kind of vestry music. Not merely a hymnal, the book began with a thirteen-page discussion of the elements of vocal music intended for the average singer.

The editor of *The American Vocalist* was D. H. Mansfield (1810–1855), a Methodist minister in Maine. Mansfield's hymnal combined elements of the elite and popular musical cultures of his day. He was especially impressed with the musical legacy of Puritan New England. While Mansfield condemned what he called "imported discord," *The American Vocalist* included representative pieces by members of Boston's European music movement, such as Lowell Mason, E. L. White, and I. B. Woodbury. Mansfield based much of his introductory essay, "Elements of Vocal Music," on Lowell Mason's method of musical instruction. At the same time, Mansfield stated that his aim was to preserve "tunes and poetry" that were "useful to thousands of illiterate persons." He transcribed many Methodist and Baptist revival hymns that were popular in his region. The Millerite religious movement had left a deep imprint in New England during the 1840s, and this too was clearly reflected in the hymns Mansfield selected for *The American Vocalist*. Almost half of the texts in the second and third sections of the hymnal were devoted to millennial themes, and many of the hymns had appeared previously in *The Millenial Harp* (1843), the Millerites' hymnal.

The lyrics to "The Warning" by Billings stress God's openness and receptivity toward the sinner but also the fearful punishment that awaits those who refuse to repent. Billings's "Jordan" is devoted to the "land of pure delight" that awaits Christian believers, depicting it in terms of the land of Canaan and the river Jordan—a Christianizing of Old Testament themes that is common in Isaac Watts and other eighteenth-century hymnodists.

The hymn "Greenwich" by Daniel Read is a typical fuguing tune, with an opening chordal phrase followed by an imitative section that highlights each of the four parts in sequence. Such works were regarded as more difficult, sophisticated, and showy than most other hymns. As in Billings's "The Warning," the lyrics of "Greenwich" speak of judgment, yet they are less a warning or invitation to the sinner than an expression of contrition: "Lord, what a tho'tless wretch was I." The imagery and language evoke the Seventy-third Psalm, with its warning against envying the wicked, who will surely be punished by God.

The unattributed hymn "Nothing True but Heaven" is presented in two very different versions on the same page of *The American Vocalist*. The first begins: "This world is all a fleeting show / For man's illusion given; / The smiles of joy, the tears of wo, / Deceitful shine, deceitful flow; / There's nothing true but Heaven." The words of the second version seem a blunt contradiction of the first: "This world's not all a fleeting show, / For man's illusion given; / He that hath soothed a widow's wo, / Or wiped the orphan's tear, doth know, / There's something here of Heaven." Perhaps the this-worldliness of the second version serves as a counterpoise to the otherworldliness of the first. Heaven is all that is true, and yet there is a foretaste of it here and now. On the other hand, the second version could be read as an index of shifting attitudes. The present world, rather than a realm beyond, was becoming the locus of religious attention and action.

"O Come, Come Away" is a piece done in a popular mid-nineteenth-century style. The lyrics are both an invitation to worship and a testimony to the singer's devout resolution: "While others may seek for vain and foolish pleasures, / The Sabbath school shall be my choice."

Protestant hymnody would continue to undergo important changes in the nineteenth century. Revivalism would stress the emotional appeal of religion, and lively choruses and sentimental lyrics would appeal to popular tastes. The solo singer who could capture an audience's wills and affections and thus carry the message of conversion and salvation would complement the work of the preacher. Yet eighteenth-century hymns would retain their prominent place in Protestant religious life—in church services, Sunday schools, camp meetings, and around the hearth or parlor organ at home. The theological themes that shaped the hymns may have faded from the minds of the singers, but the images of sin, judgment, justice, devotion, and love remained.

The four versions of the First Psalm are from *The Authorized Version* (1611), Henry Ainsworth's *The Book of Psalmes* (1612), *The Bay Psalm Book* (1640), and *The New England Psalm Book* (1651) as found in George Hood, *A History of Music in New England* (Boston: Wilkins, Carter, 1846), pp. 14–15, and Henry Wilder Foote, *Three Centuries of American Hymnody* (Cambridge: Harvard University Press, 1940), p. 50. Isaac Watts's "Crucifixion to the World by the Cross of Christ" and "Salvation by Grace in Christ" are from Selma L. Bishop, *Isaac Watts: Hymns and Spiritual Songs, 1707–1748: A Study in Early Eighteenth-Century Language Changes* (London: Faith Press, 1962), pp. 353, 129. Charles Wesley's "Oh, for a Thousand Tongues to Sing" and "Love Divine All Loves Excelling" are from Frank Whaling, ed., *John and Charles Wesley: Selected Prayers, Hymns, Journal Notes, Sermons, Letters, and Treatises*, The Classics of Western Spirituality (New York: Paulist Press, 1981), pp. 177–78, 227–28. William Billings's "The Warning" and "Jordan," Daniel Reed's "Greenwich," and the unattributed "Nothing True but Heaven" and "O Come, Come Away" are all from *The American Vocalist* (Boston: W. J. Reynolds, 1849), pp. 271, 104, 25, 273, 10, 304–5.

Further Reading

The American Vocalist: Spirituals and Folk Hymns, 1850–1870 (CD recording, Erato Disques, 1992); *A Land of Pure Delight, William Billings Anthems and Fuguing Tunes* (CD recording, Harmonia Mundi, 1992); Ian Bradley, ed., *The Book of Hymns* (Woodstock, N.Y.: Overlook, 1989); Richard Crawford, ed., *The Core Repertory of Early American Psalmody*, Recent Researches in American Music, Volumes 11 and 12 (Madison, Wisc.: A-R Editions, 1984); Orpha Ochse, *The History of the Organ in the United States* (Bloomington and Indianapolis: Indiana University Press, 1975); Peter Williams, *The King of Instruments: How Churches Came to Have Organs* (London: SPCK, 1993); Samuel J. Rogal, *A General Introduction to Hymnody and Congregational Song*, ATLA Monograph Series, No. 26 (Metuchen, N.J., and London: American Theological Library Association and Scarecrow, 1991);

Erik Routley, *The Music of Christian Hymns* (Chicago: G.I.A. Publications, 1981);
Percy A. Scholes, *The Puritans and Music in England and New England* (New York:
Russell and Russell, 1962); Paul Westermeyer, "Religious Music and Hymnody,"
in Charles H. Lippy and Peter W. Williams, eds., *Encyclopedia of the American Religious Experience: Studies of Traditions and Movements*, vol. 3 (New York: Scribners,
1988), pp. 1,285–1,305.

Psalm One
The Authorized Version, or King James Version (1611)

Blessed is the man that walketh not in the counsel of the ungodly
Nor standeth in the way of sinners,
Nor sitteth in the seat of the scornful.
But his delight is in the law of the Lord;
And in his law doth he meditate day and night.
And he shall be like a tree planted by the rivers of water,
That bringeth forth his fruit in his season;
His leaf also shall not wither;
And whatsoever he doeth shall prosper.
The ungodly are not so:
But are like the chaff which the wind driveth away.
Therefore the ungodly shall not stand in the judgment,
Nor sinners in the congregation of the righteous.
For the Lord knoweth the way of the righteous:
But the way of the ungodly shall perish.

Henry Ainsworth, The Book of Psalmes (1612)

O Blessed man, that doth not in
    the wickeds consell walk:
nor stand in sinners way; nor sit
    in seat of scornful-folk.
But setteth in Jehovahs law
    his pleasureful delight
and in his law doth meditate,
    by day and eke by night.
And he shall be, like-as a tree,
    by water brooks planted;
which in his time, shall give his fruit
    his leaf eke shall not fade;
and whatsoever he shall doe,
    it prosp'rously shall thrive.

Not so the wicked: but as chaff,
   which winde away-doth drive.
Therefore, the wicked shall not in
   the judgment stand-upright:
and in th' assembly of the just,
   not any sinfull-wight.
For, of the just, Iehovah he
   acknowledgeth the way:
and way of the ungracious
   shall utterly-decay.

The Bay Psalm Book (1640)

O Blessed man, that in th' advice
   of wicked doth not walk:
nor stand in sinners way, nor sit
   in chayre of scornful folk.
But in the law of Iehovah
   is his longing delight:
and in his law doth meditate,
   by day and eke by night.
And he shall be like to a tree
   planted by water-rivers:
that in his season yeilds [*sic*] his fruit,
   and his leaf never withers.
And all he doth shall prosper well,
   the wicked are not so:
but they are like unto the chaffe,
   which winde drives to and fro.
Therefore shall not ungodly men,
   rise to stand in the doome,
nor shall the sinners with the just,
   in their assemblie come.
For of the righteous men, the Lord
   acknowledgeth the way:
but the way of ungodly men,
   shall utterly decay.

The New England Psalm Book (1651)

O Blessed man that walks not in
   th' advice of wicked men,

Nor standeth in the sinners way
　　nor scorners seat sit in,
But he upon Jehovah's law
　　doth set his whole delight,
And in his law doth meditate
　　both in the day and night.
He shall be like a planted tree
　　by water-brooks which shall
In his due season yield his fruit,
　　whose leaf shall never fall.
And all he doth shall prosper well,
　　the wicked are not so:
But they are like unto the chaff
　　which wind drives to and fro.
Therefore shall not ungodly men
　　in judgment stand upright,
Nor in the assembly of the just
　　shall stand the sinful wight.
For of the righteous men, the Lord
　　acknowledgeth the way:
Where as the way of wicked men
　　shall utterly decay.

Crucifixion to the World by the Cross of Christ

When I survey the wond'rous Cross
On which the Prince of Glory dy'd,
My richest Gain I count but Loss,
And pour Contempt on all my Pride.

Forbid it, Lord, that I should boast
Save in the Death of Christ my God;
All the vain things that charm me most,
I sacrifice them to his Blood.

See from his Head, his Hands, his Feet,
Sorrow and Love flow mingled down;
Did e're such Love and Sorrow meet?
Or Thorns compose so rich a crown?

His dying Crimson like a Robe
Spreads o're his Body on the Tree,
Then am I dead to all the Globe,
And all the Globe is dead to me.

Were the whole Realm of Nature mine,
That were a Present far to [sic] small;
Love so amazing, so divine
Demands my Soul, my Life, my All.

Salvation by Grace in Christ

Now to the Power of God Supreme
Be everlasting Honours giv'n,
He saves from Hell, (we bless his Name)
He calls our wand'ring Feet to Heav'n.

Not for our Duties or Deserts,
But of his own abounding Grace,
He works Salvation in our Hearts,
And forms a People for his Praise.

'Twas his own Purpose that begun
To rescue Rebels doom'd to die;
He gave us Grace in Christ his Son
Before he spread the Starry Sky.

Jesus the Lord appears at last,
And makes his Father's Counsels known;
Declares the great Transactions past,
And brings Immortal Blessings down.

He dies; and in that dreadful Night
Did all the Pow'rs of Hell destroy;
Rising, he brought our Heaven to light,
And took possession of the Joy.

Oh, for a Thousand Tongues to Sing

Oh, for a thousand tongues to sing
 My dear Redeemer's praise!
The glories of my God and King,
 The triumphs of his grace!

My gracious Master, and my God,
 Assist me to proclaim,
To spread through all the earth abroad
 The honors of thy name.

Jesus, the name that charms our fears,
    That bids our sorrows cease—
'Tis music in the sinner's ears,
    'Tis life, and health, and peace.

He breaks the power of canceled sin,
    He sets the prisoner free;
His blood can make the foulest clean—
    His blood availed for me.

Hear him, ye deaf; his praise, ye dumb,
    Your loosened tongues employ;
Ye blind, behold your Savior come,
    And leap, ye lame, for joy!

Look unto him, ye nations, own
    Your God, ye fallen race;
Look, and be saved through faith alone,
    Be justified by grace.

See all your sins on Jesus laid:
    The Lamb of God was slain,
His soul was once an offering made
    For every soul of man.

Awake from guilty nature's sleep,
    And Christ shall give you light,
Cast all yours sins into the deep,
    And wash the Ethiop white.

Love Divine All Loves Excelling

Love divine, all loves excelling,
    Joy of heaven, to earth come down,
Fix in us thy humble dwelling,
    All thy faithful mercies crown!
Jesus, thou art all compassion,
    Pure, unbounded love thou art;
Visit us with thy salvation!
    Enter every trembling heart.

Come, almighty to deliver,
    Let us all thy grace receive;
Suddenly return, and never,
    Never more thy temples leave.

Thee we would be always blessing,
  Serve thee as thy hosts above,
Pray, and praise thee without ceasing,
  Glory in thy perfect love.

Finish then thy new creation,
  Pure and spotless let us be;
Let us see thy great salvation
  Perfectly restored in thee;
Changed from glory into glory,
  Till in heaven we take our place,
Till we cast our crowns before thee,
  Lost in wonder, love, and praise.

The Warning

Ah, guilty sinner, ruined by transgression,
What shall thy doom be, when, arrayed in terror,
God shall command thee, covered with pollution,
Up to the judgment? Up to the judgment.

Will thou escape from his omniscient notice,
Fly to the caverns, seek annihilation?
Vain thy presumption; justice still shall triumph
In thy destruction, in thy destruction.

Stop, thoughtless sinner, stop awhile and ponder,
Ere death arrest thee, and the Judge, in vengeance,
Hurl from his presence thine affrighted spirit,
Swift to perdition, swift to perdition.

Oft has he called thee, but thou wouldst not hear him,
Mercies and judgments have alike been slighted;
Yet he is gracious, and with arms unfolded,
Waits to embrace thee.

Come, then, poor sinner, come away this moment,
Just as you are, but come with heart relenting,
Come to the fountain open for the guilty;
Jesus invites you.

But, if you trifle with his gracious message,
Cleave to the world and love its guilty pleasures,
Mercy, grown weary, shall in righteous judgment
Leave you forever.

Oh! guilty sinner, hear the voice of warning;
Fly to the Saviour, and embrace his pardon;
So shall your spirits meet, with joy triumphant,
Death and the judgment!

Jordan

There is a land of pure delight,
Where saints immortal reign;
Infinite day excludes the night,
And pleasures banish pain.

Sweet fields beyond the swelling flood,
Stand dressed in living green;
So to the Jews old Canaan stood,
While Jordan rolled between.

Greenwich

Lord, what a tho'tless wretch was I,
To mourn and murmur and repine,
To see the wicked placed on high,
In pride and robes of honor shine.

But O their end, their dreadful end,
Thy sanctuary taught me so;
On slipp'ry rocks I see them stand,
And fiery billows roll below.

Nothing True but Heaven

First Version

This world is all a fleeting show
For man's illusion given;
The smiles of joy, the tears of wo,
Deceitful shine, deceitful flow;
There's nothing true but Heaven.

As false the light on glory's plume,
As fading hues at even;
And genius' bud and beauty's bloom,

Are blossoms gathered for the tomb,
There's nothing bright but heaven.

Poor wanderers on a stormy sea,
From wave to wave we're driven;
And fancy's flash, and reason's ray
Serve but to light us on the way;
There's nothing calm but heaven.

And where's the hand held out to cheer
The heart with anguish riven?
For sorrow's sigh, and trouble's tear
Have never found a refuge here;
There's nothing kind but Heaven.

In vain do mortals sigh for bliss,
Without their sins forgiven;
True pleasure, everlasting peace,
Are only found in God's free grace;
There's nothing good but Heaven.

From such as walk in wisdom's road,
Corroding fears are driven;
They're washed in Christ's atoning blood,
Enjoy communion with their God,
And find their way to Heaven.

Second Version

This world's not all a fleeting show,
For man's illusion given;
He that hath soothed a widow's wo,
Or wiped the orphan's tear, doth know,
There's something here of Heaven.

And he that walks life's thorny way,
With feelings calm and even;
Whose path is lit from day to day
By virtue's bright and steady ray,
Hath something felt of Heaven.

He who the Christian's course hath run,
And all his foes forgiven—
Who measures out life's little span,
In love to God, and love to man,
On earth has tasted Heaven.

O Come, Come Away

O come, come away! the Sabbath morn is passing,
Let's hasten to the Sabbath school;
O come, come away!
The Sabbath bells are ringing clear,
Their joyous peals salute my ear,
I love their voice to hear,
O come, come away!

My comrades invite to join their happy number,
And gladly will I meet them there;
O come, come away!
'Tis there we meet to sing and pray,
To read God's word on his glad day,
Then joyful haste away,
O come, come away!

While others may seek for vain and foolish pleasures,
The Sabbath school shall be my choice;
O come, come away!
How dear to hear the plaintive strain
From youthful voices rise amain,
With sweetest tones again,
O come, come away!

'Tis there I may learn the ways of heavenly wisdom,
To guide my steps to join on high;
O come, come away!
The flow'ry paths of peace to tread,
Where rays of heavenly bliss are shed,
My wand'ring steps to lead,
O come, come away!

I there hear the voice in heavenly accents speaking,
"Let little children come to me:
O come, come away!
Forbid them not their hearts to give,
Let them on me in youth believe,
And I will them receive,"
O come, come away!

With joy I accept the gracious invitation,
My heart exults with rapt'rous hope;
O come, come away!
My deathless spirit when I die,

Shall on the wings of angels fly,
To mansions in the sky,
O come, come away!

—8—

The 1842 Hymnal of Penina Moise

Dianne Ashton

In 1842 the first hymnal written by an American Jew was published in Charleston, South Carolina, by the members of congregation Beth Elohim (House of God). These hymns proved so popular that the congregation reissued the volume in 1856 and that volume went through four more printings. Largely the work of one woman, Penina Moise, the hymnal reflected not only her own religious vision but that of the members of her extraordinary synagogue. More than one hundred years later, Reform Jews in America continued to sing her hymns. The Reform hymnal, used across the country into the l960s, included more hymns by Moise than by any other Jewish author. According to one historian, some of her poems were included in every English language hymnal used by Jews in the United States and abroad.

Born in Charleston in 1797, Moise (pronounced mō-é-zeh) was the sixth child of Abraham and Sarah Moise. Her father died when she was only twelve years old, and so Penina Moise came of age in a poor family. Her brothers and sisters augmented the family income in various ways with Penina helping through selling her needlework. We know little about her early efforts at writing except that she began writing poetry in earnest after about 1830 when perhaps she felt more confident about her skills. The small payment she received for her poems no doubt helped her family. She may also have received a small stipend from her synagogue when she took over the reins of its Sunday School, which had been organized by women of the congregation in 1838. Only the second such school in the country, it was guided by the advice sent by Philadelphia's Rebecca Gratz, who had established the first Jewish Sunday school in America earlier that year.

Penina Moise soon earned a reputation as the poet laureate of Charleston. Much of her work was published in local newspapers but also in publications in places as distant as Boston, Washington, and New Orleans, and in prestigious national magazines like *Godey's Lady's Book*. In 1833 she published a collection of her poetry called *Fancy's Sketch Book*. Moise probably had written most of the items included in the l842 hymnal sometime before then, because she had stopped writing a few years earlier to tend her mother, who had become paralyzed in old age; she died that same year. Over the course of her life, Penina Moise produced over 190 hymns based on her own original poetry.

During the Civil War, Penina, along with her widowed sister, Rachel, and Rachel's daughter, Jacqueline, moved to Sumter, South Carolina, to be near their brother, Abraham, who lived there. In Sumter the three women shared a two-room cottage where they supported themselves by running a school for girls in their home. By then, Penina Moise's eyesight was failing, and as she aged she relied more and more on her niece. In the last years of her life, Moise depended largely on the small stipend left to her by her brothers (who she outlived by many years) and on Jacqueline's kindness and skill in continuing their small school.

It seems likely that her hymns became a central part of her congregation's devotions in the early 1840s. A fire in 1838 had destroyed the synagogue, and three years passed before the community was able to rebuild. Moise wrote a poem for the new synagogue's dedication. Her 1842 hymnal may have been part of the congregation's acclimation to the new building, which included an organ for instrumental accompaniment—a radical new step in synagogue music.

Beth Elohim was the first Jewish group in America to dedicate itself to what came to be called Reform Judaism. Reformers changed Jewish worship in several ways, hoping to inspire those Jews who did not understand Hebrew or the reasons behind many practices. Reformers shortened and simplified devotional worship and used everyday language, instead of Hebrew, for many prayers. Many later American Reform leaders were educated in western philosophy and wanted to emphasize the universals within Judaism rather than the ideas and practices unique to it. Thus, they focused their teachings and worship on the biblical prophets rather than on rabbinical traditions explaining the commandments of Moses. As early as 1855, congregations in New York, Cincinnati, Albany, and Baltimore had joined Charleston in experimenting with Reform. By 1877, 277 American synagogues had joined the Reform movement.

Although American Jewish hymnals have been associated largely with the Reform movement, liturgical poetry has a long history in Judaism. The psalms of the Bible, written between about 950 B.C.E. and 600 B.C.E., first served Jews as hymns. Later hymn writers often took inspiration from these oldest religious poems. During the fifth century, Jews living on the eastern shore of the Mediterranean and its surrounding hillsides circumvented Justinian's imperial ban on teaching the Bible by creating poems with hidden religious teachings that could be sung in congregational worship. Called *piyyutim*, these hymns proved enormously popular. Since that time, more than thirty-five thousand such liturgical poems have been written by Jews living throughout the Middle East, North Africa, and in all parts of Europe.

Despite their wide variety, Jewish liturgical poems share similar purposes. They praise God, commemorate historical events believed to have religious meaning, or teach a moral or religious lesson. The experience of singing also raises the spirit and enhances communal identity. Particularly moving poems were often incorporated into worship services. For instance, some of the oldest piyyutim became part of the Sabbath and holiday versions of the Amidah, one of the central and most important prayers in Jewish worship. Similarly, Psalms 113 through 118, collectively called the Hallel, are often sung after the Amidah on Sabbaths and festivals. Other liturgical poems, those more rooted in biblical imagery and language that asked forgiveness of sins, were inserted into the worship services for Rosh Hashanah and Yom Kippur, the most solemn Jewish holidays. In the synagogue, piyyutim are usually found woven into worship services in prayer books rather than in separate volumes.

Music seems to have always been a part of Jewish worship. Although we do not know the earliest melodies, it seems that by about 700 B.C.E. the choir for the Temple in Jerusalem numbered at least twelve and that this number could be expanded significantly on special occasions. By 50 B.C.E. the Levites who provided music in the Second Temple had developed techniques of virtuoso singing. Instrumental music was complex as well. The Temple's musical tradition did not extend to worship in synagogues, however. Rabbis of the early period created the synagogue as a place where Bible study and worship of God could be combined. After the Romans destroyed the Second Temple in 70 C.E., the synagogue took center stage as the site for Jewish communal worship. The rabbis banned instrumental music from Jewish worship as an expression of mourning for the loss of the Temple. They discouraged women, who were already seated apart from men, from singing aloud as a means to ensure that Jews would not be drawn to promiscuity during worship by the delights of congregational mixed singing.

Consequently, the synagogue developed its own musical traditions. First, the chanting of scripture according to specific melodic patterns became standard as the Torah was read aloud each Thursday, Monday, Saturday, new moon, holy day, and fast day. The Torah is the first five books of the Hebrew Bible, sometimes called the "five books of Moses." In handwritten scroll form, Torahs are considered sacred and are stored in a special cabinet on the eastern wall of synagogues. The Torah is read ceremonially in many worship services. In an era when many people lacked sophisticated reading and writing skills, chanting made the texts easier for both the singers and the listeners to remember. That was especially true for the Torah, which lacked both punctuation and vowels in its original text. The first chanted tunes were probably based on older melodies. After the invention of a bound text with punctuation and vowels in the ninth century, simple recitation of the text was permitted at some points in the service. The bound text also included markings above and below the words to indicate proper chanting. Over time, communities in various parts of the world differed in interpreting the vowel markings and chanting notations. Today, no Jewish community can claim it sings the original tunes.

The synagogue also developed a new religious musical actor, that of cantor or prayer leader. In the early days of the synagogue, the cantor was selected for his religious learning and piety because he acted as the "agent of the congregation" to speak to God, not necessarily because he had a good voice. Soon, larger congregations relied on two readers for the longer morning services, and at some point it became customary that the second reader would be the better singer. Thus the role of cantor developed into a primarily musical position in the synagogue. Eventually, two very different cantorial customs developed. In Sephardi congregations (those in and around the Mediterranean Sea and in Arabic cultures) cantors emphasized accurate Hebrew pronunciation and meter rather than musical embellishment. On the other hand, in the Ashkenazi tradition (developed by Jews in northern Europe), where Jews were often segregated from the larger population, musical ornamentation of the text by cantors grew to such a degree that rabbis and congregations viewed it with mixed feelings. Although the beauty of great cantorial singing inspired many listeners, some rabbis suspected that it also led to vanity among cantors and opened the door to foreign music. More complex musical renditions by the cantor also discouraged congregational singing, and thus inhibited the real purpose and goal of communal worship. Nonetheless, the cantor was a beloved figure in many congregations. Both cantorial traditions are widely practiced in the state of Israel today.

The third musical tradition of the synagogue is a distinctive kind of harmony, dating back to the sixth and seventh centuries when the classical piyyutim were written and sung. Those early hymns were based on what were then new principles of rhyming and strophe, or the arrangement of stanzas, that varied the number of syllables in a verse. The result was heterophony, in which the congregation never sings in exact unison and each individual contributes his or her own private version of melody and harmony to the chant. Later Sephardi congregations continued to emphasize this rich musical communal effort. In Ashkenazi congregations, however, where cantorial embellishment of the text sometimes intimidated the congregation, heterophony was sometimes the result of the congregation's inability to follow the cantor's musical lead.

By the early Middle Ages, Ashkenazi and Sephardi customs had developed their own distinctive musical cultures. First, piyyutim sung by Ashkenazi Jews in Northen Europe differed considerably from those popular among Sephardi Jews. Ashkenazi poetry grew out of local feelings and situations, sometimes with simple hidden messages or the author's name in acrostic patterns. Sephardi poetry was far better literature. Second, polyphony, or music with two or more melodic parts sounded together, was sung in Jewish communities throughout Europe by the sixteenth and seventeenth centuries. This may have emerged from the standard vocal trio found in larger congregations: cantor, boy soprano, and either a tenor, baritone, or bass voice that complemented the cantor's lead. By the eighteenth century, baroque cantatas were sung in some synagogues in Italy, and traveling cantors spread that musical form to other congregations. Organ music was permitted on occasions other than Sabbath worship. By the nineteenth century, cantorial embellishment, heard to a greater extent in Ashkenazi synagogues, was inspired by Italian opera. At the same time, despite this innovation, other melodies had become so standard that they were treated as if Moses had handed them down from Mount Sinai.

Jewish hymns are also sung outside of the synagogue. Families often sing liturgical poetry at home, during and after the Sabbath meal on Friday evening and after other meals, to praise and thank God. These songs are often published in easy-to-read collections for domestic use. Jews differ in their favorites; songs popular in one part of the world may be unknown or disliked elsewhere. There is no fixed order to these songfests and everyone may sing whatever they wish. Among Hassidim (Jews who follow mystical traditions that emerged in eastern Europe in the 1700s) a wordless musical tradition emerged. These wordless melodies are believed to express a pure music similar to pure souls. Hassidim believe that singing them not only lifts the human spirit but also helps to return the cosmos to its pure, pristine state as God created it. These wordless melodies are often sung at table fellowship in homes, at worship in the synagogue, and on special occasions.

Jewish hymnody underwent significant changes during the Reform movement that began in the Germanic lands of western Europe. Napoleon's conquest opened the ghetto gates, but his defeat in 1815 brought with it a resurgence of anti-Jewish laws. German political debates throughout the nineteenth century aired a wide variety of perspectives as to how to integrate a minority religious population into a country that viewed itself as homogenous. Before Jews could acquire entry into schools, professions, and trades, and access to public cultural centers and voting rights, German society and politics demanded that Jews blend into the German culture. Thus challenged to view their own culture through the eyes of outsiders who were utterly ignorant of its meaning, Jews in Germanic lands began to adapt Judaism's style to look more like German Lutheranism. Reformers hoped that they could modify the form of Judaism while leaving its substance unchanged.

But form and substance are closely linked, and synagogue music, an early focus for change, quickly became a controversial issue. Between 1810 and 1817, three breakaway congregations abolished piyyutim to shorten the worship service. They also introduced choirs and replaced the cantorial chant of Torah in its original Hebrew with recitations from a German translation of the Bible. The polyphony and heterophony of traditional congregational chanting sounded like noisy confusion to Germans, who told Jews of their disdain. Jews who wanted reform therefore wrote new German hymns, found gentile composers who could write arrangements for both new and traditional poetry that sounded like Lutheran hymns, replaced minor chords with major chords, and sang these new songs in unison, rather than in a polyphonic manner. Organs and choirs were used to set the cadence for prayer. Although these early efforts were dramatic, they did not produce good music.

A decade later, talented Jewish musicians in Vienna began to compose new music for the synagogue using the Austrian standards of musical taste then in vogue. Trained in both Judaism and western music, they successfully reshaped congregational polyphony into choir music using four-part harmony. Their new arrangements often inserted melodic congregational responses into the choir's songs. To train future congregants they wrote songbooks for children. For smaller and more traditional congregations who wanted to modernize their music, simpler musical arrangements in two-part harmony for cantor and choir, without organ music, were written. Finally, the Viennese Jewish musicians made the new music widely adaptable to congregations, who differed in wealth and in attitudes toward reform, by writing organ music that simply echoed one of the choir's harmonic lines.

Eastern European congregations also developed new musical styles in the nineteenth century, although they were far less eager to change synagogue traditions than were Jews in western Europe. Jews in the East did not face the same pressure to change that challenged Jews in Germanic lands. Indeed, eastern Jews were still restricted to certain geographic areas, banned from many public cultural centers, and barred from many schools, professions, and trades.

Among eastern European Jews, cantorial singing flourished to a degree that rivaled operatic performances. Many of those cantors learned complex modern singing styles while visiting Odessa, a seaside city outside the area of western Russia, where most eastern Jews were confined. In Odessa, Jews could attend public musical performances alongside non-Jews. Through Odessa's influence, the opera, the symphony, and the music hall inspired synagogue music. Yet tradition dictated that women would almost never sing in synagogue choirs and that instrumental music was seldom allowed.

American Jews also contributed to changing trends in Judaism. In 1824 a small group calling themselves the Reformed Society of Israelites organized in Charleston, South Carolina. Members of Congregation Beth Elohim, the Society tried to convince the congregation to adopt their ideas for change. After failing at that, the Society formed a separate group. Their motives for change differed in part from those changing Jewish worship in Germany. Charleston's reformers worried that too many local Jews were so unfamiliar with Hebrew and Jewish tradition that they were beguiled by the arguments of Christian missionaries. The changes the Charleston reformers had in mind would, they hoped, so accommodate Jewish worship to the sensibilities of American-born Jews in the South that evangelists would be resisted and attendance at worship would increase. Their action made Charleston's Jewish community the first in the country to form a second congregation because of doctrinal disagreements rather than differences in national origins.

The Reformed Society of Israelites was also the first American Jewish congregation to transform its liturgical music. Yet, as with the reformers in Germany, the members viewed synagogue style through the eyes of their Christian neighbors, who set the standard for American culture and who could not fathom polyphonic chants. Indeed, Christian Americans who visited synagogues sometimes found the chants confusing and insufficiently solemn. They published their conclusions in local and national newspapers and magazines and told their Jewish neighbors of their opinions. Although American Jews enjoyed religious freedom, they, like Jews in Germany, found themselves challenged by local gentiles to change their traditions to suit Christian tastes. Moreover, many of Charleston's Jews, born and raised as a small minority in the South, shared the tastes of the larger culture. Thus, Charleston's reformers hoped to bring "order and decency . . . harmony and beauty in chanting" to Jewish worship.

Penina Moise's brother, Abraham, was probably the most ardent member of the new society and served for a time as its president. He helped to write new prayers and hymns sung in unison by the congregation at worship and on special occasions, when instrumental music and mixed choirs often were heard.

Although the project quickly attracted fifty members, it collapsed a few years later. Yet, within fifteen years, Beth Elohim adopted its ideas. For many members, the fact that similar changes were being made to Jewish worship in Europe legitimated the reformers' more radical efforts.

Penina Moise undoubtedly participated in the religious creativity that so engaged her brother. Abraham Moise wrote a handful of hymns and edited a prayer book used by the Reformed Society of Israelites. Although no other congregation adopted that text, many congregations who did not know her name sang Penina's hymns. In her hymns, language and meaning effectively blended Jewish religious and American cultural values and styles. Although her hymns display the taste and language shared by many Victorian female Christian poets, Moise, like writers of piyyutim throughout history, was also deeply inspired by the synagogue service and its psalms. As with other Jewish creators of religious poetry, she expressed her own religious vision. And, as with other poets, she often used a teaching voice and hoped to instill her own piety in others. Finally, as with those ancient piyyutists, she gave Jewish meaning to words from the surrounding culture. Her use of terms such as "grace" and "first elected nation" displays her understanding of the literature and religion of her surrounding culture, just as ancient psalmists incorporated Greek and Aramaic and the great Sephardi writers incorporated Arabic meter.

Most members of Reform congregations had come to the United States from western Europe between 1825 and 1870. By and large, these immigrants were less concerned with maintaining religious traditions than were the Jews who remained in Europe. For many immigrants, American individualism meant a willingness to break with the past. Some of them were already familiar with European reforms similar to those carried out by Reform Judaism in America. European changes included shortened worship services, unison singing, four-part harmony by choirs, and prayers in German. The Protestant worship style, on which American Reform modeled itself, was similar to the German Lutheranism that influenced Jews in Germany. Finally, the movement for reform in nineteenth-century America reshaped its worship to integrate Torah reading with the sermon of the rabbi and the hymnody of the congregation in a manner similar to Protestant worship.

By the time of the Civil War, Isaac Mayer Wise, the leader of the Reform movement in America, published a prayer book and hymnal in hopes of unifying diverse practices used by over one hundred congregations who participated in Jewish reform. Throughout the second half of the nineteenth century, new Reform prayer books and hymnals continued to appear in various cities around the country, reflecting the efforts of local gifted rabbis and their congregations. Some of the new hymnals were designed to be used by Sunday school children. Their simple melodies appealed to children, and their lyrics instilled basic beliefs and explained the meaning of many holidays and symbols.

But in many congregations, the splendid sounds of the choir and organ did not inspire the congregants—they intimidated them. Rabbis serving those congregations sought a means to modify Reform hymns so that people felt invited to participate. In 1897, Reform rabbis published the Union Hymnal, which helped to unify Reform worship and encourage participation. By 1905, over sixty-two thousand copies were being used by 183 congregations. The hymnal included not only hymns with texts by American poets John Greenleaf Whittier and James Russell Lowell but also hymns first published in 1842 by Penina Moise.

By the late nineteenth century, Reform Jews had dramatically changed their singing patterns. In the synagogue, mixed seating replaced sex-segregation and singing in unison replaced polyphonic chant. At the same time, an increasing number of women attended religious services. In some synagogues, singing thus came to provide an experience of unity among all Jews of the local community, male and female together. In larger congregations, choirs and cantors provided much of the music sung by congregants elsewhere. Reform Jews rarely sang domestic, after-meal praise songs, so that synagogue experiences comprised a higher percentage of their worship activities than they did for more traditional Jews. Yet, though Moise's hymns were sung in unison or by a choir in the synagogue, because they were originally written as poems, they could also serve to guide private devotions at home.

Although Reform was the most popular movement in American Judaism in the nineteenth century, by 1920 it served only a minority of American Jews. We can point to two reasons for this change. First, congregations began to feel that Reform had grown cold and intimidating. The largest Reform congregations had built large, impressive synagogues presided over by rabbis who lectured their congregants in weekly sermons. In some synagogues, robed choirs, strengthened by professional singers, marched with dignity to their assigned places. Historians have noted that, generally, when organs and formal choirs were introduced into synagogues, congregational participation in singing waned. Reform rabbis sought ways to improve participation among their congregants. Congregations also tried to address the problem themselves. For example, in 1911, one Houston Reform congregation instructed its choir director to teach members of the congregation how to sing, rather than hiring professional singers.

The second reason for the decline in Reform's popularity was that between 1880 and 1924, 2.3 million Jews came to America from eastern Europe. Those new immigrants had had no contact with Reform in Europe. Indeed, most of these immigrants were intimately familiar with Judaism's historically complex and rich worship traditions. For them, Reform did not look like Judaism at all. Those eastern European immigrants and their descendants found the formality and quiet of most Reform synagogues unappealing.

By the mid twentieth century, Moise's hymns were seldom heard because they expressed a worldview and used language intimately tied to the nineteenth century. As Victorian culture died in World War I, hymns that expressed Victorian values fell out of favor. At the dawn of the twenty-first century, hymns sung in American synagogues include traditional psalms and piyyutim, melodies written by contemporary Jewish songwriters, ditties composed for Jewish summer camps, tunes from Jewish folk music, and popular Israeli songs. Today's vibrant cross-fertilization in Jewish liturgical music is nurtured by the close contact among Jews from communities long separated but who today find themselves neighbors in America and especially in Israel.

The three hymns included here typify Moise's themes, writing style, and point of view. Together, they illustrate her own beliefs and help us understand the world she lived in. The first, "Religion," is a lesson about the benefits of a religious life. In it we see Moise as a teacher of religion. Perhaps her years as a Sunday school teacher inspired the verses. The hymn argues that religion helps us cope with life's difficulties and disappointments, protects us from being seduced by worldly goods, and helps us to be good to others and to face death calmly. Even though the hymn speaks of religion in general, we know that Moise means Judaism.

While many writers throughout history and in many cultures have written of religion's power to help us cope with life's difficulties, we can also discover specific elements in "Religion" that point to Moise's pen. These elements identify its author as a Jewish woman living in a seaport town, part of a minority population who worked to keep good relations with the larger non-Jewish world. Her vivid opening metaphor, of being tossed on breakers by a tempest when the guiding beacon has gone out, conjures up an image of disaster familiar to everyone living in her seaport city of Charleston, South Carolina. Immediately after explaining that religion alone enables us to cope with disaster, she points out that religion also helps us appreciate good times. Finally, religion should guide our relationships with non-Jews as well, returning insults with kindness. Although Judaism teaches the importance of kindness, Moise's choice of phrase hints that in Charleston, Jewish relations with non-Jews could sometimes be tense.

Because the hymn presents Judaism as a religion of the heart, the home, and the mind, we may conjecture that its author was a Victorian woman. Victorian culture of the mid nineteenth century not only typified women's lives as home-centered, it also claimed that women were especially spiritual, because they were more emotional than men. In that view, religious activities that could be conducted at home were especially important to women. Just as Judaism teaches, Moise insists that we should enjoy the blessings of life and acknowledge them with prayers of thanks at rising and before going to sleep. She mentions Judaism's private prayers rather than its communal prayers or rituals. According to Judaism, to the Enlightenment philosophy still influential in early-nineteenth-century America, and to Moise, human reason can conclude that the laws of nature were put in place by God not only to keep the world running smoothly but also to teach us lessons about God's power. Thus, the hymn says not only that religion in general strengthens courage and comforts anxiety but that Judaism and its private rituals fortify Jews (and especially Jewish women) to face life as minorities while fully living their religion.

The second piece, "Hymn," offers some of the same lessons as "Religion," but from a more personal point of view. This poem is also a prayer, and that is what makes it especially vivid as a hymn. Its primary theme is that faith transformed Moise's emotions from despair to calm. By seeing life's disasters as part of God's plan, she could resign herself to hardship because she believed that, although God might punish her as a father, God would ultimately reward her goodness. That idea filled many pages of literature written by and for women in Victorian America and England. Her hymn places Jewish faith in the midst of other faiths, just as her own life as a Jew was lived in the midst of other religions. First, she speaks of God as the shield of faith divine, alluding to Jewish prayers that speak of God as the "shield of Abraham." Toward the end of the hymn, she talks of her membership in the "first elected nation," an allusion to Jews, who, according to biblical record, established a relationship with God long before Christianity's birth. But the word "first" implies that there might be a second or third, thus opening up the Jews' status from the unique people to one among others.

Moise's "Hymn" is especially interesting because in it we can see how she adapted ideas and images from Christianity and from American culture to express her Judaism. Indeed, we can even see in it her own answer to Charleston's Christian evangelists, who insisted that Christianity alone was the source of true faith, America's liberties, and eternal life. Moise speaks of lifting her hands in prayer, a gesture common in Christian iconography but not especially used in Judaism. It works in her "Hymn" because it is a private gesture that indicates personal piety. She talks of God's grace, a Christian concept that refers to Jesus coming into one's life to instill and help maintain faith. For Moise, however, God's grace comes not from Jesus but from God the father, the God of the Hebrew Bible and the focus of Jewish worship. To her, God's grace not only instills faith but also is the source of all life's goodness. She declares that "Light, being, liberty and joy" are gifts of that God, not of Jesus. Finally, she proclaims that after granting life, liberty, all the goodness of the earth, and faith, God grants eternal life. That last claim especially refutes the evangelical assertion that only Christianity offers eternal life for the soul.

In "Feast of Esther," a hymn composed for the celebration of the Jewish holiday of Purim, Moise's rhymes are simpler. Purim's rituals blend a children's carnival with synagogue prayer, and she probably intended this hymn to be sung by children. The hymn avoids all talk of adult themes such as coping with despair. Instead, it tells the events that Purim celebrates in a simple manner and assures children that God watches over them. Here, too, Moise uses the Christian term "grace" to describe God's relationship with Jews, called the "Hebrew race," a term that focuses on Jewish identity based on family descent. The term "race" was applied to all sorts of national and ethnic groups in the early nineteenth century.

The Purim story tells how Jews living in Persia (Susa in Moise's poem) during the fifth century B.C.E. were saved from mass execution. Moise's poem refers to the main characters in that salvation: Mordecai, "the mourner at the palace-gate," and his niece, Esther, "the maiden on the throne." In several ways throughout the poem, Moise repeats the idea that God defends Jews and never allows their enemies to destroy them. Although the adults in the congregation no doubt understood the dangers of living as a religious minority, in this child's hymn Moise builds confidence that God protects those who remain faithful.

For over one hundred years, American Jews found Moise's hymns appealing and inspiring. Children sang her simpler works at holiday celebrations and in religious schools. As late as 1929, the Hebrew Sunday School in Philadelphia, which then served over three thousand students each year, included one of her pieces in their then newly printed hymnal, which was used for more than twenty years throughout the United States. Their blending of Jewish ideas with ideas about religion common in American culture, whether from Christian sources, Enlightenment philosophy, or Victorian ideals, solved religious questions for many American Jews. Yet most American Jews have never heard of Penina Moise. Often, as in the case of the Philadelphia hymnal, her name was not included as author of the hymn she had written. Victorian values often erased women's accomplishments. But even without fame, Moise helped generations of American Jews give voice to their faith.

The hymns printed here are from *Hymnal*, Beth Elohim Congregation, (Charleston, S.C.: Levin and Tavel, 5602 [1842]). From the Klau Library, Hebrew Union College, Cincinnati, Ohio.

Further Reading

Lawrence Hoffman and Janet Walton, eds., *Sacred Sounds and Social Change: Liturgical Music in Jewish and Christian Experience* (Notre Dame: University of Notre Dame Press, 1992); Michael Meyer, *Response to Modernity: A History of the Reform Movement* (New York: Oxford University Press, 1988); Harold Moise, *The Moise Family of Charleston* (Columbia: University of South Carolina Press, 1961); Alan Silverstein, *Alternatives to Assimilation: The Response of Reform Judaism to American Culture 1840–1930* (Hanover, N.H.: Brandeis University Press, 1994); Ellen Umansky and Dianne Ashton, *Four Centuries of Jewish Women's Spirituality* (Boston: Beacon, 1992); Sharona Wachs, *American Jewish Liturgies: A Bibliography of American Jewish Liturgy from the Establishment of the Press in the Colonies through 1925* (Cincinnati: Hebrew Union College Press, 1997); Jack Wertheimer, ed., *The American Synagogue: A Sanctuary Transformed* (Cambridge: Cambridge University Press, 1987); Gary Zola, *Isaac Harby of Charleston 1788–1828: Jewish Reformer and Intellectual* (Tuscaloosa: University of Alabama Press, 1984).

Religion

To smile when we on life's breakers are tossed
And serenely its tempest survey;
To say, though the beacon of hope is lost:
"Mercy's star will direct our way";
Such trust in trial's hour,
Springs from Religion's pow'r

At morn, with cheerful emotions to rise
Glorifying the Giver of rest:
Ne'er to let sleep our senses surprise,
Ere the world's benefactor is blest,
Such is the righteous course,
Man's reason should enforce.

With high resolve in duty's path to tread,
Though it may our fondest wish frustrate;
Nor ever, by temptation to be led,
Virtue's sacred laws to violate;
Faith only nerves the soul
To this great self-control.

To live in harmony with all mankind;
Injuries with favors to requite
To hold God's image in the heart enshrined
Nor by sin its purity to blight;
Now, and forevermore.

Undazzled by gold, by menace unmoved,
One sole Being Supreme to cherish;
To be firm in the faith our fathers loved,
Though for this, as martyrs we perish;
To piety alone
Such fortitude is known.

To make decay familiar to the mind,
And in death God's messenger perceive,
Who, when the mortal breath has been resigned,
Will the soul to its Redeemer leave;
What but Religion can
Reveal this gracious plan?

Hymn

I weep not now as once I wept
At Fortune's stroke severe;
Since faith hath to my bosom crept,
And placed her buckler there.

Lightly upon this holy shield
Falls sorrow's thorny rod;
And he who wears it, learns to yield
Submissively to God.

It breaks the force of ev'ry dart,
By disappointment hurled
Against the shrinking human heart,
In this cold, callous world.

Wrestling with this, I have defied
All that my peace assailed;
Passion subdued hath turned aside,
And sin before it quailed.

How many wounds would now be mine;
How many pangs intense!
But for the shield of faith divine,
My spirit's strong defence.

Oh! When in prayer my hands I lift
To Thee Almighty God!
The excellence of this Thy gift,
With fervor will I laud.

O God! To Thy paternal grace,
That ne'er its bounty measures,
All gifts Thy grateful children trace,
That constitute Life's treasures.

Light, being, liberty, and joy,
All to Thee are owing;
Nor can another hand destroy
Blessings of Thy bestowing.

None, save our own! For in man's heart
Such passions are secreted,
That peace affrighted weeps apart,
To see Thy aim defeated.

LIGHT is made dim by human guile;
EXISTENCE doth but languish;
And FREEDOM loses her bright smile
'Mid scenes of strife and anguish.

Father! Though forfeited by sin
Are all Thy tender mercies;
There is TRUSTING FAITH within,
That ev'ry fear disperses.

Honour and praise to Thee belong,
O God of our salvation!
Who will defend from shame and wrong,
Thy first elected nation.

Protector of the quick and dead!
Thy love THIS WORLD o'erfloweth;
And when the "vital spark" hath fled,
Eternal Life bestoweth.

Feast of Esther

Almighty God! Thy special grace
In seasons of distress;
Hath ever by the Hebrew race,
Been gratefully confest.

When lots were cast with evil aim
Thy people to destroy;
From Thee the great decision came,
That turned their tears to joy.

Earth's mightiest at thy decree,
E'en to the frailest yield;
And Susa's shore, and Egypt's sea,
Proclaim Thee Israel's shield.

The mourner at the palace-gate,
The maiden on the throne,
Were but the instruments of fate,
To make God's mercy known.

To Thee alone the praise belongs,
Who with a father's hand,
From Judah's race averts
The wrongs, By adversaries planned.

Let proud, ungodly man elate,
With trumpets of an hour;
Remember heaven can frustrate
Each dark device of pow'r.

Sov'reign of worlds! Thou will extend
The scepter to the just;
The rights of innocence defend,
And bring its foes to dust.

9

Catholic Song in the Antebellum United States

Robert R. Grimes, S. J.

The Reformation of the sixteenth century radically transformed the nature and practice of Christianity throughout Europe. In England the Anglican Church supplanted Roman Catholicism and emerged in the seventeenth century as the dominant form of British Christianity. The practice of Roman Catholicism was outlawed throughout England and its colonies, and Catholics were disenfranchised at best, imprisoned and executed at worst. Thus, when the British made settlements on the eastern coast of North America, various forms of Protestantism were soon established as the official religion.

The ban on the practice of their religion did not stop Catholics from immigrating to the American colonies. In 1634 a group of largely upper-class Catholics and working-class Protestants founded the colony of Maryland under a charter obtained by George Calvert, Lord Baltimore. His hope was for a colony in which there would be toleration for all forms of Christianity. The hope became law with the passage by the Maryland Assembly of the Toleration Act of 1649; the same hope was dashed with the law's repeal in 1692 and the establishment of the Anglican Church in Maryland. The public practice of Roman Catholicism would be illegal in all thirteen British colonies until they declared independence from Britain in 1776. Nevertheless, Catholics continued to arrive in the colonies from many lands, including England, Ireland, Acadia, and France. In the more tolerant atmosphere of Quaker Pennsylvania, public Catholic chapels, if discreet, were allowed as early as 1734. After independence from Britain, Catholics erected churches in many cities and towns, including Boston, New York, and Baltimore.

Although Catholicism was no longer illegal, many citizens of the new United States were wary of the religion. They often viewed Catholics' allegiance to the Pope, the bishop of Rome, as a threat to American democracy and its freedoms. Their fears were also fueled by what they regarded as the strange and elaborate rituals of Catholicism, which were conducted in Latin and founded on what many Americans considered superstition and idolatry. Fears began to be expressed in violence. In 1834 a Catholic convent school in Massachusetts was burned in the middle of the night by a Protestant mob. In the 1840s huge numbers of Catholic immigrants from Ireland and Germany began landing in the United States, and fear and violence escalated. The city of Philadelphia suffered anti-Catholic riots in the spring and summer of 1844. The American Catholic experience of the mid-nineteenth century was molded by many factors, including longing for the "old country" that many immigrants departed due to poverty or oppression, and hopes for the future in spite of the hostility and challenges faced in the United States.

Many leaders in the American Catholic community perceived public institutions as a threat to Catholic identity. In response they founded not only churches but Catholic schools, colleges, and orphanages. Catholic social organizations—political clubs, temperance leagues, and musical organizations—became numerous in the first half of the nineteenth century. The historical evidence indicates that music was performed in many of these. The Catholic Church itself, however, under the influence of late-nineteenth- and early-twentieth-century liturgical reforms, had forgotten most of its earlier songs, with a few notable exceptions. The words for the first Catholic hymns published in what would become the United States were included in two devotional manuals printed in Philadelphia in 1774: *A Manual of Catholic Prayers* and *The Garden of the Soul*. By 1787 the first collection of Catholic music with notation, *A Compilation of Litanies, Vesper Hymns and Anthems as They are Sung in the Catholic Church,* appeared under the auspices of Philadelphia silversmith and music engraver John Aitken. It is considered the first collection of sacred music published for a specific religious denomination in English-speaking America. By the outbreak of the American Civil War, over seventy hymnals and collections of Catholic music had been printed in the United States.

The existence of vernacular song in early American Catholic worship is clear, in spite of the mandated use of Latin in the worship of the Roman Catholic Church. The vast majority of texts in *A Manual of Catholic Prayers* and *The Garden of the Soul* are English texts. John Carroll, the first Catholic Bishop of the United States, noted in 1784 that few American Catholics understood Latin. Furthermore, missals—books that explained Catholic rituals and contained English translations of some of the Latin texts used in services—were unavailable to most church members, many of whom were illiterate. Under Carroll's leadership the first diocesan synod in the United States (1791) recommended the use of the vernacular for some hymns and prayers during the Catholic mass and vesper service. In response to European criticism of the practice, Carroll argued that songs in English were not sung as part of the official liturgy but were used between parts of the service in the same way that instrumental and choral music was used in Italian churches. Vernacular songs embellished the service and allowed the congregation a role parallel to the official ritual being performed by the priest. Vernacular song would also become a part of Catholic religious and social organizations as well as Catholic schools. While English was by far the most common language used, collections of Catholic songs in French appeared as early as 1798 in Baltimore and in German by 1820 in Pennsylvania.

The expressed motivations behind the work of the compilers and composers of these collections varied greatly. John Lefebvre de Cheverus, the future bishop of

Boston, was tremendously impressed by the role of music among the Passamaquoddy tribe of the present-day state of Maine, a tribe Cheverus had visited in
1797. Converted to Catholicism by French missionaries but long without contact
with Catholic clergy, the Passamaquoddy gathered each Sunday to sing the music
taught them by the missionaries many years earlier. Cheverus attributed their
retention of Catholicism to the power of music and shortly thereafter published a
collection of music for New England Catholics who were often unable to attend
Catholic services. He included instructions on when certain hymns should be
sung, both within Catholic services and when Catholics gathered without a priest
to perform the ceremonies. Philip Kirk, compiler of the 1844 collection entitled
The Catholic Harp, warned that Catholic children attending public schools
learned Protestant hymnody that might prove a danger to their Catholic faith. His
collection was designed to ensure that Catholic children sang Catholic songs.
Other writers stressed the pedagogical function of song, as in Jeremiah Cum-
mings's 1860 collection *Songs for Catholic Schools and Aids to Memory for the Catechism.* While a few Catholic churches in large urban centers such as New York
City or Philadelphia developed elaborate musical programs employing professional musicians, collections such as *Rohr's Collection of Favorite Catholic Music for
Church, School and Home* (1854) were the most widely used; they were described
as "adapted to the wants of small choirs, sodalities, and Sunday Schools."

A writer for a Boston newspaper, *The Literary and Catholic Sentinel,* penned a
romantic explanation of the power of music for the immigrant: "When the Irish exile,
in a far distant clime, hears the music of his native land, his heart feels transport; the
image of his country floats on every note, and its voice speaks audibly in every sound.
. . . It is music that fires the soul of the hero and the minstrel" (September 26, 1836).
Another journalist, in the *Freeman's Journal* (an Irish Catholic New York newspaper),
noted a link between music and Catholicism, writing that the "Catholic Church
speaks not from the pulpit alone. She speaks through all her solemn ceremonies. The
music, the incense, the processions, of her festivals, all speak,—and when rightly
performed, these speak with power and effect" (May 24, 1856).

The songs of antebellum American Catholicism can still speak today. While
one can never know how any individual interpreted or related to a particular
song, the music and lyrics of the most popular and enduring hymns provide a
glimpse into major themes within the community's understanding of itself. The
songs Catholics sang and listened to at the time can provide insight into the
hopes and beliefs, the sentiments and fears of a people. Four songs popular in
American Catholic circles in the early and middle years of the 1800s serve as
examples. Each represents different forces operating within Catholic culture
and various influences that stem from Ireland, Germany, America, and the creative impulses of the song's creators.

In 1826 appeared a Catholic song, "Like the Children of Sion," that captured
Catholic imagination and soon became an important part of the Catholic repertory
in antebellum America. New printing processes developed in the 1820s allowed
for the cheap and mass production of sheet music, the most marketable product of
the music industry before the advent of recorded sound. Songs published in this

format were often printed on a large sheet of paper folded once to form a four-page booklet. The first page frequently functioned as a cover and included the name of the song, its creators, and sometimes an illustration. The music and lyrics were printed on pages two, three, and four. Shorter songs appeared on a single sheet printed on one or two sides, whereas longer songs might take six or eight pages. "Like the Children of Sion" was sheet music created by two notable Catholics of the age. The composer was Philadelphia musician Benjamin Cross, an important figure in the musical life of Philadelphia. Charles Constantine Pise, a young Catholic priest who would become the first Catholic to serve as chaplain of the United States Senate, penned the words. He was a noted Catholic speaker and author who, over his career, worked in Baltimore, Washington, New York City, and Brooklyn. The lyrics are based on a type of imagery often found in immigrant writings of the time, images of exile and loneliness that reflected the experiences reported by many immigrants in their first years in America.

Pise's text is based on an image from Psalm 137: "By the waters of Babylon, there we sat down and wept." The psalm reflects the feelings of the Jewish people exiled in Babylon after their defeat in 586 B.C. The first stanza of Pise's text is one great simile, mirroring the psalm. The dominant images throughout the hymn focus on the idea of exile and loneliness. The Babylon of verse one becomes "this valley of life" in the second stanza. Jerusalem becomes "my country above," that is, heaven, in the third stanza. The "sorrows and fears" of life are contrasted with "contentment and love" in heaven. The condition of the speaker is one of passivity ("I recline me and think") and impotence ("Had I wings" and "Who will restore me").

Pise created a strophic text in four-line stanzas with a regular meter, although the rhyme scheme in stanza two differs from that of the other stanzas. Given the form, Benjamin Cross could easily have composed a hymn setting similar to those of Protestant composers of the period. But in his musical setting, Cross repeats part of the third line in each stanza, intensifying the phrases "and wet with their tears," "I should fly from this strife," and "from the storms shall I flee." The last word of each of these phrases is further intensified by the addition of a short cadenza, a musical device that stops the regular metrical pattern of the music and allows the performer an opportunity for a freer form of expression. The cadenzas, along with the elaborate melody and embellishments, reflect an Italian operatic style popular with many American composers in the early years of the nineteenth century.

"Like the Children of Sion" conveys the Christian belief in heaven and a new life after death that will heal all the sufferings of the present world. One can also interpret the song sociologically. Although both Pise and Cross were American-born and educated (Pise at Georgetown and Cross at The University of Pennsylvania), the song reflects images common among immigrants of the time: exile, loneliness, and the harshness of daily life. Hymns frequently contained dual religious and worldly meanings. The practical realities of life were thus raised to a higher meaning, and traditional theological concepts in turn were enlivened by everyday experiences. (See next page.)

Like the Children of Sion

Like the chil-dren of Si - on on Ba - by - lon's shore, When Je-rus'-lem their coun-try smil'd round them no more; Their harps were all lone-ly and wet with their tears, and wet with their tears - - - - And their bo - soms were har-row'd with sor - rows and fears.

Although the popularity of "Like the Children of Sion" may have been influenced by the immigrant experience, "Hail Glorious Apostle" is a direct reflection of the growing tide of Irish Catholic immigration in the 1830s. The hymn to Saint Patrick, the patron of Ireland, debuted at the Catholic cathedral in Boston on Saint Patrick's Day, 1833. The tune was familiar to the Irish immigrant as the traditional Irish air "St. Patrick's Day," arranged and harmonized by Boston composer and opera impresario Thomas Comer. The text was reported to have been written by a nun in the Ursuline Convent in Charlestown, Massachusetts, the convent that would be burned to the ground by an angry mob the following year. The bishop of Boston privately recorded that the nun was Sister Mary Austin. Born in County Cork, Ireland, in 1811 as Frances O'Keeffe, Austin had immigrated to Massachusetts and in 1830 had entered the Ursuline Convent.

The nine stanzas of the hymn follow the life of Saint Patrick, with a refrain that ends each stanza: "Hail glorious apostle selected by God, To enlarge the bless'd pale of Christ's faithful believers," but Irish immigrants could find many phrases in the text that reflected their own experience: "thy country and kindred to leave," "nor his freedom regained, / Till he'd suffer'd hardships and misery," "go forth to dwell among strangers," and "menac'd by infidels." There are also phrases that mirror the hopes of the institutional Catholic Church in America: the many conversions to Catholicism and the choice of priesthood by "men who were holy and learned" in stanza six, and the foundation of monasteries and schools in stanza seven. In sharp contrast with "Like the Children of Sion," this hymn, with its energetic Irish tune, is an expression of pride and vigor in the Catholic community. "Hail Glorious Apostle" is also an example of both the traditional Catholic veneration of the saints and the adaptation of that practice to changing circumstances. It was frequently sung at Catholic church services and concerts over its first thirty years and was published in numerous editions both as sheet music and in broadside format (a single page with words only). (See next page.)

"Mother Dear, O Pray for Me" did not originate as a Catholic, or even a religious, song. Although one of the most popular Catholic songs for over a century, it was the creation of Isaac Baker Woodbury, a Protestant composer of secular ballads and parlor songs (popular music that could be performed by amateurs in the "parlors" of their homes). First published as sheet music in 1850, the song dealt with a son addressing his mother:

> Mother dear, O pray for me,
> When fresh in youth's bright home,
> Or when afar thy child from thee,
> Feels oft the cold world's frown;
> O bow thy knee in earnest pray'r
> As none but parents know,
> That I may in temptation's hour,
> Be kept where'er I go.
> Mother dear remember me,

ROBERT R. GRIMES, S. J.

Hail Glorious Apostle

In thy constant pray'r;
Pray O pray most earnestly
That Heav'n may for me care.

The song was a typical example of sentimental parlor songs in a time when the theme of "mother" was especially popular.

It was also a time when it was common for individuals to create new lyrics to popular songs, changing the original focus for comic, political, religious, or social reasons. For example, William Dempster's tremendously popular "Lament of the Irish Emigrant" (1843) tells the story of a young man leaving Ireland after the death of his wife and child. An 1849 adaptation printed in a newspaper changed the story from one of poverty to one of alcoholism. New lyrics appear to have been composed for "Mother Dear, O Pray for Me" during the 1850s, most likely by someone connected to the sodality movement. Sodalities were Catholic religious organizations of laypeople that fostered prayer and good works among their members. The sodalities were particularly devoted to Mary, the Mother of Christ, and sought forms of devotion that would be popular with large groups of people. Woodbury's lyrics were transformed into a hymn to Mary and first printed in an 1861 sodality manual entitled *The Sacred Wreath*.

The first stanza is almost entirely rewritten, the second contains many changes, but the third stanza is almost identical in both versions. Two Philadelphia priests, Edward Sourin and Felix Barbelin, were closely associated with the manual, and one or both of them may have been the authors. Whether they initially retained Woodbury's melody is unclear, but when the song was first printed with musical notation in *Peters' Catholic Harp* (1863)—with the altered opening "O Virgin Mother, pray for me"—a new melody appeared with the text, along with the subtitle "Sodality Hymn." It is possible that the compiler of the collection, William Cumming Peters, composed the new melody. Peters was a Catholic musician tremendously successful as both a music publisher (he published Stephen Foster's early songs) and composer of both secular song and Catholic church music. The style of the 1863 version is not incompatible with that of Peters's parlor songs. Filled with images of frailty, danger, and loneliness, the text seems to express a deep-seated feeling within the Catholic immigrant community. The traditional Catholic belief in the care and intercession of the Mother of Christ is expressed here in a form similar to many secular "mother" songs popular at the time. Its sentimental nature spoke to generations of American Catholics before the liturgical reform of the Second Vatican Council in the 1960s. (See next page.)

The final example of antebellum Catholic song is the most enduring: "Holy God, We Praise Thy Name." The hymn first appeared in a collection of Catholic hymns published in Austria in the 1770s and was entitled "Grosser Gott! Wir loben Dich" ("Great God, We Praise You"). It is a metrical hymn, similar to Lutheran hymns of the period, based on the ancient Latin hymn of thanksgiving, "Te Deum Laudamus" ("We Praise You, O God"). The hymn was probably introduced into America through German Catholic immigrants and first appears in German language hymn collections. A number of attempts were made to translate the

Mother Dear, Oh! Pray for Me

Mo - ther dear, pray for me, Whilst far from heav'n and thee I wan - der in a fra - gile bark, On life's tem - pes - tuous sea. O vir - gin Moth - er, from thy throne, So bright in bliss a - bove, Pro - tect thy child, and cheer my path With thy sweet smile of love.

Moth - er dear, re - mem - ber me, And nev - er cease thy care Till in heav'n e - ter - nal - ly Thy love and bliss I share.

German text into English, such as one by the Reverend W. J. Barry that begins "God of Might! We sing Thy praise." But the hymn did not become popular until a Redemptorist priest, Clarence Walworth, penned the text that would be central to American Catholic hymnody up to the present day. Walworth was an early organizer of parish missions—what might be called a Catholic form of the Methodist revival—designed to increase the religious fervor of parish communities. A traveling team of priests would come into a Catholic parish for a week or more and conduct a series of services and devotions, for either the men or the women of the area, punctuated by powerful sermons. At the end of the mission, participants were asked to make some sort of commitment to increased religious practice. It is likely that Walworth wrote "Holy God, We Praise Thy Name" for use at the end of the missions he preached in the 1850s. His translation of the text began to appear in hymnals around 1860.

Avoiding the sentimentality so common to hymn texts of the period, the words are a strong affirmation of the belief of the American Catholic community in the sovereignty of God. The hymn connects an English-speaking congregation to an ancient and important hymn of the Christian Church. Perhaps a reflection of the melody's popularity, vocal embellishments were added to the fifth phrase and help build to a musical climax in the sixth and final phrase. The embellishments proved so popular that they began to be included in printed versions (as they are here: the notes with an asterisk above them are the embellishments). "Holy God, We Praise Thy Name" became the standard closing hymn in the Catholic service of Benediction. It survived the reforms of the Second Vatican Council and remains popular among American Catholics. (See next page.)

The tunes of these four songs—two sentimental, two triumphant—stem from different sources: Irish and German tunes and more recently composed American ones. The four texts are also influenced by various sources: Christian Scripture, Irish legend, American sentiment, and ancient Christian prayer. Two of the songs are quite personal, and two focus on the community, yet none of them is a part of the official worship of the Catholic Church. They provide, however, significant clues about the piety of the average churchgoer. The variety of sources and sentiments from which they were created reflect the variety of forces that shaped the antebellum American Catholic community, a group of diverse immigrants who found themselves in a sometimes hostile but always new and challenging environment. Just as the immigrants formed a new repertory of song, so too did they forge a new expression of Catholicism.

The lyrics of "Like the Children of Sion" are by Charles Constantine Pise (Philadelphia: George Willig, 1826). "Hail Glorious Apostle: A Hymn for St. Patrick's Day" was published in Boston by C. H. Keith in 1833. "Mother Dear, O Pray for Me" is from Laudis Corona: The New Sunday School Hymn Book (New York: D. & J. Sadlier, 1885). There are many variants in published versions of the song, further evidence of its popular origins. The author has corrected a few typographical errors in keeping with earlier printed versions. "Holy God, We Praise Thy Name" is from Anthony Werner, Cantate (Boston: Oliver Ditson, 1863).

ROBERT R. GRIMES, S. J.

Holy God We Praise Thy Name

Further Reading

Sandra Sizer Frankiel, *Gospel Hymns and Social Religion: The Rhetoric of NineteenthCentury Revivalism* (Philadelphia: Temple University Press, 1978). Although the book deals exclusively with Protestant song, it offers valuable insights into interpreting hymns and hymn texts. Robert R. Grimes, *How Shall We Sing in a Foreign Land? Music of Irish Catholic Immigrants in the Antebellum United States* (Notre Dame: University of Notre Dame Press, 1996). J. Vincent Higginson, *History of American Catholic Hymnals: Survey and Background* ([Springfield, Ohio]: Hymn Society of America, 1982).

LIKE THE CHILDREN OF SION

Like the children of Sion on Babylon's shore,
When Jerus'lem their country smil'd round them no more;
Their harps were all lonely and wet with their tears,
And their bosoms were harrow'd with sorrows and fears.

So in the dark shade of this valley of life,
I recline me and think of my country above,
Had I wings like the dove I should fly from this strife,
And repose in the arms of contentment and love.

O, when to thy beautiful visions I turn,
For thee like the love stricken turtle I mourn:
Oh! when from the storms of this world shall I flee,
And who will restore me Jerus'lem to thee.

HAIL GLORIOUS APOSTLE

Hail glorious apostle selected by God,
To enlarge the bless'd pale of Christ's faithful believers,
Accept our weak efforts to honor thy virtues,
And chiefly thy wonderful charity.
For t'was the bright flame of love seraphic
which moved thee thy Country and Kindred to leave,
All earthly enjoyment and comforts to part with.

Repeat: Hail glorious apostle . . .

Th' Almighty was pleased that our saint should be seized,
And led captive to Ireland by cruel barbarians.
He was long detained, nor his freedom regained,
Till he'd suffer'd hardships and misery.

He, during that time, laid up a store,
Of meekness, humility, patience and zeal;
His love for our Savior, increased beyond measure.

Repeat: Hail glorious apostle . . .

Six months thus elapsed, when St. Patrick at last,
Was deliver'd by Providence, from his hard bondage.
Grateful to Jesus for all his past favors,
He serves him with perfect fidelity.
God made known to him in diverse ways
That he was the person appointed on high,
To draw from idolatry the Irish nation.

Repeat: Hail glorious apostle . . .

Although to obey, he must every thing leave,
And like Abraham, go forth to dwell among strangers;
Burning with ardor, and heavenly fervor,
He yields to God's orders most generously.
With diligent care, did he prepare,
His soul for a mission so great and sublime;
Resolv'd to acquit himself of it most faithfully.

Repeat: Hail glorious apostle . . .

To Ireland he goes, in this manner dispos'd,
And for forty years, labor'd with zeal for that people,
Who had been buried in the grossest errors,
In all that regarded eternity.
He visited the remotest parts,
Without being daunted by dungeons or death,
With which he was frequently menac'd by infidels.

Repeat: Hail glorious apostle . . .

St. Patrick took care to ordain ev'ry where,
In his diocess, men who were holy and learned.
He consecrated great numbers to Jesus,
Who chose the state of chaste virginity.
God gave such a blessing to his zeal,
That infinite multitudes join'd the true church;
And many were models of virtue and fervor.

Repeat: Hail glorious apostle . . .

The saint well aware, how important is pray'r,
To succeed in the gaining of souls to th' Almighty,
Himself did unite with the source of all light,
In that exercise, most assiduously.

The glory of God to propagate,
He zealously founded three monasteries;
And schools did establish in ev'ry quarter.

Repeat: Hail glorious apostle . . .

At length did the Lord, ever true to his word,
Call our saint to receive the reward of his labors;
With joy he'd have giv'n his blood for religion,
Had he met with an opportunity.
For sake of his servant, God did free,
From venomous reptiles, the island of saints,
Which Patrick had sanctifi'd and rendered blessed.

Repeat: Hail glorious apostle . . .

Ah! now thou art plac'd in the kingdom of peace,
O most holy Apostle! our faithful protection;
Look down on Ireland, that once happy island,
But now persecuted and suffering.
Obtain for that nation ev'ry grace,
Which may draw upon it the blessing of heav'n;
And may all the nations be peaceful and happy!

Repeat: Hail glorious apostle . . .

MOTHER DEAR, O PRAY FOR ME

Mother dear, O pray for me,
Whilst far from heav'n and thee
I wander in a fragile bark,
On life's tempestuous sea.
O virgin Mother, from thy throne,
So bright in bliss above,
Protect thy child, and cheer my path
With thy sweet smile of love.

Refrain: Mother dear, remember me,
And never cease thy care
Till in heav'n eternally
Thy love and bliss I share.

Mother dear, O pray for me,
Should pleasure's syren lay
E'er tempt thy child to wander far
From Virtue's paths away:
When thorns beset life's devious way,

And darkling waters flow,
Then, Mary, aid thy weeping child,
Thyself a Mother show.

Refrain: Mother dear, remember me . . .

Mother dear, O pray for me,
When all looks bright and fair,
That I may all my danger see,
For surely then 'tis near;
A Mother's pray'r how much we need,
If prosperous be the ray,
That paints with glow the flow'ry mead
Which blossoms in our way.

Refrain: Mother dear, remember me . . .

HOLY GOD, WE PRAISE THY NAME

Holy God, we praise Thy Name!
Lord of all, we bow before Thee!
All on earth Thy sceptre claim,
All in heav'n above adore Thee:
Infinite Thy vast domain,
Everlasting is Thy Reign.

Hark! the loud celestial hymn,
Angel choirs above are raising!
Cherubim and Seraphim,
In unceasing chorus praising:
Fill the Heav'ns with sweet accord,
Holy! Holy! Holy Lord.

Let the apostolic train
Join Thy sacred Name to hallow!
Prophets swell the loud refrain,
And with white-robed martyrs follow,
And from morn till set of sun,
Through the Church the song goes on.

Holy Father, Holy Son,
Holy Spirit, Three we name Thee,
While in essence only One,
Undivided God we claim Thee:
And adoring bend the knee,
While we own the mystery.

Thou art King of Glory Christ!
Son of God, yet born of Mary,
For us sinners sacrificed,
And to death a tributary:
First to break the bars of death,
Thou hast opened Heav'n to Faith.

— 10 —

African American Spirituals

Paul Harvey

Beginning in the late eighteenth century, black slaves (and free people of color) converted to Christianity in significant numbers. Whites had begun proselytizing efforts earlier in the eighteenth century but with limited success. By the later eighteenth century, however, the growing evangelical movement of Baptists and Methodists preached a message appealing not only to ordinary whites but to black slaves as well. In the nineteenth century, white evangelicals led missions to the slaves, attempting to bring the Gospel to slaves while reassuring slave owners that this message would teach obedience and humility to their captive workers.

Many slaves accepted Christianity but adapted it to suit their own purposes. As evangelicalism spread throughout the South, white slave owners often brought slaves to church with them. Many antebellum churches in the South were filled with whites on the main floor and slaves in the balcony. In some cases, especially in urban centers in the South such as Richmond and Charleston, black congregants formed a majority in "white" churches. In some cases, blacks were allowed to attend their own churches, provided that whites remained in a supervisory capacity. Since slaves could not hold property, church buildings and other property for slave churches were held by white trustees, who also participated in the selection of pastors for the churches.

Beyond this visible church lay the "invisible institution"—slave religion. Enslaved Christians might have attended white-sanctioned and supervised services, sung the hymns of whites, and listened to white ministers advise them to practice obedience, patience, and humility. They also created their own covert religious culture, however, one with its own distinctive theology and rituals. In services held in slave cabins, in the woods at night, and in "hush harbors," enslaved African Americans developed a religious culture that brought together elements of their African past and their American evangelical training into a whole that ultimately was a unique creation of American religious culture. After the Civil War, the invisible church would become visible as African Americans formed thousands of their own churches and denominational institutions. Before the war, however, when such independent institutions were impossible, black religious life emerged most clearly in the religious rituals of their own services, including ring shouts, spirituals, and chanted sermons.

The spirituals have inspired much excellent historical, theological, and musicological scholarship, as well as a fair amount of controversy over their origins and meaning. The origins of the spirituals are vague, as is true of much folk music. Generally, they came from a mixture of white evangelical hymnology, black traditional song (and dance), and black southern folklore. The spirituals cannot be attributed to individual authors but instead emerged as a sort of communal voice of slave believers. Some lines of the spirituals clearly borrowed from folk tunes and hymns from the Anglo-American tradition. Other words and phrases seem to be derived from African American folklore, some traceable to Africa.

More importantly, the call-and-response pattern of the spirituals, and their rhythmically complex and antiphonal structure, clearly have roots in African and African American music. The very singing of the spirituals also indicates the African musical heritage. In 1862 a folklorist from the Sea Islands despaired of being able to "express the entire character of these negro ballads by mere musical notes and signs. The odd turns made in the throat; and that curious rhythmic effect produced by single voices chiming in at different irregular intervals, seem almost as impossible to place on score, as the singing of birds of the tones of an Aeolian Harp." In religious ritual, moreover, spirituals were accompanied by dance, swaying, foot stamping, hand clapping, and other physical exertions. Song and dance were always combined in the slave religious rituals. Thus, the experience of seeing the spirituals reproduced on the page conveys only a vague sense of what one gets from hearing the spirituals sung, even when performances attempt to recreate their antebellum "sound."

More important than the origins of the spirituals are their meanings. Meanings embedded in the ritual context—the hush arbors and secret meetings—of slave religion. Much debate has centered on the degree to which the spirituals contained encoded messages. To what degree was the spiritual freedom referred to in so many songs in effect a code for freedom from slavery? The spirituals, as poetry and literature set in musical form, could take on many meanings, depending on the time, circumstance, and individual. For generations of slaves, there was simply no viable hope that freedom would come in this life. In times of turmoil and war, however, when the very future of slavery was in question, freedom took on more obvious meanings. During the Civil War, slaves in South Carolina were jailed for singing what had become obviously subversive lines, such as "We'll soon be free." Recording these lines, a white army officer who commanded a black regiment wrote that "though the chant was an old one, it was no doubt sung with redoubled emphasis during the new events." As one of his soldiers told him, "De tink *de Lord* mean for say *de Yankees*," and they considered the final river to cross as not really being the Jordan of biblical times but the Potomac River near Washington. Another example often used by those who emphasize the double meaning of the spirituals is "Steal Away to Jesus," with its obvious connotation of stealing oneself away from the slave master into freedom: "Steal away, steal away home / I ain't got long to stay here." Finally, the remarkable rapidity with which slaves took up the story of the enslaved Israelites in Egypt as their own (despite the attempts of slave masters to prevent these passages in the Bible from being taught) shows that many had to be aware of the multiple meanings of what they sang. "Go down Moses," with its exhortation to tell Pharaoh to release the captives in Egypt, is the best example here.

At the same time, for much of the antebellum era, temporal freedom was simply beyond the grasp of most enslaved Americans. A few notable slaves managed to escape, and some even penned autobiographies following their successful ventures into freedom (the most notable being Frederick Douglass). The vast majority of slaves, however, faced the prospect of unending hard work, without recompense, for one or several masters, and the reality that their marriage partners or their children could be separated from them by sale. The slaves' religious expressions were, in part, an assertion of humanity against the dehumanizing system of treating humans as property. And they were more besides; they were an assertion of many slaves' deeply spiritual religious views from the Old Testament. The spirituals exalted Old Testament heroes, such as Moses and more obscure figures, and often turned New Testament figures such as Jesus into Old Testament–style avenging heroes. These biblical heroes became available then, for the slaves' sacred world invoked a kind of constant present. Sacred time merged with real time—hence the eagerness with which slaves in Richmond, Virginia, at the conclusion of the Civil War, greeted the arrival of President Lincoln as tantamount to the coming of Moses. He had "come way down in Egyptland" at last.

Slaves learned Christianity first from whites and later from their own preachers. They were not, however, passive receivers of this Christianity, as the spirituals themselves make abundantly clear. As one Alabaman noted in her diary, "When Baptist Negroes attended the church of their masters, or when their mistress sang with them, they used hymn books, but in their own meetings they often made up their own words and tunes. They said their songs had 'more religion than those in the books'." Many spirituals have some basis in the white popular evangelical tunes that were making their way (in the form of shape-note hymn books) to churches through the newly settled and developed areas. Whites also employed a variety of lyric books from the eighteenth century, setting the texts to familiar tunes. Slaves learned this music, and thus much of the evangelical imagery made its way into the slave spirituals. Whites and slaves sang of sin, conviction, redemption, salvation, and eternal life. At funerals for slaves, participants often sang a slave version of the white evangelical funeral hymn "Hark from the Tomb a Doleful Sound." Whites and slaves sang of how "this world is not my home" and retold biblical narratives such as the story of Joshua and the battle of Jericho.

Slaves also brought their own images and literary devices into the spirituals, which spoke as much of their African heritage as of their white Christian training. For example, the frequent call-and-response choruses found in the spirituals (and other black religious music) have a clear antecedent in the antiphonal music of their African ancestors. These practices were reinforced by the common practice in antebellum American singing of "lining out" hymns, with a leader calling out verses and congregants responding. The devil portrayed in the spirituals bears a more striking resemblance to the conjuring trickster of West African folklore than to the unambiguously evil Satan of Christian tradition. The slave spirituals, moreover, speak much less of individual sin and wretchedness, and much more of communal triumph, than the music favored by whites. "Amazing Grace," with its second line, "That saved a wretch like me," seems to have never taken hold in the slave community, or in postbellum black religion for that matter. Slaves had little use for white Calvinist cosmology, recognizing that southern whites theologically justified slavery as God's predestined fate for black people. Indeed, one of the remarkable attributes of the "sorrow songs," as the great black scholar W. E. B. Du Bois called the spirituals, is how much hope and jubilation may be found in their lyrics.

Thomas Wentworth Higginson, the white commander of a black Army regiment, recorded the beautiful lyrics to "I Know Moon-Rise," a spiritual that, on its surface, is about the peace that death will bring: "I'll lie in de grave and stretch out my arms; Lay dis body down." As Higginson wrote upon recording these lines, "Never, it seems to me, since man first lived and suffered, was his infinite longing for peace uttered more plaintively than in that line." And yet, through the turmoil and tribulation prominently featured in the spirituals, there is hope, and a powerful sense of self-worth and transcendence, that bursts through even the most troubled songs. Even in "I Know Moon-Rise," the lyrics attest to the conquering of death, to a self still able to stretch out arms and gaze at the canopy of the night sky. Even in one of the darker spirituals, "Sometimes I Feel Like a Motherless Child," lines such as "Sometimes I feel like an eagle in de air. . . . Spread my wings and / Fly, fly, fly" interrupt the sorrowful mood of the lyrics.

But the most important evidence of the African contribution to the spirituals is in the ritual that accompanied the singing: the moans, shuffles, and ring shouts central to African American religious expression. Most of the best observations of ring shouts come from the post–Civil War era, but it is clear they emerged in full form much earlier, during slavery times. In slave cabins (oftentimes with great secrecy, including turning a pot upside down at the door to "catch" the sound, a tradition probably derived from African folklore), in the hush harbors, or in other secluded settings, slaves would form a circle and begin singing. A leader would sit in the middle and become the caller, the lead singer, often singing the main lines with the rest of the group singing out the chorus and refrain in call-and-response form. Gradually the group would begin a slow shuffle, clapping their hands and moving rhythmically counterclockwise in a circle around the leader. Because evangelicals proscribed dancing, Christian slaves shuffled around the circle without crossing their feet, as feet-crossing was the barrier between proscribed dancing and perfectly acceptable forms of religious expression. Sometimes, after hours of the singing, the ring shout grew in intensity, picking up the tempo with successive verses and refrains of familiar tunes. Participants called out new verses that included local names and locations. By such means, stock phrases were turned over again and again to produce new material, some of which found its way into the versions of the spirituals recorded by observers such as Higginson. It is also for this reason that the spirituals cannot be said to have any author; they were, instead, communally (and anonymously) authored, and constantly revised and extemporized through the years. Finally, the intensity of the ring shout waned, and the informal services were finished off with slower and more solemn spiritual tunes. White observers of the ring shout, dating from the early nineteenth century, were fascinated with the ritual, as in this account: "The fascination of the music and the swaying motion of the dance is so great that one can hardly refrain from joining the magic circle in response to the invitation of the enthusiastic clappers, 'No, brudder!' 'Shout, sister!' 'Come, belieber!'"

In 1867, white collectors published the first "songbook" of the spirituals, *Slave Songs of the United States*, and introduced many Americans to the spirituals as a genre. Soon thereafter, concert hall performances of the spirituals swept the nation. In 1871 the "Jubilee Singers" of Fisk University, a black college in Nashville, set out on a fund-raising tour and brought the spirituals into American concert halls. By singing the African American spirituals in European concert form, the Jubilee Singers dissociated the music from the ritual context out of which it had emerged. Whites in America and England flocked to the performances, making the Jubilee Singers the single best fund-raising device that any black college president could have used. By the early twentieth century, most black colleges boasted their own version of the Jubilee Singers, and the performances receded further and further from the authentic music of the slave period. The musicians arranged the spirituals to European classical musical form, with precisely pitched notes and well-articulated consonants.

During these same years, black college students and faculty members at Hampton Institute in Virginia collected folklore and music of the freed people in heavily black-populated Southside Virginia. They published their work in the *Southern Workman,* one of the first academic journals to study Negro folklore as a distinctive contribution to the disciplines of folklore and anthropology. The purpose of their study was to document these "old traditions" before they passed away. The *Southern Workman* scholars collected much valuable material, including the lyrics to spirituals and all manner of black religious songs, providing an invaluable record for future scholars. Little did they know, however, that the spirituals would not die out with the older generation. In the twentieth century, spirituals lived on in rural churches and were incorporated into newer forms of black sacred song such as gospel music. Much later in the twentieth century, the spirituals took on new life as freedom songs, anthems of the black freedom struggle of the 1950s and 1960s. Today, musical groups such as Sweet Honey in the Rock have revived traditional ways of singing the spirituals, rescuing the musical form from the innovations brought to it by the Jubilee Singers and other similar groups. Scholars have studied the spirituals extensively, bringing the best historical, anthropological, and musicological methods to bear on these old and powerful musical texts.

The Selections here come from Deirdre Mullane, *Crossing the Danger Water: Four Hundred Years of African-American Writing* (New York: Anchor, 1993), pp. 274–92; Thomas Wentworth Higginson, *Army Life in a Black Regiment* (Reprint, New York: Norton, 1984, orig. 1867), pp. 187–213; and James Cone, *The Spirituals and the Blues* (New York: Seabury, 1972), p. 45.

Further Reading

Jon Cruz, *Culture on the Margins: The Black Spiritual and the Rise of American Cultural Interpretation* (Princeton University Press, 1999), Cheryl A. Kirk-Duggan, *Exorcizing Evil: A Womanist Perspective on the Spirituals* (Maryknoll, N.Y.: Orbis Books,1997); James Cone, *The Spirituals and the Blues* (New York: Seabury Press, 1972); John Lovell, *The Forge and the Flame: The Story of How the Afro-American Spiritual Was Hammered Out* (New York: Macmillan, 1972). On the Jubilee Singers, see Andrew Ward, *Dark Midnight When I Rise: The Story of the Jubilee Singers, Who Introduced the World to the Music of Black America* (New York: Farrar, Straus, and Giroux, 2000); for a recent compilation of the lyrics to spirituals, see Erskine Peters, ed., *Lyrics of the Afro-American Spiritual: A Documentary Collection* (Westport, Conn.: Greenwood Press, 1993).

Go Down, Moses

Refrain: Go down, Moses,
Way down in Egyptland
Tell old Pharaoh
To let my people go

When Israel was in Egyptland
Let my people go
Oppressed so hard they could not stand
Let my people go

Refrain: Go down, Moses . . .

"Thus saith the Lord," bold Moses said,
"Let my people go;
If not I'll smite your first-born dead
Let my people go.
No more shall they in bondage toil,
Let my people go;
Let them come out with Egypt's spoil,
Let my people go."

Refrain: Go down, Moses . . .

The Lord told Moses what to do
Let my people go;
To lead the children of Israel through,
Let my people go.

Refrain: Go down, Moses . . .

Roll, Jordan, Roll

Roll, Jordan, roll
Roll, Jordan, roll
I wanter go to heav'n when I die
To hear ol' Jordan roll.
O, Bretheren,
Roll Jordan, roll
Roll Jordan, roll,
I wanter go to heav'n when I die,
To hear ol' Jordan roll.
Oh brothers you oughter been dere,
Yes my Lord a sittin' up in de kingdom
To hear ol' Jordan roll,
Sing it ovah,
Oh, sinner you oughter been dere,
Yes my Lord a sittin' up in de kingdom.
To hear ol' Jordan roll.
O, Roll Jordan, roll,
Roll Jordan, roll,
I wanter go to heav'n when I die,
To hear ol' Jordan roll.

Steal Away to Jesus

Steal away, steal away, steal away to Jesus!
Steal away, steal away home.
I ain't got long to stay here.

Steal away, steal away, steal away to Jesus!
Steal away, steal away home.
I ain't got long to stay here.

My Lord, He calls me, He calls me by the thunder,
The trumpet sounds within-a my soul,
I ain't got long to stay here.

Steal away, steal away, steal away to Jesus!
Steal away, steal away home,
I ain't got long to stay here.

Steal away, steal away, steal away to Jesus!
Steal away, steal away home.
I ain't got long to stay here.

Green trees a-bending, po' sinner stand a-trembling,
The trumpet sounds within-a my soul,
I ain't got long to stay here,
Oh, Lord, I ain't got long to stay here.

I Know Moon-Rise

I know moon-rise, I know star rise,
   Lay dis body down.
I walk in de moonlight, I walk in de starlight,
   To lay dis body down.
I'll walk in de graveyard, I'll walk through de graveyard,
   To lay dis body down.
I'll lie in de grave and stretch out my arms;
   Lay dis body down.
I go to de judgment in de evenin' of de day,
   When I lay dis body down;
And my soul and your soul will meet in de day
   When I lay dis body down.

Deep River

Deep river, my home is over Jordan,
Deep river, Lord; I want to cross over into camp ground.

O, don't you want to go to that gospel feast,
That promised land where all is peace?

Deep river, my home is over Jordan,
Deep river, Lord, I want to cross over into camp ground.

My Army Cross Over

My army cross over,
   My army cross over,

O, Pharaoh's army drownded!
  My army cross over.

We'll cross de mighty river,
  My army cross over.
We'll cross de river Jordan,
  My army cross over,
We'll cross de danger water,
  My army cross over.
We'll cross de might Myo,
  My army cross over.

My army cross over,
  My army cross over,
O, Pharaoh's army drownded!
  My army cross over.

My Way's Cloudy

O, bretheren, my way, my way's cloudy, my way,
Go sen'a dem angels down,
O, bretheren, my way, my way's cloudy, my way,
Go sen'a dem angels down.

Dere's fire in de eas' an' fire in de wes',
Sen dem angels down,
Dere's fire among dem Methodis',
Oh sen'a dem angels down.

Old Satan is mad an' I'm so glad,
Sen dem angels down,
He missed de soul he thought he had,
Oh, sen'a dem angels down.

O, bretheren, my way, my way's cloudy, my way,
Go sen'a dem angels down.
O, bretheren, my way's cloudy, my way,
Go sen'a dem angels down.

Many Thousand Gone

No more peck o' corn for me,
  No more, no more,
No more peck o' corn for me,
  Many thousand gone.

No more driver's lash for me,
  No more, no more,
No more driver's lash for me,
  Many thousand gone.

No more pint o' salt for me,
  No more, no more,
No more pint o' salt for me,
  Many thousand gone.
No more hundred lash for me,
  No more, no more,
No more hundred lash for me,
  Many thousand gone.

No more mistress' call for me,
  No more, no more,
No more mistress' call for me,
  Many thousand gone.

We'll Soon Be Free

We'll soon be free,
We'll soon be free
We'll soon be free
  When de Lord will call us home.

My brudder, how long,
My brudder, how long,
My brudder, how long,
  'Fore we done sufferin' here?

It won't be long,
It won't be long,
It won't be long,
  'Fore de Lord will call us home.

We'll walk de miry road,
We'll walk de miry road,
We'll walk de miry road,
  Where pleasure never dies.

We'll walk de golden street,
We'll walk de golden street,
We'll walk de golden street,
  Where pleasure never dies.

My brudder, how long,
My brudder, how long,
My brudder, how long,
    'Fore we done sufferin' here?

We'll soon be free,
We'll soon be free,
We'll soon be free,
    When Jesus sets me free.

We'll fight for liberty,
We'll fight for liberty,
We'll fight for liberty,
    When de Lord will call us home.

Ride in, Kind Saviour

Ride in, kind Saviour!
    No man can hinder me.
O, Jesus is a mighty man!
    No man can hinder me.
We're marching through Virginny fields.
    No man can hinder me.
O, Satan is a busy man,
    No man can hinder me.
And he has his sword and shield,
    No man can hinder me,
O, old Secesh done come and gone!
    No man can hinder me.

I Thank God I'm Free at Last

Free at las', free at las',
I thank God I'm free at las'.
Free at las' free at las',
I thank God I'm free at las'.

Way down yonder in de graveyard walk,
I thank God I'm free at las'.
Me an' my Jesus gwineter meet an' talk,
I thank God I'm free at las'.

On-a my knees when de light pass by,
I thank God I'm free at las'.
Thought my soul would arise and fly,
I thank God I'm free at las'.

Some o'dese mornin's bright and fair,
I thank God I'm free at las',
Gwineter meet my Jesus in de middle of de air,
I thank God I'm free at las'.

Slavery Chain Done Broke at Last

Slavery chain done broke at last,
    Broke at last, broke at last,
Slavery chain done broke at last,
Going to praise God till I die.

Way down in-a dat valley,
Praying on my knees;
Told God about my troubles,
And to help me ef-a He please.

I did tell him how I suffer,
In de dungeon and de chain,
And de days I went with head bowed down,
And my broken flesh and pain.

I did know my Jesus heard me,
Cause de spirit spoke to me,
And said, 'Rise my child, your chillun,
And you shall be free.

I done 'p'int on might captain
For to marshall all my hosts,
And to bring my bleeding ones to me,
And not one shall be lost.

Slavery chain done broke at last,
    Broke at last, broke at last.
Slavery chain done broke at last,
Going to praise God till I die.

— 11 —

Ojibwe Funerary Hymn Singing

Michael D. McNally

Beginning in the 1830s, Protestant missionaries began promoting translations of evangelical hymns into the Ojibwe language as part of their larger effort to dismantle the structures, beliefs, and practices of Ojibwe tradition and to inculcate Protestant Christianity and Anglo-American culture. Ironically enough, the hymns emerged over time to become emblematic of the very culture that missionaries tried to eradicate. The same translated hymns took root in Ojibwe communities and grew to have a life of their own such that, today, the elders who sing those native language hymns are considered by many to be the more traditional Ojibwe people. The hymns were by and large faithful translations of the evangelical theologies of the missionaries and the tunes remained European in origin, but in the ritualized practice of singing them, Ojibwe people made them their own.

The Ojibwe were, and are, one of the largest of the native North American peoples whose traditional lands enveloped the western Great Lakes in Minnesota, Wisconsin, Michigan, Manitoba, and Ontario. By the time Protestant missionaries arrived in the old Northwest, many Ojibwe communities had more than one hundred years experience with the beliefs and practices of Catholicism, initially presented by Jesuit missionaries prior to their ordered removal from North America and maintained at fur-trading posts by métis of mixed French and Ojibwe descent. Yet it was Protestant missionaries who made a more necessary link between conversion to Christianity and cultural revolution. For these missionaries, to be Christian was to abandon subsistence from the seasonal round for the family farm, to leave the clan system and extended kin networks for the patriarchal nuclear family, and to forgo the traditions of the land and drum for those of the evangelical home.

Frustrated that preaching alone was insufficient to ignite this cultural revolution, missionaries embraced the translated hymn with great expectations. Consistent with the prevailing educational theory of the day, evangelicals believed the lessons sung in hymns could best transform even the most intractable of children. Missionaries similarly seized on hymns as useful for the transformation of the native peoples they considered to be like children. "The *wild* Indian voice is harsh," wrote Episcopalian Bishop Henry Whipple, "nothing could be more discordant than their wild yell and hideous war song. The religion of Christ softened this; their voices became plaintive, and as they sing from the heart their hymns are full of emotion."

From the missionaries' perspective, hymn singing marked a sharp departure from the shrill voicings of traditional Ojibwe music, from the dancing that typically accompanied it, and most importantly, from the drum, long the sine qua non of sacred music in the Ojibwe tradition. In traditional Ojibwe religious thought, the drum was more than an instrument; it was a sacramental vehicle for sung prayer. Drums were considered animate beings, powerful persons, coded grammatically as "he/she" rather than "it." The drum societies, groups of men who acted as stewards of particular drums, took their role very religiously, honored the drum by singing with it in the right spirit and by aspiring to higher standards of ethical and ritual conduct. Most traditional Ojibwe songs were considered to be sacred gifts from various spirits presented in dreams, whose performance constituted a kind of generation of sacred power. In such a cultural idiom, music was no casual matter. Melodies and texts of particular songs were, and are, respectfully passed on in the oral tradition by people considered to be stewards of their power. Even if the originating dreams presented songs with "meaningless" syllables, these were memorized verbatim and sung with utmost care. Given this posture toward song, it is not surprising that missionaries found Ojibwe people to be attentive listeners to their own sacred music, hymnody. "It is said that the early missionaries won the attention of the Ojibways more by hymn tunes than by exhortation," observed Frederick Burton, a turn-of-the-century composer who spent his summers among the Ojibwes living on the narrows between Lake Superior and Lake Huron.

In the earliest encounters with Protestant missionaries, in the early nineteenth century when a still viable fur trade enabled Ojibwe communities to conduct their affairs with relative autonomy, Ojibwes simply incorporated these missionary songs into their broader musical repertory alongside traditional drum songs and métis fiddle music. But as the nineteenth century wore on, the fur trade wore out and the more thoroughgoing dispossession and disease set in. By the 1880s, when most Ojibwes were concentrated on reservations too small or too fully logged out to support subsistence from the seasonal round, some came, as a strategy for survival, more thoroughly under missionary influence. Not coincidentally, it was in these latter decades of the nineteenth century that missionaries observed how hymn singing had captured the imagination of Ojibwes trying to make a new living for themselves on the reservation. Singing of these songs in the Ojibwe language accompanied nearly every interaction missionaries had with the Ojibwes, whether in church or in the wigwams and tarpaper shacks of the community. But missionaries often remarked about the formal, stylized feel of the performance, for Ojibwes were ritualizing the practice of singing the hymns even as they made them their own.

Episcopalians in Minnesota had trained a number of Ojibwe deacons to lead indigenous mission churches at the White Earth, Red Lake, and Leech Lake reservations, and hymn singing appeared to have set the tone for just about every gathering of these semiautonomous communities. Hymns were sung in the mission church on Sunday morning, but they were sung with greater urgency and frequency at the peripheries of missionary influence, such as in the evening prayer meetings where these communities gathered several nights per week to share food and devise strategies for survival amid the depleted resources and undercapitalized farms on the reservation. Even more particularly, the hymns became identified as a music of grief and mourning, sung at sickbeds, deathbeds, and especially at all-night funeral wakes in the community. With time, even ardently non-Christian Ojibwes would associate these songs with such occasions and come to respect them as appropriate and, for some, even "traditional."

Like other forms of Ojibwe music, the ritualized hymns were not sung casually. They became the province of discrete groups of singers, led not by clergy but by traditional elders, and these singers became the effective stewards of a distinctive Ojibwe Christianity. As with the drums and the drum societies, the musical performance of hymns became ensconced in the social relations of these singing groups. The elders and their singers were stewards of the music for the community, were expected to lead lives of extraordinary generosity and respect, and carried the songs' blessing to moments of crisis in the life of the community.

The music came to be associated with these elders and singing groups, and with occasions of grief. The hymns were most at home in performances at night, in Ojibwe homes during evening prayer meetings and all-night funeral wakes. They were sung slowly, deliberately, like laments that rose and fell not according to a piano, organ, or metronome, but to the spirit established in the room. Between hymns were long periods of silence, and often elders or singers would rise in such pauses to address the gathering.

Those Ojibwes who sang hymns were, in effect, performing a departure from established tradition, especially given the conspicuous absence of the drum. The songs they sang were in the Ojibwe language but were faithful translations of Christian concepts set to European tunes. In the context of reservation life, such performances were very much on display to the missionaries, Indian agents, and others who exercised increasing control over the people's livelihood. And yet, the way that Ojibwe singers ritualized the practice of singing the hymns folded into the missionary songs cherished Ojibwe ways of hearing, seeing, listening, and knowing. Within the tight confines of reservation life, and especially in times of mourning, when communal survival seemed most uncertain indeed, the ritualized singing of hymns by elders in the original language made room for a new life blending old and new, significantly, if not completely, on Ojibwe terms.

The following document describes hymn singing in the old tradition by elders at a funeral wake. The author, Frederick Burton, was a composer who sought to incorporate Native American themes into his music. At the turn of the twentieth century, Burton spent several summers near native communities along the narrows between Lakes Superior and Huron, researching Ojibwe music and culture. He published his observations in 1909 as *American Primitive Music, with Especial Attention to the Songs of the Ojibways*. The following passage from that book takes as its scene a small cabin in Ontario's Garden River Reserve, the home of three elderly sisters mourning the death of a fourth, whose body was laid out in the home. Here is a detailed description of the ritualized practice of hymn singing in the mourning process, a practice that knitted a seamless garment of both Christian and traditional Ojibwe elements. It seemed to matter little to the scene that two of the sisters were Episcopalian, the others Roman Catholic, or that a "staunch Episcopalian" elder presided over the singing at the wake of the deceased, who was a Catholic. In this native community, such distinctions did not seem so significant in the realm of practice.

The second text, an English retranslation of the Ojibwe version of a hymn by Charles Wesley (1762), reveals the distance at certain points between the English and the Ojibwe language. The Ojibwe translation, though rendered by a Christian Ojibwe who did not wish to subvert the message of the hymn, does modify the theology of the English original, particularly in the last line, where Wesley's text charts the consequences of a betrayed commitment to keep the charge of the Christian life—"I shall forever die"—and where the Ojibwe translation simply says "I will live." Nevertheless, a comparison of the English and Ojibwe hardly does justice to the refashioning of the hymn in ritualized practice. For the song amounted to far more than a translated text set to music. The Ojibwe syllables were, as Burton notes, sung so slowly that they could lose their narrative or discursive coherence altogether, in a manner that reflects traditional Ojibwe song.

The first two texts printed here are from Frederick R. Burton, *American Primitive Music, with Especial Attention to the Songs of the Ojibways* (New York: Moffat, Yard, 1909), pp. 132–39, 279–80. The Ojibwe language text comes from the *Ojibwa Hymnal*, compiled by Edward C. Kah-O-Sed (Minneapolis: Protestant Episcopal Church, Diocese of Minnesota, 1910). The translation of the hymn was made by the author with the late Larry Cloud Morgan, a Minnesota Ojibwe elder, artist, and poet, with some assistance from John Nichols.

Further Reading

Beverley Diamond, M. Sam Cronk, and Franziska von Rosen, *Visions of Sound: Musical Instruments of First Nations Communities in Northeastern America* (Chicago: University of Chicago Press, 1994); Michael McNally, *Ojibwe Singers: Hymns, Grief, and a Native Culture in Motion* (New York: Oxford University Press, 2000); Christopher Vecsey, *Traditional Ojibwa Religion and Its Historical Changes* (Philadelphia: American Philosophical Society, 1983); Thomas Vennum, Jr., *The Ojibwa Dance Drum* (Washington, D.C.: Smithsonian Institution Press, 1982).

Funerary Hymn-Singing

At sunset came Megissun, "the singer" as he is called, a staunch Episcopalian and older by a long span than she who had departed. He brought with him his Protestant hymnal, a collection of hymns translated into Ojibway, but with no note of music between the covers, and sat beside the dead. The surviving sisters took their places near. No word of greeting had passed, no comment of any kind was uttered, no moan of grief escaped the lips. Upon the table at Megissun's elbow was a lamp, and beside it a saucer of lozenges and a plate of plain cakes. Shortly after Megissun's entrance three neighbors, a man and two women, drifted in, more silently, more unobtrusively than if they had been autumn leaves impelled by an idle wind. By not so much as a nod, or a glance from the eyes, did they recognize the presence of the singer or the bereaved sisters. Megissun stirred not, neither did the mourners. Presently another silent figure blotted out the doorway for an instant and joined the expectant group, and then still others, till the narrow room was full. All these, Christians every one, were there to go part way with their friend upon her long journey to the land of the hereafter. In the presence of death, sectarian differences were forgotten, the new faith itself faded and fluttered before the persistence of ancient custom.

Megissun did not wait for the room to fill. In his own good time he opened the hymnal and began to sing. Through nearly the whole of the first line his wavering voice bore the tune alone; then one and another joined in unison and sang the hymn through all its slowly toiling stanzas to the end. A pause ensued while Megissun turned the pages of his book. Presently he selected another hymn and began. As before the assembled neighbors joined as soon as they recognized the tune. Now and again a single voice stumbled over the words of an ill remembered line, but nobody was disturbed or abashed thereby, least of all the person who committed the error. While yet the hymns was sounding, other neighbors drifted in. Some of them had walked miles from the far end of the Reservation. Silently, unobtrusively, recognizing nobody, they found their places. Between hymns the clatter of crickets beat noisily upon the ear, and the sudden hoot of an owl shocked as might profanity before the altar. There was no uneasy rustle of garments or shuffling of feet to indicate that the unbidden visitors had wearied; they seemed not to breathe. Only Megissun stirred, and he all but inaudibly turned the pages of his oft-thumbed hymnal.

Some time between ten and eleven o'clock, two of the guests arose and, without word or glance of parting, drifted out into the darkness and came not again that night. By midnight others had gone, but the places of a few were filled by late comers. At rare intervals as the night wore on with its succession of hymns, Megissun relieved his throat with a lozenge, and such guests as were so minded sought the table for a piece of cake. When the sun rose, the room was no longer crowded, but a loyal handful of neighbors yet remained singing a final hymn for the comfort of their friend upon her journey through the darkness. With the full light of day Megissun closed his book and went home, and the others, with no word to him or the sisters, departed also.

To the wondering Yankee who observed and heard this ceremony, the musical interest lay in the unwitting perversion of the tunes by Megissun and the older singers. So dominating was Megissun's voice that at first I did not realize that some of the others were not keeping strictly with him; and at that time I was hard put to it to know whether the tunes were aboriginal, or the product of civilization. . . . Regarding Megissun's voice alone, I might have persuaded myself that he was singing the Christian words to an ancient Ojibway tune, so completely did he cover and disguise it with the mannerisms I had become familiar with as characteristic of ancient Ojibway song. The older people kept with the leader easily, for he harked them back to childhood when, perhaps, to every one the Christian faith and its music were unknown; but the others, who had learned their hymns from the lips of a white missionary while they were young enough to receive and retain strange impressions, found the old leader's manner disconcerting.

This [an Ojibwe translation of Charles Wesley's "A Charge to Keep I Have"] was Chief Bukwujjinini's [Garden River Ojibwe leader, 1811–1900] favorite hymn, and the Garden River Indians still sing it occasionally. Shingwauk, grand nephew of the chief, and other well informed Ojibways, believe that the tune is aboriginal. "It is very old," they say, "and was made over for this hymn by Chief Bukwujjinini himself." I think they are mistaken in this. Up to the present I have not been able to identify the tune with any in the hymn books, but it appeals to me as a white man's tune made over rather than an Indian's. Whether or no, it was sung at Bukwujjinini's bedside by the members of his family while he lay dying, the incident illustrating another conventional use of music among the Ojibways, for every Indian has his death song, one that he will sing himself, if possible, at the every moment of dissolution; and if voice fails him, his friends sing it for him. In the old days the words of death songs befitted the occasion, being expressive of courage, faith, doubt, defiance, as the case might be. I am thinking of the non-Christian Indian when I use the term "old days," the fact being that the pagans of the present adhere to the custom. United States Army officers have told me that when it is necessary to execute an Indian, the victim marches to his place before the firing squad singing his death song, and that his voice never falters till the bullets stop it forever. The Christianized Ojibway tends to modify this striking custom as he does all else that belonged to his ancient life, but not infrequently he preserves the poetic atmosphere.

I have alluded to the struggle that took place between Indian and civilized music when the Ojibways were converted by Protestant missionaries. The two styles did not mix well or permanently. The hymn tune could not be grafted on the Indian stock, nor the Indian melody on the hymn tune. Shingwauk has told me that the chiefs tried to make over the tunes taught them by the missionaries, seeking to adapt them to the Indian manner. He and other Indians believe that some of the tunes still used in the church service are "half Indian and half white," and he sang several to me as examples. . . . The words are a translation into Ojibway of the hymn beginning, "A charge to keep I have, a God to glorify." Our notation is incapable of expressing with absolute exactness the manner of singing the hymns. It is so slow that it seems to be drawled rather than sung; time values are disregarded, and the voice slurs up and down from one tone to another in the most extraordinary fashion. I have tried to suggest the extreme portamento by a generous use of slurs and small notes.

A Charge to Keep I Have
English Original

A charge to keep I have,
A God to glorify,
A never dying soul to save,
And fit it for the sky.

To serve the present age,
My calling to fulfill;
O may it all my powers engage
To do my Master's will!

Arm me with jealous care,
As in thy sight to live,
And oh, thy servant, Lord, prepare
A strict account to give.

Help me to watch and pray
And on thyself rely,
Assured, if I my trust betray,
I shall forever die.

Ojibwa Hymnal

Che anokitonan
Nose, nind ayanan,
Che wi-gijitad ninchichag
Ishpiming wi-ijad

Ki nundawenim su
Che anokitonan,
O mano anguamiishin
Guayuk che anam'ayan.

Wawejiishin su
Che agasen'moyan,
Che de-gijitayan, Nose,
Api naquesh konan.

Widokawishin su
Che akawabiyan
Gaye che anamiayan
Wi-bimadiziyan

Translation

I will work for you
My Father, have I,
My soul will finish at last
My soul wants to go to heaven

You want me
to work for you
Let it be so, make me hopeful
That I pray correctly.

Accompany me
When I feel overwhelmed
[Until] at last I am done,
When Father, I meet you

Help me!
That I will wait and watch
And also that I pray
I would live.

— 12 —

Temperance Songs and Hymns

Carolyn DeSwarte Gifford

The nineteenth century was an era of reform in the United States. Inspired by several currents of thought and belief abroad in the country at the time—among them liberal political ideals, evangelical Protestant perfectionism, and a spirit of buoyant optimism among many Americans—reformers agitated for a great variety of causes. Anti-slavery, women's rights, peace, abolition of the death penalty, prison and asylum reform, health and dietary reforms, and educational improvements claimed the energy of all kinds of Americans hoping, through reform activity, to make their country a perfect society.

One of the most popular and widespread of the many reforms that flourished during the period was the temperance movement. The issue of temperance, moderation in or even total abstinence from drinking alcoholic beverages, was raised toward the close of the eighteenth century, most notably by Dr. Benjamin Rush, a signer of the Declaration of Independence and a leader in shaping the educational institutions of the new republic. Rush saw some of the disturbing results of alcoholism in his medical practice and strongly advised against imbibing distilled liquor. Like most Americans of the time, however, Rush thought cider, beer, and wine promoted good health. The admonitions of Rush and others had little effect on curbing the drinking habits of the nation. By the early nineteenth century the nation was, as one historian has dubbed it, an "alcoholic republic."

In response to what growing numbers of Americans perceived as the scandal of national insobriety, the temperance movement began during the 1810s and grew rapidly during the 1820s and after. Particularly in New England, numerous local temperance societies were formed at the urging of preachers and other temperance advocates. As the movement took hold, it spread beyond the Northeast to other parts of the country and to all social classes. Temperance societies banded together to form powerful national organizations such as the American Temperance Society (founded 1826), the Washington Society, or Washingtonians (1840), the Sons of Temperance (1843), the Independent Order of Good Templars (1851), the

Woman's Christian Temperance Union (1874), and the Anti-Saloon League (1893). Although the movement was predominantly a Protestant one, some Roman Catholics formed the Catholic Total Abstinence Society (1840), modeled after a successful organization in Ireland. Temperance novels and short stories, drama and poetry, sermons and Sunday school lessons, public school readers, tracts and pamphlets, and newspapers and magazines appeared, beginning in the 1830s, as the temperance reform movement gained ground. In 1919, after more than a century of growth, the work of the temperance movement culminated with the passage of the Eighteenth Amendment, which established Prohibition as the law of the land.

If in the early nineteenth century the United States was a nation of drinkers, it was also a nation of singers. When Americans met together, inevitably they sang. Church services, revivals, camp meetings, political rallies, and meetings of voluntary associations were all accompanied by rousing music. Reform movements produced lively songs and hymns that expressed their goals, strategies, and hopes for the eventual triumph of their causes. Beginning in the 1840s, for example, the Hutchinson family quartette sang numbers such as "The Slave's Appeal" and "Get Off the Track" at hundreds of antislavery gatherings. The women's suffrage movement also generated songs sung at national conventions and local rallies. At the turn of the nineteenth century, a Social Gospel Hymnal was published to sound that movement's call for reform of unjust economic structures. Throughout the twentieth century, labor organizing inspired many rousing songs that protested poor working conditions and vilified management and strike breakers. Folksingers like Woody Guthrie and the Weavers became troubadours of the labor movement, lending their voices and guitars to the fight for fair employment and popularizing labor songs such as "Which Side Are You On" and "Union Maids." By the 1950s and 1960s, songs and hymns such as "We Shall Overcome" and "Keep Your Eyes on the Prize" buoyed up the long struggle for African-American civil rights.

Like these reforms, the temperance movement was accompanied by music. Temperance hymns and songs were printed in magazines, newspapers, hymnals, and songbooks. Temperance tunes were also increasingly published in inexpensive formats and thus were affordable to large numbers of temperance supporters. The songbooks were very popular and were often reprinted many times to meet the rising demand for them.

Reform leaders understood well the potential of music to aid in recruiting supporters. Frances Willard, longtime president of the Woman's Christian Temperance Union, expressed the opinion of many reformers when she wrote in *Do Everything* (1897), a handbook for her organization, "Song is a sentiment maker and . . . every chorus rendered at a public entertainment ought to add new converts to the cause of Temperance. . . . We have not appreciated the magic power of song to win the hearts of those whom we may have supposed to be indifferent or opposed to Temperance work" (67, 151). After recruits were won by song they were kept enthusiastic and energetic through endless parades, rallies, and organizational meetings. Singing had the power to inspire flagging spirits and recapture wandering attention.

Over the temperance movement's long development, both its aims and its methods changed. These changes were evident in the lyrics of its hymns and songs. In the early years, its participants believed that moral suasion was the way to convince people to moderate their drinking or, better, give it up entirely. Drunkenness was understood as sin, and individuals were urged to foreswear drinking as they should other forms of sinful behavior. In the evangelical context in which the early movement flourished, "coming to Christ" and thereby being freed from sin certainly included giving up liquor. Those who continued to drink were seen to be in Satan's grasp and thus in grave moral danger. Family and friends of the person captured by the devil prayed and wept over the tempted one, hoping for a change of heart. Sober citizens as well as reformed drunks joined temperance societies for mutual support. "Away the Bowl," an early temperance song, suggests the enticing and dangerous qualities of drinking and dramshops and describes the strength that could be gained from joining a temperance group. It also reveals a changing notion of what drinks were dangerous since it adds wine to the list of those to be avoided.

By the 1850s, temperance reformers had shifted from total reliance on prayer and moral suasion toward pushing for legislative action to regulate the sale of liquor or prohibit it entirely. Attention also shifted from saving individuals to attacking what reformers now identified as a powerful interlocking economic and political system bent on destroying the lives of vulnerable individuals. Hymns addressed the growing liquor industry and its allies: politicians and the men who voted them into office, and businessmen intent on making money no matter what the cost to the morals of society. "An Incident True" indicts this system, pointing the finger not only at the drunkard but at all those who play a role in maintaining the powerful liquor industry. "Vote As You Pray" makes clear that praying, while necessary, is no longer a weapon sufficient to defeat the liquor foe. "Let us wake from the delusion that praying will win the day," the song warns. Every weapon in the temperance reformers' arsenal should be used. Prayer must be accompanied by the ballot to ensure victory over alcohol.

In reformers' changing analysis of the situation it was not only the drunkard himself who was responsible for his condition. Although nineteenth-century temperance reformers were aware of some female drinking, they saw drunkenness primarily as a male problem. As the lyrics of "An Incident True" recount in melodramatic fashion, not only did the drunkard suffer, but so did his wife and children. The themes of the drunkard's suffering family and ruined home were featured in many temperance hymns and songs during the century and with good reason. Most women and children were dependent on men's earnings for their support, and if a man spent his wages at the saloon his wife and children went hungry, ill clothed, and ill housed. Often they were physically abused as well.

The 1870s saw the entry of large numbers of women into the ranks of temperance reform. Although there had been women's auxiliaries earlier and women leaders of the Good Templars, the Ohio Women's Crusade of winter 1873–1874 mobilized women to an unprecedented extent in spontaneous demonstrations against local saloon keepers. "The Crusade Hymn" was sung by Crusaders from Hillsboro, Ohio, as they marched toward the town's saloons to plead with saloon keepers to stop selling liquor to their husbands, brothers, and sons. The hymn is not, strictly speaking, a temperance hymn, because its lyrics mention nothing at all about the reform but rather are based on verses from Psalm 146. As the Hillsboro women gathered to march, their leader asked the town's Methodist minister to choose a familiar hymn that all of them could sing. He asked for a hymn that would rally them to their task and aid them in overcoming the fear of stepping out of their usual sphere of the home into the alien territory of the saloon. The minister's choice was a sound one, and as the Crusade women marched down the main street singing the hymn, they testified that they felt the power of God uplifting them and making them bold.

The Crusade spread rapidly across the northern United States as women took to the streets to protect their homes and families from the dangers of alcohol. To consolidate the work of the Crusade, a permanent organization, The Woman's Christian Temperance Union (WCTU), was established in fall 1874. "The Crusade Hymn" became the rallying cry of the WCTU. It became part of the ritual of the organization and was sung at national, state, and local meetings to remind members of the WCTU's formative event and to inspire them in their continuing effort to eradicate the liquor industry.

The WCTU's publishing arm produced numerous collections of hymns and songs and attracted songwriters who wrote specifically for the organization. Anna A. Gordon, for years personal secretary to Frances Willard, the organization's most famous president, and herself the president of the WCTU during the 1910s and 1920s, was a prolific writer who compiled a number of songbooks used and distributed by the organization. "Saloons Must Go," published in one of Gordon's most popular collections, was a collaboration between the two women. A lively march, it weaves the WCTU's motto, "For God and Home and Native Land," into its lyrics. In addition to the familiar theme of the protection of home and family from drink, it contains another favorite theme of temperance reformers: a concern for the nation and the hope that, by purifying America from alcohol, reformers would be helping to bring in the Kingdom of God on Earth.

The WCTU, like other temperance groups, sought to bring children and young people into its ranks. From the earliest decades of the reform, the education of youth in temperance beliefs and aims was seen as crucial to the continuation of the work. "The Future Lawmakers," included in a WCTU songbook for children, is an example of a temperance song geared to youngsters as future voters. The first line of the song looks forward to the time when women as well as men can cast ballots. From the early 1880s, the WCTU supported woman suffrage, devising the slogan "The Ballot for Home Protection." It saw the women's vote as a powerful tool in both the temperance reform and a host of other reforms the organization championed.

By the 1890s the push for total constitutional prohibition was becoming strong. A third party, the national Prohibition Party, was organized in 1869, and though it never gathered enough supporters to win a national election, it succeeded in gaining many state and local offices. It also kept the issue of prohibition in the forefront of the national consciousness and forced the Republican Party to take prohibition seriously. The goal of total prohibition had been voiced as early as the 1860s, when the song "Prohibition" was published. Its chorus proclaimed, "Nought will cure our sad condition short of total prohibition." For fourteen years, from 1919 until the Eighteenth Amendment's repeal in 1933, a majority of the nation's citizens agreed.

"Away the Bowl" is found in George W. Ewing, *The Well-Tempered Lyre: Songs and Verse of the Temperance Movement* (Dallas: Southern Methodist University Press, 1977), p. 25; "An Incident True" is in *Silver Tones: A New Temperance and Prohibition Song Book*, compiled by Rev. C. H. Meade, G. E. Chambers, and Rev. W. A. Williams (Warnock, Ohio: W. A. Williams, 1892), no. 4; "Vote As You Pray" is in J. N. Stearns and H. P. Main, *Trumpet Notes for the Temperance Battlefield* (New York: National Temperance Society and Publication House, 1892), no. 40; "The Crusade Hymn" is in *The White Ribbon Hymnal, or Echoes of the Crusade,* compiled by Anna A. Gordon (Chicago: Ruby I. Gilbert, 1904), p. 107; "Saloons Must Go" is in Anna A. Gordon, *The Temperance Songster* (Cincinnati: Fillmore Music House, n.d., after 1904), no. 93; "Future Lawmakers" is in Anna A. Gordon, *Temperance Songs for Children* (Evanston, Ill.: NWCTU Publishing, 1916), p. 5; and "Prohibition" is in George F. Root, ed., *The Musical Fountain* (Chicago: Root and Cady, 1866), as published in George Ewing, *The Well-Tempered Lyre,* p. 156.

Further Reading

For background on the temperance movement in the United States, see William Rorabaugh, *The Alcoholic Republic: An American Tradition* (New York: Oxford University Press, 1979); Norman H. Clark, *Deliver Us from Evil: An Interpretation of American Prohibition* (New York: W. W. Norton, 1976); and Jack S. Blocker, Jr., *American Temperance Movements: Cycles of Reform* (Boston: Twayne, 1989). For a discussion of temperance hymns and songs, see George W. Ewing, *The Well-Tempered Lyre: Songs and Verse of the Temperance Movement* (Dallas: Southern Methodist University Press, 1977), and "A Bibliography of American Temperance Hymnals, 1835–1934," in *The Hymn: A Journal of Congregational Song* 51 no. 2 (April 2000): 28–36. For a brief discussion of the Catholic temperance movement and its music, see Robert F. Grimes, *How Shall We Sing in a Foreign Land: Music of Irish Catholic Immigrants in the Antebellum United States* (Notre Dame: Notre Dame University Press, 1996), pp. 139–43.

Away the Bowl

Our youthful hearts with temp'rance burn, Away, away the bowl;
From dramshops all our steps we turn, Away, away the bowl;
Goodbye to rum and all its harms, Farewell the winecup's boasted charms.

See how the staggering drunkard reels, Away, away the bowl;
Alas! the misery he reveals, Away, away the bowl;
Goodbye to rum and all its harms, Farewell the winecup's boasted charms.

No alcohol we'll buy or sell, Away, away the bowl;
The tippler's offer we repel, Away, away the bowl;
United in a temperance band, We're joined in heart, we're joined in hand.

An Incident True

If you'll listen I'll tell you an incident true,
Which occurred in a high license place,
Where five thousand saloons pay a large revenue,
For the right to breed crime and disgrace.

Chorus: Oh, what shall we do with this terrible curse,
And when will deliverance come?
O God, we turn our eyes to Thee,
Protect, protect our home.

In the city Chicago, a poor drunken man,
In his wrath seized his dead infant child;
With its body he beat his own poor dying wife;
Licensed rum made him frantic and wild.

Chorus: Oh, what shall we do with this terrible curse . . .

But who sold him the drink? Who enacted the laws
That allowed the saloonist to sell?
And who made him saloonist?
And who was the cause of this horrible deed,
Can you tell?

Chorus: Oh, what shall we do with this terrible curse . . .

Shall we say that the man who elects by his vote,
Those who make just such laws ev'ry time,
And supports party platforms that license denote,
Has no part in this terrible crime?

Chorus: Oh, what shall we do with this terrible curse . . .

Can we tell at what price all that's dear shall be sold,
And just what is the worth of a soul?
Can the sum that would meet all the damage be told—
That would make ev'ry broken heart whole?

Chorus: Oh, what shall we do with this terrible curse . . .

Vote as You Pray

Can you go on thus my brother,
While praying day by day,
"Thy kingdom come, thy will be done,"
And yet not vote as you pray?

Chorus: Oh, vote as you pray, vote as you pray,
Vote as you pray, my friends;
Oh, vote as you pray, 'twill hasten the day
When the rum fiend's work shall end.

Can you see your neighbor falling
Around you in the fray,
And pray that God may speed the right,
And yet not vote as you pray?

Chorus: Oh, vote as you pray, vote as you pray, . . .

Do not cease from prayer; no never!
But pray on while you may;
But if you would know your pray'r is heard,
Be sure to vote as you pray.

Chorus: Oh, vote as you pray, vote as you pray, . . .

Let us wake from this delusion,
That praying will win the day;
Unless our prayer and votes agree,
Then always vote as we pray.

Chorus: Oh, vote as you pray, vote as you pray, . . .

The Crusade Hymn (Give to the Winds Thy Fears)

Give to the winds thy fears;
Hope and be undismayed;
God hears thy sighs and counts thy tears,
God shall lift up thy head.

Thro' waves and clouds and storms,
He gently clears the way;
Wait thou His time; the darkest night
Shall end in brightest day.

Far, far above thy thought
His counsel shall appear,

When fully He the work hath wrought,
That caused thy needless fear.

Saloons Must Go

List to the tread of many feet, from home and playground, farm and street,
They talk like tongues, their words we know:
"Saloons, saloons must go!"

Chorus: Saloons must go, saloons must go,
Of home sweet home the deadliest foe;
With pray'r and work the world we'll show,
Saloons must go!

For God they lift their flag of white,
His name is on their banners bright;
His law of purity doth show,
"Saloons, saloons must go!"

Chorus: Saloons must go, saloons must go, . . .

For Home's sweet sake they move in line,
With mother love their faces shine;
Their loyal hearts will have it so,
"Saloons, saloons must go!"

Chorus: Saloons must go, saloons must go, . . .

For Native Land their drums they beat,
Quick time they keep with marching feet;
America, for thee they know,
"Saloons, saloons must go!"

Chorus: Saloons must go, saloons must go, . . .

Thy kingdom come, O Saviour great,
In hearts and home, in church and state;
But ere it comes, full well we know,
"Saloons, saloons must go!"

Chorus: Saloons must go, saloons must go, . . .

The Future Law-Makers

I'm a little "Loyal" Legion boy/girl,
I'm only ten years old,

But in the cause of temperance
My name has been enrolled.

Chorus: We are growing up you see,
And we'll help the temp'rance cause;
When we're twenty-one, you know, then we'll make the laws,
Oh! then we'll make the laws, Oh! then we'll make the laws,
Yes, when we're twenty-one, Oh! then we'll make the laws.

I don't know much about the curse,
But this I know full well:
That wine and cider, gin and rum,
They nevermore should sell.

Chorus: We are growing up you see, . . .

The broken hearts of mothers dear,
The cries of little ones,
Plead earnestly for help from us,
The daughters and the sons.

Chorus: We are growing up you see, . . .

We are coming, coming, one and all,
To fight against the wrong;
We all are "Loyal Legioners,"
Three hundred thousand strong.

Chorus: We are growing up you see, . . .

Prohibition

Hark! the world is hoarse with wailing,
Lamentation unavailing,
For today is heap'd with sorrow,
And there's more to come tomorrow.

Chorus: Prohibition, prohibition,
O! 'tis worth all repetition;
Nought will cure our sad condition
Short of total prohibition.

Oh, thou earth and thou great heaven,
Are no means of rescue given?
Yes, there are on one condition,
Yes, there are with prohibition.

Chorus: Prohibition, prohibition, . . .

Talk no more of mere restriction,
Do not trifle with conviction,
We may fence with regulation,
It must come to prohibition.

Chorus: Prohibition, prohibition, . . .

Teaching: Learning How to Live Correctly

— 13 —

The Celebration of Marriage in the
Dutch Reformed Church

Daniel James Meeter

Within just a few decades of the Protestant Reformation, the various Reformed churches (without seeming to pay much attention to it) arrived at a fair consensus about what a ritual for matrimony should be. This consensus is remarkable, since the Roman Catholic Church, in spite of regarding marriage as a sacrament, had been unable to establish any regularity or uniformity in its matrimonial practice. The marriage forms of the Reformed churches are, for the most part, attempts to bring chastity and discipline to a situation of extreme disorder. The Reformed churches repudiated the sacramental idea, but they did consider marriage to be close enough to the heart of religion to warrant the inclusion of rites for it in all their liturgical books.

The Dutch version of Reformed Protestantism came to the New World in the middle of the seventeenth century. After a few years of exploratory voyages, the Dutch West India Company established the colony of New Netherland in 1621, in what is now New York, New Jersey, and parts of Delaware and Connecticut. The Company provided for the spiritual needs of its colonies by employing special lay ministers, who were called "Comforters of the Sick." The first such Comforter to arrive in New Netherland in 1624 was Bastian Krol. At first he was only allowed to read official prayers from the liturgical books and printed sermons from authorized collections. Soon Krol also gained authorization to baptize infants and perform marriages. Krol was instructed to study and read the appropriate liturgy but not to interject any of his own words into either the rituals or the sermons. Krol's ministry marks the first use of the Dutch Reformed marriage liturgy in North America.

Four years later the first regular pastor was sent to serve the growing village of New Amsterdam at the tip of Manhattan Island. Domine Jonas Michaelius immediately organized a congregation according to the rules of the Dutch Church Order, formed a consistory to govern the congregation, and celebrated a service of Holy Communion. Thus by 1628 the Netherlands Liturgy—a text originally compiled between 1566 and 1619—was fully in use in North America.

In spite of neglect and mismanagement by the West India Company, the colony of New Netherland quietly grew. Land was cleared around the forts and along the rivers. A few small villages were settled by farmers, and new congregations were organized. Eventually, little churches could be found at Fort Orange (Albany), Brooklyn, Flatbush, Flatlands, Harlem, Kingston, Bergen (Jersey City), and Staten Island. By the time of the English conquest in 1664, there were about a dozen congregations served by six pastors.

The English takeover immediately threatened the religious settlement of the Dutch population, the status of their church, and its connection with the mother church's government in Amsterdam. Dutch settlers feared that by becoming subjects of the British government they would be forced to contribute to the financial support of the Church of England. They feared that the British would not allow them to be obedient to a church whose leaders lived in Holland. The West India Company had paid the salaries of the pastors; who would pay them now? And most importantly, would the British insist that the Dutch adopt the Anglican liturgy? Fortunately for the Dutch, the terms of surrender in the Articles of Capitulation were generous. They guaranteed that the Dutch living in the colonies would enjoy full liberty of conscience in religion and church discipline. They also would be permitted to keep their church property and buildings.

Consequently, the Dutch Reformed Church flourished in the colonies. Although English became the government language after 1664, Dutch was retained for almost all other functions. The schools were run by the church, and Dutch was used in both—this served to preserve the language. One book that every colonial family was certain to possess was a *kerkboekje* (church book)—containing the Dutch metrical Psalter (with the Genevan tunes), the Heidelberg Catechism, and the Netherlands Liturgy—which they carried with them to church each Sunday. In more well-to-do families, every person had a kerkboekje of his or her own. Because of their high birth rate, the Dutch Americans were able to maintain their language and culture under the English regime for another century. Their culture was so tenacious that the French and German immigrants who later settled in the Hudson Valley adopted Dutch as their new language rather than English.

After a hundred years of English rule, however, Dutch eventually lost its place as the common language of New York and New Jersey. Consequently, after much hesitation, the consistory of the New York City church decided to introduce English-language preaching in 1763. This decision required the further step of also translating the kerkboekje. In 1767 the New York consistory published an English version of the church book for the use of its own congregation, entitled *The Psalms of David, with Hymns and Spiritual Songs, Also the Catechism, Confession of Faith, Liturgy &c.* This book represents the first English translation of the full Netherlands Liturgy, and it was accomplished by a committee of New York merchants who had no theological training other than their own church involvement. After the American Revolution and the establishment of a nation independent from England, the one hundred or so Dutch Reformed congregations in North America followed the lead of the New York City church and introduced English-language services. Eventually the New York Liturgy became the official liturgy of the whole Dutch Reformed Church in North America (and the other English-speaking Dutch Reformed churches in Africa, Asia, and Australia).

The New York Liturgy contains the texts of prayers appropriate for many occasions, both public and private, at church and at home. These range from prayers to be said at Sunday worship, prayers before and after catechism, prayers before and after meals, prayers at rising and at sleeping, and prayers for sick or tempted persons. The liturgy contains the precise wording to be used in administering baptism and the Lord's Supper and in ordaining pastors, elders, and deacons. The liturgy even provides a unique section called "The Consolation of the Sick, To Prepare Believers to Die Willingly." The New York Liturgy was the indispensable guide to religious observance for all the Dutch Reformed faithful. The Dutch American worshipers could follow from their own little books the complete texts of the rituals, but they probably knew most of them by heart anyway.

The marriage ceremony reprinted here constitutes one part of the New York Liturgy. The Reformed churches called marriage a divine "ordinance" (although they never defined the word "ordinance" as carefully as they defined "sacrament"). As soon as an engagement was made public, the banns were announced in church for three successive Sundays, and the marriage was celebrated with dispatch. The Dutch American authorities tended to be compassionate and lenient toward couples needing to be married for whatever reason. From the Reformed perspective, matrimony should be celebrated on Sunday amid the whole congregation as part of public worship. The liturgy explains the reasons for this: first, God himself gave Eve to Adam, second, the new couple, and those already married, should be exhorted by God's Word, and third, the whole congregation ought to call upon God for his blessing on the union. Marriage was not merely a contract between individuals or a sign of personal affection. The marriage ceremony was a chance for the whole community to reflect on the ways that God had ordered the world.

Therefore, as with all Reformed liturgy, the marriage ceremony was understood as a time for teaching and exhortation. The Reformed churches harbored a skeptical distrust of ceremony. The Dutch Reformed tradition used liturgy for catechetical purposes; it sought to teach good doctrine and reinforce godly behavior as much as it sought to praise and thank God. Consequently, the "Form for the Confirmation of Marriage, before the Church" is a careful and richly detailed discussion of why a man and woman should marry, what they should do in order to live a godly marriage, and how God will bless a marriage that is honorable. Every sentence addressed to the couple was understood to be of value to the whole congregation as well.

The marriage ceremony opens with a startlingly pessimistic introduction: "Married persons," the minister begins, "are generally, by Reason of Sin, subject to many Troubles and Afflictions." This first sentence serves to remind both the couple and the congregation of the basic Reformed assumption that sin is everywhere and sorrow is unavoidable. However, God has great love for his people, and so the congregation "may also be assured in your Hearts of the certain Assistance of God in your Afflictions." The opening words tell the congregation what they already know, that God approves of marriage and that he will bless and assist married people. The minister also tells the community, as prescribed in the liturgy, that "on the Contrary [God will] judge and punish Whoremongers and Adulterers." The message taught by the ritual is clear: married people can have the support of God, while those who transgress the natural order of God's world will be punished. The opening of the marriage ceremony is a somber reminder of the division between good and evil in the world.

The ritual then moves on, in typical Reformed fashion, to establish the doctrine by means of quoting a series of biblical texts. After a paraphrase of Genesis 1:26, Genesis 3:18 is quoted, followed by 3:21–24. The creation ordinance of the Old Testament is taken to have been confirmed in the New Testament by Christ's presence at the marriage in Cana. Just as typically Reformed is the assumption that to "live godly in this state, you must know the reasons wherefore God hath instituted the same." Here again is the Dutch Reformed emphasis on liturgy as a tool for instruction, especially for the couple. The liturgy specifically states that God's reasons for marriage are three: first, that both spouses provide for each other the "meet help" of Genesis 2; second, that they raise their children in true religion; and third, that sexual morality be preserved in keeping with 1 Corinthians 3:17 and 7:1–9.

The ritual then moves to address the bridegroom and to teach him where he fits into God's order. Here the controlling idea is that of headship, modeled upon Christ's headship of the church, using scriptures from 1 Corinthians 11, Ephesians 5, 1 Peter 3, and Genesis 3:19. The husband is the head of the wife, and he is required to lead her with discretion, to teach and comfort her, and to protect her. The minister warns the groom not to be "bitter against her" but to live with her "as a man of understanding." He must give honor to his wife "as the weaker vessel," since the couple together are "joint heirs of the Grace of Life." Finally, recalling Adam's sin, the liturgy explains that the new husband will have to work diligently and faithfully in whatever the special calling is that God has given him. This will enable the husband to provide for his household and to have something left over to give to the poor. The marriage ceremony teaches that the man has responsibilities not only to his wife but to God and the community as well.

The catechesis of the bride is directly complementary, using parallel scriptures from the same passages in the letters of Paul and Peter, along with 1 Timothy 2:11–13 and Genesis 3:16. The liturgy instructs the bride to love her husband, and this includes honoring and fearing him. She should obey him as she would God, just as the Church obeys Christ. "You shall not exercise any Dominion over your Husband," the minister reads, "but be silent, for Adam was first created, and then Eve to be an Help to Adam." When children come, the wife should look to her family. She should live her life in honesty and virtue, without worldly pride, "that you may give an Example to others of Modesty." Although the ideas taught in this section are not congenial to today's thinking, one cannot deny that they are a reasonable interpretation of the cited ancient scriptures. For the Dutch community of colonial America, the wedding ceremony clearly described the duties of husband and wife toward each other, toward their community, and toward God.

The next part of the ritual consists chiefly of three vows read by the minister; these are derived from the liturgy that John Calvin wrote for Geneva. The movment of the ritual action at this point follows the same pattern as in the instruction—the attention moves from the couple to the bridegroom to the bride. The first vow is asked of the couple, and it concerns their understanding of God's institution and their public consent to be married. They answer with a simple "Yes." Then the minister declares to the congregation that all is legal and exhorts the couple to continue in God's name. At this point the couple joins hands in order to make its marital vows, and such a joining of hands is considered to be a ritual act. The first vow is asked of the groom and the second of the bride, to which, again, each simply answers "Yes." These two vows are made not partner to partner but in the manner of a public confession before God and the church. The vows are quickly followed by the minister giving the couple God's blessing.

It is typical of the Netherlands Liturgy that each of the ceremonies ends with a closing exhortation and a prayer. The marriage form is unique in that the closing exhortation is, for the most part, a direct quotation of scripture, the teaching of Jesus in Matthew 19:3–9. Coming at this point in the ceremony, it again brings in a rather pessimistic tone. "Believe these Words of Christ" the minister tells the couple. "You are therefore to receive, whatever befalls you therein with Patience and Thanksgiving, as from the Hand of God. . . ." God did not intend for man to be alone in the world, and so he made woman as a "Help meet" for him, and the two would join as one. The couple are reminded of Jesus' warnings against divorce, fornication, and adultery. The Holy Spirit will help the couple live piously together and resist wickedness. And they are instructed, should they come to have children, to educate them in godliness, to the glory of God's holy Name, to the edification of the Church, and to the spreading of the Gospel.

At this point comes the only real prayer in the whole marriage ritual. It is mostly borrowed from the writings of Calvin. Remarkably, the couple are bidden to kneel during this prayer, the single example of kneeling in the whole Netherlands Liturgy. The prayer is a petition; first, for the Holy Spirit, and second, for a blessing on any family that the couple might have, that they might inherit the Abrahamic covenant. As with all the other liturgical forms, the prayer concludes with the Lord's Prayer, although, atypically, this is not the last item in the form. After the prayers a double blessing is given to the couple. First comes the promise of marital blessing to those who "fear the Lord and walk in his ways," quoting Psalm 128:1–6. The second blessing is a benediction taken from Calvin, offering God's "grace" and a "long life together in all godliness and holiness." Thus, the ending of the Form is as cheerful as its beginning is somber.

We lack enough primary sources to determine the actual social and emotional flavor of this ritual in the colonial era. We know from historian Joyce Goodfriend's research that the great majority of Dutch Americans tended to marry relatively young, before the age of twenty-five, and that they tended to marry within their own ethnic and religious group. We can surmise that their weddings were great affirmations of the intricate extended family network of Dutch Americans, and that the bond of the couple served to strengthen the kinship of the group. We can also surmise that the matrimonial union was more of a mutual contract between the groom and bride than an exchange of property between the groom and his father-in-law. Indeed, in this rite the father does not "give away" the bride. We know that Dutch women enjoyed stronger inheritance rights and a more elevated status than did their English peers. In cases of Dutch-English intermarriage, the couples usually ended up Dutch Reformed.

A Dutch American wedding feast was a community event, and, in spite of our modern estimations of Calvinism, they were hardly puritanical affairs. Complaints about carousing and excessive drinking were not uncommon. Undoubtedly a great deal of business was conducted of all kinds—social, economic, and ecclesiastical—and one wonders how the beverages might have enhanced negotiations. In 1642 Adrian van der Donck, an officer of the West India Company, recorded this story about a wedding in New Amsterdam [New York City]: The Director of the West India Company had decided to build a church, but people wondered where he would get the funds. It happened at this time that Pastor Everardus Bogardus "should marry off his daughter." The Director judged that the wedding would be the perfect time to raise money for the church. So, "after the fourth or fifth drink took effect," he set a good example by making a pledge to donate money for the church. Then he called the wedding guests to pledge, and "each of them, lightheaded, pledged richly away, the one above the other. And though they were sorry by sunrise at home, they had to pay, or be in trouble." [*Ecclesiastical Records of the State of New York,* vol. 1 p. 165.]

The text below is from "The Form for the Confirmation of Marriage, before the Church," in Daniel James Meeter, ed., *"Bless the Lord, O My Soul": The New-York Liturgy of the Dutch Reformed Church, 1767* (Lanham, Md.: Scarecrow, 1998), pp. 154–160.

Further Reading

Daniel James Meeter, ed., *"Bless the Lord, O My Soul": The New-York Liturgy of the Dutch Reformed Church, 1767* (Lanham, Md.: Scarecrow, 1998); Gerald De Jong, *The Dutch Reformed Church in the American Colonies* (Grand Rapids, Mich.: Eerdmans, 1978); Joyce D. Goodfriend, *Before the Melting Pot: Society and Culture in Colonial New York City, 1661–1730* (Princeton: Princeton University Press, 1992); Ellis Lawrence Raesly, *Portrait of New Netherland* (New York: Columbia University Press, 1945).

The Form for the Confirmation of Marriage, before the Church

WHEREAS MARRIED PERSONS are generally, by Reason of Sin, subject to many Troubles and Afflictions; to the End that you N[ame of groom] and N[ame of bride] (who desire to have your Marriage Bond publickly confirmed, here in the Name of God, before his Church) may also be assured in your Hearts of the certain Assistance of God in your Afflictions, Hear therefore from the Word of God, how honourable the married State is, and that it is an Institution of God, which is pleasing to him. Wherefore he also will (as he hath promised) bless and assist the Married Persons, and on the Contrary judge and punish Whoremongers and Adulterers.

In the first Place you are to know, that God our Father, (after he had created Heaven and Earth, and all that in them is) made Man *in his own Image and Likeness, that he should have Dominion over the Beasts of the Field, over the Fish of the Sea,* and over the Fowls of the Air. And after he had created Man, he said, *It is not good that Man should be alone, I will make him an Help meet for him. And the Lord caused a deep Sleep to fall upon Adam, and he slept, and he took one of his Ribs, and closed up the Flesh instead thereof. And the Rib which the Lord God had taken from Man, made he a Woman, and brought her unto the Man. And Adam said, this is now Bone of my Bone, and Flesh of my Flesh: She shall be called Woman, because she was taken out of Man. Therefore shall a Man, leave his Father, and his Mother, and shall cleave unto his Wife, and they two shall be one Flesh.* Therefore ye are not to doubt but the married State is pleasing to the Lord, since he made unto Adam his Wife, brought, and gave her himself to him to be his Wife; witnessing thereby that he doth yet as with his Hand bring unto every Man his Wife. For this Reason the Lord Jesus Christ did also highly honour it with his Presence, Gifts and Miracles in Cana of Galilee, to shew thereby, that this holy State ought to be kept honourable by all, and that he will, aid and assist the married Persons even when they are least expecting it.

But that ye may live godly in this State, you must know the Reasons wherefore God hath instituted the same. The first Reason is, that each faithfully assist the other in all Things that belong to this Life, and a better.

Secondly. That they bring up the Children which they shall get, in the true Knowledge and Fear of God, to his Glory, and their Salvation.

Thirdly. That each of them avoiding all Uncleanness and evil Lusts, may live with a good and quiet Conscience. *For to avoid Fornication, let every Man have his own Wife, and every Wife her own Husband;* insomuch that all who are come to their Years, and have not the Gift of Continence, are bound by the Command of God, to enter into the married State, with Knowledge and Consent of Parents, or Tutors and Friends; *that so the Temple of God, which is our Body, may not be defiled, for, whosoever defileth the Temple of God, him shall God destroy.*

Next, you are to know, how each is bound to behave respectively towards the other, according to the Word of God.

First. You who are the Bridegroom, shall know, that God hath set you to be the Head of your Wife, that you, according to your Ability, shall lead her with

Discretion; instructing, comforting, protecting her, as the Head rules the Body; yea, as Christ is the Head, Wisdom, Consolation, and Assistance to his Church. Besides, *you are to love your Wife as your own Body, as Christ hath loved his Church: You shall not be bitter against her, but dwell with her as a Man of Understanding, giving Honour to the Wife as the weaker Vessel, considering that ye are joint Heirs of the Grace of Life, that your Prayers be not hindered;* And since it is God's Command, *that the Man shall eat his Bread in the Sweat of his Face,* therefore you are to labour diligently and faithfully, in the calling wherein God hath set you, that you may maintain your Household honestly, and likewise have something to give to the Poor.

In like Manner shall you, who are the Bride, know how you are to carry yourself towards your Husband, according to the Word of God: You are to love your lawful Husband, to honour and fear him, as also to be obedient unto him in all lawful Things, as to your Lord, *as the Body is obedient to the Head, and the Church to Christ. You shall not exercise any Dominion over your Husband, but be silent; for Adam was first created, and then Eve to be an Help to Adam;* and after the Fall, God said to Eve, and in her to all Women, *Your Will shall be subject to your Husband:* You shall not resist this Ordinance of God, but be obedient to the Word of God, and follow the Examples of godly Women, who trusted in God, and were subject to their Husbands; *as Sarah was obedient to Abraham, calling him her Lord:* You shall also be an Help to your Husband in all good and lawful Things looking to your Family and walking in all Honesty and Virtue, without worldly Pride, that you may give an Example to others of Modesty.

Wherefore you N. and you N. having now understood that God hath instituted Marriage, and what he commands you therein; Are ye willing thus to behave yourselves in this holy State, as you here do confess before this Christian Assembly, and are desirous that you be confirmed in the same?

Answer. Yes.

Whereupon the Minister shall say to the Assembly,

I take you all, who are met here, to witness, that there is brought no lawful Impediment:

Further to the married Persons,

Since then it is fit that you be furthered in this your Work, the Lord God confirm your Purpose, which he hath given you; and your Beginning be in the Name of the Lord, who made Heaven and Earth.

Hereupon they shall join Hands together, and the Minister speak first to the Bridegroom,

N. Do you acknowledge here before God, and this his holy Church, that you have taken, and do take to your lawful Wife N. here present, promising her never to forsake her; to love her faithfully, to maintain her, as a faithful and pious

Husband is bound to do to his lawful Wife; that you will live holily with her; keeping Faith and Truth to her in all Things according to the holy Gospel?

Answer. Yes.

Afterwards to the Bride,

N. Do you acknowledge here before God, and this his holy Church, that you have taken, and do take to your lawful Husband N. here present, promising to be obedient to him, to serve and assist him, never to forsake him, to live holily with him, keeping Faith and Truth to him in all Things, as a pious and faithful Wife is bound to her lawful Husband according to the holy Gospel?

Answer. Yes.

Then the Minister shall say,

The Father of all Mercies, who of his Grace hath called you to this holy state of Marriage, bind you in true Love and Faithfulness, and grant you his Blessing, Amen.

Hear now from the Gospel, how firm the Bond of Marriage is, as described, Matthew, Chapter 19, Verses 3, 4, 5, 6, 7, 8, 9.

The Pharisees came unto him, tempting him, and saying unto him, is it lawful for a Man to put away his Wife for every Cause? And he answered and said unto them, have ye not read, that he which made them at the Beginning, made them Male and Female? And said, for this Cause shall a Man leave Father and Mother and shall cleave to his Wife; and they twain shall be one Flesh; Wherefore they are no more twain, but one Flesh. What therefore God hath joined together, let not Man put asunder. They say unto him, Why did Moses then command to give a Writing of Divorcement, and to put her away? He saith unto them, Moses, because of the Hardness of your Hearts, suffered you to put away your Wives; but from the Beginning it was not so. And I say unto you, Whosoever shall put away his Wife, except it be for Fornication, and shall marry another, committeth Adultery: And whoso marrieth her which is put away, doth commit Adultery.

Believe these Words of Christ, and be certain and assured, that our Lord God hath joined you together in this holy State. You are therefore to receive, whatever befalls you therein with Patience and Thanksgiving, as from the Hand of God, and thus all Things will turn to your Advantage and Salvation, Amen.

Then the Minister shall bid the married Persons to kneel down, and exhort the Congregation to pray for them.

Almighty God, thou who displayest thy Goodness and Wisdom in all thy Works and Ordinances, and hast said from the Beginning, that it is not good that Man should be alone, and therefore hast made an Help meet for him, and ordained, that those who were two should be one, and likewise punishest all

Uncleanness. We beseech thee (since thou hast called these two Persons to the holy State of Marriage, and joined them together) replenish them with thy Holy Spirit, that they may piously live together according to thy divine Will in true and firm Faith, and resist all Wickedness. Vouchsafe to bless them, as thou didst send thy Blessing upon the faithful Fathers, thy Friends and Servants, Abraham, Isaac, and Jacob; that they may as Co-Heirs of the Covenant (which thou didst make with those Fathers) educate the Children which thou shalt be pleased to give them, in all Godliness, to the Glory of thy holy Name, to the Edification of thy Church, and to the Propagation of thy holy Gospel. Hear us O Father of Mercies! for Jesus Christ's sake thy beloved Son our Lord, in whose Name we conclude our Prayers, saying, Our Father, &c.

Hearken now to the Promise of God from 128 Psalm.

Blessed is every one that feareth the Lord, that walketh in his Ways.

For thou shalt eat the Labour of thine Hands; happy shalt thou be, and it shall be well with thee.

Thy Wife shall be as a fruitful Vine by the Sides of thine House; thy Children like Olive Plants, round about thy Table.

Behold, that thus shall the Man be blessed, that feareth the Lord.

The Lord shall bless thee out of Zion; and thou shalt see the Good of Jerusalem all the Days of thy Life.

Yea thou shalt see thy Children's Children, and Peace upon Israel.

The Lord our God replenish you with his Grace, grant that ye may long live together in all Godliness and Holiness, Amen.

—14—

The Visions of Plenty-coups

Joel W. Martin

"The Indians know it without a book; they dream much of God, and therefore they know it." This statement, made by a Muskogee Indian man in the early nineteenth century to a European Christian visitor, pointed to a major difference between their religions. What Christians received from the Bible and prayer, many native people gained from dreams and visions. Dreams and visions provided profound experiences to contemplate, guidance, for life and inspiration for individuals and communities. Dreams and visions revealed vital truths, what people needed to know not only to survive but to thrive.

Considered gifts from another realm of existence and thus charged with sacredness or medicine-power, dreams and visions helped healers cure the sick. Rich in meaningful symbolism, dreams and visions told communities what they should do. In their dreams and visions, Native American individuals perceived their unique powers and identified specific paths to a good life. On the basis of their dreams and visions, individuals changed their identities, took new names, altered their behavior, and gained new social roles. Among some groups, a single powerful dream could redefine the dreamer's gender. Two hundred years ago among the Winnebago and Oglala Sioux, men who dreamed of the moon were offered the option of living the life of a woman, wearing female clothing, and behaving in accordance with recognized female properties. In dreams and visions, Native American communities discerned insights into the very order of the universe, detected hints about their collective future, and derived mandates for physical, social, and political movements. In dreams and visions, Native Americans found their core values symbolized, reinforced, and even questioned. For all of these reasons, Native Americans encouraged their children to seek dreams and visions and to treat them as powerful ways of knowing.

Vision seeking, a practice among many Native American peoples in the past but less so in the present, has been called the most basic concept of American Indian religion. Although most books and articles on the subject by non–native scholars focus on the ritual practices of men, women also sought visions and the

knowledge they provided. In 1751, for example, a young Lenni Lenape, or Delaware Indian, woman living in the village of Wyoming (near the Susquehanna
river in present-day Luzerne County, Pennsylvania) received a powerful vision. It
explained the cosmic origins of the three major social groups interacting in colonial America. The young woman lived at a time when European settlers were taking vast areas of land away from native peoples in Pennsylvania and enslaving
African men, women, and children to work on farms and plantations. Her vision
attracted the attention of Lenni Lenape, Shawnee, Conoy, and Nanticoke men
and women living in the Wyoming Valley. She told them they should protect their
cultural and territorial boundaries from further assaults,   challenge Europeans
who claimed superiority, avoid practicing Christianity, and resist dispossession
and enslavement. Based on her vision, leaders of many villages organized a great
council and planned resistance to the ongoing invasion of Pennsylvania.

Many visions, although uniquely experienced by individual male and female
seekers, enjoyed a public life while affecting the seeker's personal life. Dreams
affected others. Many visions were meant to be shared, first with a trusted interpreter, quite often with a council of elders, and in many cases with the whole village. If a person hoarded such a vision or kept quiet about it, personal grief and
confusion could result. Years later, the person might feel he or she wasted his or
her life or missed the great opportunity given by the cosmos to help his or her
people. Share a vision in the proper way—ideally by enacting it in a ceremony—
and it could bring considerable personal fulfillment to oneself and curative
power to others.

This ethos, the imperative to share certain visions, shaped how members of the
Iroquois confederacy and others responded to individuals' dreams. According to
a seventeenth-century observer, the Iroquois had only a single divinity—the
dream—which they followed with the utmost exactness. The Huron, although
enemies of the Iroquois during the seventeenth century, shared this view. Huron
individuals very carefully noted their dreams and frequently tried to obtain what
was pictured to them during their sleep. If, for instance, dreamers saw a javelin in
a dream, they tried to get one; if they dreamed that they gave a feast, they would
begin the preparations to give one. This was called *ondinnonk*—the secret desire
of the soul manifested by a dream that the waking person should take very
seriously.

Great variety characterized how native peoples responded to dreams and visions,
how they interpreted them, whom they entrusted them with, and what they did with
them. Not every vision was supposed to be shared; not every dream enacted. Some
people sought but did not receive dreams. Others received them but understood that
they could not be discussed with anyone. Others misunderstood the meaning of the
dreams they received. Some misused the power donated by the vision and turned
it to bad ends. Some lied about their dreams and suffered cosmic retribution. Almost
everyone who received a powerful dream spent the rest of their lives thinking about
it, returning to it, seeing new dimensions and symbols and messages in it, and forg-
ing fresh interpretations of its meaning. In such a way, a single great dream could

become the backbone of a person's biography, the spine of one's mind, the living source that shaped an individual's identity and defined his or her core.

Important to the individuals who experienced them, dreams could also teach how communities might avoid disaster and devastation. At least this is the message presented in the book *Plenty-Coups, Chief of the Crow*. *Plenty-Coups* resulted from the collaboration of a great Crow chief named Plenty-coups (born in 1848) and Frank B. Linderman (born in 1869). Frank Linderman had led a rich life. First a hunter and trapper in late-nineteenth-century Montana, he later became an assayer, prospector, newspaper owner, state legislator, and assistant secretary of state of Montana. Linderman is considered a trustworthy source of information about Plains Indians. In 1927–1929, Linderman and Plenty-coups met at Plenty-coups's home near Pryor, Montana, and collaborated on Plenty-coups's memoir. With the help of an interpreter who translated their words and by using Plains Indian sign language, they gathered the stories and memories that would become a well-written, reliable book about the chief's life. It relays Plenty-coups's memories but also provides Linderman's observations regarding places, ideas, and practices. In the excerpt reprinted here, we have left out Linderman's editorial remarks regarding places, ideas, and practices to make the text read more clearly.

The English name Plenty-coups is a translation of the Crow or Absarokee name Aleek-chea-ahoosh, or Many Achievements. The name refers specifically to acts of defiant courage warriors performed in battle. Among the Crow and other Plains peoples, counting coups was an important male activity. For an act to count as a coup, a warrior had to come close enough to the enemy to display his bravery and cunning, while not injuring the opponent—at least at first. For instance, a warrior could strike an armed and fighting enemy with his coup-stick, quirt (a type of riding whip), or bow before otherwise harming him. Or he could take his weapons while he was yet alive; strike the first enemy in battle, no matter who killed him; touch the enemy's breastworks while under fire; or steal a horse tied to a lodge in an enemy's camp. Plenty-coups received this bold name from his grandfather, who had received a dream telling him that his grandson would count many coups, become a wise chief, and live to be an old man. All of that came to pass.

Plenty-coups helped his people navigate some of the most difficult times ever faced by Plains nations. During the late nineteenth century, the United States invaded the West, subjugated its indigenous peoples, and virtually exterminated the buffalo, the heart of Plains Indian economy, subsistence, and spiritual life. This devastation did not happen overnight. Nor did it strike each nation at the same time or in an identical way. Native communities responded to the crisis with a variety of strategies. Lakotas, who had enjoyed preeminent status on the Plains before the invasion, fought back and dominated other Plains Indians. Others, such as the Crow, hoped to avoid direct conflict with the United States. Thus Indian nations found themselves at odds with each other. All relied on dreams to help them find the right answers.

The book *Plenty-Coups* details two of Plenty-coups's greatest dreams. The first was received in 1857 when Plenty-coups was nine years old. Mourning his brother's death, he purified himself in a sweat lodge, a dome-shaped structure containing heated rocks that release cleansing steam when doused with water. After this cleansing, Plenty-coups cried for spiritual help. Supernatural beings called his name and took him to their lodge. There they told him his destiny, that he could become an important leader if he would only discipline his will and sharpen his senses. The second vision, received when he was not yet ten, exceeded his comprehension and he had to seek help to understand it.

Visions blended the familiar with the extraordinary. In all of his visions, Plenty-coups encountered standard Absarokee architecture, food, animals, colors, geographical features, symbols, words, and places. But in his visions, Plenty-coups also traveled at impossible speeds, experienced intense fear, and met the Little People face to face. These supernatural dwarves possessed superhuman abilities and wisdom. Later in the second vision, Plenty-coups witnessed enigmatic and massive movements of buffalo and other strange creatures and observed himself as an old man. His dream mystified him, escaped his grasp, and overwhelmed his powers of analysis. Visions resemble extremely condensed or compressed messages. Not easily exhausted of meaning and value, they can sustain a person throughout a lifetime. Combining the familiar with the uncanny, dreams are not transparent in meaning, even though they feature many elements that seem very close to the everyday waking life of the dreamer.

After his dream, Plenty-coups went before a council of elders to relate his vision. Experienced dreamers themselves and trusted leaders, the elders could make sense of his experience, take the measure of what seemed unfathomable, and find within it wisdom for the whole community. They could transform something deeply individual or private into a narrative useful to the whole people. To understand the lesson of his vision, Plenty-coups needed both the images of the dream and the insights of the elders. Plenty-coups's dream, they said, showed that the buffalo, the essential basis of the Crow way of life in those days, would disappear as whites invaded the Plains, killed bison, and imported cattle into the region. The Crow nation, however, could survive this violent and destructive transformation of their world, but only if it avoided warring against the United States. Thus Plenty-coups's dream, interpreted by the community leaders, became something public, effective, and authoritative. Dreams and visions helped Plenty-coups and his people anticipate and respond to this manifold crisis and helped them survive as Indians in a time when others sought to crush their culture and suppress their religion. Years later, as Frank Linderman listened, Plenty-coups expressed his joy at the miracle of his and his people's resilience: "Ho! said Plenty-coups, making the sign for finished. And here I am, an old man sitting under this tree where [an elder] sat seventy years ago when this was a different world." "We traveled by that dream," a Crow man remembered long afterwards, and indeed, the Crow people survived the deepest crisis of the nineteenth century in part because of Plenty-coups's vision.

Plenty-coups's story originally appeared in Frank B. Linderman, *American: The Life Story of a Great Indian* (New York: John Day, 1930), reprinted as Frank B. Linderman, *Plenty-Coups, Chief of the Crows* (Lincoln: University of Nebraska Press, 1962), pp. 33–44, 52–75.

Further Reading

Lee Irwin, *The Dream Seekers: Native American Visionary Traditions of the Great Plains* (Norman: University of Oklahoma Press, 1994); William K. Powers, *Yuwipi: Vision and Experience in Oglala Ritual* (Lincoln: University of Nebraska Press, 1982), pp. 11–18; Frederick Hoxie, *Parading Through History: The Making of the Crow Nation in America, 1805–1935* (New York: Cambridge University Press, 1995); Celeste River, "The Great Stillness: Visions and Native Wisdom in the Writings of Frank Bird Linderman," in Arnold Krupat, ed., *New Voices in Native American Literary Criticism* (Washington, D.C.: Smithsonian Institution Press, 1993), pp. 291–316.

Plenty-coups's Visions

FIRST VISION

When I was nine years old, a happening made me feel that I was a grown-up man, almost in a day. . . . I had a brother. I shall not speak his name, but if there were four brave, handsome young men in our tribe my brother was one of them. I loved him dearly, and he was always an inspiration to me. . . .

One morning when our village was going to move, he went on the war-trail against our enemy, the Lacota [Sioux]. All that day he was in my thoughts. Even when we crossed Elk River, where usually there was satisfying excitement, I kept thinking of my brother. Rafts had to be made for the old people and children, and these, drawn by four men on good horses, had ever given me plenty to think about. But this day nothing interested me. That night I could not sleep, even when all but the wolves were sleeping. When the village was set up on the Big River [Missouri], news reached us that my brother was gone—killed by Sioux on Powder River.

My heart fell to the ground and stayed there. I mourned with my father and mother, and alone. I cut my flesh and bled myself weak. I knew now that I must dream if I hoped to avenge my brother, and I at once began to fast in preparation, first taking a sweat-bath to cleanse my body.

Nobody saw me leave the village. I slipped away and climbed The-buffalo's-heart, where I fasted two more days and nights, without success. I saw nothing at all and gave up to travel back to my father's lodge, where I rested.

The fourth night, while I was asleep, a voice said to me, You did not go to the right mountain, Plenty-coups. I knew then that I should sometime succeed in dreaming.

The village was preparing to move to the Little Rockies, a good place for me, and before the women began to take down the lodges I started out alone. Besides extra moccasins, I had a good buffalo robe, and as soon as I reached the mountains I covered a sweat-lodge with the robe and again cleansed my body. I was near the Two Buttes and chose the south one, which I climbed, and there I made a bed of sweet-sage and ground-cedar. I was determined that no smell of man should be on me and burned some *e-say* [a root that grows in the mountains] and sweet-sage, standing in their smoke and rubbing my body with the sage.

The day was hot; and naked I began walking about the top of the mountain crying for Helpers, but got no answer, no offer of assistance. I grew more tired as the sun began to go toward the west, and finally I went to my bed, lying down so my feet would face the rising sun when he came again. Weakened by my walking and the days of fasting, I slept, remembering only the last rays of the sun as he went to his lodge. When I wakened, looking into the sky, I saw that The-seven-stars [the Big Dipper] had turned round The-star-that-does-not-move [North Star]. The night was westward. Morning was not far away, and wolves were howling on the plains far below me. I wondered if the village would reach the Little Rockies before night came again.

"Plenty-coups."

My name was spoken! The voice came from behind me, back of my head. My heart leaped like a deer struck by an arrow. "Yes," I answered, without moving.

"They want you, Plenty-coups. I have been sent to fetch you," said the voice yet behind me, back of my head.

"I am ready," I answered, and stood up, my head clear and light as air.

The night had grown darker, and I felt rather than saw some Person go by me on my right side. I could not tell what Person it was, but thought he beckoned me.

"I am coming," I said, but the Person made no answer and slipped away in a queer light that told me where he was. I followed over the same places I had traveled in the afternoon, not once feeling my feet touch a stone. They touched nothing at all where the way was rough, and without moccasins I walked in the Person's tracks as though the mountain were as smooth as the plains. My body was naked, and the winds cool and very pleasant, but I looked to see which way I was traveling. The stars told me that I was going east, and I could see that I was following the Person downhill. I could not actually see him, but I knew I was on his trail by the queer light ahead. His feet stirred no stone, nothing on the way, made no sound of walking, nor did mine.

A coyote yelped on my right, and then another answered on my left. A little farther on I heard many coyotes yelping in a circle around us, and as we traveled they moved their circle along with us, as though they were all going to the same place as we. When the coyotes ahead stopped on a flat and sat down to yelp together, the ones behind closed in to make their circle smaller, all yelping loudly, as though they wished to tell the Person something. I knew now that our destination was not far off.

The Person stopped, and I saw a lodge by his side. It seemed to rise up out of the ground. I saw that he came to it at its back, that it faced east, and that the Person reached its door by going around it to the right. But I did not know him, even when he coughed to let someone inside the lodge know he was there. He spoke no word to me but lifted the lodge door and stepped inside. "Come, Plenty-coups," he said gently. And I too stepped into the lodge.

There was no fire burning, and yet there was light in the lodge. I saw that it was filled with Persons I did not know. There were four rows of them in half-circles, two rows on each side of the center, and each Person was an old warrior. I could tell this by their faces and bearing. They had been counting coup. I knew this because before each, sticking in the ground, was a white coup-stick bearing the breath-feathers of a war-eagle. Some, however, used no stick at all, but only heavy first-feathers whose quills were strong enough to stick in the ground. These first-feathers were very fine, the handsomest I had ever seen, and I could not count them, they were so many.

"Why have you brought this young man into our lodge? We do not want him. He is not our kind and therefore has no place among us." The words came from the south side, and my heart began to fall down.

I looked to see what Persons sat on the south side, and my eyes made me afraid. They were the Winds, the Bad Storms, the Thunders, the Moon, and many Stars, all powerful, and each of them braver and much stronger than men. . . .

"Come, Plenty-coups, and sit with us." This voice was kind. It came from the north side.

"Sit," said the Person who had brought me there, and then he was gone. I saw him no more.

They, on the north side of the lodge, made a place for me. It was third from the head on the left, and I sat down there. The two parties of Persons were separated at the door, which faced the east, and again in the west, which was the head of the lodge, so that the Spirit-trail from east to west was open, if any wished to travel that way. On neither side were the Persons the same as I. All were different, but I knew now that they had rights in the world, as I had, that Ah-badt-dadt-deah had created them, as He had me and other men. Nobody there told me this, but I felt it in the lodge as I felt the presence of the Persons. I knew that to live on the world I must concede that those Persons across the lodge who had not wished me to sit with them had work to do, and that I could not prevent them from doing it. I felt a little afraid but was glad I was there.

"Take these, Plenty-coups." The Person at the head of the lodge on the north side handed me several beautiful first-feathers of a war-eagle.

I looked into his eyes. He was a Dwarf-person, chief of the Little-people who live in the Medicine-rock, which you can almost see from here, and who made the stone arrow points. I now saw that all on my side were the same as he, that all were Dwarfs not tall as my knee. . . .

"Stick one of your feathers in the ground before you and count coup," said the Dwarf-chief.

I hesitated. I had never yet counted coup, and here in this lodge with old warriors was no place to lie.

"Count coup!" commanded the Dwarf-chief.

I stuck a first-feather into the ground before me, fearing a dispute.

"That," said the Dwarf-chief, "is the rider of the *white* horse! I first struck him with my coup-stick, and then, while he was unharmed and fighting, I took his bow from him."

The Thunders, who sat at the head of the lodge on the south side, said, "Nothing can be better than that."

"Stick another feather before you, Plenty-coups," said the Dwarf-chief.

I stuck another first-feather in the ground, wondering what the Dwarf-chief would say for it. But this time I was not afraid.

"That," he said, "is the rider of the *black* horse. I first struck him with my bow. Then, while he was armed with a knife and fighting me, I took his bow from him, also his shield."

"Enough!" said the Persons on the south side. "No Person can do better than that."

"Let us leave off counting coups. We are glad you have admitted this young man to our lodge," said the Bad Storms, "and we think you should give him something to take back with him, some strong medicine that will help him."

Plenty-coups had been speaking rapidly, his hands following his spoken words with signs, acting parts, while his facial expressions gave tremendous emphasis to his story. He was perspiring and stopped to brush his face with his hand.

I had not spoken . . . and could not understand why the Dwarf-chief had ordered me to stick the feathers, nor why he had counted coups in my name before such powerful Persons.

"He will be a Chief," said the Dwarf-chief. "I can give him nothing. He already possesses the power to become great if he will use it. Let him cultivate his senses, let him use the powers which Ah-badt-dadt-deah has given him, and he will go far. The difference between men grows out of the use, or non-use, of what was given them by Ah-badt-dadt-deah in the first place."

Then he said to me, "Plenty-coups, we, the Dwarfs, the Little-people, have adopted you and will be your Helpers throughout your life on this world. We have no medicine-bundle to give you. They are cumbersome things at best and are often in a warrior's way. Instead, we will offer you advice. Listen!

"In you, as in all men, are natural powers. You have a will. Learn to use it. Make it work for you. Sharpen your senses as you sharpen your knife. Remember the wolf smells better than you do because he has learned to depend on his nose. It tells him every secret the winds carry because he uses it all the time, makes it work for him. We can give you nothing. You already possess everything necessary to become great. Use your powers. Make them work for you, and you will become a Chief." . . .

When I wakened, I was perspiring. Looking into the early morning sky that was growing light in the north, I went over it all in my mind. I saw and understood that whatever I accomplished must be by my own efforts, that I must myself do the things I wished to do. And I knew I could accomplish them if I used the powers that Ah-badt-dadt-deah *had* given me. I had a will and I would use it, make it work for me, as the Dwarf-chief had advised. I became very happy, lying there looking up into the sky. My heart began to sing like a bird, and I went back to the village, needing no man to tell me the meaning of my dream. I took a sweat-bath and rested in my father's lodge. I *knew* myself now. . . .

SECOND VISION

One windy day, the Chief went on, when the clouds touched their peaks, we came to the Beartooth Mountains. I saw many lodges among the trees there and thought at first they belonged to our enemies, the Blackfeet. But they were Crow lodges, and all the clans, even those that had been farthest away, had come to the mountains to meet the chiefs in council. I was glad to see them all. I was born a Burned-mouth, but had been raised by the Newly-made-lodges. Both were here, with the Whistling-waters, the Big-lodges, the Kicked-in-the-bellies, and the others. The sight of so large a village under the pine trees, the air-clear water racing past it to the plains, the smell of smoke from lodge-fires, the sound of war-drums and happy voices, made my heart sing. . . .

We feasted there . . . Fat meat of bighorn, deer, and elk was plentiful. The hunters had killed many of these animals because they knew there would soon be a very large village to feed. Besides, light skins were always needed for shirts and leggings. Even the dogs found more than they could eat near that village, and our horses, nearly always feasting on rich grass, enjoyed the change the mountains gave them. All night the drums were beating, and in the light of fires that smelled sweet the people danced until they were tired.

I was wakened by a crier. He was riding through the village with some message from the council of the night before. I sat up to listen. "There are high peaks in these mountains, O young men! Go to them and dream!" the crier said. "Are you men, or women? Are you afraid of a little suffering? Go into these mountains and find Helpers for yourselves and your people who have so many enemies!"

I sat there in my robe, listening till his voice was far off. How I wished to count coup, to wear an eagle's feather in my hair, to sit in the council with my chiefs, holding an eagle's wing in my hand.

I got up from my robe. The air was cool and smelled of the trees outside. Ought I to go again and try to dream?

"Go, young man!"

Another crier had started through the village. His first words answered my unspoken question. I walked out of the lodge, only half hearing the rest of his message. The sun was just coming, and the wind was in the treetops. Women were kindling their fires, and hunters were leaving the camp when I started out alone.

I decided to go afoot to the Crazy Mountains, two long days' journey from the village. The traveling without food or drink was good for me, and as soon as I reached the Crazies I took a sweat-bath and climbed the highest peak. There is a lake at its base, and the winds are always stirring about it. But even though I fasted two more days and nights, walking over the mountain top, no Person came to me, nothing was offered. I saw several grizzly bears that were nearly white in the moonlight, and one of them came very near to me, but he did not speak. Even when I slept on that peak in the Crazies, no bird or animal or Person spoke a word to me, and I grew discouraged. I could not dream.

Back in the village I told my closest friends about the high peaks I had seen, about the white grizzly bears, and the lake. They were interested and said they would go back with me and that we would all try to dream.

There were three besides myself who set out, with extra moccasins and a robe to cover our sweat-lodge. We camped on good water just below the peak where I had tried to dream, quickly took our sweat-baths, and started up the mountains. It was already dark when we separated, but I found no difficulty in reaching my old bed on the tall peak that looked down on the little lake, or in making a new bed with ground-cedar and sweet-sage. Owls were hooting under the stars while I rubbed my body with the sweet-smelling herbs before starting out to walk myself weak.

When I could scarcely stand, I made my way back to my bed and slept with my feet toward the east. But no Person came to me, nothing was offered; and when the day came I got up to walk again over the mountain top, calling for Helpers as I had done the night before.

All day the sun was hot, and my tongue was swollen for want of water; but I saw nothing, heard nothing, even when night came again to cool the mountain. No sound had reached my ears, except my own voice and the howling of wolves down on the plains.

I knew that our great Crow warriors of other days sacrificed their flesh and blood to dream, and just when the night was tearing to let the morning come I stopped at a fallen tree, and, laying the first finger of my left hand upon the log, I cut part of it off with my knife. [The end of the left index finger on the Chief's hand is missing]. But no blood came. The stump of my finger was white as the finger of a dead man, and to make it bleed I struck it against the log until blood flowed freely. Then I began to walk and call for Helpers, hoping that some Person would smell my blood and come to aid me.

Near the middle of that day my head grew dizzy, and I sat down. I had eaten nothing, taken no water, for nearly four days and nights, and my mind must have left me while I sat there under the hot sun on the mountain top. It must have traveled far away, because the sun was nearly down when it returned and found me lying on my face. As soon as it came back to me I sat up and looked about, at first not knowing where I was. Four war-eagles were sitting in a row along a trail of my blood just above me. But they did not speak to me, offered nothing at all.

I thought I would try to reach my bed, and when I stood up I saw my three friends. They had seen the eagles flying over my peak and had become frightened, believing me dead. They carried me to my bed and stayed long enough to smoke with me before going back to their own places. While we smoked, the four war-eagles did not fly away. They sat there by my blood on the rocks, even after the night came on and chilled everything living on the mountain. . . .

I dreamed. I heard a voice at midnight and saw a Person standing at my feet, in the east. He said, "Plenty-coups, the Person down there wants you now."

He pointed, and from the peak in the Crazy Mountains I saw a Buffalo-bull standing *where we* [Linderman and Plenty-coups] *are sitting now.* I got up and started to go to the Bull, because I knew he was the Person who wanted me. The other Person was gone. Where he had stood when he spoke to me there was nothing at all.

The way is very long from the Crazies to this place where we are sitting today, but I came here quickly in my dream. On that hill over yonder was where I stopped to look at the Bull. He had changed into a Man-person wearing a buffalo robe with the hair outside. Later I picked up the buffalo skull that you see over there, on the very spot where the Person had stood. I have kept that skull for more than seventy years.

The Man-person beckoned me from the hill over yonder where I had stopped, and I walked to where he stood. When I reached his side he began to sink slowly into the ground, right over there [pointing]. Just as the Man-person was disappearing he spoke. "Follow me," he said.

But I was afraid. "Come," he said from the darkness. And I got down into the hole in the ground to follow him, walking bent-over for ten steps. Then I stood straight and saw a small light far off. It was like a window in a white man's house of today, and I knew the hole was leading us toward the Arrow Creek Mountains. . . .

In the way of the light, between it and me, I could see countless buffalo, see their sharp horns thick as the grass grows. I could smell their bodies and hear them snorting, ahead and on both sides of me. Their eyes, without number, were like little fires in the darkness of the hole in the ground, and I felt afraid among so many big bulls. The Man-person must have known this, because he said, "Be not afraid, Plenty-coups. It was these Persons who sent for you. They will not do you harm."

My body was naked. I feared walking among them in such a narrow place. The burrs that are always in their hair would scratch my skin, even if their hoofs and horns did not wound me more deeply. I did not like the way the Man-person went among them. "Fear nothing! Follow me, Plenty-coups," he said.

I felt their warm bodies against my own, but went on after the Man-person, edging around them or going between them all that night and all the next day, with my eyes always looking ahead at the hole of light. But none harmed me, none even spoke to me, and at last we came out of the hole in the ground and saw the Square White Butte at the mouth of Arrow Creek Canyon. It was on our right. White men call it Castle Rock, but our name for it is The-fasting-place.

Now, out in the light of the sun, I saw that the Man-person who had led me had a rattle in his hand. It was large and painted red. . . . When he reached the top of a knoll he turned and said to me, "Sit here!"

Then he shook his red rattle and sang a queer song four times. "Look!" he pointed.

Out of the hole in the ground came the buffalo, bulls and cows and calves without number. They spread wide and blackened the plains. Everywhere I looked great herds of buffalo were going in every direction, and still others without number were pouring out of the hole in the ground to travel on the wide plains. When at last they ceased coming out of the hole in the ground, all were gone, *all*! There was not one in sight anywhere, even out on the plains. I saw a few antelope on a hillside, but no buffalo—not a bull not a cow, not one calf, was anywhere on the plains.

I turned to look at the Man-person beside me. He shook his red rattle again. "Look!" he pointed.

Out of the hole in the ground came bulls and cows and calves past counting. These, like the others, scattered and spread on the plains. But they stopped in small bands and began to eat the grass. Many lay down, not as a buffalo does but differently, and many were spotted. Hardly any two were alike in color or size. And the bulls bellowed differently too, not deep and far-sounding like the bulls of the buffalo but sharper and yet weaker in my ears. Their tails were different, longer, and nearly brushed the ground. They were not buffalo. These were strange animals from another world.

I was frightened and turned to the Man-person, who only shook his red rattle but did not sing. He did not even tell me to look, but I did look and saw all the Spotted-buffalo go back into the hole in the ground, until there was nothing except a few antelope anywhere in sight.

"Do you understand this which I have shown you, Plenty-coups?" he asked me.

"No!" I answered. How could he expect me to understand such a thing when I was not yet ten years old?

During all the time the Spotted-buffalo were going back into the hole in the ground the Man-person had not once looked at me. He stood facing the south as though the Spotted-buffalo belonged there. "Come, Plenty-coups," he said finally, when the last had disappeared.

I followed him back through the hole in the ground without seeing anything until we came out *right over there* [Plenty-coups points to a spot] where we had first entered the hole in the ground. Then I saw the spring down by those trees, this very house just as it is, these trees which comfort us today, and a very old man sitting in the shade, alone. I felt pity for him because he was so old and feeble.

"Look well upon this old man," said the Man-person. "Do you know him, Plenty-coups?" he asked me.

"No," I said, looking closely at the old man's face in the shade of *this* tree.

"This old man is yourself, Plenty-coups," he told me. And then I could see the Man-person no more. He was gone, and so too was the old man.

Instead I saw only a dark forest. A fierce storm was coming fast. The sky was black with streaks of mad color through it. I saw the Four Winds gathering to strike the forest, and held my breath. Pity was hot in my heart for the beautiful trees. I felt pity for all things that lived in that forest, but was powerless to stand with them against the Four Winds that together were making war. I shielded my own face with my arm when they charged! I heard the Thunders calling out in the storm, saw beautiful trees twist like blades of grass and fall in tangled piles where the forest had been. Bending low, I heard the Four Winds rush past me as though they were not yet satisfied, and then I looked at the destruction they had left behind them.

Only one tree, tall and straight, was left standing where the great forest had stood. The Four Winds that always make war alone had this time struck together, riding down every tree in the forest but *one*. Standing there alone among its dead tribesmen, I thought it looked sad. "What does this mean?" I whispered in my dream.

"Listen, Plenty-coups," said a voice. "In that tree is the lodge of the Chickadee. He is least in strength but strongest of mind among his kind. He is willing to work for wisdom. The Chickadee-person is a good listener. Nothing escapes his ears, which he has sharpened by constant use. Whenever others are talking together of their successes or failures, there you will find the Chickadee-person listening to their words. But in all his listening he tends to his own business. He never intrudes, never speaks in strange company, and yet never misses a chance to learn from others. He gains success and avoids failure by learning how others succeeded or failed, and without great trouble to himself. There is scarcely a lodge he does not visit, hardly a Person he does not know, and yet everybody likes him, because he minds his own business, or pretends to.

"The lodges of countless Bird-people were in that forest when the Four Winds charged it. Only one is left unharmed, the lodge of the Chickadee-person. Develop your body, but do not neglect your mind, Plenty-coups. It is the mind that leads a man to power, not strength of body."

I wakened then. My three friends were standing at my feet in the sunshine. They helped me stand. I was very weak, but my heart was singing, even as my friends half carried me to the foot of the mountain and kindled a fire. One killed a deer, and I ate a little of the meat. It is not well to eat heartily after so long a time of fasting. But the meat helped me to recover my strength a little. Of course we had all taken sweat-baths before touching the meat, or even killing the deer, and I was happy there beside the clear water with my friends. Toward night two of them went back to the village to bring horses for me and the man who stayed with me at the foot of the mountains. I was yet too weak to travel so far afoot.

Lying by the side of the clear water, looking up into the blue sky, I kept thinking of my dream, but could understand little of it except that my medicine was the Chickadee. I should have a small medicine-bundle, indeed. And I would call upon the Wise Ones [medicine men] of the tribe to interpret the rest. Perhaps they could tell the meaning of my dream from beginning to end.

In the middle of the third day my ears told me that horses were coming. My friend and I walked a little way to meet them, and very soon I heard the voices of my uncles, White-horse and Cuts-the-turnip. They were singing the Crow Praise Song with several others who were leading extra horses for my friend and me.

I was stronger now and could ride alone, but the way seemed very far indeed. Of course I had spoken to nobody of my dream, but when I came in sight of the village my uncles began again to sing the Praise Song, and many people came out to meet us. They were all very happy, because they knew I now had Helpers and would use my power to aid my people.

None spoke to me, not because he did not wish to be kind but because the people knew I must first cleanse myself in a sweat-lodge before going about the village with my friends. I saw my young sweetheart by her father's lodge, and although she did not speak to me I thought she looked happier than ever before.

While I was in the sweat-lodge my uncles rode through the village telling the Wise Ones that I had come, that I had dreamed and wished interpretation of my vision in council. I heard them calling this message to those who had distinguished themselves by feats of daring or acts of wisdom, and I wondered what my dream could mean, what the Wise Ones would say to me after I had told them all I had seen and heard on the peak in the Crazy Mountains. I respected them so highly that rather than have them speak lightly of my dream I would willingly have died. . . .

My father was gone . . . so that I had only my uncles to speak for me before the Wise Ones. But my uncles were both good men. Both loved me and both belonged to the tribal council, whose members had all counted coup and were leaders. No man can love children more than my people do, and while I missed my father this day more than ever, I knew my uncles looked on me as a son and that they would help me now.

Both of them were waiting, and when I was ready they led me to the lodge of Yellow-bear, where our chiefs sat with the Wise Ones. When I entered and sat down, Yellow-bear passed the pipe round the lodge, as the sun goes, from east to west. Each man took it as it came, and smoked, first offering the stem to the Sun, the father, and then to the Earth, the mother of all things on this world. But no one spoke. All in that lodge had been over the hard trail and each knew well what was in my heart by my eyes. The eyes of living men speak words which the tongue cannot pronounce. The dead do not see out of their bodies' eyes, because there is no spirit there. It has gone away forever. In the lodge of Yellow-bear that day seventy years ago I saw the spirits [souls] of my leaders in their eyes, and my heart sang loudly because I had dreamed.

When the pipe was finished, my uncle, White-horse, laid his hand on my shoulder. "Speak, Plenty-coups," he said. "Tell us your dream. Forget nothing that happened. You are too young to understand, but here are men who can help you."

At this point a rolling hoop bumped violently against the Chief's chair and fell flat beside it. The old man did not start or show the least displeasure, even when a little bright-eyed girl ran among us to recover it. He did not reprove her with so much as a look. Instead, he smiled. "I have adopted many children," he said softly. Then he went on.

I told my dream, all of it. Even a part I forgot to tell you, about trying to enter a lodge on my way back from this place to the Crazies. A Voice had spoken. "Do not go inside," it said. "This lodge contains the clothes of small babies, and if you touch them or they touch you, you will not be successful." Of course I did not enter that lodge, but went on to my bed in the mountains. This I told in the order it came in my dream.

When I had finished, Yellow-bear, who sat at the trend of the lodge which faced the east, lighted the pipe and passed it to his left, as the sun goes. Four times he lit the pipe, and four times it went round the lodge, without a word being spoken by anybody who took it. I grew uneasy. Was there no meaning in my dream.

"White-horse," the voice of Yellow-bear said softly, "your nephew has dreamed a great dream."

My heart began to sing again. Yellow-bear was the wisest man in the lodge. My ears were listening.

"He has been told that in his lifetime the buffalo will go away forever," said Yellow-bear, "and that in their place on the plains will come the bulls and the cows and the calves of the white men. I have myself seen these Spotted-buffalo drawing loads of the white man's goods. And once at the big fort above the mouth of the Elk River [Fort Union, above the mouth of the Yellowstone] on the Big River [Missouri] I saw cows and calves of the same tribe as the bulls that drew the loads.

"The dream of Plenty-coups means that the white men will take and hold this country and that their Spotted-buffalo will cover the plains. He was told to think for himself, to listen, to learn to avoid disaster by the experiences of others. He was advised to develop his body but not to forget his mind. The meaning of his dream is plain to me. I see its warning. The tribes who have fought the white man have all been beaten, wiped out. By listening as the Chickadee listens we may escape this and keep our lands.

"The Four Winds represent the white man and those who will help him in his wars. The forest of trees are the tribes of these wide plains. And the one tree that the Four Winds left standing after the fearful battle represents our own people, the Absarokees, the one tribe of the plains that has never made war against the white man.

"The Chickadee's lodge in that standing tree is the lodges of this tribe pitched in the safety of peaceful relations with white men, whom we could not stop even though we would. The Chickadee is small, so are we against our many enemies, white and red. But he was wise in his selection of a place to pitch his lodge. After the battle of the Four Winds he still held his home, his country, because he had gained wisdom by listening to the mistakes of others and knew there was safety for himself and his family. The Chickadee is the medicine of Plenty-coups from this day. He will not be obliged to carry a heavy medicine-bundle, but his medicine will be powerful both in peace time and in war.

"He will live to be old and he will be a Chief. He will some day live different from the way we do now and will sit in the shade of great trees on Arrow Creek, where the Man-person took him in his dream. The old man he saw there was himself, as he was told. He will live to be old and be known for his brave deeds, but I can see that he will have no children of his own blood. This was told him when he tried to enter that lodge on his way from Arrow Creek to the peak in the Crazy Mountains where he dreamed. When the Voice told him not to enter, that the lodge was filled with the clothes of babes, that if he touched them he would not succeed, it meant he would have no children. I have finished."

"Your dream was a great dream. Its meaning is plain," said the others, and the pipe was passed so that I might smoke with them in the lodge of Yellow-bear.

Ho! said Plenty-coups, making the sign for finished. And here I am, an old man, sitting under this tree just where that old man sat seventy years ago when this was a different world.

— 15 —

Mary Anne Sadlier's Advice for
Irish Catholic Girls

Liz Szabo Hernadi

To the millions of Irish immigrants who flocked to America in the second half of the nineteenth century, the New World was a land of promise, teeming with money, jobs, freedom, and opportunity. Yet it was also a country of religious prejudice and racial segregation, where cities were crowded with cramped, dingy tenements, where ethnic groups clashed over territory, where children labored in dangerous factories, where immigrants fleeing fear and famine at home found signs warning "No Irish Need Apply" when they looked for work. Like members of other religious minorities, many looked to their faith to help make sense of the confusion. Others began to suspect that their Catholicism was hindering their advancement in a largely Protestant society. If only America came with a survival manual!

That is exactly what Irish American author Mary Anne Sadlier set out to write—advice books in narrative form. Not long after she arrived in North America in 1844, Sadlier assigned herself the task of helping her fellow Catholic immigrants navigate the strange new American culture. She knew their hardships well. Biographers suggest that Sadlier left Ireland after her father's financial collapse and, like so many immigrants, came to the New World to start over. She found an audience in the growing tide of Catholic immigrants, who were hungry not only for guidance but for entertainment with an Irish theme. While priests and bishops preached from the pulpit, Sadlier aimed to capture readers in their leisure hours. In scores of stories, plays, textbooks, and novels, including the one to be examined here, *Bessy Conway, or The Irish Girl in America,* Sadlier sketched morality tales aimed at keeping Irish Catholics on the right path: *Stay away from dances and pubs. Say your prayers. Attend Sunday Mass. Work hard and save your money.* In admonishing the Irish to be pious and law-abiding, she hoped that immigrants would improve their lives. At the same time, Sadlier was acutely aware of anti-Irish stereotypes and the common conception of Irish immigrants as uneducated or prone to drink. In trying to alleviate various social ills, and in elevating the Irish American community, Sadlier aimed to prove its critics—and the stereotypes—wrong. Sadlier says as much in her preface to *Bessy Conway:* "I have written this book from a sincere and heartfelt desire to benefit these young country-women of mine, by showing them how to win respect and inspire confidence on the part of their employers, and at the same time, to avoid the snares and pitfalls which have been the ruin of so many of their own class. Let them be assured," she continues, "that it rests with themselves whether they do well or ill in America—whether they do honor to their country and their faith, or bring shame and reproach to both." In this way, Sadlier was following a long tradition of nineteenth-century popular fiction. Novels were crowded with earnest young heroines created to provide good examples for readers. Magazines were filled with etiquette tips and social advice. Domestic manuals, too, sought to help women establish homes that were not only tidy and well-organized, but morally uplifting.

Similarly, each of Sadlier's novels confronts a different social issue or social class. In *Bessy Conway* she addresses the lot of young women who hire themselves out as domestic servants. The following selection from *Bessy Conway* condenses some of the final chapters of the novel, which ends, as it begins, in Ireland. Earlier in the book, Bessy leaves Ireland as a teenager to see the world and try her luck in the United States. Although her family remains in Ireland, Bessy does not journey alone. She is accompanied by a host of village friends: some of them look out for Bessy; others lose their way. Bessy is also pursued across the Atlantic by her landlord's son, known as young Herbert, a vindictive, yet apparently handsome, Protestant playboy, who has determined to seduce her. In America, Bessy works hard as a house maid and—in a voice that sounds far more like that of the matronly Sadlier than that of a young girl—often reprimands her fellow servants for going out at night. Bessy, indeed, is a model of piety and obedience. She disobeys an authority figure only once, when she refuses her Protestant employer's request to join in non-Catholic prayers. Bessy quits her job in protest but quickly finds a new and better one. Her friends do not fare as well. Her old neighbor, Ned Finigan, succumbs to materialism, briefly finding success as a pub owner. But alcohol gets the best of him, and he deteriorates into a wife-beating alcoholic. Bessy's fast-living female friends also meet gruesome ends, generally marrying abusive husbands who leave them in poverty and despair.

Her message apparently resonated with many readers. Although reliable sales figures for *Bessy Conway* are difficult to find, there is evidence that Sadlier's other novels sold quite well. Scholar Charles Fanning has noted that by 1860, when Sadlier was working on *Bessy Conway*, she had become "the best known Irish Catholic voice in American letters." Her novels often went through as many as six editions. According to Sadlier's daughter, Anna, one of her mother's early works, *Willy Burke*, sold 7,000 copies in its first six weeks—not bad for 1850.

Our excerpt begins at chapter nineteen, when the action of *Bessy Conway* shifts from New York back to Ardfinnan, Bessy's hometown in Ireland. As the scene opens, Sadlier describes the effects of the Irish famine of 1845 to 1850 on Bessy's family. The famine, it should be noted, took the lives of one million people, and—over the decades that followed—sent millions more to the United States and other countries in search of a living. Bessy's family and the rest of the village suffer in the famine after the potato blight kills their crops. In an effort to steal the family's land, the landlord hides letters that Bessy's father had sent to America imploring his daughter for money. Without aid from Bessy, the Conway family seems doomed to eviction and starvation. Just as the bailiffs arrive to repossess the Conways' furniture and throw them into the street, however, Bessy miraculously materializes, her pockets filled with greenbacks. The Conways are overjoyed to find that Bessy has not forsaken them but saddened to hear that nearly everyone who emigrated to America has died or deteriorated. Bessy resolves never to return to America and advises her friends not to let their daughters emigrate.

In the final chapter of the novel, which is quite long and not included here, Bessy proves even more triumphant. The landlord's profligate son Herbert returns home to Ireland and reveals to Bessy that he has converted from Protestant to Catholic for her sake. This is a stunning reversal. Through her piety, Bessy not only is able to avoid being seduced but actually persuades the landlord's rakish son to reject his parents' faith. Bessy then marries the converted Herbert and inherits tremendous wealth, ensuring her family's security for generations to come. She succeeds, in the end, not so much by *doing* good as by *being* good. Bessy maintains her high moral character, and the world seems to change in response. Feminist literary critic Nina Baym has observed this plot in dozens of nineteenth-century didactic novels. "Women could change others by changing themselves," Baym writes, "and the phrase 'woman's sphere is in the home' could appear to mean 'woman's sphere is to reform the world.'"

Sadlier's didactic fiction paints a rich and complex portrait of Irish Catholic values and religious practices—both official church teaching and, in some cases, pre-Christian folk religion. Her advice for young immigrants illustrates the predominant moral concerns of Catholic leaders and gives us an understanding of community standards—or, at least, Sadlier's opinion of what should be community standards. Lastly, Sadlier's novels capture Irish Catholic anxieties. At times, as we shall see, her sermonizing is anything but subtle. Below the surface, however, her fiction reveals some of the more complex and gnawing problems for Irish Catholic women, for whom the demands of religion, gender, and ethnicity often created difficult, if not impossible, choices.

In *Bessy Conway,* Sadlier presents two kinds of Catholicism: that of the immigrants in America and that of the Irish back home in Ardfinnan. The Catholic New Yorkers in *Bessy Conway* inhabit a largely secular modern world. The dangers they face are not supernatural but human: poverty, domestic abuse, and the threat of sexual violence. Back home in Ireland, however, Bessy's family celebrates a Halloween dinner and gravely speaks of fairies on the hill. While the pagan rituals of the Irish peasants might seem to us to be in conflict with Catholicism, Sadlier's characters seem comfortable mixing the two traditions. Indeed, pagan mythology, populism, and anti-Protestant sentiment seem to converge smoothly in the excerpts that follow. These three elements combine to villify the Conways' Protestant landlord, for example, who oppresses the poor, hates Catholics, and even manages to insult the town fairies.

Bessy Conway, we see, is a window into the ways that Catholicism changed after the famine. According to historians Paul Wagner and Kerby Miller, most Irish peasants before the famine were not practicing Catholics—at least, not in the way that the religion is practiced today. In many cases, Irish peasants were isolated from parish life, and peasants might hope to attend Mass once a quarter rather than once a week. Before the famine, pre-Christian mythology played a far greater role in peasants' lives than it did in the later decades of the nineteenth century. Like the Conway family, many Irish still celebrated ancient spring and harvest festivals and believed in fairies, which were reported to inhabit abandoned farmhouses, ancient ruins, hills, and trees. Often, peasants attributed a child's death to fairies, who were said to have spirited the living baby away from its crib, leaving a "changeling" in its place. In Ardfinnan, Sadlier's characters live in a world where fairies, ghosts, and pagan rituals still influence peasant life.

Although fairies have a place in Sadlier's world, she has no similar affinity for Protestants. In this matter, even the fairies that exact revenge on the landlord seem to be on Sadlier's side. Yet Sadlier's anti-Protestantism takes different forms in the two different countries. Sadlier's hostility is loaded with not only religious prejudice but working-class resentment of the landed aristocracy in Ireland and of the native-born elite in the United States. In Ireland, according to *Bessy Conway*, Protestants own the land and demand exorbitant rents from their Catholic tenants. In America, Protestants are bankers, merchants, and politicians devoted as much to materialism as they are to their own religion. They threaten Irish Catholics with assimilation and moral temptation. One of Sadlier's minor characters, Ann McBride, marries a Protestant and, although she moves up in the world financially and socially, loses all notion of religion. To Sadlier, Protestants are not merely worldly, however; they are thoroughly despicable, without a single redeeming trait. Protestants are constantly scheming in *Bessy Conway* to undermine Catholics, either—in Mrs. Herbert's case—by stealing their land, or, in her son's example, by seducing their daughters and luring their young men into vice. Even simple friendship with Protestants is impossible. Protestants, to Sadlier, represent the mainstream religious majority, and they exert a powerful corrupting influence on her immigrant characters, who often are co-opted by native-born Americans into abandoning their religion to gain a place in society. Catholics, Sadlier warns, should avoid any association with them. For her readers, her message is a lesson in intolerance.

Sadlier, indeed, fought a losing battle on several fronts. To her, young women like Bessy had more to worry about than just Protestants. In America moral and spiritual dangers were everywhere. Although Bessy triumphs in the end, her fellow domestic servants, who serve as dramatic foils, meet grisly fates. Mary Mulligan, for example, is punished for sexual dalliances. Sadlier, of course, was far too proper to directly mention the idea of illicit sex or even female sexual desire. Mary's sexual transgressions, however, are suggested by her attraction to a dangerous man, whom she marries without the approval of the community. Mary's husband deserts her, and she gives birth alone to a crippled child, who later dies in a tenement fire. Mary, broken by grief, liquor, and poverty, dies in prison. Such is the fate, Sadlier suggests, for any young Catholic girl who goes astray. It is a bleak picture by any moralist's standards. In her preface, however, Sadlier was unapologetic. "Some may say that I have drawn too gloomy a picture. Such persons know little about it. The reality exceeds my powers of description."

What could have propelled Sadlier to paint such grim tales? Sadlier was motivated by a real social phenonmenon. Like many priests and prominent Catholic leaders of her day, she was worried about the growing tide of young women emigrating alone to America. The Irish were the only immigrant group in which women, especially single women, at times outnumbered men, and the only group that chose to emigrate in primarily female cliques. Domestic service, Bessy's occupation, was by far the most popular career choice; more than 60 percent of Irish-born working women labored as servants. The attraction of "living out" or "going into service" was great. Irish domestics could earn 50 percent more than saleswomen and 25 percent more than textile workers. In addition, housemaids had no expenses for food, housing, shelter, heat, water, or transportation and were able to live in pleasant, middle-class neighborhoods as opposed to the tenements occupied by factory workers. Most importantly, Irish female domestics could save up to several thousand dollars, which they invariably sent home to their impoverished Irish families. As historian Miller has noted, most of the money that flowed eastward across the Atlantic to postfamine Ireland came, in fact, not from Irish men but from women, many of whom were able to put enough aside to create their own dowries and establish families in the New World. By contrast, women in postfamine Ireland had little opportunity to find work or a husband. In flocking to America in droves, Irish women seem to have ignored Sadlier's advice.

Sadlier was not interested in merely teaching the young how to save their money. Her fiction, like so many works of popular nineteenth-century domestic literature, offer lessons in feminine propriety. As the inculcators of values in the home, women have important roles to perform, and their success as wives and mothers directly determines the health of their families and even their communities. As she writes in Bessy's preface, "Every woman has a mission, either for good or evil; and, unhappily for society, the lax, and the foolish, and the unprincipled will find husbands as well as the good and the virtuous. The sphere of influence thus extended, who can calculate the results, whether good or ill?" Sadlier's heroines must conform not only to the strict dictates of Victorian society but to Catholic doctrine. Ally Finigan, one of Sadlier's secondary characters, serves as another narrative foil for the pious Bessy. In America, Ally struggles to obey both her husband, who owns a bar, and her faith. Both Ally and her husband are entranced by the money to be made in the pub business, and set aside their qualms about purveying liquor. Their downfall, in the end, is presented as largely Ally's fault. Sadlier suggests that Ally, as a Catholic wife charged with saving her husband from sin, must assume the role of social reformer and household conscience. As a Catholic wife, however, Ally is also called to submit to her husband's authority and to never question his judgment. How can a wife reform her husband if she never challenges him? The task proves too much for Ally. Her husband Ned dies of delirium tremens, and she is ruined as well.

Sadlier's vision of the Catholic woman as domestic savior and servant was widespread. The newspaper *The Irish World* offered similar guidance: "In all the vicissitudes of fortune an Irish man clings to his wife and the wife clings to her husband, and is the joy of his life and the light of his day. If he turns out bad and comes home drunk, she says, 'I've made a bad bargain and must make the best of it'." According to Cardinal Gibbons, Sadlier's contemporary, women were "angels of expiation" who by their "prayers and mortifications" atoned for the sins of "fathers, husbands, sons and brothers."

At times Sadlier seems to place her Catholic characters in an impossible double bind. Take Bessy as an example. Sadlier holds her up as a shining example of Catholic piety and modesty, the perfect embodiment of Irish womanhood. In fact, Bessy is able to succeed economically while her unemployed fathers and brothers fail, and her money makes her father feel like a "man" again. The moral, at first, seems clear. A reader might reasonably conclude that Catholic girls, if they behave themselves, can prosper in America and even reach heroic stature. However, this is not really the case—at least in Sadlier's fiction. Bessy, when asked for advice for girls considering a trip to America, warns a neighbor to keep her daughters at home. New York is, after all, one of the "great Babylons of the West." At this point a reader might ask, What sort of survival manual is this? How can a reader, hoping to emulate Bessy's success, both succeed in America and remain safely at home in Ireland? How can a woman lift her family out of poverty if she never leaves the home? How can a Catholic woman ever respectably earn her bread without transgressing the bounds of decency? What is Sadlier really saying about Irish Catholic mores? I would argue that *Bessy Conway* is a surprisingly strong critique of Irish Catholic culture, especially for a writer who so often represents herself as a defender of propriety and the establishment. Catholic women must walk a narrow tightrope of rules and expectations, Sadlier suggests. But this is no guarantee for success. The fate of earnest, devoted Christian women, in many cases, is simply to suffer. If there is a solution to these problems, Sadlier herself cannot find it. In the end, Sadlier tells us, the moral value to which Catholic women must aspire is martyrlike endurance. Not all women agreed, of course. Sadlier's novels were moralistic lessons meant to influence behavior, not depict reality with objectivity. In real life, women did not necessarily follow Sadlier's injunctions. Even Sadlier herself chose not to take her own advice. If she had followed Bessy Conway's suggestions, Sadlier would never have left Ireland or become a successful literary woman.

Yet we see these paradoxes over and over again in Sadlier's writings and, of course, in many other works by nineteenth-century women writers. As a conservative Catholic, Sadlier advised women to stay at home under the protection of their fathers and brothers. Proper Catholic ladies, she wrote, confine their work to the home; only Protestant women dabble in business or the public sphere. And yet many of Sadlier's characters, and Sadlier herself, moved successfully into the public sphere. Like Bessy, Sadlier was an immigrant and a career woman, and quite a successful one at that. She was an editor, publisher, businesswoman, prolific writer, and translator, who authored sixty volumes of novels, short stories, plays, children's texts, and translations of French romances and religious works. Sadlier even ran her family's Catholic publishing house after her husband died. Yet Sadlier seems to have been aware of the contradictions between her writing and her life. In the novel *Tales of the Olden Time,* written in 1845 before she was married and while she was supporting herself independently, Sadlier laments that the life of a woman of "genius" often is "madness—a broken heart—an early grave." The impossible double binds of Catholic womanhood, she suggests, can take a fatal toll.

Sadlier's fiction critiques one of the most sacred institutions in Catholicism: marriage. More than half the marriages depicted in *Bessy Conway* are absolutely dreadful. In fact, all of the young women in *Bessy Conway*—Ally Finigan, Sally Murphy, Mary Murphy—end their lives as abused wives. Their husbands either desert them or beat them, and either way they die in poverty, unloved, and alone. Bessy, Sadlier tells us, lives happily ever after with her rich, newly converted husband. Given the earlier parade of abused wives, however, a reader cannot be blamed for entertaining doubts about Bessy's marriage as well. If Bessy represents an ideal, it is one that is impossible to achieve.

The following selection is condensed from chapters 19 through 21, pages 258–91, of the 1863 edition of Mary Ann Sadlier, *Bessy Conway, or The Irish Girl in America,* published by D. & J. Sadlier of New York; it was originally written in 1861.

Further Reading

Hasia R. Diner, *Erin's Daughters in America: Irish Immigrant Women in the Nineteenth Century* (Baltimore: Johns Hopkins University Press, 1983); Michele Lacombe, "Frying Pans and Deadlier Weapons: The Immigrant Novels of Mary Anne Sadlier," *Essays on Canadian Writing* 29 (Summer 1984): 96–116; Colleen McDannell, *The Christian Home in Victorian America, 1840-1900* (Bloomington: Indiana University Press, 1986); Colleen McDannell, "'The Devil Was the First Protestant': Gender and Intolerance in Irish Catholic Fiction," *U.S. Catholic Historian* 8 (1989): 51–65; Kerby Miller and Paul Wagner, *Out of Ireland: The Story of Irish Emigration to America* (Washington, D.C.: Elliott & Clark, 1994).

Bessy Conway, or The Irish Girl in America

CHAPTER 19

Full seven years had passed away since Bessy left her father's cottage, and eventful as those years had been to her they were not less so to "the old folks at home."

"The summer sun was sinking
With a mild light calm and mellow,"

and its slanting rays rested on the straw-thatched roof of Denis Conway, but
there was no beauty in the picture, for the look of comfort and neatness that
belonged to the place in former days was gone, and had left scarce a trace
behind. The thatch so trim and smooth in those by-gone days was broken in
many places, and covered with patches of moss, whilst chicken-weed and dar-
nel flaunted their unwelcome verdure on the gable-tops. The white walls
beneath were discolored and stripped here and there of the "pebble-dash" that
had covered them all so neatly. The small windows, too, were disfigured with
sundry pieces of board nailed on as substitutes for broken panes, and altogether the house had a desolate, neglected look in painful contrast with its
former appearance. The haggard was empty, and so was the byer—the horse
was gone from the stable, and even the sty had lost its tenants—the overgrown
sow was no longer there with her squeaking brood, nor the well-cared bacon
pigs, which, in other days, furnished so important a share of the winter's store
for the family. The fowl were gone from the barn-door, for no grain was there
to gather them round it. The discordant chorus of the farm-yard was no longer
heard; the very hum of the bees in the adjacent garden had ceased, and silence
sat brooding over Denis Conway's cottage. Decay, too, was there, and, beneath
its withering touch, all things were hastening to ruin.

This was the aspect of affairs without, and within it was nothing better. The
same look of desolation was everywhere visible, but its saddest imprint was on
the people. Famine and disease had found their way into that happy household,
and misery sat on the threshold. The aged father and mother sat opposite each
other in their old straw chairs, by the dull, flickering fire, watching with dis-
tended eyes the unsavory mess which Nancy was making for the family supper,
consisting of water and nettles, with a handful or so of oatmeal. Nancy herself
as she bent over the pot was a living picture of hunger, and the low, suppressed
moans which came at irregular intervals from a straw "shake-down" in the corner indicated the presence of one who suffered bodily pain. It was Ellen, the
bright-eyed, dark-haired fairy, whose laugh used to ring the loudest, whose foot
spring the lightest in days not long gone by. But the terrible fangs of hunger had
fastened on her vitals, and disease was wearing her young life away.

"Nancy dear!" said the mother, "go and see what Ellen wants. I think she's
speaking."

"What is it, astore?" said the elder sister bending over the straw pallet.

"Something to eat," murmured Ellen, only half conscious. "I'm hungry."

"You'll have it in a minute, darling in one minute," and Nancy hastened back
to her miserable cooking, and squatted down on the hearth to fan the expiring
embers into something like a blaze.

The tears ran down the mother's face, and she clasped her hands and looked
up to heaven in silent anguish.

"Don't grieve, Bridget, don't grieve, achorra!" said her husband; "God is good, you know, and He'll never desert us."

"Well, father! we're far enough gone now," said Nancy in a faint, dejected voice.

"Never mind, dear, never mind!" still said Denis; "it's only tryin' us He is—He'll change His hand with us when He sees fit. Have you the broth ready for Ellen, Nancy?—God help us! it's poor stuff for a sick weakly stomach!—well! the Lord be praised, anyhow!"

Ellen was raised on her sister's arm, and swallowed with avidity some spoonfuls of the pottage, then looked up in Nancy's face and whispered: "Have you enough for all?"

"Plenty, machree, plenty!—don't be afeard! there's a potful of it!" Ellen's face lighted, and she gulped down some spoonfuls more, then made a sign that she had enough, and sank heavily back on her pillow.

"How do you find yourself after that sleep, Ellen?" said her mother with assumed composure.

"Was I asleep, mother? I didn't know," muttered the patient sufferer as she turned her heavy eyes first on one parent then on the other with a look of unutterable fondness; "Well! I think I'm better—I'm no worse, anyhow!"

"Thank God, dear! thank God for that!" said the father with pious fervor.

"Did the boys come back from Cashel?" Ellen asked.

"Not yet—we're expectin' them every minute," said Nancy, "and then you'll have a cup of tea, Ellen darling, and some white bread, too!"

Ellen looked up eagerly in her sister's face, and a faint flush suffused her wasted cheek, it faded as quickly as it came, and the tears gushed to her eyes. "I don't want tea or bread, Nancy!—I know it's for me you get them, and I'd rather you'd buy meal with the money."

"Hush! Ellen! hush!" said her mother, "don't be talkin' so much!"

"Make your mind easy," whispered Nancy, "we're not so far gone as you thinks." Ellen shook her head and smiled sadly, then closed her eyes and appeared to sleep.

A little while after the young men came in. They placed their spades and shovels behind the door and came forward with as cheerful an aspect as they could assume, one of them handing a small bag to Nancy. The first glance of each was at the pot on the fire, and Nancy hastened to dish up the wretched substitute for a supper. The father and mother looked at each other and glanced with sorrowful meaning at the sunken cheeks and hollow eyes of their sons. It was clear that each one avoided speaking first. At last the father took courage.

"Well, boys! did you get any work?"

"Only half a day each, father!" said the elder brother, whose haggard, careworn face was more like that of middle age than the summer-time of life. "As we were brothers, they wouldn't give us any more than a day's work between us, we only worked from twelve o'clock."

"So you weren't able to get the things for Ellen," said the mother faintly.

"Not much, mother," the son replied with a heavy sigh, "the two shillings we got had to go for meal, for we knew there was none in the house, but as God would have it, a gentleman that saw us standin' there idle gave Tommy a six-penny piece for holdin' his horse, an' we got the worth of that of tea and sugar." He filled up so full that he was almost choking and could not speak another word. His brother, of somewhat a lighter spirit though equally sick at heart, undertook to finish the sentence, "and there was a penny over for which we bought bread for Ellen. Wasn't that fine dealing mother?"

"Wisha, God help you, poor boys!" said the mother tenderly. "It's a pity you'd ever want money, for it's yourselves that hadn't your hearts in it when you had it. Och! och! but they're the awful times these!"

"Well! it's one comfort," said the younger son with a poor attempt at gaiety, "it's one comfort that we're no worse than our neighbors. I saw Denny Ryan of the Hill there awhile ago carryin' home a stone of Indian meal on his back—and more by token he looked as if he was hardly able to stand with the dint of hunger!"

"Poorman! God help him!" said Denis compassionately, "him that had full and plenty of everything such a short time ago. It's little he'd think of giving more than that to a beggar goin' the road!"

"An' Jack Hagerty's wife an' two children are down with the sickness," said Tommy.

"Lord bless us and save us! what's comin' on the people, at all?" said Mrs. Conway in a desponding tone; "there's nothing for any of us, I'm afeard, but death and starvation! Och!" . . .

"What are we goin' to do for that rent?" said Tommy, suddenly starting from his reverie, "you're forgettin' Mrs. Herbert altogether, an' you know what the bailiff said the last time he came."

"Know it?" said his father, "do you think we could forget it? But never mind, children, never mind! God is good, and even if that tyrant of a woman did put us out, He'd provide us with a shelter! Boys! you forgot to ask how Ellen was!" . . .

Truly that was a dismal time in Denis Conway's cottage, and in many a cottage through the length and breadth of Ireland. It was the terrible year of the Famine, as the reader will have guessed, and the ruin which had been progressing rapidly during the previous years of dearth and commercial depression, and the failure of crops, had at length reduced the small farmers of the country, and amongst the rest Denis Conway and his family, to the pitiful state in which we have seen them. What money Denis had had was long since gone, no corn or wheat was ripening in his fields, for in the spring-time he had not the means to purchase seed, the stock could not live without eating, and one after another every hoof was taken to the fair and sold. Milk and butter, of course, went with them, and what was worse than all, the money which they brought—it was little compared with what it would have been at another time—had most of it to go to satisfy the clamorous demands of Mrs. Herbert's bailiffs. So from bad to worse things went on, till everything was wanting in the once-plentiful household, everything except the grace of God and

His holy peace. That was still there in as great abundance as ever, and faith and hope, though at times, perhaps, dimmed by the heavy clouds of suffering and privation, were never wholly obscured. The old man himself never allowed distrust or fear to enter his mind: no patriarch of old ever trusted more firmly in the Lord Almighty, and the darker the clouds that gathered around him the more steadily he fixed his eyes on the light that glimmered afar in the firmament. It was sad to see the failing old man wandering in the morning or evening twilight around his fallow fields where in other years the golden grain would, at that season, wave luxuriant, ready for the sickle, and the rugged leaves of the potato-stalk covering whole acres with their dark green hue of promise. Now the tall rag-weed nodded in the summer breeze, the dock-weed spread its broad leaves on the arid soil, and the fiery nettle grew and flourished where a weed dared not rear its head before, to dispute possession with the carefully-tended grain-stalk. As Denis noted all this, and thought how many other farms in that fertile district were like unto his own, he would sit down on a broken stile, or one of those huge boulders—geological puzzles—so common in the inland as well as the maritime counties of Ireland, and burying his face in his hands, give free vent to that natural sorrow which he could not but feel at sight of so much desolation. At home, the old man tried to conceal his feelings, for he knew that the wife of his youth and the children of his love were pining and wasting day by day under the blighting hand of misery, and he felt it incumbent on himself to set them an example of fortitude and resignation. . . .

Denis had stolen out that evening, after partaking of the sorry fare which all Nancy's culinary skill was not able to make palatable. . . .

Poor Denis Conway! his trusting heart had another hard trial to undergo. A fiery crucible was even then ready to test the purity of his faith, the firmness of his fortitude. The morning sun was shining far up in heaven's blue vault, and the world looked as bright and joyous as though it contained no aching heart within its wide circumference.

Denis Conway was sitting at his door enjoying the beauty and freshness of the morning, employing himself the while in making a potato-basket of sally-twigs, a bunch of which lay beside him on the ground. For the basket, when completed, he expected to get a few pence in the village, and with that hope he worked assiduously. All at once, however, the basket fell from his hand, his pale cheek grew paler still, and a faint cry escaped him. What sight was it that had so alarmed the usually calm old man? Alas! 'twas no uncommon one then in Ireland. Two bailiffs, with half a dozen policemen, were advancing from the village, and Denis, mindful of Mrs. Herbert's threats, was not slow to imagine that his poor dwelling was about to be honored with their official visit.

CHAPTER 20

"Well! have you the rent for us, Conway?" said the insolent bailiff who was Mrs. Herbert's factotum; the other was merely an assistant.

"'Deed I haven't, Alick!" said poor Denis Conway trembling all over; "I told the mistress I couldn't raise a penny till I'd get it from America—I'm expectin' a letter every day from my daughter Bessy that's in New York beyant."

"Fudge!" was Alick Bowman's emphatic reply. "You might as well give us a draft on the man in the moon. As you haven't the money, Conway! we have a duty to perform—you must march!"

"Why, sure, Mister Bowman! it isn't turn us out you'd be doin'—sure Mrs. Herbert wouldn't do that on an old tenant like me that's on the estate since—since the old master's time—that's Mr. Mullady, the heavens be his bed, this day!"

"Can't help it," was the man of law's curt reply. "Come, Charlie!" to his companion, "lend a hand, will you? we've got plenty of work to do before night!—it's like there's not much here to detain us."

In the bailiffs went, but Denis went in before them, trying to soothe as well as he could his wife and their daughter Nancy who were sobbing and crying and wringing their hands in a paroxysm of grief. Ellen was just sitting up for the first time, propped up in her mother's old arm-chair, and on hearing the direful news she fell back fainting, though not insensible. She had not strength enough to make any demonstration of her feelings.

The poor father had only time to say, "don't despair, for your lives don't! the darkest hour, you know, is the hour before day, and I tell you God won't desert us though the world may!"

The words were still on his lips when the two officials were hard at work turning the poor menage inside out. The beds—such as the hard times had left—chairs, tables, pots, pans, and so forth, were flying through the door-way with little regard to loss or damage on the part of those who trundled them out. The family within sat looking on in hopeless anguish waiting for the moment when they, in turn, were to be sent after their goods and chattels.

"Well! God sees all this," said the afflicted father of the family as he saw his wife wrapping a thin shawl round Ellen—the blankets were gone with the rest, "God sees all this!"

"What are you about, young woman?" cried Alick suddenly. A little hand had been laid on his arm, and a soft feminine voice bade him stop. "Who the d---l are you?"

The Conways answered the question. Father, mother, sisters—even Ellen—rushed forward with hands outstretched and the one word "Bessy!" escaped the lips of each with a thrilling cry of joy.

Bessy put them all gently aside with her hand. "Let us get the bailiff out first," said she; "oh! father, father! how did it ever come to this with you? —Ellen, darling, sit down—you're not able to stand—oh! you haven't a seat, I see—hand in a chair!" said she to the astonished bailiff.

"Can't do it," said he scratching his head, "the things are all under seizure, and they're a-going to be sold by and by."

"They're nor going to be sold," said Bessy with quite an air of authority; "give in the chair, I say!" Mechanically the man obeyed.

"Now all the other things—put them in, I tell you!"

"I tell you I won't," said Bowman doggedly, "unless the old man is ready to hand out the cash." This by way of a taunt.

"How much is it, father?" demanded Bessy.

"Oh! indeed, it's little use to tell you, astore!"

"Well! well! let us hear it, anyhow."

"Why I'll soon tell you, if you want so bad to hear it," said Bowman impudently, "it's twenty-three pounds, ten shillings, and seven pence halfpenny." He and his colleague looked as though they expected the young woman to be quite confounded by so startling an announcement. She was not, though, but appeared rather to enjoy it as something particularly amusing.

"Go up now to Mrs. Herbert," said she with a quiet smile, "and tell her she will oblige us by sending a receipt in full—in full, mind you!—for all rent and arrears of rent due on Denis Conway's farm."

"But what'll I say to her in regard of the money?" demanded Alick. "Of course, she's not such a fool as to give a receipt without knowin' for what?"

"I'll tell you what you'll do, father," said Bessy after a moment's thought, "I'll give you the money, and you can go up yourself with this man and pay Mrs. Herbert and get your receipt."

"An' have you that much money, Bessy?" said the father with tears in his eyes—tears of joy.

"Yes, and a trifle more to the back of it," said Bessy in her gayest tone.

Hearing this the two bailiffs took off their hats, and simultaneously declared that they didn't wish to put Mr. Conway or his family to any inconvenience. They weren't to be blamed, they were only poor men earning an honest penny, and so forth. In proof of their good dispositions, Alick ordered his aide-de-camp to take in the things as the decent girl said, and "be sure you put them in their places again, Toal!"

Toal, though somewhat of the roughest and gruffest, addressed himself willingly to his task, possibly influenced by a sly little whisper from Alick as he passed him to go off with Denis.

The news of Bessy's arrival had already gone out, and a crowd of the nearest neighbors were collected in front of the door, only kept from rushing in by the imperative orders of the policemen. Denis was besieged on his way out by a multitude of eager questions, very few of which he took time to answer. He did not fail, however, to publish the fact that Bessy was paying all he owed to Mrs. Herbert, and the old place was still to be theirs. "Here's the money in my pocket," said he slapping his thigh with honest exultation; "Ay! every penny of it—thank God! we're out of their power!" He looked the policemen in the face as he passed them, and held up his head with a most independent air to the great satisfaction of his delighted friends and neighbors.

"Wisha God be praised, Denis!" cried one, "it's you that wasn't out of the need of that relief, anyhow!"

"Thanks be to God, Denis!" said another, "you can hold up your head now like a man!"

"More luck to you, Denis! an' God speed you!" shouted a third—"be sure you tell Madam Herbert her own!"

Whilst Denis was gone it afforded much amusement to the spectators to see Toal McGreevy replacing the household effects with much care and attention. It was something altogether new, and they relished it exceedingly, in the full belief that he did it "against his grain." Bailiffs are always obnoxious to the people, and Toal was particularly so on account of his harsh, sullen disposition.

"That's it, Toal! put them pewter plates on the dresser! now the noggins! I declare you're doin' it beautifully!"

"Here's the beds, Toal! won't you make them up, agra? do now!"

"Well now, who'd think he was so handy?"

"He's takin' more pains puttin' them in than he did puttin' them out."

Toal looked savage, and shook his fist at the rustic wags, but they only laughed, and went on just the same. The policemen strove to silence them, but it was no use. There was no law against talking, anyhow, they knew that—and so they talked and laughed incessantly, the crowd increasing every moment till Denis came back with his receipt in his hand, and then they all pressed up to the door after him to get a sight of Bessy. The policemen no longer opposed any resistance, their duty being at an end.

The scene that followed may be better imagined than described. Whilst Bessy and her parents and sisters were exchanging their fond and joyous greeting, their friends outside were dismissing the bailiffs and policemen with derisive cheers, and sundry expressions of mock condolence for their disappointment. This was as much, perhaps, with a view to leave those within time to give expression to their feelings as anything else. That delicacy of feeling intuitive in the Irish heart in its natural state kept the people from docking in till the re-united family had enjoyed the bliss of their meeting for a few moments without witnesses, no matter how friendly. Furthermore, there was that love of fun, also inherent in the Irish nature, and which no circumstances can ever wholly destroy, and then such a glorious opportunity of having a laugh at the expense of their official tyrants could not possibly be let slip. The others bore the iron-ical merriment of the people with more good nature than might have been expected. Alick Bowman was particularly free and easy, and "humored the joke" in a way that was quite refreshing to see in a man of such high official authority. He even condescended to throw out divers "quirks and quibbles" for the amusement of the crowd as he marched away, pretty much in the same way as a bear showing off his steps to a gaping crowd at a country fair.

Meanwhile the Conways were enjoying the exquisite sense of present happi-ness, all the laughter for the cloud that had just passed. The mother sat in an ecstasy of joy silent and tearful, with the hand of her newly recovered daughter clasped in hers. Ellen was on the other side with her languid head resting on Bessy's shoulder, whilst Nancy sat at her sister's feet looking up in her face, scru-tinizing every feature with the tenderest expression of interest. The old man planted himself on a long seat behind Nancy and the tears of joy were rolling unheeded down his furrowed cheeks.

"Now, didn't I tell you, Bridget, astore!" said he, "that Bessy would bring light to us some dark day when we most needed it?—didn't I tell you God would never desert us!" . . .

"Nancy dear!" said Bessy taking her sister aside, "I want to speak to you a moment." What passed between them was a secret, though many ears were open to hear, but whatever it was, Nancy threw a shawl around her attenuated form and vanished, after in turn whispering her mother. Up rose Bridget with alacrity, and made the best fire she could and over it hung a large pot of water, bustling her way through the sitters with an air half consequential, half good-natured.

Denis watched his wife's movements with a curious eye, and so did Ellen, too, but neither asked any questions. After a little Nancy returned with a large basket of baker's bread, whilst a boy from the village carried another containing tea, sugar, butter and meat. By that time the water was boiling, and Bessy said to her mother:

"Now you sit down, and Nancy and I will do the rest!"

"'Deed an' I'll not sit down, then," said Bridget jocosely, "it's long since I had any cookery to do, an' do you think I'll let you an' Nancy have it all to yourselves, now when it is to be done?"

Bessy laughed and said, "have your own way, then!" and tucking up the sleeves and skirt of her brown merino dress, she went to work to assist her mother, telling Nancy to gather up all the cups and saucers and plates she could find, and set the table for supper.

"I want to surprise the boys," said she "and have something nice ready for them comin' in."

Many a hungry eye was cast on the savory smelling meat "fizzling" by the fire, and the piles of white bread which rose at either end of the table, with tempting looking butter in proportionate quantity. It was long since any one there had seen such preparations for a meal, and it was pitiful to see the greedy eyes with which they gazed on the sumptuous fare. Strict propriety would have urged a general move, but some how the farther the preparations advanced, the less the visitors seemed inclined to leave. Fast and faster they talked, and every one appeared to ransack his or her memory for some other question to put to Bessy, some scrap of information yet to be elicited.

Denis tried to catch his daughter's eye several times, but failed, for Bessy seemed rather to avoid meeting his glance. It seemed very strange to the hospitable old man that the girls and their mother should make such a parade of their eatables at a time when the whole country was starving. "I wish they had waited," said he to himself, "till the poor creatures were gone. That's always the way with these women, wanting to make a show."

The night was closing in when the word went round that the boys were coming up the boreen. "Run, Bessy! run and hide!" said her father—"we'll take a rise out of them, if they haven't heard of your comin'.'"

This suggestion was unanimously applauded, and Bessy, having cast a glance over the table, and the cooking apparatus, to see that all was in readiness, stationed herself just within the door of the room—at the lower end of the kitchen, opposite the fireplace, where, by keeping the door ever so little open, she had a view of all that passed.

When the young men came in they could scarce believe their eyes, and they stood looking round them like persons recovering from some strange dream. Where they expected to see only penury, and want, and woe, there was comfort and plenty and smiling faces. A bright fire burned on the hearth, the table was spread for a feast, and the place was redolent with the grateful smell of frying beef. The kitchen was full of friends and neighbors, all looking as gay as could be in anticipation of the good cheer, which they began to suspect was not all for family consumption. The young men looked at their father, then at their mother. More wonders: the wo-begone look of the morning had vanished, and hope and joy were beaming in the eyes but late so dull and heavy. There was a twinkle of sly humor, too, that brought old times vividly back, and made the brothers smile they knew not why. Even Ellen was no longer the same—the pinched, parched look was gone, and the ghastly paleness of the sweet features was tinted with a more life-like hue. Ellen was smiling, too, and smiling cheerfully and hopefully as she used to do in the days when peace and plenty were their lot. It was strange, passing strange. Every object was so changed that it seemed as if a magician's wand had waved over all.

A chorus of glad welcome greeted the bewildered brothers, but they heeded it not. Their attention was riveted on their parents.

"Father! mother! what's the meaning of this?" cried one.

"We heard as we came along," said the other, "that something had happened at home, but nobody would tell us what it was!"

"Can't you guess?" said their father pleasantly.

"Well! either Bessy's come home, or the fairies have been at work here since we left."

A shout of laughter followed and a general clapping of hands.

"You may as well come out, Bessy!" cried her mother, "these lads are too good at guessin' to be kept in the dark."

A moment more and Bessy was in the arms of the brothers so long unseen, so fondly remembered, and the tears that years of suffering and privation could not squeeze from their hearts, now gushed from their manly eyes and rolled unheeded down their cheeks. Their emotion was shared by all present. If ever there was a moment of unclouded happiness that was one. Oh! beautiful is the love that unites the sister and the brother! The human heart knows no feeling holier or more tender. . . .

And Denis rubbed his hands in a little ecstasy of hospitality; then taking his place at the table, renewed the invitation by an imperative gesture, which, of course, had the desired effect, every one protesting, however, that "they hadn't the least occasion;" most of them were "just after eatin' when they left the house," and indeed, to hear Bessy Conway's guests on that evening as they drew their seats to the table, you would think it was all a mistake about the famine, and that times were particularly good just then and provisions in the greatest abundance in that part of the country. . . .

"But what about Ned Finigan, Bessy?" said her father suddenly. "It's reported here that he doesn't know the end of his own riches."

"And is that all you know about it?" exclaimed Bessy, with a start, and the color faded from her cheek. "Ned did make some money, but I'm afraid it's little good he ever got of it. I wish to the Lord he had never left Ardfinnan!"

"Why, dear bless us! what happened him?" asked her elder brother. "What's amiss with poor Ned?"

"I'm loth to tell it," said Bessy in a husky voice. "Poor Ned!"—her voice sank to a whisper and her eyes filled with tears—"he died about a month before I left New York."

A universal chorus of lamentation followed this announcement, for Ned had been a general favorite.

"Ned Finigan dead!" said Denis Conway in a voice choking with emotion, "him that was so stout and strong! Ah, then, what did he die of, Bessy?"

"Well! it's hard to say," was the answer, and Bessy gave her father a look that made him change the subject immediately. . . .

"Don't you mind what I wrote to you, father, about Mary marrying Luky Mulligan?"

"To be sure I mind it well, Bessy! but I was forgettin' to ask you how it turned out!"

All eyes and ears were open to know what came of such a match. Nothing good could come of it, every one said.

"Well! you're not far wrong there," said Bessy, "they were only a few months married when Luky went off and 'listed, and was sent away out to Mexico, I believe it was, and Mary had no other shift but going out for a day's work, on account of a poor cripple of a little girl she had that was born after the father went away. Sometimes she used to get leave to take the poor child with her to work, and there she'd be all day trying to mind it and mind her work; if she left it in the tenement house where she had part of a room it was worse still, for she'd be fretting about it all the time. So that's the way it went on until she was fairly heart-broken, with poverty, and want, and the height of wretchedness, for the pride that was in her wouldn't let her go to her own to look for help. At last, she took to drink, and her unfortunate child was burned to death one day when she was out for something at the grocery, and she didn't live long herself after it: I believe she died over on Blackwell's Island, where prisoners are sent for stealing, or anything of that kind that doesn't entitle them to States Prison."

There was a general murmur of pity and regret on hearing this doleful tale. There was no one there that did not remember Mary Murphy, the prettiest girl about Ardfinnan, ay! and the merriest, too! Soon after the neighbors began to drop off, saddened by the fate of Ned Finigan and Mary Murphy. When the last was gone, Bessy told her father what she did not choose to tell before so many, that Ned had died a dreadful death of delirium tremens; that it took four men to hold him in the bed, and he fancying he saw all kinds of horrible shapes, and fairly out of his senses,

"And that's the way he died, Bessy?"

"That's the way he died!"

No prayer was breathed in response, nothing but sighs and groans.

CHAPTER 21

Before "the Lammas Floods" rolled that year over the sunparched holms of Tipperary Denis Conway's house had assumed more than its former appearance of comfort and neatness, and when the family sat down to their Hallow-Eve supper on the last night of October the barn had grain, and the byer had cows, and a fine young colt was munching his hay through the rack of the well-covered stable, perhaps enjoying the sense of comfort as well as his owners. The big ark was packed full of new meal, and the flitches of bacon were again pendant from the snow-white rafters. There was a fire blazing on the well-swept hearth that suggested the idea of a grand pyramidal turf-stack somewhere in the immediate vicinity.

There was no other light in the kitchen but what the fire gave, but that was so bright that every object was plainly discernible, and it needed only a glance to establish the fact that everything there was "like a new pin." The antique pewter on the dresser, and the tins on the wall hard by, were reflecting the warm fire-beam like so many mirrors, and the wooden ware beneath was as white as any one had ever seen it in the best days of the Conways.

The supper was ready, and every one seemed as ready for it. Ellen, now a site recovered, was bustling around giving the last touch to the preparations, whilst Nancy and Bessy were hurrying to put the last stitch in a new stuff dress for their mother. One brother was reading aloud a passage in Columbkille's Prophecies for the special entertainment of his father who was listening with great attention; the other was teasing the girls "on the sly" about their skill in dress making which Owen affected to rate very low. The mother sat looking at them all with her calm, sober smile of happiness, pondering in her mind how God had brought them out from such a sea of misery. "Well! I think it's all along of the faith that Denis had," she said within herself, "like Job, that the priest tells us about so often, that got to be better off after all his troubles than he ever was before, and all on account of his patience. That's just the way with Denis—he bore everything that came—ay! things that fretted the life and out in me, and now see how the Lord sent Bessy home to us with plenty of money just when we were at the lowest! It's a wonderful thing to think of, anyhow!"

Drop, drop came down the rain on the rough stones outside the door.

"Well! sure enough," said Owen with a gay laugh, "it's a hard night for the fairies!"

"Hush! Owen, hush!" whispered his mother all in a tremor; "let them alone, and they'll let you alone!—they're the best of neighbors, but it isn't safe to be namin' them at all."

"Lord save us, what's that?" cried Ellen, stopping short in her work, and standing pale as death in a listening attitude; "what's that, at all?"

"Maybe it's the fairies," put in the incorrigible Owen. He was silenced by a warning gesture from his father, and they all held in their breath to listen.

Drop, drop on the stones still went the rain, splash, splash in the puddles, but another sound was plainly heard, a small voice muttering words, the tenor of which was lost to the ear.

"I think Owen is about right," whispered Nancy.

"It's some creature—some child, maybe, that's out in the rain," said Bessy in the same low whisper.

"I'll bet my life it's Bid McGuigan," cried Tommy aloud; "I'm sure that's her voice."

He rushed to the door, but Ellen was as quick as himself, and placed her hand on the latch. "Don't, don't till we know what it is!"

"Come away, Ellen!" said her father gently, "let him open the door. Whoever's in it, we can't leave them outside such a night as this."

The door was opened, and in stumped Bid McGuigan, as doleful an object as could well be imagined. The heavy drops were dripping from her elfin locks, and everything on her was drenched with rain, yet the placid expression of her big gabby face was no whit disturbed.

The young men laughed and Owen said: "There she is now for you—the queen of the fairies, I declare!"

The other members of the family were too much occupied with Bid's pitiful state to pay much attention to Owen's dry jokes. Many questions were put to her, as to why she was abroad at such a time and in such weather, but Bid only shook her head, and smiled and said "Bid's cold."

"It was God sent her," said Denis looking at the poor idiot with tears in his eyes, "it was God sent her, for a share of our Hol'eve supper. It's an honor she's doin' us, blessed be His name! so hurry and put dry clothes on her an' we'll fix her here next the fire." . . .

"I wouldn't be in Mrs. Herbert's shoes the night for a new suit of clothes!"

"And why so, Owen?" asked Bessy with great earnestness.

"Oh! that's true, you were away in America when it happened. Why, you see, the ould madam couldn't let even the fairies alone, good people as they are—she must go and dig up the rath on the hill above."

"Dig up the rath?" cried Bessy in horror, "why, no! surely she wouldn't do that?"

"I tell you she did, and she couldn't get a man to do it, only Bill Morrow and Harry Grimes—by the same token, Bill broke his arm before ever he got home the day they finished the job, and Harry Grimes found the best cow he had lyin' dead in the byer a week or two after."

"Good for them!" chimed in Nancy. "They might have known what would come of meddlin' with them—fair may they come, and fair may they go!"

"Well! but Mrs. Herbert that was the cause of it all," said Bessy, "how well nothing came across her! maybe the good people have a respect for the rich as well as others."

"Bessy! Bessy! take care!" said her mother anxiously, holding up her finger at the same time by way of caution.

Nothing more was said at the time about Mrs. Herbert or of her eviction of the pigmy community of the rath. The merriment which usually characterizes Hallow-eve in Irish households was that night somewhat subdued on account of the miserable state of the country, and the family after saying their usual prayers in common, retired to rest early, a comfortable shake-down being made for Bid McGuigan in the chimney corner.

Next day the whole country was thrown into a state of fearful excitement. Word went out that Mrs. Herbert had been found dead in her bed that morning, and as soon as the awful news had been fully verified, it was set down as an act of fairy vengeance. People crossed themselves and looked at each other, and shook their heads.

"She knows the difference now," said one with religious solemnity.

"I'll go bail she does," said another, "and I think she has her own death to answer for—if she had let the rath alone she might be a living woman yet, for sure there wasn't a gray hair in her head, an' she always had the best of care. Ha! ha! herself an' himself are both gone now—ay faith! where they'll have no poor tenants to harry—I'm thinkin' there's more landlords than tenants there."

Such were the general feelings of the people. Even Denis Conway's family, though shocked to hear of such a death, did not fail to view it as an act of retributive justice on the part of Almighty God. . . .

Before the visitors retired, however, one of them, an ancient dame who was the mother of a large family of grown-up daughters, took occasion to ask Bessy would she advise any of her girls to go out to America. "There's Jenny and Peggy," said she, "an' they have a great notion of startin' next spring."

"Well! I'm not over fond of giving advice," said Bessy, "but as you asked my opinion I'll give it, and then you can't blame me one way or the other. America is a bad place for young girls to go to, unless they have their father, or brothers, or somebody to look after them."

"Humph! who had you to look after you?"

"Not one but myself and God's good Providence."

"Well! an' wouldn't our girls have the same?" asked the dame sharply.

"I'm not speaking of them, at all," said Bessy, "but I tell you, Mrs. O'Hare, there's many a girl that had as good a mother as ever you were—and I'm not saying but you're good enough—that leaves home a simple country girl with the fear of God in her heart, and the blush of modesty on her cheek, that turns out very bad and very indifferent in America. If they keep in the state of grace, and go regularly to their duty they're all right, and sure, thanks be to God! there's thousands of them that do, and signs on them and their friends at home—but there's just as many—perhaps more—that falls in with Protestants and Jews, and everything that way, and in the course of a little time forget themselves altogether—at least they forget that they have a soul to be saved, or a God to judge them. Dress and finery, and balls and dances is all the God they have then, and you may guess it's not a good end they make of it either for body or soul."

"Well, now, that's curious," put in another neighbor, "an' we hearin' such a different account of it from every one else. Why, there's Jemmy McBride's daughter from beyond the river that got a great match in New York or Philadelphy or some of them places—they say she doesn't know the end of her own riches."

Bessy laughed in her own quiet way. "God help your wit, Mrs. Shanaghan! it's little you know here about those great matches. Now I happen to know something about Ann McBride, for though I never saw her in America, I know them that did, and lived with her, too; she is married to a man in New York that's pretty well off—I think he's in the grocery business—she lives in a fine house and has very nice furniture and all that, and dresses in the very height of the fashion, but her husband is a Protestant—a sort of a one—and poor Ann is—nothing at all. Himself goes to church of an odd time, but Ann never troubles church or chapel. I was told by a girl that lived with her that when she caught her one night teaching her children their prayers—Catholic prayers, of course—she was very angry, and told her not to be 'bothering their brains with them old prayers, they'd have time enough to learn then.'"

Various exclamations of horror and indignation testified the feelings of the listeners. Some of them, however, were a little skeptical on the subject.

"Why, then, Bessy! it's hard to think that girls brought up Catholics could ever come to that!"

"Well! hard or easy, I tell you it's true," said Bessy.

"There's thousands of Irish girls in New York (of course that's the city I know best) that are as good Catholics as any of their people at home, but there's just as many the other way. What would you think of an Irish girl that would tell you she was seven years in America, and had never been to Communion in all that time—maybe once or twice to confession?"

"Lord save us, Bessy!" her mother exclaimed, "you're enough to frighten one!"

"I know that, mother, but I'm only telling the truth, and God knows! my heart bleeds to tell it. I knew girls myself that were just as I say, some of them that would laugh at you if you spoke to them of saying their prayers morning or night, and would never think of crossing a Church door if somebody didn't make them go. That all comes, as I told you, of their going out alone to America, without any one to advise or direct them, and them falling into bad places at the very first. Take my advice, Mrs. O'Hare, and keep your girls at home—if you can live here, so can they, and you'll find it better in the long run."

"Well I believe you're about right, Bessy!" replied Mrs. O'Hare; "it's best keep them under our own eyes. Good night, and God be with you all." The visitors then retired, wondering much at what they had heard.

16

John Humphrey Noyes, the Oneida Community,
and Male Continence

Michael J. McClymond

The name John Humphrey Noyes is inextricably linked with the community he founded in upstate New York in 1848, and with the unusual sexual and familial practices that characterized this group. Many of those who participated in the so-called Oneida Community felt that they were pioneers of a completely new way of organizing human society. In their theory and practice of "complex marriage," they were indeed innovators. Lawrence Foster, in his *Religion and Sexuality: Three American Communal Experiments of the Nineteenth Century,* compared the Oneida Community with two other religious groups that departed from the existing norms of family life in nineteenth-century America, the Shakers, who required celibacy of their members, and the Mormons, who in their first decades both allowed and encouraged polygamy (that is, multiple wives for male members). Although all three groups were countercultural, both celibacy and polygamy already existed in the various religions and cultures of the world. Yet "complex marriage" was distinctive to John Humphrey Noyes and his followers. Its rationale and mode of practice are themselves complex issues, best understood by outlining the steps that led to the emergence of the Oneida Community.

The intellectual background of Oneida lies in the doctrine of Christian perfectionism, according to which some persons are able to attain a state of holiness, or sanctification, so complete as to render them sinless and invulnerable to temptation. While studying at Yale Divinity School in 1833–34, Noyes shocked both his professors and his fellow students by declaring that he had become free from all sin. A conversation between Noyes and the redoubtable Professor Nathaniel Taylor did nothing to dissuade Noyes from his belief. Noyes left Yale, and for a number of years his life was characterized by both outward tumult and inward uncertainty. He suffered rejection by the woman he loved, his future vocation remained indefinite, and the general misunderstanding of his doctrines by the public at large compounded his difficulties. He began publication of a circular called *The Perfectionist* (followed by another known as *The Witness*), yet his teaching was rejected out of hand. At times Noyes felt himself to be under spiritual assault, as when he traveled to Brimfield, Massachusetts, to visit a group of attractive and intelligent perfectionist women who soon started the practice of mixed "bundling," or sleeping next to men, in token of their newfound spiritual freedom. In fear and trepidation, Noyes left the scene alone, traveling by foot through snow and subzero weather.

During this period Noyes was often tarred by association with the proponents of "free love," or unrestrained sexual expression, which was not in fact Noyes's position. In 1830s America, some believed that the heart, once having been cleansed from all moral impurity, would innately and instinctively choose what is right. Pure motives would guarantee pure actions. According to this line of reasoning, anything that a perfect Christian did was acceptable and blameless, however contrary it might be to the ethical standards of the day. Not surprisingly, there were many who believed that the advocates of "free love" were simply using pious phrases to cloak their sinful self-indulgence.

Noyes's understanding of Christian perfection followed a different logic. His imagination was captivated by something he called "Bible communism," a fellowship of persons in which all selfish tendencies were overcome and no one claimed anything as belonging strictly and properly to himself or herself as an individual. Along these lines, the New Testament texts describe the earliest Christians as pooling their money and sharing a common purse (Acts 4:32–35). Noyes took this idea a step further. God intended for the powerful currents of romantic and erotic love not to be confined to male-female pairs but to overflow in all directions within a community of "perfect Christians." This love transcended the narrowness and the jealousies of conventional marriage. What distinguished Noyes's outlook from that of the "free lovers" was his insistence that only a disciplined community could embody an unselfish approach to sexuality. It was one thing to act on erotic impulse, and quite another for a whole community to overcome what Noyes called "idolatrous love" or "the marriage spirit." In fact, the Oneida Community had to struggle constantly to prevent its members from forming more or less permanent pair-bonds and thus slipping out of complex marriage.

The turning point in Noyes's thinking came in the late 1830s and early 1840s. "In a holy community," he wrote, "there is no reason why sexual intercourse should be restrained by law, than why eating and drinking should be—and there is as little reason for shame in the one case as in the other." In the new heavens and the new earth that God was to create, the "jealousy of exclusiveness" was to be unknown. "I call a certain woman my wife—she is yours, she is Christ's, and in him she is the bride of all saints," he mused. "She is dear in the hand of a stranger, and . . . I rejoice. My claim upon her cuts directly across the marriage covenant of this world, and God knows the end." At the time he wrote these words, Noyes had been abandoned by his first great love, Abigail Merwin, who had married a schoolteacher. The repudiation of marital exclusiveness may have given to Noyes a certain emotional satisfaction: Abigail was his even though she was married to another. Later in life Noyes suggested that marriage to Abigail might have kept him from ever attempting the experiment with complex marriage.

Two other women also played a key role in Noyes's emerging sense of vocation. The first was Harriet Horton, three years his senior, who shared his perfectionist views and had financial resources that were invaluable to Noyes during the early years of community building. Despite Noyes's admitted lack of sentimental attachment to Harriet (in contrast with his attitude toward Abigail), he judged that Harriet was a suitable partner in his work and married her in 1838. Accused at times of marrying for wealth, he insisted that it was not the love of money but the love of truth that drew them together. They settled in Putney, Vermont, and Noyes promptly began publishing a perfectionist broadside. Among Noyes's early followers in Putney was Mary Cragin, of whom he later wrote that he "found her spirit exceedingly intoxicating—one that will make a man crazy." While Noyes had already developed his theory of "Bible communism" by the early 1840s, his passion for Mary Cragin seems to have triggered the move into complex marriage. Feeling intensely drawn to her, and yet not wanting to offend either his own wife or Mary's husband, George, Noyes brought both couples together in May 1846 and, over the initial objections of Mary's husband, secured the consent of all four persons to a complex marriage "in the quartette form." The arrangement, however, was to prove more gratifying to John and Mary than to Harriet and George. In the half decade prior to Mary Cragin's death in 1851, Harriet was jealous and never reconciled herself to her husband's passion for another woman. Indeed, Noyes's attachment to Mary Cragin was so intense and invariable that at times he seems to have become guilty of the "marriage spirit" that he deprecated in his followers.

Even at the earliest stage of Noyes's community, it was clear who was in charge. While at Putney, Noyes made his followers acknowledge his divine authority by means of a formal vow of obedience. "John H. Noyes," it read, "is the father and overseer whom the Holy Ghost has set over [us]. To John H. Noyes as such we submit ourselves in all things spiritual and temporal." Complex marriage was a closely guarded secret while Noyes remained with his followers in Putney. The leaders were afraid of giving scandal to their neighbors, and they were also convinced that any drastic departure from existing marriage and family practices had to be undertaken very cautiously. Many of Noyes's own followers at Putney were not aware that anything unusual was occurring. As the experiment in complex marriage was well underway, Noyes made the fateful decision to impart knowledge of the secret arrangement to David Hall, a convert to perfectionism and the husband of a woman who claimed to be the beneficiary of a remarkable spiritual healing. Hall did not respond favorably as expected. Instead he went to the state's attorney in Brattleboro, Vermont, and soon the county sheriff was at Noyes's door with a warrant.

In October 1847 Noyes was arrested on a charge of adultery with a woman named Fanny Leonard. While the legal issues remained unresolved, Noyes and his followers concluded that the prospects for the community in Putney were unfavorable. They left Vermont under a cloud of suspicion and disapproval and relocated to Oneida, New York, in early 1848. By the end of the calendar year, there were some eighty-seven persons in residence, and the community's numbers continued to swell. After several years of financial struggle, the Oneidans began manufacturing steel animal traps, and the income from their sale gave the community a sound economic basis. The steel traps also laid the foundation for the production of the silver plate and other tableware that continue to be produced under the Oneida name.

The early experiments in complex marriage at Putney and Oneida were based not only on new ideas regarding sexual love but also on a novel method of contraception. During the early years of his marriage, Noyes saw his wife Harriet suffer through one difficult pregnancy after another, and he resolved to find a way to prevent conception. Regarding masturbation as unnatural and rejecting coitus interruptus (advocated by the communitarian Robert Owen), Noyes developed a practice of coitus reservatus, or intercourse without male ejaculation. Part of the following excerpt from Noyes's tract on "male continence" is devoted to a description of this method of contraception, which the author colorfully compares to canoeing in the still waters above a waterfall without actually going over it.

During the years of complex marriage at Oneida, Noyes's critics charged that coitus reservatus was harmful to the men, and this led to a medical self-study that concluded there were no harmful side effects. When the community began its foray into scientific propagation, or "stirpiculture," in 1869, the men who had long been accustomed to nonejaculation were able to propagate without difficulty. As a result of the prolonged sexual contact made possible by coitus reservatus, some of the women reported increased satisfaction in their sexual lives at Oneida. Postmenopausal women, who could teach the appropriate techniques without danger of unwanted pregnancies, were responsible for the sexual initiation of inexperienced young men, who might be in greatest danger of going "over the waterfall." Implausible as it may sound, Noyes claimed that the men of Oneida learned coitus reservatus easily and found no major difficulty in practicing it. The small number of unintentional pregnancies at Oneida is an indication that the community consistently practiced effective contraceptive measures.

The girls of Oneida were customarily introduced to sex by Noyes himself at the age of puberty, which in the nineteenth century was around fourteen. Sex was seen not only as a bodily function but as a form of spiritual communion. Consequently, Noyes and the other leaders considered it important for the younger members of the community to gain spiritual benefit from sexual intercourse with their elders. This led in time to the principle of "ascending fellowship," in which the young were expected, at least on some occasions, to choose or accept sexual partners from among the older members. Younger members were thus prevented from pulling away and forming a closed circle among themselves. Yet as community morale declined in the late 1860s, the younger members began to neglect their elders, the principle of ascending fellowship was increasingly disregarded, and its abandonment accelerated the demise of complex marriage.

Oneida offered little privacy to its members, and anyone who seemed to be at odds with the rest of the community could expect to have his or her faults exposed and bemoaned during one of the scheduled sessions of "mutual criticism." Those who experienced these sessions found them to be painful but liberating—a kind of moral bathing or washing. Couples who fell in love in the traditional way and ceased to circulate sexually were excoriated for giving into "idolatrous love" and "the marriage spirit." If criticism failed to have its desired effect, such couples might be sent to one of Oneida's satellite communities. One of the most painful aspects of Oneida for many of the children was the physical and emotional separation from their parents that they experienced. Just as "the marriage spirit" was discountenanced, the community also tried to wean parents away from any special attachment to their biological children and to replace it with a generalized sense of attachment to the whole community. Often, parents were allowed to see their children only by appointment and for a limited period of time, after which the children were to be returned to the children's residence and left in the custody of their appointed caretakers.

In some respects the Oneida Community exhibited a greater measure of equality between men and women than was true of other communities of the time. Men and women shared in the daily chores, and in principle neither sex was barred from any of the many occupations needed to run the community. Even in appearance, the sexes were somewhat alike. With hair cut short and wearing a distinctive sort of pantaloon, the women of Oneida were known for their lack of feminine adornment. The cultural life of Oneida was open to men and women alike. Yet Noyes's leadership was highly paternalistic, and he was especially hard on those who spurned his authority. All requests for sexual liason had to be presented by the male to the female through intermediaries, of whom Noyes himself was chief. Thus he had implicit veto power over all requests, and by controlling access to the most desirable sexual partners he wielded influence over every adult member of the community. Moreover, Noyes asserted that women, in God's plan, were subordinate to men. Males, not females, served as stand-ins for Noyes during his absence. Promising young men were sent to Yale College, but nothing comparable was done for the education of young women. Oneida women, although they agreed that the life of a typical American housewife left much to be desired, were not prepared to claim full equality with men.

The daily life of the Oneidans was varied. Because assignment to a single job was thought to produce boredom, one's work might range between running the printing press, manufacturing springs for animal traps, milking cows, shoveling manure, and working in the community kitchen. In the evenings there were lectures on topics covering the whole spectrum of arts and sciences. Noyes had always been a man of wide intellectual interests, and he was often the featured lecturer. There were musical concerts and plays that featured community members as performers. Dances were especially popular. Members of the Oneida Community were encouraged to read secular books generally thought to be antithetical to Christian faith, including works by Auguste Comte and Charles Darwin. This intellectual openness created opportunity for members to doubt or question the foundational principles of the community. Noyes's son, Theodore, a Yale-educated physician and the person whom Noyes hoped would succeed him in leadership, came to doubt the existence of God. Noyes's support for his son's leadership caused dissent among members who wanted to see Oneida remain true to its Christian roots.

Toward the end of the period of complex marriage, the Oneidans began an effort in scientific propagation, known as "stirpiculture." Reproduction, based on a theory of the transmission of spiritual traits, was to be allowed only between approved couples. Noyes apparently considered it important for his own traits to be passed on to the next generation, and so it is not surprising that some nine of the first fifty-eight children begotten after the start of stirpiculture were sired by Noyes himself. Ironically, the practice of stirpiculture as inaugurated by Noyes may have aided in the dissolution of the community. The experience of bearing and raising children tended to draw couples closer to one another and thus lessen their emotional stake in the community at large.

The final years of the Oneida Community were tumultuous and unhappy. Internal dissension wracked the community, the issue of Noyes's successor remained in doubt, and the founder's personal magnetism and sexual vitality diminished as he approached the age of sixty. Many members turned to spiritualism in the quest for authoritative guidance, while others drifted into agnosticism or atheism. The young people had begun to disregard their elders' wishes. With so many of the community's foundational principles in doubt, some thought it would be best to allow for marriage between members who desired it. As a last resort, Noyes urged that celibacy be considered as an alternative to marriage. Yet when the tide of opposition became too strong, Noyes himself consented to allow traditional marriage, and the experiment in complex marriage came to an end in 1879.

John Humphrey Noyes had argued that marriage and communism could not be reconciled, and in the end marriage prevailed. Public spirit gave way before the quest for private happiness. Once complex marriage ended, Noyes's attitude toward the community at Oneida was ambivalent. In 1881, just a few years before his death, he wrote, "We made a raid into an unknown country, charted it, and returned without the loss of a man, woman, or child." Yet he could also be harsh, as when he declared that "communism is not for swine, but only for the sons and daughters of God." He had been unable, he said, "to carry Communism through to final visible success amid the temptations and enmities of this evil world." He struggled to transform or transcend human nature, yet human nature refused to cooperate.

The text included here is taken from John Humphrey Noyes, *Male Continence* (Oneida, N.Y.: Office of the Oneida Circular, 1872), pp. 11–17, 5–10. This work, along with others by Noyes, is photoreproduced with the original pagination in John Humphrey Noyes, *The Berean. Male Continence. Essay on Scientific Propagation* (New York: Arno Press and the New York Times, 1969). The first of the two excerpts from the 1872 publication was originally included in Noyes's earlier tract *The Bible Argument* (1848). The second of the excerpts was originally written as a letter (July 26, 1866) in response to an unnamed inquirer in New York who wanted to learn the specifics of Noyes's practice of male continence.

Further Reading

Walter Edmonds, *The First Hundred Years, 1848–1948* (Oneida, N.Y.: Oneida Community, 1880); Lawrence Foster, *Religion and Sexuality: Three American Communal Experiments of the Nineteenth Century* (New York: Oxford University Press, 1981); *Handbook of the Oneida Community: Mutual Criticism* (New York: AMS Press, 1976); Spencer Klaw, *Without Sin: The Life and Death of the Oneida Community* (London: Penguin, 1993); John Humphrey Noyes, *Home-Talks*, edited by Alfred Barron and George Noyes Miller (New York: AMS Press, 1975).

The Bible Argument

The amative and propagative functions of the sexual organs are distinct from each other, and may be separated practically. They are confounded in the world, both in the theories of physiologists and in universal practice. The amative function is regarded merely as a bait to the propagative, and is merged in it. The sexual organs are called "organs of reproduction," or "organs of generation," but not organs of love or organs of union. But if amativeness is the first and noblest of the social affections, and if the propagative part of the sexual relation was originally secondary, and became paramount by the subversion of order in the fall [as had previously been shown], we are bound to raise the amative office of the sexual organs into a distinct and paramount function. It is held in the world, that the sexual organs have two distinct functions, viz., the urinary and the propagative. We affirm that they have *three*—the urinary, the propagative, and the amative, i.e., they are conductors, first of the urine, secondly of the semen, and thirdly of the social magnetism. And the amative is as distinct from the propagative, as the propagative is from the urinary. In fact, strictly speaking, the organs of propagation are *physiologically* distinct from the organs of union in both sexes. The testicles are organs of reproduction in the male, and the uterus in the female. These are distinct from the organs of union. The sexual conjunction of male and female no more necessarily involves the discharge of the semen than of the urine. The discharge of the semen, instead of being the main act of sexual intercourse, properly so called, is really the sequel and termination of it. Sexual intercourse, pure and simple, is the conjunction of the organs of union, and the interchange of magnetic influences, or conversation of spirits, through the medium of that conjunction. The communication from the seminal vessels to the uterus, which constitutes the propagative act, is distinct from, subsequent to, and not necessarily connected with, this intercourse. On the one hand, the seminal discharge can be voluntarily withheld in sexual connection; and on the other, it can be produced without sexual connection, as it is in masturbation. This latter fact demonstrates that the discharge of the semen and the pleasure connected with it, is not essentially social, since it can be produced in solitude; it is a personal and not a dual affair. This, indeed, is evident from a physiological analysis of it. The plea-sure of the act is not produced by contact and interchange of life with the female, but by the action of the seminal fluid on the internal nerves of the male organ. The appetite and that which satisfies it are both within the man, and of course the pleasure is personal, and may be obtained without sexual intercourse. We insist, then, that the amative function—that which consists in a simple union of per-sons, making "of twain one flesh," and giving a medium of magnetic and spiritual interchange—is a distinct and independent function, as superior to the repro-ductive as we have shown amativeness to be to propagation.

We may strengthen the preceding argument by an analogy. The *mouth* has three distinct functions, viz., those of breathing, eating, and speaking. Two of these, breathing and eating, are purely physical; and these we have in common with the brutes. The third function, that of speaking, is social, and subservient to the intellectual and spiritual. In this we rise above the brutes. They are destitute of it except in a very inferior degree. So, the two primary functions of the sexual organs—the urinary and reproductive—are physical, and we have them in common with the brutes. The third, viz., the amative, is subservient to the spiritual, and is social. In this again we rise above the brutes. They have it only as a bait to the reproductive. As speech, the distinctive glory of man, is the superior function of the mouth, so the social office of the sexual organs is their superior func-tion, and that which gives man a position above the brutes.

The method of controlling propagation which results from our argument is natural, healthy, favorable to amativeness, and effectual.

First, it is *natural*. The useless expenditure of seed certainly is not natural. God cannot have designed that men should sow seed by the way-side, where they do not expect it to grow, or in the same field where seed has already been sown and is growing; and yet such is the practice of men in ordinary sexual intercourse. They sow seed habitually where they do not *wish* it to grow. This is wasteful of life and cannot be natural. So far the Shakers and Grahamites are right. Yet it is equally manifest that the natural instinct of our nature demands frequent congress of the sexes, not for propagative, but for social and spiritual purposes. It results from these opposite indications, that simple congress of sexes, *without the propagative crisis*, is the order of nature for the gratification of ordinary amative instincts; and that the act of propagation should be reserved for its legitimate occasions, when conception is intended. The idea that sexual intercourse, pure and simple, is impossible or difficult, and there-fore not natural, is contradicted by the experience of many. Abstinence from masturbation is impossible or difficult where habit has made it a second nature; and yet no one will say that habitual masturbation is natural. So absti-nence from the propagative part of sexual intercourse may seem impracticable to depraved natures, and yet be perfectly natural and easy to persons properly trained to chastity. Our method simply proposes the subordination of the flesh to the spirit, teaching men to seek principally the elevated spiritual pleasures of sexual connection, and to be content with them in their general intercourse with women, restricting the more sensual part to its proper occasions. This is certainly natural and easy to spiritual men, however difficult it may be to the sensual.

Secondly, this method is *healthy*. In the first place, it secures woman from the curses of involuntary and undesirable procreation; and, secondly, it stops the drain of life on the part of man. This cannot be said of Owen's method or of any other that merely prevents the *propagative effects* of the emission of the seed, and not the emission itself.

Thirdly, the method is *favorable to amativeness*. Owen can only say of his method that it does not *much diminish* the pleasure of sexual intercourse; but we can say of ours, that it *vastly increases* that pleasure. Ordinary sexual intercourse (in which the amative and propagative functions are confounded) is a momentary affair, terminating in exhaustion and disgust. If it begins in the spirit, it soon ends in the flesh; i.e., the amative, which is spiritual, is drowned in the propagative, which is sensual. The exhaustion which follows naturally breeds self-reproach and shame, and this leads to dislike and concealment of the sexual organs, which contract disagreeable associations from the fact that they are instruments of pernicious excess. This undoubtedly is the philosophy of the origin of shame after the fall. Adam and Eve first sunk the spiritual in the sensual, in eating the forbidden fruit; and then, having lost the true balance of their natures, they sunk the spiritual in the sensual in their intercourse with each other, by pushing prematurely beyond the amative to the propagative, and so became ashamed, and began to look with an evil eye on the instruments of their folly. On the same principle we may account for the process of "cooling off" which takes place between lovers after marriage and often ends in indifference and disgust. Exhaustion and self-reproach make the eye evil not only toward the instrument of excess, but toward the person who tempts to it. In contrast with all this, lovers who use their sexual organs simply as the servants of their spiritual natures, abstaining from the propagative act, except when procreation is intended, may enjoy the highest bliss of sexual fellowship for any length of time, without satiety or exhaustion; and thus marriage life may become permanently sweeter than courtship or even the honey-moon.

Fourthly, this method of controlling propagation is *effectual*. The habit of making sexual intercourse a quiet affair, like conversation, restricting the action of the organs to such limits as are necessary to the avoidance of the sensual crisis, can easily be established, and then there is no risk of conception without intention.

Ordinary sexual intercourse, i.e., the performance of the propagative act without the intention of procreation, is properly to be classed with masturbation. The habit in the former case is less liable to become besotted and ruinous than in the latter, simple because a woman is less convenient than the ordinary means of masturbation. It must be admitted, also, that the amative affection favorably modifies the sensual act to a greater extent in sexual commerce than in masturbation. But this is perhaps counterbalanced by the cruelty of forcing or risking undesired conception, which attends sexual commerce, and does not attend masturbation.

Our theory, separating the amative from the propagative, not only relieves us of involuntary and undesirable procreation, but opens the way for *scientific* propagation. We are not opposed, after the Shaker fashion, or even after Owen's fashion, to the increase of population. We believe that the order to "multiply" attached to the race in its original integrity, and that propagation, rightly conducted and kept within such limits as life can fairly afford, is a blessing second only to sexual love. But we are opposed to *involuntary* procreation. A very large proportion of all children born under the present system are begotten contrary to the wishes of both parents, and lie nine months in their mother's womb under their mother's curse or a feeling little better than a curse. Such children cannot be well organized. We are opposed to *excessive,* and of course oppressive procreation, which is almost universal. We are opposed to *random* procreation, which is unavoidable in the marriage system. But we are in favor of *intelligent, well-ordered procreation.* The physiologists say that the race cannot be raised from ruin till propagation is made a matter of science; but they point out no way of making it so. Propagation is controlled and reduced to a science in the case of valuable domestic brutes; but marriage and fashion forbid any such system among human beings. We believe the time will come when involuntary and random propagation will cease, and when scientific combination will be applied to human generation as freely and successfully as it is to that of other animals. The way will be open for this when amativeness can have its proper gratification without drawing after it procreation, as a necessary sequence. And at all events, we believe that good sense and benevolence will *very soon* sanction and enforce the rule that women shall bear children only when they choose. They have the principal burdens of breeding to bear, and they rather than men should have their choice of time and circumstances, at least till science takes charge of the business.

The separation of the amative from the propagative, places amative sexual intercourse on the same footing with other ordinary forms of social interchange. So long as the amative and propagative are confounded, sexual intercourse carries with it physical consequences which necessarily take it out of the category of mere social acts. If a man under the cover of a mere social call upon a woman, should leave in her apartments a child for her to breed and provide for, he would do a mean wrong. The call might be made without previous negotiation or agreement, but the sequel of the call—the leaving of the child—is a matter so serious that it is to be treated as a business affair, and not be done without good reason and agreement of the parties. But the man who under the cover of social intercourse commits the propagative act, leaves his child with the woman in a more oppressive way than if he should leave it full born in her apartment; for he imposes upon her not only the task of breeding and providing for it, but the sorrows and pains of pregnancy and childbirth. It is right that law, or at least public opinion, should frown on such proceedings even more than it does; and it is not to be wondered at that women, to a considerable extent, look upon ordinary sexual intercourse with more dread than pleasure, regarding it as a stab at their life, rather than a joyful act of fellowship. But separate the amative from the propagative—let the act of fellowship stand by itself—and sexual intercourse becomes a purely social affair, the same in kind with other modes of kindly communion, differing only by its superior intensity and beauty. Thus the most popular, if not the most serious objection, to communistic love is removed. The difficulty so often urged, of knowing to whom children belong in complex-marriage, will have no place in a Community trained to keep the amative distinct from the propagative. Thus also the only plausible objection to amative intercourse between near relatives, founded on the supposed law of nature that "breeding in and in"deteriorates offspring (which law, however, was not recognized in Adam's family) is removed; since science may dictate in this case as in all others, in regard to propagation, and yet amativeness may be free.

In society trained in these principles, as propagation will become a science, so amative intercourse will have place among the "fine arts." Indeed, it will take rank above music, painting, sculpture, etc.; for it combines the charms and benefits of them all. There is as much room for cultivation of taste and skill in this department as in any.

The practice which we propose will give new speed to the advance of civilization and refinement. The self-control, retention of life, and ascent out of sensualism, which must result from making freedom of love a bounty on the chastening of physical indulgence, will raise the race to new vigor and beauty, moral and physical. And the refining effects of sexual love (which are recognized more or less in the world) will be increased a thousand-fold, when sexual intercourse becomes an honored method of innocent and useful communion, and each is married to all.

From the Introduction to "The Bible Argument"

1. It is not immodest, in the present exigency, to affirm that the leading members of the Putney Association belonged to the most respectable families in Vermont, had been educated in the best schools of New England morality and refinement, and were by the ordinary standards irreproachable in their conduct, so far as sexual matters are concerned, till they deliberately commenced, in 1846, the experiment of a new state of society, on principles which they had been long maturing and were prepared to defend before the world.

2. It may also be affirmed without fear of contradiction, that the main body of those who have joined the Community at Oneida are sober, substantial men and women, of good previous character and position in society.

3. The principles discussed in the ensuing argument have never been carried into full practical embodiment, either at Putney or Oneida, but have been

held by the Community as the principles of an *ultimate state,* toward which society among them is advancing slowly and carefully, with all due deference to sentiments and relations established by the old order of things.

4. The Community, in respect to practical innovations, limits itself to its own family circle, not invading society around it; and no just complaint of such invasions can be found at Putney or Oneida.

Noyes's Letter of 26 July 1866

Mr. ___ ___:

Dear Sir:—Your letter addressed to the CIRCULAR, asking for information in regard to our method of controlling propagation, has been sent to me, and as it seems to come from a well-disposed person (though unknown to me), I will endeavor to give it a faithful answer—such, at least, as will be sufficient for scientific purposes.

The first question, or rather, perhaps I should say, the *previous* question in regard to Male Continence, is whether it is desirable or proper that men and women should establish intelligent voluntary control over the propagative function. Is it not better (it may be asked), to leave "nature" to take its course (subject to the general rules of legal chastity), and let children come as chance or the unknown powers may direct, without putting any restraint on sexual intercourse after it is once licensed by marriage, or on the freedom of all to take out such license? If you assent to this latter view, or have any inclination toward it, I would recommend to you the study of *Malthus on Population;* not that I think he has pointed out anything like the true method of voluntary control over propagation, but because he has demonstrated beyond debate the absolute *necessity* of such control in some way, unless we consent and expect that the human race, like the lower animals, shall be forever kept down to its necessary limits, by the ghastly agencies of war, pestilence and famine.

For my part, I have no doubt that it is perfectly proper that we should endeavor to rise above "nature" and the destiny of the brutes in this matter. There is no reason why we should not seek and hope for discovery in this direction, as freely as in the development of steam power or the art of printing; and we may rationally expect that He who has promised the "good time" when vice and misery shall be abolished, will at last give us sure light on this darkest of all problems—how to subject human propagation to the control of science.

But whether the study and invention in this direction are proper are not, they are actually at work in all quarters, reputable and disreputable. Let us see how many different ways have already been proposed for limiting human increase.

In the first place, the practice of child-killing, either by exposure or violence, is almost as old as the world, and as extensive as barbarism. Even Plato recommended something of this kind, as a waste-gate for vicious increase, in his scheme of a model republic.

Then we have the practice of abortion reduced in modern times to a science, and almost to a distinct profession. A large part of this business is carried on by means of medicines advertized in obscure but intelligible terms as embryo-destroyers or preventives of conception. Every large city has its professional abortionist. Many ordinary physicians destroy embryos to order; and the skill to do this terrible deed has even descended among the common people.

Then what a variety of artificial tricks there are for frustrating the natural effects of the propagative act. You allude to several of these contrivances, in terms of condemnation from which I should not dissent. The least objectionable of them (if there is any difference), seems to be that recommended many years ago by Robert Dale Owen, in a book entitled Moral Physiology; viz., the simple device of withdrawing immediately before emission.

Besides all these disreputable methods, we have several more respectable schemes for attaining the great object of limiting propagation. Malthus proposes and urges that all men, and especially the poor, shall be taught their responsibilities in the light of science, and so be put under inducements *not to marry*. This prudential check on population—the discouragement of marriage—undoubtedly operates to a considerable extent in all civilized society, and to the greatest extent on the classes most enlightened. It seems to have been favored by Saint Paul; (see 1st Cor. 7); and probably would not be condemned generally by people who claim to be considerate. And yet its advocates have to confess that it increases the danger of licentiousness; and on the whole the teaching that is most popular, in spite of Malthus and Paul, is that marriage, with all its liabilities, is a moral and patriotic duty.

Finally Shakerism, which actually prohibits marriage on religious grounds, is only the most stringent and imposing of human contrivances for avoiding the woes of undesired propagation.

All these experimenters in the art of controlling propagation may be reduced in principle to three classes, viz.:

1. Those that seek to prevent the intercourse of the sexes, such as Malthus and the Shakers.
2. Those that seek to prevent the natural effects of the propagative act, viz., the French inventors and Owen.
3. Those that seek to destroy the living results of the propagative act, viz., the abortionists and child-killers.

Now it may seem to you that any new scheme of control over propagation must inevitable fall to one of these three classes; but I assure you that we have a method that does not fairly belong to any of them. I will try to show you our fourth way.

We begin by *analyzing* the act of sexual intercourse. It has a beginning, a middle, and an end. Its beginning and most elementary form is the simple *presence* of the male organ in the female. Then usually follows a series of recip-rocal *motions*. Finally this exercise brings on a nervous action or ejaculatory *crisis* which expels the seed. Now we insist that the whole process, up to the very moment of emission, is *voluntary*, entirely under the control of the moral faculty, and *can be stopped at any point*. In other words, the *presence* and the *motions* can be continued or stopped at will, and it is only the final *crisis* of emission that is automatic or uncontrollable.

Suppose, then, that a man, in lawful intercourse with woman, choosing for good reasons not to beget a child or to disable himself, should stop at the primary stage and content himself with simple *presence* continued as long as agreeable? Would there be any harm? It cannot be injurious to refrain from voluntary excitement. Would there be no *good*? I appeal to the memory of every man who has had good sexual experience to say whether, on the whole, the sweetest and noblest period of intercourse with woman is not that *first* moment of simple presence and spiritual effusion, before the muscular exercise begins.

But we may go farther. Suppose the man chooses for good reasons, as before, to enjoy not only the simple *presence,* but also the *reciprocal motion,* and yet to stop short of the final *crisis*. Again I ask, Would there be any harm? Or would it do no good? I suppose physiologists might say, and I would acknowledge, that the excitement by motion *might* be carried so far that a voluntary suppression of the commencing crisis would be injurious. But what if a man, knowing his own power and limits, should not even *approach* the crisis, and yet be able to enjoy the presence and the motion *ad libitum*? If you say that this is impossible, I answer that I *know* it is possible—nay, that it is easy.

I will admit, however, that it may be impossible to some, while it is possible to others. Paul intimates that some cannot "contain." Men of certain temperaments and conditions are afflicted with involuntary emissions on very trivial excitement and in their sleep. But I insist that these are exceptional morbid cases that should be disciplined and improved; and that, in the normal condition, men are entirely competent to choose in sexual intercourse whether they will stop at any point in the voluntary stages of it, and so make it simply an act of communion, or go through to the involuntary stage, and make it an act of propagation.

The situation may be compared to a stream in the three conditions of a fall, a course of rapids above the fall, and still water above the rapids. The skillful boatmen may choose whether he will remain in the still water, or venture more or less down the rapids, or run his boat over the fall. But there is a point on the verge of the fall where he has no control over his course; and just above that there is point where he will have to struggle with the current in a way which will give his nerves a severe trial, even though he may escape the fall. If he is willing to learn, experience will teach him the wisdom of confining his excursions to the region of easy rowing, unless he has an object in view that is worth the cost of going over the falls.

You now have the whole theory of "Male Continence." It consists in analyzing sexual intercourse, recognizing in it two distinct acts, the social and the propagative, which can be separated practically, and affirming that it is best, not only with reference to remote prudential considerations, but for immediate pleasure, that a man should content himself with the social act, except when he intends procreation.

Let us see now if this scheme belongs to any of the three classes I mentioned. 1. It does not seek to prevent the intercourse of the sexes, but rather gives them more freedom by removing danger of undesired consequences. 2. It does not seek to prevent the natural *effects* of the propagative act, but to prevent the propagative act itself, except when it is intended to be effectual. 3. Of course it does not seek to destroy the living *results* of the propagative act, but provides that the impregnation and child-bearing shall be voluntary, and of course desired.

And now, to speak affirmatively, the exact thing that our theory does propose, is to take that same power of moral restraint and self-control, which Paul, Malthus, the Shakers, and all considerate men use in one way or another to limit propagation, and instead of applying it, as they do, to the prevention of the intercourse of the sexes, to introduce it at another stage of the proceedings, viz., *after* the sexes have come together in social effusion, and *before* they have reached the propagative crisis; thus allowing them all and more than all the ordinary freedom of love (since the crisis always interrupts the romance), and at the same time avoiding undesired procreation and all the other evils incident to male incontinence. This is our fourth way, and we think it the better way.

The wholesale and ever ready objection to this method is that it is *unnatural, and unauthorized by the example of other animals.* I may answer in a wholesome way, that cooking, wearing clothes, living in houses, and almost everything else done by civilized man, is unnatural in the same sense, and that a close adherence to the example of the brutes would require us to forego speech and go on "all fours!" But on the other hand, if it is natural in the best sense, as I believe it is, for rational beings to forsake the example of the brutes and improve nature by invention and discovery in all directions, then truly the argument turns the other way, and we shall have to confess that until men and women find a way to elevate their sexual performance above those of the brutes, by introducing into them moral culture, they are living in *unnatural* degradation.

But I will come closer to this objection. The real meaning of it is, that Male Continence in sexual intercourse is a difficult and injurious interruption of a natural act. But every instance of self-denial is an interruption of some natural act. The man who virtuously contents himself with a look at a beautiful woman is conscious of such an interruption. The lover who stops at a kiss denies himself a natural progression. It is an easy, descending grade through all the approaches of sexual love, from the first touch of respectful friendship, to the final complete amalgamation. Must there be no interruption of this natural slide? Brutes, animal or human, tolerate none. Shall their ideas of self-denial prevail? Nay, it is the glory of man to control himself, and the Kingdom of Heaven summons him to self-control in ALL THINGS. If it is noble and beautiful for the betrothed lover to respect the law of marriage in the midst of the glories of courtship, it may be even more noble and beautiful for the wedded lover to respect the laws of health and propagation in the midst of the ecstasies of sexual union. The same moral culture that ennobles the antecedents and approaches of marriage will some time surely glorify the consummation.

Of course, you will think of many other objections and questions, and I have many answers ready for you; but I will content myself for the present with this limited presentation.

Yours respectfully,

J. H. Noyes.

— 17 —

Is Life Worth Living?

Paul Jerome Croce

William James's essay "Is Life Worth Living?" began as a lecture, delivered on April 25, 1895, to the Young Men's Christian Association of Harvard University. Many nineteenth-century thinkers spoke to student clubs, lyceum meetings, and social and religious groups, and so James's lecture to a YMCA meeting was a characteristic intellectual activity of his time. Presenting generalizations from one's studies was also socially expected of college teachers. In the days before specialization by discipline, philosophers and psychologists such as James would regularly address "popular audiences," and in the days before electronic mass media, such events attracted large crowds of people. Like a sermon, such lectures would often explore moral and religious issues—only outside of the confines of a church organization. James often used these talks as a way to test out ideas or to offer a more generalized version of ideas he had written about more extensively elsewhere. Still, since he lived in an era when specialization was just starting, he sometimes balked at giving too many of these popular talks. Like a good minister, however, he was popular despite himself, gaining wide attention for his ability to translate big ideas into accessible form and to moderate cultural tensions about the conflicting authority of science and religion.

The written version reprinted here keeps the spoken, informal quality of James's lecture. From the lecture's vitally urgent title question to its wide-ranging examples and arresting turns of phrase, James seeks to capture and maintain first the listeners', and then the readers', attention. On one level, the lecture can be understood as a "font of wisdom" for the reflective soul wondering about the purpose of life. Or the lecture is simply a bank of quotable quotes: "our hour of triumph is what brings the void"; "our science is a drop, our ignorance a sea;" or, "you make one . . . of two possible universes true by your trust." As a modern guide to contemplation, this informal philosophical essay, which was reprinted as a pamphlet to keep up with popular demand, uses direct wording to prompt deep thinking about the mysteries of life. From this point of view, the essay is timeless, since issues of purpose, conviction, moral choice, and the limits of our knowledge appear in every age. James's support for our voluntary power can hold in check both the discouragement and the excessive pride that repeatedly tempt individuals and whole societies.

In addition to its timeless qualities, James's essay can also be understood in its context—a reading that actually adds to the richness of the insights. The essay was an apology for religion in the context of late-nineteenth-century challenges to belief. In western Europe and North America, William James was a popular intellectual and his writings circulated among educated urbanites whose religious commitments had been on the decline for generations. Even in places where church attendance had remained stable, the average citizen no longer assumed that providential ways of understanding the world were unquestionable. While it was common practice throughout the eighteenth century to attribute natural events to the hand of the divine, by the late nineteenth century it was more and more common to credit chance. The conversational use of "thank God" and "God bless you" continued to be used more as conventions than as prayers to the divine. This is not to say that religion disappeared or even became weaker, but that it became privatized in the province of personal convictions within communities of like-minded people. From the late nineteenth century onward, secularism increasingly dominated public life.

The largest single factor in the eclipse of religious conviction was the rise of science. While it was a general force in the decline of providential thinking in popular culture, scientific methods and facts had a very specific impact on intellectuals who matched up those insights against religious doctrines and often found the latter seriously wanting. This created a religious backlash against intellectuals and against science during the nineteenth century, a trend that has continued to this day. Many students of science and religion scrambled to find compromises, however, by accepting the newer views, with pictures of the divine operating through nature and even proved by scientific facts. The most ardent enthusiasts for a strictly scientific worldview, however, were the agnostic positivists who James features in his essay. Their arguments are the most immediate context for his comments.

Positivism arose as the ardently antireligious philosophy of Auguste Comte, who proposed that science's systematic inquiry would render religion and philosophy, with their uncertain knowledge and vague theories, wholly obsolete. Supporters of science in many fields rallied to a materialistic outlook on the world that seemed to be supported by the promise of scientific inquiry. Thanks to the writings of John Stuart Mill and other enthusiasts for science, especially in England and the northeast of the United States, positivism became popularized and generalized as a cultural worldview. Positivism ridiculed obscurantist religion and looked optimistically to the world-transforming—and even world-redeeming—qualities of science in the modern world. For positivists, science would present an alternative religion. Within this culture, the British biologist and ardent advocate of Darwinism, Thomas Henry Huxley, coined the term "agnosticism" in 1869 to refer to the uncertainty of all religious positions. With limits to our knowledge, ultimate questions could only be answered with frank ignorance. In fact, Huxley maintained that whenever evidence was in short supply, we have an agnostic obligation to withhold belief. With this restriction on religion, the field was clear for the increase of scientific authority.

Beginning in the middle of the nineteenth century, agnostic positivists had an influence beyond their numbers because they were taking the rising authority of science to its logical conclusion. They were articulating the implications embedded in the erosion of providential assumptions and in the scientific questions about religious doctrines. Their arguments were a particularly potent force in university settings, where James worked and where he had been teaching since 1873. The college setting and the prevailing worries about scientific challenges to religion explain his framing of the essay in terms of the difference between knowledge of facts and trust in ideals. This dichotomy expresses the tension between the authority of science and the hopes of religion. Initially, at least, he is willing to give each side its due: science looks to tangible, accurate, empirical facts, while religion answers "the craving of the heart to believe" in a purpose beyond this world.

From a factual point of view, says James, the agnostic positivists are right about religion: it is an empirical absurdity because it proposes beliefs that cannot be confirmed by the senses. This is why he speaks of "the inevitable bankruptcy of natural religion," the belief that natural facts prove religious truths through the intricate design of the created world. Positivism would be a reasonable resolution of the issue if human lives only included things that could be verified factually. But there is much that spills beyond these boundaries, including dreams, curiosity, and even natural facts not yet scientifically understood. James turns the tables on the confidence of the agnostic positivists in science by pointing out that even scientific inquiry is animated by unproven assumptions that there are "ideal logical and mathematical harmonies" beneath the chaotic diversity of nature.

In addition to this theoretical problem with the philosophy of agnostic positivism, it is also discouraging because it denies purposes any deeper than the finite concerns of this world. James therefore charges that this scientific outlook is the source of a "speculative melancholy" that can lead to world-weariness and even suicide. He admits that the scientific way of thinking does not directly cause the many suicides caused by deep pathological problems. In addition, he points out, in anticipation of his book *The Varieties of Religious Experience* (1902), that some people are so temperamentally optimistic that the worth of life is never a question. It becomes an issue, however, for those who are "sick souls" (to use the words of the later book), urgently searching for deeper meaning and never fully finding it in this troubled world.

This philosophical temptation to end life because of its pointlessness gets to the heart of James's topic. This deep pessimism, which issues in "a religious disease," actually has secular sources. The strictly scientific outlook, in a mind of reflective temper, is wholly bleak: just by examining the bare facts, life is not worth living. To this depressing conclusion, James responds that there is much more to life than just the scientifically understandable material. Those qualities of life emerge only when we live beyond verifiable facts, through risking our trust, acting with effort, and struggling against obstacles—all beliefs and actions without certainty. Where the agnostic positivists demand proof, James welcomes maybes.

For models of action taken (and life fully relished) despite uncertainty, James turns to the examples of urgent situations. He illustrates his point with the image of a mountain climber stuck "in a position from which the only escape is by a terrible leap." When in such a crisis, and especially if our life is in danger, it does not even occur to us to wait for more evidence as the positivists suggest. That is also why James refers to people who put up with enormous pains and persecutions and nevertheless thrive optimistically. They have "the cheerfulness that comes with fighting ills," struggles which often involve fighting against odds. He proposes that action based on shreds of possibility can also motivate people languishing with melancholia. Exhorting them to stop thinking and start doing, James suggests that the answers to the questions of thought will only emerge in action. And that is why he concludes that life is not necessarily worth living until we create its worth with our own commitment. Then the question is answered not in the brain but in "the liver," as he says with the double meaning of both the person doing the living and the response from the body's liver—our guts.

James's call to action was part of a widespread trend at late-nineteenth-century universities. Educators were eager to steer young people away from "mere idleness and dissipation," as one of his Harvard colleagues said, and to connect learning to broader moral and civic purposes. The student group that James first addressed with this essay, the Harvard YMCA, was one of a number of campus organizations formed in the 1880s and 1890s to foster Christian beliefs among college students. By 1895, when James delivered his lecture, the association's evangelical purposes had evolved into a focus on service to the community. Student and faculty leaders maintained that social activism had double advantages: it helped working-class people benefit from the knowledge and cultural refinements that students brought with them, and such activism helped college students to be less selfish and more well-rounded citizens. One YMCA leader at the University of Pennsylvania said of student service that it provided a "splendid opportunity . . . to drive away 'the blues.'" While James's audience at Harvard was exclusively male in 1900, the trend toward coeducation in the United States had been well established, especially in public institutions. Service to the community was important for both young men and young women.

James not only endorsed the student activists but also, at the time he wrote this essay, he was becoming more socially and politically active himself. Although his primary commitments were to teaching and writing, he also threw himself into contemporary causes. His major concern was that the country was becoming more rigid institutionally and that individual freedoms were being lost to regulations, to corporate demands, and most especially to the rise of America's ambitions for empire. He was appalled at the headlong transformation of this democratic nation, this former colony no less, into an imperialist nation. The deliberate provocation toward Spain that would lead to the Spanish-American War, the acquisition of colonies in the Pacific and the Caribbean, the long occupation of the Philippines, and American suppression of the Filipino independence movement all moved him to take action as a thinker and writer. Although he did not become involved in politics or demonstrations, he did deliver impassioned lectures, write extensive letters and essays in newspapers and magazines, and join a prominent anti-imperialist organization. His actions built on the same principles that he was advocating to the students.

For all of James's endorsement of action and conviction, he does not, in this essay, recommend specific actions. While he could be fairly charged with vagueness, his own purpose was to keep his words personal enough to deal with the individual motivations behind countless specific projects. He was playing the role of the public intellectual addressing students and the general public, and hoping that his words would inspire a range of creative individual choices. Because of his universalist goals, James also did not endorse any one religion; instead, he proposed that any religious belief that serves as an endorsement of hopes and ideals beyond empirical facts is reasonable and plausible, even in a scientific age. Religion's very uncertainty is suited to the "half-saved universe" we live in. Our struggles and the beliefs we adopt to keep our motivations well stoked will themselves help to make life worth living.

The selections here are from "An Address to the Harvard Young Men's Christian Association," which was published in the *International Journal of Ethics* (October 1895) and as a pocket volume by S. B. Weston, Philadelphia, 1896. The current text is reprinted from *The Will to Believe and Other Essays in Popular Philosophy*, vol. 6, in *The Works of William James*, Frederick H. Burkhardt, general editor; Fredson Bowers, textual editor; Ignas K. Skrupskelis, assoc. editor (Cambridge: Harvard University Press, 1979).

Further Reading

Deborah J. Coon, "'One Moment in the World's Salvation': Anarchism and the Radicalization of William James," *Journal of American History* 83 (June 1996): 70–99; Emily Mieras, "'A More Perfect Sympathy': College Students and Social Service, 1889–1914," Ph.D., College of William and Mary, 1998; Lewis O. Saum, *The Popular Mood of America, 1860–1890* (Lincoln: University of Nebraska Press, 1990); Linda Simon, *Genuine Reality: A Life of William James* (New York: Harcourt, Brace, 1998); James Turner, *Without God, Without Creed: The Origins of Unbelief in America* (Baltimore: Johns Hopkins University Press, 1985).

Is Life Worth Living?

When Mr. Mallock's book with this title appeared some fifteen years ago, the jocose answer that "it depends on the liver" had great currency in the newspapers. The answer which I propose to give to-night cannot be jocose. In the words of one of Shakespeare's prologues,

> "I come no more to make you laugh; things now,
> That bear a weighty and a serious brow,
> Sad, high, and working, full of state and woe,"

must be my theme. In the deepest heart of all of us there is a corner in which the ultimate mystery of things works sadly; and I know not what such an association as yours intends, nor what you ask of those whom you invite to address you, unless it be to lead you from the surface-glamour of existence, and for an hour at least to make you heedless to the buzzing and jigging and vibration of small interests and excitements that form the tissue of our ordinary consciousness. Without further explanation or apology, then, I ask you to join me in turning an attention, commonly too unwilling, to the profounder bass-note of life. Let us search the lonely depths for an hour together, and see what answers in the last folds and recesses of things our question may find.

With many men the question of life's worth is answered by a temperamental optimism which makes them incapable of believing that anything seriously evil can exist. Our dear old Walt Whitman's works are the standing text-book of this kind of optimism. The mere joy of living is so immense in Walt Whitman's veins that it abolishes the possibility of any other kind of feeling.

> "To breathe the air, how delicious!
> To speak—to walk—to seize something by the hand! . . .
> To be this incredible God I am! . . .
> O amazement of things—even the least particle!
> O spirituality of things! . . .
> I too carol the sun, usher'd or at noon, or as now, setting,
> I too throb to the brain and beauty of the earth and of all the growths of
> the earth . . .
> I sing to the last the equalities modern or old,
> I sing the endless finals of things,
> I say Nature continues, glory continues,
> I praise with electric voice,
> For I do not see one imperfection in the universe,
> And I do not see one cause or result lamentable at last." . . .

If moods like this could be made permanent, and constitutions like these universal, there would never be any occasion for such discourses as the present one. No philosopher would seek to prove articulately that life is worth living, for the fact that it absolutely is so would vouch for itself, and the problem disappear in the vanishing of the question rather than in the coming of anything like a reply. But we are not magicians to make the optimistic temperament universal; and alongside of the deliverances of temperamental optimism concerning life, those of temperamental pessimism always exist, and oppose to them a standing refutation. In what is called "circular insanity," phases of melancholy succeed phases of mania, with no outward cause that we can discover; and often enough to one and the same well person life will present incarnate radiance to-day and incarnate dreariness to-morrow, according to the fluctuations of what the older medical books used to call "the concoction of the humors." In the words of the newspaper joke, "it depends on the liver." . . . Some men seem launched upon the world even from their birth with souls as incapable of happiness as Walt Whitman's was of gloom, and they have left us their messages in even more lasting verse than his—the exquisite Leopardi, for example; or our own contemporary, James Thomson, in that pathetic book, *The City of Dreadful Night*, which I think is less well-known than it should be for its literary beauty, simply because men are afraid to quote its words—they are so gloomy, and at the same time so sincere. In one place the poet describes a congregation gathered to listen to a preacher in a great unillumined cathedral at night. The sermon is too long to quote, but it ends thus:

> "My Brother, my poor Brothers, it is thus;
>   This life itself holds nothing good for us,
> But it ends soon and nevermore can be;
> And we knew nothing of it ere our birth,
> And shall know nothing when consigned to earth:
>   I ponder these thoughts and they comfort me."

"It ends soon and nevermore can be," "Lo, you are free to end it when you will"—these verses flow truthfully from the melancholy Thomson's pen, and are in truth a consolation for all to whom, as to him, the world is far more like a steady den of fear than a continual fountain of delight. That life is not worth living the whole army of suicides declare—an army whose roll-call, like the famous evening gun of the British army, follows the sun round the world and never terminates. We, too, as we sit here in our comfort, must "ponder these things" also, for we are of one substance with these suicides, and their life is the life we share. The plainest intellectual integrity—nay, more, the simplest manliness and honor—forbid us to forget their case.

"If suddenly," says Mr. Ruskin, "in the midst of the enjoyments of the palate and lightnesses of heart of a London dinner party, the walls of the chamber were parted, and through their gap the nearest human beings who were famishing and in misery were borne into the midst of the company—feasting and fancy free—if, pale from death, horrible in destitution, broken by despair, body by body, they were laid upon the soft carpet, one beside the chair of every guest, would only the crumbs of the dainties be cast to them—would only a passing glance, a passing thought, be vouchsafed to them? Yet the actual facts, the real relation of each Dives and Lazarus, are not altered by the intervention of the house wall between the table and the sick bed—by the few feet of ground (how few!) which are indeed all that separate the merriment from the misery."

To come immediately to the heart of my theme, then, what I propose is to imagine ourselves reasoning with a fellow-mortal who is on such terms with life that the only comfort left him is to brood on the assurance "you may end it when you will." What reasons can we plead that may render such a brother (or sister) willing to take up the burden again? Ordinary Christians, reasoning with would-be suicides, have little to offer them beyond the usual negative "thou shalt not." God alone is master of life and death, they say, and it is a blasphemous act to anticipate his absolving hand. But can we find nothing richer or more positive than this, no reflections to urge whereby the suicide may actually see, and in all sad seriousness feel, that in spite of adverse appearances even for him life is still worth living? There are suicides and suicides (in the United States about three thousand of them every year), and I must frankly confess that with perhaps the majority of these my suggestions are impotent to deal. Where suicide is the result of insanity or sudden frenzied impulse, reflection is impotent to arrest its headway; and cases like these belong to the ultimate mystery of evil, concerning which I can only offer considerations tending towards religious patience at the end of this hour. My task, let me say now, is practically narrow, and my words are to deal only with that metaphysical *tedium vitae* which is peculiar to reflecting men. Most of you are devoted, for good or ill, to the reflective life. Many of you are students of philosophy, and have already felt in your own persons the skepticism and unreality that too much grubbing in the abstract roots of things will breed. This is, indeed, one of the regular fruits of the over-studious career. Too much questioning and too little active responsibility lead, almost as often as too much sensualism does, to the edge of the slope, at the bottom of which lie pessimism and the nightmare or suicidal view of life. But to the diseases which reflection breeds, still further reflection can oppose effective remedies; and it is of the melancholy and *Weltschmerz* bred of reflection that I now proceed to speak.

Let me say, immediately, that my final appeal is to nothing more recondite than religious faith. So far as my argument is to be destructive, it will consist in nothing more than the sweeping away of certain views that often keep the springs of religious faith compressed; and so far as it is to be constructive, it will consist in holding up to the light of day certain considerations calculated to let loose these springs in a normal, natural way. Pessimism is essentially a religious disease.

In the form of it to which you are most liable, it consists in nothing but a religious demand to which there comes no normal religious reply.

Now there are two stages of recovery from this disease, two different levels upon which one may emerge from the midnight view to the daylight view of things, and I must treat of them in turn. The second stage is the more complete and joyous, and it corresponds to the freer exercise of religious trust and fancy. There are, as is well known, persons who are naturally very free in this regard, others who are not at all so. There are persons, for instance, whom we find indulging to their heart's content in prospects of immortality; and there are others who experience the greatest difficulty in making such a notion seem real to themselves at all. These latter persons are tied to their senses, restricted to their natural experience; and many of them, moreover, feel a sort of intellectual loyalty to what they call "hard facts," which is positively shocked by the easy excursions into the unseen that other people make at the bare call of sentiment. Minds of either class may, however, be intensely religious. They may equally desire atonement and reconciliation, and crave acquiescence and communion with the total soul of things. But the craving, when the mind is pent in to the hard facts, especially as science now reveals them, can breed pessimism, quite as easily as it breeds optimism when it inspires religious trust and fancy to wing their way to another and a better world.

That is why I call pessimism an essentially religious disease. The nightmare view of life has plenty of organic sources; but its great reflective source has at all times been the contradiction between the phenomena of nature and the craving of the heart to believe that behind nature there is a spirit whose expression nature is. What philosophers call "natural theology" has been one way of appeasing this craving; that poetry of nature in which our English literature is so rich has been another way. Now suppose a mind of the latter of our two classes, whose imagination is pent in consequently, and who takes its facts "hard"; suppose it, moreover, to feel strongly the craving for communion, and yet to realize how desperately difficult it is to construe the scientific order of nature either theologically or poetically—and what result can there be but inner discord and contradiction? Now this inner discord (merely as discord) can be relieved in either of two ways. The longing to read the facts religiously may cease, and leave the bare facts by themselves; or, supplementary facts may be discovered or believed in, which permit the religious reading to go on. These two ways of relief are the two stages of recovery, the two levels of escape from pessimism, to which I made allusion a moment ago, and which the sequel will, I trust, make more clear.

Starting then with nature, we naturally tend, if we have the religious craving, to say with Marcus Aurelius, "O Universe! What thou wishest I wish." Our sacred books and traditions tell us of one God who made heaven and earth, and, looking on them, saw that they were good. Yet, on more intimate acquaintance, the visible surfaces of heaven and earth refuse to be brought by us into any intelligible unity at all. Every phenomenon that we would praise there exists cheek by jowl with some contrary phenomenon that cancels all its religious effect upon the mind. Beauty and hideousness, love and cruelty, life and death keep house together in indissoluble partnership; and there gradually steals over us, instead of the old warm notion of a man-loving Deity, that of an awful power that neither hates nor loves, but rolls all things together meaninglessly to a common doom. This is an uncanny, a sinister, a nightmare view of life, and its peculiar *Unheimlichkeit*, or poisonousness, lies expressly in our holding two things together which cannot possibly agree—in our clinging, on the one hand, to the demand that there shall be a living spirit of the whole; and, on the other, to the belief that the course of nature must be such a spirit's adequate manifestation and expression. It is in the contradiction between the supposed being of a spirit that encompasses and owns us, and with which we ought to have some communion, and the character of such a spirit as revealed by the visible world's course, that this particular death-in-life paradox and this melancholy-breeding puzzle reside. Carlyle expresses the result in that chapter of his immortal *Sartor Resartus* entitled "The Everlasting No." "I lived," writes poor Teufelsdröckh, "in a continual, indefinite, pining fear; tremulous, pusillanimous, apprehensive of I knew not what: it seemed as if all things in the Heavens above and the Earth beneath would hurt me; as if the Heavens and the Earth were but boundless jaws of a devouring monster, wherein I, palpitating, waited to be devoured."

This is the first stage of speculative melancholy. No brute can have this sort of melancholy; no man who is irreligious can become its prey. It is the sick shudder of the frustrated religious demand, and not the mere necessary outcome of animal experience. Teufelsdröckh himself could have made shift to face the general chaos and bedevilment of this world's experiences very well, were he not the victim of an originally unlimited trust and affection towards them. If he might meet them piecemeal, with no suspicion of any whole expressing itself in them, shunning the bitter parts and husbanding the sweet ones, as the occasion served, and as the day was foul or fair, he could have zigzagged towards an easy end, and felt no obligation to make the air vocal with his lamentations. The mood of levity, of "I don't care," is for this world's ills a sovereign and practical anesthetic. But, no! Something deep down in Teufelsdröckh and in the rest of us tells us that there is a Spirit in things to which we owe allegiance, and for whose sake we must keep up the serious mood. And so the inner fever and discord also are kept up; for nature taken on her visible surface reveals no such Spirit, and beyond the facts of nature we are at the present stage of our inquiry not supposing ourselves to look.

Now, I do not hesitate frankly and sincerely to confess to you that this real and genuine discord seems to me to carry with it the inevitable bankruptcy of natural religion naively and simply taken. There were times when Leibnitzes with their heads buried in monstrous wigs could compose Theodicies, and when stall-fed officials of an established church could prove by the valves in the heart and the round ligament of the hip-joint the existence of a "Moral and

Intelligent Contriver of the World." But those times are past; and we of the nineteenth century, with our evolutionary theories and our mechanical philosophies, already know nature too impartially and too well to worship unreservedly any God of whose character she can be an adequate expression. Truly, all we know of good and duty proceeds from nature; but none the less so all we know of evil. Visible nature is all plasticity and indifference—a moral multiverse, as one might call it, and not a moral universe. To such a harlot we owe no allegiance; with her as a whole we can establish no moral communion; and we are free in our dealings with her several parts to obey or destroy, and to follow no law but that of prudence in coming to terms with such of her particular features as will help us to our private ends, If there be a divine Spirit of the universe, nature, such as we know her, cannot possibly be its ultimate word to man. Either there is no Spirit revealed in nature, or else it is inadequately revealed there; and (as all the higher religions have assumed) what we call visible nature, or this world, must be but a veil and surface-show whose full meaning resides in a supplementary unseen or other world.

I cannot help, therefore, accounting it on the whole a gain (though it may seem for certain poetic constitutions a very sad loss) that the naturalistic superstition, the worship of the God of nature, simply taken as such, should have begun to loosen its hold upon the educated mind. In fact, if I am to express my personal opinion unreservedly, I should say (in spite of its sounding blasphemous at first to certain ears) that the initial step towards getting into healthy ultimate relations with the universe is the act of rebellion against the idea that such a God exists. . . .

We are familiar enough in this community with the spectacle of persons exulting in their emancipation from belief in the God of their ancestral Calvinism— him who made the garden and the serpent, and pre-appointed the eternal fires of hell. Some of them have found humaner gods to worship, others are simply converts from all theology; but, both alike, they assure us that to have got rid of the sophistication of thinking they could feel any reverence or duty towards that impossible idol gave a tremendous happiness to their souls. Now, to make an idol of the spirit of nature, and worship it, also leads to sophistication; and in souls that are religious and would also be scientific the sophistication breeds a philosophical melancholy, from which the first natural step of escape is the denial of the idol; and with the downfall of the idol, whatever lack of positive joyousness may remain, there comes also the downfall of the whimpering and cowering mood. With evil simply taken as such, men can make short work, for their relations with it then are only practical. It looms up no longer so spectrally, it loses all its haunting and perplexing significance, as soon as the mind attacks the instances of it singly, and ceases to worry about their derivation from the "one and only Power."

Here, then, on this stage of mere emancipation from monistic superstition, the would-be suicide may already get encouraging answers to his question about the worth of life. There are in most men instinctive springs of vitality that respond healthily when the burden of metaphysical and infinite responsibility rolls off. The certainty that you now may step out of life whenever you please, and that to do so is not blasphemous or monstrous, is itself an immense relief. The thought of suicide is now no longer a guilty challenge and obsession.

"This little life is all we must endure,
The grave's most holy peace is ever sure,"

says Thomson; adding, "I ponder these thoughts and they comfort me." Meanwhile we can always stand it for twenty-four hours longer, if only to see what to-morrow's newspaper will contain, or what the next postman will bring.

But far deeper forces than this mere vital curiosity are arousable, even in the pessimistically-tending mind; for where the loving and admiring impulses are dead, the hating and fighting impulses will still respond to fit appeals. This evil which we feel so deeply is something that we can also help to overthrow; for its sources, now that no "Substance" or "Spirit" is behind them, are finite, and we can deal with each of them in turn. It is, indeed, a remarkable fact that sufferings and hardships do not, as a rule, abate the love of life; they seem, on the contrary, usually to give it a keener zest. The sovereign source of melancholy is repletion. Need and struggle are what excite and inspire us; our hour of triumph is what brings the void. Not the Jews of the captivity, but those of the days of Solomon's glory are those from whom the pessimistic utterances in our Bible come. Germany, when she lay trampled beneath the hoofs of Bonaparte's troopers, produced perhaps the most optimistic and idealistic literature that the world has seen; and not till the French "milliards" [at the end of fighting after the Franco-Prussian War and the Paris Commune] were distributed after 1871 did pessimism overrun the country in the shape in which we see it there to-day. The history of our own race is one long commentary on the cheerfulness that comes with fighting ills. . . .

What are our woes and sufferance compared with these? Does not the recital of such a fight so obstinately waged against such odds fill us with resolution against our petty powers of darkness—machine politicians, spoilsmen, and the rest? Life is worth living, no matter what it bring, if only such combats may be carried to successful terminations and one's heel set on the tyrant's throat. To the suicide, then, in his supposed world of multifarious and immoral nature, you can appeal—and appeal in the name of the very evils that make his heart sick there—to wait and see his part of the battle out. And the consent to live on, which you ask of him under these circumstances, is not the sophistical "resignation" which devotees of cowering religions preach: it is not resignation in the sense of licking a despotic Deity's hand. It is, on the contrary, a resignation based on manliness and pride. So long as your would-be suicide leaves an evil of his own unremedied, so long he has strictly no concern with evil in the abstract and at large. The submission which you demand of yourself to the general fact of evil in the world, your apparent acquiescence in it, is here nothing but the conviction that evil at large is none of your business until your business with your private particular evils is liquidated and settled up. A challenge of this sort, with proper designation of detail, is one that need only be made to be accepted by men whose normal instincts are not decayed; and your reflective, would-be suicide may easily be moved by it to face life with a certain interest again. The sentiment of honor is a very penetrating thing. When you and I, for instance, realize how many innocent beasts have had to suffer in cattle-cars and slaughter-pens and lay down their lives that we might grow up, all fattened and clad, to sit together here in comfort and carry on this discourse, it does, indeed, put our relation to the universe in a more solemn light. "Does not," as a young Amherst philosopher (Xenos Clark, now dead) once wrote, "the acceptance of a happy life on such conditions involve a point of honor?" Are we not bound to take some suffering upon ourselves, to do some self-denying service with our lives, in return for all those lives upon which ours are built? To hear this question is to answer it in but one possible way, if one have a normally constituted heart.

Thus, then, we see that mere instinctive curiosity, pugnacity, and honor may make life on a purely naturalistic basis seem worth living from day to day to men who have cast away all metaphysics in order to get rid of hypochondria, but who are resolved to owe nothing as yet to religion and its more positive gifts. A poor halfway stage, some of you may be inclined to say; but at least you must grant it to be an honest stage; and no man should dare to speak meanly of these instincts which are our nature's best equipment, and to which religion herself must in the last resort address her own peculiar appeals.

And now, in turning to what religion may have to say to the question, I come to what is the soul of my discourse. Religion has meant many things in human history; but when from now onward I use the word I mean to use it in the supernaturalist sense, as declaring that the so-called order of nature, which constitutes this world's experience, is only one portion of the total universe, and that there stretches beyond this visible world an unseen world of which we now know nothing positive, but in its relation to which the true significance of our present mundane life consists. A man's religious faith (whatever more special items of doctrine it may involve) means for me essentially his faith in the existence of an unseen order of some kind in which the riddles of the natural order may be found explained. In the more developed religions the natural world has always been regarded as the mere scaffolding or vestibule of a truer, more eternal world, and affirmed to be a sphere of education, trial, or redemption. In these religions, one must in some fashion die to the natural life before one can enter into life eternal. The notion that this physical world of wind and water, where the sun rises and the moon sets, is absolutely and ultimately the divinely aimed-at and established thing, is one which we find only in very early religions, such as that of the most primitive Jews. It is this natural religion (primitive still, in spite of the fact that poets and men of science whose good-will exceeds their perspicacity keep publishing it in new editions tuned to our contemporary ears) that, as I said a while ago, has suffered definitive bankruptcy in the opinion of a circle of persons, amongst whom I must count myself, and who are growing more numerous every day. For such persons the physical order of nature, taken simply as science knows it, cannot be held to reveal any one harmonious spiritual intent. It is mere *weather,* as Chauncey Wright called it, doing and undoing without end.

Now I wish to make you feel, if I can in the short remainder of this hour, that we have a right to believe the physical order to be only a partial order; that we have a right to supplement it by an unseen spiritual order which we assume on trust, if only thereby life may seem to us better worth living again. But as such a trust will seem to some of you sadly mystical and execrably unscientific, I must first say a word or two to weaken the veto which you may consider that science opposes to our act.

There is included in human nature an ingrained naturalism and materialism of mind which can only admit facts that are actually tangible. Of this sort of mind the entity called "science" is the idol. Fondness for the word "scientist" is one of the notes by which you may know its votaries; and its short way of killing any opinion that it disbelieves in is to call it "unscientific." It must be granted that there is no slight excuse for this. Science has made such glorious leaps in the last three hundred years, and extended our knowledge of nature so enormously both in general and in detail; men of science, moreover, have as a class displayed such admirable virtues that it is no wonder if the worshippers of science lose their head. In this very University, accordingly, I have heard more than one teacher say that all the fundamental conceptions of truth have already been found by science, and that the future has only the details of the picture to fill in. But the slightest reflection on the real conditions will suffice to show how barbaric such notions are. They show such a lack of scientific imagination, that it is hard to see how one who is actively advancing any part of science can make a mistake so crude. Think how many absolutely new scientific conceptions have arisen in our own generation, how many new problems have been formulated that were never thought of before, and then cast an eye upon the brevity of science's career. It began with Galileo, not three hundred years ago. Four thinkers since Galileo, each informing his successor of what discoveries his own lifetime had seen achieved, might have passed the torch of science into our hands as we sit here in this room. Indeed, for the matter of that, an audience much smaller than the present one, an audience of some five or six score people, if each person in it could speak for his own generation, would carry us away to the black unknown of the human species, to days without a document or monument to tell their tale. Is it credible that such a mushroom knowledge, such a growth overnight as this, can represent more than the minutest glimpse of what the universe will really prove to be when adequately understood? No! Our science is a drop, our ignorance a sea. Whatever else be certain, this at least is certain—that the world of our present natural knowledge is enveloped in a larger world of some sort of whose residual properties we at present can frame no positive idea.

Agnostic positivism, of course, admits this principle theoretically in the most cordial terms, but insists that we must not turn it to any practical use. We have no right, this doctrine tells us, to dream dreams, or suppose anything about the unseen part of the universe, merely because to do so may be for what we are pleased to call our highest interests. We must always wait for sensible evidence for our beliefs; and where such evidence is inaccessible we must frame no hypotheses whatever. Of course this is a safe enough position *in abstracto*. If a thinker had no stake in the unknown, no vital needs, to live or languish according to what the unseen world contained, a philosophic neutrality and refusal to believe either one way or the other would be his wisest cue. But, unfortunately, neutrality is not only inwardly difficult, it is also outwardly unrealizable, where our relations to an alternative are practical and vital. This is because, as the psychologists tell us, belief and doubt are living attitudes, and involve conduct on our part. Our only way, for example, of doubting, or refusing to believe, that a certain thing *is*, is continuing to act as if it were *not*. If, for instance, I refuse to believe that the room is getting cold, I leave the windows open and light no fire just as if it still were warm. If I doubt that you are worthy of my confidence, I keep you uninformed of all my secrets just as if you were *unworthy* of the same. If I doubt the need of insuring my house, I leave it uninsured as much as if I believed there were no need. And so if I must not believe that the world is divine, I can only express that refusal by declining ever to act distinctively as if it were so, which can only mean acting on certain critical occasions as if it were not so, or in an irreligious way. There are, you see, inevitable occasions in life when inaction is a kind of action, and must count as action, and when not to be for is to be practically against; and in all such cases strict and consistent neutrality is an unattainable thing.

And, after all, is not this duty of neutrality where only our inner interests would lead us to believe, the most ridiculous of commands? Is it not sheer dogmatic folly to say that our inner interests can have no real connection with the forces that the hidden world may contain? In other cases divinations based on inner interests have proved prophetic enough. Take science itself! Without an imperious inner demand on our part for ideal logical and mathematical harmonies, we should never have attained to proving that such harmonies lie hidden between all the chinks and interstices of the crude natural world. Hardly a law has been established in science, hardly a fact ascertained, which was not first sought after, often with sweat and blood, to gratify an inner need. Whence such needs come from we do not know: we find them in us, and biological psychology so far only classes them with Darwin's "accidental variations." But the inner need of believing that this world of nature is a sign of something more spiritual and eternal than itself is just as strong and authoritative in those who feel it, as the inner need of uniform laws of causation ever can be in a professionally scientific head. The toil of many generations has proved the latter need prophetic. Why may not the former one be prophetic, too? And if needs of ours outrun the visible universe, why may not that be a sign that an invisible universe is there? What, in short, has authority to debar us from trusting our religious demands? Science as such assuredly has no authority, for she can only say what is, not what is not; and the agnostic "thou shalt not believe without coercive sensible evidence" is simply an expression (free to anyone to make) of private personal appetite for evidence of a certain peculiar kind.

Now, when I speak of trusting our religious demands, just what do I mean by "trusting"? Is the word to carry with it license to define in detail an invisible world, and to anathematize and excommunicate those whose trust is different? Certainly not! Our faculties of belief were not primarily given us to make orthodoxies and heresies withal; they were given us to live by. And to trust our religious demands means first of all to live in the light of them, and to act as if the invisible world which they suggest were real. It is a fact of human nature, that men can live and die by the help of a sort of faith that goes without a single dogma or definition. The bare assurance that this natural order is not ultimate but a mere sign or vision, the external staging of a many-storied universe, in which spiritual forces have the last word and are eternal— this bare assurance is to such men enough to make life seem worth living in spite of every contrary presumption suggested by its circumstances on the natural plane. Destroy this inner assurance, however, vague as it is, and all the light and radiance of existence is extinguished for these persons at a stroke. Often enough the wild-eyed look at life—the suicidal mood—will then set in.

And now the application comes directly home to you and me. Probably to almost every one of us here the most adverse life would seem well worth living, if we only could be certain that our bravery and patience with it were terminating and eventuating and bearing fruit somewhere in an unseen spiritual world. But granting we are not certain, does it then follow that a bare trust in such a world is a fool's paradise and lubberland, or rather that it is a living attitude in which we are free to indulge? Well, we are free to trust at our own risks anything that is not impossible, and that can bring analogies to bear in its behalf. That the world of physics is probably not absolute, all the converging multitude of arguments that make in favor of idealism tend to prove; and that our whole physical life may lie soaking in a spiritual atmosphere, a dimension of being that we at present have no organ for apprehending, is vividly suggested to us by the analogy of the life of our domestic animals. Our dogs, for example, are in our human life but not of it. They witness hourly the outward body of events whose inner meaning cannot, by any possible operation, be revealed to their intelligence—events in which they themselves often play the cardinal part. My terrier bites a teasing boy, for example, and the father demands damages. The dog may be present at every step of the negotiations, and see the money paid, without an inkling of what it all means, without a suspicion that it has anything to do with him; and he never can know in his natural dog's life. Or take another case which used greatly to impress me in my medical-student days. Consider a poor dog whom they are vivisecting in a laboratory. He lies strapped on a board and shrieking at his executioners, and to his own dark consciousness is literally in a sort of hell. He cannot see a single redeeming ray in the whole business; and yet all these diabolical-seeming events are often controlled by human intentions with which, if his poor benighted mind could only be made to catch a glimpse of them, all that is heroic in him would religiously acquiesce. Healing truth, relief to future sufferings of beast and man, are to be bought by them. It may be genuinely a process of redemption. Lying on his back on the board there he may be performing a function incalculably higher than any that prosperous canine life admits of; and yet, of the whole performance, this function is the one portion that must remain absolutely beyond his ken.

Now turn from this to the life of man. In the dog's life we see the world invisible to him because we live in both worlds. In human life, although we only see our world, and his within it, yet encompassing both these worlds a still wider world may be there, as unseen by us as our world is by him; and to believe in that world may be the most essential function that our lives in this world have to perform. But "*may* be! *may* be!" one now hears the positivist contemptuously exclaim; "what use can a scientific life have for maybes?" Well, I reply, the "scientific" life itself has much to do with maybes, and human life at large has everything to do with them. So far as man stands for anything, and is productive or originative at all, his entire vital function may be said to have to deal with maybes. Not a victory is gained, not a deed of faithfulness or courage is done, except upon a maybe; not a service, not a sally of generosity, not a scientific exploration or experiment or text-book, that may not be a mistake. It is only by risking our persons from one hour to another that we live at all. And often enough our faith beforehand in an uncertified result is the only thing that makes the result come true. Suppose, for instance, that you are climbing a mountain, and have worked yourself into a position from which the only escape is by a terrible leap. Have faith that you can successfully make it, and your feet are nerved to its accomplishment. But mistrust yourself, and think of all the sweet things you have heard the scientists say of maybes, and you will hesitate so long that, at last, all unstrung and trembling, and launching yourself in a moment of despair, you roll in the abyss. In such a case (and it belongs to an enormous class), the part of wisdom as well as of courage is to believe what is in the line of your needs, for only by such belief is the need fulfilled. Refuse to believe, and you shall indeed be right, for you shall irretrievably perish. But believe, and again you shall be right, for you shall save yourself. You make one or the other of two possible universes true by your trust or mistrust—both universes having been only maybes, in this particular, before you contributed your act.

Now, it appears to me that the question whether life is worth living is subject to conditions logically much like these. It does, indeed, depend on you the liver. If you surrender to the nightmare view and crown the evil edifice by your own suicide, you have indeed made a picture totally black. Pessimism, completed by your act, is true beyond a doubt, so far as your world goes. Your mistrust of life has removed whatever worth your own enduring existence might have given to it; and now, throughout the whole sphere of possible influence of that existence, the mistrust has proved itself to have had divining power. But suppose, on the other hand, that instead of giving way to the nightmare view you cling to it that this world is not the ultimatum. Suppose you find yourself a very well-spring, as Wordsworth says, of

> "Zeal, and the virtue to exist by faith
> As soldiers live by courage; as, by strength
> Of heart, the sailor fights with roaring seas."

Suppose, however thickly evils crowd upon you, that your unconquerable subjectivity proves to be their match, and that you find a more wonderful joy than any passive pleasure can bring in trusting ever in the larger whole. Have you not now made life worth living on these terms? What sort of a thing would life really be, with your qualities ready for a tussle with it, if it only brought fair weather and gave these higher faculties of yours no scope? Please remember that optimism and pessimism are definitions of the world, and that our own reactions on the world, small as they are in bulk, are integral parts of the whole thing, and necessarily help to determine the definition. They may even be the decisive elements in determining the definition. A large mass can have its unstable equilibrium overturned by the addition of a feather's weight; a long phrase may have its sense reversed by the addition of the three letters n-o-t. This life is worth living, we can say, since it is what we make it, from the moral point of view; and we are determined to make it from that point of view, so far as we have anything to do with it, a success.

Now, in this description of faiths that verify themselves I have assumed that our faith in an invisible order is what inspires those efforts and that patience which make this visible order good for moral men. Our faith in the seen world's goodness (goodness now meaning fitness for successful moral and religious life) has verified itself by leaning on our faith in the unseen world. But will our faith in the unseen world similarly verify itself? Who knows?

Once more it is a case of maybe; and once more maybes are the essence of the situation. I confess that I do not see why the very existence of an invisible world may not in part depend on the personal response which any one of us may make to the religious appeal. God himself, in short, may draw vital strength and increase of very being from our fidelity. For my own part, I do not know what the sweat and blood and tragedy of this life mean, if they mean anything short of this. If this life be not a real fight, in which something is eternally gained for the universe by success, it is no better than a game of private theatricals from which one may withdraw at will. But it feels like a real fight—as if there were something really wild in the universe which we, with all our idealities and faithfulnesses, are needed to redeem; and first of all to redeem our own hearts from atheisms and fears. For such a half-wild, halfsaved universe our nature is adapted. The deepest thing in our nature is this *Binnenleben* (as a German doctor lately has called it)[literally, "inner life" or "internal life"], this dumb region of the heart in which we dwell alone with our willingnesses and unwillingnesses, our faiths and fears. As through the cracks and crannies of caverns those waters exude from the earth's bosom which then form the fountain-heads of springs, so in these crepuscular depths of personality the sources of all our outer deeds and decisions take their rise. Here is our deepest organ of communication with the nature of things; and compared with these concrete movements of our soul all abstract statements and scientific arguments—the veto, for example, which the strict positivist pronounces upon our faith—sound to us like mere chatterings of the teeth. For here possibilities, not finished facts, are the realities with which we have actively to deal; and to quote my friend William Salter, of the Philadelphia Ethical Society, "as the essence of courage is to stake one's life on a possibility, so the essence of faith is to believe that the possibility exists."

These, then, are my last words to you: Be not afraid of life. Believe that life is worth living, and your belief will help create the fact. The "scientific proof" that you are right may not be clear before the day of judgment (or some stage of being which that expression may serve to symbolize) is reached. But the faithful fighters of this hour, or the beings that then and there will represent them, may then turn to the faint-hearted, who here decline to go on, with words like those with which Henry IV greeted the tardy Crillon after a great victory had been gained: "Hang yourself, brave Crillon! We fought at Arques, and you were not there."

— 18 —

In His Steps: A Social Gospel Novel

Janet C. Olson

The social gospel was one form of "social Christianity," a group of movements that started in the 1870s and, by the turn of the century, had changed the face of American Protestantism. The most important characteristics of social Christianity were a rejection of traditional Protestant individualism (which had led most denominations to treat such conditions as poverty and alcoholism as the result of sin) and an acceptance of social responsibility for changing the circumstances that cause misery. Some middle-class Protestants, unsatisfied with seeking individual salvation, began to work for the salvation of society as a whole. Social Christians no longer waited for the Kingdom of God as a reward of the afterlife but instead believed that it could be achieved on earth through social justice.

Social Christians shared many values and goals with the secular reformers of the time—socialists, labor organizers, Populists, and Progressives—who strove to counteract the negative impact of capitalism, industrialization, and urbanization on American society. Although social Christianity included secular writers, educators, and economists, as well as clerical leaders, it promoted a social conscience within a religious context. Social Christians recognized that the church would have to exchange its tradition of passive worship for an active living-out of the gospel message in order to meet the needs of the modern world. The social Christian motto, based on Matthew 7:12 and Luke 6:31 in the New Testament, was the Golden Rule: "Do unto others as you would have others do unto you."

Within a framework of shared assumptions about the biblical basis for social responsibility, Protestant social Christianity encompassed a range of approaches. Its radical wing, the Christian Socialists, believed that Jesus Christ was the first socialist and that an economic revolution was required in order to bring about a new heaven on earth. The more conservative members taught what came to be known as the "social gospel," which called for sacrifice and service but stopped short of the redistribution of wealth. The first denominations to promote social Christian thinking were the Episcopalians and the Congregationalists, probably because of their traditions of moral responsibility and missionizing. In later years, evangelical denominations such as the Baptists and Methodists took the lead, incorporating the social gospel into their efforts to bring salvation and regeneration to the lost.

The social Christian impulse emerged from a number of influences. In Germany, a new scientific biblical scholarship known as "higher criticism" placed scripture in historical context and paved the way for a reemphasis on Jesus' social teachings. The writings of the English Christian Socialists of the 1840s, who had perceived and reacted against social injustice in the new industrial world, were dusted off and read anew. Liberal theologians applied religion to the problems of everyday life and encouraged their students to take courses in new fields, such as sociology. Urban clergymen experienced firsthand the wretched working and living conditions of the poor and recognized the limitations of a religion that ignored injustice in the material world. Protestant clergymen were also concerned about the perceived dwindling of congregations; they realized that they needed to address topical issues in order to retain their constituents, especially among the alienated working class.

Not all Protestants sanctioned social Christianity. Traditionalists disputed liberal theology and feared that ministers actively pursuing reforms in the worldly realm were encouraging secularization. Nevertheless, by the 1890s, Protestant seminaries were teaching a liberal theology that emphasized the presence of God within the material world, not just beyond it. By the first decade of the twentieth century, the church had established itself as an agent of social as well as spiritual betterment. Settlement houses and "full-service" institutional churches were providing social services that went far beyond traditional worship services and charitable efforts aimed at the "deserving" poor. The social gospel was explicitly expressed in the creeds of the new interdenominational federations that were formed to present a united front in the face of secular pressures.

Americans were exposed to social Christianity in many ways from many sources. Sermons by popular preachers of the social gospel, such as Washington Gladden and Walter Rauschenbusch, were widely printed for those who could not hear them in person. The political platform of Toledo mayor Samuel "Golden Rule" Jones made news in the 1890s. Social Christian ideas were expressed in tracts and Bible lessons, in popular nonfiction books on economics or on applied Christianity, and, more significantly, in the form of social gospel novels.

Social gospel novels followed a tradition of pious fiction that had been part of American popular culture since the beginning of the nineteenth century. By couching a moral text within a work of fiction, writers could stir the emotions of a wide audience—a technique exemplified by Harriet Beecher Stowe in *Uncle Tom's Cabin* (1852). To the dismay of many religious leaders, novels took on an important role in teaching religion beyond the auspices of the church. Religious novels were written both by professional authors and by clergymen who had noted the success of incorporating fictional narratives into their sermons. While antebellum religious novels told of individual spiritual quests and taught conformity with the prevailing Protestant creed, post–Civil War novels treated the problems of the individual in society and taught readers that religion could help them advance in the business and social world. By the late 1880s, religious novels often preached social gospel principles with the hope of inspiring readers to action in the interest of society as a whole.

In 1902 Charles M. Sheldon (1857–1946), Congregationalist minister and author, summed up the goal of social gospel novels. He wrote that "the use of fiction for the purpose of inspiration—that is, to promote reforms, to incite to any kind of nobler action, to show up the sins of humanity, not as a critic but as a philanthropist, is the highest office of fiction. . . . there is some defect of a serious character in any book of purpose which does not leave with the reader some desire to carry that purpose out." The formula of a social gospel novel combined melo-drama with social criticism and an implicit call to arms. The typical plot introduced a protagonist whose insulated, middle-class peace of mind is shattered when he or she is dramatically confronted with the poverty and despair of a working-class char-acter. The shaken hero or heroine investigates the circumstances, acknowledges the consequences of unethical industrial capitalism and religious apathy, and finally rises to accept personal moral responsibility as a Christian and a citizen. While the main characters are practicing Christians (whose specific denominational affilia-tion is downplayed), the oppressed people they meet have been disillusioned by the hypocrisy of mainstream religion. Ultimately, the middle-class characters redis-cover the simple, Christlike messages of love and brotherhood. By devoting their services and a portion of their worldly goods to social justice, they hope to restore the workingman's faith in true Christianity.

This formula was very successful. By offering engrossing plots and characters with whom readers could identify, the authors of social gospel novels could point out errors and suggest possible solutions without explicitly indicting the audience for its own sins. Within a familiar setting, they could introduce new ideas and per-suade the reader that he or she could play a role in shaping a better world. Although the simplistic, programmatic messages, sentimental plots, and poor writing of social gospel novels were deplored by literary critics and theological traditionalists alike, they sold remarkably well in the United States and in England.

The outstanding example of the social gospel novel in terms of popularity, sales, and life span is Charles M. Sheldon's *In His Steps* (1897). The novel began its long life as a serial "sermon-story," one of many that Sheldon had composed in order to attract his Topeka, Kansas, congregation to Sunday evening services. Sheldon's sermon-stories were fictional tales that taught a moral lesson. He would read one chapter each week, holding the audience's interest with mild cliff-hangers, familiar situations, and satisfying love stories wrapped around a message of social respon-sibility. These sermon-stories were so successful that they drew listeners from other churches in Topeka and were published in religious magazines. During the summer of 1896, Sheldon entranced his congregation with a sermon-story about a minister who, along with members of his congregation, pledges to follow "in His steps" by prefacing all decisions with the question, "What would Jesus do?"

"In His Steps" was immediately published as a serial in the weekly Christian mag-azine *The Advance*. In June 1897, Advance Publishing Company issued the story in book form. It was instantly popular, selling hundreds of thousands of copies. These figures soared even higher when a number of publishing houses took advantage of a flaw in Advance's copyright terms. Multiple editions began to appear, and eventually the story was issued in every format from serial to pamphlet to hardbound book. During Sheldon's lifetime, *In His Steps* sold around eight million copies, and through the years the book has been published in over seventy editions (counting only the English-language versions), of which at least ten are still in print. Since sales figures do not reflect the number of readers per copy, the total number of people who have read the book cannot even be estimated.

In many ways, *In His Steps* is little different from the many other social gospel novels published in the last quarter of the nineteenth century and the early years of the twentieth. The plot is simplistic, the dialogue awkward, and the message heavy-handed. What accounts for the popularity and longevity of *In His Steps*? First, Sheldon's sincerity transcends the banality of his writing. Like most social Christians, Sheldon believed that people educated about problems would wish to solve them, and his optimism is manifested in the positive, hopeful ending of *In His Steps*. Second, although the book contains much moralizing and some explicit sermonizing, it is still a novel. Sheldon spins a compelling tale and peoples it with characters tailored to inspire sympathetic identification among middle-class readers. Other characters are colorful enough to sustain interest, and all are interconnected through plot twists and romance.

Most important, the lesson of *In His Steps* is uncomplicated, direct, and taught in an appealing way. Sheldon firmly believed in—and had demonstrated with his sermon-stories—the ability of fiction to inspire its readers both to improve their own lives and to better the lives of those around them. His method was to teach by example through the lives of his fictional characters. Readers and characters alike are presented with the deceptively simple challenge of asking themselves, "What would Jesus do?" Yet, taken to heart and acted on every day, the task is far from easy. The reader will ask first, "How do I know what Jesus would do in my case?" and second, "How do I go about it?" Here Sheldon's teaching technique is at its most effective. Rather than preach or spell out a standard program for facing these challenges, he is careful to show the novel's characters experiencing the same confusion about how to proceed, so that the reader can learn from their tentative efforts. He makes it clear that the process is complex, involving a growing understanding of Jesus' life and teaching, and a growing need to give something to the world. The fact that the story's fictional minister is himself working out his own salvation day by day is evidence that there are no easy answers.

Central to the theme of *In His Steps* is a reminder to readers of their own responsibility for the causes and results of poverty. As a social Christian, Sheldon rejected the assumption that poverty is the result of sin. He taught that most poor people were trapped by circumstance, and that the well-off were responsible for creating many of the barriers that obstructed the poor. Low wages and substandard housing—situations controlled by employers and tenement owners who called themselves good Christians—were as significant in perpetuating the cycle of poverty as intemperance and ignorance. Although Sheldon strongly advocated temperance throughout his life, he did not condemn the poor for drinking, but showed that tavern owners and liquor producers facilitated their addiction.

To promote the social gospel message that the causes of poverty are environmental, not inherent, Sheldon represented the poor as the mirror image of his middle-class audience, eager to adopt its middle-class values if they could. Laborers wanted to work, turning to atheism, socialism, and violence only when they were prevented from earning a living wage. Lower-class men and women became drunkards and criminals only when they were abandoned by their natural protectors in the upper classes. The issue of shared values is simplified further because there are no immigrants among Sheldon's poor. (Nor are there African-Americans, even though Sheldon worked diligently to provide religious and social services to the African-American residents of Topeka.)

Sheldon's treatment of the poor reflects the ambivalent attitude of his readers, who feared the specter of unruly masses but could not welcome the poor and the laborer as class equals. The perception that the poor were merely disadvantaged middle-class citizens minimized their menace, but eliminating class distinctions was not the goal. By acknowledging their own responsibility for the persistence of poverty, middle-class Christians could control the solution just as they had controlled the problem. Sheldon's characters connect with poor individuals by teaching them Jesus' way; they combat poverty on a larger scale by funding educational programs, refusing to own tenements and saloons, and learning to treat laborers as brothers in Christ.

Still, even the poor who are the objects of concern in the novel remain shadowy figures, and the focus is distinctly on the spiritual development of the middle-class characters. In His Steps emphasizes the unselfishness, self-sacrifice, and "joyful suffering" that Sheldon considered to be essential elements of Christian discipleship. However, the new regimen is highly individualized. It is up to each character in the novel, or to each reader of the novel, to decide how Jesus would respond in a given situation. Of course, the choices Sheldon's characters make reflect his own understanding of the problems besetting society. But throughout In His Steps, Sheldon stresses that people must do what works best for themselves. Sheldon had great faith in people's ability to do as Jesus would do, once they understood the needs of the less fortunate around them. He believed that the more people thought about Jesus' life and actions, the more they would seek opportunities to give. The simplicity of Sheldon's message and his emphasis on a personal interpretation of Christlike action go far to account for the fact that In His Steps, alone among the many such novels published during the heyday of social Christianity, is still read for its inspirational qualities.

The plot of In His Steps adheres to the typical format of a social gospel novel: awakening, challenge, decision, action, sacrifice, and success. In a dramatic opening chapter, the congregation of the prosperous First Church of Raymond is startled out of its middle-class complacency when a grimy laborer interrupts the Reverend Henry Maxwell's Sunday service. The unemployed printer delivers a poignant speech (excerpted here as Selection 1) in which he questions the sincerity of those who listen to sermons and sing songs about following Jesus but have no intention of acting as Jesus did. The nameless man then collapses and is taken to the minister's home, where he dies. Reverend Maxwell is so affected by the dying man's words that, after much soul-searching, he puts a remarkable proposition to his congregants (Selection 2). He requests that willing members of the congregation join him in pledging to approach every decision by asking themselves what Jesus would do, and then by following in His steps to the best of their abilities.

The first two-thirds of *In His Steps* tells the story of several of the members of the congregation who decide to take the pledge. They are a representative selection from middle-class society, including a newspaper editor, a professor, a wealthy young woman, a merchant, a talented singer, and a railroad executive. Much of this portion of the book depicts the characters' efforts to understand the pledge they have undertaken—first, how to decide what Jesus would do (Selection 3), and second, how to act on the decision, even when it conflicts with social norms. Sheldon shows each character discussing the difficulties and then working out an individual plan founded on a developing understanding of Jesus' life and work (Selections 4a, 4b, and 4c). In some cases, characters make lists of the steps they plan to take (Selection 4d).

The new choices involve threats to the comfortable social and financial situations of the characters. The railroad executive loses his job and alienates his family, the newspaper editor loses his advertisers, and the heiress loses her society friends. In this way, Sheldon's readers learn that these decisions are not easy to make, and that they entail a measure of suffering and sacrifice. Despite the trials that each character endures, however, all are determined to persevere along the path they have chosen.

In the last section of the book, with the initial band of followers committed to asking themselves what Jesus would do, the plot shifts to Chicago to show how the movement that changed a town could work in a big city. New characters—a speculating financier, a calculating socialite, a common criminal, and a respectable citizen who owns tenements—reflect the special problems of a metropolis. On a visit to a friend from seminary days who is now a society minister in Chicago, Henry Maxwell attends a debate at a settlement house. When he suggests that members of the audience take the pledge to do as Jesus would do, he is confronted with a torrent of negative reactions to religion from embittered laborers, including a black-bearded Socialist (Selection 5). Somehow Maxwell finds the courage to respond with a stirring speech that vividly recapitulates the message of the social gospel (Selection 6). Later, heartened by the positive response to his oration, Maxwell experiences a vision that reveals the destinies of the followers who took the pledge in Raymond and Chicago. As the book ends, Maxwell's vision has become a prophecy of far-reaching consequences for a nation of people who have chosen to follow "in His steps" (Selection 7).

The selections here are from Charles M. Sheldon, *In His Steps* (1897; reprint, Grand Rapids, Mich.: Zondervan, 1970). The title of the book comes from

1 Peter 2:21: "For hereunto were ye called: because Christ also suffered for you, leaving you an example, that ye should follow his steps."

Further Reading

Charles M. Sheldon summarized the goal of the social gospel novel in "The Use and Abuse of Fiction," *Independent* 54 (April 24, 1902): 965–67. The standard history of the social gospel in the United States is Charles Howard Hopkins, *The Rise of the Social Gospel in American Protestantism, 1865–1915* (New Haven: Yale University Press, 1940). David S. Reynolds sets the social gospel novel in the context of religious fiction in *Faith in Fiction: The Emergence of Religious Literature in America* (Cambridge: Harvard University Press, 1981). On the subject of social gospel novels as a genre, see Grier Nicholl, "The Christian Social Novel and Social Gospel Evangelism," *Religion in Life* 34 (Autumn 1965): 548–61. Paul S. Boyer provides a different perspective on *In His Steps* and, by extension, other social gospel novels in "*In His Steps*: A Reappraisal," *American Quarterly* 23 (Spring 1971): 60–78. An excellent biography of Charles Sheldon is Timothy Miller's *Following in His Steps: A Biography of Charles M. Sheldon* (Knoxville: University of Tennessee Press, 1987).

SELECTION 1

Pages 8–10

"The minister said," here the man turned about and looked up at the pulpit, "that it is necessary for the disciple of Jesus to follow His steps, and he said the steps are 'obedience, faith, love and imitation.' But I did not hear him tell you just what he meant that to mean, especially the last step. What do you Christians mean by following the steps of Jesus?

"I've tramped through this city for three days trying to find a job; and in all that time I've not had a word of sympathy or comfort except from your minister here, who said he was sorry for me and hoped I would find a job somewhere. . . . Of course, I understand you can't all go out of your way to hunt up jobs for other people like me. I'm not asking you to; but what I feel puzzled about is, what is meant by following Jesus. What do you mean when you sing 'I'll go with Him, with Him, all the way?' Do you mean that you are suffering and denying yourselves and trying to save lost, suffering humanity just as I understand Jesus did? . . . Somehow I get puzzled when I see so many Christians living in luxury and singing 'Jesus, I my cross have taken, all to leave and follow Thee,' and remember how my wife died in a tenement in New York City, gasping for air and asking God to take the little girl too. Of course I don't expect you people can prevent every one from dying of starvation, lack of proper nourishment and tenement air, but what does following Jesus mean? I understand that Christian people own a good many of the tenements. A member of a church was the owner of the one where my wife died, and I have wondered if following Jesus all the way was true in his case. . . . It seems to me there's an awful lot of trouble in the world that somehow wouldn't exist if all the people who sing such songs went and lived them out. I suppose I don't understand. But what would Jesus do? Is that what you mean by following His steps? . . . "

The man suddenly gave a queer lurch over in the direction of the communion table and laid one grimy hand on it. . . . [He] passed his other hand across his eyes, and then, without any warning, fell heavily forward on his face, full length up the aisle. Henry Maxwell spoke:

"We will consider the service closed."

SELECTION 2

Page 15

"What I am going to propose now is something which ought not to appear unusual or at all impossible of execution. Yet I am aware that it will be so regarded by a large number, perhaps, of the members of this church. But in order that we may have a thorough understanding of what we are considering, I will put my proposition very plainly, perhaps bluntly. I want volunteers from the First Church who will pledge themselves, earnestly and honestly for an entire year, not to do anything without first asking the question, 'What would Jesus do?' And after asking that question, each one will follow Jesus as exactly as he knows how, no matter what the result may be. I will of course include myself in this company of volunteers. . . . Our aim will be to act just as He would if He was in our places, regardless of immediate results. In other words, we propose to follow Jesus' steps as closely and as literally as we believe He taught His disciples to do. And those who volunteer to do this will pledge themselves for an entire year, beginning with to-day, so to act."

SELECTION 3

Pages 17–18

[Rachel asked:] "I am a little in doubt as to the source of our knowledge concerning what Jesus would do. Who is to decide for me just what He would do in my case? It is a different age. There are many perplexing questions in our civilization that are not mentioned in the teachings of Jesus. How am I going to tell what He would do?"

"There is no way that I know of," replied the pastor, "except as we study Jesus through the medium of the Holy Spirit. . . . [When] it comes to a genuine, honest, enlightened following of Jesus' steps, I cannot believe there will be any confusion either in our own minds or in the judgment of others. We must be free from fanaticism on one hand and too much caution on the other. If Jesus' example is the example for the world to follow, it certainly must be feasible to follow it."

SELECTION 4A. RACHEL WINSLOW, SINGER

Pages 55–57

[When Rachel announces that she will not pursue a career on the concert stage, her mother asks:] "Do you presume to sit in judgment on other people who go out to sing in this way? Do you presume to say they are doing what Christ would not do?"

"Mother, I wish you to understand me. I judge no one else; I condemn no other professional singer. I simply decide my own course. As I look at it, I have a conviction that Jesus would do something else."

"What else?" Mrs. Winslow had not yet lost her temper. . . . She was totally unprepared for Rachel's next remark.

"What? Something that will serve mankind where it most needs the service of song. Mother, I have made up my mind to use my voice in some way so as to satisfy my own soul that I am doing something better than pleasing fashionable audiences, or making money, or even gratifying my own love of singing. I am going to do something that will satisfy me when I ask: 'What would Jesus do?'. . ." [Rachel tells her mother that she plans to sing at revival meetings in the slums of Raymond.] "I want to do something that will cost me something in the way of sacrifice. I know you will not understand me. But I am hungry to suffer for something. What have we done all our lives for the suffering, sinning side of Raymond? How much have we denied ourselves or given of our personal ease and pleasure to bless the place in which we live or imitate the life of the Saviour of the world? Are we always to go on doing as society selfishly dictates, moving on its little narrow round of pleasures and entertainments, and never knowing the pain of things that cost?"

"Are you preaching at me?" asked Mrs. Winslow slowly. Rachel rose, and understood her mother's words.

"No. I am preaching at myself," she replied gently.

SELECTION 4B. DONALD MARSH, PRESIDENT OF LINCOLN COLLEGE

Pages 89–90

"'What would Jesus do in my place?' I have asked the question repeatedly since I made my promise. I have tried to satisfy myself that He would simply go on as I have done, attending to the duties of my college work, teaching the classes in Ethics and Philosophy. But I have not been able to avoid the feeling that He would do something more. That something is what I do not want to do. It will cause me genuine suffering to do it. I dread it with all my soul. . . .

"Maxwell, you and I belong to a class of professional men who have always avoided the duties of citizenship. We have lived in a little world of literature and scholarly seclusion, doing work we have enjoyed and shrinking from the disagreeable duties that belong to the life of the citizen. . . . 'What would Jesus do?' I have even tried to avoid an honest answer. I can no longer do so. My plain duty is to take a personal part in this coming election, go to the primaries, throw the weight of my influence, whatever it is, toward the nomination and election of good men, and plunge into the very depths of the entire horrible whirlpool of deceit, bribery, political trickery and saloonism as it exists in Raymond today.   I would sooner walk up to the mouth of a cannon any time than do this. . . . I would give almost any thing to be able to say, 'I do not believe Jesus would do anything of the sort.' But I am more and more persuaded that He would. This is where the suffering comes for me. It would not hurt me half so much to lose my position or my home. . . . I would so much prefer to remain quietly in my scholastic life with my classes in Ethics and Philosophy. But the call has come to me so plainly that I cannot escape. 'Donald Marsh, follow me. Do your duty as a citizen of Raymond at the point where your citizenship will cost you something. . . .' Maxwell, this is my cross, I must take it up or deny my Lord."

SELECTION 4C. VIRGINIA PAGE, HEIRESS

Page 95

Virginia was rapidly reaching a conclusion with respect to a large part of her money. She had talked it over with Rachel and they had been able to agree that if Jesus had a vast amount of money at His disposal He might do with some of it as Virginia planned [subsidizing the Raymond *Daily News* so that it can be published as a Christian paper]. At any rate they felt that whatever He might do in such case would have as large an element of variety in it as the differences in persons and circumstances. There could be no one fixed Christian way of using money. The rule that regulated its use was unselfish utility.

SELECTION 4D. MILTON WRIGHT, BUSINESSMAN

Page 76

"WHAT JESUS WOULD PROBABLY DO IN MILTON WRIGHT'S PLACE AS A BUSINESS MAN"

1. He would engage in the business first of all for the purpose of glorifying God, and not for the primary purpose of making money.

2. All money that might be made he would never regard as his own, but as trust funds to be used for the good of humanity.

3. His relations with all the persons in his employ would be the most loving and helpful. He could not help thinking of them in the light of souls to be saved. This thought would always be greater than his thought of making money in the business.

4. He would never do a single dishonest or questionable thing or try in any remotest way to get the advantage of any one else in the same business.

5. The principle of unselfishness and helpfulness in the business would direct all its details.

6. Upon this principle he would shape the entire plan of his relations to his employees, to the people who were his customers and to the general business world with which he was connected.

SELECTION 5

Pages 229–230

"This is all bosh, to my mind," began Carlsen [the Socialist leader], while his great bristling beard shook with the deep inward anger of the man. "The whole of our system is at fault. What we call civilization is rotten to the core. There is no use trying to hide it or cover it up. We live in an age of trusts and combines and capitalistic greed that means simply death to thousands of innocent men, women and children. I thank God, if there is a God—which I very much doubt— that I, for one, have never dared to marry and make a home. . . . And yet this city, and every other big city in this country, has its thousands of professed Christians who have all the luxuries and comforts. . . . I don't say that there aren't good men and women among them, but let the minister who has spoken to us here to-night go into any one of a dozen aristocratic churches I could name and pro- pose to the members to take any such pledge as the one he's mentioned here to- night, and see how quick the people would laugh at him for a fool or a crank or a fanatic. Oh, no! . . . We've got to have a new start in the way of government. The whole thing needs reconstructing. I don't look for any reform worth any- thing to come out of the churches. They are not with the people. They are with the aristocrats, with the men of money. The trusts and monopolies have their greatest men in the churches. What we need is a system that shall start from the common basis of socialism, founded on the rights of the common people."

SELECTION 6

Pages 235–237

"Is it true," continued Henry Maxwell, and his fine, thoughtful face glowed with a passion of appeal that stirred the people as they had seldom been

stirred, "is it true that the church of to-day, the church that is called after
Christ's own name, would refuse to follow Him at the expense of suffering, of
physical loss, of temporary gain? The statement was made at a large gathering
in the Settlement last week by a leader of workingmen that it was hopeless to
look to the church for any reform or redemption of society. On what was that
statement based? Plainly on the assumption that the church contains for the
most part men and women who think more of their own ease and luxury than
of the sufferings and needs and sins of humanity. How far is that true? Are the
Christians of America ready to have their discipleship tested? How about the
men who possess large wealth? Are they ready to take that wealth and use it as
Jesus would? How about the men and women of great talent? Are they ready
to consecrate that talent to humanity as Jesus undoubtedly would do?

"Is it not true that the call has come in this age for a new exhibition of Christian
discipleship? You who live in this great sinful city must know that better than I do.
Is it possible you can go your ways careless or thoughtless of the awful condition
of men and women and children who are dying, body and soul, for need of Christian help? Is it not a matter of concern to you personally that the saloon kills its
thousands more surely than war? Is it not a matter of personal suffering in some
form for you that thousands of able-bodied, willing men tramp the streets of this
city and all cities, crying for work and drifting into crime and suicide because they
cannot find it? Can you say that this is none of your business? Let each man look
after himself? Would it not be true, think you, that if every Christian in America
did as Jesus would do, society itself, the business world, yes, the very political system under which our commercial and governmental activity is carried on, would
be so changed that human suffering would be reduced to a minimum? . . .

"What would be the result if in this city every church member should begin
to do as Jesus would do? It is not easy to go into details of the result. But we all
know that certain things would be impossible that are now practiced by church
members. What would Jesus do in the matter of wealth? How would He spend
it? What principle would regulate His use of money? Would He be likely to live
in great luxury and spend ten times as much on personal adornment and entertainment as He spent to relieve the needs of suffering humanity? How would
Jesus be governed in the making of money? Would He take rentals from saloons
and other disreputable property, or even from tenement property that was so
constructed that the inmates had no such things as a home and no such possibility as privacy or cleanliness?

"What would Jesus do about the great army of unemployed and desperate who
tramp the streets and curse the church, or are indifferent to it, lost in the bitter
struggle for the bread that tastes bitter when it is earned on account of the desperate conflict to get it? Would Jesus care nothing for them? . . . Would He say
that it was none of His business? Would He excuse Himself from all
responsibility to remove the causes of such a condition? . . .

"It is the personal element that Christian discipleship needs to emphasize.
'The gift without the giver is bare.' The Christianity that attempts to suffer by

proxy is not the Christianity of Christ. Each individual Christian business man, citizen, needs to follow in His steps along the path of personal sacrifice to Him. There is not a different path to-day from that of Jesus' own times. It is the same path. The call of this dying century and of the new one soon to be, is a call for a new discipleship, a new following of Jesus, more like the early, simple, apostolic Christianity, when the disciples left all and literally followed the Master. Nothing but a discipleship of this kind can face the destructive selfishness of the age with any hope of overcoming it. There is a great quantity of nominal Christianity to-day. There is need of more of the real kind. We need revival of the Christianity of Christ. We have, unconsciously, lazily, selfishly, formally grown into a discipleship that Jesus himself would not acknowledge. . . .

"Are we ready to make and live a new discipleship? Are we ready to reconsider our definition of a Christian? What is it to be a Christian? It is to imitate Jesus. It is to do as He would do. It is to walk in His steps."

SELECTION 7

Pages 240–243

And this is what Henry Maxwell saw in this waking vision:

He saw himself, first, going back to the First Church in Raymond, living there in a simpler, more self-denying fashion than he had yet been willing to live, because he saw ways in which he could help others who were really dependent on him for help. He also saw, more dimly, that the time would come when his position as pastor of the church would cause him to suffer more on account of growing opposition to his interpretation of Jesus and His conduct. . . .

He saw President Marsh of the college using his great learning and his great influence to purify the city, to ennoble its patriotism, to inspire the young men and women who loved as well as admired him to lives of Christian service, always teaching them that education means great responsibility for the weak and the ignorant.

He saw Alexander Powers meeting with sore trials in his family life, with a constant sorrow in the estrangement of wife and friends, but still going his way in all honor, serving in all his strength the Master whom he had obeyed, even unto the loss of social distinction and wealth.

He saw Milton Wright, the merchant, . . . coming out of his reverses with clean Christian honor, to begin again and work up to a position where he could again be to hundreds of young men an example of what Jesus would do in business.

He saw Edward Norman, editor of the NEWS. . . creating a force in journalism that in time came to be recognized as one of the real factors of the nation to mold its principles and actually shape its policy, a daily illustration of the might of a Christian press, and the first of a series of such papers begun and carried on by other disciples who had also taken the pledge.

He saw Jasper Chase, who had denied his Master, growing into a cold, cynical, formal life, writing novels that were social successes, but each one with a sting in it, the reminder of his denial, the bitter remorse that, do what he would, no social success could remove. . . .

He saw Dr. Bruce and the Bishop going on with the Settlement work. He seemed to see the great blazing motto over the door enlarged, "What would Jesus do?" and by this motto every one who entered the Settlement walked in the steps of the Master.

He saw Burns and his companion and a great company of men like them, redeemed and giving in turn to others, conquering their passions by the divine grace, and proving by their daily lives the reality of the new birth even in the lowest and most abandoned. . . .

He thought he saw the church of Jesus in America open its heart to the moving of the Spirit and rise to the sacrifice of its ease and self-satisfaction in the name of Jesus. He thought he saw the motto, "What would Jesus do?" inscribed over every church door, and written on every church member's heart. . . .

He rose at last with the awe of one who has looked at heavenly things. He felt the human forces and the human sins of the world as never before. And with a hope that walks hand in hand with faith and love Henry Maxwell, disciple of Jesus, laid him down to sleep and dreamed of the regeneration of Christendom, and saw in his dream a church of Jesus without spot or wrinkle or any such thing, following him all the way, walking obediently in His steps.

Healing: Health, Happiness,
and the Miraculous

— 19 —

The Spiritual Meanings of Illness
in Eighteenth-Century New England

Kenneth P. Minkema

Today when we think of diseases we think of them clinically and biologically. Armed by modern science with extensive knowledge of the microscopic world of bacteria and with new and ever more potent vaccines, we have, relative to previous eras, an impressive awareness of how diseases are caused, how they are spread, and how to fight them. Thanks to great strides in medical research, the twentieth century saw the elimination of an unprecedented number of deadly diseases that had ravaged humankind for centuries. Nowadays, if you ask young people what polio, or rubella, or whooping cough is, the vast majority most likely have little or no notion of their symptoms and effects. At the same time, however, around the world we see the reappearance of diseases such as tuberculosis, and in the United States medical experts are concerned about the reintroduction of small pox. Inoculations for smallpox ended in this country decades ago, on the optimistic assumption that this excruciating disease was extinct. Now, with new strains of the smallpox bacterium reported abroad, epidemiologists fear that our stock of serum is too low and ineffective to safeguard our population.

Such reports temporarily shake our confidence in science to solve all our ills. On the whole, though, our ability to identify, contain, and even eradicate illnesses has had the effect of demystifying them. Diseases, we know, are the result of natural causes, insufficient hygiene, or the spread of viruses—of a "bug going around." To assert any spiritual significance or meaning to illness would seem, to many of us, ridiculous. Yet in some segments of our culture, disease is still seen as having religious import. This is particularly true in the case of Acquired Immune Deficiency Syndrome (AIDS); homosexuals and drug addicts who contract this disease, some judgmentally declare, are rightfully being punished by God for immorality.

Actually, attributing spiritual or religious meanings to illness was common among the first European settlers of our country, including the Puritans and their descendants who, beginning in the early seventeenth century, founded and inhabited the New England colonies. The documents presented here were written by men and women of varying ranks from that culture, whether for public consumption or personal meditation. Together, the documents reveal attitudes toward, and experiences of, illness in eighteenth-century Massachusetts and Connecticut, and provide a glimpse into a different way of viewing the natural world.

Our writers, like most of the New England colonists, were adherents to one variation or another of Calvinism, a brand of Protestantism named after John Calvin, one of the major figures of the Reformation of the early sixteenth century. Calvinism asserted the total depravity of humankind arising from original sin, contracted when Adam and Eve sinned in the Garden of Eden. The God of Calvin, and of the people of New England, was a God of absolute sovereignty, an all-powerful and all-righteous judge of the living and the dead, who demanded the implicit obedience and faith of anyone who sought to enter into heaven. Sinful human beings were totally dependent on the arbitrary and sovereign mercy of God for life, health, and salvation.

But Calvin's God was also a God of time and of history, who worked personally in the lives of individuals and of communities large and small in order to reveal divine purpose. There were many ways in which this divine activity manifested itself: through obviously supernatural occurrences such as individual conversions and large-scale revivals, but also through seemingly natural or human-made causes such as droughts, famines, wars, and, yes, illnesses and epidemics. It was up to individuals or groups of individuals to discern what God's message was in sending these things or allowing them to occur, and to model their actions accordingly.

This conception of God as intimately involved in the affairs of the world is summed up in one word that appears again and again in Puritan and post-Puritan documents: Providence. Providence identified the way in which God achieved divine will by working through events to achieve his desired outcomes. To show how important this concept was to Puritans, the word "Providence" was even used interchangeably with "God." The Puritans and their New England Calvinist descendants therefore espoused a providential view of history, which can be defined as God using or ordering temporal events in such a way as to further God's cause of redemption for believers (the Church) and bring about victory over God's enemies (the devil and his minions). In this view, history becomes nothing less than the stage on which the eternal struggle of good against evil is fought and eventually won by the forces of righteousness. Ultimately, all natural phenomena have significance in this larger drama.

Providential history could be experienced on the national, local, and even the individual level. God, it was believed, blessed obedience to divine law and punished disobedience. Nations and communities were judged collectively and given prosperity or calamity depending on how closely they followed God. The thermometer for gauging a society's spiritual health was an examination of its recent circumstances. For interpretations of events—for reading the signs of the times—

communities turned to their ministers, who would deliver sermons pronouncing the favor or judgment of God. These communal rituals were enacted several times a year on days set aside by government proclamation, such as days of fasting, election, and, as we still observe each autumn, thanksgiving. These regularly scheduled events were interspersed with specially called observations prompted by unusual occurrences such as fires, earthquakes, and epidemics.

On these occasions, crowds would turn out to hear a sermon in the way modern Americans flock to hear their favorite musical group. Our first selection illustrates the popularity of these events. The text, taken from a sermon of 1714 entitled *A Perfect Recovery,* by the famous Boston minister Cotton Mather, was preached following a measles epidemic. Mather wrote in his diary for January 21 that on the day he delivered *A Perfect Recovery* he "went forth into a vast auditory, where the glorious Lord was mightily present with me, in my beginning to discourse the things, which I thought seasonable for the town, relating to the late calamity and deliverance." The winter of 1713–14 had been a trying one in Boston. Among a population of about eleven thousand, several hundred people had died of measles. In a two-week period in November 1713, Mather himself had lost his wife and three children to the measles, with several others bedridden. Now came the opportunity to contemplate and learn from the calamity. Like doctors of the soul, ministers such as Mather would diagnose the people's sins and prescribe an antidote: repentance and reformation. Repentance meant acknowledging sinfulness, contention, envy, or another sin identified as odious. If the nation, province, or town was to thrive, the inhabitants would have to show their new awareness by reformation, changing their wicked behavior and following God's ways.

The entries in this part of this book are gathered under the rubric, "Health, Happiness, and the Miraculous." In commenting on the town's "recovery" from smallpox, Mather did not point to anything miraculous happening. In fact, according to the strictures of Puritan doctrine, he could not do so. Puritans were cessationists, which meant they believed that miracles and revelations had ended with the closing of the canon of sacred Scripture. Nonetheless, Mather's text—on Christ's healing of the blind man at the Pool of Siloam—and his exposition on it, conjure images of the miraculous. Introducing the sermon with this text set the stage for a review of extraordinary events filled with powerful meanings.

Mather's sermon was constructed in the classic Reformed mode. Following an exposition, or explanation of the biblical text on which the sermon was based, he moved into the doctrine, or pedagogical part of the sermon. Here he set forth several propositions, or things to be proved. The first proposition stated, baldly enough, that sin was the cause of sickness. Speaking at once metaphorically and in keeping with good Calvinist teachings about human nature, he asserted that "sin is the sickness of the soul." Yet (and here modern-day vilifiers of AIDS victims should take note) Mather warned that his hearers should not pass judgment on the sick, for not everyone who was ill was guilty of special sins. A case in point from the Bible was Job, who God allowed Satan to afflict. As in the instance of Job, who remained true to God throughout his ordeal, earthly disappointments, trials, pains, and other trials from God helped the sufferer grow in faith. For the afflicted's neighbors, the sick person could be a "pattern," even a hero of righteousness. Nothing happened for nothing; there was a reason and lesson in every occurrence, sent and intended by God. It was up to the persons involved to figure out what the reasons were.

The second proposition discussed how convalescents should act. First and foremost, they must acknowledge God as the author of their recovery and should offer God thanks and praise. Furthermore, they should strive to see God's "declared ends" in visiting them with sickness. Sickness, as Mather put it, was a "discipline" in which God purged what was bad in the person's body and spirit, much like alloy tried in a fire to burn away the dross and leave only pure gold. The final proposition described ways in which recovered persons should "improve," or learn from, their sickness. Here, reformation of behavior was key. Believers must try to sin no more, quit "special sins" for which God may have been particularly incensed, and learn "the skill of dying daily." If they did not, Mather warned, echoing the words of Jesus, "a worse thing will come upon you."

Having completed the doctrinal part of the sermon, Mather concluded with the application, in which the preacher "applied" the lessons to his hearers' own experiences. Here Mather adopted the sermonic formula of the jeremiad, named for the prophet Jeremiah, who denounced Israel's sins in great detail and threatened the judgment of God. Like the prophet, Puritan ministers would enumerate the people's sins and exhort them to repent and reform. Often these ministers would address themselves to segments of the congregation. On this occasion, Mather turned to the children in the audience, reminding those who had been ill of how they had resolved to improve their life if they became well.

In just a few years Mather was at the center of a controversy the likes of which New England had not seen since the Salem witchcraft trials. No doubt recalling the measles episode of 1714 and earlier epidemics, Mather advocated new countermeasures, especially inoculation, for fighting disease. These countermeasures proved to be highly contentious. To understand why, we must appreciate that the culture of colonial New England was steeped in traditional beliefs and practices, which died hard. For example, many people still operated with a Ptolemaic or earth-centered cosmology; for anyone to assert the Copernican view of a heliocentric solar system was considered controversial. Even a highly educated person like Judge Samuel Sewall, upon hearing Mather preach "of the sun being in the center of our system," remarked in his diary for December 23, 1714, "I think it inconvenient to assert such problems." In matters of health, few knew, for example, of the circulation of blood, and knowledge of bacteria was limited to tentative identification of certain "animalcules" under crude microscopes. It was assumed that humans were controlled by "humors," and that an overabundance of one humor or another was the cause of a sickness. To be ill in these times was a dangerous proposition; the treatments could be worse than the illness itself. The common remedy was "physick," which consisted of a combination of bleeding, blistering, and "purging," or induced vomiting and evacuation.

The notion of preventive medicine was hotly debated. In particular, inoculation (or "incision," as it was otherwise called), which we take for granted, was advocated in the colonies by only a few beleaguered members of the educated elite—and strenuously opposed by the majority. Cotton Mather deserves credit for being the first person in the American colonies to call for inoculation against smallpox. He had read of the success of the procedure in countries such as Turkey, and, closer to home, he had learned from Africans, such as his own slave Onesimus, that a form of incision had long been practiced in Africa. But to institute in New England a procedure that was by no means foolproof and not yet adequately proven was another story.

In Massachusetts, the inoculation controversy came to a head in 1721, when smallpox was ravaging the colony and creating widespread fear bordering on hysteria. In the town of Boston alone, half of the population contracted smallpox and nearly nine hundred people died. Newspapers printed scurrilous, accusatory letters both for and against inoculation, while pamphlets by more reasonable heads attempted to bridge the gap between the two sides. Though influential figures such as Mather endorsed inoculation, the populace resisted, unsure as to whether the practice encouraged the smallpox to spread or whether the inoculated patients might be contagious. Physicians were divided over the issue. For example, Zabdiel Boylston began by successfully inoculating his own son and two slaves, and then, with two other Boston doctors, went on to treat almost three hundred people—of whom only six died. Other doctors and apothecaries, however, objected that the constitutions of those who received inoculation would be irreparably damaged, that inoculation did not bring on smallpox but only a fever, and—most sensationally—that it could produce the most feared of contagions, the plague. So violent were the feelings on the issue that in the early morning hours of November 14, 1721, a "fired Granado"—a bomb—was thrown through the window of Mather's house, with a note attached that read: "Cotton Mather, you dog, damn you: I'll inoculate you with this, with a pox to you."

The second selection is a pamphlet published in the midst of this anxious, uncertain time. Some objections to inoculation arose from political considerations, but even more originated from religious ones. In his *Letter to a Friend in the Country*, printed in 1722, the Reverend William Cooper, a minister of the Brattle Street Church in Boston from 1715 to 1743, attempted an answer on behalf of the pro-inoculationists. The title picked up on an anonymous letter published the previous year, *A Letter from One in the Country, to his Friend in the City*, which equated inoculation with contaminating the community. What horrified the "country writer" was that mortal contagion was willfully and knowingly being spread. Such accusations highlight the extent to which faith-based convictions affected social policy. That Cooper felt it necessary to address such concerns, and the extent to which he went to do so, indicate the seriousness with which he took popular religious exceptions to inoculation. To win people over, Cooper assumed the role of a calm, impartial rationalist using logic to assuage suspicions and correct misinformation. Working from Enlightenment assumptions about nature as a

Newtonian series of causes and effects, Cooper asserted that God, the First Cause, worked through secondary or natural causes. It was the duty of reasonable beings, he argued, to discern which human advancements could be permitted and utilized. For Cooper, inoculation was a means of healing discovered by humans but provided by God, and therefore was legitimate.

He then took up a list of scruples and addressed them in turn. First, some people said that it was unlawful to make oneself sick. In 1714, even Mather had stated "for a man to make himself sick, 'tis to do a very foolish and frantic thing indeed." If I bring an illness on myself and die of it, have I not killed myself? These were ethical questions, not unrelated to modern debates over abortion and assisted suicide, to which the dogmatic religious response was that God gives life and God alone should take life away. But the solution then, as now, was not that simple. Several other objections were in a similar vein: humans should not take upon themselves the role and prerogatives of God; believers should "wait God's time," that is, wait till they were actually ill and then attempt a remedy— otherwise, by seeking to preempt the illness, they were thwarting God's will. They should therefore trust in God's ways and not humanity's, continue to hold God's power in reverence, and permit God to bring corrective punishments and, ultimately, to determine the length of one's life. The final objection—scandalous to Cooper—was that inoculation originally came from the devil. Against these scruples, Cooper asserted that God put certain discoveries into the hands of humankind, who were duty-bound to use them. To neglect them would be to doubt God's wisdom.

Deadly epidemics were regular events right up until the early part of the twentieth century. Contagion of one sort or another swept through the New England colonies every five or six years, killing hundreds and even thousands. How did the inhabitants make sense of so much suffering and death? First, they put their worldly affairs in order, but then they went about the more important task of preparing themselves spiritually: praying for deliverance while expecting to die. Back then, there were personal spiritual consequences in these episodes, consequences that could come creeping up or crashing down on a person at any time.

The final two documents, from the unpublished papers of the Edwards family of Connecticut, illuminate the more intimate familial and personal dimensions of illness. First is an excerpt from the journal of Hannah Edwards of East Windsor, Connecticut. Journal and diary writing were widely practiced rituals in early New England. They provided a record of one's spiritual highs and lows and a means of assessing progress in religion over time. Pieces of Edwards's journal are in her original hand. Most of her journal, however, is preserved in a copy made by her daughter, Lucy Wetmore Whittelsey. Copying journals was a common practice that preserved an honored family member's memory for his or her descendants.

Hannah Edwards was born in 1713 to Reverend Timothy Edwards and Esther Stoddard Edwards. She was one of ten sisters, who, because they were all tall, were referred to by their father as his "sixty feet of daughters." They had one brother, the great American theologian Jonathan Edwards. The journal excerpt presented here is from 1736, when Hannah was at her sister's house in West Springfield, Massachusetts. Therein lies a tale. Several years previous, a young man named Matthew Rockwell, a resident of East Windsor and a student of Timothy's, asked Hannah's parents for her hand in marriage; they agreed, leaving the couple alone to make the arrangements between themselves. Matthew took this for a marriage contract, which in those days was considered legally and morally binding. He set about building a new house for his prospective bride, in the process nearly spending all his money. She, however, did not return his feelings and did not consider herself betrothed to him. In late 1735 she let it be known that she did not want to marry him. For nearly a decade he repeatedly asserted her obligation to marry him, making it difficult for her to live in her hometown. News of an approaching epidemic of the "throat distemper," or diphtheria, provided a pretext for leaving town, and, with that, Hannah was packed off to live with her sister.

The entry begins with a revealing and quite detailed description of the spread and extent of the distemper, particularly its effects within the Edwards family. Epidemics could be debilitating for a family, and she recounts member after member, living in various towns, falling sick. One of her sisters, Lucy Edwards, succumbed in 1736 to diphtheria, and she was buried beside another sister, Jerusha, who had died of the same disease in 1729. Then Hannah herself became ill. She described her developing symptoms and her mental state, seeking, as the Puritans termed it, to "wean herself from the world," or minimize the attractiveness of earthly life in anticipation of heaven. As her illness worsened, she began to hear beautiful—what she must have taken for heavenly—music, including a magnificent choir and ringing bells. As the fever reached its climax, she even heard the strains of a "merry violin," at which she expressed her embarrassment—not because she was opposed to dance music, but because she did not think a sickbed was the appropriate place for such things. Because her sickness pressed upon her the importance of spiritual issues and gave her time to meditate on them, she actually took pleasure in being sick and in her "frame," or state of mind. As she felt herself recovering, she hated the thought of having to get involved in worldly business again. "'Tis better to be sick," she wrote. She became nostalgic for what she experienced during her illness, recalling, "There is no part of my life I regret the passing of so much."

For an individual who contracted a life-threatening disease, the proper duty was to come to terms with one's dependence on God for one's life, to humble oneself before God, and to resign oneself to God's will. Abasing the self is a rather foreign concept to modern Americans, with our culture of individual display, conspicuous consumption, and immediate gratification, and our often inflated notions of self-worth and self-improvement. But humility and resignation were key elements of Puritan piety and living. Humility was a state of mind and heart that involved awareness of one's small place in an eternal scheme. Resignation meant conformity not to the ways of the world but to the will of God as He gave one the light to understand that will. Together, humility and resignation meant denying one's own desires and creature comforts for higher ends: serving and seeking God, helping others.

Those who died left behind memories for their friends and loved ones, who had to ponder the meaning of the deceased's life and the way in which he or she died. A fascinating relic of the colonial New England way of death is the composition entitled "Memoranda by Mrs. Pearce within Four or Five Weeks of Mr. Pearce's Death." The text, perhaps written as late as the 1780s, is a collection of Mrs. Pearce's reminiscences of her husband's final, deathbed speeches. Since the narrative is written for the most part in the second person, an acquaintance apparently gathered together and wrote down the speeches from Mrs. Pearce's own notes or from her verbal recollections. The fragmentary nature of early records makes it impossible to positively identify Mr. and Mrs. Pearce. However, there was a couple named Joseph and Sarah Pearce of East Windsor, who had children in 1774 and 1777.

The first remarkable thing about this document is the way it is made. It is written in a minuscule but neat hand on a narrow band of paper measuring one and one-half inches wide and about eleven inches long, with the ends pasted together to form a band with a diameter of about three and one-half inches—just wide enough to be worn on the wrist, possibly over a cuff. This is an amulet, or fetish, an inscribed ornament meant to aid the wearer. Calvinist religious culture frowned on the use of symbols—churches and homes, for example, could not be decorated with crosses or images of any kind—and instead emphasized the inward, spiritual experience of worship and meditation. But, along with customs such as giving monogrammed handkerchiefs and inscribed rings at funerals— "tokens for mourners," a Puritan writer called them—the use of an amulet demonstrates that, in actual practice, some early New Englanders resorted to visible devices. In this case, the wearer—most likely Mrs. Pearce herself—could read and re-read the amulet in order to assuage her grief over her husband's death, assure herself about his salvation, and apply the words to her own religious experience.

Mr. Pearce died of an unspecified cause, but, since we know from the document that he had young children, he seems to have died unexpectedly of illness at a fairly young age. Through the speeches that the amulet preserves, he emerges as a laudable practitioner of the *ars morienda,* the "art of dying," which had its origins in the Middle Ages. Death in premodern times was not a private, lonely affair. Today we separate ourselves from the dying process by isolating the ill and aged in hospitals, hospices, and nursing homes. But then, several generations could live under the same roof, and children and grandchildren, not to mention relatives and neighbors, would take turns tending the sick and elderly, talking to them, watching them die—and writing down what they said. Fallen into obsolescence only recently, the death watch was a ritual enacted in home after home over the centuries. In religious homes, a dying person was expected to provide a model of resignation to God's will and of preparedness for death, giving proof to those around that he or she was a saint destined for heaven and inspiring them to achieve the same reward. Because they were leaving the cares of this world behind, dying persons, it was believed, were given insights into the afterlife, and they might impart these visions, and other words of wisdom and direction, to their watchers. For all of these reasons, friends and family hung on the dying person's every word.

Of course, our memories are selective; we generally choose what we wish to retain. So, too, the accounts of deaths were often discordant, even sanitized. No doubt Mr. Pearce was as flawed as the next person, but the act of commemoration transformed him into an exemplar of piety and faith—and that, for the grieving Mrs. Pearce, was the point. As eulogized in his widow's memoranda, he manifested Christian resignation of self and effusive glorification of God. Though plagued by natural doubts, he nonetheless emerged confident in God's mercy and in his place in heaven.

What is striking is the affective, experiential language in which the vignettes are couched, which went hand in hand with a new religious psychological concept, developed in the middle of the eighteenth century, known as the "sense of the heart." Through this "sixth sense," it was believed, the presence of God was felt in the heart or affections in the same manner as natural objects were detected by the five bodily senses. This "sense of the heart" was part of a new language that arose out of revivals, which were religious movements that involved emotional preaching and mass conversions. The most significant revivals occurred in the 1740s and became known collectively as the "Great Awakening." These movements would forever transform the American religious scene, and they marked a step away from established Puritan religious culture.

We can find no better expression of the intuitionist language of the revival than Pearce's last utterance. When his wife assured him that "Jesus can make a dying bed as soft as downy pillows are," he replied, "Yes, he can, he does, I feel it." This inner, almost inexpressible "feeling" or "sense" was, for Pearce and many of his contemporaries, whether in sickness or in health, the most coveted possession.

The readings below are from: Cotton Mather, *A Perfect Recovery. The Voice of the Glorious God, Unto Persons, whom His Mercy has Recovered from Sickness Exhibited in a Brief Discourse to the Inhabitants of a Place, that had pass'd thro' a very Sickly Winter, And a Time of much Adversity* . . . (Boston: T. Fleet for Samuel Gerrish, 1714, excerpts); William Cooper, *A Letter to a Friend in the Country, Attempting a Solution of the Scruples and Objections of a Conscientious or Religious Nature, commonly made against the New Way of receiving the Small-Pox* (Boston: S. Kneeland for S. Gerrish, 1722); Hannah Edwards, journal fragment, c. 1736, and Lucy Wetmore Whittelsey, copy of Hannah Edwards's journal, 1736–1739, Edwards Family Papers, General Manuscripts 151, box 24, folders 1377–78, Beinecke Rare Book and Manuscript Library, Yale University, New Haven; "Memoranda by Mrs. Pearce within Four or Five Weeks of Mr. Pearce's Death," Edwards Family Papers, General Manuscripts 151, box 24, folder 1376, Beinecke Rare Book and Manuscript Library, Yale University, New Haven.

Further Reading

The Diary of Cotton Mather, 2 vols. (New York: Frederick Ungar, 1957); Cotton Mather, *The Angel of Bethesda,* edited by Gordon W. Jones (Barre, Mass.: American Antiquarian Society and Barre Publishers, 1972); George L. Kittredge, "Introduction," in Increase Mather, *Several Reasons Proving that Inoculating or Transplanting the Small Pox, is a Lawful Practice* (1721; reprint, Cleveland, privately printed, 1921); Perry Miller, *The New England Mind: From Colony to Province* (Cambridge: Harvard University Press, 1953); *Medicine in the New World: New Spain, New France, and New England,* edited by Ronald L. Numbers (Knoxville: University of Tennessee Press, 1987); Patricia A. Watson, *The Angelical Conjunction: The Preacher-Physicians of Colonial New England* (Knoxville: University of Tennessee Press, 1991); David D. Hall, *Worlds of Wonder, Days of Judgment: Popular Religious Belief in Early New England* (Cambridge: Harvard University Press, 1989); Elizabeth Reis, *Damned Women: Sinners and Witches in Puritan New England* (Ithaca, N.Y.: Cornell UniversityPress, 1997).

Cotton Mather, *A Perfect Recovery*

John 5:14.
Behold, thou art made whole; sin no more,
lest a worse thing do come unto thee.

This is a counsel given by the best Physician that ever was in the world, yea, given by him whose name is "the Lord our healer." 'Tis a counsel given unto a man recovered from sickness, expressing the care of a good Physician to prevent a relapse and obtain a perfect recovery. Our incomparable Savior had wrought a miracle on a cripple who had languished under an infirmity for no less than eight and thirty years, and had for many years been disappointed of his expectations to be relieved by another miracle. There was a pool of a miraculous virtue, called Bethesda, near the sheep market in Jerusalem. The fountain of Siloam, called also *Gibon,* ran into two channels. The upper of these was called the Old Pool; and it was called also Solomon's. . . . God was pleased then so to impregnate this pool with a virtue from above, that upon a turbation of it from a descending angel, whoever should be the first that stepped into it should be healed of whatever malady he might labor of. . . . But our Savior, in speaking one word, conveys a miraculous cure unto him. He presently withdrew upon the miracle. The surprised man knew not his benefactor. Our Savior anon meets him in the temple. It may be, the man was got there to give thanks unto God for his deliverance from so long, and sad, and sore a malady. . . . There finding his restored patient, our compassionate Savior gives this advice unto him: "Behold, thou art made whole; sin no more, lest a worse thing do come unto thee!"

My hearers, the words of this man, who is God as well as man, are as deep waters; there is a wellspring of wisdom which flows down unto us in the brook of this excellent advice. Come to it, and find in it the blessings which the pool of Bethesda itself could not have afforded.

The doctrine of godliness, which now requires your attention, is this:

[DOCTRINE]

They that have been delivered from sickness, as well as from any other calamity, should consider the mercy of heaven in their deliverance, and, from this consideration, they should improve in their dread of sin, and of its dreadful consequences; of sin, the frequent cause of sickness, and of every calamity.

You are sensible that what I aim at is to accommodate the late works of God in this place with some words that, being spoken in season, may contribute unto the good effects thereof upon us. And the younger people in the auditory will be sensible that they are peculiarly concerned in these words, inasmuch as the most of them that have passed through the sickness of this winter are such as have not seen four sevens of years in the world. Children, do you hearken to me, that God may hearken to you another day. But then, I hope, none of the hearers will forget the rule of hearing once given by our Savior: "What I say unto you, I say unto all" [Mark 11:37].

You shall have all under three propositions.

THE FIRST PROPOSITION

We take no wrong view of things when we look upon sin as the cause of sickness. When our Savior said unto the healed cripple, "Do not sin any more," it intimates that sin had some causal influence on his malady. When the case of sickness occurs in the inspired writings, the report is made in those terms; Psalm 107:17, "Fools, because of their transgressions, and because of their iniquities, are afflicted." The punitive justice of God scourges the children of men for their sins, and sickness is one of the scourges; in that wondrous Book which miscalls nothing, 'tis called by a name of that signification. A righteous God says to sinful man, Micah 6:13, "I make thee sick in smiting thee." . . . The curse, "Thou shalt surely die" [Gen. 2:17], is owing to the sin of our first parent [Adam]. In that sin we may find the first parent of all our sin and of all our death, and of the sickness by which man, groaning under the punishment of sin, may say, "I know that thou wilt bring me to death.". . . In the divine oracles we find sin threatened with sickness. It was the tenor of the threatening, Deuteronomy 28:58–60, "If thou wilt not observe to do all the words of this law, then the Lord will make thy plagues wonderful; sore sicknesses, and of long continuance," yea, every sickness. And we have seen the threatening executed. . . . Yea, sin is very often the natural as well as the moral cause of sickness. There are sinful passions of the mind, which do very much affect the body. There is a heaviness in the heart of man that makes him stoop; a broken heart which dries the bones; a sorrow that works death; an anger that inflames the blood. By intemperance, men sicken themselves and shorten their lives. Disorderly living puts the body out of order. In gluttony, men dig their graves with their teeth. In drunkenness, men drown the lamp of life. By unchastity, men soon come to mourn that their flesh and their body are consumed.

Briefly, sin is the sickness of the soul; and one punishment of it is in sickness on the body. Thus we are instructed from above. But what improvement shall we make of this instruction?

First, we must use a due caution in passing a judgment on the sick. Let Job's friends be a little more cautious than they sometimes are [Job 3:11]. We must not judge that every sickness always comes because of some sin for which the great God is managing a special controversy. Of a sick man we read that supposition, in James 5:15, "if he has committed sins." It implies, it may be so that he has not committed sins of such a peculiar malignity as to procure the sickness. A sickness may come, not that this man hath sinned in any singular manner, but that the works of God may be made manifest. A Job, a perfect and upright man, may have the Syriac ulcers (I take those to have been his malady), wherein wearisome nights are appointed unto him. Such a thing may be to try the patience of the pious man and expose the passive hero as a pattern of patience to other men. And hence, we must not judge that there is the most of sin where we see the most of sickness. Of the most sickly persons it may be said unto us, Luke 13:2, "Suppose not that these were sinners above others, because they suffer such things." Persons that are close walkers with God may be confined by abundance of sickness. . . . So then, "judge righteous judgment" [John 7:24].

Secondly, they should be sensible that they have to do with God in what has befallen them. It is God who afflicts them; and it may be so that God, for some sin of theirs, lays their affliction upon them. For such people to say, "'Tis a chance that has happened unto us," this were a language for the mouths of none but Philistines. There can be nothing so wholesome for any sick man as to be under the power of this thought: "I am now under a visitation of God; and now God visits me, how shall I best answer his intentions?" Under sickness, whatever directions be given us, there is none more proper than this: Micah 6:9, "hear the rod"; for there is a voice of God crying in it, and a man of wisdom will hear the voice. A sick man should be concerned for nothing in the world so much as this: "O! That I may duly discern and obey the call of God in the chastisement which it pleases him to lay upon me!" . . . Alas, the most skillful men upon earth are physicians of no value when God withholds his blessing. In the eastern countries, when there was no more to be done for their sick, they would set them abroad for the sun to dart his healing beams upon them. No, sirs: 'tis God in our Jesus, who is the sun of righteousness, that has all healing in his wings. Where his rays do fall, there, there only, is health to be expected. Without him, O infirm one, thy fate will be that, "Thou shalt use many medicines, but thou shalt not be cured" [Jer. 46:11].

Thirdly, to delight in sin, what a folly! What a madness! To take pleasure in unrighteousness can be no other than an exalted folly, no other than the extremest madness. For a man to make himself sick, 'tis to do a very foolish and frantic thing indeed. That ever men should have any delight in wounding themselves! . . . A Bolognian physician thought that the picture of a man eaten up with a detestable malady, being put into the hand of a man when he was going where that malady might be met withal, would be such an effectual preservative that he could never dare to go in the way of such a fire. Truly, that you may be deterred from sin, it will be no improper expedient, that I should set a sick man before you. Step into an hospital, and think: "O thou hot pursuer of sin, here I may see what I am running into!" Draw near to a bedside: see a poor man, sweating, panting, fainting; see the man in those dolors, which render all the comforts upon earth sapless unto him; hear the groans of the man, perhaps under intolerable pains; listen to his moans—"I am come to the gates of the grave, I am deprived of the residue of my years; O Lord, I am oppressed"—then think: "All the while I am sinning, I am hastening into these cords of death, I am hastening this trouble and sorrow upon me!" But, O foolhardy sinners, will you go on to do so? I must then carry you to a more formidable spectacle, and open the bars of the pit before you. But this must be reserved for our next interview. I am stopped at present by that which first waits to be insisted on, which is:

THE SECOND PROPOSITION

They that have been delivered from sickness, and grown well again, will do well to consider the mercy of God in their deliverance. The word used by our Savior unto the healed cripple is, "Behold!" Which is as much as to say, "Observe well what is done for thee! Take a due observation of it."

There is an inquiry of practical piety to be now answered: *How ought a recovered person to consider the mercy of God in his recovery?*

If my hearers will heartily fall in and close in with the things which are now to answer this inquiry, verily, the dispensations of God among us this winter will at once be gloriously answered. Hearken, O you that would not be called ungrateful—which is indeed to be called all that is bad—hearken to the counsels of God.

First, a recovered person should consider the glorious God as the author of his recovery, and thankfully give him the glory of it. God is to be glorified by every recovered person with such acknowledgments, Psalm 30:2–3, 12, "O Lord my God, thou hast healed me; O Lord, thou hast kept me alive, that I should not go down to the pit. O Lord my God, I will give thanks unto thee forever." The recovery must not be ascribed unto second causes, with an oblivion or overlooking of the glorious God, the first cause of all, the giver of every good gift. . . . O recovered ones, now you feel yourselves well, say, "This is what God has wrought!" Say, "This is the Lord's doing!" And let it appear as a matter of marvelous thankfulness in your eyes. Let the glorious God have this acknowledgment from you: "I was brought low, and the Lord has helped me; Lord, thou hast delivered my soul from death!" Awaken your own souls unto acknowledgment of the glorious God: "Bless the Lord, O my soul, and all that is within me, bless his holy name, who heals my diseases" [Ps. 103:1, 3].

Secondly, a recovered person should consider how mercifully the glorious God has dealt with him in his recovery, and give Mercy the glory of it. They that have been sick, but are now recovered, are to have this note in their thanksgivings: Psalm 136:23, "O give thanks unto him, who remembered us in our low estate, because his mercy endureth forever." The recovery is to be assigned unto mercy; but it should also be owned what sort of mercy it is, how much of mercy there is conspicuous in it. O partakers of a merciful recovery, first you must own that you have received an undeserved mercy. In being made sick, you must see and say, "Lord, thou hast punished me less than my iniquities deserve." But what will you then say in a recovery from sickness? You cannot but say this: "Lord, had I been punished as I have deserved, I should have now been among the damned, and not among the living." My neighbor, this sparing mercy of God that has kept thee alive while thy brethren are gone down to the grave, 'tis a triumph of grace over very great unworthiness. . . . You must own that you have received a distinguishing mercy. Of the sick, all are not recovered. How many have died of the sickness? 'Tis a sovereign mercy that has made the distinction. Don't imagine that you that have been spared are any better than those that have been taken off. Say, "Lord, why am I alive, when so many better than I are taken out of the world?" The mercy which has done that for thee, my brother, which has not been done for so many as good as thou art in the neighborhood, O! let it affect thee, surprise thee, fill thee with astonishment, and compel thee to say, "O mercy, what hast thou done for me? and why for me rather than for another?". . .

Thirdly, a recovered person should comply with the declared ends of the glorious God in sending sickness upon him and granting him a recovery. The blessed God pleases to declare that, for such and such ends, he smites with sickness the children of men—at least, those of them whom he pleases to make his own children. "Behold, thou art made whole." O! let those holy ends be complied withal. I will tell you what sickness is: 'tis a discipline, under which both God and man expect that you should grow in piety. Or, you shall allow me to express it so: sickness is physick; 'tis administered for that purpose. Isaiah 27:9, "By this, iniquity is purged, and the fruit is, to take away sin.". . .

First, sickness has been ordered for you that you may better know some things which you knew not so well before. You have endured such sorrow that you may increase knowledge. The correction of such a rod has been to give you wisdom. You have been chastened that you may be the more instructed; O! let it not be said that you are no wiser now than you were before. . . . O recovered ones, 'tis to be hoped that by your sickness you have been recovered out of many mistakes, and that the right thoughts of the righteous are now shaped and lodged in you. . . .

Moreover, since you are well, you must be on all accounts better than you were before. Having your health restored, you must be more thankful for your health, and employ it more heartily for God than ever you have done heretofore. You have got your strength again. You must now apply your strength to the work of God, and be stronger in that grace which is in Christ Jesus ready for you when you ask it of him. Your time is lengthened out. You are now to be more concerned for and expert at redeeming your time, and spend it wisely in getting of good, and in doing of good. This world has been embittered unto you in the sickness, wherein you may say, "For peace I had great bitterness" [Is. 39:17]. You ought now to be more weaned from the world, and not hang on the breasts that have had so much wormwood laid on them. . . . You have been rescued from death; you must be now more prepared for death, and more advanced in the skill of dying daily.

Finally, one recovered from sickness has that question to think upon, Psalm 116:12, "What shall I render to the Lord?" Restored people, it is now vehemently demanded of you that you reach and most seriously ponder on that grateful question, "What shall I render to the Lord?". . . I will put the matter over into the hands of a preacher that shall go home with you; and one who, I hope, will drive the matter home, and will give you no rest, until you are come to such an answer as will be most agreeable. That preacher is the conscience, which the breast of every person here has flaming in it. Conscience, do thy office! Recovered man, what canst thou render to the Lord, less than thy very self? O! confess thy debt, even that thou owest no less than thy very self, thy life, thy all, unto the merciful God who has recovered thee and made thee to live. . . . It was a custom of old for a recovered person to pay unto the physician that saved his life a gratuity, which was called *sostron*, or a "salvation fee." O recovered person, I demand thy salvation fee to the glorious One who hath saved thy life. The conscience of the person is the officer who is to serve a writ for it. O thou officer of God, let him know what it is; 'tis no less than himself. Require this of the person; say, "Wilt thou be the Lord's? And though idols have had hitherto the dominion over thee, shall the glorious God now be thy only Lord?" O! let him not go till he be come unto it. . . .

But we are no longer to be detained from:

THE THIRD PROPOSITION

They that have been mercifully delivered from sickness ought to make a dread of sin, and of its dreadful consequences, the improvement of their deliverance; if they do not so, very dreadful, very dreadful will be the consequences. The advice of our Savior unto the healed cripple is to be now prosecuted, and the recovered inhabitants of this town are to have it now with all possible solemnity addressed unto them. I call to mind that when one of the shining and flaming spirits in the heavenly world cried, "Holy, holy, holy is the Lord God of hosts," then the very "posts of the door moved at the voice of him that cried" [Is. 6:3–4]. Sirs, there is a voice to be now heard among you; the cry of the voice is, "The holy Lord expects an holy, an holy improvement of what has been doing for you; an improvement in holiness upon what he has done for you. They that will not be moved at the voice of this cry are more deaf than the posts of those doors, the pillars of these galleries. It would cause that apostrophe, "O ye pillars, do you hear the word of the Lord, and stand there as witnesses of the contempt cast by the people on the word of the Lord!" But it may be my hearers will be moved at the voice of him that now cries unto them, and some will be so wise as to hear the voice of the Lord crying to the city.

'Tis this:

First, the glorious Lord your healer does now demand this of you, that you do not sin anymore as formerly. Sin no more, sin no more! This is that which the holy One does now insist upon. . . .

But there are these things implied in it:

1. Being recovered from sickness, you must no longer persist in a state and course of sin. We read, Romans 6:2, "God forbid: how shall we, that are dead in sin, live any longer therein?" This may be spoken to many that have been recovered from sickness. Hadst thou died in thy sickness, it may be thou hadst died in thy sin; but since God has given thee a new life, God forbid thou shouldest live any longer in sin against him! An ungodly life is to do nothing but sin against God. The life of an ungodly man is a life of nothing but sin, a perpetual paying to self the regards due only to God: a death rather than a life. Recovered person, turn, turn from all ungodliness; return from every way of wickedness. . . . Think, "Had my sickness carried me off in my unregeneracy, ah! what would have become of me? Had I died before I was newborn, it had been good for me that I had never been born. Wherefore now, let me dare to continue no longer in such evil circumstances, no longer continue with the wrath of God abiding on me!"

2. Being recovered from sickness, you must not again commit any special sin for which you may apprehend that you have been chastised of God. Upon a strict examination, it is possible you may see cause for some apprehension that there may be some special sin for which God might in your late sickness manage some controversy with you. Recovered from sickness, now examine yourselves: "What special sin was there, for which in my late sickness I might have my heart smiting of me? the special sin that my soul saw in my late sickness, I must vomit up?" Having discovered that special sin, O recovered person, don't return like the dog to the vomit! Sin no more; that is to say, shun that special sin and all tendencies to it, all temptations to it, all the rest of thy life. Having been brayed with the pestle of such a sickness, O! be not a fool brayed in a

mortar, still retaining all thy wretched foolishness. The obstinacy of the drunk-ard has that lively description given of it, Proverbs 23:35, "They have stricken me, and I was not sick; I will seek it yet again." O! be not thou so obstinate; and let it not be said, thou hast been stricken for a special sin and been made sick by the stroke of God, but being recovered thou wilt seek it yet again. There is all of this in that voice of God, "Sin no more."

Secondly, you have this warning from the glorious Lord your healer, that if you do sin any more a worse thing shall come unto you. Such a monstrous ingratitude will be severely and fearfully revenged; and the person who, by sinning still, does not render to the Lord according to his benefit that is done unto him, will find a wrath from the Lord upon him. Such ungrateful and incorrigible sinners are the worst of sinners, and they will infallibly, such evil men will, wax worse and worse. It is but suitable that there should be a worse thing in the revenges of God upon them. . . .

[APPLICATION]

But now for the conclusion, and as the improvement of all that has been said, the more particular expectations of God from so many of our own people, and very particularly from our young people, as in the late memorable winter have been recovered from sickness, these are now from this public place of thunder to be declared unto you. Many hundreds, perhaps thousands of our people, in this lamentable winter, have been sick and weak; some have slept: above three-score, if I mistake not, in the one dark month whereof I have most cause to remember the wormwood and the gall; and above an hundred in the month which devoured next after that. But the greater part by far are yet living before the Lord—O! that I could say living *as* before the Lord! And of these, by far the greater part are young persons, whereof I see a mighty cloud before me, waiting and, I hope, willing to hear what God the Lord has to speak unto them. Hearken, O recovered ones, hearken to the expectations and admoni-tions of heaven; hearken, as you will answer to God for your disobedience.

I will, before I go any further, confess my fear to you that this poor town has a worse thing than the last epidemical sickness to come unto it. Methinks I feel the sad presages of it; I see the multiplied invitations and introductions leading to it. But if the counsels of God now to be offered be not so received as to prevent it, yet it will be found that a good thing has been done by them that have received them, and a thing that will not be repented of. O! let not the hearts of our children be under such an obduration, that the sermon of this day shall have no more influence than a rock feels from a shower of rain that falls upon it.

First. Children, remember the resolutions of your souls, which you made in the hour of your distress; let there be an abiding remembrance of them with you, and an effectual performance of them. We read of some, Psalm 78:34, "When he slew them, then they sought him, and they returned and inquired early after God." I wish that your good resolutions do not vanish like theirs, upon the distress blowing over. A very great person once asked, "What will be my best way to order my life?" And he had this good answer given him: "Sir, order it so as in the last fit of sickness upon you it was your choice and wish to do." Dying men usually have other and righter sentiments of things than they have while dreaming of a long life and bewitched with the vanities and amusements of this life. When you had the approach of a sickness, whereof you could not foresee the issue, and the sickness was upon you, wherein you were uncertain whether it might not issue in your death: O! recollect what, what were your sentiments in the distressing hour? Doubtless, you thought of a glorious God; the favor of God is better than all the enjoyments of this world. And you resolved, "I will walk in the fear of God, that I may not lose his favor." You thought of a precious Christ; an interest in Christ is more needful than anything in this world. And you resolved, "I will make it my first and main business to secure an interest in my Savior." Your thoughts of sin were, "'Tis a most odious evil, an evil thing and a bitter, to sin, and by sin to deny the God that is above. And you resolved, "I will never venture to do anything that I take to be a wicked thing." And, concerning your time, your thoughts were, "Time is never so well spent as in the service of the eternal God." And you resolved, "I will no more throw away my time in useless impertinences, but contrive so to spend it that I may give a good account of it at the last." And, I pray, how did all things here below appear unto you? I make no doubt that you thought the people very miserable who are put off with a portion in these things, and you resolved, "It shall be my grand care to make sure of a better portion." Well, don't now lay aside these resolutions. O! let these things be kept forever in the imagination of the thoughts of your hearts, and let your hearts be established in these resolutions; and let your conversations be always ordered according to these resolutions. It was of old said, "Blessed are they that keep judgment, and he who doth righteousness at all times" [Ps. 106:3]. At *all* times—not only just when a cry for mercy or a sense of mercy puts them upon it, but all the days of their lives.

Secondly, you must live now at such a rate that you may without blushing hold up your face before heaven when the hours of a new distress may come upon you. Notorious delinquencies, especially after notable deliverances, will produce that confusion, Ezra 9:6, "I am ashamed, and blush to lift up my face unto thee, my God." Being brought out of one adversity, how disingenuous a thing will it be if that complaint must be made of you, "Thou hast not glorified the God in whose hand thy breath is, and who has prolonged thy breathing time, and whose are all thy ways!" And how must you be ashamed, and blush to lift up your face unto God, when you find yourselves going into a new adversity? A delivered but unrepenting sinner, going into a fresh distress, will not be able to bear the force of that thunderclap from the mouth of an offended God: "Go now to the idols which thou hast served; let them help thee! I know thee not; my help does not belong unto thee." My friends, you must not imagine that the storms are all blown over with you and that you are come to a perfect and final rest from adversity. No, no; you will see the clouds return after the rain, and there will another distressing hour come upon you. . . .

Thirdly, the deaths which you have lately seen, while you have yourselves outlived them, you should now make your profitable remarks upon them. There have those died lately among us, with circumstances whereof wisdom would say what we read of a funeral: Ecclesiastes 7:2, "the living should lay such things to his heart." I will a little particularize the observations on which the loud call of heaven unto you has been, "Come and see!"

You have seen many die by a blow which was generally thought very unlikely to have proved a deadly one. A contagion whereof they generally make very light in other countries; a contagion that generally goes off exceeding easily, generally no more than a little disorder: how many have you seen fall down slain before it? The remark you make upon it should be this: "How frail, how frail a thing is the life of man? and how little to be depended on! How easily this poor vapor [is] dissipated, this poor candle extinguished!"

Again, you have seen many die when everyone thought the bitterness of death was over with them. Some appeared on the mending hand, in an hopeful way; they and their attendants hoped the worst was past. But some latent poison, or some unforeseen accident, utterly dashed those hopes and carried them off. The remark you make upon it should be this: "Man knoweth not his time. As a bird is taken in the snare, or a fish in the net, so suddenly may the evil time come upon me. O! Let me not be so unprepared for it as to make it an evil time. When I feel my health and strength at the best, and I most flatter myself with a prospect of many years, this night my soul may be required of me."

Once more: the dying agonies of some that have died in youth ought never to be forgotten by the survivors, especially by the surviving young ones. There have been very affecting lamentations and ejulations from the deathbeds of some whom our charity must leave with the boundless mercy of God. No tongue is able to utter the anguish wherewith some have bewailed the faults of their lives, when they had the dimness of the anguish of death upon them. With the groans of a deadly wounded man they have bewailed their prayerless neglects of God, and their forsaking the religion of the closet [private prayer, meditation, and reading]; they have bewailed their vile backslidings from good beginnings, and their coming to scoff at the instructions for which they once had more of reverence; they have bewailed their entanglements with vicious company, and the snares of death which they have by vicious company been drawn into. You should make a remark upon these things, and it should be this: "O! let me not be wicked over much, lest I die before my time! O! let me do none of those wicked things which will make my deathbed uneasy to me!" If there be any sons of Belial among our sons, O! let them hear solemn tidings from God in his way brought unto them. . . .

Let it be thoroughly considered what we and our fathers have done, that so the dispensations of God may not be lost upon us. There is a word which I must now leave with you, and wish that the awful sound of it may last with you! My neighbors, 'tis that word, Ezra 9:13–14, "After all that is come upon us for our evil deeds, and seeing that thou our God hast given us such deliverance as this, should we again break thy commandments, wouldest thou not be angry with us till thou hadst consumed us?" We have seen much evil; O! that by the good we fetch out of it we may see a sign, that God will "make us glad according to the days wherein he has afflicted us, and the months wherein we have seen evil" [Ps. 90:15].

William Cooper, *A Letter to a Friend in the Country*

Sir,

The new method of receiving the small pox by incision (or inoculation, as 'tis commonly called) has been, you know, the subject not only of plentiful discourse, but of angry debate and fierce contention among us in this town [Boston]. And it is a very unhappy circumstance attending us here, that almost everything that is now done or doing among us, if it be at all of a public nature, creates heats and animosities. I am in hopes our good people will by and by be sensible of the folly and mischief of this, and come to such a temper as will suffer them to differ from one another without being angry with one another. In the meantime, I hope that the people in other towns where the distemper has made its entrance will preserve a better temper, if any among them should put this method into practice.

However some among us may appear against it out of party and prejudice, or make an engine of it to serve designs not friendly to the peace and true interest of the place, yet there are many who are conscientiously averse to it, I believe; and, if these preserve the meekness of wisdom, they are . . . greatly to be commended and honored in that they will not act against a doubting conscience.

I perceive that the scruples and objections commonly offered by people here have such a force upon your mind as keeps you from going into this method which may be your safety and preservation. Now friendship (the offices of which should be sacredly regarded by us) obliges me to attempt to relieve and help you in a matter wherein your life, so precious in itself, and deservedly dear to me, is so much concerned. . . .

That which you want satisfaction about is the scruples and objections of a conscientious or religious nature which are commonly offered by people against this method. These I shall endeavor to answer and resolve, as I am able, in a few words; and if they afford you any light or satisfaction respecting the same, you may communicate them to whom you please; and if it should be thought worthwhile to make them public, I think none can censure me for starting out of my line or meddling with what is none of my business, since the thing I am now upon relates to religion and conscience.

One great thing urged against this practice is, *That it is not lawful for me to make myself sick when I am well, or voluntarily to bring a distemper upon myself.*

To bring sickness upon one's self for its own sake is what no man in his right wits would do. But to make myself sick in such a way as may probably serve my health and save my life, and with such a design, is certainly fitting and reasonable, and therefore lawful. This is every day practiced among people without any scruple, in purges and vomits, and other things in medical use. Now, if I may lawfully make myself sick by taking something in at my mouth, why not by putting something in at my arm? Or, if I may lawfully make myself sick for one day, why not for two days, or more, as the case may require? *Aye, but this is to bring a distemper upon myself.* I think it can hardly be called bringing it upon myself, when the case is so with me (not having had the distemper, and living in an infected air) that I can't but expect to undergo it in a very little time. I know indeed God can preserve me from the infection, but when my neighbors all round me are visited, I know of no warrant that any particular person has to expect an extraordinary preservation. He that has no reason to think but that he is as liable to the small pox as other people are, and yet keeps in the way of it, expecting that God will preserve him untouched, however some may give it the name of trust and faith and the like, I cannot but look upon it and call it presumption. In short, I can't but think, when I am in such circumstances that I cannot rationally nor warrantably expect to escape the distemper, it is then lawful for me to bring upon myself a lesser degree of it to prevent a greater. I'll put the case thus: if I have not had the small pox, it is to be supposed there is in my body what I'll call the fuel of that distemper, and there only wants the lighting of a spark to set this fuel on burning. The air I breath in is full of these sparks; and I may expect every breath I fetch to draw some of them in. If now it appears upon daily experience that making an incision in my arm, and letting the spark in that way, the fuel will burn with less fierceness and consequently danger, why mayn't I take it in that way? Why must I needs stay till it come in at my mouth or nostrils, or through some of the porous parts of my body? For my part, I think the law of self-preservation, which is God's law, requires me to take this method of safety, whereby . . . the disease is, through God's common blessing, happily converted into a remedy.

What then, will you not wait God's time for it?, they ask. I think then is the time Providence calls me to this method of safety, when I am in imminent and immediate danger of the distemper, the other way. Should anyone go into the practice of inoculation out of a fancy or bravado, without his being in known hazard of the distemper by the common way of infection, I should not think it warrantable. But then is God's time for us to use means of safety, when we are in apparent danger of any deadly or destructive evil.

But then, 'tis asked again, *Why can't you trust God?* I suppose everybody will allow that the use of means is not inconsistent with trust in God; and why there can't be trust in God in the use of this means, as well as others, I cannot imagine. *Why, it is a going from God to man,* some say. What then, can't we make use of men and means in a time of danger without going from God? If any, like Asa, look to the physician and not the Lord [2 Chron. 16:12], they are very irreligious and profane therein. But if any do principally and in the first place seek to God, may they not then innocently and lawfully make use of the best human help the providence of God affords them? I must profess and declare on the part of many of the inoculated, that they and their friends concerned in them have gone into the practice with many prayers to God and other suitable expressions of trust and devotion.

But still some say, *This practice looks to them like taking God's work out of his hand.* Indeed this distemper can arrest none without a commission from God. But yet it is not inflicted by God's immediate hand; we receive it in a natural way, and by means of second causes; and this we do in the way of inoculation, as well as of common infection. If we have the small pox in either of these ways, it is still the work of God: for all second causes depend on and act under him, the first cause. And the application of means natural for this or that end, is it not an application to the God of nature? If God does not cooperate by his actual providence, can the effect be produced? For, "who is he that saith, and it cometh to pass, when the Lord commandeth it not?" [Lam. 3:37]. What is there of the hand or power of man in this work after the incision is made and the matter applied? The work is still left with God, and we must wait upon him for his actual influence and blessing, even as the husbandman does for the rain and shines of heaven after the seed is thrown into the earth.

But the small pox is a judgment of God, sent to punish and humble us for our sins; and what, shall we so evade it, and think to turn it away from us? I fully agree to it, that it is a sore judgment of God upon us for our sins, which we have much deserved: and it is greatly to be lamented that it has no better effect upon the hearts of men. But is it unlawful to use means for our preservation from a desolating judgment? Especially, if at the very time that God sends the judgment, he shows us a way to escape the extremity and destruction at least, if not the touch of it. If a gracious God shows us so much mercy as this under the judgment, does it become us to put it away from ourselves, or rather should we not accept it with adoring thankfulness? If this town was to suffer an inundation, that would be a more terrible judgment than this, and we should look upon it too as a righteous punishment for our sins; yet would any refuse to make use of a boat or a plank that might providentially come in his way, thinking that to do it would be a criminal evading the judgment? I trow not.

But, some have said to me, *This method tends to take off the fears of this distemper from the minds of people, and who knows of what spiritual advantage these fears might be to them?* In answer to it I ask them, whether God cannot make the mercy of their preservation and recovery in this way of spiritual advantage to them also, and by that lead them to repentance? And, I truly hope, the salvation of God bestowed upon some in this way, as well as the other, will have a gracious sanctifying effect upon them under the powerful working of the Spirit of grace. I was glad to see the serious frames some of them were in at the very time: how much affected they seemed to be with the favor of God to them, what a good profession of holy resolution some of them made. And I would take this opportunity to call upon them from God to remember the same, and to be daily performing their vows.

Some object against the practice because of *the unhappy consequent of it among us; the feuds and contention, sin and mischief that it has occasioned.* Of this, I hope, I am a mournful spectator; and it has made me sundry times ready to take up that wish, "Oh that I had wings like a dove!" [Ps. 55:6]. And I must freely declare that I look upon that spirit of party and division that is reigning among us to be a sorer judgment of God upon us than the distemper which has so distressed us. But yet I am far from thinking that the badness of the thing in itself is to be argued or inferred from this effect of it. For does not the same effect attend many other things unquestionably good in themselves, such as the building of houses for the worship of God, the choice of ministers, and of persons to serve in the state, etc.? Nay, the very preaching of the gospel in the world, though it be the gospel of peace, and the gospel of salvation too, has been, and is, accidentally, through the corruption of men's hearts, and under the influence of the envious Enemy of mankind, the occasion of all this; according as our Savior has foretold that it would be, saying, as Matt. 10:34–35, "Think not that I am come to send peace on earth: I came not to send peace but a sword. For I am come to set a man at variance with his father, and the daughter against her mother, and the daughter-in-law against her mother-in-law. And a man's foes shall be they of his own house."

Some frame an objection against this practice from the decrees of God. They say that *God has predetermined and fixed the period of everyone's life, beyond which nothing shall protract it; so that if this time be come, inoculation will not save the person's life.* But this argument may as well be urged against the use of physick, nay, even of food, as against this practice. I truly believe, as my Bible teaches me, that God has fixed the period of everyone's life; but I also believe that he has done it with a regard to second causes, or that course of nature which he has established, so the ends and means are determined together. He that has fixed in his own counsel how long we shall live, has also determined that by such and such means our lives shall be continued to that period of time. And how does anyone know, but this is to be the appointed means of their preservation in life?

Some have asked, *Whether we could assure them their lives in this way?* It is strange that any should put the question! When there is none can give the assurance of this, not in the most innocent and common means that are every day made use of, why then should they demand it in this? I know of one who died under a vomit. Another, whom I also knew, died by pulling out a tooth; the bleeding at the gums after the extraction of the tooth could not be stopped, and in a few hours he died. And for my own part, as much as I am now for inoculation, I am not at all shy to say that a person may miscarry under it: for God is sovereign, and will keep us in a dependence upon him in the use of all means. But if it be safe under the common blessing of God, that is sufficient to warrant me to venture upon it, when there is occasion—nay, if one in an hundred should die in this way, while there is demonstration (as there then would be) that it is ten times as safe as the common way of infection. This, I humbly conceive, would be sufficient to justify my going into it: though I must confess, in this particular, I was once of another mind.

But suppose I should die in the way of inoculation: would it not make a dying hour very dark to me, to think that I used means to bring it upon myself? This is a question, I must confess, has been the most affecting to me, of any that have related to this matter. But after the most serious consideration I have bestowed upon it, I thus think: if a person should die under inoculation, he dies in the use of the most *likely* means he knew of, to save his life in a time of common peril; he dies then in the way of duty, and so in God's way. If the blessing is denied, he must humbly resign this his frail life unto the God of it, "looking for the mercy of our Lord Jesus Christ unto eternal life" [Jude 21].

There is one thing more said against this practice, which I am loath to take notice of, because of the [damnableness] of it; but it being so frequently in the mouths of people, I cannot but name it. 'Tis this, *that it is originally from the Devil.* Surely this is the effect of transport, etc. I will return a better answer to it than it deserves. If it be a method of safety and a benefit to mankind, as hitherto it appears to be, how came the Devil to be the author of it? Was he ever a benefactor to mankind? No, but he is "a murderer from the beginning" [John 8:44]. Every age of the world produces some new and useful discoveries in one profession, art, and science or another: and, if this discovery be reserved for our day, why should it not be accepted in all places with all thankfulness? In a word, I cannot but think its original derived elsewhere, because my Bible teaches me that "every good and perfect gift comes down from the father of lights" [James 1:17].

As to that objection of *the danger of others catching the distemper of the inoculated*, there needs only this be said: that as 'tis to be supposed the practice will not be gone into till the danger of infection becomes common in a place, so there may be methods easily taken to prevent its hazarding others that can't yet come to it. And I think there ought to be a prudent care in this respect.

Thus, my friend, I have freely given you my thoughts about this practice so much spoken against. I must now leave you to judge for yourself, praying God to show you his way. If you come into the practice, I know you will not do it in carnal security; for that may provoke God to deny the blessing. And, if God please to give it the desired success, you'll religiously give glory to him, not only for delivering you from death, but for saving you from such a bed of corruption, as others have many wearisome days and nights appointed them in; you'll think yourself the more obliged to thank and praise your kind Physician (I mean the Great One) who has wrought your cure by so gentle a method.

I have no more to add but my prayers that you and I may be made meet for, and, in God's time, brought safe to that world where there shall be no more sickness, nor any more death; where sin, and all the penal consequences of it, shall be done away forever.

I am,

Your hearty friend and servant,
[William Cooper]

Boston, Nov. 20, 1721.

Hannah Edwards, Journal

The year 1736 was filled up with remarkable passages of Providence towards the country in general, but more especially towards our family. Sometime the year before, we heard of the throat distemper's proving so very mortal at the eastward, and in the winter '36, we frequently heard of its proceeding and raging exceedingly: which made our hearts to bleed for those so visited, and to tremble, fearing what the ensuing year would bring upon us. We were in expectation of, and did as it were, wait for the judgments of God, which seemed in some measure to solemnize the minds of people. It continued to come nearer and nearer, but as it approached it lost some of its terror, growing more mild and less mortal. In the spring it reached Wethersfield, Hartford and several towns near us, and appeared at its first coming in a terrible shape. The next summer and autumn following, it overspread this part of the country: scarce any town escaped, at some towns proving very mortal and terrible, and at others very gentle; and to families in the same town, to some very terrible and the effects awful, and to others but light. As for our family and myself in particular:

I being under melancholy and difficult circumstances at home on some accounts, it occasioned me [to] spend great part of my time that spring and summer at Springfield. I went first at the beginning of April and returned the beginning of May, and found my brother [John] Ellsworth dangerously sick, and in a few days his child was also taken very ill. In about a week's time I was obliged to return to Springfield again, left my brother and his child both in a doubtful state, though with hopes the worst was past with them. I went from home from prudential considerations, but 'twas with many relentings, and with a heavy heart I left my friends. I had not been gone long before I heard of my mother's being laid up and suffering much pain with the rheumatism, which made me very uneasy and more long to go home; but was, as I thought, providentially forbid. I was soon after siezed with the throat distemper, but it proved but a light visitation, and soon passed off. And after some time I heard of the amendment of my mother [Esther Stoddard Edwards], my brother Ellsworth and his child, but was presently made sorrowful by learning my sister [Eunice Edwards] Backus was dangerously sick of the throat distemper and had lost her infant child. And the messenger had scarce done speaking, as it were, before we heard again that sister Molly [Mary Edwards], who went to be helpful to sister Backus, was there taken with the same distemper, and it was hard upon her, and sister's oldest daughter had it exceeding bad at the same time, and that poor family was in a distressed condition for some time. In the meantime, my brother Edwards's wife [Sarah Pierpont Edwards] fell into great and, as they feared, a dangerous weakness. Of some of these sorrowful things my sister Lucy informed me in a letter, and also that she was much overdone to that degree that she had a settled weakness and pain in her breast. It was very unnatural to me to be absent from home at such a time; my soul did long after my father's house. But I felt as if I was banished, for some circumstances relating to [Matthew Rockwell] forbid my going home, but took care to ease my sister of the [burden] of business that lay upon her; and I soon heard she had recovered her health, and the rest of [my] friends were better. But in the meantime, Mr. [Samuel] Hopkins and his eldest daughter were taken with a very bad fever and ague, which held them till I heard of sister Lucy's sickness three days before her death. And just about that time, Mr. Hopkins's family were taken with the throat distemper, and five of them had it, and some of 'em considerably bad; and at the time of sister Lucy's sickness and after, our family was in the most distressed condition, worn out with grief and terror, and with a great burden which lay upon them for want of help, my mother and sister Molly not being fully recovered from their own sickness; the neighbors being frighted and almost as shy as if it had been the small pox. My sister died August 21st, on Saturday morning, at which time my sister Nabby [Abigail Edwards] lay, as was feared, at the point of death with the same throat distemper. The next Tuesday morning I was siezed with it, and in less than a week's time was brought to death's door; at which time, on Saturday night, sister Betty [Elizabeth Edwards] was violently siezed with the same distemper, and my sister Nabby, though better of her distemper, in the utmost distress and horror in her mind, and in a manner harried out of her reason, which of itself would have been a sore affliction.

Hannah Edwards's original entry ends here, and Lucy Wetmore Whittelsey's copy of her mother's diary begins. Lucy Whittelsey interpolates: "After her return from Springfield, she writes thus. She did not return until after her sister was buried."

On Monday evening, went to Lucy's grave and found it at Jerusha's left hand, a place I had often laid out for myself. The next morning I awaked ill, and by noon was convinced it was with the same distemper; and began to take care, to put things in such order, as it would be best to leave them. At night I grew very ill for the time, but was not under any amazement at all; but felt a calmness that I cannot account for, which did not seem [to] arise from a satisfaction that my soul was safe, nor altogether from senselessness and stupidity. But as my distemper prevailed upon me, I was apt to be lost, and found it difficult to free my thoughts; and I soon grew delirious at turns. But though my distemper was hard upon me, yet my courage kept up. My spirits seemed generally in a pleasing posture, and [I] always hoped for the best. My mind was much solemnized; I seemed to be set at great distance from this world, and to have no concern with it. It then appeared to me a vain, toilsome place, and that the inhabitants were strangely wandered, lost and bewildered. And it seemed a comfort to me that I was so separated from the confusions of worldly affairs by my present affliction and danger; my mind in general, though melancholy, was yet in a quiet frame. When I thought of the danger I [was] in, it was not without a deep concern, for fear I was not prepared for death, and did set myself to seek for mercy as well as I could, though very much unfitted for it: but always hoped to get well. And when I thought of dying, I had some hopes of going to rest, though I feared. On Wednesday night I was much out of my head; and though I was rational a great deal of my time after that, yet my mind was full of strange ideas. By Thursday night, I grew very bad, my fever raged exceedingly, and after that my spirits were (as the doctor said) much raised by my distemper; and I thought myself better. And about that time I began to hear the sound, or rather to have strong and exceeding lively ideas, of music; the finest, most exalted and solemn by far, that I had ever any conception of before. My ideas were of its being the voice of a vast number of beings in the air. It solemnized my mind, and carried my ideas much into the other world. I used to be very much ravished with it, and sometimes felt lost or in a sort of trance: had scarce any distinct ideas, hardly knew who or what I was, but felt like a wave in the air, held there by the music; and though I was something delerious and sometimes lost, yet I was to a considerable degree rational, and consulted with myself about it, and concluded it was in my imagination only. I [had] thoughts of speaking of it to those about me, but forbore, lest that should abate the pleasure I took in it, or occasion the ideas to leave me. At times I endeavored to give a close attention to it, discern the notes more particularly, and then it would vanish from me. When anybody spoke to me, or when I was talking, I should lose the ideas; but when I lay still again, they would instantly return. This held a day or two, and then began to change to the ringing and tolling of bells, and at last, against my will, to the merriest notes of a violin, exceeding lively and distinct, and the finest of the sort I ever heard—but strove against it. It seemed to raise my spirits in a different manner, and made me feel airy and light as if I could fly, which made me uneasy and afraid I should be so in reality. Then I was in some degree out of my head, which made me talk of it to those about, and then it left me. This, I think, was on Saturday night.

Lucy Wetmore interpolates: "She writes some account of the state of her mind in her sickness as follows, though a considerable part is torn off."

My heart was moved to love and gratitude to my Redeemer and Great Benefactor, but my ideas at this time were somewhat confused, and I [was] unable to examine the acts of my mind. But I held this confidence, or hope, some time: and when I was out of my head, and thought myself sick and lost, or at a river side, and among strangers that would not direct me home, I longed to get home, that I might be in quiet and have leisure to exercise my thoughts and be trusting in and loving Jesus Christ; and thought that if [I] did die, I should be safe enough, if they would let me get home and be in the exercise of faith and dependence upon him.

But all my notions of these things were somewhat confused. On Monday I grew sensibly better; on Tuesday was got out of bed, which I had not been for six days before, and came steadily to reason, and began to find myself capable of attention in my devotion and found more pleasure in religion than I had ever done before, and a great desire my life should become one continued act of devotion. And though I could not depend on my late supposed faith as true, yet it had left a grateful sense upon my mind. It was pleasant to me on many accounts to find myself growing better, especially because I was not in such present danger of death, and because I might not be so burdensome to my parents and my sister Molly, who were almost worn out with grief and tending. Yet I came back into this restless world again (from which I had seemed to be set at so great a distance) with a constant regret. I shrunk at the thought of being exposed to snares and temptations, and having my mind filled with trifling but vexatious cares of it. I had almost ever since I had been sick (notwithstanding my great affliction and distressing circumstances of the family) enjoyed a calmness and quiet, and indeed a sweetness and exaltation of mind, which I was very loath to lose; but as I grew well I found it necessary, and in some degree natural, to concern myself with the world. And the business and cares of it would sometimes engage, vex and debase [my] mind, which I have ever since groaned under and said to myself, 'tis better to be sick. There is no part of my life I regret the passing of so much, nor that I reflect upon with so much pleasure. I begrudge myself my past privilege of being so free from the world and confusions of it. But I must, and am in a great measure, got into them again. I find myself more and more engaged in the business, and affected with the accidents of this world, every week, if not every day, which against my will takes up my thoughts and fills my mind with anxiety. A sense of the reality, nearness and importance of the things of another world daily abates.

Nov. 1, 1736. Magnify the Lord. I received the greatness and sovereignty of God with delight; and though his taking away my sister Lucy by death under such affecting circumstances was a bitter dispensation to me, yet I found no disposition to fault the providence of God, but flattered myself I could see him entirely just therein, and take pleasure in his sovereign disposal of all things. I see myself entirely in his hands, and that it was of his mere mercy that I was spared. It grieved me to think how formal and slack I had been in religion, and was ready [to] shrink at the thoughts of being so again. I see that happiness was in God and religion only, and the world appeared like an empty, troublesome place, so full of snares. I did as it were dread to come into it again, lest I should be snared with these vanities. Everything that treated of the vanity of the world, of the greatness and excellency of the things of religion, immediately touched my heart. I sensibly apprehended the truth of it. The spiritual part of the Scripture was my delight; the Book of Psalms seemed as a mouth unto me.

Memoranda by Mrs. Pearce

"I have been in darkness two or three days, crying, 'O when wilt thou comfort me?'; but last night the mist was taken from me, and the Lord shone in upon my soul. O that I could but speak, I would tell a world to trust a faithful God. Sweet affliction! now it worketh glory, glory!"

After telling him the various anxieties of my mind, he replied, "O trust the Lord; if he lifts up the light of his countenance upon you, as he has done upon me this day, all your mountains will become molehills. I feel your situation, I feel your sorrow; but he who takes care of sparrows will care for you, and my dear children."

When scorching with burning fever, he said, "Hot and happy." On a Lord's day morning, he said, "Cheer up, my dear, think how much will be said today of the faithfulness of God. Though we are called to separate, he will never separate from you. I wish I could tell the world what a good and gracious God he is, and never need they who trust in him to be afraid of trials. He has promised to give strength for the day; that is his promise. O what a lovely God—and he is *my* God and yours! He will never leave us nor forsake us, no, never. I have been thinking that this and that medicine will do me good, but what have I to do with it? It is in my Jesus's hands; he will do it all, and there I leave it. What a mercy is it: I have a good bed to lie upon; you, my dear Sarah, to wait upon me, and friends to pray for me. And how thankful should I be for all my pains; I want for nothing, all my wishes are anticipated. O I have felt the force of those words of David, 'Unless thy law (my gracious God) had been my delights, I should have perished in mine affliction' [Ps. 119:92]. Though I am too weak to read it, or hear it, I can think upon it, and O! how good it is. I am in the best frame I can be in, in the hands of my dear Lord and Savior, and he will do all things well; yes, he cannot do wrong."

One morning, Mrs. Pearce asked him how he felt. "Very ill, but unspeakably happy in the Lord and my dear Lord Jesus."

On beholding one grieving: "O my dear Sarah, do not be so anxious, but leave me entirely in the hands of Jesus, and think if you were as wise as he, you would do the same by me. If he takes me, I shall not be lost, I shall only go a little before; we shall meet again, never to part." After a violent fit of coughing, he said, "It is all well. O what a good God is he! If it's done by him, then it must be well. If I ever recover, I shall pity the sick more than ever. And if I do not, I shall go to sing delivering love. So you see, it will be all well. O for more patience! Well, my God is the God of patience, and he will give me all I need. I rejoice it is [in] my Jesus's hands to communicate, and it cannot be in better. It is my God who gives me patience to bear all his will."

When, after a restless night, Mrs. Pearce asked him what she should do for him: "You can do nothing but pray for me, that I may have patience to bear all my Lord's will." After taking a medicine, he said, "If it be the Lord's will, to bless it for your sake and for the sake of the dear children, [then let him bless it]; but the Lord's will be done. O I fear I sin, I dishonor God, by impatience; but I would not for a thousand worlds sin in a thought if I could avoid it." Mrs. Pearce replied, she trusted the Lord would still keep him; seeing the Lord had brought him thus far, he would not desert him at last. "No, no," he said, "I hope he will quit, as a father pitieth his child. Why do I complain? My dear Jesus's sufferings were much sorer and [more] bitter than mine. And did he thus suffer, and shall I repine? No, I will cheerfully suffer my Father's will."

One morning after being asked how he felt, he replied, "I have but one more pain about me. What a mercy! O how good is God to afford some intervals of so much pain! He is altogether good! Jesus lives, my dear, and that must be our final consolation." After taking a medicine which operated very powerfully, he said, "This will make me so much lower. Well, let it be. Multiply my pains thou good God, so thou art glorified. I care not what I suffer; all is right."

Asking how he felt after a restless night, he replied, "I have so much weakness and pain, I have not had much enjoyment; but I have a full persuasion the Lord is doing all things well. If it was not for strong confidence in a lovely God, I must sink; but all is well. O blessed God, I would not love thee less! O support a sinking worm! O what a mercy to be assured that all things are working together for good!"

Mrs. Pearce saying, "If we must part, I trust the separation will not be forever": "Oh no," he replied, "we sorrow not as those who have no hope." She said, "Then you can leave me and your dear children with resignation, can you?" He replied, "My heart was pierced through with many sorrows before I could give you and the dear children up, but the Lord has heard me say, Thy will be done, and I can now say, Blessed is his name, I have none of my own."

His last day was very happy. Mrs. Pearce repeated this verse:

> Since all that I meet shall work for my good,
> The bitter is sweet, the medicine is food;
> Though painful at present, 'twill cease before long,
> And then, O! how pleasant the conqueror's song.

He repeated, with an inexpressible smile, the last line, "the conqueror's song."

He said, "O my dear, what shall I do? But why do I complain? He makes all my bed in my sickness." I repeated those lines, "Jesus can make a dying bed as soft as downy pillows are." "Yes," he replied, "he can, he does, I feel it."

—20—

Supernaturalism and Healing in the Church of Jesus Christ of Latter-day Saints

Grant Underwood

From one vantage point, to note that early members of the Church of Jesus Christ of Latter-day Saints (Mormons) believed in the supernatural says little. Almost by definition, religious people of every stripe have some notion that things occur beyond natural explanation. To add that early Mormons were vibrant in their faith in the supernatural intervention of God places them in a long line of Christian "enthusiasts," literally those "inspired by God." The Church of Jesus Christ of Latter-day Saints continues the trend of charismatic Christianity that spans from the second-century Montanists through a luxuriant undergrowth of "heresy" in the Middle Ages to the Radical Reformation, the Quakers, the French Prophets, the primitive Methodists, and a variety of evangelical, "democratic" Christians in the nineteenth century. Despite the impact of rationalism and the Enlightenment, charismatic Christianity has never died. Indeed, it has thrived. Before the onset of Pentecostalism a century ago, however, few religious communities had been as emphatic in their emphasis on spiritual giftedness as the Latter-day Saints.

The Church of Jesus Christ of Latter-day Saints was born into a world of biblical primitivism. For the period between the Revolution and the Civil War, "No creed but the Bible" was the distinctive feature of American Protestantism. Ironically, the supposed perspicuity of scriptural truth that was to free back-to-the-Bible Christians from the accretions of the ages only amplified the cacophony of competing voices. Little wonder that, like numerous other antebellum Americans, Joseph Smith, the church's prophet, exclaimed, "In the midst of this war of words, and tumult of opinions, I often said to myself, what is to be done? Who of all these parties are right? Or are they all wrong together? And if any one of them be right which is it? And how shall I know it?" From the Mormon perspective, only an individual or individuals divinely empowered to settle doctrinal disputes, a sort of Supreme Court of Christianity, could end the confusion. When Latter-day Saints turned to the Bible, they argued that apostles, prophets, and evangelists were essential to lead the earthly followers of Christ. The Mormon answer was to bridge the centuries by announcing the return of resurrected ancients, such as John the Baptist and the apostles Peter, James, and John, who would pass on their power and authority to latter-day successors. Here was apostolic succession at its purest.

Hand in hand with apostolic authority went the apostolic gifts. These gifts, promised in Scripture, were the certifying marks of that authority. As emphatically as the Latter-day Saints affirmed the unique legitimacy of their priesthood, they pointed to the pervasive presence of the gifts of the Spirit in their midst. The linchpin passage for them was Mark 16:17–18: "And these signs shall follow them that believe; in my name shall they cast out devils; they shall speak with new tongues; they shall take up serpents; and if they drink any deadly thing, it shall not hurt them; they shall lay hands on the sick and they shall recover." Not surprisingly, the Latter-day Saints made ready proclamation of their own spiritual giftedness. Included in the catalog of charismata that they claimed to enjoy were speaking in tongues, prophecy, revelation, visions, healing, and the interpretation of tongues. Despite the care they took to tally such triumphs of their faith, consistent efforts were made to guard against excesses. Joseph Smith reminded his followers that the gifts of God are all useful in their place, but when they are applied incorrectly, they could prove an injury, a snare, or a curse instead of a blessing.

A full restoration of all the spiritual gifts and miracles portrayed in the New Testament was beyond what most other evangelical Christians were willing to expect, and they often spoke against Mormon charismatic activities. For most Protestant theologians of the day, the miraculous healings and extraordinary spiritual gifts of Jesus' early followers had ended long ago. Regardless of whatever else they might have shared with fellow evangelical Christians, though, Latter-day Saints could not compromise on this point. Visible signs of faith were the sine qua non of authentic Christianity. Individuals might, on their own, be able to imitate certain New Testament forms of godliness, but without the demonstration of spiritual power, all was vain. Indeed, Joseph Smith wrote that, by the gauge of spiritual giftedness, one could look at the Christian world and see how far Christians had strayed from the Bible. Their frequent refrain that "the age of miracles was past" was wrong. From the Latter-day Saint perspective, Protestants had simply constructed an unscriptural distinction between ordinary and extraordinary gifts of the Spirit to camouflage its own impotence.

Mormonism offered to antebellum Americans a vital Christianity that accepted the continued presence of the miraculous. Perhaps chief among the manifestations of divine power displayed by the Latter-day Saints was the gift of healing. Mormon leaders generally sought to root out the age-old assumption, which later undergirded healing in certain branches of the Holiness and Pentecostal movements, that sickness was primarily related to sin and Satan. As early as 1834, Latter-day Saint leaders warned against teaching that disease was of the devil or that it was wrong to administer medicine because the sick in the church ought to live by faith. Despite official disapproval, such sentiments were slow to die. Several years later, Joseph Smith described how, when Latter-day Saint Apostle Willard Richards had been brought to the borders of the grave by illness, many were tempted to believe that he must have been transgressing God's law or else he would not have been afflicted. Smith, however, rejected such speculation, calling it "an unhallowed principle" to say people must have transgressed because they were threatened by disease or untimely death.

Finding the proper relationship, however, between the use of medicine and the exercise of faith in the healing process is always difficult. The Saints, many of them converted Methodists, tended to follow the lead of John Wesley and his "primitive physic." Like the Methodists, Mormons stressed the need for a balance between self-doctoring (utilizing God's natural remedies) and exercising faith to bring about a restoration of health. Latter-day Saints also participated in the cultural revolution taking place in the new American republic that pitted ordinary citizens against mediating elites. With rhetorical flourish, Joseph Smith declared that he would strike with accelerated force against religious bigotry, priestcraft, lawyercraft, doctorcraft, and lying newspaper editors. Such populist sentiment abounds in the Book of Mormon and in early Latter-day Saint literature. Their antiestablishment sentiment led them to believe that in medicine, as in religion and politics, Americans should act for themselves. Latter-day Saints cited a passage in the Book of Mormon that mentions the "excellent qualities of the many plants and roots which God had prepared to remove the cause of diseases" (Alma 46:40) as proof of God's concern for the health of his people. By opening up healing to both faith and physical treatments, Mormons cultivated an integrative approach to health.

During the nineteenth century, Latter-day Saint leader Orson Pratt argued that the spiritual gifts, including healing, were intended more or less for the whole church not only for elders or those in the Latter-day Saint priesthood. He read the promise in Mark 16:18 as authorization for both men and women to participate in the healing process. Sick children could have the benefit of both fathers and mothers laying their hands on them and asking Heavenly Father, in the name of Jesus, to heal them. If the father was not a believer or was absent, the mother had the right to lay her hands upon her sick child. On the other hand, following James 5:14–15, only ordained Latter-day Saint elders anointed with oil in the healing process. While only the Lord could heal, and did so at his pleasure, Mormons understood that they had the privilege of calling upon his name for health. Pratt affirmed that Latter-day Saints had known since the establishment of the church that "the Lord really does stretch forth his hand to heal the sick, and that he does raise them up from the very point of death, and restore them, almost instantly, to health and strength" (*Journal of Discourses* 16:289–90). Pratt articulated the established Mormon view that while not all will be healed, despite the presence of God's authority and spiritual gifts in the latter-day church, many will be.

Miracles of restoring health began within weeks after the church was officially organized in April 1830, and the first one was Joseph Smith's dramatic exorcism of the devil. In the selection reprinted here, Newel Knight, who would be one of Smith's earliest converts from upstate New York, had been possessed by the devil after trying to pray alone in the woods. Feeling uneasy in mind and body, he asked his wife to bring Smith to their home and eventually requested that Smith cast out the devil. The successful restoration of Knight to health led Joseph Smith to write that "this was the first miracle which was done in this church or by any member of it."

The second selection is more typical of early Mormon healing narratives. Drawn from the detailed journal of Wilford Woodruff, it shows a moving progression from despair, to dependence on God, to the ultimate performance of a healing miracle following the Mormon-embraced biblical pattern of anointing with oil and laying on hands. Wilford Woodruff had joined the church in 1833 in Richland, New York. By 1838, Woodruff and his wife, Phebe, were on their way to "gather" with the Latter-day Saints in western Missouri. While en route, Phebe became deathly ill, and the journal entries relate her restoration to health. Phebe would live nearly another fifty years, dying in 1885. Wilford was ordained an Apostle of the Church in 1839 and traveled widely as a missionary, making two successful missionary trips to England in the early 1840s. With the community of Latter-day Saints, he migrated to Utah, eventually becoming president of the Twelve Apostles of the Church in 1880 and church president in 1889.

The third selection illustrates the impact of healing miracles on ordinary people. Mr. and Mrs. Shamp were members of the Mormon community in Batavia, New York, and are unknown except for this letter published in the Latter-day Saint newspaper, *Times and Seasons*. Yet it is clear that they experienced remarkable healings after the manner of the New Testament, convincing them that the Latter-day Saint faith represented a full restoration of biblical practice. It was accounts like this that spread the news of the power of the new religion while reinforcing the beliefs of those who were already members.

The final selection describes what is arguably one of the most extensive and dramatic examples of healing in Mormon history. In 1839, after being driven from a variety of locations, the Saints settled in Illinois along the Mississippi River at a place they eventually called Nauvoo. Malarial fever (at the time called "ague") seized a great many of the refugees. The situation was pathetic. Joseph Smith responded with a healing crusade that would live in Mormon memory for years. Especially noteworthy is the biblical mimesis apparent in the account. Joseph Smith does the same things Jesus did. He uses almost the same language. He even imitates Paul's sending out handkerchiefs to heal the sick (Acts 19:11–12). It is a poignant example of the organic relationship between Biblical primitivism and Mormon charismata.

The Church of Jesus Christ of Latter-day Saints today seems removed from the populist and charismatic character that once epitomized it. As an institution, the Church has taken on the coloration of modernity. When it comes to the world of thought, beliefs, and values, however, modernity takes a backseat. The nineteenth-century sense of the miraculous endures and continues to ground members in moral absolutes and the supernatural. As much as any other factor, what makes this possible for Latter-day Saints today is their core conviction that they are still led by a living prophet and living apostles and still enjoy the gifts of the spirit, albeit suited to contemporary circumstances. Through a current prophet and continuing revelation, Latter-day Saints are prepared to respond to change without succumbing to the desacralization characteristic of much of American society. The continuing affirmation of spiritual gifts, especially in the area of healing, provides a connection to the church's founding period. Latter-day Saints today regularly, if quietly, proclaim the presence of healing miracles in their lives.

The selections below are from Dean C. Jessee, ed., *The Papers of Joseph Smith*, Volume 1; *Autobiographical and Historical Writings* (Salt Lake City: Deseret Book, 1989), pp. 304–7, 316; Scott G. Kenney, ed., *Wilford Woodruff's Journal, 1833–1898*, typescript, 10 volumes (Midvale, Utah: Signature Books, 1983), 1:304–6; J. Shamp and Margaret Shamp, *Times and Seasons* 2 (August 1841): 516–17; Wilford W. Woodruff, *Leaves from My Journal: Third Book of the Faith-Promoting Series* (Salt Lake City: Juvenile Instructor, 1881), pp. 62–65. Spelling has been corrected in all selections.

Further Reading

Lester E. Bush, *Health and Medicine among the Latter-day Saints: Science, Sense, and Scripture* (New York: Crossroad, 1993); Robert T. Divett, *Medicine and the Mormons: An Introduction to the History of Latter-day Saint Health Care* (Bountiful, Utah: Horizon Publishers, 1981); Jill Mulvay Derr, Janath R. Cannon, and Maureen Ursenbach Beecher, *Women of Covenant* (Salt Lake City: Deseret Book, 1992); Grant Underwood, *The Millenarian World of Early Mormonism* (Urbana: University of Illinois Press, 1993).

Newel Knight Exorcism
From Jessee, ed., *The Papers of Joseph Smith*

During this month of April [1830] I [Joseph Smith] went on a visit to the residence of Mr. Joseph Knight, of Colesville, Broom Co N.Y. with whom and his family I had been previously acquainted, and of whose name I have above mentioned as having been so kind and thoughtful towards us, while translating the Book of Mormon. Mr. Knight and his family were Universalists, but were willing to reason with me upon my religious views, and were as usual friendly and hospitable. We held several meetings in the neighborhood, we had many friends, and some enemies. Our meetings were well attended, and many began to pray fervently to Almighty God, that he would give them wisdom to understand the truth.

Amongst those who attended our meetings regularly, was Newel Knight son to Joseph Knight. He and I had many and serious conversations on the important subject of man's eternal salvation; we had got into the habit of praying much at our meetings and Newel had said that he would try and take up his cross, and pray vocally during meeting; but when we again met together he rather excused himself . . . he deferred praying until next morning, when he retired into the woods; where (according to his own account afterwards) he made several attempts to pray but could scarcely do so, feeling that he had not done his duty, but that he should have prayed in the presence of others. He began to feel uneasy, and continued to feel worse both in mind and body, until, upon reaching his own house, his appearance was such as to alarm his wife very much. He requested her to go and bring me to him. I went and found him suffering very much in his mind, and his body acted upon in a very strange manner. His visage and limbs distorted and twisted in every shape and appearance possible to imagine; and finally he was caught up off the floor of the apartment and tossed about most fearfully. His situation was soon made known to his neighbors and relatives, and in a short time as many as eight or nine grown persons had got together to witness the scene. After he had thus suffered for a time, I succeeded in getting hold of him by the hand, when almost immediately he spoke to me, and with great earnestness requested of me, that I should cast the devil out of him, saying that he knew he was in him, and that he also knew that I could cast him out. I replied "if you know that I can it shall be done," and then almost unconsciously I rebuked the devil; and commanded him in the name of Jesus Christ to depart from him; when immediately Newel spoke out and said that he saw the devil leave him and vanish from his sight. This was the first miracle which was done in this church or by any member of it, and it was done not by man nor by the power of man, but it was done by God, and by the power of godliness: therefore let the honor and the praise, the dominion and the glory be ascribed to the Father, Son, and Holy Spirit for ever and ever Amen.

The scene was now entirely changed, for as soon as the devil had departed from our friend, his countenance became natural, his distortions of body ceased, and almost immediately the spirit of the Lord descended upon him, and the visions of eternity were opened to his view. He afterwards related his experience as follows: "I now began to feel a most pleasing sensation resting upon me, and immediately the visions of heaven were opened to my view. I felt myself attracted upward, and remained for some time enrapt in contemplation, insomuch that I knew not what was going on in the room. By and by I felt some weight pressing upon my shoulder and the side of my head; which served to recall me to a sense of my situation and I found that the spirit of the Lord had actually caught me up off the floor, and that my shoulder and head were pressing against the beams."

All this was witnessed by many to their great astonishment and satisfaction, when they saw the devil thus cast out; and the power of God and his holy spirit thus made manifest. So soon as consciousness returned, his bodily weakness was such that we were obliged to lay him upon his bed and wait upon him for some time. As may be expected, such a scene as this contributed much to make believers of those who witnessed it, and finally, the greater part of them became members of the Church.

Several months later when he returned to the area, Joseph Smith recorded that he was arrested on a charge of "being a disorderly person" and "setting the country in an uproar by preaching the Book of Mormon." At the trial, Newel Knight was called up as a witness.

So soon as Mr. Knight had been sworn, Mr. Seymour proceeded to interrogate him as follows: Q. Did the prisoner, Joseph Smith, jr. cast the devil out of you? Ans. No sir. Q. Why, have not you had the devil cast out of you? A. Yes sir. Q. And had not Joe Smith some hand in its being done? A. Yes sir. Q. And did he not cast him out of you? A. No sir; it was done by the power of God, and Joseph Smith was the instrument in the hands of God, on the occasion. He commanded him out of me in the name of Jesus Christ. Q. And are you sure that it was the devil? A. Yes sir. Q. Did you see him, after he was cast out of you? A. Yes sir, I saw him. Q. Pray, what did he look like? (Here one of my lawyers informed the witness that he need not answer the question.) The witness replied, I believe I need not answer your last question, but I will do it provided I be allowed to ask you one question, first, and you answer me, viz: Do you, Mr. Seymour, understand the things of the spirit! No, (answered Mr. Seymour) I do not pretend to such big things. Well then, (replied Knight,) it would be of no use to tell you what the devil looked like, for it was a spiritual sight, and spiritually discerned; and of course you would not understand it. The lawyer dropped his head, whilst the loud laugh of the audience proclaimed his discomfiture.

The Healing of Phebe Woodruff
From Kenney, ed., *Wilford Woodruff's Journal*

This is the first day of winter. The weather is pleasant but oh the winter of sorrow trying to roll over my soul. Our whole company is much afflicted. We passed Br[other] Thomas by the way side mending his wagon that had broke down. Brother Townsend is quite sick.

I had not passed this afflicted company but few miles before I was called to stop my horses for the purpose to all appearance to Behold my wife my Companion give up the [ghost] to breathe her last while lying in the wagon in the midst of the street. But while two of our sister were standing around her bedside to behold the scene the Lord was very merciful & notwithstand[ing] to all human appearance her breath had left her body it again returned & she began to revive. I then drove the horses a few rods further & put up for the night at an inn in Eaton. I spent the night taking care of Phebe & the babe. O I pray the Lord to spare the life of my wife.

Dec 2d [1838] Sunday. Our Circumstances were of such a nature we were obliged to remove from the inn where we spent the night. Phebe feels as though she had but a breath of life left in her body. I carried her into the wagon & drove 2 miles at the house of Mr. Makinzie & put up for the present at least until Phebe recovers her health in some degree or departs this life. We went into a house by ourselves which was much better than to be crowded by other families. How long we shall tarry here the Lord only knows.

Brother Thomas passed us again to day. Brother Townsend was quite sick. After getting my wife & things into the house & my horses put out I confined myself to the taking Care of my wife which to human appearance is at the gate of death. She called me to her bedside in the evening & said she felt as though a few moments more would end her existence in this life & manifested great confidence in the cause she had embraced & exhorted us to confidence & in God & to keep his commandments & to appearance was a dying but she again revived as on the day before. I prayed with her & laid hands upon her & commended [her] unto God. She revived & slept some during the night.

[Dec.] 3rd. I spent the day taking Care of my companion who is still alive. These are days of trial but may the Lord sanctify them to my good I pray.

[Dec.] 4th Phebe is still very feeble & low. I returned to Eaton to get some necessarys for her. I felt the power of the destroyer resting upon me in the fore part of the day.

In the evening Phebe for the first time during her sickness began to lay hold on faith for her recovery. Her faith was strong in God. We laid hold on faith together repented of all our sins & confessed them before God & covenanted to keep his Commandments. I had some oil that was Consecrated for my anointing while in Kirtland [Ohio]. I again consecrated it before God for anointing the sick. I bowed myself down before the Lord & prayed with my companion & anointed her [with] oil in the name of the Lord. I laid my hands upon her in the name of JESUS CHRIST and rebuked the fever the destroyer the deadly malady that was praying upon her system & thank God we both obtained a great blessing in so doing & according to her faith her fever left her & praised be the name of GOD for we will ever keep his commandments & trust in him. Praise the Lord O my soul for all of his wonderful acts.

[Dec.] 5th I spent the day in reading meditation & prayer.

Dec 6th The voice of the spirit of the Lord was unto us arise & be going & through the mercy of God Phebe was enabled to rise & walk & continue her journey after being confined here 4 days. . . .

J. Shamp and Margaret Shamp Testimonial
From Shamp and Shamp, *Times and Seasons*

Batavia, N. Y. May 19th, 1841.

To the Saints scattered abroad, and to all whom it may concern:

GREETING.

Be it known that on or about the first of December, last, we J. Shamp and Margaret Shamp of the town of Batavia, Gennessee County, N. Y. had a daughter that had been deaf and dumb four and a half years, and was restored to her hearing the time aforesaid by the laying on of the hands of the elders of the Church of Jesus Christ of Latter Day Saints, commonly called Mormons, through the power of Almighty God, and faith in the Lord Jesus Christ, as believed and practiced by them in these last days.

The circumstances attending her restoration were these. It was asked, as a sign in a meeting of the Latter Day Saints by an Elder of the Baptist Church of the name of Stimson in an insolent manner, and he said if they would heal the child, he would be a Mormon, and he would guarantee that the whole congregation would be Mormons too. When the sign was asked, it was manifest to me by the spirit of God, that if I would believe and obey the fullness of the gospel it should be done. Soon after we had obeyed the gospel, Elders Nathan R. Knight and Charles Thompson came to our house, and they administered to her by the laying on of hands and she was restored to her hearing, and now she both hears and speaks and is improving very fast in talking; for which we feel to thank God for the blessings and power of the gospel as manifest in my family at three different instances, and in a number of instances in our neighborhood. Those affected with numbness have been restored—a fever sore on the ankle that medicine had no effect upon was healed by the laying on of hands. Another case in our vicinity of a disease in the chest—a severe case indeed, and given over by the physicians, and the night previous to the lady having hands laid on her by the Elders her friends thought she would not survive until morning—she was immediately restored by the laying on of hands and faith in Jesus Christ.

We had a child attacked with the inflammation of the lungs, for which we applied to medical aid but it got no relief; then we called upon Elder Knight and he laid hands on her in the name of Jesus Christ, and she was instantly healed and in fifteen minutes appeared as well as ever she did.

My wife had a swelling in her side internally, of two years standing, to relieve which medical aid had been sought for and tried but in vain. It had become very alarming so that she was unable to do much, and we had given up all hopes of her recovery, but to our great joy she was restored, immediately, by the laying on of hands, by the miraculous power of God, to the glory and honor of his name. Brethren let us take courage, notwithstanding that persecutions and afflictions await us, and we are doomed to be cast out and set at nought by the sects of the day; and to have the finger of scorn and derision pointed at us, and to have all manner of evil spoken against us falsely for Christ's sake. Let us keep humble, knowing that God exalteth the humble but bringeth to naught the proud and scornful. Our Savior said, "He that believeth on me, greater works than these shall he do," speaking of the miracles he had done at a certain time; and truly we are witnessing daily his mighty power by the signs which he said should follow his believing children. . . .

We are witnesses, and subscribe our hands in testimony of the truths of the everlasting gospel as taught and believed by the Latter Day Saints.

J. SHAMP
M. SHAMP

Nauvoo Healing
From Woodruff, *Leaves from My Journal*

WHILE I was living in [a] cabin in the old barracks, we experienced a day of God's power with the Prophet Joseph. It was a very sickly time and Joseph had given up his home in Commerce [soon to become Nauvoo, Illinois] to the sick, and had a tent pitched in his door-yard and was living in that himself. The large number of Saints who had been driven out of Missouri, were flocking into Commerce; but had no homes to go into, and were living in wagons, in tents, and on the ground. Many, therefore, were sick through the exposure they were subjected to. Brother Joseph had waited on the sick, until he was worn out and nearly sick himself.

On the morning of the 22nd of July, 1839, he arose reflecting upon the situation of the Saints of God in their persecutions and afflictions, and he called upon the Lord in prayer, and the power of God rested upon him mightily, and as Jesus healed all the sick around Him in His day, so Joseph, the Prophet of God, healed all around on this occasion. He healed all in his house and door-yard, then, in company with Sidney Rigdon and several of the Twelve, he went through among the sick lying on the bank of the river and he commanded them in a loud voice, in the name of Jesus Christ, to come up and be made whole, and they were all healed. When he had healed all that were sick on the east side of the river, they crossed the Mississippi River in a ferry boat to the west side, to Montrose, where we were. The first house they went into was President Brigham Young's. He was sick on his bed at the time. The Prophet went into his house and healed him, and they all came out together. As they were passing by my door, Brother Joseph said; "Brother Woodruff, follow me." These were the only words spoken by any of the company from the time they left Brother Brigham's house till we crossed the public square, and entered Brother Fordham's house. Brother Fordham had been dying for an hour, and we expected each minute would be his last.

I felt the power of God that was overwhelming His Prophet.

When we entered the house, Brother Joseph walked up to Brother Fordham, and took him by the right hand; in his left hand he held his hat.

He saw that Brother Fordham's eyes were glazed, and that he was speechless and unconscious.

After taking hold of his hand, he looked down into the dying man's face and said: "Brother Fordham, do you not know me?" At first he made no reply; but we could all see the effect of the Spirit of God resting upon him.

He again said: "Elijah, do you not know me?"

With a low whisper, Brother Fordham answered, "yes!"

The Prophet then said, "Have you not faith to be healed?"

The answer, which was a little plainer than before, was: "I am afraid it is too late. If you had come sooner, I think I might have been."

He had the appearance of a man awaking from sleep. It was the sleep of death.

Joseph then said: "Do you not believe that Jesus is the Christ?"

"I do, Brother Joseph," was the response.

Then the Prophet of God spoke with a loud voice, as in the majesty of the Godhead: "Elijah, I command you, in the name of Jesus of Nazareth, to arise and be made whole!"

The words of the Prophet were not like the words of man, but like the voice of God. It seemed to me that the house shook from its foundation.

Elijah Fordham leaped from his bed like a man raised from the dead. A healthy color came to his face, and life was manifested in every act.

His feet were done up in Indian meal poultices. He kicked them off his feet, scattered the contents, and then called for his clothes and put them on. He asked for a bowl of bread and milk, and ate it; then put on his hat and followed us into the street, to visit others who were sick. . . .

As soon as we left Brother Fordham's house, we went into the house of Joseph B. Nobel, who was very low and dangerously sick.

When we entered the house, Brother Joseph took him by the hand, and commanded him, in the name of Jesus Christ, to arise and be made whole. He did arise and was immediately healed. . . .

This case of Brother Noble's was the last one of healing upon that day. It was the greatest day for the manifestation of the power of God through the gift of healing since the organization of the Church.

When we left Brother Noble, the Prophet Joseph went, with those who accompanied him from the other side, to the banks of the river, to return home.

While waiting for the ferry-boat, a man of the world, knowing of the miracles which had been performed, came to him and asked him if he would not go and heal two twin children of his, about five months old, who were both lying sick nigh unto death.

They were some two miles from Montrose.

The Prophet said he could not go; but, after pausing some time, he said he would send some one to heal them; and he turned to me and said: "You go with the man and heal his children."

He took a red silk handkerchief out of his pocket and gave it to me, and told me to wipe their faces with the handkerchief when I administered to them, and they should be healed. He also said unto me: "As long as you will keep that handkerchief, it shall remain a league between you and me."

I went with the man, and did as the Prophet commanded me, and the children were healed.

I have possession of the handkerchief unto this day.

— 21 —

Christian Physiology and Diet Reform

Peter Gardella

As industry and transportation transformed the colonial economy, American Protestants launched a crusade for plain food. Eating, intoxication, and sex have religious significance in every human culture, but the United States of the early nineteenth century saw simultaneous and related movements for diet reform, abstinence from alcohol, and limits on sexual practice that continue to influence American life and thought today. Some reformers called themselves "Christian physiologists" and made diet the center of a mission to redeem the world.

For Dr. William Andrus Alcott (1798–1859), whose advice about eating whole foods and reducing both cooking and spices is reprinted here, Christian physiology was the only true Gospel. "When will the world understand the whole intention of Christianity?" Alcott asked in 1839. "When will it be fully and clearly seen, that the salvation and sanctification of man includes his whole being—body, soul, and spirit . . . and that, until man is in this respect fully redeemed, the whole object of the divine mission to our earth will not be accomplished?" Such sweeping statements expressed the breadth of this movement for health. For nearly two millennia, Christians were more likely to mortify the flesh with whips and fasting than to strengthen and civilize it with exercise and diet. Protestant Americans rejected Catholic monasticism but created their own ascetic cultures. Christian physiologists of antebellum America were a part of a cultural and social transformation that would eventually include exercise at the YMCA and the assumption that anyone who drank alcohol or smoked tobacco could not be a proper Christian. Though it may seem odd that a religion of health should claim authority from Jesus—who "came eating and drinking" wine (Luke 7:33–34) and who died in his thirties—Christian physiologists saw themselves completing the incarnation and redemption.

The writings of two individuals, Sylvester Graham (1794–1851) and William Andrus Alcott, best typify the ideals of the movement. Graham was born in West Suffield, Connecticut, and, like Alcott, was a sickly child. He entered the Presbyterian ministry in 1829 and acquired the skills of a powerful and successful evangelist. After a period as a temperance lecturer, he started speaking on the importance of correct physiology, diet, and morality. His contributions included Graham flour and the Graham cracker. Alcott was also a Connecticut native and cousin of transcendentalist Bronson Alcott (father of Louisa May). After a period of teaching school, Alcott was led by his illnesses to attend Yale Medical School. Although he established a medical practice, he soon left it to preach on how his own health was restored through diet and proper living. Alcott became the equivalent of a minister in the health reform movement. Both men and their followers believed in the importance of studying science and the Bible. No longer was disease the result of God's punishment or a test by God to purify believers. By understanding the laws of nature and the laws of God, people could achieve salvation.

Diet reformers participated in a revolution in cooking that began around 1650. Before that time, European doctors and scientists thought of life as a kind of cooking: seeds cooked into plants, people cooked food, the stomach cooked whatever it ingested to make the four humors of the body. Under this theory, it was generally thought healthier to eat things cooked for a long time in many different ways and including many ingredients to balance the humors. Sugar and flour, boiled meat and fat, sprinkled with fried items, as in a blancmange or meat pudding, made up the ideal foods, served with cooked and spiced drinks. The curries and samosas of India and the moles of Mexico still resemble this late medieval cuisine. Around 1650 came a shift, based on empirical chemistry, to fermentation as the model for life. Fresh foods that spoiled quickly now seemed healthier and more digestible. Roasted meats, salads and fruits, and clear or sparkling wine dominated the tables of the West, as they still do today. Sugar, once thought good as a glaze or main ingredient in many dishes, became relegated to desserts. But the Christian physiologists of the United States carried the ideal of simplicity farther and made more sweeping claims.

The Christian physiology movement appeared while multitudes declared their faith in Christ during what historians have called the Second Great Awakening. Beginning with revivals under President Timothy Dwight at Yale in the 1790s, the Awakening included a meeting of thousands of believers and dozens of ministers at Cane Ridge, Kentucky in 1801, the preaching of evangelist Charles Grandison Finney (1792–1875) in cities across upstate New York from 1824 to 1832, and camp meetings that promoted both conversion to Christ and abolition of slavery in the 1840s. Unlike evangelists of the first Awakening, in the 1740s, who worked by convicting their audiences of sin and inducing despair in order to lead them to confess their need for a savior, preachers of the Second Awakening urged action. Finney's great innovation, resisted by many in his day, was to teach that revivals should be planned and advertised, not just prayed for; this new attitude seems to have been effective. Along with rapid increases in church membership, especially among Methodists, the antebellum decades gave rise to dozens of voluntary associations, including the American Bible Society, the American Missionary Society, the Temperance Union, the Sunday School Union, and the first

American chapters of the YMCA. An organization called the American Physiology Association, founded by Alcott and Graham, gave diet reform a place among the new agencies of social organization. Though APA membership never numbered more than a few hundred, most members of the other groups and most preachers of the Awakening also believed in diet reform.

Charles Grandison Finney never saw himself as a medical doctor or a Christian physiologist, but he taught doctrines similar to those of Dr. Alcott about food. In the chapter on "Sanctification" from his *Systematic Theology,* Finney connected spiritual and physical health. Woe be it to those who "indulge themselves in a stimulating diet, and in the use of those condiments that irritate and rasp the nervous system." They would find that their bodies became "so fierce and overpowering a source of temptation to the mind, as inevitably to lead it into sin" through the constant pressure of "evil tempers and vile affections." Christians may be saved by grace, but they "cannot be too careful to preserve the nervous system from the influence of every improper article of food or drink." Believers have a positive duty "to acquire information in regard to the laws of life and health."

While today many doctrines on diet and health compete in the American marketplace, the American nineteenth century knew nothing of macrobiotics or the Atkins diet, nor were the Jewish kosher laws or Islamic *halal* standards widely known or practiced. Instead, an overwhelming consensus on what constituted a healthy diet united Christian physiologists and other health reformers. Writers on diet held that most food was too heavy and above all too "stimulating," which meant that it was too spicy and too full of animal energy. Butter and cheese, beef and salt pork, gravies and pastries, fried foods and coffee all fell under nearly universal condemnation.

Because the food and drink forbidden by Christian physiologists formed the center of the nineteenth-century American diet, the crusades of people like Graham and Alcott had an evangelical tone resembling that of the movement to abolish slavery in an economy based on cotton. Scholars have long identified the nineteenth century as an era of national indigestion when a disease called "dyspepsia," no longer known today, was frequently cited as a cause of death. For most of the year, fresh fruits and salads were hard to find, and even when available they were not in fashion among the non-elite classes; it was the American ideal to have gravy and meat at three meals of the day, washed down with coffee, beer, or whiskey. A tradition of what we would now call "alcohol abuse," not only unchallenged by religion but even associated with it, went back to colonial days. At Harvard College in the 1630s, students awoke to bread and beer. The Puritans of colonial New England had laws against public drunkenness but considered it a sign of manliness to drink all day while continuing to conduct business. On festive occasions, especially the ordinations of ministers, barrels of rum were consumed in the same meetinghouses where services were held. Around 1825, with the *Six Sermons on Temperance* by the Reverend Dr. Lyman Beecher, the father of Harriet Beecher Stowe, the tide began to turn against alcohol.

Once that tide turned, it went out with a rush. Nearly all the new religious movements of the day, from the Seventh-Day Adventists to the Latter-day Saints, had strict rules about food and drink. Temperance hotels and boarding houses offering the Graham diet sprang up. When Finney became the president of Oberlin College, he made all students sign a pledge to eat only plain, healthy food and to abstain from tobacco, alcohol, coffee, and tea. The vegetarian diet prescribed by Graham became mandatory at Oberlin for ten months in 1840, though a protest by faculty and students led to the return of an elective meat table.

The consensus for diet reform reached beyond revivalists. In *Christian Nurture* (1847; expanded edition, 1861), a book describing how Christian childrearing could make revivals unnecessary, Hartford pastor Horace Bushnell traced alcohol abuse and sexual excess to a childhood pattern of "vicious feeding," by which he meant the use of sugar, spices, and coffee instead of plain food, milk, and water. "False feeding genders false appetites," wrote Bushnell. Exposing children to "the captivating flavor of some dainty or confectionery" leaves them "lusting in every kind of excess" so that "the vice of impurity is taught, how commonly, at the mother's table."

Behind this terror of excess stood a general theory of "stimulation" as the key to life that was common in eighteenth-century medicine. In such thinking, Protestant theologians found support for their general suspicion that nature had become corrupted by original sin. For example, John Wesley, the founder of Methodism, recommended "abstinence and plain food, with due labor" in his *Primitive Physick* (1730). "The sun and moon shed unwholesome influences from above," he wrote about nature after the Fall. The earth was a poisonous prison that "exhales poisonous damps from beneath; the beasts of the field, the birds of the air, the fishes of the sea, are in a state of hostility; the air itself that surrounds us on every side, is replete with the shafts of death; yea, the food we eat, daily saps the foundation of that life which cannot be sustained without it." Nature itself could not be trusted.

Alcott, Graham, and other nineteenth-century Americans agreed with Wesley about plain food, but unlike Wesley, they saw nature as good. According to Alcott, natural foods were "the good things of God," and he advised women to avoid "an expenditure of time in attempting to alter or amend such things as God has already perfected." People could corrupt their tastes, then pass these on to their children; this changed the meaning of sin. As Horace Bushnell wrote in *Nature and the Supernatural* (1858), "The doctrine of physiology therefore is the doctrine of original sin, and we are held to inevitable orthodoxy by it, even if the scriptures are cast away." To locate sin exclusively in humanity implied that human action could overcome it. Even Wesley, with all his pessimism about nature, taught abstinence from alcohol and plain eating as part of a path to spiritual perfection. In the Romantic and optimistic culture of antebellum America, the path toward perfection through diet became much clearer.

Communities seeking perfection while consuming plain food sprang up across the land. Alcott's cousin Bronson Alcott ran a vegetarian enclave called Fruitlands. When the transcendentalist commune at Brook Farm had to forego meat, subsisting on turnips and squash one winter, a resident wrote that she supposed "we shall have fewer headaches, etc." Disciples of Fourier, several settlements of Shakers, and the Oneida Community all experimented with vegetarianism.

Absolutely crucial to bringing about a perfect body and a perfect world was the establishment of a lifestyle that was in harmony with natural law. People should not merely think about how to be right, they should live in a proper way. Christian physiologists, such as Alcott and Graham, set about writing books, giving lectures, and establishing boardinghouses that would specifically explain how to live a physically and spiritually healthy life. While the documents included here focus on diet, health reformers took a holistic approach to well-being. They condemned the tight-fitting clothes of the day, especially corsets on women. They encouraged exercise and living in an environment of fresh air. Sleeping no more than seven hours a day on a hard bed with plenty of ventilation was recommended for good sleep. Alcott thought that sleep accomplished before midnight was better than that after, so he told people to be in bed by ten. Once in bed, married couples were to show sexual restraint because overstimulation led to disease and debility. Both Alcott and Graham thought that having sexual intercourse once a month would be sufficient for the young; older couples could get by on less. Sex was like eating and drinking—too much would ruin one's taste.

The selections reprinted here are from the writings of Alcott, who was a more prolific and versatile Christian physiologist than Graham. In 1831, after leaving medicine, Alcott moved to Boston, where he edited an educational magazine and a periodical for children. One of his earliest books, *The House I Live In* (1834), was a collection of articles for children that provided them with basic physiological and anatomical information. His books, *The Young Man's Guide* (1833), *Vegetable Diet* (1838), *Tea and Coffee* (1839), *The Use of Tobacco* (1844), and *The Physiology of Marriage* (1856), were widely read and appreciated. Alcott was convinced that too many Americans believed that health was an unpredictable act of Providence beyond human control. He wrote and lectured in order to change that opinion and to emphasize that God had endowed people with a free will and responsibility for their own salvation. Physical salvation, like spiritual salvation, was achieved through effort, not luck. Poor health was a result of ignorance, not a punishment. To help dispel ignorance, Alcott published his many advice books addressed to old and young, male and female.

The texts reprinted here are from *The Laws of Health*, which was the sequel to *The House I Live In*. As with all of Alcott's writings, the book contains a variety of health reform issues of which proper diet is merely one part. In the section "Abuses in Cookery," Alcott agrees that some processing of food is necessary to render it more nutritious and digestible. However, Americans tend to overcook and over-season food, which not only makes the food less tasty but can make it injurious to the health. The section typifies Alcott's commitment to investing food with moral importance. Eating improperly cooked food is not merely unappealing and unhealthy, it is a "moral abuse." The section also reveals something of Alcott's sense of humor, which made his writing appealing to the general public.

The next section, "Cookery as It Should Be," is specifically addressed to the women who were responsible for preparing America's food. In trying to understand the psychology of cooking, Alcott speculates as to why women prepare food the way that they do. In his opening example he asks a rhetorical question, the answer to which is not entirely obvious to the modern reader: Would a woman prefer to prepare cooked green fruits for guests or put uncooked ripe ones on the table? The answer in the nineteenth century was: cooked green fruits. According to Alcott, women cooked fruit in order to demonstrate their domestic skills and receive the positive comments of those who ate their preparations. They transgress one of the natural laws, in effect, by trying to improve on a substance designed by God to be eaten raw. Rather than glorifying God, who produced the natural world, a woman merely glorified herself by overcooking food. In this section, Alcott adds another reason why food should be eaten without elaborate preparations: it saves time. Improper cooking not only is unhealthful and irreligious, but it monopolizes a woman's time such that she cannot perform her Christian duties. How many bodies and how many souls might she save, Alcott muses, if a woman was freed to be an angel of mercy?

In the visions of Christian physiologists and their allies, transformed roles for women and millennial hopes mixed with ideals of economic efficiency. Cooking was "a useless waste of health, and of woman's time," as Alcott says in the passage below. A woman "fully imbued with the spirit of Christian cookery," and therefore cooking little, could personally prepare food for 250 people, William Alcott asserted. Because cooks insisted on making cheese and pastries instead of serving milk and apples, the labor of ten women was required. "These things ought not so to be," concluded the doctor, and they would not long continue. "A better day is coming, or Scripture and science are mere humbuggery." Though Alcott was no feminist, many feminists and women writers were interested in diet reform. Susan B. Anthony and Amelia Bloomer attended the American Vegetarian Association convention at which Alcott presided in 1853. Ellen Gould White (1827–1915), the prophetess of Seventh-Day Adventism, not only taught vegetarianism as a way to overcome original sin and help God usher in the millennium but also paid for the medical education of John Harvey Kellogg (1851–1943), who, with his brother, founded the cereal industry.

Although reading Alcott on "abuses in cookery" may provoke more than one laugh, readers should also recall that in many ways, the ideals of twenty-first-century Americans descend directly from the Christian physiologists. Many religious people—from Baptists to New Age seekers to Mormons to Orthodox Jews—argue that regulating what one drinks and eats supports spiritual and physical health. Antebellum health reformers turned away from the bleedings and harsh "medicines" of their time and looked for other ways for Americans to reclaim and control their own well-being.

The selections below are from William Alcott, *The Laws of Health* (Boston: J. P. Jewett, 1857), pp. 171–172; 184–186.

Further Reading

Catherine L. Albanese, *Nature Religion in America: From the Algonkian Indians to the New Age* (Chicago: University of Chicago Press, 1990); Ruth Clifford Engs, *Clean Living Movements: American Cycles of Health Reform* (Westport, Conn.: Praeger, 2000); Rachel Laudan, "Birth of the Modern Diet," *Scientific American* 283, no. 2 (August 2000): 76–81; James C. Whorton, *Crusaders for Fitness: The History of American Health Reformers* (Princeton: Princeton University Press, 1982).

Abuses in Cookery

We need not be afraid of that kind of cookery which makes an article of food at once more agreeable, more nutritious, and more digestible. Thus, the potato, by cookery, is improved in all these three particulars. The apple is made more digestible, and some kinds of this fruit more nutritious; while its agreeableness is but little diminished. So the Indian corn. If not made more agreeable, it is little less so; while its digestibility is increased. Such cookery I call legitimate.

But it is not so with many things. Take milk, for example; or the banana, or the strawberry, or the melon. Now, we cannot bring any known processes of cookery to bear upon these without injuring them in one or more of the three points above named—agreeableness, nutrition, and digestibility—while they are improved in no one of those particulars, nor in any way whatever.

The taste of a few fruits, I grant, may be improved by cookery. Many, however, carry this notion so far as to be unwilling to eat so much as a raw apple. But such preferences are never born with us; they are always acquired. They are, moreover, always unnatural, entirely so.

Some things are injured by partial cookery, or by cookery which is excessive; while they are improved by being cooked thoroughly, or in a truly scientific manner. Rice, peas, beans, and chestnuts, only half cooked, are injured. Thus I have known rice, half cooked, produce disease. Over-cooked eggs have induced the same results. Bread, moreover, but half cooked is not so good, in any particular, as the raw grain; while, rightly prepared it is, emphatically the staff of life.

I have alluded to the egg. There is but one good method of cooking this article. Cooked at a heat above 165°, the albuminous part becomes coagulated, and is nearly or quite insoluble in the human stomach; but, cooked below that point, it is perfectly soluble. It may be cooked at 160°, as long as is preferred—fifteen minutes or fifty. If not cooked in this precise way, it should be eaten raw.

Many processes of cookery prove injurious, by being carried too far. Thus, in toasting bread, we are liable to make it bitter. In these circumstances, an empyreumatic property seems to be developed, which is slightly injurious. An empyreumatic oil is also developed during the process of preparing fatty substances; as in frying pork, preparing doughnuts, cooking buckwheat cakes, etc. Some individuals, with weak lungs, cannot endure the vapor of burnt oil or fat.

Frying, by which is usually meant the fashionable process of preparing food in fat or grease, is always objectionable. Nothing is improved by it, and many things are greatly injured; such as the onion, the apple, and the potato, and cakes and puddings. Com[mander] Nicholson, of Revolutionary memory (as I am informed by his daughters), would never allow a frying-pan or spider to come into his house.

In general, we cook too much, and cook erroneously. Seasonings for food, if applied at all, should never be applied till the food is on the table. Even then, it were well if custom required us to make the additions supposed to be needful on our own plates. The idea of compelling everybody to the same conventional law, in this particular is, to say the least, quite unrepublican.

There is a good story told of a foreigner at a table in New York. One man had besprinkled the platter of hash with pepper, saying, at the same time, "I take it, gentlemen, you all like pepper." Another had added mustard, with the same assurance and the same remark. The foreigner, not a little vexed, took out his snuff-box and in his turn sprinkled its contents on the food, saying, "I take it, gentlemen, you all like snuff!"

All unnecessary cookery is, in one important sense, an abuse. It is a *moral* abuse. It involves a useless waste of health, and of woman's time. On the latter point, much might be said, if this were the place for it. Time is too valuable and life too short to be squandered or made useless; above all, on pernicious cookery.

Cookery as It Should Be

Most of the little talent woman possesses at invention, so far as the culinary art is concerned, is manifested in taking very indifferent or insipid articles, and making them not only palatable, but positively agreeable. The great question, with her, is not whether she can make changes, by her art, favorable to health, or even to Christian economy; but rather whether she can render them more agreeable to our fallen standard of taste. She does not inquire whether God will be pleased with the changes she makes, but whether man will be.

Thus, suppose green apples, currants, etc., to be in the garden at the same time with ripe ones, and both in the greatest abundance, so as to render it entirely optional with the housekeeper which she uses. We will still further suppose them equally accessible. Which will she prefer to place upon the table for her guests,—the cooked green fruits, or the uncooked ripe ones? Except in the case of a very few, who have of late dared to oppose the fashions, can there be a doubt.

In the one instance, woman would have no opportunity to evince her skill, or secure either approbation or admiration. The food prepared by Heaven's own culinary processes, so to call them, would be simply eaten without note or comment. But making sour, bitter, or insipid green articles into sauces, pies, tarts, puddings, etc., by various and tedious admixture and combination, may perhaps gain her a little reputation.

Now, few housekeepers will do this in ignorance of the general fact that green fruits are unhealthy. And yet, unaddicted to reflection on this subject, and to have any higher standard of action than a regard to the good opinion of their fellow creatures, they seem to flatter themselves that they can actually improve the condition of the substances they take in hand. They improve a little, they would seem to think, upon the handiwork of the Creator.

But it is not so; and it is high time they should know it. They make them worse rather than better. They are, we know, more palatable. They pass the mouth and throat very quietly, to perform their work of destruction in the stomach and intestines. Woman, during all this, professes Christianity, perhaps,— which requires us to do all things to the glory of God, preparing food as well as anything else. This she has not done; she has glorified herself!

Who is not aware that thousands of bushels of green fruit of various kinds, are swallowed in New York and Boston, every day, at certain seasons of the year; not merely by the poor and necessitous, who can hardly afford to buy that which is better, but by the comfortable, and even the opulent? Yet some of these fruits contain the deadly prussic acid, in small quantity: whether cooked, or uncooked, makes little difference.

Another case is that of the potato. Thousands of families will turn away from the use of the boiled or baked perfect potato, to eat a miserably poor, unripe, watery thing, in the shape of the genuine article; when they know, or might know, that it is as unfit for the stomach as a mass of common putty. Why do they make the exchange? First, because they must have something *new*. Secondly, because the seasonings of the imperfect article delight them more than the natural excellences of the perfect one. How long shall cookery, by Christians, be prostituted to such unworthy and unhallowed purposes?

The true preparation of food, on Christian principles, would neither require nor permit a waste of valuable time on things in themselves indifferent, even though it should effect a slight improvement in their condition; nor an expenditure of time in attempting to alter or amend such things as God has already perfected. It would allow us to take the good things of God, and, if possible to do so cheaply, improve them. Art should adorn nature,—it should never be a substitute for it.

Thus, we may lawfully take wheat, corn, rice, apples, and other simple articles of food, and, by healthful processes of preparation, try to make them better. Then we may combine things which are not greatly dissimilar, such as rice and wheat, rye and wheat, potatoes and arrow-root, etc. These combinations of farina with farina would not be as objectionable in themselves as the combination or union of opposites.

One danger to which we are liable, in making up our mixtures of various sorts of food which are unlike each other, is that of bringing into play new chemical affinities, whose results may, for anything most housekeepers can know, be virulent poison. Such things as this have happened a thousand times, and have resulted, many a time, in the loss of health and life.

But, above all the rest, cookery, except on Christian and scientific principles, is a wicked waste of time. For example, a housekeeper, or dairy-woman, in changing milk into cheese, requires equal to three months of valuable time to make *three thousand pounds of cheese*. Now, the latter, when made, is neither so agreeable to a correct taste, nor so digestible, as the former; nor is there, in the aggregate, so much nutriment.

These three months, expended to no valuable purpose, by woman, who was destined, not to make cheese, but to be an angel of mercy, are they not worse than wasted? How much [more] might a female . . . intent on doing good— instructing the ignorant, feeding the hungry, clothing the naked, or visiting the prisoner— . . . perform in three months? How many bodies might she, perhaps, save; and perchance, how many souls?

It can be demonstrated, beyond doubt, that an active woman, who is fully imbued with the spirit of Christian cookery, is perfectly competent to prepare food for two hundred or two hundred and fifty individuals, such as usually make up our families. Whereas, now, the energy spent in cooking for two hundred and fifty persons is equal to the whole time of from six to ten efficient laborers. These things ought not so to be. They will not be so always. A better day is coming, or Scripture and science are mere humbuggery.

22

Sickness, Death, and Illusion in Christian Science

Craig R. Prentiss

The Church of Christ, Scientist, deriving from the practice known as Christian Science, has proven to be among the most successful nineteenth-century religious movements to have originated in the United States. Its founder, Mary Baker Eddy (1821–1910), published *Science and Health with Key to the Scriptures* in 1875, which has remained the cornerstone of Christian Science ever since. Though Eddy herself explicitly rejected the claims of those who viewed her as divine, Eddy and Christian Scientists impart a sacred status to *Science and Health* as divinely revealed. Christian Science ritual is built around the intensive study and recitation of Eddy's text in addition to the Bible. Ceremonial usage of *Science and Health* was codified by Mary Baker Eddy in her *Manual of the Mother Church* (1895), which has remained nearly unchanged for over a century.

Though founded officially as a church in 1879, the practice of Christian Science emerged as a response to orthodox theologies, the lingering effects of the Civil War, horrific medical practices, and the suffrage movement, to name a few. It developed within the cultural and intellectual climate of the nineteenth century, which included such mental practices as hypnosis and mesmerism. Anton Mesmer (1734–1815), an Austrian physician and spiritualist, was one of the earliest practitioners of hypnosis. Mesmer toured the United States and promoted his belief that in the process of hypnosis we enter into an active spiritual realm with tremendous power over our lives. This mysterious energy affected our thoughts and our physical health, and hypnosis allowed us to tap into it. Mesmer called this energy "animal magnetism." His work received much publicity, and while rejected by mainstream medicine, a large number of middle- and upper-middle-class Protestants fixated on the apparent healing powers of Mesmer's hypnosis.

An early disciple of mesmerism, Phineas P. Quimby (1802–66), modified Mesmer's teachings by rejecting the need for entering a trance-like hypnotic state in order to connect the mind with a river of spiritual energy. All that was needed, instead, was cognitive readjustment. With a proper change in thought, the human mind would be adequate to heal illness and any forms of psychological distress. By the 1840s and 1850s, Quimby was performing his own healings and concluded that the human mind was tied into a larger spiritual force, which he called "Mind." Though he is often credited with being the first to use the term "Christian Science," his focus was decidedly on the *science* of healing rather than the Christian aspect. The same could not be said for Quimby's most famous patient, Mary Baker Eddy.

Mary Baker Eddy was born and raised in New Hampshire to a family of some wealth. Throughout her early life she suffered from anxiety and pain from a spinal disorder. The death of her first husband, George W. Glover, only months after their marriage, and a troubled relationship with her second husband, a dentist named Daniel Patterson, only added to her problems. It was during her marriage to Patterson that Eddy encountered Phineas P. Quimby. In October of 1862, Quimby began a successful treatment of the chronic pain that Eddy had suffered for many years. For the first time in decades she was able to engage in rigorous physical activity without pain. Their close relationship lasted until Quimby's sudden death in 1866. His death left Eddy devastated, though his absence did allow her to recognize her own power to heal herself. In fact, Eddy realized the mental nature of health before her encounter with Quimby. She experimented with many healing systems, including allopathy, homeopathy, hydropathy, and various dietary systems. With each, especially homeopathy, she realized that the mental states of the patient and healer were the determining factors in the case. That is why Quimby's work was so meaningful to her. A short time after Quimby's death, Eddy slipped on ice and injured her back. Bedridden, depressed, and suffering, Eddy turned to the Bible for comfort. On the third day after her fall, she read Matthew 9:2–7, which told of Jesus healing a paralyzed man and forgiving him his sins as a result of the man's faith. Upon reading this passage, Eddy arose from her bed and was healed. This was the turning point in the creation of Christian Science.

The term "Christian" was fitting for this new religion because Jesus Christ was seen as the ultimate exemplar of its theology and practice, while the term "Science" applied because the religion's proof rested on the actual practice of healing itself. In an age when faith in science and immutable laws of nature dominated intellectual circles, it was only fitting that this movement would appeal to the positivistic tendencies of the day by grounding itself in demonstration.

For the next decade Mary Baker Eddy engaged in a life of itinerant healing. During these years, until the publication of *Science and Health with Key to the Scriptures*, Eddy developed a theology that distinguished her from Quimby in many ways. Though raised in the Calvinist Congregationalist tradition, she had long since rejected the Calvinist doctrine of predestination. She remained deeply influenced, however, by the all-important Calvinist teaching on God's sovereignty, a concept that Eddy spiritualized by rejecting traditional anthropomorphic conceptions of deity. For Eddy, God was understood and spoken of as pure Spirit. Furthermore, God was seen as the only reality and, in keeping with the biblical precedent of using many names for God, could be referred to synonymously as Mind, All-in-all, I AM, Life, Love, Mother, Father, Principle, Soul, Spirit, Supreme Being, Elohim, and Truth. Men and women were the image and likeness of the Divine Mind, as described in Gen. 1:26. This being the case, reasoned Eddy, they were purely spiritual as God is pure spirit. Rather than being individual and distinct, people were merely expressions of the one Spirit. In *Science and Health* she wrote that "God expresses in man the infinite idea forever developing itself, broadening and rising higher and higher from a boundless basis. Mind manifests all that exists in the infinitude of Truth" (258:13–16).

Christian Science theology in *Science and Health* appeared to subscribe to a radical Platonic dualism between spirit and matter. Upon closer inspection, however, Christian Science rejected the dualism by rejecting the reality of matter. Matter was simply illusion, the product of a false consciousness endemic to human beings. Exposing this essential truth was the heart of Jesus of Nazareth's mission. Jesus, whom Scientists take to be only human, demonstrated the illusory nature of matter and therefore the illusory nature of the death of the body, with his own crucifixion and apparent resurrection. Yet "resurrection" was a misnomer from the Christian Science perspective, because he never suffered death. However, as mortals needed evidence to be convinced of the power that spirit and mind had over death, the demonstration of surviving crucifixion was necessary. The Christian Scientist position on the matter is best summarized in the Scientific Statement of Being: "There is no life, truth, intelligence, nor substance in matter. All is infinite Mind and its infinite manifestation, for God is All-in-all. Spirit is the real and eternal; matter is the unreal and temporal. Spirit is God, and man is His image and likeness. Therefore man is not material; he is spiritual" (468:8–15). As such, Eddy rejected the presuppositions of both Mesmer and Quimby, who accepted the reality of matter.

All Christian Science doctrine and practice springs from this central assumption, which Eddy propagated with some success. The laws of nature were, after all, the laws of God. Armed with knowledge of God's spiritual reality and a commitment to shedding false consciousness, Eddy believed that the temporal problems of humankind could be transcended. She gained a loyal following, including her third husband, Asa Gilbert Eddy, who helped promote her metaphysical teachings until his death in 1882, five years after their wedding. She formed the Massachusetts Metaphysical College with a curriculum built around her insights. Courses typically lasted three weeks and were devoted to the understanding and practice of healing. In 1879, The Church of Christ, Scientist was officially chartered and based in Boston, Massachusetts. The Scientists had no creed, though their faith was grounded in the Bible and *Science and Health with Key to the Scriptures*.

Their message soon spread into the frontier states of the West. Everywhere the Church grew, however, controversy followed. Cynicism towards the Scientists' rejection of what most Americans deemed objective reality was pervasive, and many were simply scandalized by the leadership role that Eddy, as a woman, maintained in the movement.

There were also internal divisions that persistently plagued Christian Science. Several of Eddy's students came to reject the direction she was taking the Church and deliberately sought to subvert the movement's success. Eddy frequently complained that she was being subjected to mental assault stemming from the hostile thoughts of her enemies. In a world where Mind is the only reality, these psychological attacks were understood to be as real for Eddy as a physical assault would be for a non-Scientist. Even the death of Mary Baker Eddy's husband, Asa, was attributed to a mental assassination perpetrated by an angry ex-student, though the medical report listed the cause of death as heart disease.

As Christian Science expanded, Mary Baker Eddy became concerned that her teachings were sometimes being distorted. In its first decades, Christian Science churches were voluntary associations connected with one another only in their commitment to the teachings of *Science and Health with Key to the Scriptures.* Though Eddy was always considered the one official pastor of the Church, services would include sermons and commentary that were beyond Eddy's control. By the 1890s, however, it became clear to Eddy that her message was susceptible to distortion, both innocent and malicious. She resolved to centralize her authority in 1895 by creating the Mother Church of Christ, Scientist, in Boston.

From that point on, nearly all Christian Science churches became branches of the one Mother Church. Though individual churches were allowed to govern themselves in theory, Eddy's *Manual of the Mother Church* (1895) spelled out the organization and ritual of Christian Science in such exhaustive detail that there was little room for variation. Furthermore, the *Manual* stipulated that the Bible and *Science and Health with Key to the Scriptures* alone would serve as both pastor and preacher in Christian Science churches, rather than having individual people fulfill those functions. In essence, readers rather than clergy led services. The Mother Church, under Eddy's rule, prescribed many details down to the ceremonial laying of a cornerstone for a new church. By making her personal approval a necessity for any alterations in the *Manual,* Eddy ensured that the Church would forever be preserved according to her beliefs after her death. Underlying this regimentation, however, was her understanding that the science operated by fixed rules which, if not followed, would lead to failure.

The ritual life of a Christian Scientist was built around three primary functions: daily reading of *Science and Health with Key to the Scriptures,* Sunday services, and Wednesday Evening meetings, where Scientists could testify to the impact of *Science and Health* on their own lives. The *Christian Science Quarterly* spelled out the daily readings by placing weekly Bible lessons side by side with a set of related passages from *Science and Health with Key to the Scriptures.* Each week was devoted to specific topics such as Mind, reality, matter, or Life. At the end of the week, the readers in the Sunday service read the passages that the Scientists had been meditating on in the six days before. Scientists were to listen attentively as the passages were read.

A male and a female reader led Sunday services. The services began with organ music as the attendees arrived, followed by an opening hymn by the congregation. Shortly thereafter, the first reader of a church would lead the congregation in the Lord's Prayer, though each line would be followed by an explanatory statement taken from *Science and Health.* The pinnacle of the service was the reading of each week's lesson. One reader was assigned Bible verses, while the other reader would recite the corresponding *Science and Health* passages. The words were to be read in a straightforward manner, and a premium was placed on clarity and good diction. Typically, anywhere from two to five biblical passages would be read at a time, followed by as many as five sections *of Science and Health* illuminating the previously read biblical passages. A total of six sets of paired readings, one set for each day of the week leading up to Sunday, would be completed before the readers led the congregation toward the closing of the service. Services were designed to last no longer than one hour.

The Wednesday evening meeting was less structured and focused more on the participation of those in attendance. The first reader of the Church would still begin the evenings with selections from the Bible and *Science and Health,* but testimonials made by those who had been healed or affected in some way by Eddy's insights in *Science and Health* were at the heart of these meetings. These testimonials ranged from the mundane to the profound. What they all shared in common was the realization that the illusory nature of their mortal minds had nothing to do with the truth of God's all-pervading Spirit, of which we were simply a reflection. The mortal mind was that ordinary human perception continually being deceived by the senses. Mortal mind imagined pain, disease, and death when there was none. Reality and Truth were pure Spirit rendering the appearance of physical ailments and mortality powerless over the continuous spiritual existence we all shared with God.

In many cases a Christian Science practitioner, someone recognized by the Mother Church to care for health, would assist in the healing process. Practitioners functioned both as teachers who led individuals to the right thinking necessary to rid themselves of the illusion of their illness, and as healers whose mental alignment with God would overcome an apparent ailment, particularly when treating a nonbeliever. In keeping with Eddy's own ideas about both the positive and negative power of mind, Scientists believed that their own false thinking could result in harm to others, particularly their loved ones. As such, when somebody they were in contact with experienced him- or herself to be sick or injured, the logical place to begin was with a self-assessment. In the process, Scientists often found that a renewed focus on the truth of Spirit as the only reality protected not only themselves but also those around them from suffering.

The growth of Christian Science in the nineteenth century is attributable in large measure to the fact that people experienced its healing practices to work for them and for others. An entire chapter of *Science and Health,* entitled "Fruitage," documented dozens of testimonies of healing. The confidence that came with knowing that disease, pain, and other matter-based causes for displeasure were nothing more than manifestations of an error in thinking provided Scientists with a sense of peace and contentment that they were eager to share with others. Death itself lost its power over the Scientists, who viewed it as an illusion of mortal mind that concealed the reality of the ever present life of the Spirit. When Eddy died in 1910, some of her followers believed that she would return to them as Jesus had returned to his apostles. Eddy, however, had never predicted such an event, and her apparent mortality was in line with her eschatological teaching that humankind would continue to experience the illusion of death until that day when all had shed the beliefs of mortal mind and recognized that there was no life in matter.

The following excerpts include a selected testimony from a 1899 version of the *Christian Science Sentinel* that illustrates how Christian Science was applied in practice, as well as a variety of selections from *Science and Health with Key to the Scriptures*. These passages from *Science and Health* address healing and the fundamental presuppositions that make healing possible. They are taken from various sections throughout the text and are referenced by page number and line number.

Mary Baker Eddy, *Science and Health with Key to the Scriptures* (1875; reprint Boston: First Church of Christ, Scientist, 1994).

"Broken Arm Healed by Christian Science" from *Christian Science Sentinel* 2 (December 28, 1899): 277–278.

Further Reading

Stephen Gottschalk, *The Emergence of Christian Science in American Religious Life* (Berkeley and Los Angeles: University of California Press, 1973); John K. Simmons, "Christian Science and American Culture," in *America's Alternative Religions*, edited by Timothy Miller (Albany: State University of New York Press, 1995), pp. 61–68; Robert Peel, *Mary Baker Eddy*, vols. 1–3 (New York: Holt, Rinehart & Winston, 1977); Carl B. Becker, "Religious Healing in 19th Century 'New Religions': The Cases of Tenrikyo and Christian Science," *Religion* 20 (1990): 199–215; Gillian Gill, *Mary Baker Eddy* (Cambridge: Perseus Books, 1998).

Science and Health with Key to the Scriptures

16:26–17:15

The recitation of the Lord's Prayer went as follows:

> Our Father which art in heaven,
> *Our Father-Mother God, all-harmonious*
> Hallowed be Thy name.
> *Adorable One.*
> Thy kingdom come.
> *Thy kingdom is come; Thou art ever-present.*
> Thy will be done in earth, as it is in heaven.
> *Enable us to know,—as in heaven, so on earth,—*
> *God is omnipotent, supreme.*
> Give us this day our daily bread;
> *Give us grace for to-day; feed the famished affections;*
> And forgive us our debts, as we forgive our debtors.
> *And Love is reflected in love;*

And lead us not into temptation but deliver us from evil;
 *And God leadeth us not into temptation, but deliver us from sin, disease,
 and death.*
For Thine is the kingdom, and the power, and the glory, forever.
 For God is infinite, all-power, all Life, Truth, Love, over all, and All.

13:20–14:24

If we pray to God as a corporeal person, this will prevent us from relinquishing
the human doubts and fears which attend such a belief, and so we cannot
grasp the wonders wrought by infinite, incorporeal Love, to whom all things
are possible. Because of human ignorance of the divine Principle, Love, the
Father of all is represented as a corporeal creator; hence men recognize themselves as merely physical, and are ignorant of man as God's image or reflection
and of man's eternal incorporeal existence. The world of error is ignorant of
the world of Truth—blind to the reality of man's existence—for the world of
sensation is not cognizant of life in Soul, not in body.

If we are sensibly with the body and regard omnipotence as a corporeal, material person, whose ear we would gain, we are not "absent from the body" and
"present with the Lord" in the demonstration of Spirit. We cannot "serve two
masters." To be "present with the Lord" is to have, not mere emotional ecstasy
of faith, but the actual demonstration and understanding of Life as revealed in
Christian Science. To be "with the Lord" is to be in obedience to the law of God,
to be absolutely governed by divine Love—by Spirit, not by matter.

Become conscious for a single moment that life and intelligence are purely
spiritual,—neither in nor of matter—and the body will then utter no complaints. If suffering from a belief in sickness, you will find yourself suddenly
well. Sorrow is turned into joy when the body is controlled by spiritual Life,
Truth, and Love. Hence the hope of the promise Jesus bestows: "He that believeth on me, the works that I do shall he do also; . . . because I go unto my
Father," [because the Ego is absent from the body, and present in Truth and
Love.] The Lord's Prayer is the prayer of the Soul, not of material sense.

26:28–27:16

Our Master taught no mere theory, doctrine, or belief. It was the divine Principle
of all real being which he taught and practiced. His proof of Christianity was no
form or system of religion or worship, but Christian Science, working out of the
harmony of Life and Love. Jesus sent a message to John the Baptist, which was
intended to prove beyond question that Christ had come: "Go your way, and tell
John what things ye have seen and heard; how the blind see, the lame walk, the
lepers are cleansed, the deaf hear, the dead are raised, to the poor the gospel is
preached." In other words: Tell John what the demonstration of divine power is,
and he will at once perceive that God is the power in the Messianic work.

That Life is God, Jesus proved by his reappearance after the crucifixion in
strict accordance with his scientific statement: "Destroy this temple [body], and

in three days I [Spirit] will raise it up." It is as if he had said: "The I—the Life, substance, and intelligence of the universe—is not in matter to be destroyed."

42:15–29

The resurrection of the great demonstrator of God's power was the proof of his final triumph over body and matter, and gave full evidence of divine Science,—evidence so important to mortals. The belief that man has existence or mind separate from God is a dying error. This error Jesus met with divine Science and proved its nothingness. Because of the wondrous glory which God bestowed on his anointed, temptation, sin, sickness, and death had no terror for Jesus. Let men think they had killed the body! Afterwards he would show it to them unchanged. This demonstrates that in Christian Science the true man is governed by God—by good, not evil—and is therefore not a mortal but an immortal. Jesus had taught his disciples the Science of his proof.

70:1–11

Mortal existence is an enigma. Every day is a mystery. The testimony of the corporeal senses cannot inform us what is real and what is delusive, but the revelations of Christian Science unlock the treasures of Truth. Whatever is false or sinful can never enter the atmosphere of Spirit. There is but one Spirit. Man is never God, but spiritual man, made in God's likeness, reflects God. In this scientific reflection the Ego and the Father are inseparable. The supposition that corporeal beings are spirits, or that there are good and evil spirits, is a mistake.

73:19–74:2

The belief that material bodies return to dust, hereafter to rise up as spiritual bodies with material sensations and desires, is incorrect. Equally incorrect is the belief that spirit is confined to the finite, material body, from which it is freed by death, and that, when it is freed from the material body, spirit retains the sensations belonging to that body.

It is a grave mistake to suppose that matter is any part of the reality of intelligent existence, or that Spirit and matter, intelligence and non-intelligence, can commune together. This error Science will destroy. The sensual cannot be made the mouthpiece of the spiritual, nor can the finite become the channel of the infinite. There is no communication between so-called material existence and spiritual life which is not subject to death.

79:1–28

The act of describing disease—its symptoms, locality, and fatality—is not scientific. Warning people against death is an error that tends to frighten into death those who are ignorant of Life as God. Thousands of instances could be cited of health restored by changing the patient's thoughts regarding death.

A scientific mental method is more sanitary than the use of drugs, and such a mental method produces permanent health. Science must go over the whole ground, and dig up every seed of error's sowing. . . . Jesus cast out evil spirits, or false beliefs. The Apostle Paul bade men have the Mind that was in the Christ. Jesus did his own work by the one Spirit. He said: "My Father worketh hitherto, and I work." He never described disease, so far as can be learned from the Gospels, but he healed disease.

The unscientific practitioner says: "You are ill. Your brain is overtaxed, and you must rest. Your body is weak and it must be strengthened. You have nervous prostration, and must be treated for it." Science objects to all this, contending for the rights of intelligence and asserting that Mind controls body and brain.

108:19–109:10

When apparently near the confines of mortal existence, standing already within the shadow of the death-valley, I learned these truths in divine Science: that all real being is God, the divine Mind, and that Life, Truth, and Love are all-powerful and ever-present; that the opposite of Truth—called error, sin, sickness, disease, death,—is the false testimony of false material sense, of mind in matter; that this false sense evolves, in belief, a subjective state of mortal mind which this same so-called mind names *matter,* thereby shutting out the true sense of Spirit.

My discovery, that erring, mortal, misnamed *mind* produces all the organism and action of the mortal body, set my thoughts to work in new channels, and led up to my demonstration of the proposition that Mind is All and matter is naught as the leading factor in Mind-science.

Christian Science reveals incontrovertibly that Mind is All-in-all, that the only realities are divine Mind and idea. This great fact is not, however, seen to be supported by sensible evidence, until its divine Principle is demonstrated by healing the sick and thus proved absolute and divine. This proof once seen, no other conclusion can be reached.

113:9–114:31

The fundamental propositions of divine metaphysics are summarized in the four following, to me, *self-evident* propositions. Even if reversed, these propositions will be found to agree in statement and proof, showing mathematically their exact relation to Truth. De Quincey says mathematics has not a foot to stand upon which is not purely metaphysical.

1. God is All-in-all.
2. God is good. Good is Mind.
3. God, Spirit, being all, nothing is matter.
4. Life, God, omnipotent good, deny death, evil, sin, disease.—Disease, sin, evil, death, deny good, omnipotent God, Life.

Which of the denials in proposition four is true? Both are not, cannot be true. According to Scripture, I find that God is true, "but every [mortal] man a liar."

The divine metaphysics of Christian Science, like the method in mathematics, proves the rule by inversion. For example: There is no pain in Truth, and no truth in pain; no nerve in Mind, and no mind in nerve; no matter in Mind, and no mind in matter; no matter in Life, and no life in matter; no matter in good; and no good in matter.

Usage classes both evil and good together as *mind;* therefore, to be understood, the author calls sick and sinful humanity *mortal mind*—meaning by this term the flesh opposed to Spirit, the human mind and evil in contradistinction to the divine Mind, or Truth and good. The spiritually unscientific definition of mind is based on the evidence of the physical senses, which makes minds many and calls *mind* both human and divine.

In Science, Mind is *one,* including noumenon and phenomena, God and His thoughts.

Mortal mind is a solecism in language, and involves an improper use of the word *mind.* As Mind is immortal, the phrase *mortal mind* implies something untrue and therefore unreal; and as the phrase is used in teaching Christian Science, it is meant to designate that which has no real existence. Indeed, if a better word or phrase could be suggested, it would be used; but in expressing the new tongue we must sometimes recur to the old and imperfect, and the new wine of the Spirit has to be poured into the old bottles of the letter.

Christian Science explains all cause and effect as mental, not physical. It lifts the veil of mystery from Soul and body. It shows the scientific relation of man to God, disentangles the interlaced ambiguities of being, and sets free the imprisoned thought. In divine Science, the universe, including man, is spiritual, harmonious, and eternal. Science shows that what is termed matter is but the subjective state of what is termed by the author *mortal mind.*

118:26–119:24

The definitions of material law, as given by natural science, represent a kingdom necessarily divided against itself, because these definitions portray law as physical, not spiritual. Therefore they contradict the divine decrees and violate the law of Love, in which nature and God are one and the natural order of the heaven comes down to earth.

When we endow matter with vague spiritual power—that is, when we do so in our theories, for of course we cannot really endow matter with what it does not and cannot possess—we disown the Almighty, for such theories lead to one of two things. They either presuppose the self-evolution and self-government of matter, or else they assume that matter is the product of Spirit. To seize the first horn of this dilemma and consider matter as a power in and of itself, is to leave the creator out of His own universe; while to grasp the other horn of the dilemma and regard God as the creator of matter, is not only to make Him responsible for all disasters, physical and moral, but to announce Him as their source, thereby making Him guilty of maintaining perpetual misrule in the form and under the name of natural law.

In one sense God is identical with nature, but this nature is spiritual and is not expressed in matter. The lawgiver, whose lightning palsies or prostates in death the child at prayer, is not the divine ideal of omnipresent Love. God is natural good, and is represented only by the idea of goodness; while evil should be regarded as unnatural, because it is opposed to the nature of Spirit, God.

142:26–144:2

Which was first, Mind or medicine? If Mind was first and self-existent, then Mind, not matter, must have been the first medicine. God being All-in-all, He made medicine, but that medicine was Mind. It could not have been matter, which departs from the nature and character of Mind, God. Truth is God's remedy for error of every kind, and Truth destroys only what is untrue. Hence the fact that, to-day, as yesterday, Christ casts out evils and heals the sick.

It is plain that God does not employ drugs or hygiene, nor provide them with human use; else Jesus would have recommended and employed them in his healing. The sick are more deplorably lost than the sinning, if the sick cannot rely on God for help and sinning can. The divine Mind never called matter *medicine,* and matter required a material and human belief before it could be considered as medicine.

Sometimes the human mind uses one error to medicine another. Driven to choose between two difficulties, the human mind takes the lesser to relieve the greater. On this basis it saves from starvation by theft, and quiets pain with anodynes. You admit that mind influences the body somewhat, but you conclude that the stomach, blood, nerves, bones, etc., hold the preponderance of power. Controlled by this belief, you continue in the old routine. You lean on the inert and unintelligent, never discerning how this deprives you of the available superiority of divine Mind. The body is not controlled scientifically by a negative mind.

Mind is the grand creator, and there can be no power except that which is derived from Mind. If Mind was first chronologically, is first potentially, and must be first eternally, then give to Mind the glory, honor, dominion, and power everlastingly due its holy name. Inferior and unspiritual methods of healing may try to make Mind and drugs coalesce, but the two will not mingle scientifically. Why should we wish to make them do so, since no good can come of it?

164:17–29

If you or I should appear to die, we should not be dead. The seeming decease, caused by a majority of human beliefs that man must die, or produced by mental assassins, does not in the least disprove Christian Science; rather does it evidence the truth of its basic proposition that mortal thoughts in belief rule the materiality miscalled life in the body or in matter. But the forever fact remains paramount that Life, Truth, and Love save from sin, disease, and death. "When this corruptible shall have put on incorruption, and this mortal shall have put on immortality [divine Science], then shall be brought to pass the saying that is written, Death is swallowed up in victory" (St. Paul).

173:17–29

Anatomy declares man to be structural. Physiology continues this explanation, measuring human strength by bones and sinews, and human life by material law. Man is spiritual, individual, and eternal; material structure is mortal.

Phrenology makes man knavish or honest according to the development of the cranium; but anatomy, physiology, phrenology, do not define the image of God, the real immortal man.

Human reason and religion come slowly to this recognition of spiritual facts, and so continue to call upon matter to remove the error which the human mind alone has created.

174:22–175:3

Mortal belief is all that enables a drug to cure mortal ailments. Anatomy admits that mind is somewhere in man, though out of sight. Then, if an individual is sick, why treat the body alone and administer a dose of despair to the mind? Why declare that the body is diseased, and picture this disease to the mind, rolling it under the tongue as a sweet morsel and holding it before the thought of both physician and patient? We should understand the cause of disease obtains in the mortal human mind, and its cure comes from the immortal divine Mind. We should prevent images of disease from taking form in thought, and we should efface the outlines of disease already formulated in the minds of mortals.

177:25–178:7; 178:13–178:27; 178:32–179:4

If a dose of poison is swallowed through mistake, and the patient dies even though physician and patient are expecting favorable results, does human belief, you ask, cause this death? Even so, and as directly as if the poison had been intentionally taken.

In such cases a few persons believe the potion swallowed by the patient to be harmless, but the vast majority of mankind, though they know nothing of this particular case and this special person, believe the arsenic, the strychnine, or whatever the drug used, to be poisonous, for it is set down as a poison by mortal mind. Consequently, the result is controlled by the majority of opinions, not by the infinitesimal minority of opinions in the sick-chamber. . . . Perhaps an adult has a deformity produced prior to his birth by the fright of his mother. When wrested from human belief and based on Science or the divine Mind, to which all things are possible, that chronic case is not difficult to cure.

Mortal mind, acting from the basis of sensation in matter, is animal magnetism; but this so-called mind, from which comes all evil, contradicts itself, and must finally yield to the eternal Truth, or the divine Mind, expressed in Science. In proportion to our understanding of Christian Science, we are freed from the belief of heredity, of mind in matter or animal magnetism; and we disarm sin of its imaginary power in proportion to our spiritual understanding of the status of immortal being. . . . Whoever reaches the understanding of Christian Science in its proper signification will perform the sudden cures of which it is capable; but this can be done only by taking up the cross and following Christ in the daily life.

188:3–27

What is termed disease does not exist. It is neither mind nor matter. The belief of sin, which has grown terrible in strength and influence, is an unconscious error in the beginning—an embryonic thought without motive; but afterwards it governs the so-called man. Passion, depraved appetites, dishonesty, envy, hatred, revenge ripen into action, only to pass from shame and woe to their final punishment.

Mortal existence is a dream of pain and pleasure in matter, a dream of sin, sickness, and death; and it is like the dream we have in sleep, in which every one recognizes his condition to be wholly a state of mind. In both the waking and the sleeping dream, the dreamer thinks that his body is material and the suffering is in that body.

The smile of the sleeper indicates the sensation produced physically by the pleasure of a dream. In the same way pain and pleasure, sickness and care, are traced upon mortals by unmistakable signs.

Sickness is a growth of error, springing from mortal ignorance or fear. Error rehearses error. What causes disease cannot cure it. The soil of disease is mortal mind, and you have an abundant or scanty crop of disease, according to the seedlings of fear. Sin and fear of disease must be uprooted and cast out.

388:31–390:26

If mortals think that food disturbs the harmonious functions of mind and body, either the food or this thought must be dispensed with, for the penalty is coupled with the belief. Which shall it be? If this decision be left to Christian Science, it will be given in behalf of the control of Mind over this belief and every erroneous belief, or material condition. The less we know or think about hygiene, the less we are predisposed to sickness. Recollect that it is not the nerves, not matter, but mortal mind, which reports food as undigested. Matter does not inform you of bodily derangements; it is supposed to do so. This pseudo-mental testimony can be destroyed only by the better results of Mind's opposite evidence.

Our dietetic theories must first admit that food sustains the life of man, and then discuss the certainty that food can kill man. This false reasoning is rebuked in Scripture by the metaphors about the fount and the stream, the tree and its fruit, and the kingdom divided against itself. If God has, as prevalent theories maintain, instituted laws that food shall support human life, He cannot annul these regulations by an opposite law that food shall be inimical to existence.

Materialists contradict their own statements. Their belief in material laws and in penalties for their infraction is the ancient error that there is fraternity between pain and pleasure, good and evil, God and Satan. This belief totters to its falling before the battle-axe of Science.

A case of convulsions, produced by indigestion, came under my observation. In her belief the woman had chronic liver-complaint, and was then suffering from a complication of symptoms connected with this belief. I cured her in a few minutes. One instant she spoke despairingly of herself. The next minute she said, "My food is all digested, and I should like something more to eat."

We cannot deny that Life is self-sustained, and we should never deny the everlasting harmony of Soul, simply because, to the mortal senses, there is seeming discord. It is our ignorance of God, the divine Principle, which produces apparent discord, and the right understanding of Him restores harmony. Truth will at length compel us all to exchange the pleasures and pains of sense for the joys of Soul.

When the first symptoms of disease appear, dispute the testimony of the material senses with divine Science. Let your higher sense of justice destroy the false process of mortal opinions which you name law, and then you will not be confined to a sick-room nor laid upon a bed of suffering in payment of the last farthing, the last penalty demanded by error. "Agree with thine adversary quickly, whiles thou art in the way with him." Suffer no claim of sin or of sickness to grow upon the thought. Dismiss it with an abiding conviction that it is illegitimate, because you know that God is no more the author of sickness than He is of sin. You have no law of His to support the necessity either of sin or sickness, but you have divine authority for denying that necessity and healing the sick.

392:11–393:8

The physical affirmation of disease should always be met with mental negation. Whatever benefit is produced on the body, must be expressed mentally, and thought should be held fast to this ideal. If you believe in inflamed and weak nerves, you are liable to an attack from that source. You will call it neuralgia, but we call it a belief. If you think that consumption is hereditary in your family, you are liable to the development of that thought in the form of what is termed pulmonary disease, unless Science shows you otherwise. If you decide that climate or atmosphere is unhealthy, it will be so to you. Your decisions will master you, whichever direction they take.

Reverse the case. Stand porter at the door of thought. Admitting only such conclusions as you wish realized in bodily results, you will control yourself harmoniously. When the condition is present which you say induces disease, whether it be air, exercise, heredity, contagion, or accident, then perform your office as porter and shut out these unhealthy thoughts and fears. Exclude from mortal mind the offending errors; then the body cannot suffer them. The issues of pain and pleasure must come through mind, and like a watchman forsaking his post, we admit the intruding belief, forgetting that through divine help we can forbid this entrance.

The body seems to be self-acting, only because mortal mind is ignorant of itself, of its own actions, and of their results—ignorant that the predisposing, remote, and exciting cause of all bad effects is a law of so-called mortal mind, not matter. Mind is the master of the corporeal senses, and can conquer sickness, sin, and death.

411:3–12

My first discovery in the student's practice was this: If the student silently called the disease by name, when he argued against it, as a general rule the body would respond more quickly,—just as a person replies more readily when his name is spoken; but this was because the student was not perfectly attuned to divine Science, and needed the arguments of truth for reminders. If Spirit or the power of divine Love bear witness to the truth, this is the ultimatum, the scientific way, and the healing is instantaneous.

411:27–412:1

Always begin your treatment by allaying the fear of patients. Silently reassure them as to their exemption from disease and danger. Watch the result of this simple rule of Christian Science, and you will find that it alleviates the symptoms of every disease. If you succeed in wholly removing the fear, your patient is healed.

412:16–31

To prevent disease or to cure it, the power of Truth, of divine Spirit, must break the dream of the material senses. To heal by argument, find the type of ailment, get its name, and array your mental plea against the physical. Argue at first mentally, not audibly, that the patient has no disease, and conform the argument so as to destroy the evidence of disease. Mentally insist that harmony is the fact, and that sickness is a temporal dream. Realize the presence of health and the fact of harmonious being, until the body corresponds with the normal conditions of health and harmony.

If the case is that of a young child or infant, it needs to be met mainly through the parent's thought, silently or audibly on the aforesaid basis of Christian Science.

418:26–419:7

Include moral as well as physical belief in your efforts to destroy error. Cast out all manner of evil. "Preach the gospel to every creature." Speak the truth to every form of error. Tumors, ulcers, tubercles, inflammation, pain, deformed joints, are waking dream-shadows, dark images of mortal thought, which flee before the light of Truth.

A moral question may even hinder the recovery of the sick. Lurking error, lust, envy, revenge, malice, or hate will perpetuate or even create the belief in disease. Errors of all sorts tend in this direction. Your true course is to destroy the foe, and leave the field to God, Life, Truth, and Love, remembering that God and His ideas alone are real and harmonious.

427:13–25

Death is but another phase of the dream that existence can be material. Nothing can interfere with the harmony of being nor end the existence of man in Science. Man is the same after as before a bone is broken or the body guillotined. If man is never to overcome death, why do the Scriptures say, "The last enemy that shall be destroyed is death?" The tenor of the Word shows that we shall obtain the victory over death in proportion as we overcome sin. The great difficulty lies in ignorance of what God is. God, Life, Truth, and Love make man undying. Immortal Mind, governing all, must be acknowledged as supreme in the physical realm, so-called, as well as in the spiritual.

Broken Arm Healed by Christian Science

A few weeks ago, one Friday afternoon, a lady came hurriedly into my office, saying, "Mrs. ___ wishes you to come to her as soon as possible; her daughter, little Ruth, about five years old, has broken her arm." I replied that it was impossible for me to go at once, but to tell the mother that I would commence treatment immediately and come over as soon as I could. To outward appearances I was very much engaged in other work, yet the thought of Truth was above it all, and I so clearly realized God's presence and all-powerfulness that a feeling of peace came to me and I knew that all was well with God's child.

In this sweet realization I remained, and about an hour later I went to the home of the little girl and found, as I expected, that she had gone to sleep. The mother told me that several little children had been playing on a fence and one of them pushed Ruth and she fell to the ground, striking her arm on a stone. The children ran to Ruth's mother and told her that Ruth was hurt. The mother hurried to her, and as she picked her up she pushed up the sleeve of her dress and noticed a protrusion on one side of her arm and a corresponding indentation on the other side, which looked as though the bone was broken and pushed out of place. She immediately pressed down the lump and took Ruth into the house and bound a strip of flannel around her arm and sent for me. Then she took *Science and Health with Key to the Scriptures*, and declared the Truth with all her might and tried to quiet the child with the assurance that divine Love watches over all, and no harm could come to her. In a little while she fell asleep.

I read a little more from *Science and Health* with the mother, and then we silently realized the presence of infinite Mind and the nothingness of matter. Soon little Ruth awoke and came running to me full of joy, bringing to me her latest picture-books to show me, saying nothing about her arm and paying no attention to it whatever, merely allowing it to hang limp at her side. In a short while I took her upon my knee, and while talking with her I felt of her arm and found that there was no swelling and no claim of fever, and harmony seemed to reign.

Ruth's father had not returned from business yet, so I waited for him to see what he would wish to have done. He has not as yet declared himself to be a believer in Christian Science, although he makes no objection to it and attends our meetings frequently. Upon his return the case was explained to him and I suggested that he send for a physician and have the bone set, and then, if he wished Christian Science treatment to bring about speedy healing, I was willing to give the treatment. He said, "According to your belief, a doctor should not be necessary, and besides, how do I know that it is broken." I quoted him the instruction from our text-book, *Science and Health*, with reference to having broken bones set by a surgeon, and told him that he might take the child to a surgeon and explain the case to him and have the bone set. He replied that he would leave it all with his wife, saying she could do as she thought best and he would not interfere. The child's mother is one of our loyal church members, and she at once declared that God is the Great Physician, and we need no other.

Little Ruth has been taught that divine Love heals all disease and overcomes all error, and has had many beautiful proofs of it before this, so she also chimed in that she didn't want a doctor. I said that this decision must be entirely their own responsibility and by no means by my advice; then if they wished me to take charge of the case I was ready to do so. They said they wanted no other help than Christian Science, and for me to take charge of the case. I gave another treatment and went home. The next day (Saturday) I called and found that Ruth had slept all night as harmoniously as a babe, and was playing around during the day. Sunday morning, just before the beginning of church services, Ruth's mother came to me and said that they had been battling with error all night, and Ruth had slept but little, and there was much discord manifested. I also learned that there had been many harsh things said in the neighborhood against Christian Science and what would happen. This only uncovered the error and showed me how to work. During the reading of the Lesson-Sermon the Truth was so clearly revealed that before the service was over I knew the error had been overcome. And thus it proved to be. Sunday night little Ruth slept peacefully all night, and in the morning, when her mother went to her crib, she found her sleeping sweetly with her arm (the one that had been broken) up over her head. From that time there was no further trouble. She was kept at home from school a few days, lest the jostling of the children might cause more to demonstrate over. In less than a week she commenced to use her arm a little, and in about two weeks she was all right again. Truly our God is a great God, and greatly to be praised. We give everlasting thanks for the glorious revelation of Truth to this age through our dear Mother and Leader, Rev. Mary Baker G. Eddy, Discoverer and Founder of Christian Science.

Charles Rockwell, Mt. Vernon, N. Y.

— 23 —

The Miracles of St. Anthony of Padua

Timothy J. Meagher

Devotions to the saints extend far back into the history of the Christian church, but these devotions, like many other Christian rituals, have had an episodic history, rising and falling through periods of indifference and neglect, revival and interest. In the middle and late nineteenth century, for example, a "devotional revolution" erupted in the Catholic Church in the West and devotions to many saints suddenly became more widely popular than they had ever been. This revolution was encouraged by the Vatican in Rome, made possible by new technologies of cheap printing and lithography, and welcomed by many Catholics confronting the economic and social dislocations caused by urbanization and industrialization.

Devotion to St. Anthony of Padua was one of the most popular of the rituals revitalized in this Catholic religious revival. Born in Portugal to a noble family in 1195, Anthony made his name as a powerful preacher for St. Francis of Assisi's new Franciscan friars in northern Italy and southern France. Many of the miracle stories linked to Anthony played on the theme of his preaching skills; one told, for example, that while he was rehearsing his sermon near a stream one day, the fish were so moved by his eloquence that they jumped and frolicked in appreciation. Such stories notwithstanding, Anthony was a serious figure and his preaching a powerful weapon in the bitter and sometimes bloody religious controversies of his day. He became known as the "hammer of the heretics" for his work against the Cathars of northern Italy and the Albigensians of southern France. A grateful Pope Gregory IX, who knew Anthony and appreciated his efforts in these disputes, canonized him but a year after the saint's death in 1231.

Devotions to St. Anthony began almost immediately after his death and new ones were invented and old ones revived intermittently over the next seven centuries. Yet Anthony's cult only became broadly popular and well organized at the end of the nineteenth century and the beginning of the twentieth. It was then that Pope Pius IX and his successor, Leo XIII, endorsed devotion to Anthony and granted indulgences to all who prayed to him. In the 1890s the Vatican also approved the organization of a Pious Union of St. Anthony, headquartered in Rome, a Guild of St. Anthony, based in England, and revived a Confraternity of St. Anthony. By the second decade of the twentieth century, the Union had over 100,000 members and the Guild over 200,000. Gifts to the poor or clerical students given in St. Anthony's name were organized as "St. Anthony's Bread" at Toulon in 1888, and within a few years that charity was raising hundreds of thousands of francs for those causes.

St. Anthony was no less popular in the United States. In some cities, Italian immigrants celebrated his feast day (June 13) as an ethnic holiday, but Anthony's popularity transcended ethnic boundaries. Indeed, St. Anthony was one of a small number of widely popular saints, including St. Theresa of Lisieux and St. Jude. Their devotions became the core of a new panethnic or supraethnic American Catholic devotionalism emerging in the early twentieth century and persisting until the Second Vatican Council. In Worcester, Massachusetts, for example, a group of Irish Sisters of Mercy imported a statue of Anthony in the late 1890s and established a devotion to him. By the early twentieth century, devotion to St. Anthony in Detroit, encouraged by Capuchin friars, rivaled that of St. Anne's, the long time patron of the city's Catholics. About the same time, Franciscans established shrines to St. Anthony in Butler, New Jersey, and Mount Airy, Ohio, attracting thousands of visitors. In 1893 the Franciscans founded a magazine, *St. Anthony's Messenger,* to encourage devotions and raise money for their seminarians. Letters printed in the magazine reflect the nationwide interest in the saint. Letters came from towns and cities as diverse as Dixie, Arkansas; Springfield, Massachusetts; Lincoln, Nebraska; Lockport, New York; Lemon City, Florida; and Sacramento, California.

St. Anthony of Padua is the patron of lovers, marriage, women in confinement, people sick with fever, miners and, perhaps most notably, the patron saint of the search for lost objects. Some of the letters below testify to St. Anthony's time-honored role as the finder of lost objects: A.H. from Campbelltown, Ohio, for example, thanked Anthony for help in locating a lost satchel, and T.C. from Calumet, Michigan for finding "my paybook." Yet, as in devotions to other saints or Mary, Mother of Christ, Catholic men and women in America petitioned St. Anthony for all sorts of reasons. Many, including J.C. from Dixie, Arkansas, N.N. from Tiffin, Ohio, M.H. from Lincoln, Nebraska, and S.G. from Madison, Indiana, thanked St. Anthony for his aid in overcoming illnesses. They found in St. Anthony, as Robert Orsi suggests many Catholic women later found in St. Jude, a power greater than the power of medical science, a power that freed them from dependence on an emerging medical establishment. For example, S.G. from Madison boasted of St. Anthony's ability to "relieve me without being obliged to go to a doctor," and J.C. from Dixie exulted in "a wonderful cure for a sore limb, which had baffled the skill of excellent physicians." As these letters show, however, Anthony's power extended beyond healing the body or finding lost objects. Anthony's intercessions, as revealed in these letters, ranged across almost the entire spectrum of human need, from buying a home and finding better tenants, to finding a long lost brother, bringing a son back to the church, or securing music students. Though their needs were diverse, all of the correspondents wanted the same thing: the saint's miraculous help to solve a concrete problem. The letters do not ask St. Anthony to make them better Christians, build character in the face of adversity, or learn to accept God's will in their fates. As Colleen McDannell has noted about participants in the devotion at Lourdes, petitioners to St. Anthony clearly sought, and believed they had received, neither comfort nor education, but his miraculous, almost magical intervention in their lives. For example, C. from Bradley, Illinois, pointed out his/her prayers were answered on the very day the family ended their novena, and M.O'S. from Peoria speaks of the implausible accidents that led to her finding her brother.

The petitioners also seemed to share a common vision of St. Anthony and an understanding of the proper ways in which they should relate to him. They seemed, first of all, to think of him as a "friend," an extension of their networks of family and friends, of their community into the heavenly sphere. Such networks were critical to the bulk of American Catholics, whose communal values originated in peasant pasts and were nourished by the economic constraints of the working-class present. The bonds of reciprocity and mutual obligation that tied family and friends on earth reached through the heavenly friend, St. Anthony, to his friend, Christ himself. Petitioners thus did not simply ask for help by reciting this prayer; they offered money, prayers, or good deeds in return, nourishing the bonds of mutuality that tied them and Anthony together in a network of friendship. The very act of writing him in gratitude was a critical element in maintaining those bonds. Several letter writers noted their promises to thank St. Anthony, should he fulfill their request. If the petitioners did not keep their promises and express such thanks, the bonds of reciprocity and friendship might be broken and the evils might return. For example, B. from Covington, Kentucky, confessed regretfully: "I neglected to make the announcement as promised, and the favors have, practically, been taken from me."

Even if these letters of thanksgiving were reaffirmations of bonds of mutuality with heavenly friends, they were much more than that. The letters themselves were, as Orsi and McDannell have suggested of other Catholic devotions, rituals of worship. St. Anthony could have been thanked privately, but these petitioners felt compelled to express their gratitude publicly. In this respect, McDannell suggests, such letters were like Catholic ex votos, reproductions of limbs in wax or other substances, left at shrines by the cured as testaments to a saint's power to heal their illnesses and injuries. The letters are testaments, and the *Messenger* is the shrine where they are made visible. Spread far and wide through publication, these thanksgivings became, Orsi argues, "narratives of grace," a means of converting others to the cult of the saint.

The responsory prayer included here has been attributed to St. Bonaventure. It was first part of the Franciscan prayers for St. Anthony's feast before becoming a prayer of popular devotion. Taking advantage of new printing technologies, pious societies devoted to St. Anthony all produced holy cards bearing his figure with the responsory on the back. These cards were widely distributed in the late nineteenth and early twentieth centuries. Petitioners were encouraged to use the responsory in several ways. By decree of Leo XIII, they could receive a plenary indulgence by attending mass on thirteen consecutive Tuesdays and reciting the responsory. By decree of Pius IX, they could receive such an indulgence if they said this prayer, attended mass, received communion, and prayed for the intentions of the pope every day for a month. The Pious Union encouraged its members to say the prayer, "Glory be to the Father, Son and Holy Ghost, as it was in the beginning, is now and ever shall be, world without end. Amen," three times daily, recite the responsory once a day, go to mass, and receive communion on St. Anthony's feast day of June 13.

The following selections are from *St. Anthony's Messenger*: Responsory: 1 no.1 (June 1893): 23; Letters: 1 no. 8 (January 1894): 287; 2 no.1 (June 1894): 35; 2 no. 9 (February 1895): 326; 7 no. 2 (June 1899): 71; 8 no. 1 (June 1900): 34; 8 no. 2 (July 1900): 71; 8 no. 4 (September 1900): 142; 8 no. 5 (October 1900): 178; 15 no. 4 (September 1907): 143; 15 no. 8 (January 1908): 287; and 15 no. 10 (March 1908): 359.

Further Reading

Ann Taves, *Household of Faith: Roman Catholic Devotions in Mid-Nineteenth-Century America* (Notre Dame: University of Notre Dame Press, 1986); Joseph P. Chinnici, *Living Stones: The History and Structure of Catholic Spritual Life in the United States* (New York: Macmillan, 1989); Hugh McLeod, *Piety and Poverty: Working Class Religion in Berlin, London and New York, 1870–1914* (New York: Holmes and Meier, 1996); Robert A. Orsi, *Thank You St. Jude: Women's Devotion to the Patron Saint of Hopeless Causes* (New Haven: Yale University Press, 1996); Colleen McDannell, *Material Christianity: Religion and Popular Culture in America* (New Haven: Yale University Press, 1995).

Responsory
June 1893

If Miracles thou fain would see:
Lo! Error, death, calamity,
The leprous stain, the demon flies:
From beds of pain the sick arise

The hungry seas forego their prey,
The prisoner's cruel chains give way
While palsied limbs and treasures lost
Both young and old recovered boast

And perils perish, plenty's hoard
Is heaped on hunger's famished board
Let those relate, who know it well,
Let Padua of her patron tell

The hungry seas forego their prey,
The prisoner's cruel chains give way
While palsied limbs and treasures lost
Both young and old recovered boast

The Father, Son, may glory be
And Holy Ghost eternally

V. Pray for us St. Anthony
R. That we may be made worthy of the promises of Christ.

Let Us pray

Almighty and eternal God, who didst glorify thy faithful Confessor Anthony
with the perpetual gift of working miracles, graciously grant, that we confi-
dently seek through his merits, we may surely receive through his intercession. Through Christ Our Lord Amen.

The Letters

Waterford, New York, November 2, 1893. Some time ago our store was entered by
a thief and $100 worth of goods stolen. Naturally we were in great excitement, but
we prayed to St. Anthony and, behold, the next day some of the goods were found
and the thief caught, for which we return sincere thanks to our great patron.

G.H.

Baltimore, Maryland [nd]. My father had neglected the sacraments for many
years and belonged to several secret societies. As he was dangerously ill and gave
no sign of repentance, I had a mass offered for his conversion at St. Anthony's
shrine, Butler, New Jersey, on the 20th of April. The same day he asked for a
priest, received the sacraments, after giving up all connections with the secret
societies, and died in the evening. Thanks to the powerful intercession of St.
Anthony.

Dr. K.

Boston, Massachusetts, December 27, 1894. Twenty six years ago my uncle left
for the far West. For the last 22 years we had not heard from him and all our
efforts to learn his whereabouts were in vain. Discouraged, we gave up all
hopes, thinking our uncle had died. Upon the advice of a good Franciscan we
prayed fervently to St. Anthony. A short time after and in the most unexpected
manner I found a book, which enabled me to correspond with one of the

Fathers in whose parish my uncle was. You may imagine our happiness at once more being in communication with one, loved so dearly. Thanks to St. Anthony for this intercession.

C.A.

Cleveland, Ohio, May 29, 1899. Last Tuesday there was a runaway; horses ran on the sidewalk and one of them run [sic] into the iron-railing with such speed that I was not able to get out of the way. The horse struck my right foot and threw me to the pavement, and one horse fell with its back on my lower limbs quite badly bruising them. I escaped without broken bones, and as I had been making the Nine Tuesdays in honor of St. Anthony. I feel that the Saint saved me from death or serious injuries. For this great favor I wish to give public thanks to St. Anthony.

N.H.

Dixie P.O. Ark., May 12, 1900. Glory and praise to dear St. Anthony for a wonderful cure of a sore limb, which had baffled the skill of excellent physicians. We had recourse to dear St. Anthony, and in his name used an ordinary remedy, and can say that within two weeks all pain had ceased. Thanks to the great and glorious St. Anthony!

J.C.

Springfield, Mass., May 15, 1900. I had requested from St. Anthony to let me have a good tenant, and rid me of a bad one. Both of my requests having been granted, I beg to return sincere thanks to dear St. Anthony for this great favor.

C.McC.

Calumet, Mich., May 23, 1900. I had lost my pay-book, which meant a great deal to me. I had recourse to St. Anthony in prayer, and am happy to say the book was found in a mysterious way. Thanks to God, and praise to dear St. Anthony.

T.C.

Sacramento City, Cal., May 28, 1900. Glory to God, and thanks to dear St. Anthony of Padua, through whose intercession I have received a great favor of being cured completely of the itch, which for twenty five years had annoyed me and would not yield to all medical treatment.

M.A.M.

Tiffin O., August 17, 1900. I had made a promise to St. Anthony if I would get over a sickness in a certain time and not be obliged to suffer too much. I would publish it in the Messenger in every respect, and we have now a little son whom we named in honor of the Saint. With many thanks to St. Anthony we fulfil our promise.

N.N.

Madison, Ind., July 18, 1900. Several weeks ago I was eating and something stuck in my throat. I at once took refuge to the Blessed Virgin and St. Anthony to relieve me without being obliged to go to a doctor, and promised to give thanks through the Messenger. Many thanks to the Blessed Virgin and St. Anthony, my prayer has been answered in a short time.

S.G.

Peoria, Ill., September 13, 1900. For the honor of God and His glorious St. Anthony please publish the following: "Six years ago my brother left home without letting us know where he intended to go. Not hearing from him for four years, I thought he had died, but still a little hope was left in me, and so I made several novenas to great St. Anthony at St. Boniface Church, and had three masses said. On labor-day, the 3rd of September, I accidently (sic) met a friend who keeps a boarding house, who told me that she had heard one of her boarders speaking about my brother, and so I learned that he was in Massachusetts, working for some railroad, looking and doing well. Many sincere thanks, therefore, to great St. Anthony, for letting me hear of my lost brother."

M.O'S.

Bradley, Ill., October 19, 1900. I and my family were in a most pressing need and there was no earthly mortal to whom I could have recourse. I told my entire family to put all our trust in Almighty God, knowing He would not desert us. We all began a Novena to the Sacred Heart, to Our Lady of Perpetual Help and St. Anthony, and thanks be to God we received more than we looked for. The day our novena ended—the 13th of June—was indeed remarkable because on St. Anthony's day a man entered my home telling me the needed assistance was to come. For this and several other requests I wish to return my sincerest thanks to the Sacred Heart, Our Lady of Perpetual Help, St. Joseph and St. Anthony.

C.

Campbellstown, O., July 26, 1907. Last spring I lost my satchel containing very valuable papers and other articles which I prized very highly. I placed my trust in St. Anthony, and in a few weeks I received my treasures. I wish to give public thanks to St. Anthony, and recommend all go to him to find both spiritual and temporal assistance.

A.H.

Omaha, Neb., July 27, 1907. I promised to have it published in St. Anthony's Messenger, in honor of the great Saint, if my son, who had neglected the Sacraments for some time, should return to his religion. I am thankful to say he died a most penitent and happy death. I cannot say too much in praise of dear St. Anthony, he has done so much for me.

K.F.

Lincoln, Neb., August 14, 1907. I wish to express my sincerest gratitude to St. Anthony for my recovery, after two operations, and hereby fulfill my promise to have it published in St. Anthony's Messenger.

M.H.

Soldiers Grove, Wis., Dec. 15, 1907. Last winter my mother sent a petition to be placed at the foot of St. Anthony's statue in your Oratory for the restoration of my health. I was so sick that, in spite of three doctors trying their utmost to keep me alive, all seemed in vain. I grew weaker from day to day and could not retain the medicine they had prescribed. I was almost at the point of death, when suddenly a marked change came over me, and in a few days I was able to get up and walk about, after another relapse I got better and remained so until two months ago, when I got worse again. I am afraid it is in punishment of having neglected to publish it, after I had been restored to health. If so I beg your pardon, and request you to pray for me, so God will give me health again, if it is His holy will.

A.V.F.

Covington, Ky., Feb. 2, 1908. I desire, through the Messenger, to return thanks to good and dear St. Anthony for favors obtained for me during and at the end of a novena of the nine Tuesdays in his honor. In return I had promised to make a donation and public announcement of thanks through the Messenger. I neglected to make the announcement of thanks as promised, and the favors have, practically, been taken from me.

B.

Imagining: The Unseen World

—24—

The Life and Death of
Mother Marie de Saint Joseph

Julia Boss

Marie Savonnières de la Troche was born in 1616 in the Anjou region of France. As a girl she gave away her food to the poor; in her youth she saw visions, took the veil of an Ursuline nun and the name of St. Joseph; in her twenties she sailed as a missionary to North America; at age thirty-five she died in Quebec, ending her years of suffering for Christ. Her life was crowned with virtues, her death with miracles: apparitions, miraculous rescues, flesh that refused to decay. This is the story that Marie de l'Incarnation tells in the "Account of the life, virtues, and death of Mother Marie de Saint Joseph" that she sent to the Ursulines of Tours in the spring of 1652. It is in some ways a familiar European story, sharing many of its details with the biographies of saints and other holy persons that had been part of Christian literature since the days of the early church. But here the old genre is adapted to a new North American setting.

Like other early modern European powers, France cited religious motives to justify its colonization of North America—the moral obligation to convert the continent's indigenous population to Christianity, more precisely, to the Roman Catholicism threatened by the rise of Protestantism in Europe. In 1534 Jacques Cartier planted a cross to enact France's possession of Canada, and by the mid-seventeenth century missionaries of several different religious orders had begun work in the nascent colony. Until late in the century, French colonial activities, and therefore missionary efforts, were concentrated in the St. Lawrence River Valley (Quebec, and farther south into territory that would later become New York state) and in Acadia (later Nova Scotia, New Brunswick, and Maine). By 1700 France asserted its ownership of a vast geographical area extending from Canada down the Mississippi River to the Gulf of Mexico. Missionaries traveled with explorers from Quebec into Louisiana.

Ursuline nuns came to New France in 1639 in response to a request by Jesuit missionaries for women to instruct French and Native American girls. The

Ursulines had been founded in Italy in the mid-sixteenth century. By the 1590s they were established in France, and the "company" of women soon assumed the more formal character of a cloistered "congregation." The Ursulines were among more than a dozen new women's religious orders created during the sixteenth and seventeenth centuries. These new orders of the Catholic Reformation allowed women to pursue active vocations such as hospital work or (as in the case of the Ursulines) teaching. The new foundations offered an alternative to the traditional contemplative prayer role to which religious women had previously been restricted. By the end of the seventeenth century, there were ten thousand French Ursulines living in 320 communities in France and Quebec. In 1727 another North American Ursuline mission would be founded in New Orleans.

Marie de Saint Joseph arrived in Quebec in August 1639. She was part of the founding mission led by the laywoman Marie-Madeleine de Chauvigny de la Peltrie and by Marie Guyart (called de l'Incarnation), who would serve as the Quebec community's first superior. With Madame de la Peltrie and the two sisters from Tours traveled a third Ursuline from the community at Dieppe and another laywoman who would herself later become a member of the order. The group dedicated their foundation to St. Joseph, who had been designated the patron saint of Canada. They built a monastery high on the bluff above the St. Lawrence River. They studied the Huron and Algonkian languages, taught French boarding pupils (*pensionnaires*) and Indian girls (whom they called *séminaristes*), and catechized adult Indian converts of both genders. By 1650 the community had grown to fourteen sisters, teaching anywhere from twenty to fifty girls. In that year a fire destroyed their monastery, and they worried that the mission might have to be abandoned. But benefactors in Quebec and France responded to the crisis with gifts of money, food, linens, books, rosaries, and "little devotions" to replace all that had been lost in the fire. By the date of Marie de Saint Joseph's death, reconstruction was nearly completed.

Marie de l'Incarnation's letter of 1652 about Marie de Saint Joseph and the letter of 1663 also translated here partake of two literary traditions: colonial promotional literature and sacred biography. As letters sent from a colonial missionary to readers in France, the texts have a clear promotional purpose. They demonstrate to European benefactors that the mission has been entrusted to dedicated hands, and they display evidence of progress in converting and instructing North America's native peoples. Partly in the service of this agenda, the Jesuit Paul Le Jeune edited the biographical letter for publication in the "Jesuit Relations" (an annual series reporting the year's events in French North America). The letter's content and structure, however, belong to the tradition of hagiography. Marie de l'Incarnation wrote the 1652 account to serve as the obituary notice (*notice nécrologique*) by which the superior of an Ursuline monastery customarily informed other communities of a member's death. In this commemorative capacity circulation was limited, but the letters about Marie de Saint Joseph reached a wider audience when Claude Martin later edited them for inclusion in *Lettres de la Vénérable Mère Marie de l'Incarnation*. With the publication of that collection in

1681, readers from outside the Ursuline order had a chance to read this early contribution to the hagiography of New France.

Hagiography, defined literally as "writing about saints," is as old as the church itself. In the early church, Christians compiled lists of martyrs killed for their faith and used these lists to commemorate the anniversaries of the martyrs' deaths. By the Middle Ages, martyred saints were joined by other saints who had not died for their faith but had lived in an exemplary manner. Simple lists of names had grown into complete life narratives (called "lives") that described a full cycle of birth, growth in virtue, sufferings, and death.

By the time Marie de l'Incarnation wrote her biography of Marie de Saint Joseph, the canonization of saints had become a highly standardized practice. Following the death of an exemplary "servant of God," acquaintances composed accounts of the holy person's life and virtues. If demonstrations of heroic virtue were substantial, favors from God sufficiently numerous and miraculous, and the deceased's "reputation for sanctity" enduring, Rome might eventually pursue the process for canonization that was officially required to declare someone a saint. Seventeenth-century French Catholics—wherever they lived—hoped to add French names to a canon of saints then dominated by Italians and Spaniards, and new religious orders sought canonization for their founders and members. This quest for inclusion may have been intensified among missionaries seeking recognition for their efforts overseas. Writing "lives" of fellow colonial missionaries helped New France's authors demonstrate to European readers that their subjects— despite their exile in the North American wilderness—had not been barbarized by the experience but remained firmly in the world of European Catholicism and no less directly connected to divine favor.

The correlation of literary genre (hagiography) and canonical status (actual sainthood) was not exact. Lives of Catholic Reformation saints like Teresa of Avila were so widely read during the seventeenth century that they inevitably became models for writing about any notable religious person. Most biographies that followed the hagiographic model (including that of Marie de Saint Joseph) did not trigger official canonization processes. But narratives of holy lives served other purposes for their readers—who included the laity as well as members of religious orders. Because saints were expected to demonstrate "heroic virtue," these biographies devoted many pages to illustrating their subjects' piety, modesty, charity, and the like. Although laypeople might be cautioned against imitating saints' more extreme behaviors (severe fasting or other bodily mortifications), the heroically virtuous life of a figure like St. Teresa could inspire more modest sacrifices in an ordinary reader's life. Saints' lives also helped readers to construct a relationship between the material world that surrounded them in the present and the spiritual world that awaited them in the future.

Early modern Catholics saw frequent evidence of interaction between the parallel worlds of heaven and earth, spirit and matter. Most obviously and officially, at the moment of consecration in the Eucharist, God was believed to intervene directly to transform earthly bread and wine into the body and blood of Christ.

The window between mundane and celestial worlds could also open without priestly assistance: religious and laity saw visions of the saints or the Virgin Mary, or they heard inner voices directing their actions. When a holy person died, the fortunate few present at his or her deathbed might share a glimpse of the heavenly reward beyond. The relics of saints—entire bodies, bones, oils and unguents distilled from holy flesh, or "secondary relics" such as books and rosaries used by the deceased—could also be sites where matter and spirit came together.

In Catholic spirituality, saints in heaven maintained an ongoing relationship with believers on earth; a saint might use his or her proximity to God to intercede on behalf of earthly counterparts. Theologians were careful to distinguish between the worship (*latria*) owed to God alone and the veneration (*dulia*) appropriate to the saints, and they argued over the precise significance of saints' relics. In popular practice, however, physical proximity to a saint's relic was understood to mean greater access to that holy person's intercessory power before God. The unearthly fragrances and healing powers attached to these objects made heavenly presence available to human sensory perception. The miraculous protections and healings described in the "lives" of God's favored people demonstrated to more ordinary readers and listeners that God could intervene to right the wrongs of the material world. These sacred biographies also demonstrated that—in the absence of miraculous deliverance—virtuous suffering in the material world would be rewarded in the spiritual realm.

Marie de l'Incarnation's life of Marie de Saint Joseph conforms closely to the conventions of the hagiographic genre. Lives of female saints typically described an early vocation and a gradual growth in virtue and piety. In this account Marie shows an early inclination toward charity (secretly giving away her meals to the poor), and a firm commitment to modesty and sexual purity. In the complete text from which the translated excerpts are taken, the author includes a lengthy catalogue of her subject's virtues: attachment to the Ursuline Rule; dedication to prayer; love of suffering and poverty; humility, obedience, and purity. The narrative's first half chronicles Marie's life in France, where she demonstrates her virtue by renouncing food, the vanities of aristocratic life, marriage, and the comforts of family. In the story's second half, set in North America, self-imposed suffering is no longer required. New France is presented as a purer alternative to France, where the temptation to vanity is reduced and the opportunity for imitating Christ's suffering greatly increased. Marie's special relationship to the Virgin Mary, her protection by Canadian patron St. Joseph (whose name she assumes "in religion"), and the miracles later performed through her own intercession demonstrate the active reciprocal relationships possible between members of the earthly and heavenly dimensions of the communion of saints.

Given the highly formulaic character of hagiography—and the miracles that to modern readers seem more bizarre than edifying—historians have often shied away from using such documents as evidence. Rather than trying to understand what "really happened," we might better ask what the miracles and visions meant in their historical context. As suggested above, the life of Marie de Saint

Joseph reveals the importance that its author and readers attached to their relationships with members of the heavenly community of saints—whether unseen, pictured in visions, or perceived through the human senses in miraculous paintings or unearthly fragrances. The document may also say something about bonds of community on earth. It was highly unusual in this period for women to travel as missionaries. Those who did go to New France expected never to return to the country of their birth. One might suggest that it was her departure for North America rather than her death that most significantly changed Marie de Saint Joseph's relationship to Ursulines in France. The narrative also reveals French hopes and fears for their colony in New France. As an intercessor, Marie de Saint Joseph seems especially concerned with protecting the vulnerable from New France's special dangers, such as icy rivers or dechristianization in Indian captivity.

The miracle of incorruptible flesh described in the letter of 1663 deserves particular mention. When she died, Marie de Saint Joseph left behind a body invaded by gangrene. Nevertheless, a decade later that same body reportedly retained a miraculously preserved heart and brain. By the seventeenth century, it had become a hagiographic commonplace that a holy person's corpse, or important portions of it, should remain intact and should exude not the stench of corruption but a sweet fragrance termed "the odor of sanctity." Yet in life this particular heart had "carried" both French colonists and Indian converts. And Marie de Saint Joseph's death took place at a time when New France's Catholics were particularly concerned over issues of fragmentation and disintegration: What was their relationship to the European Catholic world they had left behind? Would North America's French colony be wiped out by some disaster? How should they define the relationship between the French colonial church and Native American converts, who even when they became Christian never ceased to be "savage"? (Like most seventeenth-century French writers, Marie de l'Incarnation consistently uses the word *sauvage* as a generic term for North America's indigenous people.) The miraculous incorruptibility of Marie de Saint Joseph's heart might seem to promise a similar preservation for the church in New France.

The question of Native American response to Catholic mission efforts has received extensive scholarly attention: How many converted? How many resisted? Were those conversions genuine? To what extent were ostensibly religious decisions influenced by demographic crisis after European diseases decimated indigenous populations? What role did conversions play in further dividing Indians into opposing groups of Christians and traditionalists? These are difficult questions to answer, especially because most surviving documents that describe converts' beliefs and devotional practices were written in the service of the French mission. In the letters translated here, the Indian role is instrumental to the sanctification of Marie de Saint Joseph. Her dream of Indians who tell her, "It is by us you will be saved," casts North America's people in a role that in European hagiography is more often assigned to "the poor" or "the sick." Their own salvation or subjective participation in Christianity is less at issue than their function as objects of education, conversion, and charity. Yet, in other texts from late-seventeenth-century New France, native converts (the best known being the Mohawk Kateri Tekakwitha) occupy the central saintly role, living out the same patterns of virtue and renunciation that appear in the life of Marie de Saint Joseph or any other European saint.

It was still true in the seventeenth century that women rarely wrote biographies or autobiographies, especially for publication. French women were still less likely than men to be literate, although orders like the Ursulines had begun to address this educational imbalance. For religious women who did write, publication was deemed inconsistent with pious modesty (the same modesty that prompted Marie de l'Incarnation to leave her own spiritual autobiography to burn in the Ursulines' 1650 fire). Texts authored by cloistered women typically reached print only after editorial intervention by some male authority. Thus, the version of the 1652 "life" of Marie de Saint Joseph printed in the "Jesuit Relations" was heavily rewritten; Paul Le Jeune, who had served as Marie de Saint Joseph's spiritual director, freely mixed his own observations with those he received from Marie de l'Incarnation. The text of the 1681 edition (on which the following translations are based) is considered much closer to the original. Nevertheless, editor Claude Martin—Marie de l'Incarnation's son, and a member of the Benedictine order—did "improve" his mother's writings to meet his own literary and theological standards. He also added long footnotes to these letters, in part to lend his own religious authority to testimony regarding the "few miraculous events." Thus, Marie de Saint Joseph's story, like her relics, grew ever more saintly in the years that followed her death.

The translation is based on the text in *Lettres de la Vénérable Mère Marie de l'Incarnation Première Supérieure des Ursulines de la Nouvelle France* (Paris, 1681), pp. 464–503, 587–88. The most recent French edition is Marie de l'Incarnation, *Correspondance,* edited by Guy Oury (Solesmes, France: Abbaye Saint-Pierre, 1971), pp. 436–73, 721–22. The account of Marie de Saint Joseph's life published in the "Jesuit Relations" for 1651–1652 can be found in *The Jesuit Relations and Allied Documents,* edited by Reuben Gold Thwaites (Cleveland: Burrows Brothers, 1896–1901), vol. 38, pp. 68–165.

Further Reading

Peter Burke, "How to be a Counter-Reformation Saint," in *Religion and Society in Early Modern Europe, 1500–1800,* edited by Kaspar von Greyerz (London: George Allen & Unwin, 1984), pp. 45–55; Carolyn Walker Bynum, "Bodily Miracles and the Resurrection of the Body in the High Middle Ages," in *Belief in History: Innovative Approaches to European and American Religion,* edited by Thomas Kselman (Notre Dame: University of Notre Dame Press, 1991), pp. 68–106;

Natalie Zemon Davis, *Women on the Margins: Three Seventeenth-Century Lives* (Cambridge: Harvard University Press, 1995); Carlos M. N. Eire, *From Madrid to Purgatory: The Art and Craft of Dying in Sixteenth-Century Spain* (Cambridge and New York: Cambridge University Press, 1995); Allan Greer, "Colonial Saints: Gender, Race, and Hagiography in New France," *William and Mary Quarterly*, 3rd series, 67 (2000): 323–48; Peter N. Moogk, "Reluctant Exiles: Emigrants from France in Canada before 1760," *William and Mary Quarterly*, 3rd series, 46 (1989): 463–505; Elizabeth Rapley, *The Dévotes: Women and Church in Seventeenth-Century France* (Montreal, Quebec, and Kingston, Ontario: McGill–Queen's University Press, 1990).

Letter from Marie de l'Incarnation to the Community of Ursulines in Tours

She gives them an account of the life, virtues, and death of Mother Marie de Saint Joseph.

My Reverend Mothers. In my plan to describe to you the life and virtues of Mother Marie de Saint Joseph, my very dear and very faithful Companion, Professed Religious of your house, and Assistant of ours, I will consider it a very particular grace from Heaven if I can remember all that I know of her: but there are so many things to tell, that I fear something will escape my memory. I will mention nothing that I did not witness during the twenty-two years that I had the happiness to know her and converse with her, or that I have not learned either from her in the familiar and confidential conversations we had together, or from spiritual persons to whom she confided her inner secrets and the extraordinary graces she had received from God. But whatever I might be able to say will be little, compared to that which her humility has kept hidden from us, in the view she had of pleasing only God and being known only to him. I will try nonetheless to tell all that I know of her, as much to console our Mothers in France as to serve as an example to those who in the future will succeed us in this Monastery.

1. On her birth, childhood, and education

God caused her to be born in Anjou the seventh of September in the year 1616. Her father was Monsieur de la Troche Saint Germain, and her mother Madame Jeanne Raoul, equally admirable for their nobility and their piety. From the moment she was delivered into the world, Madame her mother was strongly inspired to dedicate her to God's service, and to put her under the protection of the very holy Virgin Mary, that the Virgin herself might take charge of her care and conduct, and might give her as a bride to her son. It soon became clear that our Lord had accepted this gift; for while she was still in the hands of her wet-nurse, he hastened her understanding, and gave her an extraordinary inclination toward virtue. . . .

The pious mother took this consecrated child nearly everywhere with her, and set her a great example of piety and charity toward the poor. She, on her side, benefited from the example; for she loved the poor so tenderly that she privately gave them all she could. She sometimes told me that neither she nor Mesdemoiselles her sisters dared to leave their room without permission, yet she often slipped away to bring to the poor her lunch, breakfast, and whatever she could take from the kitchen. There was a good old man whom Messieurs her parents lodged in a tower at the Portico of their house. It was this man she visited, and to whom she gave her little presents, consoling him in the infirmities of his old age. She performed these deeds in secret, furtively, for as she was spoiling her clothes, she feared her Governess would accuse her, and she would thereafter be forbidden these little acts of charity. She was finally discovered, and someone reported her activities to her pious mother, who far from reprimanding her was thrilled to see such noble inclinations in her amiable daughter. Seeking to inspire the girl further, her mother granted her a general permission to give alms and to accompany her whenever she went, as was her custom, to visit the poor. She even gave her money, which she used with a singular pleasure in her heart to feed and raise several poor children, and to perform many other works of charity. Once she had obtained this permission and was freed from her former constraints, she felt her heart flying as she visited the poor, to console them and to dress their wounds and ulcers.

As soon as this dear daughter began to have use of her reason, Madame her mother wanted to teach her herself, not wishing to confide to anyone else the responsibility for her education. She inspired in her daughter above all things a great love for the very holy Virgin, and she became so attached to this devotion that when she heard herself called Marie, she felt a particular joy to bear this name, and she gloried in it over those who had another. Thus it seemed that this mother of piety had indeed taken her into her protection, giving her an inclination toward piety, and making her despise the world's vanities: for she had a unique hatred for the insignificant trifles and vain ornaments of girls belonging to her age and rank, and she could not bear to keep the things that were given to her for adornment. She thought the little shepherd girl she saw tending sheep must be much happier than she was, because she had neither gloves, nor mask, nor anything of the kind to care for.

All this made her parents understand that God approved the plan they had formed at her birth, to consecrate her to him. This recognition gave them great spiritual comfort, although on the side of nature they were rightly aware that the loss of such a dear daughter would otherwise have been very painful to them.

2. Her parents send her to board with the Ursulines at Tours, where she shows signs of her piety, wisdom, and her zeal for the Religious life   3. She is received into the Novitiate   4. She receives the veil of a Novice. Her faithfulness to the practice of the Rule and her devotion to the very holy Virgin

5. On her profession and her zeal for the salvation of souls

She thus made her profession [took her vows] at the age of sixteen years, and this commitment made her quicken her pace and practice virtue even more purely and simply than during her Novitiate. Above all else she possessed an extraordinary zeal for advancing God's glory and for saving souls. It had been remarked since her childhood that her heart was inclined in this direction, and this was why her mother had sent her to board with the Ursulines rather than elsewhere, thinking this order, which devoted itself to the instruction of girls, would best fit her temperament. She was employed in this activity during her Novitiate, because it had been observed when she was among the boarders [pensionnaires] that she had a particular grace for it. After her Profession, she was again assigned to this holy exercise, in which she displayed an extraordinary zeal. One day I held in my hands the life of Saint François Xavier, to whom she had been especially devoted since her childhood, because of his zeal for converting nations to the Faith of Jesus Christ. Her heart itself felt drawn to imitate him, but she did not know how she could do so. She took the book from me, and with the permission of our Reverend Mother I gave it to her gladly. This reading lit a new fire in her heart, and the examples she saw nourished the flame of her zeal, as she waited until God might provide opportunities to serve him in the instruction of souls redeemed by his Son's blood.

At this time began to appear the relations of what had happened in New France and the great conversions being made there [the "Jesuit Relations"]: the Reverend Father Poncet [who would later accompany the Ursulines to New France], or some other of the Reverend Fathers, sent me one every year, knowing they treated a subject that was to my taste. This reading warmed her heart, and renewed her desires: And as she knew that I sighed after the joy of sacrificing myself for the salvation of sauvage girls, she finally revealed to me the secrets of her soul. But she was sad to foresee many obstacles, because of her parents, as well as her gender, her condition, and her youth. Confronting these difficulties, which occupied her mind, she could not persuade herself that her vocation would ever be realized. Thus she contented herself with offering up to our Lord the Missionaries' labors, believing by this means to fulfill her vocation as much as it was in her power.

In the meantime, she believed she must devote herself completely to that which God asked of her in the present—that is, to the practice of the rules, and to the functions of the Institute. Indeed, she accomplished this, for there could be seen no more exacting regularity. Her modesty was completely Angelic, and her gravity sent everyone into raptures. One day a certain Religious, but one more so in name and habit than in fact, as I will explain, paid her a visit because he knew Messieurs her parents. After some conversation that she did not much appreciate, he urged her to unveil her face in front of him. She begged him with much humility for dispensation from this request, saying that she did not have permission to do so, besides that for conversation, she needed only ears to hear him speak, and a tongue to answer him, and she had the one and the other, without being obliged to uncover her face. This refusal did not appease him, but he insisted anew, adding that no one would know anything about it, and that she should not fear to give him this satisfaction, for which he would be greatly indebted to her. This request, resting on such base and human motives, so horrified this young Religious, that she answered him severely, that God was present, that it was to him she bore respect, and that she wanted no other witness of her actions than he. At these words the man was left very ashamed; she, saying farewell, went away.

6. On her devotion toward Saint Joseph and her vocation for Canada

In her tenderness of heart toward the very holy Virgin, she felt a great interior sorrow for her complete lack of a similar inclination—or so she believed—for Saint Joseph. She felt that she could not love this divine Mother, if she did not also love her very chaste Spouse. Thus she asked often if she would not take pity on her, and consecrate her to this holy Patriarch, fearing that it might be a mark of reprobation in her that she did not belong to him. It was not that deep in her heart she did not love this great Saint very much; but as she said, she did not feel his protection as she felt that of the holy Virgin.

At this time the Mother Prioress of the Loudon Ursulines went to Anessi [Annecy] by the order of Monseigneur the Bishop of Poitiers, to pay her respects at the sepulcher of Blessed François de Salles. She traveled by way of our Monastery of Tours, bringing with her the holy Unguent with which Saint Joseph had cured her of a mortal illness when she was at the point of death. This unguent gave off an unearthly fragrance and possessed a miraculous and completely celestial property. The Community kissed it, and breathed the sweetness of its fragrance, and at the same time felt its effect carried into the depths of the soul. Only our dear Sister could not sense at all either the fragrance or its effect. This singularity afflicted her anew, and sent her into new fears. Meanwhile the Reverend Mother continued her voyage, and on her return trip she again passed by our Monastery. All the Community begged her to give them again the consolation of seeing and kissing the holy Unguent. She granted this wish very obligingly. Our dear Sister presented herself in her turn with a spirit humbled to the last degree, but nevertheless full of confidence that the holy Virgin would not reject her but would consecrate her to her spouse. Her wish was granted: for not only did she experience the fragrance of this holy balm, but she was also penetrated to the bottom of her soul with the effect of the grace she had requested. This celestial operation sent her into such transports of spirit that the Reverend Mother noticed it, and said to her smiling, "Here is a heart completely in the hands of God." In fact, he so touched her heart that she secretly broke away from the Community and went to shut herself into the grotto of Saint Joseph [in the garden of the convent], where she remained hidden for some two hours. During that time our Lord gave her to understand that he wanted Saint Joseph to be her Father and special Protector, and that she should be his daughter as she was that of the Holy Virgin. At the same time, she dissolved in tears, and she felt in her soul the outpouring of the graces that worked in her this affiliation, with so much certainty that she could not doubt it. This certainty remained with her all her life, during which she experienced the very particular aid of this holy Patriarch.

Something utterly extraordinary happened to her a year before our departure for Canada, at a time when no one thought this intention would ever be executed. One night she found herself in spirit at the entrance of a very beautiful and spacious square, completely surrounded by houses and shops filled with all the instruments of vanity, where worldly people used to fall under the influence of vanity and be lost. She stood at the entrance to this place, utterly terrified to see that all who entered were unconsciously attracted to these shops, where they were charmed by the false glittering of their vanities, and fell victim to their traps. What most terrified her was to see a Religious go astray there and so succumb to temptation that he disappeared from view. Not knowing where to walk in order to reach her destination, especially because there was no path other than that where one risked becoming lost, she could not decide what to do. While in this perplexity, she perceived all along the square a great number of young people—very brave, if rather unattractive, and dressed like *Sauvages*. They divided themselves into two bands, like two hedges between which she safely walked. As she passed, she heard distinctly these words: "It is by us you will be saved." But glancing at the guidon or standard, she noticed that it was written in an unknown language, which she could not understand. She could not recognize more clearly to whom she owed her escape from such a great peril (some believed that these were the guardian Angels of the *Sauvages*). She noticed, however, that the Religious who was lost there was the one I mentioned who had been so curious to see her uncover her face, and who indeed has since twice apostasized his Religion.

Although she did not at all recognize the *Sauvages* who had preserved her from the dangers in which she had found herself, and though then she was not thinking at all about Canada, God nonetheless secretly disposed her heart and her spirit, to go there when the occasion presented itself, to consume her life in the service of these forsaken souls. This is why in the course of time she asked me in our private conversations, if I knew whether we would go there one day, if I myself were not destined for this purpose, and who would accompany me. "Ah!" she said, "How contented I would be, how happy to dedicate my life to such a holy expedition. Just one thing worries me: the Relations say the *Sauvages* are nearly naked, and I fear this might have some harmful consequences for purity. Nonetheless, be assured that if you take me with you, I will cling to you so strongly that nothing will ever separate me from you. Death, sorrows, labors, sea, storms, deprivation of parents, separation from our Mothers and our Sisters, in a word nothing will be able to break the tie with which God will unite us together." See the disposition of this generous girl for the salvation of souls; in which she gives at the same time a striking proof of her love for purity. Nothing in this enterprise could distress her except the risk that she might happen to see something that could cause harm to this Angelic virtue.

At the time she had the mysterious dream I mentioned, she was on a very slippery path, potentially leading her into the way of vanity under an apparent pretext of virtue. She often discussed this with me, and in speaking to me of it, she never tired of blessing God for guiding her past the traps held out by the demon, and for giving her courage to flee by a different path that could lead her to holiness. I knew more clearly than ever that the hand of God guided her, to make her a subject worthy of his grace in the Canada mission: I will report here none of the particulars for reasons of charity, which oblige me to remain silent.

7. Ursulines from Tours are requested, in order to found a Monastery in Canada

My dear companion's vocation and my own having reached the point of maturity, it pleased our Lord to provide the means for fulfilling them. Madame de la Pelletrie [Marie-Madeleine de Chauvigny de la Peltrie], who has since become our Founder, went to Tours to honor our house by requesting from it Religious women for the foundation she wished to make. The Reverend Fathers Binet and de la Haye, the first of whom was then Provincial of the Company of Jesus, took the lead, writing to Monseigneur the Archbishop about the noble qualities of Madame de la Pelletrie, and assuring him that her project had been examined by the most spiritual and capable persons in Paris, and had been deemed solid and founded on the grace and will of God. . . . [The Archbishop] entered into the project, happy that God had cast his eyes on his daughters, rather than others, for such a glorious undertaking. He sent an order to our Reverend Mother, the Mother Françoise de Saint Bernard, to welcome Madame de la Pelletrie into the house, to present me to her (since she had done me the honor of requesting me), and to choose for me a companion from the members of the Community. . . .

8. The lot falls upon Mother Marie de Saint Joseph
9. On her departure from Tours for New France; and on her modesty and zeal during the voyage

One cannot imagine greater modesty and restraint than were shown by this dear companion. During our voyage she was more readily taken for a person of consummate perfection than for a girl of twenty-three years, and I did not once see her depart from this humble gravity. Several persons of rank and virtue came to visit us in the cities where we stayed: We were sometimes even obliged to go to the Court, as the Queen had expressed a desire to see us, and everywhere she spoke only of virtue and contempt for the world; doing so with such grace that all who met her admired and were touched by her.

She was not at all frightened by the dangers of the sea; instead, in the storms that threatened us with nothing less than shipwreck, it was she who began the prayers, performing them with such piety that it was easy to see her heart was not at all frightened. She always had some word to say to lift the courage of those who were demoralized. To instruct the ignorant was her joy. In sum, during all the ocean navigation she displayed the effect of the fire embracing her heart, and showed clear evidence of her vocation to consume her life in saving souls.

10. She arrives in Quebec, where she learns Sauvage *languages and performs the functions of her vocation with marvelous success*

From the day after our arrival in Quebec, we were sent all the girls who could be found, French as well as *Sauvage*, to instruct them in piety and good morals. The principal responsibility for this instruction was given to Mother Marie de Saint Joseph, who accepted it with incredible zeal and fervor; and as our Lord had given her a very particular grace and talent for this task, she made a noteworthy profit from the beginning. . . .

She soon learned the Huron and Algonkian languages, and she used them with great facility. Our Lord had given her a particular grace for winning hearts, not only of girls, but also of the men and women of these two Nations. They addressed themselves to her with marvelous simplicity, exposing to her the sorrows and difficulties of their conscience; with no less admirable submission, they obeyed her as children do their Mother. The name of Marie Joseph (it was thus that they called her) was famous in the country of the Hurons and the Algonkins; and these good Neophytes spoke of her with esteem and love to those not yet acquainted with her, and by this means, she was soon known to all. They called her the holy girl. As for myself, I would gladly have called her the holy Mother; because she loved them, and consoled them as a Mother does her children; and she regarded them as creatures made in the image of God, for whose salvation she would have wished to give her life, had it been in her power. Each year she made her best effort to obtain from Madame her Mother, and from several other high-ranking persons, alms for her dear Neophytes. They sent alms liberally, and she procured for them in exchange mediators near to God; she continued this practice until her death.

For several years our Lord had given her an extraordinary vocation to seek from him conversion for the Peoples of this American country, strength for the French colony, and holiness for our Community. These three things were very much in her heart and entirely occupied her spirit when she was in conversation with God. She offered herself as a victim to his divine Majesty, without cease and without reserve, if only he might be pleased to answer these prayers. She sometimes told me, in confidence: "It is impossible for me to do anything in my inner soul that is not for this poor country, and it seems that God expects only this from me." She felt that she carried in her heart all the French and all the *Sauvages*. She felt their joys and their sorrows more than anything that could touch her in this world. Nothing was more painful to her than hearing that some disaster threatened to destroy the country. On these occasions, in her ordinary conversations with God, she spoke the words Moses used when God threatened his people with destruction. "My God, erase me from the Book of Life, and even remove me from this world, rather than allow the rupture of the French Colony." She devoted herself to God, offering to suffer for him and burning with love at his feet, to win his heart and oblige him to grant her prayer by a motion of his grace.

After the Huron Mission was scattered, the Iroquois had ravaged all their country, and our holy Missionaries had suffered martyrdom, it was a mortal blow to this Mother's heart to see the remnant of this desolate Nation seeking shelter nearby. Her only consolation was that in her interaction with these miserable fugitives she would have the means to exercise what she knew of their language, to teach them our holy Mysteries and teach them to love God. This she did with an incomparable fervor. I served as her Companion in this work: where I was overjoyed to hear and see around her forty or fifty Hurons, men as well as women and children, who listened to her with incredible eagerness and made it quite clear from their postures and their uncivilized gestures that they liked what she said. Her love for this holy exercise made her forget her illness in the midst of her duty; only later would she become so exhausted, and suffer such great pains in her chest, that one would have said she was at the point of death. . . .

11. Her virtues   12. Her final illness, and the virtues she displayed therein

13. Her joyful death, and a few miraculous events that followed it

Our Lord, who had permitted for his glory and for the sanctification of his servant that she would endure by so many crosses, interior and exterior, the space of more than four and a half years, and had greatly increased these sufferings in her final illness, wanted her to end her life in the delights of his grace and charity. Three days before her death, he filled her soul with a peace that gave her a foretaste of Paradise, and that dismissed all earthly sights. We saw her body agonizing, and the gangrene gaining everywhere, but she did not seem to notice it. She answered all the questions posed to her, until she was ready to expire; even though she was in the agony of death for twenty-four hours, she never ceased to perform the actions recommended to her. Even in dying she gave signs that she was attentive to what was desired from her. She died so quietly that one could only with difficulty perceive it; and in dying, her face was so soft and angelic that instead of being left with sadness at her departure, we felt joy, with an interior anointing so penetrating, that it gave us a taste of the glory she was going to enjoy. Not one of us failed to sense the effect of an utterly extraordinary grace, with a kind of certainty that we would have a good Advocate close to God. One felt led to invoke her, and in invoking her one felt the effect of her request; since her death several have had this experience. In conclusion, we bless the memory of this dear Mother. She died the 4th of April of this year 1652, at eight hours in the evening, Thursday of the Easter Octave. We carried her that evening into our newly reconstructed building, where we were not yet living, in order to perform her obsequies more easily, and this was the building's first use. She was buried the next day, and the Reverend Father Lallemant performed the ceremonies with the greatest solemnity. There has not been such a handsome funeral procession in this country since it was first inhabited: Everyone of importance attended, the great and the small, the French and the *Sauvages*. The Hurons on their Island had already celebrated a feast for her burial as a mark of their gratitude toward her. In short, as she was universally loved and esteemed, on this occasion there was no one who did not wish to show some sign of his affection, and bear witness to his regret for the loss of such a holy and beloved person.

An hour after her burial a person who had rendered great assistance to her for some years was going to perform an act of charity at a league's distance from Quebec. As he passed near our Monastery, she appeared to him in the road by means of a mental vision. She had a grave and majesterial bearing, and there emanated from her face, and especially from her eyes, rays of light capable of slaying a soul and consuming a heart. She so possessed the heart of this person, and she imprinted him with such strong sensations of God's grace and love, that although he continued on his way he could not divert his attention. He assured me that he thought he would die from the violence of her assaults, and from the excess of love for God kindled in his heart by the force of her luminous eyes. She accompanied him thus to his destination, and again on his return by an interior presence equally certain and effective.

The next day when this same person was going to the Isle d'Orleans, called Saint Mary's, to give some aid to the Hurons who had established themselves there after their defeat by the Iroquois, he came to a river crossing that he would have to make over the ice. All winter the ice had supported him, but as spring was coming it was now melted and weakened beneath the surface, so that there remained no more than a little shiny crust that had formed during the night. He thought that under this thin layer of ice a thicker was hidden, that the thicker layer still existed. He thus continued on his way without fear, but when he had gone some distance our dear departed (who accompanied him everywhere, as I have described) spoke to him inwardly this word: "Stop!" He came to his senses and, opening his eyes, found himself completely surrounded by water: He struck his walking-stick on the thin crust of ice, looking for a stronger layer beneath it, but he found only water. He was very surprised to see himself in such an inescapable danger. Hoping nevertheless to escape this situation, he addressed himself to the one who had so charitably stopped him. He commended himself to her, and retraced his steps, but with such surprising and extraordinary ease that it felt like walking on air. He assured me that he made his way more than three hundred paces over the water, thanks to the favor of his dear Benefactor, who, as he said, brought him from a place he could not have escaped without a miracle. Since that time he has referred to her only as his Angel, and she for her part has remained in communion with him ever since the first apparition of which I spoke.

There, my Reverend Mothers, is what I can tell you for your consolation, of your dear daughter and my very faithful and very lovable companion. But what I say to console you is to me no small cause for shame and confusion, when I think that while I am considerably more advanced in age, she infinitely surpassed me in virtue and merit. I urge you to pray to our Lord that he might take me into his grace, that as she has been my companion in my small labors, I may merit to be hers in the tranquility of his glory and joy.

Note in the 1681 edition

The person mentioned at the end of this letter is Brother Bonnemer, a Jesuit, who had rendered great services to this Religious during her illnesses. He wrote and signed these two acts, and his attestation has been sent to France. . . .

A Carpenter from Quebec named Philippes Estienne has likewise declared and signed that once when he was mounted on scaffolding at the third floor of the Monastery, the platform collapsed under his feet. Mother Marie de Saint Joseph, who was watching him, saw that the scaffolding had given out, and that the man was falling over backwards. Raising her eyes toward Heaven, she said in a loud voice, "Jesus, Mary, Joseph," and at these words the Carpenter found himself on his feet without any injury, on another scaffolding lower down.

When fire destroyed her parents' house, her portrait, which had been rolled on a piece of wood and tied with ribbons, was stored on top of a cupboard containing gunpowder (which was the cause of the blaze). House, cupboard, the scroll on which the painting was rolled, and the ribbons that tied it—all were entirely burned: Only the portrait remained intact, the fire respecting the image of such a holy person, by the will of the One who commands the Elements.

A girl named Anne Baillagon, nine years old, was taken by the Iroquois, and sent into their country, where she lived for nearly nine years. She so liked the customs of these *Sauvages* that she decided to spend the rest of her life with them. When Monsieur de Traci [Alexandre de Prouville de Tracy, French lieutenant-general for the Americas] compelled this Nation to return all the French people they held as captives, the girl retreated into the woods, for fear of returning to her country. Just when she thought she was safe, a Religious appeared to her, and threatened to punish her if she did not return with the French. Her fear sent her running out of the woods to join the other captives who were being set free. On her return Monsieur de Traci gave her fifty *écus* as a dowry, but he wanted her first to be put with the Ursulines, to relearn the Christian spirit that had been greatly weakened among the Iroquois. When she saw the painting of Mother Marie de Saint Joseph, she cried, "Ah! It was she who spoke to me, and she wore the same habit." Living among Pagans during her long captivity, it was impossible that she would not have committed many sins against the sanctity of Christianity: She had nonetheless always maintained a very great purity; and it was believed that this Mother had been made her Angel to conserve her in this integrity. . . .

There have been observed several like apparitions of this faithful Spouse of Jesus Christ to diverse persons, but the most remarkable of all was that by which she took leave of her good Mothers of Tours, almost at the moment she died. There was an excellent lay sister named Sister Elizabeth de Sainte Marthe, who had been a kind of nurse to her and had particular responsibility for her when she was a boarder at the convent. In gratitude for these good offices, Mother Marie de Saint Joseph had contracted with her a completely religious and holy friendship in which they held in common all the merits and spiritual goods they could acquire during their lives. Now she appeared to her and exhorted her to prepare herself to follow her, that their souls joined in this world by charity would be united again in Heaven by the enjoyment of a shared glory. This good Sister immediately got up, and although it was an unreasonable hour she went to find her Superior, and told her that Mother Marie de Saint Joseph had appeared to her and ordered her to prepare herself for death, and that assuredly she would die in a few days. Having said this, she returned to bed and spent the rest of the night in great peace. The next day at recreation, Sister Elizabeth imposed silence on those present, and when she had their attention said, "Last night I saw something beautiful, which you will be very happy to know about: I saw my Mother de Saint Joseph all resplendent with light, with a ravishing beauty and an incomparable majesty. She said, gesturing toward me, 'My sister, follow me, it is time to leave, that we may be united together in the same place.'" The following Thursday this good Sister was seized by such a violent pain in her side that the illness seemed incurable, and it was easy to see that the effect of this apparition would come to pass: and indeed she died the seventeenth of the same month, thirteen days after the Mother Marie de Saint Joseph. . . .

Letter from Marie de l'Incarnation to Benedictine Mother Gabrielle de l'Annonciation (de la Troche)

She describes the translation of the body of her sister, Mother Marie de Saint Joseph, from old into new coffins.

My Reverend Mother. You have had the goodness to be willing to remember me, and to continue to honor me with your affection. For myself, I assure you that I preserve my affection for your dear person, that as you wish I regard you as I did my dear Mother Marie de Saint Joseph your very lovable Sister and my very faithful companion. I shall tell you something you will not be grieved to know: when our little Church was finished, we removed her body from the place where it had been laid to place it in a crypt we had had excavated under our Choir. We were drawn by curiosity, or rather by devotion, to see the state of her body. Our plan was abetted by the need for a change of coffin: although the body was encased in two coffins, the first of these was rotten; the other, made of cedar, was not. We found all her flesh consumed and changed into a paste white as milk, a finger's thickness in depth. Her heart, which had sustained so many holy transports for her Spouse, and her brain, the instrument for so many holy thoughts, were still intact. All her bones were in place, each in its natural position: The remains were without any foul odor. At the moment that we performed the opening, we felt ourselves filled with a joy and a sweetness so great that I cannot express it to you. Fearing to discover decomposition or something that might frighten our young Sisters, we had wanted to visit the remains in secret. But finding things in the state I have just described, our Reverend Mother had all the Community summoned, to share in the consolation that penetrated us so deeply. To render to this dear departed our final duties of charity and affection, we set ourselves to washing the bones. The hands of those who touched them exuded a fragrance of irises. The bones were as if covered in oil; after they were washed and wiped, hands and linens gave off the same fragrance. Neither the sight nor the handling of the bones, nor of this white mass or consumed flesh, inspired the least fear, as the cadavers of the dead might ordinarily have done; rather these inspired sentiments of union and love for the departed. Each wanted to be the first to kiss her bones, and to render her this last pious duty. After we had satisfied our affection, we replaced her bones in a new coffin with an inscription on parchment describing this dear Mother's principal virtues, her zeal for the conversion of souls, her family, and her parents. Then, having enclosed this coffin in another, we lowered it into the building's foundation, so that if one day by some reversal of fortune we had to return to France, we could easily retrieve it. At the service celebrated on this occasion, the Reverend Father Superior of Missions preached a very beautiful exhortation on this change of coffin, on the odor of the bones, on the white paste, and especially on the heroic virtues of this holy soul. She is the only one of our Community to have died in this country in the twenty-four years we have lived here. I thought of sending you some of her bones to be mixed with yours when you go to your own grave, but I worried they would be lost before reaching you. Dear Mother, I had to give you this account for your consolation and for the consolation of your illustrious family, on the subject of my very dear companion, whose memory will always remain precious to us and in an odor of benediction. I finish by assuring you of the sincerity of my heart and the affection with which I remain.

Note in the 1681 edition

The coffin of this excellent Religious was opened the 3rd of November 1661, by the permission of the Bishop. Besides the things reported in the letter, it was remarked that the white paste, when placed over a hot iron or burning coals, melted like wax or incense, and exuded a very sweet fragrance. It was the same with pieces of her heart, when they were placed over the fire. A Religious who had helped to wash her bones took a piece of her heart to wear over her own, as an act of devotion. When she wore it, whoever came near her detected the scent of irises. At the ceremony the Reverend Father Lallement made a touching exhortation in which he took as his theme these words from the 16th chapter of the Epistle to the Romans: *Let us give thanks to Mary who has worked hard among us.* After relating the heroic virtues of this girl and giving a moral explanation of the white paste, the odor of iris, and the four knots in her sash (which were the symbols of her four vows, and which also remained free from corruption), he did not hesitate to call her holy, saying he believed her to be in Heaven in a very high state of glory. A few years later, the occasion again presenting itself to open her coffin, no corruption was found in the substance of her brain, but it had shrunk to two small balls as hard as rocks.

— 25 —

Possession, Witchcraft, and the Demonic in Puritan Religious Culture

Kenneth P. Minkema

Mention the Puritans and, chances are, the first thing that comes to most people's minds are the infamous witchcraft trials that occurred at Salem, Massachusetts, in 1692–1693, which resulted in the imprisonment of hundreds of people and the execution of nineteen (though none of them, contrary to popular belief, were burned at the stake). We are at once repelled and fascinated by the episode and by the phenomena that gave rise to it: purported demonic activity, the practice of witchcraft, and witch-hunting. The observance of the Salem trials tercentenary in 1992 and 1993 issued in a variety of books, edited documents, museum exhibits, conferences, and a television documentary. Tourist centers, such as those at Salem, continue to attract tens of thousands of visitors every year. Movies such as *The Blair Witch Project* attract huge audiences. Meanwhile, the New Age spirituality movement has lent legitimacy to what formerly were viewed as occult beliefs and practices, to the extent that they are acquiring new adherents in surprising numbers. To one degree or another, these practitioners claim—whether rightfully or not—to be reviving centuries-old folk teachings that were misunderstood and condemned by western Christianity. So accepted has nature- and goddess-worship become that in 1999 the Oregon senate had a Wiccan priestess perform opening prayers, and Wiccan ceremonies have been sanctioned and practiced on U.S. Army bases. Primetime television features shows whose central characters are young female witches or—in a modern version of the professional demon hunter—vampire slayers. Driving down the highways, one can even see bumper stickers that proudly declare, "My other car is a broom."

In modern America, with its broad toleration of religious and quasi–religious beliefs and practices, we look back on the witch-hunting Puritans of the late seventeenth century as benighted, bigoted, and superstitious. Our sympathies lie with the victims—and correctly so, since there was no real evidence that any of them were guilty. But in condemning the supposed ignorance of people in the past, we must be careful of smugly congratulating ourselves on how much more enlightened we are than our predecessors. As historians, playwrights, and journalists have pointed out, witch-hunts come in many varieties and can arise at any time, with religious or political leaders exploiting widespread suspicions and whipping the populace into a vengeful frenzy. Arthur Miller, for example, compared the anticommunist vendetta of Senator Joseph McCarthy and the House Committee on Un-American Activities in the early 1950s to a modern-day witch-hunt, replete with its own cast of judges, accusers, and victims. Since then, the term "witch-hunt" has entered common parlance to describe attempts to play on people's irrational fears by blaming innocent individuals or groups for fabricated crimes.

For their part, the Puritans of seventeenth-century New England believed that there were witches in league with the devil, that they were intentionally harmful to others, and that, according to the scriptural rule, "Thou shalt not suffer a witch to live," they were to be tracked down and killed. One of the first truths of the Calvinist religious culture of New England was the existence of supernatural beings such as Satan and demons, and that their human agents—witches and wizards—carried out their diabolical directions. To deny the existence of such beings implied denying the existence of good angels and, ultimately, of a God intimately involved in creation. In a time when Puritan and other religious writers were intent on fighting materialist thought, witchcraft ironically provided the best means of "proving" the reality of the supernatural and of affirming that the spiritual world impinged on the natural world. Demons and witches were but one side of the larger picture of existence, in which the forces of God were pitted against the forces of evil. Eventually, God and his followers would win out over their enemies, but in the meantime the devil would use every device to thwart God's plans, steal souls, and afflict the godly. These teachings were inculcated and perpetuated through sermons, tracts, catechisms, poetry, and other means. They were as integral a part of the Puritans' shared worldview as space travel is for modern Americans. While there were those who at the time were critical of the Salem trials, even these critics never doubted that there were such things as demons and witches, because demons and witches were part of a shared system of assumptions that, for the Puritans, made sense of the world. To appreciate this is to begin to understand—if not have complete sympathy for— why people back then acted and reacted in the ways they did.

The documents printed below illustrate Puritan conceptions and descriptions of demonic activity. The first, by the Reverend Increase Mather of Boston, is an excerpt from a lengthy treatise entitled *An Essay for the Recording of Illustrious Providences*. The work was a comprehensive statement on the varieties of supernatural phenomena, punctuated by "illustrious providences." Both terms were significant. "Illustrious" meant illustrative, or representative, instances. "Providences" identified occurrences arranged or allowed by God to provide a lesson— a blessing or punishment—for the subjects and observers. For Mather, such a treatise was necessary for explaining the seemingly inexplicable in a way that was acceptable to the worldview that he shared with his fellow colonists.

Dismissing as fools any who doubt the world of spirits, Mather unequivocally affirmed that there were demons and that they were at large in the world. Generally, God restrained them with a "chain" of divine power. But on occasion, for various reasons, God "lengthened" the chain and gave them more freedom to wreak misery. One way they did so was to possess the bodies of individuals, whether believers or unbelievers. They could torment their victims through psychological temptations, through bodily pain, or both. Sometimes they even spoke through their victims in a phenomenon known as "ventriloquism."

Mather also presented a list of "signs" of a possessed person that include the ability to reveal sophisticated or secret knowledge and the manifestation of unusual bodily contortions. The Puritans, as these documents demonstrate, were great compilers of "signs" and "wonders." No fewer than three of our four selections have such lists, giving evidence of possession, witches, and bewitchment. Such lists were important in a culture that stressed the importance of education and the acquisition of personal knowledge, for they conveyed useful information for religious leaders and laypeople alike who lived in isolated settings and worshiped in independent churches. Even more, in a time when the nature of scientific inquiry was being changed by the likes of Francis Bacon and Sir Isaac Newton, gathering observations on the supernatural lent a certain empirical authority to them.

If demons could mediately operate through possession, they could also operate at secondhand through "confederates," or witches. Mather offered several points to clinch his argument. In true Puritan style, the premier source of proof was Scripture, which had numerous instances of witchcraft and sorcery. Other means of proof included experience as well as confessions by persons who admitted to being witches—though Mather allowed that some people suffered from a "deluded fancy."

Yet another type of activity was the appearance of apparitions or specters— "ghosts," we call them today. Again, Mather believed many reports were no more than "frightful apprehensions," but this did not explain away the numerous accounts of specters appearing to "mortals" in biblical times and afterward. Sometimes these apparitions were believed to be holy angels who would offer timely advice or warnings. But it was "exceeding dangerous" to seek an angelic visitation. Angels, as portrayed in the Bible and in Puritan culture, were powerful, terrifying beings. They wielded flaming swords and sharp sickles. When they did not bring death and destruction, they bore disturbing messages. After an encounter with an angel, so the Bible relates, Jacob was left crippled, and Zacharias, the father of John the Baptist, was struck dumb. These were the sort of beings Mather had in mind—not the chubby little cherubs or kindly guardians that we think of today when we think of angels.

Appearances by good angels were rare. The world was sinful, and it was, for the nonce, the playground of the devil and his minions. Believers had to be cautious that what they took for a good angel was not actually a cacodemon, which could assume the guise of a good angel (or "white man") or of a deceased person but underneath was, as its name literally meant, a "shit-demon." For that matter, even Satan himself could appear as an "angel of light" or in the likeness of ordinary saints.

Ancient folk belief that certain objects or plants could ward off demons and witches' spells were still very strong in the seventeenth century, even in a thoroughgoing Protestant culture such as that of New England. Mather addresses some of these practices as "cases of conscience." First, he criticizes the custom of using herbs and potions to fend off evil spirits. Demons, Mather points out, are incorporeal, spiritual, and cannot be affected by material substances. The same argument applies to the use of written symbols, such as runes, or of spoken incantations (as when we say "God bless you" to someone who has sneezed, a response which is today viewed simply as a common courtesy but has its origins in the ancient belief that a sneeze was caused by an evil spirit attempting to enter one's body). Other practices that Mather condemned were those used when it was feared that a milkless cow, or poor crops, or some other mishap was due to bewitchment. In cases such as these, people would, among other things, collect the blood of the person suspected of witchcraft, or bottle his or her urine, or nail a horseshoe above a door. Mather noted that using such devices, though meant to fend off the devil, merely used the devil's own devices and lead to irrational superstition, if not worse.

Stretching far back in European culture, too, was a tradition of herbology and natural remedies. The practitioners of this tradition, usually women, were called "white witches" and were accorded much respect in the community. After the Reformation, however, with the development of a patriarchal society that relegated women to the domestic sphere and saw the growth of a male-dominated doctoring profession, these "wise women" were deprived of their station. Those who practice witchcraft today frequently portray themselves as advocates of good health and preservers of the environment, and so could be likened to the white witches of old. But Puritans such as Mather would brook no such distinctions; to him, the malevolent witch and the white witch were equally evil, and he discouraged his readers from seeking their assistance.

In compiling his *Essay,* Mather referred to the case of Elizabeth Knapp of Groton, Massachusetts. A description of her experience had been written down and distributed by Rev. Samuel Willard, the minister of Groton. His "Brief Account of a Strange and Unusual Providence Befallen to Elizabeth Knapp" is one of the most remarkable descriptions of demonic possession in the annals of early American history.

In October 1671, Knapp began experiencing excruciating pains and dramatic mood swings, and she saw and spoke to people no one else could see. Her symptoms only grew worse. At first, according to prescribed procedures, a doctor was called in to give a standard diagnosis. But eventually, she was judged to be possessed. Her behavior was marked by "violent fits," screaming, frenzied activity and bodily motions, trances, and talking without use of "the organ of speech." Modern psychologists would probably diagnose Knapp's condition as conversion hysteria, or intrapsychic conflict, or some other form of psychopathology, but, for Willard, Knapp's family and neighbors, and other onlookers, there was little doubt that they were dealing with the devil embodied.

Possession narratives, as with many other genres in Puritan literature, have a distinctive morphology, or mode of progression. In this sense, possession was a cultural performance, or, as one scholar has described it, a "symbolic religious ritual through which a series of shared meanings were communicated." These shared meanings included what the devil looked like, how he spoke, how he would manifest himself in the victim's body, and how he would inevitably be forced to concede. Once it was ascertained that the origin of the victim's ailments was diabolical, the minister and community would gather to support her and attempt to relieve her. At first, Knapp tried to blame two of her neighbors of performing witchcraft on her. When the neighbors were called in, however, it quickly became obvious that witchcraft was not at the root of the problem. The alternative was possession. In Puritan culture, fasting and praying were the accepted means of driving out the devil, and we see Willard, area ministers, and the townspeople employing these means. More important, however, the minister and others would interrogate the victim to find out the possible cause of the possession. Had the victim done something to encourage the devil to enter her? Willard plied Knapp again and again, trying to get the truth out of her. The more she was asked, the more ferocious her symptoms would become. In time, Puritans believed, confession and prayer forced the devil to leave. When this occurred, the victim would resume her place as a "proper" woman. For Knapp, this occurred when she was married in 1674, apparently living out her life in anonymous normality.

At the time Knapp was "taken," she was a young woman of sixteen. In the seventeenth century, this was the period of life in which women went through several important rites of passage: entering adulthood, joining the church, marrying, and bearing children. Women entering society were expected to be retiring, modest, soft-spoken, and deferential. Possession provided an opportunity to loosen these restraints, to express hidden anxieties, and to act out resentments. At the same time, however, the victim was not blamed for her behavior and speech. In contrast to the witch, who was voluntarily in a satanic covenant and therefore punishable, the possessed was innocent, an object of sympathy, because Satan forcibly inhabited her body.

Knapp identified the occasion for the devil's incursion as her "discontent." She had been shuttled around from family to family as a serving girl, ending up finally in the minister's home. It is no coincidence that Willard himself, her master and pastor, whom she (or her demonic persona) repeatedly calls a "black rogue," is the main target of her rage. Other sources of discontent could have included her unhappiness at the prospect of marriage, confusion over sexual tensions (possibly between her and Willard), and rebellion against gender arrangements. Whatever the cause or causes, her possession episode gave her the opportunity to break out of the mold of Puritan womanhood, however briefly. When in a possession fit, she was loud, insulting, physical, and exhibitionistic. In a period in which personal privacy was almost unheard of, it is not surprising to find her constantly attended by a roomful of people—"spectators," Willard calls them at one point—and she theatrically plays to her audience. At points, the watchers even become part of the drama, as they address the devil inside her. So, for the woman who was counseled from birth not to draw attention to herself, her possession made her the center of attention and concern. In this fashion she, too, became a part of the cosmic drama of providential history; she herself became an "illustrious providence."

As Knapp's case indicates, possessed individuals were usually women, as were those accused of—and executed for—witchcraft. Scholars have noted a striking gender differentiation in witch-hunting. Some estimate that between 1560 and 1760 as much as 80 percent of all witchcraft accusations in Euro-America were against women. Of the 200,000 women accused of witchcraft, it is calculated, fully half of them were executed, which means that 85 percent of those executed were women.

These are sobering figures. They testify to systematic fear of, and violence against, women. Much of it stemmed from shifting definitions of witchcraft and gender roles and, ultimately, to a struggle over power relations between the sexes. Prior to the seventeenth century, a man could be accused of witchcraft as readily as a woman could. Only since then had the identification of witchcraft with women come into vogue. This redefinition, along with the threat of accusation that accompanied it, evolved as a means of enforcing new roles for women not as interdependent with their spouses, but as inferiors. Culturally and socially speaking, women were not only being deprived of traditional roles, such as healers, but also of legal and economic opportunities that they had long enjoyed. Men asserted primacy in occupational choices, while the description of the "good woman" became that of the subservient housewife. Not until the twentieth century was this sexual division of labor into separate and unequal spheres challenged through the efforts of the suffragist and later feminist movements.

The majority of those executed at Salem were women, but the accusers were also mostly women. In fact, if we take premodern Euro-American witch-hunting as a whole, we find that women were twice as likely as men to be accusers. However, it would be too easy to dismiss these accusing women as conformists and dupes of patriarchy. The issues surrounding accusation were much more complicated than that. As accusers, women could exercise power of their own, even if it was against other women. Customarily, as at Salem, those first accused were elderly, single, widowed, or impoverished—in other words, those who were most looked down upon in the community and most unable to defend themselves. In making such accusations, women gained a sort of power and prestige by giving voice to, and affirming, community fears and prejudices. Also, witchcraft accusations have to be seen as part of a larger trend of defamation suits in which women resorted to words as a means of attacking neighboring enemies. By this strategy, they could protect themselves from their rivals or get revenge against them. Finally, accusing was a means for a woman to work out the internalized religious message that she was more evil and more subject to sin than a man because she was more emotional and thus more irrational.

The remaining selections arose out of the Salem witchcraft hysteria. These documents, one a sermon preached in the midst of the accusations and trials, the other a narrative of events, were written by two of the town's ministers. Both had intimate knowledge of the town and of the events that transpired, and so their accounts, and their interpretations of what happened, are of great importance. Both knew that the inhabitants had been feuding for decades. Family factions within Salem Village argued over land, inheritances, and public offices among each other and with families in Salem Town, located on the coast. What the clergymen could not fully comprehend was that Salem Village, an inland hamlet dependent on agriculture, was being challenged by the more cosmopolitan merchants and seagoing interests of Salem Town. Here, writ small, the challenge of change in Puritan society was being enacted. But in contrast to other areas, where the transition from a traditional, local, farming-based economy to transatlantic mercantilism was made smoothly, in Salem the uncertainties and resentments lashed out in dark and bloody fashion.

Samuel Parris was the minister of Salem Village during the notorious outbreak. While he was by no means "the cause" of the outbreak—indeed, we cannot point to one person, one event, or one happenstance as *the* cause—he was, as the town's minister, decisive in shaping how people in the vicinity perceived and reacted to abnormal behavior. Parris had come to the hamlet in 1689 after failing as a landowner and merchant in Barbados. From the beginning of his pastorate, he had encountered contentious townspeople and a less-than-unanimous show of support for himself as minister. His sermons from the beginning dwelt on the presence of hidden evil in the church, ongoing struggles between the forces of Christ and Satan, and the dangers of an imminent invasion of devils. In his efforts to gain intellectual legitimacy and spiritual authority, he amplified Puritan assumptions about demonic activity and created an atmosphere of fear and suspicion. So, when several young women in town—including his own daughter, Elizabeth Parris, and niece, Abigail Williams—began exhibiting strange behavior, it was a self-fulfilling prophecy for Parris and his listeners to reach the conclusion that "the evil hand was upon them."

Parris's preoccupation with spiritual warfare reached a high pitch in early 1692, spurred no doubt by the torments his daughter and niece were undergoing and by the burgeoning trials. On September 11, 1692, he preached the sermon entitled "These Shall Make War with the Lamb," delivered after six witches had been sentenced to death. Here Parris struck an apocalyptic note when he depicted the struggle of the forces of Satan with the Lamb and his followers. Exhibiting typical Protestant animus against Catholics and ambivalence toward Jews, he identified both groups with the Antichrist. This was an ongoing conflict that would end, Parris assured his flock, with the Lamb's victory. However, the devil and his servants would make war "as long as they can." There were, he told his congregation, "no neuters" in this warfare; they were on one side or the other, and they had to decide which side they were on. He exhorted them not to fight against the Lamb, because they would inevitably lose and thereby aggravate their sin above the sins of devils. Disobedience to God, in short, was the way to utter ruin. He ended by urging believers to be good soldiers for Christ, enduring and persevering without fear.

So far, all of this was good Puritan doctrine. But in the sermon, Parris reproved those who were "amazed at the war the Devil has raised among us by wizards and witches." He pronounced the infamous words: "If ever there were witches, men and women in covenant with the Devil, here are multitudes in New England." In the misguided hands of Parris and other leaders of the witch-hunt, Puritan teachings and the shared set of assumptions about the demonic were distorted. Now, there were "multitudes" of demons and witches running rampant and assuming guises not thought possible before. Even church members in full communion, such as the convicted witch Martha Corey, could be servants of Satan.

There were several important ritual aspects to Parris's sermon that made it a central event in Salem's religious life as well as in the witch-hunt. First, the sermon was prefatory to serving the sacrament of the Lord's Supper, or Communion. This sacrament consisted of the minister's serving consecrated bread and wine—representing the body and blood of Christ—to those select members who, to the satisfaction of their minister and fellow churchgoers, were true saints. In Puritan churches, Communion was served once every several weeks and was a pivotal event—at once private and public—for focusing individual and church-wide piety. In the context of the witch craze, the Sacrament service heightened communicants' awareness of themselves as a small band of true Christians assaulted within and without by their foes. Just as he delivered this sermon, which referred to the convicted witches, on a Sacrament day, so Parris had previously chosen similar symbolic occasions to maximize the effect of church practices. For example, he had admonished a church member named Mary Sibly for instructing Parris's slaves, Tituba and John Indian, to make a witch cake (containing the urine of the afflicted and fed to a dog). In the ritual of admonition, the minister recited the offense, and the censured person publicly apologized to the assembled church. Parris also excommunicated Martha Corey on a Sacrament day. Excommunication meant rescinding the individual's membership in the church, forbidding church members to associate with her till she repent, and consigning her soul to the devil.

The importance of the Lord's Supper to Parris was readily obvious to the afflicted women, and they played upon their minister's earnestness. They told of "witches' Sabbaths," a parody of the Lord's Supper in which assembled witches ate red bread and drank blood. Such events were described by another minister who witnessed the beginning of the afflictions, Deodate Lawson.

Lawson had been the pastor of Salem Village until 1688, but in the years following he came back on occasion to preach to his former parishioners. Such was the case in early 1692, when he entered Salem Village only to find it in chaos. In the first two homes he visited, he found young women acting in the strangest manner, one complaining of being bitten by an unseen person, and another of being tormented by the spectral likeness of a local matron, Rebecca Nurse.

More surprising exhibitions awaited him and the inhabitants. The next day, a Sunday, the church was gathered for worship. This was traditionally the place for the highest decorum and silence; the only time parishioners opened their mouths was to sing. Puritans took very seriously the apostle Paul's injunction that women were not to speak in church. We can only imagine, then, the horror of the congregation when, right in the middle of the service, several young women began screaming and having "sore fits." Shaken but resolved to continue, Lawson prepared to deliver his sermon. Before he could start, however, Abigail Williams arose boldly and said, "Now stand up and name your text." Well might the congregation have collectively drawn in a breath! Whatever its reaction, Lawson, as was the custom, read the Scripture passage on which he would base his sermon, upon which Williams said sarcastically, "It is a long text." Yet no one reprimanded her. Encouraged by this, other young women began doing the same, interrupting the sermon because they claimed to see an apparition of Goodwife Corey "suckling her yellow bird," or familiar spirit, "betwixt her fingers."

To the congregation, this was clearly witchcraft. The following day the magistrates met to examine Goodwife Corey. She denied bewitching the afflicted, but they in turn, again encouraged because no one was criticizing them, tried to outdo each other in their statements. They testified that Corey tormented them, that they saw her likeness, or specter, and that they saw her with another familiar beside her yellow bird that they described as a "black man." Such "spectral evidence," as it was called, was accepted unquestioningly at the Salem trials, though this was a departure from past practice, and ministers such as Increase Mather had warned that demons can appear in the likeness of individuals. In this way, and in others, the Salem trials took on an inner logic that, though blatantly contradictory, was inexorable. Only with repeated admonitions from ministers and others regarding accepting spectral evidence did the accusation and trial process begin to fall apart.

In a similar manner to Knapp, the afflicted young women at Salem seemed to relish their newfound celebrity and the audiences that surrounded them. It gave them an opportunity to act on their jealousies of other people in town, to bring family feuds to a new and potentially deadly level, and to associate with powerful ministers and judges. It also gave them a chance to prove their holiness publicly by speaking defiantly to demons and apparitions. For example, Anne Putnam, Sr., in the midst of her torments—supposedly at the hands of Rebecca Nurse's specter—delivered a long speech in which she declared that her soul was out of the reach of witches and demons and "clothed with the white robes of Christ's righteousness."

Not surprisingly, Nurse was soon examined and committed to jail. The following Sabbath day, Parris was once again back in the pulpit. The church members looked to him to tell them what was happening and, it was hoped, to restore peace and order. Most anxious was Sarah Cloyse, Rebecca Nurse's sister, who relied on Parris to utter words of healing that would end the hysteria. But Parris came with a sword. His text for his sermon stated, "One of them is a devil." For Cloyse, these words could only refer to her innocent sister. She rose, strode to the back of the church, and, Lawson related, "flung the door after her violently, to the amazement of the congregation."

Lawson made no judgment of Cloyse's action except to say that she, too, was soon to be accused by the young women. Predictably, she was brought up before the magistrates and imprisoned. Her plight, and that of her sisters Rebecca Nurse and Mary Easty, both executed, galvanized members of her family along with others in the area to begin questioning the proceedings. But the process would be long and difficult, and it would not end before hundreds of people, from the highest to the lowest ranks, had been affected, and nineteen had needlessly lost their lives. Only after many years did some of those involved, judges and accusers alike, realize and publicly acknowledge their error. By then, however, the Salem witchcraft hysteria had already been firmly established as one of the most infamous events in our national experience.

The texts below are from the following sources: Increase Mather, *An Essay for the Recording of Illustrious Providences, Wherein an Account is given of many Remarkable and very Memorable Events, which have happened in this last Age; Especially in New-England* (Boston: Samuel Green for Joseph Browning, 1684, excerpts); Samuel Willard, "A briefe account of a strange & unusuall providence of God befallen to Elizabeth Knap of Groton," c. 1672, MS AM 1502, vol. 2, no. 3, Boston Public Library, Boston, Mass.; Samuel Parris, sermon on Revelation 17:14, 11 September 1692, from "Sermon Notebook, 1689–1694," Connecticut Historical Society, Hartford; Deodate Lawson, *A brief and true narrative of some remarkable passages relating to sundry persons afflicted by witchcraft, in Salem Village: which happened from the nineteenth of March, to the fifth of April, 1692* (Boston: Benjamin Harris, 1692).

Further Reading

Paul Boyer and Stephen Nissenbaum, *Salem Possessed: The Social Origins of Witchcraft* (Cambridge: Harvard University Press, 1974); *The Salem Witchcraft Papers: Verbatim Transcripts of the Legal Documents of the Salem Witchcraft Outbreak of 1692*, edited by Paul Boyer and Stephen Nissenbaum (New York: Da Capo, 1977); John Demos, *Entertaining Satan: Witchcraft and the Culture of Early New England* (New York: Oxford University Press, 1982); Carol F. Karlsen, *The Devil in the Shape of a Woman: Witchcraft in Colonial New England* (New York: W. W. Norton, 1987); Bernard Rosenthal, *Salem Story: Reading the Witch Trials of 1692* (New York: Cambridge University Press, 1993); Richard B. Trask, *The Devil Hath Been Raised: A Documentary History of the Salem Village Witchcraft Outbreak of March 1692* (Danvers, Mass.: Yeoman, 1997).

Increase Mather, *An Essay for the Recording of Illustrious Providences*

CHAPTER VI

That there are demons and possessed persons

The Sadduccees of th[e]se days . . . say that there are no spirits, and that all stories concerning them are either fabulous or to be ascribed unto natural causes. Amongst many others, the learned [Gijsbert] Voetius (in *Disputatione de Operationibus Daemonum*) has sufficiently refuted them. And as to the experience of other ages and places of the world, so the things which divine providence hath permitted and ordered to come to pass amongst ourselves (if the Scriptures were silent) make it manifest beyond all contradiction that there are devils infesting this lower world. Most true it is that Satan and all his wicked angels are limited by the providence of God, so as that they cannot hurt any man or creature, much less any servant of his, without a commission from him whose kingdom is over all. . . . Nevertheless, the Lord doth for wise and holy ends sometimes lengthen the chain which the infernal lions are bound fast in. And as there are many tremendous instances confirming the truth hereof, so that of Satan's taking bodily possession of men is none of the least.

Signs of such

Sometimes indeed it is very hard to discern between natural diseases and satanical possessions, so as that persons really possessed have been thought to be only molested with some natural disease, without any special finger of the evil spirit therein. . . . There are sundry authors . . . who have endeavored to describe and characterize possessed persons. And such particulars as these following are by them mentioned as signs of possession:

1. If the party concerned shall reveal secret things, either past or future, which without supernatural assistance could not be known, it argueth possession.
2. If he does speak with strange languages, or discover skill in arts and sciences never learned by him.
3. If he can bear burthens and do things which are beyond human strength.
4. Uttering words without making use of the organs of speech, when persons shall be heard speaking, and yet neither their lips nor tongues have any motion, 'tis a sign that an evil spirit speaketh in them.
5. When the body is become inflexible.
6. When the belly is on a sudden puffed up, and instantly flat again. . . .

That there are witches, proved by three arguments

There are [those] that acknowledge the existence of spirits, and that the bodies of men are sometimes really possessed thereby, who nevertheless will not believe there are any such woeful creatures *in rerum natura* [in the natural order of things] as witches, or persons confederate with the Devil. . . . Nevertheless, that there have been such, the following arguments do manifest:

1. The argument by many insisted on from the Scriptures is irrefragable. Therein witchcrafts are forbidden. And we often read in the Scripture of metaphorical bewitchings (Nahum 3:4, Galatians 3:1), which similitudes are undoubtedly taken from things that have a real existence *in rerum natura*. Yea, the Scripture makes particular mention of many that used those cursed arts and familiarities with the Devil, for example, Jannes, and Jambres, Balaam, Manasseh, Simon, Elymas. Nor is the relation which the Scripture giveth of the witch of Endor [1 Sam. 28], and the reasons from thence deduced to prove the being of witches, sufficiently confuted by any of our late witch advocates. Though (as one speaketh) some men to elude the argument from that instance, play more hocus-pocus tricks in the explication of that passage than the witch herself did in the raising deceased Samuel. It is a poor evasion in those who think to escape the dint of this argument, by pretending that the witches and familiar spirits spoken of in the Scripture were only jugglers, or men that by legerdemain would do strange feats of activity. The divine law requires that such witches should be cut off by the sword of justice; which may not be affirmed of everyone that shall, without any confederacy with the Devil, play tricks of legerdemain.

2. Experience has too often made it manifest that there are such in the world as hold a correspondence with hell. There have been known wizards, yea, such as have taught others what ceremonies they are to use in maintaining communion with devils. . . . In a word, it is a thing known that there have been men who would discourse in languages and reason notably about sciences which they never learned; who have revealed secrets, discovered hidden treasures, told whither stolen goods have been conveyed, and by whom; and that have caused brute creatures, nay, statues or images, to speak, and give rational answers. . . . Such things as these cannot be done by the help of mere natural causes. It must needs be, then, that the practicers of them are in confederacy with Satan.

3. There have been many in the world who have, upon conviction, confessed themselves guilty of familiarity with the Devil. . . . That divers [persons] executed for witches have acknowledged things against themselves which were never so, I neither doubt or deny. And that a deluded fancy may cause persons verily to think they have seen and done these things which never had any existence, except in their own imaginations, is indisputable. . . . This notwithstanding, that persons whose judgment and reason has been free from disturbance by any disease should not only voluntarily acknowledge their being in cursed familiarities with Satan but mention the particular circumstances of those transactions, and give ocular demonstration of the truth of what they say by discovering the stigmata made upon their bodies by the Devil's hand, and that when more than one or two have been examined apart they should agree

in the circumstances of their relations: and yet that all this should be the mere effect of melancholy or frenzy, cannot, without offering violence to reason and common sense, be imagined. . . .

CHAPTER VII

Concerning apparitions

As yet, no place nor any person in New England have been troubled with apparitions. Some indeed have given out, that I know not what specters were seen by them; but upon inquiry, I cannot find that there was anything therein more than fancy and frightful apprehensions without sufficient ground. Nevertheless, that spirits have sometimes really (as well as imaginarily) appeared to mortals in the world, is amongst sober men beyond controversy. And that such things were of old taken notice of, we may rationally conclude from that Scripture, Luke 24:37, where it is said that the disciples "were terrified and affrighted, and supposed that they had seen a spirit." It is observable, that such frightful specters do most frequently show themselves in places where the light of the gospel hath not prevailed. . . . It is, moreover, sometimes very difficult to pass a true judgment of the specters which do appear, whether they are good or evil angels, or the spirits of deceased men.

That good angels do sometimes visibly appear

That holy angels were frequently seen in old times, we are from the Scriptures of truth assured. And that the angelical ministration doth still continue is past doubt (Hebrews 1:14). But their visible appearance is less frequent than formerly. They do invisibly perform many a good office for the heirs of salvation continually. Nor is it to be questioned but they may still appear visibly when the work which they are sent about cannot otherwise be performed. . . .

One Samuel Wallas of Stamford in Lincolnshire, having been in a consumption for thirteen years, was worn away to a very skeleton and lay bed-rid for four years. But April 7, 1659, being the Lord's day, about six p.m., finding himself somewhat revived, he got out of the bed, and, as he was reading a book entitled *Abraham's Suit for Sodom*, he heard somebody knock at the door. Whereupon (there being none then in the house but himself) he took a staff in one hand, and, leaning to the wall with the other, came to the door and, opening it, a comely and grave old man of a fresh complexion, with white curled hair, entered; and, after walking several times about the room, said to him, "Friend, I perceive you are not well." To whom Wallas replied, he had been ill many years, and that the doctors said his disease was consumption, and past cure, and that he was a poor man, and not able to follow their costly prescriptions, only he committed himself and life into the hands of God, to dispose of as he pleased. To whom the man replied, "Thou sayest very well; be sure to fear God, and serve him, and remember to observe what now I say to thee. Tomorrow morning, go into the garden, and there take two leaves of red sage, and one of bloodwort; and put those three leaves into a cup of small beer, and drink thereof as oft as need requires. The fourth morning, cast those leaves away and put in fresh ones. Thus do for twelve days together, and thou shalt find ere these twelve days be expired, through the help of God, thy disease will be cured, and the frame of thy body altered." . . . Having spoken these things, he again charged Samuel Wallas to remember the directions given to him, but above all things to fear God, and serve him. Wallas asked him if he would eat anything, unto whom he answered, "No, friend, the Lord Christ is sufficient for me. Seldom do I drink anything but what cometh from the Rock." So, wishing the Lord of heaven to be with him, he departed. . . . Wallas beheld the man passing in the street, but none else observed him, though some were then standing in the doors opposite to Wallas his house. And though it rained when this grave person came into the house, and had done so all that day, yet he had not one spot of wet or dirt upon him. Wallas followed the directions prescribed, and was restored to his health within the days mentioned. The fame of this strange providence being noised abroad, sundry ministers met at Stamford to consider and consult about it, who concluded that this cure was wrought by a good angel, sent from heaven upon that errand.

That caco-demons oftentimes pretend to be good angels

However it is not impossible that holy angels may appear and visibly converse with some, yet for any to desire such a thing is unwarrantable, and exceeding dangerous. For thereby some have been imposed upon by wicked demons, who know how to transform themselves into angels of light. . . .

[Remigio] Remegius (and from him others) write of a young man whose name was Theodore Maillot, unto whom a demon appearing, advised him to reform his life, to abstain from drunkenness, thefts, uncleanness, and the like evils; and to fast twice a week, to be constant in attendance upon public worship, and to be very charitable to the poor. The like pious advice did another demon follow a certain woman with, unto whom he appeared. Could a good angel have given better counsel? But this was Satan's policy, hoping that thereby he should have gained an advantage to take silly souls alive in his cruel snare. Like as thieves upon the road will sometimes enter into religious discourse, that so their fellow travelers may have good thoughts of them, and be the more easily despoiled by them.

That Satan may appear in the likeness of holy men

And as the evil spirit will speak good words, so doth he sometimes appear in the likeness of good men, to the end that he may the more effectually deceive and delude all such as shall be so unhappy as to entertain converses with him.

No doubt but that he knows how to transform himself into the shape not only of an ordinary saint, but of an apostle, or holy prophet of God (II Corinthians 1:13–14). This we may gather from the sacred history of dead Samuel's appearing to Saul. Some are of opinion that dead Samuel spake to Saul, his soul being by magical incantations returned into his body, . . . but Tertullian and Justin Martyr are of the judgment that a lying demon appeared to Saul in Samuel's likeness. Our Protestant divines generally are of this judgment. It was customary amongst the Gentiles for magicians and necromancers to cause dead persons to appear, and they would bring whomsoever they were desired to call for. . . . Those apparitions were caco-demons, which feigned themselves to be the spirits of men departed. . . . Upon which account men had need be exceeding wary what credit they give unto, or how they entertain communion with, such specters. I do not say that all such apparitions are specters, only that many of them are so. . . .

CHAPTER VIII

The preceding relations about witchcrafts and diabolical impostures gives us too just occasion to make inquiry into some cases of conscience respecting things of this nature. And in the first place, the query may be:

Whether it is lawful to make use of any sort of herbs or plants to preserve from witchcrafts, or from the power of evil spirits? The answer unto which is, that it is in no wise lawful, but that all attempts of that nature are magical and diabolical, and therefore detestable superstition. As appears,

1. In that if the devils do either operate or cease to do mischief upon the use of such things, it must needs be in that they are signs which give notice to the evil spirits what they are to do. Now for men to submit to any of the Devil's sacraments is implicitly to make a covenant with him. Many who practice these nefarious vanities little think what they do. They would not for the world (they say) make a covenant with the Devil, yet by improving the Devil's signals, with an opinion of receiving benefit thereby, they do the thing which they pretend to abhor. For,

2. Angels (bad as well as good) are by nature incorporeal substances. . . . And thence it is that they are not visible or palpable or any way incurring the outward senses. . . . It is not to be doubted but that spirits may make use of vehicles that are subject to the outward senses; nevertheless, a mere spirit cannot be touched by human hands. Moreover, we read of a legion of demons possessing one miserable body (Luke 8:30). A legion is at least 6,000. Now if they were corporeal substances, it could not be so that so many of them should be in the same person at the same time. And if they are incorporeal substances, then it is not possible that herbs or any sensible objects should have a natural influence upon them, as they have upon elementary bodies. . . .

3. God in his holy Word has forbidden his people to imitate the heathen nations. He requires that those who profess his name should not learn the way

of the heathen, nor do after their manners (Leviticus 20:33, Jeremiah 10:2). But to attempt the driving away of evil spirits by the use of herbs, fumes, etc., is an heathenish custom. . . .

It is no less superstitious when men endeavor by characters, words or spells to charm any witches, devils, or diseases. Such persons do . . . fence themselves with the Devil's shield against the Devil's sword. . . . There cannot be a greater vanity than to imagine that devils are really frighted with words and syllables: such practices are likewise of diabolical and heathenish original. . . .

A second case, which we shall here take occasion to inquire into, is *Whether it be lawful for bewitched persons to draw blood from those whom they suspect for witches, or to put urine into a bottle, or to nail an horseshoe at their doors, or the like, in hopes of recovering health thereby?* . . .

1. They that obtain health in this way, have it from the Devil. The witch cannot recover them but by the Devil's help. Hence it is unlawful to entreat witches to heal bewitched persons, because they cannot do this but by Satan. So is it very sinful by scratching, or burnings, or detention of urine, etc., to endeavor to constrain them to unbewitch any, for this is to put them upon seeking to the Devil. The witch does neither inflict nor remove the disease but by the assistance of the Devil; therefore either to desire or force thereunto is to make use of the Devil's help. The person thus recovered cannot say, "The Lord was my healer," but, "The Devil was my healer." Certainly it were better for a man to remain sick all his days, yea (as Chrysostom speaks), he had better die than go to the Devil for health. Hence,

2. Men and women have, by such practices as these mentioned, black commerce and communion with the Devil. They do (though ignorantly) concern and involve themselves in that covenant which the Devil has made with his devoted and accursed vassals. For, whereas it is pleaded that if the thing bewitched be thrown into the fire, or the urine of the sick stopped in a bottle, or an horseshoe nailed before the door, then by virtue of the compact which is between the Devil and his witches, their power of doing more hurt ceaseth; they that shall for such an end so practice, have fellowship with that hellish covenant. . . . To use any ceremonies invented by the Devil to attain a supernatural end implies too great a concernment with him. Yea, such persons do honor and worship the Devil by hoping in his salvation. They use means to obtain health which is not natural, nor was ever appointed by God, but is wholly of the Devil's institution; which he is much pleased with, as being highly honored thereby. Nay, such practices do imply an invocation of the Devil for relief, and a pleading with him the covenant which he hath made with the witch, and a declaration of confidence that the father of lies will be as good as his word. . . .

3. Let such practitioners think the best of themselves, they are too near akin to those creatures who commonly pass under the name of "white witches." They that do hurt to others by the Devil's help are called "black witches"; but there are a sort of persons in the world that will never hurt any, but only by the

power of the infernal spirits they will unbewitch those that seek unto them for relief. . . . How persons that shall unbewitch others by putting urine into a bottle, or by casting excrements into the fire, or nailing of horseshoes at men's doors, can wholly clear themselves from being white witches, I am not able to understand.

4. Innocent persons have been extremely wronged by such diabolical tricks. For sometimes . . . the Devil does not only himself inflict diseases upon men, but present the visages of innocent persons to the fancies of the diseased, making them believe that they are tormented by them, when only himself does it. And in case they follow the Devil's direction, by observing the ceremonies which he has invented, he'll afflict their bodies no more. So does his malice bring the persons accused by him (though never so innocent) into great suspicion. And he will cease afflicting the body of one, in case he may ruin the credit of another, and withal endanger the souls of those that hearken to him. If the Devil upon scratchings, or burnings, or stoppings of urine, or the nailing of an horseshoe, etc., shall cease to afflict the body of any, he does this either as being compelled thereto, or voluntarily. To imagine that such things shall constrain the evil spirit to cease afflicting, whether he will or no, is against all reason. But if he does this voluntarily, then instead of hurting their bodies, he does a greater mischief to souls.

Samuel Willard, "A Brief Account of a Strange and Unusual Providence of God"

This poor and miserable object, about a fortnight before she was taken, we observed to carry herself in a strange and unwonted manner. Sometimes she would give sudden shrieks, and, if we inquired a reason, would always put it off with some excuse, and then would burst forth into immoderate and extravagant laughter, in such wise, as sometimes she fell onto the ground with it. I myself observed oftentimes a strange change in her countenance, but could not suspect the true reason, but conceived she might be ill; and therefore divers times inquired how she did, and she always answered, "Well," which made me wonder.

But the tragedy began to unfold itself upon Monday, October 30, 1671, after this manner (as I received by credible information, being that day myself gone from home): in the evening, a little before she went to bed, sitting by the fire, she cried out, "Oh my legs!" and clapped her hand on them; immediately, "Oh my breast!" and removed her hands thither; and forthwith, "Oh I am strangled!" and put her hands on her throat. Those that observed her could not see what to make of it, whether she was in earnest or dissembled, and in this manner they left her (excepting the person that lay with her) complaining of her breath being stopped.

The next day she was in a strange frame (as was observed by divers [persons]), sometimes weeping, sometimes laughing, and many foolish and apish gestures. In the evening, going into the cellar, she shrieked suddenly, and being inquired of the cause, she answered that she saw two persons in the cellar. Whereupon some went down with her to search, but found none, she also looking with them; at last she turned her head, and, looking one way steadfastly, used the expression, "What cheer, old man?" Which they that were with her took for a fancy, and so ceased. Afterwards (the same evening), the rest of the family being in bed, she was (as one lying in the room saw, and she herself also afterwards related) suddenly thrown down into the midst of the floor with violence and taken with a violent fit; whereupon the whole family was raised, and with much ado was she kept out of the fire from destroying herself. After which time she was followed with fits from thence till the sabbath day, in which she was violent in bodily motions, leapings, strainings and strange agitations, scarce to be held in bounds by the strength of three or four; violent also in roarings and screamings, representing a dark resemblance of hellish torments, and frequently using in these fits divers words, sometimes crying out "Money, money," sometimes, "Sin and misery," with other words.

On Wednesday [November 1], being in the time of intermission questioned about the case she was in with reference to the cause or occasion of it, she seemed to impeach one of the neighbors, a person (I doubt not) of sincere uprightness before God, as though either she, or the devil in her likeness and habit, particularly her riding hood, had come down the chimney [and] stricken her that night she was first taken violently, which was the occasion of her being cast into the floor. Whereupon those about her sent to request the person to come to her, who, coming unwittingly, was at the first assaulted by her strangely: for though her eyes were (as it were) sealed up (as they were always, or for the most part, in those fits, and so continue in them all to this day), she yet knew her very touch from any other, though no voice were uttered, and discovered it evidently by her gestures, so powerful were Satan's suggestions in her. Yet afterwards God was pleased to vindicate the case and justify the innocent, even to remove jealousies, from the spirits of the party concerned, and [to the] satisfaction of the bystanders: for after she had gone to prayer with her, she confessed that she believed Satan had deluded her, and hath never since complained of any such apparition or disturbance from the person. These fits continuing (though with intermission), divers (when they had opportunity) pressed upon her to declare what might be the true and real occasion of these amazing fits. She used many tergiversations and excuses, pretending she would [talk] to this and that young person, who coming, she put it off to another, till at the last, on Thursday night, she brake forth into a large confession in the presence of many, the substance whereof amounted to thus much: that the Devil had oftentimes appeared to her, presenting the treaty of a covenant and proffering largely to her, viz., such things as suited her youthful fancy—money, silks, fine cloths, ease from labor, to show her the whole world, etc.; that it had been then three years since his first appearance, occasioned by her discontent; that at first his apparitions had been more rare, but lately more frequent, yea, those few weeks that she had dwelt with us, almost constant; that she seldom went out of one room into another but he appeared to her, urging of her, and that he had presented her a book written with blood of covenants made by others with him, and told her such and such (of some whereof we hope better things) had a name there; that he urged upon her constant temptations to murder her parents, her neighbors, our children, especially the youngest, tempting her to throw it into the fire, on the hearth, into the oven; and that once he put a billhook into her hand to murder myself, persuading her I was asleep, but coming about it, she met me on the stairs, at which she was affrighted—the time I remember well, and observed a strange frame in her countenance, and saw she endeavored to hide something, but I knew not what, neither did I at all suspect any such matter; and that often he persuaded her to make away with herself: and once she was going to drown herself in the well, for, looking into it, she saw such sights as allured her, and was gotten within the curb, and was by God's providence prevented. Many other like things she related, too tedious to recollect: but being pressed to declare whether she had not consented to a covenant with the Devil, she with solemn assertions denied it, yea, asserted that she had never so much as consented to discourse with him, nor had ever but once before that night used the expression, "What cheer, old man?" And this argument she used, that the providence of God had ordered it so that all his apparitions had been frightful to her; yet this she acknowledged (which seemed contradictory, viz.), that when she came to our house to school, before such time as she dwelt with us, she delayed her going home in the evening till it was dark (which we observed), upon his persuasion to have his company home, and that she could not, when he appeared, but go to him. One evident testimony whereof we can say something to, viz., the night before the thanksgiving, October 19, she was with another maid that boarded in the house, where both of them saw the appearance of a man's head and shoulders, with a great white neckcloth, looking in at the window, at which they came up affrighted both into the chamber where the rest of us were. They declaring the case, one of us went down to see who it might be, but she ran immediately out of the door before him: which she hath since confessed was the Devil coming to her. She also acknowledged the reason of her former sudden shriekings was from a sudden apparition, and that the Devil put these excuses into her mouth, and bid her so to say, and hurried her into those violent (but she saith feigned and forced) laughters. She then also complained against herself of many sins—disobedience to parents, neglect of attendance upon ordinances, attempts to murder herself and others—but this particular (of a covenant) she utterly disclaimed: which relation seemed fair, especially in that it was attended with bitter tears, self-condemnations, good counsels given to all about her, especially the youth then present, and an earnest desire of prayers. She sent to Lancaster for [Rev.] Mr. Rowlandson who came and prayed with her and gave her serious counsels. But she was still followed, all this notwithstanding, with these fits; and in this state (coming home on Friday) I found her, but could get nothing from her. Whenever I came in [her] presence, she fell into those fits. Concerning which fits, I find this noteworthy: she knew and understood what was spoken to her, but could not answer nor use any other words but the forementioned, "Money," etc., as long as the fit continued; for when she came out of it, she could give a relation of all that had been spoken to her. She was demanded a reason why she used those words in her fits, and signified that the Devil presented her with such things to tempt her, and with sin and misery to terrify her; she also declared that she had seen the devils in their hellish shapes, and more devils than anyone there ever saw men in the world. Many of these things I heard her declare on Saturday at night.

On the sabbath [November 5] the physician came, who judged a main part of her distemper to be natural, arising from the foulness of her stomach and corruptness of her blood, occasioning fumes in her brain and strange fancies. Whereupon (in order to further trial and administration) she was removed home, and the succeeding week she took physick, and was not in such violence handled in her fits as before, but enjoyed an intermission, and gave some hopes of recovery; in which intermission she was altogether senseless (as to our discovery) of her state, held under security and hardness of heart, professing she had no trouble upon her spirits—she hoped Satan had left her. A solemn day [of fasting and prayer] was kept with her, yet it had then (as I apprehend) little efficacy upon her. She that day again expressed hopes that the Devil had left her, but there was little ground to think so because she remained under such extreme senselessness of her own estate. And thus she continued, being exercised with some moderate fits in which she used none of the former expressions, but sometimes fainted away, sometimes used some strugglings, yet not with extremity, till the Wednesday following [November 15]; which day was spent in prayer with her, when her fits something more increased, and her tongue was for many hours together drawn into a semicircle up to the roof of her mouth, and not to be removed, for some tried with their fingers to do it. From thence till the sabbath seven night following she continued alike, only she added to former confessions of her twice consenting to travel with the Devil in her company between Groton and Lancaster, who accompanied her in form of a black dog with eyes in his back, sometimes stopping her horse, sometimes leaping up behind, and keeping her (when she came home with company) forty rods at least behind, leading her out of the way into a swamp, etc. But still no conference would she own, but urged that the Devil's quarrel with her was because she would not seal a covenant with him, and that this was the ground of her first being taken. Besides this, nothing observable came from her, only one morning she said, "God is a father," the next morning, "God is my father"; which words (it is to be feared) were words of presumption, put into her mouth by the adversary. I, suspecting the truth of her former story, pressed whether she never verbally promised to covenant with him, which she stoutly denied, only acknowledged that she had had some thoughts so to do. But on the forenamed November 26 she was again with violence and extremity seized by her fits, in such wise that six persons could hardly hold her, but she leaped and skipped about the house perforce roaring and yelling extremely, and fetching deadly sighs, as if her heartstrings would have broken, and looking with a frightful aspect, to the amazement of all the beholders, of which I was eyewitness.

The physician being then again with her, consented that the distemper was diabolical, refused further to administer, [and] advised to extraordinary fasting, whereupon some of God's ministers were sent for. She meanwhile continued extremely tormented night and day, till Tuesday about noon, having this added, on Monday and Tuesday morning, that she barked like a dog and bleated like a calf, in which her organs were visibly made use of; yea (as was carefully observed), on Monday night and Tuesday morning, whenever any came near the house, though they within heard nothing at all, yet would she bark till they were come into the house. On Tuesday [November 28], about twelve of the clock, she came out of the fit which had held her from sabbath day about the same time, at least forty-eight hours, with little or no intermission; and then her speech was restored to her and she expressed a great seeming sense of her state: many bitter tears, sighings, sobbings, complainings she uttered, bewailing of many sins forementioned, begging prayers, and in the hour of prayer expressing much affection. I then pressed if there were anything behind in reference to the dealings between her and Satan, when she again professed that she had related all, and declared that in those fits the Devil had assaulted her many ways: that he came down the chimney and she essayed to escape him, but was seized upon by him; that he sat upon her breast and used many arguments with her, and that he urged her at one time with persuasions and promises of ease, and great matters; told her that she had done enough in what she had already confessed, she might henceforth serve him more securely; anon told her her time was past, and there was no hopes unless she would serve him: and it was observed in the time of her extremity, once when a little moment's respite was granted her of speech, she advised us to make our peace with God and use our time better than she had done. The party advised her also to bethink herself of making her peace; she replied, "It is too late for me."

The next day was solemnized, when we had the presence of [Revs.] Mr. Bulkeley, Mr. Rowlandson, and Mr. Estabrook; whither coming, we found her returned to a sottish and stupid kind of frame. Much was pressed upon her, but no affection at all discovered, though she was little or nothing exercised with any fits, and her speech also continued—though a day or two after, she was melancholy, and, being inquired of a reason, she complained that she was grieved that so much pains were taken with her, and did her no good. But this held her not long, and thus she remained till Monday [December 4], when to some neighbors there present she related something more of her converse with the Devil, viz., that it had been five years or thereabouts since she first saw him, and declared methodically the sundry apparitions from time to time till she was thus dreadfully assaulted, in which the principal was that, after many assaults, she had resolved to seal a covenant with Satan, thinking she had better do it than be thus followed by him; that once, when she lived at Lancaster, he presented himself and desired of her blood, and she would have done it but wanted a knife—in the parlay she was prevented by the providence of God interposing my father; a second time in the house he met her and presented her a knife, and as she was going about it my father stepped in again and prevented, that when she sought and inquired for the knife it was not to be found, and that afterwards she saw it sticking in the top of the barn; and some other like passages she again owned. An observable passage, which she also had confessed in her first declaration but is not there inserted, viz., [was] that the Devil had often proffered her his service, but she accepted not; and once in particular to bring her in chips for the fire, [yet] she refused, but when she came in she saw them lie by the fireside, and was afraid. And this I remark: I, sitting by the fire, spake to her to lay them on, and she turned away in an unwonted manner. She then also declared against herself her unprofitable life she had led, and how justly God had thus permitted Satan to handle her, telling them they little knew what a sad case she was in. I after asked her concerning these passages, and she owned the truth of them, and declared that now she hoped the Devil had left her; but being pressed whether there were not a covenant, she earnestly professed that, by God's goodness, she had been prevented from doing that which she of herself had been ready enough to assent to, and she thanked God there was no such thing. The same day she was again taken with a new kind of unwonted fit, in which, after she had been exercised with violence, she got her a stick and went up and down, thrusting and pushing here and there; and anon looking out at a window, and cried out of a witch appearing in a strange manner, in form of a dog downward, with a woman's head, and declared the person other whiles, that she appeared in her whole likeness, and described her shape and habit, [and] signified that she went up the chimney and went her way. What impression we read in the clay of the chimney, in similitude of a dog's paw, by the operation of Satan, and in the form of a dog's going in the same place she told of, I shall not conclude, though something there was, as I myself saw in the chimney in the same place where she declared the foot was set to go up.

In this manner was she handled that night and the two next days, using strange gestures, complaining by signs when she could not speak, explaining that she was sometimes in the chamber, sometimes in the chimney, and anon assaults her, sometimes scratching her breast, beating her sides, strangling her throat; and she did oftentimes seem to our apprehension as if she would forthwith be strangled. . . .

Whereupon I was sent for to her, and understanding how things had passed, I found that there was no room for privacy in a matter already made by her so public. I therefore examined her concerning the matter, and found her not so forward to confess as she had been to others; yet thus much I gathered from her confession:

That after she came to dwell with us, one day, as she was alone in a lower room, all the rest of us being in the chamber, she looked out at the window and saw the Devil, in the habit of an old man, coming over a great meadow lying near the house; and, suspecting his design, she had thoughts to have gone away, yet at length resolved to tarry it out and hear what he had to say to her. When he came, he demanded of her some of her blood, which she forthwith consented to, and with a knife cut her finger; he caught the blood in his hand, and then told her she must write her name in his book. She answered, she could not write, but he told her he would direct her hand, and then took a little sharpened stick and dipped [it] in the blood, and put it into her hand and guided it, and she wrote her name with his help. What was the matter she set her hand to, I could not learn from her; but thus much she confessed, that the term of time agreed upon with him was for seven years: one year she was to be faithful in his service, and then the other six he would serve her, and make her a witch. She also related that the ground of contest between her and the Devil, which was the occasion of this sad providence, was this, that after her covenant [was] made the Devil showed her hell and the damned, and told her if she were not faithful to him she should go thither and be tormented there; she desired of him to show her heaven, but he told her that heaven was an ugly place and that none went thither but a company of base rogues whom he hated, but if she would obey him it should be well with her. But afterward she considered with herself that the term of her covenant was but short, and would soon be at an end, and she doubted (for all the Devil's promises) she must at last come to the place he had shown her, and withal feared if she were a witch she should be discovered and brought to a shameful end, which was many times a trouble on her spirits. This the Devil perceiving, urged upon her to give him more of her blood and set her hand again to his book, which she refused to do; but partly through promises, partly by threatenings, he brought her at last to a promise that she would sometime do it, after which he left not incessantly to urge her to the performance of it. Once he met her on the stairs, and often elsewhere, pressing her with vehemency; but she still put if off, till the first night she was taken, when the Devil came to her and told her he would not tarry any longer. She told him she would not do it; he answered she had done it already, and what further damage would it be to do it again, for she was his sure enough. She rejoined she had done it already, and if she were his sure enough, what need he to desire any more of her. Whereupon he struck her the first night, and again more violently the second, as is above expressed.

This is the sum of the relation I then had from her, which at that time seemed to be methodical. These things she uttered with great affection, overflowing of tears, and seeming bitterness. I asked of the reason of her weeping and bitterness; she complained of her sins, and some in particular— profanation of the sabbath, etc.—but nothing of this sin of renouncing the government of God and giving herself up to the Devil. I therefore (as God helped) applied it to her and asked her whether she desired not prayers with and for her; she assented with earnestness, and in prayer seemed to bewail the sin, as God helped, then in the aggravation of it, and afterward declared a desire to rely on the power and mercy of God in Christ. She then also declared that the Devil had deceived her concerning those persons impeached by her: that he had in their likeness or resemblance tormented her, persuading her that it was they, that they bare her a spleen, but he loved her and would free her from them, and pressed on her to endeavor to bring them forth to the censure of the law. . . .

Thus she continued till the next sabbath [December 17] in the afternoon, on which day in the morning, being something better than at other times, she had but little company tarried with her in the afternoon, when the Devil began to make more full discovery of himself. It had been a question before, whether she might properly be called a demoniac, or person possessed of the Devil, but it was then put out of question: he began (as the persons with her testify) by drawing her tongue out of her mouth most frightfully to an extraordinary length and greatness, and many amazing postures of her body, and then by speaking vocally in her; whereupon her father and another neighbor were called from the meeting, on whom (as soon as they came in) he railed, calling them rogues, charging them for folly in going to hear a black rogue who told them nothing but a parcel of lies, and deceived them, and many like expressions. After exercise I was called, but understood not the occasion, till I came and heard the same voice—a grum, low, yet audible voice it was. The first salutation I had was, "Oh! you are a great rogue." I was at the first something daunted and amazed, and many reluctances I had upon my spirits, which brought me to a silence and amazement in my spirits, till at last God heard my groans and gave me both refreshment in Christ, and courage. I then called for a light, to see whether it might not appear a counterfeit, and observed not any of her organs to move: the voice was hollow, as if it issued out of her throat. He then again called me "great black rogue." I challenged him to make it appear, but all the answer was, "You tell the people a company of lies." I reflected on myself, and could not but magnify the goodness of God not to suffer Satan to bespatter the names of his people with those sins which he himself hath pardoned in the blood of Christ. I answered, "Satan, thou art a liar and a deceiver, and God will vindicate his own truth one day." He answered nothing directly, but said, "I am not Satan, I am a pretty black boy; this is my pretty girl; I have been here a great while." I sat still, and answered nothing to these expressions; but when he directed himself to me again, "Oh! you black rogue, I do not love you," I replied, "Through God's grace, I hate thee." He rejoined, "But you had better love me." These manner of expressions filled some of the company there present with great consternation; others put on boldness to speak to him, at which I was displeased, and advised them to see their call clear, fearing lest by his policy, and many apish expressions he used, he might insinuate himself and raise in them a fearlessness of spirit of him. I no sooner turned my back to go to the fire, but he called out again, "Where is that black rogue gone?" I seeing little good to be done by discourse, and questioning many things in my mind concerning it, I desired the company to join in prayer unto God. When we went about that duty and were kneeled down, with a voice louder than before something he cried out, "Hold your tongue, hold your tongue! Get you gone, you black rogue! What are you going to do, you have nothing to do with me," etc., but through God's goodness was silenced, and she lay quiet during the time of prayer; but as soon as it was ended began afresh, using the former expressions. At which some ventured to speak to him, though I think imprudently: one told him, God had him in chains; he replied, "For all my chains, I can knock thee on the head when I please." He said he would carry her away that night. Another answered, "But God is stronger than thou." He presently rejoined, "That's a lie; I am stronger than God." At which blasphemy I again advised them to be wary of speaking, counseled them to get serious persons to watch with her, and left her, commending her to God.

On Tuesday [December 19] following she confessed that the Devil entered into her the second night after her first taking: that when she was going to bed, he entered in (as she conceived) at her mouth, and had been in her ever since, and professed that if there were ever a Devil in the world, there was one in her, but in what manner he spake in her she could not tell. . . .

Since that time she hath continued for the most part speechless, her fits coming upon her sometimes often, sometimes with greater intermission and with great varieties in the manner of them, sometimes by violence, sometimes by making her sick, but (through God's goodness) so abated in violence that now one person can as well rule her, as formerly four or five. She is observed always to fall into her fits when any strangers go to visit her, and the more go, the more violent are her fits. As to the frame of her spirits, she hath been more averse lately to good counsel than heretofore, yet sometime she signifies a desire of the company of ministers. . . .

On Friday in the evening she was taken with a passion of weeping and sighing, which held her till late in the night; at length she sent for me, but the unseasonableness of the weather and my own bodily indisposedness prevented. I went the next morning, when she strove to speak something but could not, but was taken with her fits, which held her as long as I tarried, which was more than an hour, and I left her in them. And thus she continues speechless to this instant, January 15, and followed with fits: concerning which state of hers I shall suspend my own judgments, and willingly leave it to the censure of those that are more learned, aged, and judicious. Only I shall leave my thoughts in respect of two or three questions which have risen about her, viz.,

1. Whether her distemper be real or counterfeit? I shall say no more to that but this: the great strength appearing in them, and great weakness after them, will disclaim the contrary opinion; for though a person may counterfeit much, yet such a strength is beyond the force of dissimulation.

2. Whether her distemper be natural or diabolical? I suppose the premises will strongly enough conclude the latter, yet I will add these two further arguments: first, the actings of convulsion, which these come nearest to, are (as persons

acquainted with them observe) in many, yea, the most essential, parts of them quite contrary to these actings; second, she hath no ways wasted in body or strength by all these fits, though so dreadful, but gathered flesh exceedingly, and hath her natural strength when her fits are off, for the most part.

3. Whether the Devil did really speak in her? To that point, which some have much doubted of, thus much I will say to countermand this apprehension. First, the manner of expression I diligently observed, and could not perceive any organ, any instrument of speech (which the philosopher makes mention of), to have any motion at all, yea, her mouth was sometimes shut without opening, sometimes open without shutting or moving; and then both I and others saw her tongue (as it used to be when she was in some fits, when speechless) turned up circularly to the roof of her mouth. Second, the labial letters, divers of which were used by her, viz., "b," "m," "p," which cannot be naturally expressed without motion of the lips, which must needs come within our ken if observed, were uttered without any such motion; if she had used only linguals, gutturals, etc., the matter might have been more suspicious. Third, the reviling terms then used were such as she never used before nor since, in all this time of her being thus taken; yea, hath been always observed to speak respectively concerning me. Fourth, they were expressions [by] which the Devil (by her confession) aspersed me, and others withal, in the hour of temptation; particularly she had freely acknowledged that the Devil was wont to appear to her in the house of God and divert her mind, and charge her she should not give ear to what that black-coated rogue spake. Fifth, we observed, when the voice spake, her throat was swelled formidably as big at least as one's fist. These arguments I shall leave to the censure of the judicious.

4. Whether she have covenanted with the Devil or no? I think this is a case unanswerable; her declarations have been so contradictory one to another that we know not what to make of them, and her condition is such as administers many doubts. Charity would hope the best, love would also fear the worst.

But thus much is clear: she is an object of pity, and I desire that all that hear of her would compassionate her forlorn state. She is (I question not) a subject of hope, and therefore all means ought to be used for her recovery. She is a monument of divine severity, and the Lord grant that all that see or hear may fear and tremble. Amen.

Samuel Parris, *These Shall Make War with the Lamb*

After the condemnation of six witches at a court at Salem,
one of the witches, viz., Martha Corey, in full communion with our church

Revelation 17:14.
These shall make war with the Lamb, and the Lamb shall overcome them: for he is the Lord of lords, and King of kings; and they that are with him are called, and chosen, and faithful.

In these words, two things are observable:

1. A war prophesied of.
2. The victory that this war shall issue in.
1. Here is mention made of a war. "These shall make war," etc.
Now in all wars are two parties. And so here.

(1) Here is the offending party. Namely these, viz., Antichrist (the spiritual whore) and all her assistants, instruments of Satan, and instigated by that Dragon to this war (Revelation 13:1–2), namely by sorceries and witchcrafts (plentiful among the Papacy), doing lying wonders, whereby multitudes were deluded.

(2) Here is the offended party, viz., the Lamb and his followers. Text: ["These shall make war with the Lamb . . ."]. With these they make war.

2. Here is the victory, and the reason of the victory.

(1) The victory. Devils and idolaters will make war with the Lamb and his followers. But who shall have the victory? Why, the Lamb (i.e. Christ) and his followers. Text.

(2) Here is the reason of it, and that is twofold:

First, and main reason, is taken from the Lamb (Christ). "For he is Lord of lords," etc.

Second reason is taken from the saints' three victorial properties:

1. They are chosen.
2. They are called.
3. Last, they are faithful. Of all which, hereafter.

Doctrine.
The Devil and his instruments will be making war with the Lamb and his followers as long as they can.

Here are two things in this doctrine, namely:

1. The Devil and his instruments will be warring against Christ and his followers.
2. This war will be as long as they can. It will not be forever. There will be a time when they shall war no longer.

(1) The Devil and his instruments will be warring against Christ and his followers. Text: "These shall make war with the Lamb." Revelation 11:2—the Beast shall make war against them. Chap. 12:7, 17, "[And there was] war in heaven: the Dragon fought and his angels." Chap. 13:7, "It was given to him to make war with the saints," etc. Chap. 19:19.

We may farther confirm this point by instances and reasons.

1. For instances. We find the Devil assaulting the Lamb as soon as he was born to the end of his days, as we see in his instrument, Herod (Matthew 2:7, etc.); and afterwards by his manifold temptations of Christ in the wilderness (Matthew 4); and afterwards by his stirring up the chief of the Jews to kill Christ (Matthew 26:3–4). And to help forward that murder, the Devil puts it into the heart of one of Christ's disciples to betray him (John 13:2). And after all, though the Lamb be killed, but yet liveth forever, and no advantage got by the Devil by the murder of

Christ, why, now he seeks to destroy his church: and for this end influenceth bloody Saul to lay all waste (Acts 8:3, 9:1–2). But now when the Lamb had conquered this bloody instrument, and of a Saul made him Paul, a preacher of righteousness, why, now the Devil as much opposeth Paul (Acts 13:4, etc.). Yea, the Scripture is full of such instances. Church history abounds also with evidences of this truth. Yea, and in our days, how industrious and vigorous is the bloody French monarch [Louis XIV] and his confederates against Christ and his interest? Yea, and in our land (in this and some neighboring places) how many, what multitudes of witches and wizards has the Devil instigated with utmost violence to attempt the overthrow of religion?

2. The reason: and that, in a word, is from the enmity of the Devil and his instruments to religion. Acts 13:10, "Thou child of the Devil, thou enemy of all righteousness." Now the seed of the Devil will do the works of the Devil. John 8:44, "Ye are of your father the Devil, and the lusts of your father ye will do," etc. "Satan, . . . is called the god of this world, because as God at first did but speak the word and it was done, so if the Devil do but hold up his finger, give the least hint" of his mind, his servants and slaves will obey.

(2) This war shall be as long as they can. It shall not be forever and always. Here,

1. Sometimes the Devil loseth his volunteers in war. The lawful captive, the captives of the mighty, are sometimes delivered (Isaiah 49:24–25). We have an instance in bloody Saul (Acts 9:3, etc.).

2. Sometimes the Devil is chained up, so that he cannot head and form an army as otherwise he would against the saints (Revelation 20:1–3).

3. Last, after this life the saints shall no more be troubled with war from Devils and their instruments. The city of heaven, provided for the saints, is well-walled, and well-gated, and well-guarded, so that no devils nor their instruments shall enter therein (Revelation 21:10, etc.).

Use 1. It may serve to reprove such as seem to be amazed at the war the Devil has raised amongst us by wizards and witches against the Lamb and his followers, that they altogether deny it. If ever there were witches, men and women in covenant with the Devil, here are multitudes in New England. Nor is it so strange a thing there should be such: no, nor that some church members should be such. The Jews, after the return of their captivity, woefully degenerated even unto the horrible sin of sorcery and witchcraft (Malachi 3:5). Pious Bishop Hall saith, "The Devil's prevalency in this age is most clear in the marvelous number of witches abounding in all places. Now hundreds" (says he) "are discovered in one shire, and if fame deceive us not, in a village of fourteen houses in the north are found so many of this damned brood. Heretofore only barbarous deserts had them, but now the civilest and religious parts are frequently pestered with them. Heretofore some silly ignorant old woman," etc., "but now we have known those of both sexes, who professed much knowledge, holiness, and devotion, drawn into this damnable practice." . . .

Use 2. We may see here who they are that war against the Lamb and his followers: why, they are Devils, or Devil's instruments. Here are but two parties in the world: the Lamb and his followers, and the Dragon and his followers, and they are contrary one to the other. Well now, they that are against the Lamb, against the peace and prosperity of Zion, the interest of Christ, they are for the Devil. Here are no neuters. Everyone is on one side or the other.

Use 3. It calls us all (especially those that would be accounted followers of the Lamb) to mourn that the Devil has had so many assistants from amongst us, especially that he should find, or make such, in our churches. If so be, churches are deeply to mourn the dishonor done to Christ and religion by fornicators among them (I Corinthians 5:1, etc.) How much more, when witches and wizards are amongst them.

Use 4. It may show us the vileness of our natures, and that we should be ever praying that we be not left to our own lusts: for then we shall by and by fall in with devils, and with the Dragon make war with the Lamb and his followers.

Use 5. Caution and admonition to all and everyone of us, to beware of making war with the Lamb.

(1) Consider so to do, is to fight for the Devil. 'Tis to fight for an enemy. 'Tis to fight for him who will pay you no other wages than of being your eternal torturer (I Peter 5:8).

(2) Consider it is to take the weakest side. The Lamb shall most certainly overcome (text; Revelation 19:17–18, etc.).

(3) Consider this will aggravate thy sin above the sin of devils. To fight against the Lamb is to fight against thy Savior: which the damned devils never had an offer of. Hebrews 2:16, "He took not on him the nature of angels."

(4) Last, it is the way to utter ruin. I say, it is the way, the high way, to utter ruin. It is true, Christ may conquer thee when thou art hot in the battle, as he did Saul, and make thee throw away thy weapons of rebellion. But who can tell that he will do so? This is not ordinary; and if thou shouldst die a rebel in the fight, then thou art damned forever. Therefore, be we cautioned against making war with the Lamb.

Objection. But you may say, what is it to make war with the Lamb? And when do men make war with the Lamb?

First Answer. In general, all disobedience to Christ is a making war against him. As,

1. Disobedience to his laws. You know those that do not obey the king's laws are justly called rebels (I Kings 12:19). So here, not to do what Christ commands is to rebel against him, and to make war with him (Deuteronomy 9:22–24, Isaiah 1:19–20).

2. Disobedience to Christ's ordinances is rebellion against Christ, and making war with him, as warring against magistrates, opposing them in their duties. In this sense, Korah and his company are called rebels (Numbers 17:10), and the mutinous and murmuring Israelites are called rebels (Numbers 20:10). Hence, resisters of authority are resisters of God, because they resist the ordinance of God (Romans 13:1, etc.). But,

Second Answer. More especially to fight against the Lamb, and so to side with the Devil, is,

1. To fight against the gospel, or to war against the gospel. When men will not receive the gospel, and do what they can to hinder the course of the gospel, this is to make war with the Lamb.

(1) When men will not receive the gospel themselves, then they fight against the Lamb; as the Jews (Acts 13:46). Not to accept of terms of peace is to proclaim war, etc.

(2) When they will not suffer others to receive it, as those Jews (Acts 13:44, etc.), and the sorcerer (Acts 13:8), and those [mentioned in] II Timothy 3:8. And they that forbid preaching (Acts 5:28).

2. They make war against the Lamb, who oppose the Holy Spirit. Acts 7:51, "Ye do always resist the Holy Ghost."

3. Last, they make war against the Lamb, who do oppose the doctrine of Christ. As,

(1) Either the person of Christ, his deity or his humanity. He must be man, that he might die of us; he must be God, that he might conquer death for us. Now to deny either of these is to deny the Lamb, and so to make war with the Lamb.

(2) Or the offices of Christ as a Savior, both prophetical, sacerdotal, or regal. His office of prophet, to teach; of priest, to atone for us; of king, to govern us, as might in particular be shown.

Use 6. Last, may be of encouragement to all Christians, in the words of the apostle, to "endure hardness, as good soldiers of Christ" (II Timothy 2:3). For encouragement hereto, devils and instruments shall not war against us always. Revelation 2:10, "Fear none of those things which thou shalt suffer: behold, the Devil shall cast some of you into prison, that ye may be tried; and ye shall have tribulation ten days: be thou faithful unto death, and I will give thee a crown of life."

Deodate Lawson, *A Brief and True Narrative*

On the nineteenth day of March last [1692], I went to Salem Village and lodged at Nathaniel Ingersoll's near to the minister, Mr. Parris's, house. And presently after I came into my lodging, Capt. Walcot's daughter Mary came to Lieut. Ingersoll's and spake to me, but suddenly after, as she stood by the door, was bitten, so that she cried out of her wrist; and looking on it with a candle, we saw apparently the marks of teeth, both upper and lower set, on each side of her wrist.

In the beginning of the evening, I went to give Mr. Parris a visit. When I was there, his kinswoman, Abigail Williams (about twelve years of age), had a grievous fit; she was at first hurried with violence to and fro in the room (though Mrs. Ingersoll endeavored to hold her), sometimes making as if she would fly, stretching up her arms as high as she could, and crying, "Whish, whish, whish!" several times. Presently after she said, there was Goodwife Nurse, and said, "Do you not see her? Why, there she stands!" and [that] the said Goodwife Nurse offered her the book, but she was resolved she would not take it, saying often, "I won't, I won't, I won't take it, I do not know what book it is: I am sure it is none of God's book, it is the

Devil's book, for aught I know." After that she run to the fire, and begun to throw fire brands about the house, and run against the back, as if she would run up [the] chimney; and, as they said, she had attempted to go into the fire in other fits.

On Lord's Day, the twentieth of March, there were sundry of the afflicted persons at meeting, as Mrs. Pope and Goodwife Bibber, Abigail Williams, Mary Walcot, Mary Lewis and Doctor Griggs's maid. There was also at meeting Goodwife Corey (who was afterward examined on suspicion of being a witch). They had several sore fits in the time of public worship, which did something interrupt me in my first prayer, being so unusual. After psalm was sung, Abigail Williams said to me, "Now stand up and name your text." And after it was read, she said, "It is a long text." In the beginning of the sermon, Mrs. Pope, a woman afflicted, said to me, "Now there is enough of that." And in the afternoon, Abigail Williams, upon [my] referring to my doctrine, said to me, "I know no doctrine you had; if you did name one, I have forgot it."

In sermon time, when Goodwife Corey was present in the meeting house, Abigail Williams called out, "Look where Goodwife Corey sits on the beam, suckling her yellow bird betwixt her fingers!" Anne Putnam, another girl afflicted, said there was a yellow bird sat on my hat as it hung on the pin in the pulpit, but those that were by restrained her from speaking loud about it.

On Monday the twenty-first of March, the magistrates of Salem appointed to come to examination of Goodwife Corey. And about twelve of the clock, they went into the meeting house, which was thronged with spectators. Mr. Noyes began with a very pertinent and pathetic prayer; and Goodwife Corey being called to answer to what was alleged against her, she desired to go to prayer, which was much wondered at, in the presence of so many hundred people. The magistrates told her they would not admit it; they came not there to hear her pray but to examine her in what was alleged against her. The worshipful Mr. Hathorne asked her, why she afflicted those children. She said, she did not afflict them. He asked her, who did then? She said, "I do not know; how should I know?" The number of the afflicted persons were about that time ten, viz., four married women: Mrs. Pope, Mrs. Putnam, Goodwife Bibber and an ancient woman named Goodall; three maids: Mary Walcot, Mercy Lewis at Thomas Putnam's, and a maid at Dr. Griggs's; [and] there were three girls from nine to twelve years of age, each of them, or thereabouts, viz., Elizabeth Parris, Abigail Williams, and Anne Putnam. These were, most of them, at Goodwife Corey's examination, and did vehemently accuse her in the assembly of afflicting them by biting, pinching, strangling, etc.; and that they did in their fit see her likeness coming to them, and bringing a book to them. She said she had no book. They affirmed she had a yellow bird that used to suck betwixt her fingers, and being asked about it, if she had any familiar spirit that attended her, she said she had no familiarity with any such thing; she was a gospel woman, which title she called herself by; and the afflicted persons told her, "Ah! she was a gospel witch." Ann Putnam did there affirm that one day, when Lieut. Fuller was at prayer at her father's house, she saw the shape of Goodwife Corey and, she thought, Goodwife Nurse, praying at the same time to the Devil; she was not sure it was Goodwife Nurse—she thought it was—but was very sure she saw the shape of Goodwife Corey. The said Corey said they were poor, distracted children, and no heed [was] to be given to what they said. Mr. Hathorne and Mr. Noyes replied, it was the judgment of all that were present, they were bewitched, and only she, the accused person, said they were distracted. It was observed several times that if she did but bite her underlip in time of examination, the persons afflicted were bitten on their arms and wrists, and produced the marks before the magistrates, ministers and others; and being watched for, that if she did but pinch her fingers or grasp her hand hard in another, they were pinched, and produced the marks before the magistrates and spectators. After that, it was observed that if she did but lean her breast against the seat in the meeting house (being the bar at which she stood), they were afflicted. Particularly Mrs. Pope complained of grievous torment in her bowels, as if they were torn out. She vehemently accused said Corey as the instrument, and first threw her muff at her; but that flying not home, she got off her shoe and hit Goodwife Corey on the head with it. After these postures were watched, if said Corey did but stir her feet, they were afflicted in their feet, and stamped fearfully. The afflicted persons asked her why she did not go to the company of witches which were before the meeting house mustering? Did she not hear the drum beat? They accused her of having familiarity with the Devil in the time of examination, in the shape of a black man whispering in her ear. They affirmed that her yellow bird sucked betwixt her fingers in the assembly; and order being given to see if there were any sign, the girl that saw it said it was too late now—she had removed a pin and put it on her head, which was found there sticking upright.

They told her she had covenanted with the Devil for ten years; six of them were gone and four more to come. She was required by the magistrates to answer that question in the catechism, "How many persons be there in the Godhead?" She answered it but oddly, yet was there no great thing to be gathered from it. She denied all that was charged upon her, and said they could not prove a witch. She was that afternoon committed to Salem prison, and after she was in custody she did not so appear to them and afflict them as before.

On Wednesday, the twenty-third of March, I went to Thomas Putnam's, on purpose to see his wife. I found her lying on the bed, having had a sore fit a little before. She spake to me, and said she was glad to see me. Her husband and she both desired me to pray with her, while she was sensible; which I did, though the apparition said I should not go to prayer. At the first beginning she attended, but after a little time was taken with a fit, yet continued silent, and seemed to be asleep. When prayer was done, her husband, going to her, found her in a fit: he took her off the bed to set her on his knees, but at first she was so stiff she could not be bended; but she afterwards set down, but quickly began to strive violently with her arms and legs. She then began to complain of and, as it were, to converse personally with Goodwife Nurse, saying, "Goodwife Nurse, be gone! be gone! Are you not ashamed, a woman of your profession, to afflict a poor creature so? What hurt did I ever do you in my life! You have but two years to live, and then the Devil will torment your soul. For this your name is blotted out of God's book, and it shall never be put in God's book again. Be gone for shame; are you not afraid of that which is coming upon you? I know, I know what will make you afraid: the wrath of an angry God, I am sure that will make you afraid. Be gone, do not torment me. I know what you would have" (we judged she meant her soul), "but it is out of your reach; it is clothed with the white robes of Christ's righteousness." After this, she seemed to dispute with the apparition about a particular text of Scripture. The apparition seemed to deny it (the woman's eyes being fast closed all this time). She said she was sure there was such a text, and she would tell it; and then the shape would be gone, for said she, "I am sure you cannot stand before that text!" Then she was sorely afflicted, her mouth drawn on one side and her body strained for about a minute, and then said, "I will tell, I will tell; it is—it is—it is—," three or four times, and then was afflicted to hinder her from telling. At last she broke forth and said, "It is the third chapter of the Revelations." I did something scruple the reading it, and did let my scruple appear, lest Satan should make any superstitious lie to improve the Word of the eternal God. However, though not versed in these things, I judged I might do it this once for an experiment. I began to read, and before I had near read through the first verse, she opened her eyes and was well. This fit continued near half an hour. Her husband and the spectators told me she had often been so relieved by reading texts that she named, something pertinent to her case, as Isaiah 40:1, Isaiah 49:1, Isaiah 50:1, and several others.

On Thursday, the twenty-fourth of March (being in course the lecture day at the Village), Goodwife Nurse was brought before the magistrates, Mr. Hathorne and Mr. Corwin, about ten of [the] clock, in the forenoon, to be examined in the meeting house. The Reverend Mr. Hale begun with prayer, and, the warrant being read, she was required to give answer, why she afflicted those persons? She pleaded her own innocency with earnestness. Thomas Putnam's wife, Abigail Williams, and Thomas Putnam's daughter accused her that she appeared to them and afflicted them in their fits, but some of the other said that they had seen her but knew not that ever she had hurt them—amongst which was Mary Walcot, who was presently after she had so declared, bitten, and cried out of her in the meeting house, producing the marks of teeth on her wrist. It was so disposed that I had not leisure to attend the whole of examination, but both magistrates and ministers told me that the things alleged by the afflicted, and defenses made by her, were much after the same manner as the former was. And her motions did produce like effects as to biting, pinching, bruising, tormenting at their breasts by her leaning, and, when bended back, were as if their backs were broken. The afflicted persons said the black man whispered to her in the assembly, and therefore she could not hear what the magistrates said unto her. They said also that she did then ride by the meeting house behind the black man. Thomas Putnam's wife had a grievous fit in the time of examination, to the very great impairing of her strength and wasting of her spirits, insomuch as she could hardly move hand or foot when she was carried out. Others also were there grievously afflicted, so that there was once such an hideous screech and noise (which I heard as I walked at a little distance from the meeting house) as did amaze me. And some that were within told me the whole assembly was struck with consternation, and they were afraid that those that sat next to them were under the influence of witchcraft. This woman also was that day committed to Salem prison.

The magistrates and ministers also did inform me that they apprehended a child of Sarah Good, and examined it, being between four and five years of age. And as to matter of fact, they did unanimously affirm that when this child did but cast its eye upon the afflicted persons, they were tormented; and [so] they held their head, and yet so many as her eye could fix upon were afflicted. Which they did several times make careful observation of. The afflicted complained they had often been bitten by this child, and produced the marks of a small set of teeth. Accordingly, this [child] was also committed to Salem prison. The child looked hale and well as other children; I saw it at Lieut. Ingersoll's.

After the commitment of Goodwife Nurse, Thomas Putnam's wife was much better, and had no violent fits at all from that twenty-fourth of March to the fifth of April. Some others also said they had not seen her so frequently appear to them, to hurt them.

On the twenty-fifth of March (as Capt. Stephen Sewall of Salem did after-wards inform me), Elizabeth Parris had sore fits at his house, which much troubled himself and his wife, so, as he told me, they were almost discouraged. She related that the great black man came to her and told her if she would be ruled by him, she should have whatsoever she desired and go to a golden city. She relating this to Mrs. Sewall, she told the child it was the Devil, and he was a liar from the beginning, and bid her tell him so if he came again; which she did accordingly at the next coming to her in her fits.

On the twenty-sixth of March, Mr. Hathorne, Mr. Corwin, and Mr. Higgin-son were at the prison keeper's house to examine the child. And it told them there it had a little snake that used to suck on the lowest joint of its fore finger; and when they inquired where, pointing to other places, it told them, not there, but there, pointing on the lowest point of the fore finger, where they observed a deep red spot about the bigness of a flea bite. They asked, who gave it that snake, whether the black man? It said no, its mother gave it.

[On] the thirty-first of March there was a public fast kept at Salem on account of these afflicted persons. And Abigail Williams said that the witches had a sac-rament that day at an house in the Village, and that they had red bread and red drink. The first of April, Mercy Lewis, Thomas Putnam's maid, in her fit said they did eat red bread like man's flesh, and would have had her eat some: but she would not, but turned away her head and spit at them, and said, "I will not eat, I will not drink; it is blood," etc. She said, "That is not the bread of life, that is not the water of life; Christ gives the bread of life, I will have none of it!" This first of April also, Mercy Lewis, aforesaid, saw in her fit a white man, and was with him in a glorious place which had no candles nor sun yet was full of light and brightness, where was a great multitude in white glittering robes, and they sung the song in the fifth of Revelations, the ninth verse, and the 110th Psalm, and the 149th Psalm; and said with herself, "How long shall I stay here? Let me go along with you." She was loath to leave this place, and grieved that she could tarry no longer. This white man hath appeared several times to some of them, and given them notice how long it should be before they had another fit, which was sometimes a day, or day and [a] half, or more or less: it hath fallen out accordingly.

The third of April, the Lord's day, being a sacrament day at the Village, Goodwife Cloyse, upon hearing Mr. Parris's naming his text—John 6:70, "One of them is a devil"—the said Goodwife Cloyse went immediately out of the meeting house and flung the door after her violently, to the amazement of the congregation. She was afterwards seen by some in their fits, who said, "O Goodwife Cloyse, I did not think to see you here"; and ([she] being at their red bread and drink) said to her, "Is this a time to receive the sacrament? You ran away on the Lord's day and scorned to receive it in the meeting house"; and, "Is this a time to receive it? I wonder at you!"

This is the sum of what I either saw myself, or did receive information from persons of undoubted reputation and credit.

Remarks of things more than ordinary about the afflicted persons

1. They are in their fits tempted to be witches, are showed the list of the names of others, and are tortured because they will not yield to subscribe, or meddle with, or touch the book, and are promised to have present relief if they would do it.

2. They did in the assembly mutually cure each other, even with a touch of their hand, when strangled and otherwise tortured; and would endeavor to get to their afflicted to relieve them.

3. They did also foretell when another's fit was a-coming, and would say, "Look to her! she will have a fit presently"; which fell out accordingly, as many can bear witness that heard and saw it.

4. That at the same time when the accused person was present, the afflicted persons saw her likeness in other places of the meeting house, suckling her familiar, sometimes in one place and posture, and sometimes in another.

5. That their motions in their fits are preternatural, both as to the manner, which is so strange as a well person could not screw their body into; and as to the violence also it is preternatural, being much beyond the ordinary force of the same person when they are in their right mind.

6. The eyes of some of them in their fits are exceeding fast closed, and if you ask a question they can give no answer; and I do believe they cannot hear at that time, yet do they plainly converse with the appearances, as if they did discourse with real persons.

7. They are utterly pressed against any persons praying with them, and told by the appearances they shall not go to prayer. So Thomas Putnam's wife was told I should not pray, but she said I should; and after I had done, [she] reasoned with the appearance, "Did not I say he should go to prayer?"

8. The forementioned Mary Walcot, being a little better at ease, the afflicted persons said she had signed the book, and that was the reason she was better. [This was] told me by Edward Putnam.

Remarks concerning the accused

1. For introduction to the discovery of those that afflicted them, it is reported Mr. Parris's Indian man and woman made a cake of rye meal and the children's water, baked it in the ashes, and gave it to a dog: since which they have discovered and seen particular persons hurting of them.

2. In time of examination, they seemed little affected, though all the spectators were much grieved to see it.

3. Natural actions in them produced preternatural actions in the afflicted, so that they are their own image, without any puppets of wax or otherwise.

4. That they are accused to have a company of about twenty-three or twenty-four, and they did muster in arms, as it seemed to the afflicted persons.

5. Since they were confined, the persons have not been so much afflicted with their appearing to them, biting or pinching of them, etc.

6. They are reported by the afflicted persons to keep days of fast and days of thanksgiving, and sacraments. Satan endeavors to transform himself to an angel of light, and to make his kingdom and administrations to resemble those of our Lord Jesus Christ.

7. Satan rages principally amongst the visible subjects of Christ's kingdom and makes use (at least in appearance) of some of them to afflict others, that Christ's kingdom may be divided against itself, and so be weakened.

8. Several things used in England at trial of witches, to the number of fourteen or fifteen, which are wont to pass instead of or in concurrence with witnesses, at least six or seven of them are found in these accused. . . .

9. Some of the most solid afflicted persons do affirm the same things concerning seeing the accused out of their fits as well as in them.

10. The witches had a fast, and told one of the afflicted girls she must not eat because it was fast day. She said she would; they told her they would choke her then, which when she did eat, was endeavored.

26

Speech of Sose-Há-Wä and the Code
of Handsome Lake

Matthew Dennis

In June of 1799 in a small settlement along the Allegheny River in southwestern New York, a dissolute Seneca league chief named Handsome Lake took to bed, a sick and broken man. His community, as well as other Seneca and Iroquois people, found themselves in a difficult predicament as they sought to cling to the remnants of their homeland. The Senecas were one of six constituent Indian nations, also known as the People of the Longhouse, or Hodenosaunee. From west to east—in what is today New York State—the Six Nations included the Senecas, Cayugas, Onondagas, Tuscaroras, Oneidas, and Mohawks. Metaphorically speaking, they all lived under one roof, arrayed in a house with expanding endwalls, a longhouse, the traditional Iroquoian dwelling. Clinging to the remnants of their homeland, the Senecas found themselves in a difficult predicament. Peace and diplomatic success had allowed the Six Nations of the Iroquois to prosper throughout much of the eighteenth century. Since the end of the French and Indian War in 1763, however, they had seen their strategic position crumble, their lands invaded and expropriated, their society, culture, and religion undermined, and their sovereignty and autonomy imperiled. The American Revolution proved the crushing blow—an anticolonial war fought for national independence for the United States promoted a new colonialism and dependency among the Six Nations and other native people now encompassed by the expanding republic. By the end of the war, the Iroquois population had been reduced by half, its refugee people stricken by famine, exposure, disease, and dispersion. The Iroquois League had been divided, with some Six Nations people regrouping in Canada while others remained in small and shrinking reserves in New York. Conditions became so desperate that one historian has felt compelled to call these communities "slums in the wilderness."

When Handsome Lake collapsed outside the door of his daughter's cabin on that summer morning in 1799, he appeared to die, leaving a world filled with drunkenness, recrimination, brawling, and little hope. But within an hour or two, Handsome Lake awoke. Revived from his trancelike state, he announced a fabulous vision. Subsequent visions—and relations of cosmic journeys while the prophet was entranced—continued in the following months and years until his death in 1815. The power of those visions motivated Handsome Lake to inaugurate a new religion, the Longhouse faith.

Holy messengers, representing the Creator, appeared to Handsome Lake and communicated to him the religious and moral obligations expected of his people. Particularly vexing to the Creator was Iroquois drunkenness, their insidious use of witchcraft, their troubled family lives, and their neglect of traditional rituals and ceremonies. During Handsome Lake's second vision, angelic intermediaries conducted him on a tour of heaven and hell. Approaching the Iroquois paradise, the prophet encountered the recently deceased George Washington, who resided in a village just outside of heaven, and Jesus Christ, who endorsed the revitalizing message of Handsome Lake and the Creator while bemoaning his own lack of followers: "You are more successful than I for some believe in you but none in me. . . . Now tell your people that they will become lost when they follow the ways of the white man." In hell, Handsome Lake witnessed the excruciating punishments reserved for various transgressors. Drunkards ceaselessly poured molten metal down their throats, gamblers painfully shuffled and played red hot cards, and wicked musicians hacked at their own arms with burning fiddle bows. Witches (here represented as female, though witchcraft had been traditionally understood as a crime committed equally by men and women) suffered repeated immersions in cauldrons of boiling liquid. Women transgressors were similarly punished for the newly identified sins of employing love magic and abortion.

Following his visions, Handsome Lake assumed a new status as a sort of high priest among Senecas, and for a time he wielded considerable power. His apocalyptic message—underscored by his own "death," rehabilitation, and revival—commanded attention in the context of crisis and demoralization that Seneca and other Iroquois people faced. Drastic measures were critical; only immediate reform could forestall their destruction. The witch-hunting campaigns of Handsome Lake and his followers, which erupted soon after the prophet's rise to prominence, similarly displayed the tumult of early-nineteenth-century Seneca life as well as the apocalypticism of Handsome Lake's new religion. The prophet's witch-hunting proved divisive as it set individuals and kin groups against each other in a destructive binge of internecine violence. Witch-hunting nearly precipitated large-scale bloodshed between two native communities. Senecas pulled back from this precipice and the hunts eventually subsided.

A new social gospel emerged more gradually from Handsome Lake's visions and the developing Longhouse religious practice, a gospel largely consistent with the recommendations of Quaker missionaries present at the Seneca reserve along the Allegheny River since 1798. Among its most controversial aspects was Handsome Lake's effort to encourage more patriarchal arrangements among Senecas as a means of promoting their acculturation and survival. The Iroquois were a people committed to greater gender equality than was typical in the white communities surrounding them, and they traditionally accorded considerable status and power to women. As a result, they were often unwilling to reconstruct households, work patterns, and land ownership into the patriarchal forms that white reformers and Handsome Lake prescribed. Nonetheless, we see in the ritual recitation of the prophet's visions and in the Code of Handsome Lake clear efforts to stabilize family life. For Handsome Lake and others, injunctions against easy divorce, interference of mothers-in-law in home life, gossip, love magic, abortion, and infanticide, as well as male transgressions against the family, such as drunkenness and wife-beating, were the key to social survival. Such rules seemed to threaten traditional female power, since the Iroquois pattern of residence in extended maternal households and easy access to divorce through the expulsion of unsatisfactory husbands clearly offered women greater autonomy and authority than they would enjoy in the male-headed, nuclear families typical of white family farms. Eventually, the new religion became the Old Way of Handsome Lake and in practice came to represent both an accommodation to the new world that surrounded the Iroquois and a conservation of their more ancient religious beliefs and traditions, including those related to gender organization.

Quickly, the Longhouse religion itself became tradition, especially because it offered the basis for protecting and expressing Iroquois identity through a religious practice that was non-Christian, an alternative to the Protestant and Catholic denominations proselytizing among the Iroquois. Moreover, Handsome Lake ardently opposed the alienation of native land, and with his followers he made the Longhouse religion not merely a means of asserting Iroquois ethnic identity and integrity but of promoting the preservation of Indian lands on which physical survival depended.

A key rite of the Longhouse religion is a long speech known as the Code of Handsome Lake, which is recited each fall over several mornings during the "Six Nations meetings" and in a cycle of visitations to Longhouses occurring over the following weeks throughout Iroquoia.

The narrative recounts Handsome Lake's visions and the Creator's instructions, details the prohibitions imposed by the Creator to ensure the people's survival, and describes, in gruesome terms, the punishments designed for transgressors. Finally, it sanctions the celebration of critical festivals devoted particularly to offerings of thanksgiving to the Creator and other beings or spirit forces in their world, throughout the year. The Code blends apocalypticism with Handsome Lake's social gospel so as to teach and motivate adherents while sanctifying their creed, ordaining the spiritual cycle of their lives, and instructing them about their faith's mythical-historical origins.

The transformation of Handsome Lake's teachings into a religion—a formal system of beliefs, practices, and institutions—occurred gradually in a complex process. Much of the history of this transformation is unavailable to outsiders. However, an unusual opportunity to observe an important moment in this development and codification of the Longhouse religion (which remains vital in

Iroquois communities today) presents itself in the speech of the Seneca chief and grandson of Handsome Lake, Sose-há-wä, or Jemmy Johnson. In 1848 Lewis H. Morgan, a pioneer of American ethnology who had begun a study of the Iroquois that would be published in 1851, commissioned the young Seneca man Ely S. Parker to write a full report of Johnson's annual speech at Tonawanda, another Seneca community in western New York. In late 1850 the report arrived, and Morgan included it in his groundbreaking book.

Jemmy Johnson died in 1856, just before the United States Supreme Court ordered restoration of some seventy-five hundred acres of land for Senecas at Tonawanda, where reservation lands had been completely alienated in 1838. Ironically, following the death of Jemmy Johnson and the restoration of these Seneca lands, a number of Tonawandas rejected the Longhouse religion of Handsome Lake and converted to Christianity, becoming Baptists. With these events, the leadership and locus of the new religion diversified, as a council of preachers from other Iroquois reservations and communities replaced Johnson. These new sages did not seek to establish a single authoritative version of the Code, which remained fundamentally an oral rather than a written narrative. Agreement between them avoided schism, while it ensured that the *Gai'wiio'*, or "good message," would function as a living, not a static, creed. Therefore, the version offered by Jemmy Johnson, collected by Parker and set in print by Morgan, does not likely mirror in precise fashion the current Longhouse religion's Code, since practitioners have sought to maintain the truth of their sacred tradition through the collective, evolving practice of reciting Handsome Lake's Code. We should regard Sose-há-wä's speech not as if it were a passage from the Bible, then, but as an important textual record of a growing oral, religious tradition.

The text below constitutes Lewis H. Morgan's extended quotation of notes taken and translated by Hä-sa-no-an´-dä, or Ely S. Parker, compiled at a general Mourning Council held at Tonawanda on October 4–6, 1848; Lewis H. Morgan, *League of the Ho-De-No-Sau-Nee, Iroquois* (Rochester: Sage & Brothers, 1851), pp. 233–59.

Further Reading

Matthew Dennis, "Seneca Possessed: Colonialism, Witchcraft, and Gender in the Time of Handsome Lake," in *Spellbound: Women and Witchcraft in America,* edited by Elizabeth Reis (Wilmington, Del.: Scholarly Resources, 1998), pp. 121–43; Elisabeth Tooker, "On the Development of the Handsome Lake Religion," *Proceedings of the American Philosophical Society* 133 no. 1 (1989): 35–50; Elisabeth Tooker, "Iroquois since 1820," and Anthony Wallace, "Origins of the Longhouse Religion," in *Northeast,* edited by Bruce G. Trigger (Washington, D.C., Smithsonian Institution Press, 1978), vol. 15 of *Handbook of North American Indians,* edited by William C. Sturtevant, pp. 449–65, 442–48; Anthony Wallace F.C., *The Death and Rebirth of the Seneca* (New York: Alfred A. Knopf, 1970).

Sose-há-wä's Ritual Discourse on Handsome Lake and His New Faith

The Mohawks, the Onondagas, the Senecas, and our children (the Oneidas, Cayugas and Tuscaroras) have assembled here to-day to listen to the repetition of the will of the Great Spirit, as communicated to us from heaven through his servant, *Gä-ne-o-di-yo* [Handsome Lake].

Chiefs, warriors, women and children:—We give you a cordial welcome. The sun has advanced far in his path, and I am warned that my time to instruct you is limited to the meridian sun. I must therefore hasten to perform my duty. Turn your minds to the Great Spirit, and listen with strict attention. Think seriously upon what I am about to speak. Reflect upon it well, that it may benefit you and your children. I thank the Great Spirit that he has spared the lives of so many of you to be present on this occasion. I return thanks to him that my life is yet spared. The Great Spirit looked down from heaven upon the sufferings and the wanderings of his red children. He saw that they had greatly decreased and degenerated. He saw the ravages of the fire-water among them. He therefore raised up for them a sacred instructor, who having lived and traveled among them for sixteen years, was called from his labors to enjoy eternal felicity with the Great Spirit in heaven. Be patient while I speak. I cannot at all times arrange and prepare my thoughts with the same precision. But I will relate what my memory bears.

It was in the month of *O-nike'-ya* (June), that Handsome Lake was yet sick. He had been ill four years. He was accustomed to tell us that he had resigned himself to the will of the Great Spirit. "I nightly returned my thanks to the Great Spirit," said he, "as my eyes were gladdened at evening by the sight of the stars of heaven. I viewed the ornamented heavens at evening, through the opening in the roof of my lodge, with grateful feelings to my Creator. I had no assurance that I should at the next evening contemplate his works. For this reason my acknowledgments to him were more fervent and sincere. When night was gone, and the sun again shed his light upon the earth, I saw, and acknowledged in the return of day his continued goodness to me, and to all mankind. At length I began to have an inward conviction that my end was near. I resolved once more to exchange friendly words with my people, and I sent my daughter to summon my brothers *Gy-ant'-wä-ka*, (Cornplanter) and *Ta-wan'-ne-ars*, (Blacksnake). She hastened to do his bidding, but before she returned, he had fallen into insensibility, and apparent death. *Ta-wan'-ne-ars*, upon returning to the lodge, hastened to his brother's couch, and discovered that portions of his body were yet warm. This happened at early day, before the morning dew had dried. When the sun had advanced half-way to the meridian, his heart began to beat, and he opened his eyes. *Ta-wan'-ne-ars* asked him if he was in his right mind; but he answered not. At meridian he again opened his eyes, and the same question was repeated. He then answered and said, "A man spoke from without, and asked that some one might come forth. I looked, and saw some men standing without. I arose, and as I attempted to step over the threshold of my door, I stumbled, and should have fallen had they not caught me. They were three holy men who looked alike, and were dressed alike. The paint they wore seemed but one day old. Each held in his hand a shrub bearing different kinds of fruit. One of them addressing me said, 'We have come to comfort and relieve you. Take of these berries and eat; they will restore you to health. We have been witnesses of your lengthened illness. We have seen with what resignation you have given yourself up to the Great Spirit. We have heard your daily return of thanks. He has heard them all. His ear has ever been open to hear. You were thankful for the return of night, when you could contemplate the beauties of heaven. You were accustomed to look upon the moon, as she coursed in her nightly paths. When there were no hopes to you that you would again behold these things, you willingly resigned yourself to the mind of the Great Spirit. This was right. Since the Great Spirit made the earth and put man upon it, we have been his constant servants to guard and protect his works. There are four of us. Some other time you will be permitted to see the other. The Great Spirit is pleased to know your patient resignation to his will. As a reward for your devotion, he has cured your sickness. Tell your people to assemble to-morrow, and at noon go in and speak to them.'" After they had further revealed their intentions concerning him they departed.

At the time appointed Handsome Lake appeared at the council, and thus addressed the people upon the revelations which had been made to him: "I have a message to deliver to you. The servants of the Great Spirit have told me that I should yet live upon the earth to become an instructor to my people. Since the creation of man, the Great Spirit has often raised up men to teach his children what they should do to please him; but they have been unfaithful to their trust. I hope I shall profit by their example. Your Creator has seen that you have transgressed greatly against his laws. He made man pure and good. He did not intend that he should sin. You commit a great sin in taking the fire-water. The Great Spirit says that you must abandon this enticing habit. Your ancestors have brought great misery and suffering upon you. They first took the fire-water of the white man, and entailed upon you its consequences. None of them have gone to heaven. The fire-water does not belong to you. It was made for the white man beyond the great waters. For the white man it is a medicine; but they too have violated the will of their Maker. The Great Spirit says that drunkenness is a great crime, and he forbids you to indulge in this evil habit. His command is to the old and young. The abandonment of its use will relieve much of your sufferings, and greatly increase the comfort and happiness of your children. The Great Spirit is grieved that so much crime and wickedness should defile the earth. There are many evils which he never intended should exist among his red children. The Great Spirit has, for many wise reasons, withheld from man the number of his days; but he has not left him without a guide, for he has pointed out to him the path in which he may safely tread the journey of life.

"When the Great Spirit made man, he also made woman. He instituted marriage, and enjoined upon them to love each other, and be faithful. It is pleasing to him to see men and women obey his will. Your Creator abhors a deceiver and a hypocrite. By obeying his commands you will die an easy and a happy death. When the Great Spirit instituted marriage, he ordained to bless those who were faithful with children. Some women are unfruitful, and others become so by misfortune. Such have great opportunities to do much good. There are many orphans, and many poor children whom they can adopt as their own. If you tie up the clothes of an orphan child, the Great Spirit will notice it, and reward you for it. Should an orphan ever cross your path be kind to him, and treat him with tenderness, for this is right. Parents must constantly teach their children morality, and a reverence for their Creator. Parents must also guard their children against improper marriages. They, having much experience, should select a suitable match for their child. When the parents of both parties have agreed, then bring the young pair together, and let them know what good their parents have designed for them. If at any time they so far disagree that they cannot possibly live contented and happy with each other, they may separate in mutual good feeling; and in this there is no wrong. When a child is born to a husband and wife, they must give great thanks to the Great Spirit, for it is his gift, and an evidence of his kindness. Let parents instruct their children in their duty to the Great Spirit, to their parents, and to their fellow-men. Children should obey their parents and guardians, and submit to them in all things. Disobedient children occasion great pain and misery. They wound their parents' feelings, and often drive them to desperation, causing them great distress, and final admission into the place of Evil Spirits. The marriage obligations should generate good to all who have assumed them. Let the married be faithful to each other, that when they die it may be in peace. Children should never permit their parents to suffer in their old age. Be kind to them, and support them. The Great Spirit requires all children to love, revere and obey their parents. To do this is highly pleasing to him. The happiness of parents is greatly increased by the affection and the attentions of their children. To abandon a wife or children is a great wrong, and produces many evils. It is wrong for a father or mother-in-law to vex a son or daughter-in-law; but they should use them as if they were their own children. It often happens that parents hold angry disputes over their infant child. This is also a great sin. The infant hears and comprehends the angry words of its parents. It feels bad and lonely. It can see for itself no happiness in prospect. It concludes to return to its Maker. It wants a happy home, and dies. The parents then weep because their child has left them. You must put this evil practice from among you, if you would live happy.

"The Great Spirit, when he made the earth, never intended that it should be made merchandise; but he willed that all his creatures should enjoy it equally. Your chiefs have violated and betrayed your trust by selling lands. Nothing is now left of our once large possessions, save a few small reservations. Chiefs, and aged men—you, as men, have no lands to sell. You occupy and possess a tract in trust for your children. You should hold that trust sacred, lest your children are driven from their homes by your unsafe conduct. Whoever sells lands offends the Great Spirit, and must expect a great punishment after death."

Here Sose-há-wă suspended his narration of Handsome Lake's discourse. He continued the next day.

Counselors, warriors, mothers and children:—Listen to good instruction. Consider it well. Lay it up in your minds, and forget it not. Our Creator, when he made us, designed that we should live by hunting. It sometimes happens that a man goes out for the hunt, leaving his wife with her friends. After a long absence he returns, and finds that his wife has taken another husband. The Great Spirit says that this is a great sin, and must be put from among us.

The four Messengers further said, that it was wrong for a mother to punish a child with a rod. It is not right to punish much, and our Creator never intended that children should be punished with a whip, or be used with any violence. In punishing a refractory child, water only is necessary, and it is sufficient. Plunge them under. This is not wrong. Whenever a child promises to do better, the punishment must cease. It is wrong to continue it after promises of amendment are made. Thus they said.

It is right and proper always to look upon the dead. Let your face be brought near to theirs, and then address them. Let the dead know that their absence is regretted by their friends, and that they grieve for their death. Let the dead know, too, how their surviving friends intend to live. Let them know whether they will so conduct themselves, that they will meet them again in the future world. The dead will hear and remember. Thus they said.

Continue to listen while I proceed to relate what further they said:—Our Creator made the earth. Upon it he placed man, and gave him certain rules of conduct. It pleased him also to give them many kinds of amusements. He also ordered that the earth should produce all that is good for man. So long as the earth remains, it will not cease to yield. Upon the surface of the ground berries of various kinds are produced. It is the will of the Great Spirit, that when they ripen, we should return our thanks to him, and have a public rejoicing for the continuance of these blessings. He made everything which we live upon, and requires us to be thankful at all times for the continuance of his favors. When Our Life (corn, etc.) has again appeared, it is the will of the Great Ruler that we assemble for a general thanksgiving. It is his will also that the children be brought and made to participate in the Feather dance. Your feast must consist of the new production. It is proper at these times, should any present not have their names published, or if any changes have been made, to announce them then. The festival must continue four days. Thus they said. Upon the first day must be performed the Feather dance. This ceremony must take place in the early day, and cease at the middle day. In the same manner, upon the second day, is to be performed the Thanksgiving dance. On the third, the Thanksgiving concert, *Ah-do'-weh*, is to be introduced. The fourth day is set apart for the

Peach-stone game. All these ceremonies, instituted by our Creator, must be commenced at the early day, and cease at the middle day. At all these times, we are required to return thanks to our Grandfather *He'-no* [the Thunder God, who controls rain] and his assistants. To them is assigned the duty of watching over the earth, and all it produces for our good. The great Feather and Thanksgiving dances are the appropriate ceremonies of thanksgiving to the Ruler and Maker of all things. The Thanksgiving concert belongs appropriately to our Grandfathers. In it, we return thanks to them. During the performance of this ceremony, we are required also to give them the smoke of tobacco. Again, we must at this time return thanks to our mother the earth, for she is our relative. We must also return thanks to Our Life and its Sisters. All these things are required to be done by the light of the sun. It must not be protracted until the sun has hid his face, and darkness surrounds all things.

Continue to listen:—We have a change of seasons. We have a season of cold. This is the hunting season. It is also one in which the people can amuse themselves. Upon the fifth day of the new moon, *Nis-go-wuk'-na*, (about Feb. 1st) we are required to commence the annual jubilee of thanksgiving to our Creator. At this festival all can give evidence of their devotion to the will of the Great Spirit, by participating in all its ceremonies.

Continue to listen:—The four Messengers of the Great Spirit have always watched over us, and have ever seen what was transpiring among men. At one time, Handsome Lake was translated by them to the regions above. He looked down upon the earth and saw a great assembly. Out of it came a man. His garments were torn, tattered and filthy. His whole appearance indicated great misery and poverty. They asked him how this spectacle appeared to him. He replied that it was hard to look upon. They then told him that the man he saw was a drunkard. That he had taken the firewater, and it had reduced him to poverty. Again he looked, and saw a woman seated upon the ground. She was constantly engaged in gathering up and secreting about her person her worldly effects. They said, the woman you see is inhospitable. She is too selfish to spare anything, and will never leave her worldly goods. She can never pass from earth to heaven. Tell this to your people. Again he looked, and saw a man carrying in each hand large pieces of meat. He went about the assembly giving to each a piece. This man, they said, is blessed, for he is hospitable and kind. He looked again, and saw streams of blood. They said, thus will the earth be, if the fire-water is not put from among you. Brother will kill brother, and friend friend. Again they told him to look towards the east. He obeyed, and as far as his vision reached, he saw the increasing smoke of numberless distilleries arising, and shutting out the light of the sun. It was a horrible spectacle to witness. They told him that here was manufactured the firewater. Again he looked, and saw a costly house, made and furnished by the palefaces. It was a house of confinement, where were fetters, ropes and whips. They said that those who persisted in the use of the fire-water would fall into this. Our Creator commands us to put this destructive vice far from us. Again he looked, and saw various assemblages. Some of them were unwilling to listen to instruction. They were riotous, and took great pride in drinking the strong waters. He observed another group who were half inclined to hear, but the temptations to vice which surrounded them allured them back, and they also reveled in the fumes of the fire-water. He saw another assemblage which had met to hear instructions. This they said was pleasing to the Great Spirit. He loves those who will listen and obey. It has grieved him that his children are now divided by separate interests, and are pursuing so many paths. It pleases him to see his people live together in harmony and quiet. The fire-water creates many dissensions and divisions among us. They said that the use of it would cause many to die unnatural deaths; many will be exposed to cold, and freeze; many will be burned, and others will be drowned while under the influence of the firewater.

Friends and Relatives:—All these things have often happened. How many of our people have been frozen to death; how many have been burned to death; how many have been drowned while under the influence of the strong waters. The punishments of those who use the fire-water commence while they are yet on the earth. Many are now thrown into houses of confinement by the pale faces. I repeat to you, the Ruler of us all requires us to unite and put this evil from among us. Some say that the use of the firewater is not wrong, and that it is food. Let those who do not believe it wrong, make this experiment. Let all who use the firewater assemble and organize into a council; and those who do not, into another near them. A great difference will then be discovered. The council of drunkards will end in a riot and tumult, while the other will have harmony and quiet. It is hard to think of the great prevalence of this evil among us. Reform, and put it from among you. Many resolve to use the firewater until near death, when they will repent. If they do this, nothing can save them from destruction, for then medicine can have no power. Thus they said.

All men were made equal by the Great Spirit; but he has given to them a variety of gifts. To some a pretty face, to others an ugly one; to some a comely form, to others a deformed figure. Some are fortunate in collecting around them worldly goods. But you are all entitled to the same privileges, and therefore must put pride from among you. You are not your own makers, nor the builders of your own fortunes. All things are the gift of the Great Spirit, and to him must be returned thanks for their bestowal. He alone must be acknowledged as the giver. It has pleased him to make differences among men; but it is wrong for one man to exalt himself above another. Love each other, for you are all brothers and sisters of the same great family. The Great Spirit enjoins upon all, to observe hospitality and kindness, especially to the needy and the helpless; for this is pleasing to him. If a stranger wanders about your abode, speak to him with kind words; be hospitable towards him, welcome him to your home, and forget not always to mention the Great Spirit. In the morning, give thanks to the Great Spirit for the return of day, and the light of the sun; at night renew your thanks to him, that his ruling power has preserved you from harm during the day, and that night has again come, in which you may rest your wearied bodies.

The four Messengers said further to Handsome Lake:—Tell your people, and particularly the keepers of the faith, to be strong-minded, and adhere to the true faith. We fear the Evil-minded will go among them with temptations. He may introduce the *fiddle*. He may bring *cards*, and leave them among you. The use of these are great sins. Let the people be on their guard, and the keepers of the faith be watchful and vigilant, that none of these evils may find their way among the people. Let the keepers of the faith preserve the law of moral conduct in all its purity. When meetings are to be held for instruction, and the people are preparing to go, the Evil-minded is then busy. He goes from one to another, whispering many temptations, by which to keep them away. He will even follow persons into the door of the council, and induce some, at that time, to bend their steps away. Many resist until they have entered, and then leave it. This habit, once indulged, obtains a fast hold, and the evil propensity increases with age. This is a great sin, and should be at once abandoned. Thus they said.

Speak evil of no one. If you can say no good of a person, then be silent. Let not your tongues betray you into evil. Let all be mindful of this; for these are the words of our Creator. Let all strive to cultivate friendship with those who surround them. This is pleasing to the Great Spirit.

Counselors, warriors, women and children:—I shall now rest. I thank you all for your kind and patient attention. I thank the Great Spirit, that he has spared the lives of so many of us to witness this day. I request you all to come up again tomorrow at early day. Let us all hope, that, until we meet again, the Creator and Ruler of us all may be kind to us, and preserve our lives. *Na-ho'*.

The council, on the following day, opened as usual with a few short speeches, from some of the chiefs or keepers of the faith, returning thanks for the privileges of the occasion, after which Sose-há-wă resumed his discourse.

Friends and Relatives, uncover now your heads:—Continue to listen to my rehearsal of the sayings communicated to Handsome Lake by the four Messengers of the Great Spirit. . . .

In discoursing yesterday upon the duties of the keepers of the faith, I omitted some things important. The Great Spirit created this office. He designed that its duties should never end. There are some who are selected and set apart by our Maker, to perform the duties of this office. It is therefore their duty to be faithful, and to be always watching. These duties they must ever perform during their lives. The faithful, when they leave this earth, will have a pleasant path to travel in. The same office exists in heaven, the home of our Creator. They will take the same place when they arrive there. There are dreadful penalties awaiting those keepers of the faith, who resign their office without a cause. Thus they said.

It was the original intention of our Maker, that all our feasts of thanksgiving should be seasoned with the flesh of wild animals. But we are surrounded by the palefaces, and in a short time the woods will be all removed. Then there will be no more game for the Indian to use in his feasts. The four Messengers said, in consequence of this, that we might use the flesh of domestic animals. This will not be wrong. The palefaces are pressing you upon every side. You must therefore live as they do. How far you can do so without sin, I will now tell you. You may grow cattle, and build yourselves warm and comfortable dwelling-houses. This is not sin; and it is all that you can safely adopt of the customs of the palefaces. You cannot live as they do. Thus they said.

Continue to listen:—It has pleased our Creator to set apart as our Life, the Three Sisters [corn, beans, squash, the basis of Iroquoian subsistence]. For this special favor, let us ever be thankful. When you have gathered in your harvest, let the people assemble, and hold a general thanksgiving for so great a good. In this way you will show your obedience to the will and pleasure of your Creator. Thus they said.

Many of you may be ignorant of the Spirit of Medicine. It watches over all constantly, and assists the needy whenever necessity requires. The Great Spirit designed that some men should possess the gift of skill in medicine. But he is pained to see a medicine man making exorbitant charges for attending the sick. Our Creator made for us tobacco. This plant must always be used in administering medicines. When a sick person recovers his health, he must return his thanks to the Great Spirit by means of tobacco; for it is by his goodness that he is made well. He blesses the medicine; and the medicine man must receive as his reward whatever the gratitude of the restored may tender. This is right and proper. There are many who are unfortunate, and cannot pay for attendance. It is sufficient for such to return thanks to the medicine man upon recovery. The remembrance that he has saved the life of a relative, will be a sufficient reward.

Listen further to what the Great Spirit has been pleased to communicate to us: He has made us, as a race, separate and distinct from the pale-face. It is a great sin to intermarry, and intermingle the blood of the two races. Let none be guilty of this transgression.

At one time the four Messengers said to Handsome Lake, lest the people should disbelieve you, and not repent and forsake their evil ways, we will now disclose to you the House of Torment, the dwelling-place of the Evil-minded. Handsome Lake was particular in describing to us all that he witnessed; and the course which departed spirits were accustomed to take on leaving the earth. There was a road which led upwards. At a certain point it branched; one branch led straight forward to the Home of the Great Spirit, and the other turned aside to the House of Torment. At the place where the roads separated were stationed two keepers, one representing the Good, and the other the Evil Spirit. When a person reached the fork, if wicked, by a motion from the Evil keeper, he turned instinctively upon the road which led to the abode of the Evil-minded. But if virtuous and good, the other keeper directed him upon the straight road. The latter was not much traveled; while the former was so frequently trodden, that no grass could grow in the pathway. It sometimes happened that the keepers had great difficulty in deciding which path the person should take, when the good and bad actions of the individual were nearly balanced. Those sent to the House of Torment sometimes remain one day, (which is there one of our years.) Some for a longer period. After they have atoned for their sins, they pass to heaven. But when they have committed either of the great sins, (witchcraft, murder, and infanticide,) they never pass to heaven, but are tormented forever. Having conducted Handsome Lake to this place, he saw a large and dark-colored mansion covered with soot, and beside it stood a lesser one. One of the four then held out his rod, and the top of the house moved up, until they could look down upon all that was within. He saw many rooms. The first object which met his eye, was a haggard-looking man; his sunken eyes cast upon the ground, and his form half consumed by the torments he had undergone. This man was a drunkard. The Evil-minded then appeared, and called him by name. As the man obeyed his call, he dipped from a caldron a quantity of red-hot liquid, and commanded him to drink it, as it was an article he loved. The man did as he was directed, and immediately from his mouth issued a stream of blaze. He cried in vain for help. The Tormentor then requested him to sing and make himself merry, as was his wont while on earth, after drinking the firewater. Let drunkards take warning from this. Others were then summoned. There came before him two persons, who appeared to be husband and wife. He told them to exercise the privilege they were so fond of while on the earth. They immediately commenced a quarrel of words. They raged at each other with such violence, that their tongues and eyes ran out so far they could neither see nor speak. This, said they, is the punishment of quarrelsome and disputing husbands and wives. Let such also take warning, and live together in peace and harmony. Next he called up a woman who had been a witch. First he plunged her into a caldron of boiling liquid. In her cries of distress, she begged the Evil-minded to give her some cooler place. He then immersed her in one containing liquid at the point of freezing. Her cries then were, that she was too cold. This woman, said the four Messengers, shall always be tormented in this manner. He proceeded to mention the punishment which awaits all those who cruelly ill-treat their wives. The Evil-minded next called up a man who had been accustomed to beat his wife. Having led him up to a red-hot statue of a female, he directed him to do that which he was fond of while he was upon the earth. He obeyed, and struck the figure. The sparks flew in every direction, and by the contact his arm was consumed. Such is the punishment, they said, awaiting those who ill-treat their wives. From this take seasonable warning, He looked again and saw a woman, whose arms and hands were nothing but bones. She had sold firewater to the Indians, and the flesh was eaten from her hands and arms. This, they said, would be the fate of rum-sellers. Again he looked, and in one apartment he saw and recognized *Ho-ne-yä'-wus*, (Farmer's Brother) his former friend. He was engaged in removing a heap of sand, grain by grain; and although he labored continually, yet the heap of sand was not diminished. This, they said, was the punishment of those who sold land. Adjacent to the house of torment was a field of corn filled with weeds. He saw women in the act of cutting them down; but as fast as this was done, they grew up again. This, they said, was the punishment of lazy women. It would be proper and right, had we time, to tell more of this place of torment. But my time is limited, and I must pass to other things.

The Creator made men dependent upon each other. He made them sociable beings; therefore, when your neighbor visits you, set food before him. If it be your next door neighbor, you must give him to eat. He will partake and thank you.

Again they said:—You must not steal. Should you want for anything necessary, you have only to tell your wants, and they will be supplied. This is right. Let none ever steal anything. Children are often tempted to take things home which do not belong to them. Let parents instruct their children in this rule.

Many of our people live to a very old age. Your Creator says that your deportment towards them must be that of reverence and affection. They have seen and felt much of the misery and pain of earth. Be always kind to them when old and helpless. Wash their hands and face, and nurse them with care. This is the will of the Great Spirit.

It has been the custom among us to mourn for the dead one year. This custom is wrong. As it causes the death of many children, it must be abandoned. Ten days mourn for the dead, and not longer. When one dies, it is right and proper to make an address over the body, telling how much you loved the deceased. Great respect for the dead must be observed among us.

At another time the four Messengers said to Handsome Lake, they would now show him the "Destroyer of Villages," (George Washington) of whom you have so frequently heard. [Washington had died December 14, 1799.] Upon the road leading to heaven he could see a light, far away in the distance, moving to and fro. Its brightness far exceeded the brilliancy of the noonday sun. They told him the journey was as follows: First, they came to a cold spring, which was a resting-place. From this point they proceeded into pleasant fairy grounds, which spread away in every direction. Soon they reached heaven. The light was dazzling. Berries of every description grew in vast abundance. Their size and quality were such, that a single berry was more than sufficient to appease the appetite. A sweet fragrance perfumed the air. Fruits of every kind met the eye. The inmates of this celestial abode spent their time in amusement and repose. No evil could enter there. None in heaven ever transgress again. Families were reunited, and dwelt together in harmony. They possessed a bodily form, the senses, and the remembrances of the earthly life. But no white man ever entered heaven. Thus they said. He looked, and saw an inclosure upon a plain, just without the entrance of heaven. Within it was a fort. Here he saw the "Destroyer of Villages," walking to and fro within the inclosure. His countenance indicated a great and a good man. They said to Handsome Lake: the man you see is the only pale-face who ever left the earth [that is, who had approached heaven]. He was kind to you, when on the settlement of the great difficulty [the War for Independence, 1775-1783] between the Americans and the Great Crown [Great Britain, specifically the king of England] you were abandoned to the mercy of your enemies. The Crown told the great American, that as for his allies, the Indians, he might kill them if he liked [many Iroquois had allied themselves with Great Britain]. The great American judged that this would be cruel and unjust. He believed they were made by the Great Spirit, and were entitled to the enjoyment of life. He was kind to you, and extended over you his protection. For this reason, he has been allowed to leave the earth. But he is never permitted to go into the presence of the Great Spirit. Although alone, he is perfectly happy. All faithful Indians pass by him as they go to heaven. They see him, and recognize him, but pass on in silence. No word ever passes his lips.

Friends and Relatives:—It was by the influence of this great man, that we were spared as a people, and yet live. Had he not granted us his protection, where would we have been? Perished, all perished.

The four Messengers further said to Handsome Lake, they were fearful that, unless the people repented and obeyed his commands, the patience and forbearance of their Creator would be exhausted; that he would grow angry with them, and cause their increase to cease.

Our Creator made light and darkness. He made the sun to heat, and shine over the world. He made the moon, also, to shine by night, and to cool the world, if the sun made it too hot by day. The keeper of the clouds, by direction of the Great Spirit, will then cease to act. The keeper of the springs and running brooks will cease to rule them for the good of man. The sun will cease to fulfil its office. Total darkness will then cover the earth. A great smoke will rise, and spread over the face of the earth. Then will come out of it all monsters, and poisonous animals created by the Evil-minded; and they, with the wicked upon the earth, will perish together.

But before this dreadful time shall come, the Great Spirit will take home to himself all the good and faithful. They will lay themselves down to sleep, and from this sleep of death, they will rise, and go home to their Creator. Thus they said.

I have now done. I close thus, that you may remember and understand the fate which awaits the earth, and the unfaithful and unbelieving. Our Creator looks down upon us. The four Beings from above see us. They witness with pleasure this assemblage, and rejoice at the object for which it is gathered. It is now forty-eight years since we first began to listen to the renewed will of our Creator. I have been unable, during the time allotted to me, to rehearse all the sayings of *Gä-ne-o-di'-yo*. I regret very much, that you cannot hear them all.

Counselors, Warriors, Women and Children:—I have done. I thank you all for your attendance, and for your kind and patient attention. May the Great Spirit, who rules all things, watch over and protect you from every harm and danger, while you travel the journey of life. May the Great Spirit bless you all, and bestow upon you life, health, peace and prosperity; and may you, in turn, appreciate his great goodness *Na-ho'*.

27

A Methodist Dream of Heaven and Homeland

A. Gregory Schneider

Rev. James B. Finley (1781–1856) was a prominent minister of the Methodist Episcopal Church. During his lifetime, Methodism grew from a small and somewhat disreputable sect into the largest denomination in the country, prompting historians of American religion to designate the nineteenth century as "the Methodist Age" in American church history. Finley promoted and chronicled western Methodism. In his time, of course, "western" meant the regions west of the Appalachian mountains, principally the Ohio valley region. He and his parents joined the great migrations in the early American republic from eastern states such as Virginia into territory that would become the states of Kentucky, Ohio, Indiana, and Illinois. His formative years and early career were spent in the midst of frontier settlements. Whether in the central eastern states or on the frontier, the Methodist style of religion proved distinctively effective in recruiting members and forming congregations.

Methodism itself was an English invention, a movement begun in the 1740s and led for decades by John Wesley, a minister of the Church of England who wished to revive the church from what he saw as its spiritually moribund condition. Methodism, he declared, was nothing more than Christianity in earnest. The name "methodist" began as a term of derision used by some of Wesley's fellow students at Oxford University to make fun of the overly earnest and methodical way in which he and a small band of sympathetic students practiced their religion. Wesley's movement was noted for its appeal to common folk of middle- and working-class backgrounds, for whom elite-dominated, state-supported churches had little place or purpose. He and the preachers who followed him made a point of taking religion out of the parish churches and into the fields. This popular appeal continued to be a Methodist trait in the New World, where Wesley's movement was transplanted just as the American colonies were moving toward revolution and the founding of the new American republic.

Many elements of Methodism's popular style were shared among most evangelical Protestants of the nineteenth century. The style included a belief in the ability of human beings to seek and secure salvation, in contrast to the Calvinist theological assertion that humans were predestined by God to salvation or damnation. Methodist style also included a focus on the feelings of the heart in the search for God's acceptance, a belief the individual could attain a certain kind of spiritual perfection, and a concern more with practical results than with creedal orthodoxy. This search for practical results helped establish some of the enduring patterns of evangelical Protestant revivalism. An emotionally charged sermon followed by an altar call to sinners to come forward and be prayed for in front of the congregation is certainly one of the best known of these patterns. Just as important, however, were practices of "social religion" that helped generate a community of feeling in congregations, moving members to work together for the conversion of others. Social religion among the lay members generated favorable conditions for the preachers to preach their revival sermons and issue altar calls.

The distinctively Methodist forms of these practices were called the "class meeting" and the "love feast." Class meetings were weekly meetings of small groups of believers, where one member was designated the class leader and all were expected to speak of their religious experience and practice. The leader was to provide encouragement, rebuke, and counsel, as seemed appropriate. Love feasts brought together larger groups. Members from the many local societies on what was called a "circuit" gathered for a weekend of meetings, some spiritual and evangelistic, others focused on administrative affairs of the circuit. The love feast was usually held on Sunday morning before administering the sacrament of the Lord's Supper. Members had bread and water together in a meal symbolic of Christian fellowship, and then the floor was opened to anyone who wished to recount his or her religious experience. Central to both practices was testimony as to what believers felt God was doing in their souls. This speaking out about inward states of feeling frequently generated intense conditions for shared emotion among participants. This community of feeling not only revived the faithful in their desires to serve God; it often engulfed unconverted souls in a spiritual tide that helped precipitate their conversions. Lay members would frequently return home from such events and turn traditional family prayer or table blessings into yet another occasion for social religion, catching up their unconverted relatives in the contagion of their religion of the heart.

The camp meeting where Finley spoke of his dream represents a practice in which many evangelical denominations in the early nineteenth century shared, but which also had strong continuities with the Methodist quarterly meeting. As congregations and circuits grew larger and administration became more complex, the spiritual community-building and evangelistic functions of the Methodist quarterly meeting became harder to combine with denominational business functions. The practice of holding camp meetings evolved as a means of separating out and elaborating the community-building functions of large public gatherings of the faithful. Contrary to popular notions that still persist today, camp meetings were not just a frontier phenomenon but were held as regularly in the east as in the west. They continued to have a prominent place in Methodist practice in places where the frontier had become a distant memory. Camp meetings were held in the summer, when days were long and weather favorable. They brought together hundreds, even thousands of believers, who camped in tents for longer periods of time than the weekend quarterly meetings. They consisted of rounds of general meetings for preaching in the center of the encampment and of smaller meetings for prayer and testimony in the surrounding tents. For the faithful, the meetings were rituals of reenactment and renewal of religious experience and commitment. They were also acts of aggressive evangelism addressed to the many indifferent and even antagonistic observers who showed up simply because camp meetings were one of the bigger and more interesting social events on the local calendar. The camp meeting was a natural venue for a preacher such as Finley to tell a story such as that of his illness, dream, and divine healing.

For practices such as class meetings and love feasts to be effective, Methodists had to know how to tell a good story and to give a testimony that would move fellow believers and catch the attention of the unconverted. These testimonial rituals ensured that all members would develop their skills of persuasion. Those who were especially effective storytellers very often found themselves pushed by their fellow believers, and drawn out by the preachers, into leadership roles. Another feature of the popular religion of early Methodism was that its ministers were drawn from among the common people, to whom Methodism most appealed. Because the ordained ministry was still reserved for men, a woman's leadership was usually local and informal. Men with a gift for telling their religious experience frequently ended up, as Reverend Finley did, in the brotherhood of itinerant ordained Methodist ministers. Ministerial recruits, moreover, were sent directly to preach and save sinners, not to take years in advanced professional schooling that might build up class barriers between preachers and people. A common counsel given to inexperienced and stage-frightened new preachers was, if they forgot their sermon outlines, to simply "tell their experience."

A primary purpose of telling one's experience, be one preacher in the pulpit or layperson in the class meeting, was to induce a similar experience in others, in a word, to convert them. Conversion was an experience of figurative death and resurrection. It began with an awareness of one's sinfulness, an awareness that soon deepened into a profound, emotionally wrenching conviction that as a sinner one was justly condemned by God and bound for eternal death. The terror, despair, and emotional darkness of conviction often caused bodily reactions like falling to the ground, uncontrollable weeping, convulsions, and the like. Thus Jacob Young, a contemporary of Finley's on the Kentucky frontier, fell to the floor when he was finally convicted of his sins. He was unable to speak, and he cried and trembled uncontrollably. This negative pole of the conversion process, however, soon gave way to a positive pole. After some hours of distress, laying on the floor of the home of some pious neighbors who prayed for him, Young felt the grace of God. "God, in mercy, lifted up the light of his countenance upon me, and I was translated from the power of darkness into the kingdom of God's dear son, and rejoiced with joy unspeakable and full of glory" (*Autobiography of a Pioneer* [Cincinnati: Swormstedt and Poe, 1857], pp. 38–43). The conversion experience, then, consisted in an emotional pattern expressed in metaphors of movement from heaviness to lightness, depths to heights, and, especially, darkness to light. Methodist converts often shouted aloud for joy when they converted or when they witnessed or heard stories of such transformations. "Shouting Methodist," in some parts of the early republic, became a byword among those who disdained such outward demonstrations.

The mythic foundation of the conversion pattern was the death and resurrection of Jesus Christ. Believers understood themselves to be following Christ in seeking and undergoing conversion. Furthermore, hearts and minds shaped by the story of Christ and by recapitulation of the divine story in the conversion experience learned to interpret the whole of experience in terms of crucifixion and resurrection. To live life in this way was to follow the "way of the cross." The everyday frustrations and privations of life became occasions to practice the way of the cross in one's soul. Pride, anger, fear, resentment, greed, or lust were common responses to life's problems, then as now. Evangelical believers sought to mortify such motives, to die to them, in order that they might rise to a peaceable tranquility in their hearts, a state of mind and affections that symbolized, indeed partook of heaven. Illness, in particular, came to be viewed as a "crucifixion" to be endured with fortitude and faith, as Christ endured the cross. If illness led to death, as it often did in those times, then believers strove to die well, giving evidence of their steadfast, even joyful belief in Christ's life-giving power in the face of death. When Christians died well, their death-beds became way stations on the verge of heaven for the friends and family who witnessed their deaths, and the testimony and exhortations given by dying believers were especially effective evangelistic appeals.

Telling one's religious experience and giving witness to the ways in which God had dealt with one's soul was a form of piety that all members were expected to practice in some degree. The common form of such practice was oral, but many also wrote down their experiences, some in private journals and diaries, others with intent to publish. Bishop Francis Asbury, father of American Methodism, wrote an extensive journal with the clear intent that it be published. In a similar vein, but a somewhat different genre, very many lesser preachers wrote and published their autobiographies, and others had friends or relatives who wrote and published ministerial biographies. The intent of such publication was the same as the intent of telling one's experience in class meetings: to edify and encourage the believers, and, perhaps, to aid in the conversion of sinners. Reverend Finley is one obvious example of this kind of spiritual autobiographer. The purchase and reading of such literature was an act of piety that gave financial support to the work of the church and often to a dead preacher's widow and orphans, even as it edified the faithful.

In this culture of storytelling in service of the cross, Reverend Finley's account of his dream may be understood as a good story, the kind that would satisfy the spiritual yearnings of his readers—and maybe even boost sales. Clearly it is one more instance of the pattern of death, or near-death, leading to resurrection or an anticipation of resurrection. Finley is sick nearly unto death in this story, but his dream of heaven results not only in ecstatic joy but also in healing. The story appears in his autobiography because his narration so moved his fellow believers that they insisted he put it in print. It functioned to exemplify and reinforce the pattern by which Finley's community of believers attempted to live their lives. Indeed, his narrative was successful enough in this regard to stimulate the characteristic Methodist shouts of joy.

The fact that this story is a dream narrative further enhanced its power for Finley and his hearers. As a movement of popular religion that appealed to common folk, American Methodism reflected the assumptions about reality, both natural and supernatural, that were current among its people. The supernatural world was very real to these people, and access to it was commonly by inner impressions, trances, visions, and dreams. To hear instructions from God, or to encounter an angel and converse with it, or to otherwise have some interaction with the supernatural realm while in a dream, was to give those things heard and seen an aura of divine authority. Finley's account further underscores the narrative's authority by the claim that he was healed, apparently miraculously, as he woke from the dream.

Appeal to direct encounter with the supernatural, furthermore, fit well with what some historians have seen as a trend toward democratization in American Christianity in the early republic. Testimony to divine encounter, whether in the common form of conversion narrative or in the more exotic dream narrative, was self-validating. It was difficult for anyone else to contradict or condemn a personal testimony to one's own private encounter with the divine. One did not need the blessing of a priest or the approval of the parish minister to make one's story plausible to one's audience. If one had the experience and could recount it with conviction and emotional power, one could command the attention and respect of one's peers. Thus, popular religion in the early republic could circumvent established religious authorities, be they the gentry-dominated parish vestries and priests of the Episcopalian South or the learned and settled clergy of the Congregationalist or Presbyterian northern states. Such openness to supernatural manifestations also allowed marginalized categories of people such as women and blacks to command a greater degree of attention, respect, and even, within existing legal and social limits, authority.

There were cultural limits also, of course, as Finley's description of the heavenly realm demonstrates. His dream images accord more or less with those accepted among Christians who read their Bibles and knew the vision of John recorded in the book of Revelation. Finley, out of a desire for a somewhat learned and literary allusion, seems to conflate biblical imagery with images from Greek mythology in his own published account. Thus, he gives his readers the emerald gates attributed by the poet to the Greek Elysian fields, instead of the gates of pearl specified in the Biblical account. It is unlikely that Finley's readers would have begrudged this bit of syncretism. Allusions to the classical world were still the mark of learning in the mid-nineteenth century, when Finley published his story, and including them in his story allowed him and his readers to feel as though they and their once-despised denomination had achieved a degree of social elevation. Such ambition for respectability was the other side of the coin of democratization.

The familial metaphor in the dream is intended to be instructive. The bishops led the brotherhood of traveling preachers by a strongly paternalistic form of administration. As God was father to all humankind, so the preachers were spiritual fathers to their children in the gospel. Members addressed each other as brother, sister, father, and mother, and they felt themselves to be a family of God, bound by ties of common religious experience and feeling. The dominant metaphors for Methodist religious community had more to do with domestic affection than with political populism.

In heaven he finds not only ministering angels but a human family: a father, mother, and child. This is a dream about family and family ties. Finley wants to comfort bereaved mothers with the knowledge of what he has seen: that their dead infants are transfigured into beautiful, joyful cherubs in heaven. Clearly, the response he elicited from his hearers suggests that they were eager to receive such comfort. Methodists and many other nineteenth-century evangelicals frequently portrayed heaven as the place where families were reunited forever. They filled sermons, exhortations, and testimonies with images of departed loved ones.

This domestication of heaven was part of a much larger nineteenth-century cultural trend that increasingly identified religious feeling with domestic affections and sacred space with the family circle. Women, furthermore, were understood to be the natural specialists in domestic affections. The rising ideology of domesticity assigned women a key function in culture and society. By means of their affectionate influence they were to tame the passions of their husbands and children. Thus women ensured individual virtue in their family members so as to provide the foundations of public order in the new American republic, where those controls previously provided by a royal court and an aristocracy were gone. The image of the family as a haven in a heartless world, as a circle of affection centered around the virtuous mother, and as a bulwark for democracy was gaining popular cultural ascendancy at the time of Finley's dream.

The family had not always been seen in such terms. A more traditional and patriarchal vision had defined family in less psychological and more political and economic terms. A family had been seen as an estate that comprised all those dependent upon the productive activity of the household as it was ruled and protected by the head of the household, the father. In such a vision, family relationships were understood in terms of the sovereignty of the patriarch and the deference, and dependence, of his wife, children, and servants. During the nineteenth century in America, especially among the emerging commercial and professional middle classes, this more traditional and patriarchal vision of family was subverted and eclipsed to a significant degree by the more affection-centered vision. Religious movements such as early American Methodism were an important force in promoting this transformation.

The text below is from James B. Finley, *Autobiography of Rev. James B. Finley,* edited by W. P. Strickland (Cincinnati: Methodist Book Concern, 1854), pp. 375–78.

Further Reading

Nathan Hatch, *The Democratization of American Christianity* (New Haven: Yale University Press, 1989); Colleen McDannell, *The Christian Home in Victorian America, 1840–1900* (Bloomington: Indiana University Press, 1986); Russell E. Richey, *Early American Methodism* (Bloomington: Indiana University Press, 1991); A. Gregory Schneider, *The Way of the Cross Leads Home: The Domestication of American Methodism* (Bloomington: Indiana University Press, 1993); John H. Wigger, *Taking Heaven by Storm: Methodism and the Rise of Popular Christianity in America* (New York: Oxford University Press, 1998).

A Dream of Heaven

During my labors on the Dayton district an incident occurred which I must relate, because it is due to the many to whom I promised an account of it that it should be published in my biography.

It was in the summer of 1842. Worn down with fatigue, I was completing my last round of quarterly meetings, and winding up the labors of a very toilsome year. I had scarcely finished my work till I was most violently attacked with bilious fever, and it was with great difficulty I reached home. The disease had taken so violent a hold on my system that I sank rapidly under its power. Every thing that kind attention and medical skill could impart was resorted to, to arrest its ravages; but all was in vain, and my life was despaired of. On the seventh night, in a state of entire insensibility to all around me, when the last ray of hope had departed, and my weeping family and friends were standing around my couch waiting to see me breathe my last, it seemed to me that a heavenly visitant entered my room. It came to my side, and, in the softest and most silvery tones, which fell like rich music on my ear, it said, "I have come to conduct you to another state and place of existence." In an instant I seemed to rise, and, gently borne by my angel guide, I floated out upon the ambient air. Soon earth was lost in the distance, and around us, on every side were worlds of light and glory. On, on, away, away from world to luminous worlds afar, we sped with the velocity of thought. At length we reached the gates of paradise; and O, the transporting scenes that fell upon my vision as the emerald portals, wide and high, rolled back upon their golden hinges! Then, in its fullest extent, did I realize the invocation of the poet:

> "Burst, ye emerald gates, and bring
>   To my raptured vision
> All the ecstatic joys that spring
>   Round the bright Elysian."

Language, however, is inadequate to describe what then, with unveiled eyes, I saw. The vision is indelibly pictured on my heart. Before me, spread out in beauty, was a broad sheet of water, clear as crystal, not a single ripple on its surface, and its purity and clearness indescribable. On each side of this lake, or river, rose up the most tall and beautiful trees, covered with all manner of fruits and flowers, the brilliant hues of which were reflected in the bosom of the placid river.

While I stood gazing with joy and rapture at the scene, a convoy of angels was seen floating in the pure ether of that world. They all had long wings, and, although they went with the greatest rapidity, yet their wings were folded close by their side. While I gazed I asked my guide who they were, and what their mission. To this he responded, "They are angels, dispatched to the world from whence you came on an errand of mercy." I could hear strains of the most entrancing melody all around me, but no one was discoverable but my guide. At length I said, "Will it be possible for me to have a sight of some of the just made perfect in glory?" Just then there came before us three persons; one had the appearance of a male, the other a female, and the third an infant. The appearance of the first two was somewhat similar to the angels I saw, with the exception that they had crowns upon their heads of the purest yellow, and harps in their hands. Their robes, which were full and flowing, were of the purest white. Their countenances were lighted up with a heavenly radiance, and they smiled upon me with ineffable sweetness.

There was nothing with which the blessed babe or child could be compared. It seemed to be about three feet high. Its wings, which were long and most beautiful, were tinged with all the colors of the rainbow. Its dress seemed to be of the whitest silk, covered with the softest white down. The driven snow could not exceed it for whiteness or purity. Its face was all radiant with glory; its very smile now plays around my heart. I gazed and gazed with wonder upon this heavenly child. At length I said, "If I have to return to earth, from whence I came, I should love to take this child with me, and show it to the weeping mothers of earth. Methinks, when they see it, they will never shed another tear over their children when they die." So anxious was I to carry out the desire of my heart, that I made a grasp at the bright and beautiful one, desiring to clasp it in my arms, but it eluded my grasp, and plunged into the river of life. Soon it rose up from the waters, and as the drops fell from its expanding wings, they seemed like diamonds, so brightly did they sparkle. Directing its course to the other shore, it flew up to one of the topmost branches of one of life's fair trees. With a look of most seraphic sweetness it gazed upon me, and then commenced singing in heaven's own strains, "To Him that hath loved me, and washed me from my sins in his own blood, to him be glory both now and forever. Amen." At that moment the power of the eternal God came upon me, and I began to shout, and, clapping my hands, I sprang from my bed, and was healed as instantly as the lame man in the beautiful porch of the temple, who "went walking, and leaping, and praising God." Overwhelmed by the glory I saw and felt, I could not cease praising God. The next Sabbath I went to camp meeting, filled with the love and power of God. There I told the listening thousands what I saw and felt, and what God had done for me, and loud were the shouts of glory that reverberated through the forests.

Though years have rolled away since that bright, happy hour, yet the same holy flame is burning in my heart, and I retain the same glorious victory. "Halleluiah! for the Lord God omnipotent reigneth."

— 28 —

African American Vision Stories

Elizabeth Reis

During the eighteenth and nineteenth centuries, most African American slaves who turned to Christianity embraced Protestantism, often becoming Baptists and Methodists. In the midst of the bondage of slavery, African Americans blended revivalist evangelicalism with rituals of Africa that resonated with Christian symbolism, and they looked to religion as a source of identity, solidarity, endurance, and joy in the present, even when that present involved enormous suffering.

Two of the conversion narratives reprinted here, "God Struck Me Dead" and "I Am Blessed but You Are Damned," were culled from interviews conducted between 1927 and 1929 by Andrew Polk Watson, then a graduate student in anthropology at Fisk University. It is nearly impossible to determine exactly when and from where each account was derived; nevertheless, this collection is an invaluable source of information about nineteenth-century slave religious life, especially regarding conversion experiences. There is a long tradition of conversion experiences in America, beginning with the seventeenth-century Puritan requirement in Congregational churches, and an even longer legacy extends from the period of early Christianity. Conversion represented an inward expression of piety and a turning toward God. The narratives also came to have a more public meaning in America, as evangelical Protestants expected each other to testify to their path to salvation.

Emotional ecstasy characterized black conversion experiences in the nineteenth-century South, radically differentiating black and white revival experience. In the segregated spaces of the camp meetings during the Second Great Awakening of the mid nineteenth century, physical expressions known as "bodily exercises" were introduced that included jumping, dancing, groaning, and shaking. Ritual forms that blacks had begun to create in earlier religious revivals developed, fusing elements that were both Christian and African. New religious music and an outpouring of emotional singing, shouting, and ritual hand-clapping, foot-stamping, and ring-shouting came to be associated with black worship. While the public ritual of conversion often included physical signs of sinners anguishing under the weight of sin, hoping for emotional release in Christ, the written narratives of conversion that have survived convey a different sort of ecstatic experience. Christian biblical teachings and African supernaturalism blended, offering the faithful spiritual power and immediacy that could not easily be denied. Nineteenth-century African American conversion narratives frequently included the story of a supernatural vision of either an angel or Christ. Believers described how angels appeared to them, offering renewed health on this earth and an eventual afterlife with Christ in heavenly comfort.

Because these narratives were recorded in interviews years later, we have no way of knowing how the stories were told at the time. We can only speculate that when the events occurred, believers told others about their experiences in ways consistent with these versions. The significance of these tales may have been, in part, in the telling. The narratives took on lives of their own and no doubt instructed and inspired listeners. How believers interpreted what happened to them is revealing, and so we must consider the ways in which these narrators conveyed their stories and made them true for others. What we might think of now as "supernatural" events—a visit from an angel or from Christ, a tour through heaven and hell, or a transformative out-of-body experience—were, to believers, compatible with their Protestantism.

Male and female slave narratives are filled with angels, visions, and voices that subjects saw or heard when they were at death's door, offering them bodily as well as spiritual renewal. When the power of God struck one female slave, she declared, "I died. I fell flat out on the floor flat on my back. I could neither speak nor move, for my tongue stuck to the roof of my mouth; my jaws were locked and my limbs were stiff." This woman was taken on a tour of heaven and hell and followed Jesus until she met God sitting in a big armchair. Then she saw the "Lamb's book of life and my name written in it." Still not quite convinced of her salvation, but commanded by God to return to earth with this knowledge, the woman disobeyed God by doubting. God sent her an affliction, and she suffered physically for her disbelief. Her narrative explains that her "limbs were all swollen so that I could hardly walk." She interpreted this sickness as punishment for her doubt and resolved to renew her faith. Finally, God revealed himself in two more ways. The woman asked God if he was pleased with how she had told the people of her experience in heaven. She requested as a sign that God would make the sun shine on the day of her baptism, and God complied. When the woman asked if she might feel the spirit when she was down by the river, her "soul caught on fire." She had been using a cane but was now able to discard it and walk without even a limp. An angel's voice told her how to heal her legs. Thereafter, she reported, she never paid more than three dollars for doctor bills for herself, her children, or her grandchildren.

A close look at these incredible stories reveals a set of literary conventions meant to justify and authenticate the experience, as well as the narrative itself. Recovery from severe illness or bodily distress was one way in which these stories were authenticated. The more dramatic the recuperation, the more convincing the tale. Observers could not see the trip to heaven, but they could surely vouch for a person's physical well-being. Believers either saw or heard about the woman slave who stepped haltingly with her cane but who afterwards walked unaided.

Believers became empowered in ways other than the physical. These ways were consistent with their particular social situations. A slave named Morte feared at first that his master would "whip him unmercifully" because his horse had run off with the plow during all the excitement of his spiritual encounter. But a "deep feeling of satisfaction" swept over Morte, and he no longer dreaded the anticipated whipping. When fear returned and overcame him, and he fell into a trance, the angel Gabriel came to him, reassured him that he would remain with him until the world ended, and encouraged him to "speak to multitudes." Not only did Morte learn from the angel that he was a "chosen vessel unto the Lord" but he escaped a whipping and earned from his master the elevated status of preacher, fit even to address the master's white friends and family. Obviously, we have no way of knowing if stories such as these are "true." Perhaps more typically, masters would have punished unusual behavior and may have viewed slave preachers as subversive. Nonetheless, such stories no doubt encouraged and empowered slaves and free blacks.

Some of the narrators recognized that readers or listeners might doubt their tales, as we see in the published account by Zilpha Elaw. A free African American Methodist woman, Zilpha Elaw saw Jesus in 1807, inspiring her to join the church the following year. Her narrative speaks directly to her readers' potential incredulity: "Dear reader, whoever thou art, into whose hands this narrative may fall, I will try to gratify thee by endeavouring to describe his manifestation." She admitted that at first she thought "it had been a vision presented merely to the eye of my mind," but when even the cow she was milking turned her head, "bowed her knees and cowered down upon the ground," she knew "the thing was certain and beyond all doubt." Elaw insisted that everything she wrote was "with conscientious veracity and scrupulous adherence to truth."

These spiritual stories often strike us today as utterly fantastic. Yet it is important to note that such narratives of otherworldly journeys often were credible to contemporaries and successfully blended into believers' ordinary lives. The familiarity of their voices helped to accomplish this goal. When slaves mentioned their uncommonly low doctor bills or their master's change of heart, listeners could imagine themselves in similar situations. A supernatural experience—especially one that seemed to guarantee one's salvation—was not so unbelievable; it could happen at any time to anyone, even to a slave.

As with conversion narratives, many African American sermons similarly revealed an active search for redemption through divine intervention, from a position of relative powerlessness. They also use a highly visual language that creates a vivid world beyond the sorrows of everyday life. The idea that God would personally deliver slaves from their suffering appeared frequently. In a sermon of 1808 celebrating the end of the slave trade, for example, the African American community leader and lay preacher Absalom Jones equated black slaves with the biblical children of Israel escaping from Egypt. He preached that God would do more than simply "issue a command to the armies of angels that surrounded him to fly to the relief of his suffering children." He would "come down from heaven in his own person, in order to deliver them out of the hands of the Egyptians." Deliverance was something that would likely happen in this life, Jones and others preached, not something for which slaves necessarily had to wait for Judgment Day. Thus, as scholars have shown, slaves identified with the Israelites of the Hebrew Bible and hoped for a similar redemption in their own time. As one African American spiritual intoned, "And the God dat lives in Moses' time is jus' de same today." Another spiritual asked, "He delivered Daniel from the lion's den, / Jonah from de belly ob de whale, / And de Hebrew children from de fiery furnace, / And why not every man?"

The common cultural images expressed in African-American sermons and conversion narratives convey the blend of religious beliefs that characterized African American religion: Christian images adapted from the Hebrew Bible and the Book of Revelation, revivalistic expressions of the Spirit working in one's heart, and African traditions that include a belief in human access to an unseen world. The syncretic religious world of African American slaves sustained and empowered its adherents, as these conversion narratives and corresponding sermon literature confirm.

"God Struck Me Dead" and "I Am Blessed but You Are Damned" are from Clifton H. Johnson, ed., *God Struck Me Dead: Voices of Ex-Slaves* (Cleveland: Pilgrim Press 1969), pp. 58–60, 15–18. *The Memoirs of the Life, Religious Experience, Ministerial Travels, and Labours of Mrs. Elaw, An American Female of Colour; Together with Some Account of the Great Religious Revivals in America (Written by Herself)* was originally published as a pamphlet in London in 1846 and reprinted in William L. Andrews, ed., *Sisters of the Spirit: Three Black Women's Autobiographies of the Nineteenth Century* (Bloomington: Indiana University Press, 1986), pp. 53–57. Absalom Jones's sermon "On Account of the Abolition of the African Slave Trade" is taken from Philip S. Foner and Robert James Branham, eds., *Lift Every Voice: African American Oratory, 1787–1900* (Tuscaloosa: University of Alabama Press), pp. 74–79.

Further Reading

Sylvia R. Frey and Betty Wood, *Come Shouting to Zion: African American Protestantism in the American South and British Caribbean to 1830* (Chapel Hill: University of North Carolina Press, 1998); Albert Raboteau, *Slave Religion: The "Invisible Institution" in the Antebellum South* (New York: Oxford University Press, 1978); Mechal Sobel, *The World They Made Together: Black and White Values in Eighteenth-Century Virginia* (Princeton: Princeton University Press, 1987).

God Struck Me Dead

I have always been a sheep. I was never a goat. I was created and cut out and born in the world for heaven. Even before God freed my soul and told me to go, I never was hell-scared. I just never did feel that my soul was made to burn in hell.

God started on me when I wasn't but ten years old. I was sick with the fever, and he called me and said, "You are ten years old." I didn't know how old I was, but later on I asked my older sister and she told me that I was ten years old when I had the fever.

As I grew up I used to frolic a lot and was considered a good dancer, but I never took much interest in such things. I just went many times to please my friends and, later on, my husband. What I loved more than all else was to go to church.

I used to pray then. I pray now and just tell God to take me and do his will, for he knows the every secret of my heart. He knows what we stand most in need of before we ask for it, and if we trust him, he will give us what we ought to have in due season. Some people pray and call on God as if they think he is ignorant of their needs or else asleep. But God is a time-God. I know this, for he told me so. I remember one morning I was on my way home with a bundle of clothes to wash—it was after my husband had died—and I felt awfully burdened down, and so I commenced to talk to God. It looked like I was having such a hard time. Everybody seemed to be getting along well but poor me. I told him so. I said, "Lord, it looks like you come to everybody's house but mine. I never bother my neighbors or cause any disturbance. I have lived as it is becoming a poor widow woman to live and yet, Lord, it looks like I have a harder time than anybody." When I said this, something told me to turn around and look. I put my bundle down and looked towards the east part of the world. A voice spoke to me as plain as day, but it was inward and said, "I am a time-God working after the counsel of my own will. In due time I will bring all things to you. Remember and cause your heart to sing."

When God struck me dead with his power I was living on Fourteenth Avenue. It was the year of the Centennial. I was in my house alone, and I declare unto you, when his power struck me I died. I fell out on the floor flat on my back. I could neither speak nor move, for my tongue stuck to the roof of my mouth; my jaws were locked and my limbs were stiff.

In my vision I saw hell and the devil. I was crawling along a high brick wall, it seems, and it looked like I would fall into a dark, roaring pit. I looked away to the east and saw Jesus. He called to me and said, "Arise and follow me." He was standing in snow—the prettiest, whitest snow I have ever seen. I said, "Lord, I can't go, for that snow is too deep and cold." He commanded me the third time before I would go. I stepped out in it and it didn't seem a bit cold, nor did my feet sink into it. We traveled on east in a little, narrow path and came to something that looked like a grape-arbor, and the snow was hanging down like icicles. But it was so pretty and white that it didn't look like snow. He told me to take some of it and eat, but I said, "Lord, it is too cold." He commanded me three times before I would eat any of it. I took some and tasted it, and it was the best-tasting snow I ever put into my mouth.

The Father, the Son, and the Holy Ghost led me on to glory. I saw God sitting in a big armchair. Everything seemed to be made of white stones and pearls. God didn't seem to pay me any attention. He just sat looking into space. I saw the Lamb's book of life and my name written in it. A voice spoke to me and said, "Whosoever my son sets free is free indeed. I give you a through ticket from hell to heaven. Go into yonder world and be not afraid, neither be dismayed, for you are an elect child and ready for the fold." But when he commanded me to go, I was stubborn and didn't want to leave. He said, "My little one, I have commanded you and you shall obey."

I saw, while I was still in the spirit, myself going to my neighbors and to the church, telling them what God had done for me. When I came to this world I arose shouting and went carrying the good news. I didn't do like the Lord told me, though, for I was still in doubt and wanted to make sure. Because of my disobedience, he threw a great affliction on me. I got awfully sick, and my limbs were all swollen so that I could hardly walk. I began to have more faith then and put more trust in God. He put this affliction on me because it was hard for me to believe. But I just didn't want to be a hypocrite and go around hollering, not knowing what I was talking and shouting about. I told God this in my prayer, and he answered me saying, "My little one, my grace is sufficient. Behold! I have commanded you to go, and you shall go."

When I was ready to be baptized I asked God to do two things. It had been raining for days, and on the morning of my baptism it was still raining. I said, "Lord, if you are satisfied with me and pleased with what I have told the people, cause the sun to shine this evening when I go to the river." Bless your soul, when we went to the river, it looked like I had never seen the sun shine as bright. It stayed out about two hours, and then the sky clouded up again and rained some more.

The other thing I asked God was that I might feel the spirit when I went down to the river. And I declare unto you, my soul caught on fire the minute I stepped in the carriage to go to the river. I had been hobbling around on a stick, but I threw it away and forgot that I was ever a cripple.

Later the misery came back, and I asked God to heal me. The spirit directed me to get some peach-tree leaves and beat them up and put them about my limbs. I did this, and in a day or two that swelling left me, and I haven't been bothered since. More than this, I don't remember ever paying out but three dollars for doctor's bills in my life for myself, my children, or my grandchildren. Doctor Jesus tells me what to do.

I Am Blessed but You Are Damned

One day while in the field plowing I heard a voice. I jumped because I thought it was my master coming to scold and whip me for plowing up some more corn. I looked but saw no one. Again the voice called, "Morte! Morte!" With this I stopped, dropped the plow, and started running, but the voice kept on speaking to me saying, "Fear not, my little one, for behold! I come to bring you a message of truth." Everything got dark, and I was unable to stand any longer. I began to feel sick, and there was a great roaring. I tried to cry and move but was unable to do either. I looked up and saw that I was in a new world. There were plants and animals, and all, even the water where I stooped down to drink, began to cry out, "I am blessed but you are damned! I am blessed but you are damned!" With this I began to pray, and a voice on the inside began to cry, "Mercy! Mercy! Mercy!"

As I prayed an angel came and touched me, and I looked new. I looked at my hands and they were new; I looked at my feet and they were new. I looked and saw my old body suspended over a burning pit by a small web like a spider web. I again prayed, and there came a soft voice saying, "My little one, I have loved you with an everlasting love. You are this day made alive and freed from hell. You are a chosen vessel unto the Lord. Be upright before me, and I will guide you unto all truth. My grace is sufficient for you. Go, and I am with you. Preach the gospel, and I will preach with you. You are henceforth the salt of the earth."

I then began to shout and clap my hands. All the time, a voice on the inside was crying, "I am so glad! I am so glad!" About this time an angel appeared before me and said with a loud voice, "Praise God! Praise God!" I looked to the east, and there was a large throne lifted high up, and thereon sat one, even God. He looked neither to the right nor to the left. I was afraid and fell on my face. When I was still a long way off I heard a voice from God saying, "My little one, be not afraid, for lo! many wondrous works will I perform through thee. Go in peace, and lo! I am with you always." All this he said but opened not his mouth while speaking. Then all those about the throne shouted and said, "Amen," then came to myself again and shouted and rejoiced. After so long a time I recovered my real senses and realized that I had been plowing and that the horse had run off with the plow and dragged down much of the corn. I was afraid and began to pray, for I knew the master would whip me most unmercifully when he found that I had plowed up the corn.

About this time my master came down the field. I became very bold and answered him when he called me. He asked me very roughly how I came to plow up the corn, and where the horse and plow were, and why I had got along so slowly. I told him that I had been talking with God Almighty, and that it was God who had plowed up the corn. He looked at me very strangely, and suddenly I fell for shouting, and I shouted and began to preach. The words seemed to flow from my lips. When I had finished I had a deep feeling of satisfaction and no longer dreaded the whipping I knew I would get. My master looked at me and seemed to tremble. He told me to catch the horse and come on with him to the barn. I went to get the horse, stumbling down the corn rows. Here again I became weak and began to be afraid for the whipping. After I had gone some distance down the rows, I became dazed and again fell to the ground. In a vision I saw a great mound and, beside it or at the base of it, stood the angel Gabriel. And a voice said to me, "Behold your sins as a great mountain. But they shall be rolled away. Go in peace, fearing no man, for lo! I have cut loose your stammering tongue and unstopped your deaf ears. A witness shalt thou be, and thou shalt speak to multitudes, and they shall hear. My word has gone forth, and it is power. Be strong, and lo! I am with you even until the world shall end. Amen."

I looked, and the angel Gabriel lifted his hand, and my sins, that had stood as a mountain, began to roll away. I saw them as they rolled over into a great pit. They fell to the bottom, and there was a great noise. I saw old Satan with a host of his angels hop from the pit, and there they began to stick out their tongues at me and make motions as if to lay hands on me and drag me back into the pit. I cried out, "Save me! Save me, Lord!" And like a flash there gathered around me a host of angels, even a great number, with their backs to me and their faces to the outer world. Then stepped one in the direction of the pit. Old Satan and his angels, growling with anger and trembling with fear, hopped back into the pit. Finally again there came a voice unto me saying, "Go in peace and fear not, for lo! I will throw around you a strong arm of protection. Neither shall your oppressors be able to confound you. I will make your enemies feed you and those who despise you take you in. Rejoice and be exceedingly glad, for I have saved you through grace by faith, not of yourself but as a gift of God. Be strong and fear not. Amen."

I rose from the ground shouting and praising God. Within me there was a crying, "Holy! Holy! Holy is the Lord!"

I must have been in this trance for more than an hour. I went on to the barn and found my master there waiting for me. Again I began to tell him of my experience. I do not recall what he did to me afterwards. I felt burdened down and that preaching was my only relief. When I had finished I felt a great love in my heart that made me feel like stooping and kissing the very ground. My master sat watching and listening to me, and then he began to cry. He turned from me and said in a broken voice, "Morte, I believe you are a preacher. From now on you can preach to the people here on my place in the old shed by the creek. But tomorrow morning, Sunday, I want you to preach to my family and neighbors. So put on your best clothes and be in front of the big house early in the morning, about nine o'clock."

I was so happy that I did not know what to do. I thanked my master and then God, for I felt that he was with me. Throughout the night I went from cabin to cabin, rejoicing and spreading the news.

The next morning at the time appointed I stood up on two planks in front of the porch of the big house and, without a Bible or anything, I began to preach to my master and the people. My thoughts came so fast that I could hardly speak fast enough. My soul caught on fire, and soon I had them all in tears. I told them that God had a chosen people and that he had raised me up as an example of his matchless love. I told them that they must be born again and that their souls must be freed from the shackles of hell.

Ever since that day I have been preaching the gospel and am not a bit tired. I can tell anyone about God in the darkest hour of midnight, for it is written on my heart. Amen.

Memoir of the Life, Religious Experience, Ministerial Travels, and Labours of Mrs. Elaw

I was born in the United States of America, in the State of Pennsylvania, and of religious parents. When about six years of age, my mother's parents, who resided on their own farm, far in the interior of America, at a distance of many hundred miles, came to visit us. My parents had three children then living; the eldest, a boy about twelve years of age, myself, and a younger sister. On his return, my grandfather took my brother with him, promising to bring him up to the business of his farm; and I saw him not again until more than thirty years afterwards.

At twelve years of age I was bereaved of my mother, who died in childbirth of her twenty-second child, all of whom, with the exception of three, died in infancy. My father, having placed my younger sister under the care of her aunt, then consigned me to the care of Pierson and Rebecca Mitchel, with whom I remained until I attained the age of eighteen. After I had been with the above-mentioned persons one year and six months, it pleased God to remove my dear father to the world of spirits; and, being thus bereft of my natural guardians, I had no other friends on earth to look to but those kind benefactors under whom my dear father had placed me.

But that God whose mercy endureth for ever, still continued mindful of me; but oh, what a change did I experience in my new abode from that to which I had been accustomed. In my father's house, family devotion was regularly attended to morning and evening; prayer was offered up, and the praises of God were sung; but the persons with whom I now resided were Quakers, and their religious exercises, if they observed any, were performed in the secret silence of the mind; nor were religion and devotion referred to by them in my hearing, which rendered my transition from home the more strange; and, being very young, and no apparent religious restraint being laid upon me, I soon gave way to the evil propensities of an unregenerate heart, which is enmity against God, and heedlessly ran into the ways of sin, taking pleasure in the paths of folly. But that God, whose eyes are ever over all his handy works, suffered me not unchecked to pursue the courses of sin. My father's death frequently introduced very serious reflections into my mind; and often was I deeply affected, and constrained to weep before God, when no human eye beheld my emotion. But, notwithstanding these seasons of serious contrition, my associations with the juvenile members of the family were too generally marked by the accustomed gaities of a wanton heart. Our childish conversations sometimes turned upon the day of judgment, and our appearance in the presence of the great God on that portentous occasion, which originated in my breast the most solemn emotions whenever I was alone; for I felt myself to be so exceedingly sinful, that I was certain of meeting with condemnation at the bar of God. I knew not what to do; nor were there any persons to whom I durst open my mind upon the subject, and therefore remained ignorant of the great remedy disclosed by the plan of salvation afforded by the gospel, and incapable of religious progress. I was at times deeply affected with penitence, but could not rightly comprehend what it was that ailed me. Sometimes I resolutely shook off all my impressions, and became more thoughtless than before; one instance, in particular, is so riveted on my memory, that I shall never forget it when ever I glance back upon my youthful life. On this occasion I was talking very foolishly, and even ventured to take the name of God in vain, in order to cater to the sinful tastes of my companions; it well pleased their carnal minds, and they laughed with delight at my profanity; but, whilst I was in the very act of swearing, I looked up, and imagined that I saw God looking down and frowning upon me: my tongue was instantly silenced; and I retired from my frolicsome companions to reflect upon what I had said and done. To the praise of divine mercy, that God who willeth not the death of a sinner, but rather that all should turn unto him and live [Ezek. 18:32], did not even now abandon me, but called me by an effectual call through the following dream. It was a prevailing notion in that part of the world with many, that whatever a person dreamed between the times of twilight and sunrise, was prophetically ominous, and would shortly come to pass; and, on that very night, after I had offended my heavenly Father by taking His name in vain, He aroused and alarmed my spirit, by presenting before me in a dream the awful terrors of the day of judgment accompanied by its terrific thunders. I thought that the Angel Gabriel came and proclaimed that time should be no longer; and he said, "Jehovah was about to judge the world, and execute judgment on it." I then exclaimed in my dream, "Oh, Lord, what shall I do? I am unprepared to meet thee." I then meditated an escape, but could not effect it; and in this horrific dilemma I awoke: the day was just dawning; and the intense horror of my guilty mind was such as to defy description. I was now about fourteen years of age; and this dream proved an effectual call to my soul. I meditated deeply upon it, my spirits became greatly depressed, and I wept excessively. I was naturally of a very lively and active disposition, and the shock my feelings had sustained from this alarming dream, attracted the attention of my mistress, who inquired the reason of so great a change. I related my dream to her, and also stated my sentiments with respect to it: she used every endeavour to comfort me, saying that it was only a dream; that dreams have nothing ominous in them; and I ought not to give myself any more concern respecting it: but she failed in her attempt to tranquilize my mind, because the convictions of my sinfulness in the sight of God, and incompetency to meet my Judge, were immoveable and distressing. I now gave myself much to meditation, and lisped out my simple and feeble prayers to God, as well as my limited apprehensions and youthful abilities admitted. About this time, the Methodists made their first appearance in that part of the country, and I was permitted to attend their meetings once a fortnight, on the Sabbath afternoons, from which I derived great satisfaction; but the divine work on my soul was a very gradual one, and my way was prepared as the dawning of the morning. I never experienced that terrific dread of hell by which some Christians appear to have been exercised; but I felt a godly sorrow for sin in having grieved my God by a course of disobedience to His commands. I had been trained to attend the Quaker meetings; and, on their preaching occasions, I was pleased to be in attendance, and often found comfort from the word ministered by them; but I was, notwithstanding, usually very much cast down on account of my sins before God; and in this state I continued many months before I could attain sufficient confidence to say, "My Lord and my God." But as the darkness was gradually dispelled, the light dawned upon my mind, and I increased in knowledge daily; yet I possessed no assurance of my acceptance before God; though I enjoyed a greater peace of mind in waiting upon my heavenly father than at any previous time; my prayer was daily for the Lord to assure me of the forgiveness of my sins; and I at length proved the verification of the promise, "They that seek shall find" [Luke 11:9]; for, one evening, whilst singing one of the songs of Zion, I distinctly saw the Lord Jesus approach me with open arms, and a most divine and heavenly smile upon his countenance. As He advanced towards me, I felt that his very looks spoke, and said, "Thy prayer is accepted, I own thy name." From that day to the present I have never entertained a doubt of the manifestation of his love to my soul.

Yea, I may say further than this; because, at the time when this occurrence took place, I was milking in the cow stall; and the manifestation of his presence was so clearly apparent, that even the beast of the stall turned her head and bowed herself upon the ground. Oh, never, never shall I forget the scene. Some persons, perhaps, may be incredulous, and say, "How can these things be, and in what form did He appear?" Dear reader, whoever thou art, into whose hands this narrative may fall, I will try to gratify thee by endeavouring to describe his manifestation. It occurred as I was singing the following lines:—

"Oh, when shall I see Jesus,
    And dwell with him above;
And drink from flowing fountains,
    Of everlasting love.
When shall I be delivered
    From this vain world of sin;
And, with my blessed Jesus,
    Drink endless pleasures in?"

As I was milking the cow and singing, I turned my head, and saw a tall figure approaching, who came and stood by me. He had long hair, which parted in the front and came down on his shoulders; he wore a long white robe down to the feet; and as he stood with open arms and smiled upon me, he disappeared. I might have tried to imagine, or persuade myself, perhaps, that it had been a vision presented merely to the eye of my mind; but, the beast of the stall gave forth her evidence to the reality of the heavenly appearance; for she turned her head and looked round as I did; and when she saw, she bowed her knees and cowered down upon the ground. I was overwhelmed with astonishment at the sight, but the thing was certain and beyond all doubt. I write as before God and Christ, and declare, as I shall give an account to my Judge at the great day, that every thing I have written in this little book, has been written with conscientious veracity and scrupulous adherence to truth.

After this wonderful manifestation of my condescending Saviour, the peace of God which passeth understanding was communicated to my heart; and joy in the Holy Ghost, to a degree, at the last, unutterable by my tongue and indescribable by my pen; it was beyond my comprehension; but, from that happy hour, my soul was set at glorious liberty; and, like the Ethiopic eunuch [Acts 8:26ff], I went on my way rejoicing in the blooming prospects of a better inheritance with the saints in light.

This, my dear reader, was the manner of my soul's conversion to God, told in language unvarnished by the graces of educated eloquence, nor transcending the capacity of a child to understand.

On Account of the Abolition of the African Slave Trade

EXODUS, iii. 7, 8: And the Lord said, I have surely seen the affliction of my people which are in Egypt, and have heard their cry by reason of their taskmasters; for I know their sorrows; and I am come down to deliver them out of the hand of the Egyptians.

These words, my brethren, contain a short account of some of the circumstances which preceded the deliverance of the children of Israel from their captivity and bondage in Egypt.

They mention, in the first place, their affliction. This consisted in their privation of liberty: they were slaves to the kings of Egypt, in common with their other subjects; and they were slaves to their fellow slaves. They were compelled to work in the open air, in one of the hottest climates in the world; and, probably, without a covering from the burning rays of the sun. Their work was of a laborious kind: it consisted of making bricks, and travelling, perhaps to a great distance, for the straw, or stubble, that was a component part of them. Their work was dealt out to them in tasks, and performed under the eye of vigilant and rigorous masters, who constantly upbraided them with idleness. The least deficiency in the product of their labour, was punished by beating. Nor was this all. Their food was of the cheapest kind, and contained but little nourishment: it consisted only of leeks and onions, which grew almost spontaneously in the land of Egypt. Painful and distressing as these sufferings were, they constituted the smallest part of their misery. While the fields resounded with their cries in the day, their huts and hamlets were vocal at night with their lamentations over their sons; who were dragged from the arms of their mothers, and put to death by drowning, in order to prevent such an increase in their population as to endanger the safety of the state by an insurrection. In this condition, thus degraded and oppressed, they passed nearly four hundred years. Ah! who can conceive of the measure of their sufferings, during that time? What tongue, or pen, can compute the number of their sorrows? To them no morning or evening sun ever disclosed a single charm: to them, the beauties of spring, and the plenty of autumn had no attractions: even domestick endearments were scarcely known to them: all was misery; all was grief; all was despair.

Our text mentions, in the second place, that, in this situation, they were not forgotten by the God of their fathers, and the Father of the human race. Though, for wise reasons, he delayed to appear in their behalf for several hundred years, yet he was not indifferent to their sufferings. Our text tells us that he saw their affliction, and heard their cry: his eye and his ear were constantly open to their complaint: every tear they shed was preserved, and every groan they uttered was recorded, in order to testify, at a future day, against the authors of their oppressions. But our text goes further: it describes the judge of the world to be so much moved, with what he saw and what he heard, that he rises from his throne—not to issue a command to the armies of angels that surrounded him to fly to the relief of his suffering children—but to come down from heaven in his own person, in order to deliver them out of the hands of the Egyptians. Glory to God for this precious record of his power and goodness: let all the nations of the earth praise him. Clouds and darkness are round about him, but righteousness and judgment are the habitation of his throne. O sing unto the Lord a new song, for he hath done marvelous things: his right hand and his holy arm hath gotten him the victory. He hath remembered his mercy and truth toward the house of Israel, and all the ends of the earth shall see the salvation of God.

The history of the world shows us that the deliverance of the children of Israel from their bondage is not the only instance in which it has pleased God to appear in behalf of oppressed and distressed nations, as the deliverer of the innocent, and of those who call upon his name. He is as unchangeable in his nature and character as he is in his wisdom and power. The great and blessed event, which we have this day met to celebrate, is a striking proof that the God of heaven and earth is the same, yesterday, and today, and forever. Yes, my brethren, the nations from which most of us have descended, and the country in which some of us were born, have been visited by the tender mercy of the Common Father of the human race. He has seen the affliction of our countrymen, with an eye of pity. He has seen the wicked arts, by which wars have been fomented among the different tribes of the Africans, in order to procure captives, for the purpose of selling them for slaves. He has seen ships fitted out from different ports in Europe and America, and freighted with trinkets to be exchanged for the bodies and souls of men. He has seen the anguish which has taken place when parents have been torn from their children, and children from their parents, and conveyed, with their hands and feet bound in fetters, on board of ships prepared to receive them. He has seen them thrust in crowds into the holds of those ships, where many of them have perished from the want of air. He has seen such of them as have escaped from that noxious place of confinement, leap into the ocean, with a faint hope of swimming back to their native shore, or a determination to seek an early retreat from their impending misery, in a watery grave. He has seen them exposed for sale, like horses and cattle, upon the wharves; or like bales of goods, in warehouses of West India and American sea ports. He has seen the pangs of separation between members of the same family. He has seen them driven into the sugar, the rice, and the tobacco fields, and compelled to work—in spite of the habits of ease which they derived from the natural fertility of their own country—in the open air, beneath a burning sun, with scarcely as much clothing upon them as modesty required. He has seen them faint beneath the pressure of their labours. He has seen them return to their smoky huts in the evening, with nothing to satisfy their hunger but a scanty allowance of roots; and these, cultivated for themselves, on that day only, which God ordained as a day of rest for man and beast. He has seen the neglect with which their masters have treated their immortal souls; not only in withholding religious instruction from them, but, in some instances, depriving them of access to the means of obtaining it. He has seen all the different modes of torture, by means of the whip, the screw, the pincers, and the red-hot iron, which have been exercised upon their bodies, by inhuman overseers: overseers, did I say? Yes: but not by these only. Our God has seen masters and mistresses, educated in fashionable life, sometimes take the instruments of torture into their own hands, and, deaf to the cries and shrieks of their agonizing slaves, exceed even their overseers in cruelty. Inhuman wretches! though You have been deaf to their cries and shrieks, they have been heard in Heaven. The ears of Jehovah have been constantly open to them: He has heard the prayers that have ascended from the hearts of his people; and he has, as in the case of his ancient and chosen people the Jews, *come down to deliver* our suffering countrymen from the hands of their oppressors. He *came down* into the United States, when they declared, in the constitution which they framed in 1788, that the trade in our African fellowmen should cease in the year 1808: He *came down* into the British Parliament, when they passed a law to put an end to the same iniquitous trade in May, 1807: He *came down* into the Congress of the United States, the last winter, when they passed a similar law, the operation of which commences on this happy day. Dear land of our ancestors! thou shalt no more be stained with the blood of thy children, shed by British and American hands: the ocean shall no more afford a refuge to their bodies, from impending slavery: nor shall the shores of the British West India islands, and of the United States, any more witness the anguish of families, parted for ever by a publick sale. For this signal interposition of the God of mercies, in behalf of our brethren, it becomes us this day to offer our united thanks. Let the song of angels, which was first heard in the air at the birth of our Savior, be heard this day in our assembly: Glory to God in the highest, for these first fruits of peace upon earth, and good-will to man: O! let us give thanks unto the Lord: let us call upon his name, and make known his deeds among the people. Let us sing psalms unto him and talk of all his wonderous works.

Having enumerated the mercies of God to our nation, it becomes us to ask, What shall we render unto the Lord for them? Sacrifices and burnt offerings are no longer pleasing to him: the pomp of public worship, and the ceremonies of a festive day, will find no acceptance with him, unless they are accompanied with actions that correspond with them. The duties which are inculcated upon us, by the event we are now celebrating, divide themselves into five heads.

In the first place, Let not our expressions of gratitude to God for his late goodness and mercy to our countrymen, be confined to this day, nor to this house: let us carry grateful hearts with us to our places of abode, and to our daily occupations; and let praise and thanksgivings ascend daily to the throne of grace, in our families, and in our closets, for what God has done for our African brethren. Let us not forget to praise him for his mercies to such of our colour as are inhabitants of this country; particularly, for disposing the hearts of the rulers of many of the states to pass laws for the abolition of slavery; for the number and zeal of the friends he has raised up to plead our cause; and for the privileges we enjoy, of worshiping God agreeably to our consciences, in churches of our own. This comely building, erected chiefly by the generosity of our friends, is a monument of God's goodness to us, and calls for our gratitude with all the other blessings that have been mentioned.

Secondly, Let us unite, with our thanksgiving, prayer to Almighty God, for the completion of his begun goodness to our brethren in Africa. Let us beseech him to extend to all the nations in Europe, the same humane and just spirit towards them, which he has imparted to the British and American nations. Let us, further, implore the influences of his divine and holy Spirit, to dispose the hearts of our legislatures to pass laws, to ameliorate the condition of our brethren who are still in bondage; also, to dispose their masters to treat them with kindness and humanity; and, above all things, to favour them with the means of acquiring such parts of human knowledge, as will enable them to read the holy scriptures, and understand the doctrines of the Christian religion, whereby they may become, even while they are the slaves of men, the freemen of the Lord.

Thirdly, Let us conduct ourselves in such a manner as to furnish no cause of regret to the deliverers of our nation, for their kindness to us. Let us constantly remember the rock whence we were hewn, and the pit whence we were digged. Pride was not made for man, in any situation; and, still less, for persons who have recently emerged from bondage. The Jews, after they entered the promised land, were commanded, when they offered sacrifices to the Lord, never to forget their humble origin; and hence, part of the worship that accompanied their sacrifices consisted in acknowledging, that a Syrian, ready to perish, was their father: in like manner, it becomes us, publickly and privately, to acknowledge, that an African slave, ready to perish, was our father or our grandfather. Let our conduct be regulated by the precepts of the gospel; let us be sober-minded, humble, peaceable, temperate in our meats and drinks, frugal in our apparel and in the furniture of our houses, industrious in our occupations, just in all our dealings, and ever ready to honour all men. Let us teach our children the rudiments of the English language, in order to enable them to acquire a knowledge of useful trades; and, above all things, let us instruct them in the principles of the gospel of Jesus Christ, whereby they may become wise unto salvation. It has always been a mystery, why the impartial Father of the human race should have permitted the transportation of so many millions of our fellow creatures to this country, to endure all the miseries of slavery. Perhaps his design was that a knowledge of the gospel might be acquired by some of their descendants, in order that they might become qualified to be the messengers of it, to the land of their fathers. Let this thought animate us, when we are teaching our children to love and adore the name of our Redeemer. Who knows but that a Joseph may rise up among them, who shall be the instrument of feeding the African nations with the bread of life, and of saving them, not from earthly bondage, but from the more galling yoke of sin and Satan.

Fourthly, Let us be grateful to our benefactors, who, by enlightening the minds of the rulers of the earth, by means of their publications and remonstrances against the trade in our countrymen, have produced the great event we are this day celebrating. Abolition societies and individuals have equal claims to our gratitude. It would be difficult to mention the names of any of our benefactors, without offending many whom we do not know. Some of them are gone to heaven, to receive the reward of their labours of love towards us; and the kindness and benevolence of the survivors, we hope, are recorded in the book of life, to be mentioned with honour when our Lord shall come to reward his faithful servants before an assembled world.

Fifthly, and lastly, Let the first of January, the day of the abolition of the slave trade in our country, be set apart in every year, as a day of publick thanksgiving for that mercy. Let the history of the sufferings of our brethren, and of their deliverance, descend by this means to our children to the remotest generations; and when they shall ask, in time to come, saying, What mean the lessons, the psalms, the prayers and the praises in the worship of this day? let us answer them, by saying, the Lord, on the day of which this is the anniversary, abolished the trade which dragged your fathers from their native country, and sold them as bondmen in the United States of America.

Oh thou God of all the nations upon the earth! we thank thee, that thou art no respecter of persons, and that thou hast made of one blood all nations of men. We thank thee, that thou hast appeared, in the fullness of time, in behalf

of the nation from which most of the worshipping people, now before thee,
are descended. We thank thee, that the sun of righteousness has at last shed
his morning beams upon them. Rend thy heavens, O Lord, and come down
upon the earth; and grant that the mountains, which now obstruct the perfect
day of thy goodness and mercy towards them, may flow down at thy presence. Send thy gospel, we beseech thee, among them. May the nations, which
now sit in darkness, behold and rejoice in its light. May Ethiopia soon stretch
out her hands unto thee, and lay hold of the gracious promise of thy everlasting covenant. Destroy, we beseech thee, all the false religions which now prevail among them; and grant, that they may soon cast their idols, to the moles
and the bats of the wilderness. O, hasten that glorious time, when the knowledge of the gospel of Jesus Christ, shall cover the earth, as the waters cover
the sea; when the wolf shall dwell with the lamb, and, the leopard shall lie
down with the kid, and the calf and the young lion and the fatling together,
and a little child shall lead them; and, when, instead of the thorn, shall come
up the fir tree, and, instead of the brier, shall come up the myrtle tree: and it
shall be to the Lord for a name and for an everlasting sign that shall not be cut
off. We pray, O God, for all our friends and benefactors in Great Britain, as
well as in the United States: reward them, we beseech thee, with blessings
upon earth, and prepare them to enjoy the fruits of their kindness to us, in
the everlasting kingdom in heaven; and dispose us, who are assembled in thy
presence, to be always thankful for thy mercies, and to act as becomes a people who owe so much to thy goodness. We implore thy blessing, O God, upon
the President, and all who are in authority in the United States. Direct them
by thy wisdom, in all their deliberations, and O save thy people from the
calamities of war. Give peace in our day, we beseech thee, O thou God of
peace! and grant, that this highly favoured country may continue to afford a
safe and peaceful retreat from the calamities of war and slavery, for ages yet to
come. We implore all these blessings and mercies, only in the name of thy
beloved Son, Jesus Christ, our Lord. And now, O Lord, we desire, with angels
and arch-angels, and all the company of heaven, ever more to praise thee, saying, *Holy, holy, holy, Lord God* Almighty: *the whole earth is full of thy glory.*
Amen.

Persuading:
Witnessing, Controversies,
and Polemics

—— 29 ——

Native American Visionary Experience
and Christian Missions

Michael D. McNally

Although quite a few Native American peoples accepted baptism and the other sacraments offered by Christian missionaries, and although some even embraced more fully Anglo-, Franco-, or Spanish-American Christian cultures, many native people rejected outright the missionary message and cultures. The religious life of many contemporary Native American communities testifies to the continuity of non-Christian religious beliefs and practices. Historians have frequently pointed to this phenomenon from a distance, but the available documentary record provides little detailed insight into the internal dynamics of the maintenance of tradition because that record was largely shaped by the interests of the missionaries themselves. More recently, ethnohistorians have paid increasing attention to the way that missionaries described the practices of those who styled themselves as opponents to the Christianizing project.

Downstream from the confluence of Native American religious traditions and the beliefs of various Christian missionaries, many swirls and eddies of religious change have formed. The process defies reduction to a singular pattern of accommodation, resistance, conversion, acculturation, or nativism. Even the traditional religions, notwithstanding the remarkable continuities they maintained, were freshly articulated in light of the dramatic changes of microbial, social, and cultural interaction with Europeans and/or other native peoples already in contact with Europeans. New boundaries were expressed that set off traditional ways more clearly from the "dangerous" ways of Christianity. Since the oral traditions of Native American religions seldom found expression in the religious idiom of creed or systematic theology, the boundaries were primarily defined and maintained not in the elaborated codes of right belief but in terms of rhetorical and ritual practices.

The two documents that follow bear witness to the place of polemic and ritual in the Ojibwes' articulation of boundaries that set off native religions from those of missionaries. Both were penned by Christians—the first a nonnative, the second native—but each bears witness to the rhetorical and ritual practices of resolutely non-Christian Ojibwes. In each case, visions provided the sacred authority for the rejection of the Christian missionaries' message.

The first text is a polemic rooted in a visionary experience that we moderns might label as a "near-death" experience. Though very brief, the story captured native imaginations and circulated widely among different native peoples in the nineteenth century. These people often expressed confusion about the contradictions between the gospel proclaimed by missionaries and the behavior missionaries exhibited with respect to their native hosts. The text is an apocryphal story of an Indian convert whose visionary journey to the afterlife persuaded him to abandon Christianity and to proclaim his vision to others, lest they be deceived.

Missionaries and native Christians were frequently confronted with this story, and it spread like fireweed in the devastated social terrain of nineteenth-century Ojibwe life. In particular, the vision conveyed a bitter truth that native converts, no matter how well they conformed to what missionaries considered "civilized," were destined to be viewed as "not quite white." Color mattered in this story. So, too, did religious affiliation, and the story traces the outlines of an emerging critique of native Christianity within many sectors of the Ojibwe population.

Although the story circulated widely in the oral tradition, it was noted here among the Ojibwes of the southwestern shore of Lake Superior. The recorder was Sherman Hall, a missionary in the Reformed tradition at a post of the American Board of Commissioners for Foreign Missions at LaPointe, in what is now northern Wisconsin. The story speaks to the continued belief in the power of visionary experience to interpret the world.

The second story concerns the message of Tenskwatawa, the Shawnee prophet whose visions provided the religious authority behind the anticolonial movement typically attributed to his brother Tecumseh. The movement offered a significant ally to the British in the War of 1812, but American victory prevented the movement from halting American expansion. The movement is nonetheless significant historically for the way it fused militant anticolonial resistance with an attempt to bridge cultural and linguistic differences among tribes in favor of an intertribal "red" identity. Although it was one among many such prophetic intertribal movements in the eighteenth and nineteenth centuries, it was the most significant because of its enormous reach. At the height of his influence in the years before 1811, Tenskwatawa claimed an enthusiastic following among Shawnee, Miami, Delaware, Wendat, Ojibwe, Odawa, and Potawatomi peoples, as well as others from what is now Michigan, Illinois, Wisconsin, Minnesota, Iowa, Ohio, and Kentucky. Under Tecumseh's ministrations, the movement formed ties to militant Cherokees and Muskogees, or Creeks, far to the south, but it proved less formidable than the divide-and-conquer tactics of a well-armed, expansionist United States.

In this account William Warren (1825–1853), a government interpreter and early legislator in Minnesota Territory, recalls how the message of "Shawano Prophet," as Warren refers to Tenskwatawa, was received in 1808 by Ojibwes living many days' journey away. Warren writes rather dismissively of Tenskwatawa as a charlatan, but although some Ojibwes clearly shared this point of view, it is important to remember that a number of Ojibwes participated in Tecumseh's movement.

At that time, Tenskwatawa held court at a community known as Prophetstown, near the confluence of Indiana's Wabash River and Tippecanoe Creek. Prophetstown itself was an artifact of Tenskwatawa's visions, designed expressly in accordance with the dictates of the Great Spirit and placed provocatively in territory that already had been ceded to the United States by accommodationist native leaders. Once a ne'er-do-well, Tecumseh's brother fell into a trance in the winter of 1804–5 and emerged to tell of a visionary sojourn with the "Master of Life" to behold a heavenly paradise of "a rich, fertile country, abounding in game, fish, pleasant hunting grounds and fine corn fields"—a place that would be off-limits to sinful native peoples, who would be consigned to a hell of eternal fire (Edmunds, p. 33). As a result of this first in his series of visions, Tecumseh's brother took a new name, Tenskwatawa, or "the Open Door," signaling the importance of his teachings as a portal to paradise. In subsequent visions, the Open Door would elaborate on the cosmic distinctions between the native, or "red," peoples and Europeans, who were revealed to be the offspring of an evil spirit. In light of the experienced dispossession and chaos of colonialism and expansion, native peoples were called through Tenskwatawa's visions to emphasize their common identity as "red" and to define themselves in contrast to Europeans, their cultures, and their religions.

Tenskwatawa's distinctions did not, however, correspond fully to what we might consider the racial or ethnic boundaries distinguishing native Americans and Europeans. In one respect, the anti-European message was directed more at Americans than at the British or other potential European allies. In another respect, the polemic was also directed against native people deemed to be sellouts, treaty makers, Christian converts, or "mission Indians," who settled into the agrarian life promoted by—and protected by—missionaries. What is more, as the following account details, the polemic was also directed at those traditional religions deemed impure because of their contamination by colonizing influences. Most of the native leaders whose treaty making Tenskwatawa decried were hardly enthusiastic Christians but rather traditionalist elder leaders themselves, often associated with tribal-specific religious societies, and shamans who often turned out to be Tenskwatawa's worst critics. Some years after the following account, Tenskwatawa's visions turned inward, provoking witch-hunts that led to the execution of native opponents.

And yet, the prophet's overall message was an ethical one; it expressed the spiritual urgency of bridging cultural and linguistic barriers in a sacred alliance with the "Master of Life." Tenskwatawa called his followers back to an ethic of sobriety, harmony, and peace with one another. They were to bury the hatchets of inter-tribal hostilities and to refrain from the domestic violence associated with lives under colonialism. They were to shun the values of the market, wealth accumulation, and class distinction and return to the economic ethics of subsistence and communalism. Followers were directed to abandon exploitative practices and to reaffirm aboriginal ethical commitments to the "nonhuman persons" of the land, especially animals overexploited in the fur trade.

The polemical distinctions asserted through the prophet's visions were to be reiterated through ritualized practices that erected and maintained boundaries separating order from chaos, "indigenous" from "European," purity from danger. Anchored in the prophet's cosmic visions of the polygenesis of white and red people, the practices were incumbent on followers to help usher in a divine restoration of cosmic balance. Intermarriage was prohibited. Those obeying the prophet (and through him the Great Spirit) were to purify themselves from the contamination of colonial contact by eating foods and drinking fluids indigenous to the land—and refusing foods introduced by Europeans, especially bread, pork, beef, and alcohol. They were to phase out usage of technologies introduced by Europeans. They were to extinguish all fires potentially derived from flint and steel and to restart fires from sacred fires ritually ignited by the rubbing of sticks.

Tenskwatawa's message articulated clear boundaries between Christianity and Native American traditions; it also articulated boundaries between the religion of the prophet and the religious traditions of the Ojibwes more directly associated with the Grand Medicine Lodge, or the Midéwiwin religious society. Thus, what was ostensibly a movement to bring unity across the "red race" in fact brought a level of religious discord within communities like the Ojibwe. Lines of division frequently accentuated differences in age, pitting enthusiasts of the prophet and his militant message among the "young men" against traditional elder "chiefs and headmen" and elder leaders of the Midéwiwin society.

Because Tenskwatawa did not commit his prophetic instructions to print, our record of the practices that distinguished his movement from both the Christianity of the missionaries and the tribal traditions of the Ojibwe must be obtained through the narrative of observers. The observer in this case is William Warren, one of several educated Ojibwes who in the later nineteenth century documented the Ojibwe culture and history of the earlier years of the century. Although Warren's narrative remains skeptical of Tenskwatawa's teachings, it faithfully relates the details of the movement's practices as they were taught in the field.

The first text is in a letter from Sherman Hall to David Greene, October 17, 1834, Papers of the American Board of Commissioners for Foreign Missions, reproduced in the Grace Lee Nute Collection, box 3, folder 7, Minnesota Historical Society, St. Paul. The second selection is from William W. Warren, *History of the Ojibway People,* in *Collections of the Minnesota Historical Society,* vol. 5 (St. Paul: Minnesota Historical Society, 1885); pp. 321–325.

Further Reading

Gregory Evans Dowd, *A Spirited Resistance: The North American Indian Struggle for Unity, 1745–1815* (Baltimore: Johns Hopkins University Press, 1992); R. David Edmunds, *The Shawnee Prophet* (Lincoln: University of Nebraska Press, 1983); Joel Martin, *Sacred Revolt: the Muskogees' Struggle for a New World* (Boston: Beacon, 1991); James Mooney, *The Ghost Dance Religion and Wounded Knee* (New York: Dover, 1973).

Heavenly Vision, Recorded by Hall

One day an Indian, of whom we entertain some hope that he has not listened in vain to the Gospel invitation, came to our house, and said that the chiefs had reported the case of a pious, or in their dialect, a praying Indian, who died far away to the North. He had prayed a long time. On his death, he went to heaven, but was refused admittance on the ground that no praying *Indians* were admitted there. He then went to the place where the white people go, but was not received. He next went to the place where the Indians go, but was there told he had been a praying Indian, and had forsaken the customs of his fathers, and they would not receive him, and ordered him away. After these repulses he came back again to this world, and assumed the body which he had before inhabited. . . . Some were very much afraid of having anything said to them on religious subjects, after the circulation of this story.

Shawnee Prophet Tenskwatawa's Vision

In the year 1808, during the summer while John B. Corbin had charge of the Lac Coutereille post, messengers, whose faces were painted black, and whose actions appeared strange, arrived at the different principal villages of the Ojibways. In solemn councils they performed certain ceremonies, and told that the Great Spirit had at last condescended to hold communion with the red race, through the medium of a Shawano [Shawnee] prophet, and that they had been sent to impart the glad tidings. The Shawano sent them word that the Great Spirit was about to take pity on his red children, whom he had long forsaken for their wickedness. He bade them to return to the primitive usages and customs of their ancestors, to leave off the use of everything which the evil white race had introduced among them. Even the fire-steel must be discarded, and fire made as in ages past, by the friction of two sticks. And this fire, once lighted in their principal villages, must always be kept sacred and burning. He bade them to discard the use of fire-water [alcohol]—to give up lying and stealing and warring with one another. He even struck at some of the roots of the Me-da-we [Midéwiwin] religion, which he asserted had become permeated with many evil medicines, and had lost almost altogether its original uses and purity. He bade the medicine men to throw away their evil and poisonous medicines, and to forget the songs and ceremonies attached thereto, and he introduced new medicines and songs in their place. He prophesied that the day was nigh, when, if the red race listened to and obeyed his words, the Great Spirit would deliver them from their dependence on the whites, and prevent their being finally down-trodden and exterminated by them. The prophet invited the Ojibways to come and meet him at Detroit, where in person, he would explain to them the revelations of the "Great Master of Life." He even claimed the power of causing the dead to arise, and come again to life.

It is astonishing how quickly this new belief obtained possession in the minds of the Ojibways. It spread like wild-fire throughout their entire country, and even reached the remotest northern hunters who had allied themselves with the Crees and Assiniboines. The strongest possible proof which can be adduced of their entire belief, is in their obeying the mandate to throw away their medicine bags, which the Indian holds most sacred and inviolate. It is said that the shores of Sha-ga-waum-ik-ong [LaPointe, on Wisconsin's shore of Lake Superior] were strewed with the remains of medicine bags, which had been committed to the deep. At this place, the Ojibways collected in great numbers. Night and day, the ceremonies of the new religion were performed, till it was at last determined to go in a body to Detroit, to visit the prophet. One hundred and fifty canoes are said to have actually started from Pt. Shag-a-waum-ik-ong for this purpose, and so strong was their belief, that a dead child was brought from Lac Coutereille to be taken to the prophet for resuscitation. This large party arrived on their foolish journey, as far as the Pictured Rocks, on Lake Superior [on Michigan's Upper Peninsula], when meeting with Michel Cadotte [an influential trader at LaPointe], who had been to Sault Ste. Marie for his annual outfit of goods, his influence, together with information of the real motives of the prophet in sending for them, succeeded in turning them back. The few Ojibways who had gone to visit the prophet from the more eastern villages of the tribe, had returned home disappointed, and brought back exaggerated accounts of the suffering through hunger, which the proselytes of the prophet who had gathered at his call, were enduring, and also giving the lie to many of the attributes which he had assumed. It is said that at Detroit he would sometimes leave the camp of the Indians, and be gone, no one knew whither, for three and four days at a time. On his return he would assert that he had been to the spirit land and communed with the master of life. It was, however, soon discovered that he only went and hid himself in a hollow oak which stood behind the hill on which the most beautiful portion of Detroit City is now built. These stories became current among the Ojibways, and each succeeding year developing more fully the fraud and warlike purpose of the Shawano, the excitement gradually died away among the Ojibways, and the medicine men and chiefs who had become such ardent believers, hung their heads in shame whenever the Shawano was mentioned. At this day it is almost impossible to procure any information on this subject from the old men who are still living, who were once believers and preached their religion, so anxious are they to conceal the fact of their once having been so egregiously duped. The venerable chiefs Buffalo of La Pointe, and Esh-ke-bug-e-coshe of Leech Lake [in Minnesota], who have been men of strong minds and unusual intelligence, were not only firm believers of the prophet, but undertook to preach his doctrines.

One essential good resulted to the Ojibways through the Shawano excitement—they threw away their poisonous roots and medicines; and poisoning, which was formerly practiced by their worst class of medicine men, has since become almost entirely unknown. So much has been written respecting the prophet and the new beliefs which he endeavored to inculcate amongst his red brethren, that we will no longer dwell on the merits or demerits of his pretended mission. It is now evident that he and his brother Tecumseh had in view, and worked to effect, a general alliance of the red race, against the whites, and their final extermination from the "Great Island which the great spirit had given as an inheritance to his red children."

In giving an account of the Shawano excitement among the Ojibways, we have digressed somewhat from the course of our narrative. The messengers of the prophet reached the Ojibway village at Lac Coutereille, early in the summer of 1808, and the excitement which they succeeded in raising, tended greatly to embitter the Indians' mind against the white race. There was a considerable quantity of goods stored in Michel Cadotte's storehouse, which was located on the shores of the lake, and some of the most foolish of the Indians, headed by Nig-gig (The Otter)—who is still living [in 1852]—proposed to destroy the trader's goods, in accordance with the prophet's teachings to discard the use of everything which the white man had learned them to want. The influence of the chief Mons-o-ne at first checked the young men, but the least additional spark to their excitement caused his voice to be unheard, and his influence to be without effect. John Baptiste Corbin, a young Canadian of good education, was in charge of the post, and through his indiscretion the flame was lighted which led to the pillage of the post, and caused him to flee for his life, one hundred miles through a pathless wilderness, to the shores of Lake Superior. As was the general custom of the early French traders, he had taken to wife a young woman of the Lac Coutereille village, related to an influential family. During the Shawano excitement, he found occasion to give his wife a severe beating, and to send her away almost naked, from under his roof, to her parents' wigwam. This act exasperated the Indians; and as the tale spread from lodge to lodge, the young men leaped into their canoes and paddling over to the trading house, which stood about one mile opposite their village, they broke open the doors and helped themselves to all which the storehouses contained.

American Anti-Catholic Pornography

Peter Gardella

A pregnant eighteen-year-old came to New York in 1835, claiming she had escaped from a convent in Canada where Roman Catholic priests regularly raped and tortured nuns. With help from three Protestant ministers, the woman, Maria Monk, soon became a best-selling author. Before the Civil War, her *Awful Disclosures of the Hotel Dieu Nunnery* sold 300,000 copies to a total U.S. population of less than thirty million. The book sold more than any other yet printed in the United States. No American book would surpass it until 1852, when Harriet Beecher Stowe wrote *Uncle Tom's Cabin*. *Awful Disclosures* served the anti-Catholic movement in the same way that *Uncle Tom's Cabin* served the antislavery cause, with new editions continuing well into the twentieth century. In antebellum America, everyone would either have read Maria Monk or at least heard the most exciting and horrific things she wrote.

Modern readers may feel puzzled by the urgent interest that Maria Monk's text inspired in Americans of her time. Sensational images, such as nuns murdering newborn infants immediately after baptism and disposing of their bodies in a pit of lye, do appear, but the narrative offers few details. "In a private apartment, he treated me in a brutal manner," Monk writes of her first violation by a priest, "and, from two other priests, I afterwards received similar usage that evening." She does not linger over what this "usage" entailed. Sometimes Monk's *Awful Disclosures* do not disclose at all but only allude to acts that were "loathsome and indecent in the highest possible degree." Penances such as gagging, bondage, and imprisonment may be described more vividly, as in the following selection, but often are merely mentioned. On the other hand, *Awful Disclosures* included accounts of how the rooms were laid out in the convent Monk claimed to have fled.

Both Monk's reticence and the details she provided made her seem a reluctant witness to the truth. She was not supposed to be a novelist or a journalist but a victim giving testimony, and on that level her narrative seemed plausible. Even today, the first question most students ask about *Awful Disclosures* is whether it was true; as with all the most effective examples of persuasive literature, it connected with truth in some ways while distorting truth in others. For example, nuns did take vows to obey their superiors, nuns lived cloistered lives in convents to which the public was not admitted, and the penances administered in those convents extended to the mortification of the flesh, sometimes by means of whips. But when the book first appeared, most Protestants assumed the truth of Monk's most lurid charges. A distinguished novelist, James Fenimore Cooper, wrote to his wife that Monk presented convents as no better than brothels and as places where murder is a common pastime. Samuel F. B. Morse, the inventor of the telegraph and founder of the New York Academy of Design, thought for a time of marrying Maria Monk. Within months after Monk's book appeared, two ministers and a newspaper editor responded to the public outcry by going to the convent Monk named in Montreal and searching for the lye pit, the dungeons, and the tunnel for priests that she described.

When the investigators found nothing, some accused them of Catholic sympathies or said that the nuns and priests had hidden evidence, but Monk's story began to unravel. A second woman claiming to be an escaped nun arrived in New York, and her lack of credibility weakened public acceptance of Monk. Contacted in Canada, Monk's mother said that her daughter had been insane since a childhood accident and had been confined not in a convent but in a prison hospital for prostitutes that was run by nuns. Monk's most modern editor, Nancy Schultz, suggests that she may have first used the escaped nun story as a way to gain sympathy, and perhaps higher fees, from her customers when she lived on the streets of Montreal. By 1838 Monk was pregnant again, and she died in prison in 1849 while serving a sentence for picking the pockets of a customer in a New York brothel. One of Monk's daughters later became a nun and wrote a book repudiating her mother.

However thoroughly Maria Monk's charges were refuted, her book helped to begin a tradition of writing on Catholic immorality that flourished in the United States because it reflected a real crisis in history and culture. According to one scholarly estimate, twenty-five newspapers, thirteen magazines, and about three hundred books devoted exclusively to attacks on the Roman Catholic Church appeared in the United States before 1860. A magazine editor of the time remarked that abuse of Catholics was "part of the regular industry of the country, as much as the making of nutmegs, or the construction of clocks."

Authors of specifically anticonventual literature ranged in prominence from George Bourne, famed as the first to advocate the immediate abolition of slavery, who wrote an elaborate narrative called *Lorette, the History of Louise, Daughter of a Canadian Nun, Exhibiting the Interior of Female Convents* in 1833, to the obscure "Mrs. L. Larned," who published *The American Nun; or the Effects of Romance* in 1836. Benjamin Barker's lurid melodrama, *Cecilia; or the White Nun of the Wilderness: A Romance of Love and Intrigue*, went through many editions between 1833 and 1845. Later and more professional efforts, such as *The Beautiful Nun* (Philadelphia, 1866) by well-known dime novelist Ned Buntline and Julia MacNair Wright's *Secrets of the Convent and Confessional* (Cincinnati, Memphis, Atlanta, and Chicago,

1873), offered more entertainment value but carried less conviction. The decades following Monk's *Awful Disclosures* produced purportedly factual convent exposes of many kinds, including several by former priests such as William Hogan of Philadelphia, who wrote *Auricular Confession and Popish Nunneries* (Hartford, 1847) and the Italian Alessandro Gavazzi, whose *Lectures Complete of Father Gavazzi* appeared in New York in 1854. Among the anti-Catholic newspapers featuring convent exposes was *The Downfall of Popery*, edited by a former priest named Samuel B. Smith, who sponsored public appearances by Maria Monk and by the other woman who had supposedly escaped from the same convent.

To understand why this flood of anti-Catholic and anticonventual literature flowed through American culture demands a perspective unavailable in most secondary schools and colleges, partly because the separation of church and state results in reluctance to deal with religion as a factor in history. Students can take many courses without learning that, before the 1830s, the United States was the most Protestant nation in the history of the world. Even Calvin's Geneva and Presbyterian Scotland had cathedrals and cities named for saints and folk memories of a Catholic past, but the English colonies of North America were settled by those who found the Anglican church too Catholic. Generations of their descendants lived in an almost purely Protestant culture for two hundred years. Then, between 1830 and 1860, immigrants from Ireland, Germany, and Austria transformed the country. Driven by famine and political unrest, and lured by the need for labor and the availability of land, millions crossed the Atlantic. Lyman Beecher, the president of Lane Seminary in Cincinnati and father of Harriet Beecher Stowe, wrote in the same year Maria Monk came to New York that "the world has never witnessed such a rush of dark-minded population from one country to another, as is now leaving Europe and dashing upon our shores" (Beecher, p. 68). The number of immigrants quadrupled from 150,000 in the 1820s to 600,000 in the 1830s, nearly tripled to 1,700,000 in the 1840s, and reached 2,500,000 in the 1850s before the temporary pause caused by the Civil War. Because most of these immigrants were Catholic, the Roman Catholic Church went from a negligible presence to the status of the largest single church in the country. By 1854 about one-quarter of the people in the United States called themselves Roman Catholics. The foreign-born held majorities in Boston and St. Louis; Chicago and Cincinnati were about half immigrant. The whole state of Ohio had no Catholic churches in 1816; by 1834 Ohio had twenty-two Catholic churches, a Catholic newspaper, a Catholic college, and a Catholic seminary. Reactions against the change became so violent that a score of Protestants and Catholics killed each other in one Philadelphia riot.

Convents were the focus of many issues raised by this cultural invasion. Although Protestants had churches and a male clergy, they had no nuns. Convents embodied the Catholic values of celibacy, poverty, and obedience, all of which flatly contradicted Protestant ideals. Catholic sisters often taught, as well as boarded, children from the Protestant upper classes. Convent education introduced girls and their families to Catholic beliefs, rituals, and customs. This intimate introduction of an alternative religious worldview combined with the rise in immigration to cause hostility against American convents and Catholic churches. A convent was burned to the ground by a mob in Charlestown, Massachusetts, the home of Bunker Hill, in 1834. During the height of anti-Catholic violence in the mid 1850s, when about a dozen Catholic churches were burned, convents from New Orleans to Charleston, South Carolina, to Providence, Rhode Island, came under attack. Maria Monk's *Awful Disclosures* and other anticonventual literature expressed distinct Protestant responses to the Catholic challenge with regard to politics, religious doctrine, sexual morality, and the continuing debate over the role of women.

Politically, Protestants feared the obedience taught in convents. According to Monk, nuns were constantly urged "to obey the priests in all things" and told that, no matter what priests commanded or did, they could not sin. Having doubts about such loyalty was evidence of sin that must be confessed. If nuns schooled in this absolute obedience taught American citizens in schools, would they not inculcate the same slavish doctrines in those who should support democracy? Similar arguments lay at the heart of Samuel F. B. Morse's *Foreign Conspiracy against the Liberties of the United States*. Morse thought that the migration of Catholics to America formed part of an international plot, including the Austrian emperor and the pope, to extirpate democracy in the United States and the world.

At the root of the tyranny exemplified by convents, according to anti-Catholic writers, lay a false religion. Protestant fear on this point grew from the conviction that Roman Catholicism did not represent a branch of Christianity at all but the religion of the Antichrist, the last and most subtle plot of Satan to prevent the Word of God—whether incarnate in Jesus or written in the Bible—from redeeming humanity. As Maria Monk said to explain her obedience, her Catholic education had left her "ignorant of the Scriptures"; she had been taught as a child, long before she took her vows, that the laity should not read the New Testament because "the mind of man is too limited and weak to understand what God has written." Instead of Scriptures, Catholics read histories of the church and lives of the saints. They relied on the magic of candles, scapulars, and miracles caused by relics of saints and holy water. Consequently, they had no moral standard against which to judge what their superiors commanded. Their depraved behavior expressed the sinful human nature that had not undergone a new birth in faith.

Such judgments of Catholicism extended well beyond Maria Monk and now unknown anti-Catholic writers to the elite of American letters. In *The Marble Faun* (1860), Nathaniel Hawthorne had his heroine, a young New England woman visiting Rome, kidnapped and held in a convent; the hero was left to reflect grimly on the vices of a city corrupted since ancient times but which "a perverted Christianity had made more noisome." Protestants from the sixteenth through the twentieth centuries routinely saw the pope as the Antichrist, the church as the whore of Babylon from Revelation 17, and average Catholics as worse than pagans, in the sense that the demonically possessed would be worse than those damned through ignorance.

This false Catholic religion perverted sexuality by means of celibacy and the confessional, both of which affected life in convents. As Hawthorne reflected on Catholic clergy, "here was a priesthood, pampered, sensual" who lived "in an unnatural relation with women, and thereby lost the healthy, human conscience" of those "who own the sweet household ties connecting them with wife and daughter." In the confessional, these priests asked women questions about sex that could never be uttered anywhere else. Maria Monk recalled, "When quite a child" in Catholic schools, "I heard from the mouths of priests at confession what I cannot repeat." During her novitiate, the priests moved on to questions "of the most improper nature, naming crimes both unthought of, and inhuman."

In fact, Catholic doctrine on sexuality differed drastically from Protestant teaching, which in Victorian days came primarily from doctors. Catholics had a tradition of moral theology extending from the Bible through the Greek and Roman medicine of Hippocrates and Galen, through churchmen from Augustine to Albertus Magnus and Thomas Aquinas. St. Alphonsus Liguori systematized that tradition in the eighteenth century. In an age when Protestants denounced the theater, Catholic tradition allowed attendance at operas with nudity. Liguori called the use of prostitutes by ignorant peasants venial (nonmortal) sin. While Protestant doctors warned that orgasm caused epilepsy, the repeated consensus of Catholic moral texts gave married women the right to bring themselves to orgasm by hand if their husbands had not done so during intercourse. Though these doctrines were published by Catholics only in Latin, for the education of confessors, Protestants of the nineteenth century published many editions of them, with as much translation as the mores of the time allowed.

Sexual fear and fear of sex directly affected American Protestant literature about convents. In *Agnes of Sorrento,* a novel that sold through sixteen editions in twenty-one years after it first appeared in 1862, Harriet Beecher Stowe centered her plot on a nude statue of St. Agnes in a fountain at the center of a courtyard in a convent built on the site of a temple of Venus, where a beautiful Italian maid would be nearly ruined by the priest who served as chaplain. More sensational writers, such as Ned Buntline in *The Beautiful Nun* (1866) and Julia McNair Wright in *Secrets of the Convent and Confessional* (1872), not only pictured women imprisoned, raped, and tortured in convents but also showed disguised nuns emerging from convents as spies to report on anti-Catholic politicians, to use sexual allure to break up Protestant families, and to attract Protestant women to Catholicism.

Beyond the political, religious, and sexual threats that convents represented, they posed a more fundamental challenge regarding the role of women. No separate realm for women existed in the United States of Maria Monk's day. The religious role of women in Protestant cultures found its original pattern when Luther married the former nun Katherine von Bora and declared that women after the Fall should confine themselves to *Kinder, Kirche, und Küche* (the children, the church, and the kitchen), but the growth of the middle class and the shift of production from home and farm to factory in the Industrial Revolution led to questions.

Antebellum America saw challenges to the exclusion of women from the public sphere, first from the Grimké sisters in the antislavery movement and then at Seneca Falls, New York, where Elizabeth Cady Stanton convened the first conference on women's rights in 1848. Without directly advocating for political or religious rights, other women were making their marks in the mass market for literature made possible by the steam press. Through *Uncle Tom's Cabin,* Harriet Beecher Stowe may have had more impact on the coming of war between the states than Senator John C. Calhoun of South Carolina or any abolitionist from William Lloyd Garrison to John Brown.

Meanwhile, a proliferation of religious orders for women took place in the Catholic world, and American Protestant women were drawn into these orders in numbers that alarmed all the Protestants who noticed them. Converts like Elizabeth Seton, who became the first Catholic saint born in the United States, Cornelia Connolly, and Katherine Drexel all founded orders of nuns to work in hospitals, schools, and colleges. This new field of action for women grew rapidly. The number of nuns active in the United States went from about 200 in 1820 to 88,773 in 1920. Academies for girls run by nuns grew from 47 in 1840 to 709 in 1910. Thirty-eight new orders of nuns were founded in the United States between 1790 and 1920, while many of the 119 new orders that appeared in Europe also sent nuns to America. Though scholars have not generally considered the growth of convents in the nineteenth and twentieth centuries as part of the feminist movement, nuns certainly formed part of the "feminization" of religious life that many have seen in the Victorian era. Catholic religious orders gave women an opportunity to exert authority, to build institutions, to live more independently of male control, and to affect the world more directly than any form of social organization available in the Protestant or secular realms.

As reactions against the mass movement of Victorian and Catholic women into convents, *Awful Disclosures* and other anticonventual books reinforced patriarchy by presenting communities of women, often founded and run by women, as dens of sin and slavery. Maria Monk's male handlers, from the ministers who helped write her story to the Harper brothers who set up a dummy firm to publish it and who took all profits for themselves, were no feminists but exploiters of women, as were the many men who presumably read Monk's book in part for its prurient interest. Harriet Beecher Stowe, Nathaniel Hawthorne, and the many lesser authors in the anticonventual genre set up marriage and family, not education or independence, as the alternatives to Catholic degradation.

On the other hand, along with Maria Monk's charges, the readers of *Awful Disclosures* read about more Latin prayers and Catholic practices than they ever had before. Both in *Uncle Tom's Cabin* and in *Agnes of Sorrento,* Harriet Beecher Stowe expressed far more sympathy with Catholicism than her father ever had. Nathaniel Hawthorne's daughter Rose, who lived with him as a child in Rome as he gathered the experience that informed *The Marble Faun,* later became a Catholic and founded an order of Dominican nuns that still serves cancer patients.

Perhaps by expressing and exposing the fears of Protestant patriarchs, anticonventual literature helped to subvert both Protestantism and patriarchy. It provided the most explicit scenes of sex that most Protestants were allowed to read, undermining Victorian repression. And as Nancy Schultz has pointed out in her introduction to *Veil of Fear* (1999), a volume that includes both Rebecca Reed's *Six Months in a Convent* (1834) and Monk's *Awful Disclosures,* anticonventual books included many "madwomen in the attic." Not only did the main female characters not fit within the domestic ideal but minor characters—mischievous nuns, evil Mothers Superior, and saintly old celibates—also fell outside of patriarchal control. Schultz argues that the anticonventual books found a spiritual successor in Toni Morrison's *Paradise* (1998), a novel about four women who are attacked by men after they set up a commune in a former convent.

To consider *Awful Disclosures* in comparison with *Uncle Tom's Cabin* reveals large patterns in American religious history and something of the relations between polemic and art. Both books tried to create sensations and succeeded, and both used tales of innocent victims, brutalized by inhuman masters, to urge Americans to eliminate a system of slavery from their midst. Both claimed to be truthful, although Stowe admitted to weaving true reports of the abuse of slaves into a fictional plot. While both affirmed Protestant domesticity, both also undermined the domestic ideal in some of the characters they presented and in their own authorship. Finally, *Awful Disclosures* stood revealed as a poisonous tissue of lies, while *Uncle Tom's Cabin* emerged as one of the great American novels. But to understand the fascinating power of Monk's book can help us to appreciate the deep fears and limits informing the culture from which writers such as Stowe and Hawthorne and Toni Morrison have made their literature.

In the following pages from *Awful Disclosures,* Monk describes her first realization that nuns were to serve as concubines for priests and the principles of absolute obedience that led her to accept this. A section on penance uses real Catholic doctrine, that the flesh should be mortified to weaken temptation and to atone for sin, to serve a Protestant polemic. In the 1830s, liberal Protestant thinking was rejecting corporal punishment of children and minimizing the wrathful aspect of God. Meanwhile, fictions about frontier life and crime in the cities became increasingly violent. Images of Maria Monk bound and gagged in the convent made Catholics the equivalent of criminals and hostile Indians. At the same time, they also updated the most traditional source of violent imagery in Protestant homes, the accounts of torture of reforming faithful by the Catholic Inquisition in John Foxe's *Acts and Monuments of the Christian Church* (commonly known as the *Book of Martyrs*).

The selections below are from Maria Monk, *Awful Disclosures of the Hotel Dieu Nunnery* (1836; reprint, Hamden, Conn.: Archon Books, 1962), pp. 56–59, 62–63, 196–200, 231.

Further Reading

Lyman Beecher, *A Plea for the West* (Cincinnati: Truman and Smith, 1835); Ray Allen Billington, *The Protestant Crusade, 1800–1860: A Study of the Origins of American*

Nativism (1938; reprint, Chicago: Quadrangle Books, 1964); Eileen Mary Brewer, *Nuns and the Education of American Catholic Women, 1860–1920* (Chicago: Loyola University Press, 1987); Jenny Franchot, *Roads to Rome: The Antebellum Protestant Encounter with Catholicism* (Berkeley and Los Angeles: University of California Press, 1994); Peter Gardella, *Innocent Ecstasy: How Christianity Gave America an Ethic of Sexual Pleasure* (New York: Oxford University Press, 1985); Laura McCall, "Armed and More or Less Dangerous: Women and Violence in American Frontier Literature, 1820–1860," in *Lethal Imagination: Violence and Brutality in American History,* edited by Michael A. Bellesiles (New York: New York University Press, 1999); Nancy Lusignan Schultz, *Veil of Fear: Nineteenth-Century Convent Tales by Rebecca Reed and Maria Monk* (West Lafayette, Ind.: Purdue University Press, 1999); Barbara Welter, "From Maria Monk to Paul Blanshard," in *Uncivil Religion: Interreligious Hostility in America* edited by Robert N. Bellah and Frederick E. Greenspahn (New York: Crossroad, 1987).

Awful Disclosures of the Hotel Dieu Nunnery

The Superior now informed me, that having taken the black veil, it only remained that I should swear the three oaths customary on becoming a nun; and that some explanations would be necessary from her. I was now, she told me, to have access to every part of the edifice, even to the cellar, where two of the sisters were imprisoned for causes which she did not mention. I must be informed, that one of my great duties was, to obey the priests in all things; and this I soon learnt, to my utter astonishment and horror, was to live in the practice of criminal inter-course with them. I suppressed some of the feelings which this announcement excited in me, which came upon me like a flash of lightning; but the only effect was to set her arguing with me, in favour of the crime, representing it as a virtue acceptable to God, and honourable to me. The priests, she said, were not situated like other men, being forbidden to marry; while they lived secluded, laborious, and self-denying lives for our salvation. They might, indeed, be considered our saviours, as without their service we could not obtain pardon of sin, and must go to hell. Now it was our solemn duty, on withdrawing from the world, to con-secrate our lives to religion, to practice every species of self-denial. We could not be too humble, or mortify our feelings too far; this was to be done by opposing them, and acting contrary to them; and what she proposed was, therefore, pleas-ing in the sight of God. I now felt how foolish I had been to place myself in the power of such persons as were around me.

From what she said, I could draw no other conclusions but that I was required to act like the most abandoned of beings, and that all my future asso-ciations were habitually guilty of the most heinous and detestable crimes. When I repeated my expressions of surprise and horror, she told me that such feelings were very common at first, and that many other nuns had expressed themselves as I did, who had long since changed their minds. She even said, that on her entrance to the nunnery, she had felt like me.

Doubts, she declared, were among our greatest enemies. They would lead us to question every point of duty, and induce us to waver at every step. They arose only from remaining imperfections, and were always evidences of sin. Our only way was to dismiss them immediately, repent and confess them. Priests, she insisted, could not sin. It was a thing impossible. Everything that they did, and wished, was of course right. She hoped I would see the reasonableness and duty of the oaths I was then to take, and be faithful to them.

She gave me another piece of information, which excited feelings in me, scarcely less dreadful. Infants were sometimes born in the convent, but they were always baptized, and immediately strangled. This secured their everlasting happiness; for the baptism purifies them from all sinfulness, and being sent out of the world before they had time to do anything wrong, they were at once admitted into heaven. How happy, she exclaimed, are those who secure immortal happiness to such little beings! Their souls would thank those who kill their bodies, if they had it in their power.

Into what a place, and among what society, had I been admitted! How different did a convent now appear from what I supposed it to be. The holy women I had always fancied the nuns to be, the venerable Lady Superior, what are they? And the priests of the Seminary adjoining (some of whom, indeed, I had reason to think were base and profligate men), what were they all? I now learned that they were often admitted into the nunnery, and allowed to indulge in the greatest crimes, which they and others call virtues.

And having listened for some time to the Superior alone, a number of the nuns were admitted, and took a free part in the conversation. They concurred in everything she told me, and repeated, without any signs of shame or compunction, things which incriminated themselves. I must acknowledge the truth, and declare that all this had an effect upon my mind. I questioned whether I might not be in the wrong, and felt as though their reasoning might have some just foundation. I had been several years under the tuition of the Catholics, and was ignorant of the Scriptures, and unaccustomed to the society, example, and conversation of Protestants; had not yet heard any appeal to the Bible as authority, but had been taught both by precept and example, to receive as truth everything said by the priests. I had not heard their authority questioned, nor anything said of any other standard of faith but their declarations. I had long been familiar with the corrupt and licentious expressions which some of them use at confessions, and believed that other women were also. I had no standard of duty to refer to, and no judgment of my own which I knew how to use, or thought of using.

All around me insisted that my doubts proved only my own ignorance and sinfulness; that they knew by experience that they would soon give place to true knowledge, and an advance in religion; and I felt something like indecision.

Still there was so much that disgusted me in the discovery I had now made, of the debased characters around me, that I would most gladly have escaped from the nunnery, and never returned. But that was a thing not to be thought of. I was in their power, and this I deeply felt, while I thought there was not one among the whole number of nuns to whom I could look for kindness. There was one, however, who began to speak to me at length in a tone that gained something of my confidence—the nun whom I have mentioned before as distinguished by her oddity, Jane Ray, who made us so much amusement when I was a novice. Although, as I have remarked, there was nothing in her face, form, or manners, to give me any pleasure, she addressed me with apparent friendliness; and while she seemed to concur with a few things spoken by them, took an opportunity to whisper a few things in my ear, unheard by them, intimating that I had better comply with everything the Superior desired, if I would save my life. I was somewhat alarmed before, but I now became much more so, and determined to make no further resistance. The Superior then made me repeat the three oaths; and, when I had sworn them, I was shown into one of the community-rooms, and remained some time with the nuns, who were released from their usual employments, and enjoying a recreation day, on account of the admissions of a new sister. My feelings during the remainder of the day I shall not attempt to describe. . . .

Nothing important occurred till late in the afternoon, when, as I was sitting in the community-room, Father Dufresne called me out, saying, he wished to speak with me. I feared what was his intention; but I dared not disobey. In a private apartment, he treated me in a brutal manner; and, from two other priests, I afterward received similar usage that evening. Father Dufresne afterwards appeared again; and I was compelled to remain in company with him until morning.

I am assured that the conduct of priests in our Convent had never been exposed, and it is not imagined by the people of the United States. This induces me to say what I do, notwithstanding the strong reasons I have to let it remain unknown. Still I cannot force myself to speak on such subjects except in the most brief manner. . . .

Penances.—I have mentioned several penances, in different parts of this narration, which we sometimes had to perform. There is a great variety of them; and, while some, though trifling in appearance, became very painful, by long endurance, or frequent repetition; others are severe in their nature, and would never be submitted to unless through fear of something worse, or a real belief in their efficacy to remove guilt. I will mention here such as I recollect, which can be named without offending a virtuous ear; for some there were, which, although I have been compelled to submit to, either by a misled conscience, or the fear of severe punishments, now that I am better able to judge of my duties, and at liberty to act, I would not mention or describe.

Kissing the floor, is a very common penance; kneeling and kissing the feet of the other nuns, is another; as are kneeling on hard peas, and walking with them in the shoes. We had repeatedly to walk on our knees through the subterranean passage, leading to the Congregational Nunnery; and sometimes to eat our meals with a rope around our necks. Sometimes we were fed only with such things as we most disliked. Garlic was given to me on this account, because I had a strong antipathy against it. Eels were repeatedly given to some of us, because we felt an unconquerable repugnance to them, on account of reports we had heard of their feeding on dead carcasses, in the river St. Lawrence. It was no uncommon thing for us to be required to drink the water in which the Superior had washed her feet. Sometimes we were required to brand our-selves with a hot iron, so as to leave scars; at other times to whip our naked flesh with several small rods, before a private altar, until we drew blood. I can assert with perfect knowledge of the fact, that many of the nuns bear the scars of these wounds.

One of our penances was to stand for a length of time with our arms extended, in imitation of the Saviour on the cross. The *Chemin de la Croix,* or Road to the Cross, is, in fact, a penance, though it consists of a variety of pros-trations, with the repetition of many prayers, occupying two or three hours. This we had to perform frequently, going into the chapel, and falling before each chapelle in succession, at each time commemorating some particular act or circumstance reported of the Saviour's progress to the place of this crucifix-ion. Sometimes we were obliged to sleep on the floor in the winter, with noth-ing over us but a single sheet; and sometimes to chew a piece of window-glass to a fine powder, in the presence of the Superior.

We had sometimes to wear leathern belts stuck full of sharp metallic points, round our waists, and the upper part of our arms, bound on so tight that they penetrated the flesh, and drew blood.

Some of the penances were so severe, that they seemed too much to be endured; and when they were imposed, the nuns who were to suffer them, sometimes showed the most violent repugnance. They would often resist, and still oftener express their opposition by exclamations and screams.

Never, however, was any noise heard from them for a long time, for there was a remedy always ready to be applied in cases of the kind. The gag which was put into the mouth of the unfortunate Saint Francis [a nun killed earlier by several sisters and a priest] had been brought from a place where there were forty or fifty others, of different shapes and sizes. These I have seen in their depository, which is a drawer between two closets, in one of the community-rooms. Whenever any loud noise was made, one of these instruments was demanded, and gagging commenced at once. I have known many, many instances, and sometimes five or six nuns gagged at once. Sometimes they would become so excited before they could be bound and gagged, that consid-erable force was necessary to be exerted; and I have seen the blood flowing from mouths into which the gag had been thrust with violence.

Indeed I ought to know something on this department of nunnery disci-pline: I have had it tried upon myself, and I can bear witness that it is not only most humiliating and oppressive, but often extremely painful. The mouth is kept forced open, and the straining of the jaws at their utmost stretch, for a considerable time, is very distressing.

One of the worst punishments which I ever saw inflicted, was that with a cap; and yet some of the old nuns were permitted to inflict it at their pleasure. I have repeatedly known them to go for a cap, when one of our number had transgressed a rule, sometimes though it were a very unimportant one. These caps were kept in a cupboard in the old nuns' rooms, whence they were brought when wanted.

They were small, made of a reddish looking leather, fitted closely to the head, and fastened under the chin with a kind of buckle. It was the common practice to tie the nun's hands behind and gag her before the cap was put on, to prevent noise and resistance. I never saw it worn by any for one moment, without throwing them in severe sufferings. If permitted, they would scream in the most shocking manner; and always writhed as much as their confinement would allow. I can speak from personal knowledge of this punishment, as I have endured it more than once; and yet I have no idea of the cause of the pain. I never examined one of the caps, nor saw the inside, for they are always brought and taken away quickly; but although the first sensation was that of coolness, it was hardly put on my head before a violent and indescribable sensation began, like that of a blister, only much more insupportable; and this continued until it was removed. It would produce such an acute pain as to throw us into convulsions, and I think no human being could endure it for an hour. After this punishment, we felt its effects through the system for many days. Having once known what it was by experience, I held the cap in dread, and whenever I was condemned to suffer the punishment again, felt ready to do any thing to avoid it. But when tied and gagged, with the cap on my head again, I could only sink upon the floor, and roll about in anguish until it was taken off.

This was usually done in about ten minutes, sometimes less, but the pain always continued in my head for several days. I thought it might take away a person's reason if kept on a much longer time. If I had not been gagged, I am sure I should have uttered awful screams. I have felt the effects for a week. Sometimes fresh cabbage leaves were applied to my head to remove it. Having had no opportunity to examine my head, I cannot say more.

This punishment was occasionally resorted to for very trifling offenses, such as washing the hands without permission; and it was generally applied on the spot, and before the other nuns in the community-rooms.

I have mentioned before, that the country, as far down as Three Rivers, is furnished with priests by the Seminary of Montreal; and that these hundred and fifty men are liable to be occasionally transferred from one station to another. Numbers of them are often to be seen in the streets of Montreal, as they may find a home in the Seminary.

They are considered as having an equal right to enter the Black Nunnery whenever they please; and then, according to our oaths, they have complete control over the nuns. To name all the works of shame of which they are guilty in that retreat, would require much time and space, neither would it be necessary to the accomplishment of my object, which is, the publication of but some of their criminality to the world, and the development, in general terms, of scenes thus far carried on in secret within the walls of that Convent, where I was so long an inmate.

Secure against detection by the world, they never believed that an eyewitness would ever escape to tell of their crimes, and declare some of their names before the world; but the time has come, and some of their deeds of darkness must come to the day. I have seen in the nunnery, the priests from more, I presume, than a hundred country places, admitted for shameful and criminal purposes: from St. Charles, St. Denis, St. Marks, St. Antoine, Chambly, Bertier, St. John's, &c &c.

How unexpected to them will be the disclosures I make! Shut up in a place from which there has been thought to be but one way of egress, and that the passage to the grave, they considered themselves safe in perpetrating crimes in our presence, and in making us share in their criminality as often as they chose, and conducted [themselves] more shamelessly than even the brutes. These debauchees would come in without ceremony, concealing their names, both by night and day. Being within the walls of that prison-house of death, where the cries and pains of the injured innocence of their victims could never reach the world, for relief or redress for their wrongs, without remorse or shame, they would glory, not only in sating their brutal passions, but even in torturing, in the most barbarous manner, the feelings of those under their power; telling us, at the same time, that this mortifying the flesh was religion, and pleasing to God. The more they could torture us, or make us violate our own feelings, the more pleasure they took in their unclean revelling; and all their brutal obscenity they called meritorious before God.

We were sometimes invited to put ourselves to voluntary sufferings in a variety of ways, not for a penance, but to show our devotion to God. A priest would sometimes say to us—

"Now, which of you have love enough for Jesus Christ to stick a pin through your cheeks?"

Some of us would signify our readiness, and immediately thrust one through up to the head. Sometimes he would propose that we should repeat the operation several times on the spot, and the cheeks of a number of nuns would be bloody.

There were other acts occasionally proposed and consented to, which I cannot name in a book. Such the Superior would sometimes command us to perform; many of them things not only useless and unheard of, but loathsome and indecent in the highest possible degree. How they could ever have been invented I never could conceive. Things were done worse than the entire exposure of the person, though this was occasionally required of several at once, in the presence of priests.

The Superior of the Seminary would sometimes come and inform us, that he had received orders from the Pope, to request that those nuns who possessed the greatest devotion and faith, should be required to perform some particular deeds, which he named or described in our presence, but of which no decent or moral person could ever endure to speak. I cannot repeat what would injure any ear, not debased to the lowest possible degree. I am bound by a regard to truth, however, to confess, that deluded women were found among us, who would comply with those requests. . . .

The last words of the book:

I realize, in some degree, how it is, that the Scriptures render the people of the United States so strongly opposed to such doctrines as are taught in the Black and the Congregational Nunneries of Montreal. The priests and nuns used often to declare, that of all heretics, the children of the United States were the most difficult to be converted; and it was thought a great triumph when one of them was brought over to "the true faith." The first passage of Scripture that made any serious impression upon my mind, was the text on which the chaplain preached on the Sabbath after my introduction to the house— "Search the Scriptures."

—— 31 ——

The Christian Doctrine of Slavery

Paul Harvey

As evangelicalism spread into the South in the late eighteenth century, slavery became an issue among the Methodists, Baptists, and Presbyterians who came to dominate the region. Black converts who joined the fold began to attend churches with their masters or, in some cases, independently. Trouble also arose when a number of early evangelicals expressed opposition to, or at least ambivalence about, slavery. John Wesley, the founder of Methodism, decried the institution of slavery, and a number of early evangelicals followed his lead. At the same time, evangelical leaders knew that, if they were to spread the gospel message to all classes, they would have to preach to slaveholders as well as common whites. If they were to form strong denominational institutions, presses, and colleges, they would need the intellectual and financial resources of the wealthy and educated whites. To gain this support, they would have to make the necessary theological adjustments to explain and justify slavery. The sermon in defense of slavery became a religious ritual of self-defense in the antebellum South. James Henley Thornwell's 1850 sermon, "The Christian Doctrine of Slavery," presents the genre at its intellectual peak.

As early as the 1820s, a series of aborted and real slave revolts frightened whites in the region and led to a suppression of free speech about slavery. By the 1830s, attacking slavery in public was virtually impossible in the South, and southern divines were well on their way to preparing a defense of slavery. Some argued that slavery was a necessary evil, foisted on the South by Yankee slavers in the colonial era, and now a living emblem of man's sinful and fallen state. They suggested that slavery could not be abolished without bringing even greater evils (anarchy, sedition, or even "race mixing") in its wake. Some theologians saw slavery as a kind of Christian way station, educating Negroes in Christianity so that, in future generations, they could carry the message back to Africa. Others attempted to show that slavery was part of God's curse on the Negro as a race, in the so-called "curse of Ham" theory. They constructed elaborate narratives based on the Old Testament to demonstrate their dubious thesis. Still others, early

Social Darwinists and pseudoscientists, simply wrote Africans and African Americans out of the human race, suggesting that black people represented a lower order of animal than humans.

Thornwell's generation, however, represented the high point of antebellum defenses of slavery. Its members argued that slavery was not just a necessary evil but could be a positive good in itself, provided that slaves received proper Christian treatment from their masters and paid due obedience to masters in return. They suggested that slavery was not so much a good or bad thing in and of itself, reasoning that any social order was godly or not depending on the extent to which men made it conform to God's image. If southern slaveholders indeed abused their slaves, broke up families with impunity, and denied the gospel message to their slaves, then slavery in the United States should be abolished. This was not the case, Thornwell argued. Instead, slaveholders had come to recognize their God-given duties to their social inferiors. They cared for slaves, treated them as part of the family, and extended to them the same blessed message of Gospel freedom that whites received. Slaveholders were fulfilling the gospel mandate to care for others in a Christian manner, and slaves responded in turn by paying obedience to those who were superior in social station. This did not mean that slavery was in and of itself good for all people and all times. Slavery was one of the curses that man's sin had brought into the world. Slavery could be turned into a blessing, however, when the institution worked to inculcate a strong sense of the cheerful and obedient performance of social duties, the virtue necessary for civilization.

Thornwell and his colleagues, then, were essentially social conservatives. They believed that human institutions had been passed down for good reason and could not be changed without inviting social disorder and chaos (such as they increasingly saw in the North). They relied on a literalist reading of the Bible together with the predominant moral philosophy of their time to portray their region's social institution in the best light possible.

Thornwell was a southern gentleman theologian. A well-educated, urbane college president, he represented the height of clerical achievement in the Old South. Born in 1812 to a slave overseer in South Carolina, he took a degree from South Carolina College and briefly studied theology in New England. Throughout his life, he defended Presbyterian and Calvinist orthodoxy against the inroads of theological innovation. He also defended his native land against abolitionist attacks and became known as the foremost intellectual defender of slavery.

Abolitionists such as William Ellery Channing had argued that slavery denied man his humanity, turning him into an object, a "thing." This transformation was a theologically indefensible action. God could not countenance such an action. Slavery was wrong because it denied the basic humanity of the slave. Thornwell, in response, insisted that the slave enjoyed "the same humanity in which we glory as the image of God." Slaves had a conscience, the fundamental constitutive element of human nature. Their conscience could not be owned, bartered, or exchanged. Just as slaves "owned" their arms and legs, so they owned their minds. Thus, slavery could not divest slaves of their humanity.

What, then, was slavery? It was, Thornwell said, the obligation to "labour for another, determined by the Providence of God, independently of the provisions of a contract." Slaveholders owned not slaves but the labor of their servants. Slavery remained a relationship between two sentient and moral beings each endowed with the conscience with which God fitted all humanity. Slavery was a relationship of "man to man," not "man to things."

What, then, were the social obligations imposed by this human relationship? Thornwell answered that men's duties depended on their particular social station in life. Thus, in the New Testament the apostle Paul suggested to slaves that their duties to their masters were the same as duties to God, "that a moral character attaches to their works, and that they are the subjects of praise or blame according to the principles upon which their obedience is rendered." And slaveholders had their own moral obligation "of rendering to their bondmen that which is just and equal." Thornwell argued that New Testament writings recognized both the humanity and responsibilities of servants and masters. God's law was written on the conscience and the heart, and it was man's obligation to discover and follow it. For slaveholders the just treatment of slaves was dictated by conscience. Likewise for slaves, the conscientious following of duties should arise naturally from the moral conscience. Thornwell was convinced that a fair and strict reading of the Bible demanded such an interpretation. "We are neither to question nor to doubt," he said, "but simply to interpret and believe." By following the law of God, slavery could be sanctified; that is, it could be cast in the image of God.

Thornwell's work arose from the dominant philosophical tradition of his era, Scottish common-sense realism. In antebellum colleges throughout the nation, the capstone course for senior students was Moral Philosophy, generally taught by the president of the college. All other work was intended to lead to this culminating moment, when philosophy, the queen of the sciences, would produce a fully intellectually matured student. The moral philosophy of the time emphasized rights, duties, and obligations. Moral philosophers in the United States were really theologians, as they sought to give a rational and philosophical exposition of God's moral law. They relied on the common-sense realist notion of conscience, the innate sense in all humans of what is right and good. Common-sense realists were spread throughout the nation, and certainly many were antislavery. In fact, abolitionists often made oblique reference to common-sense realist arguments, insisting that slavery violated the moral conscience of man. Yet southerners particularly came to rely on moral philosophy and common-sense realism to provide an intellectual foundation for the proslavery argument. They fought against what they perceived to be the radical individualism of abolitionists and their allies.

By the 1830s and 1840s, more theologically liberal northerners had begun to break away from the heritage of conservative moral philosophy and to embrace broader readings of the Bible. Hence they argued that though certain passages in the Bible did literally suggest that slaves should obey their masters, God's higher law, which humans could understand through a deeper and less literalist reading of the Bible, demanded an end to inequitable human relations. Accordingly, many abolitionists fought not only against slavery but also for women's rights and suffrage. They also participated in the huge variety of reform movements and utopian dreams that arose in the antebellum North, ranging from reform of mental institutions, to social experiments in communal living, to spiritualism and other religious practices outside the Protestant mainstream. Southern conservatives, repelled by this social and theological experimentation, returned again and again to the Bible and common-sense realist assumptions to defend social order, evangelical theology, patriarchy, and slavery.

The ritual settings of sermons such as Thornwell's highlight the importance of the preached sermon not only for its intellectual content but also for its ability to reassure a threatened southern society. In places such as Charleston, carriages pulled up to urban churches, and slaves—honored with the privilege of being carriage drivers and manservants—assisted the white ladies and gentlemen out of their coaches and into the sanctuary. The centerpiece of Protestant worship was the sermon, and southern churchgoers were particularly thrilled when their sermon presenter was a well-known regional theologian, author, and spokesman such as Thornwell. Like most urban Presbyterian ministers, Thornwell would have delivered an address that would be rarely less than one hour and often closer to two hours in length. Sermons were similar to political discourses of the time. Ministers prided themselves on undergirding their addresses with logical and biblical rigor, showing themselves to be not only deeply learned in the scriptures but also well informed on contemporary intellectual currents in the West. Thornwell himself was certainly conversant in literature, philosophy, and the sciences of his day, an accomplishment he demonstrated to good effect in his sermons. In such settings, white southerners felt themselves to be in the intellectual and social forefront of the striving nation rather than its backwaters. The well-composed sermon defended the tenets of the faith while educating both the congregation's adults and its children to the highest of contemporary intellectual standards.

The sermon reproduced here, "The Doctrine of Christian Slavery," was delivered in honor of a new church structure erected in 1850 in Charleston. Thornwell noted that the construction of the church showed that nothing would deter southerners from "providing the Negro with the armor of salvation." He reminded listeners that in Charleston—site of an 1822 abortive slave revolt led by a black Methodist named Denmark Vesey—whites had been "warned by experience to watch, with jealous care, all combinations of blacks." He suggested that black religious assemblies had been "so often prostituted to the unhallowed purposes of anarchy and crime, that good men began to apprehend that religion itself might be ultimately excluded as a measure of police." On this occasion, however, Charlestonians made known their commitment to "make known His Gospel, in its simplicity and purity, without any checks or hindrances," recognizing that "the doctrines of Jesus are doctrines according to godliness." Time would show, Thornwell assured his listeners, that the church would "prove a stronger fortress against insubordination and rebellion than weapons of brass or iron."

Thornwell's sermon was set in the context of the political controversies of that era. In 1846, at the beginning of the Mexican-American War, a northern congressman named David Wilmot introduced a resolution suggesting that any territories gained from Mexico in the war become "free soil," that slavery be excluded from them. Americans gained huge chunks of new land from the war, but the celebration of American victory was tempered by the ferocious controversy about slavery that it inevitably created. At the time of Thornwell's address, Congress was debating what became known as the Compromise of 1850, a bill that attempted to effect a political resolution to the slavery controversy. In fact, as Thornwell repeatedly recognizes in his sermon, slavery had become a moral crusade for both sides—one that could not be contained by political compromises. Abolitionism or free-soil ideas had gained the support of a significant section of the northern public, and it would be up to the southern clergy to mount defenses of slavery to answer the institution's critics. Thornwell's address came at a key moment in the years before the Civil War, when he could reasonably hope to persuade members of the Christian public to adopt his view. In 1850, southern clerics could pronounce proslavery views with confidence and without the extreme defensiveness that characterized such sermons just before the Civil War.

Thornwell's writings and sermons were deeply influential, as was his eventual declaration of support for southern secession. Thornwell provided the divine imprimatur that many white southerners sought for their peculiar institution, and later for their momentous decision to fight the bloodiest war in the nation's history to defend that institution. Thornwell died in 1862, three years before he could have witnessed God's verdict on slavery in the United States.

The sermon printed here is in James Henley Thornwell, "The Christian Doctrine of Slavery," in *The Collected Writings of James Henley Thornwell, D.D., LL.D.*, edited by John B. Adger and John L. Giradeau (Richmond, Va.: Presbyterian Committee of Publication, 1873), pp. 398–436.

Further Reading

Mitchell Snay, *Gospel of Disunion: Religion and Separatism in the Antebellum South* (Cambridge: Cambridge University Press, 1993); John McCardell, *The Idea of a Southern Nation: Southern Nationalists and Southern Nationalism, 1830–1860* (New York: W. W. Norton, 1979); E. Brooks Holifield, *The Gentlemen Theologians: American Theology in Southern Culture, 1795–1860* (Durham, N.C.: Duke University Press, 1978); Anne Loveland, *Southern Evangelicals and the Social Order, 1800–1860* (Baton Rouge: Louisiana State University Press, 1980); Eugene Genovese, *The Slaveholders' Dilemma: Freedom and Progress in Southern Conservative Thought* (Columbia: University of South Carolina Press, 1991); William W. Freehling, "James Henley Thornwell's Mysterious Antislavery Moment," *Journal of Southern History* 57 (August 1991): 383–406.

The Christian Doctrine Of Slavery

The slaveholding States of this confederacy have been placed under the ban of the public opinion of the civilized world. The "philanthropy" of Christendom seems to have concentrated its sympathies upon us. We have been denounced, with every epithet of vituperation and abuse, as conspirators against the dignity of man, traitors to our race, and rebels against God. Overlooking, with a rare expansion of benevolence, the evils which press around their own doors, the vices and crimes and sufferings of their own neighbours and countrymen, the "philanthropists" of Europe and this country can find nothing worth weeping for but the sufferings and degradation of the Southern slave, nothing worth reviling but the avarice, inhumanity and cruelty of the Southern master, and nothing worth labouring to extirpate but the system which embodies these outrages and wrongs. So monstrous are the misrepresentations which ignorance, malice and fanaticism are constantly and assiduously propagating in regard to this relation among us, that if our names were not actually written under the pictures, we should never suspect that they were intended for us. In the grave discussions of philosophy, the solemn instructions of the pulpit, the light effusions of the poet, in popular assemblies and legislative halls, among all classes and conditions of men, we are held up to execration and contempt; and our society is shunned as scrupulously as if the taint of leprosy adhered to us. . . .

This insane fury of philanthropy has not been content with speculating upon our degradation and wretchedness at a distance. It has aimed at stirring up insurrection in the midst of us. In the sacred names of religion and liberty, private efforts have been made to turn the hearts of servants against their masters; and public institutions, which the implied faith of the country should render only vehicles of convenience, have been treacherously converted into engines of sedition and organs of tumult. Outlaws from humanity, the Constitution of the Country has been unable to protect us from the machinations of those who, according to the legitimate use of language, can be much more appropriate styled *manstealers* than ourselves. At this moment the Union is shaken to its centre by the prevalence of sentiment over reason and truth; and the remarkable spectacle is exhibited of a people constrained in conscience to violate the faith of treaties, the solemnity of contracts, and the awful sanctity of an oath—constrained in conscience to trample in the dust the plainest obligations of duty, rather than infringe the speculative rights of man. A spurious charity for a comparatively small class in the community is dictating the subversion of the cherished institutions of our fathers, and the hopes of the human race. The utter ruin of this vast imperial Republic is to be achieved as a trophy to the progress of human development.

That we should be passive spectators of these scenes of madness and confusion, that we should be indifferent to the condemnation of the civilized world, and especially to efforts to put in jeopardy our lives as well as our property, is not to be expected. The fear of good men among ourselves has been, that the natural exasperation, which so much unmerited censure and such extraordinary interference with our affairs have a tendency to produce, would provoke us to extremities resulting rather from the violence of resentment than the dictates of prudence. Perhaps, at the first alarming indications of our moral position in the estimate of the world, we indulged too much in the language of defiance, and permitted ourselves to yield to suggestions of policy, which, in our calmer moments, neither the reason nor the conscience of the country should approve. It is useless to deny that we were tempted to resort to measures of legislation which, while they contribute nothing to our security, have given a pretext to the calumnies of our enemies, and embarrassed our defence in the hands of our friends. But . . . under the extraordinary pressure which has been spent upon us, it is a matter of astonishment and of devout thanksgiving to God, that we have been able, in the regulation of our domestic institutions, to preserve so much moderation, prudence, humanity and caution . . . . With infidelity on the one hand, suggesting the short reply to the indictment of the world, that our Negroes are "not of the same blood with ourselves"—a plea which, if it had been admitted, would have justly drawn down the curse of God, as well as the execrations of the race; with the dictates of a narrow expediency on the other, suggesting that our safety depended upon the depression and still lower degradation of the black race; with Scylla on the one side and Charybdis on the other, the wonder is, that we have not been frightened from our propriety, and driven to the adoption of more measures that would seem to justify the censures of our enemies.

The inception and successful progress of this enterprise encourage the hope that we mean to maintain our moderation. It is a public testimony to our faith that the Negro is of one blood with ourselves, that he has sinned as we have, and that he has an equal interest with us in the great redemption. Science, falsely so called, may attempt to exclude him from the brotherhood of humanity. Men may be seeking eminence and distinction by arguments which link him with the brute; but the instinctive impulse of our nature, combined with the plainest declarations of the Word of God, lead us to recognize in his form and lineaments, in his moral, religious and intellectual nature, the same humanity in which we glory as the image of God. We are not ashamed to call him our *brother.* The subjugation of the fears and jealousy which a systematic misrepresentation of religion, on the part of its inveterate opposers, has had a tendency to produce, is a public declaration to the world, that, in our philosophy, right is the highest expedience, and obedience to God the firmest security of communities as well as individuals. We have not sought the protection of our property in the debasement of our species; we have not maintained our own interests in this world by the deliberate sacrifice of the eternal interests of the thousands who look to us for the way of salvation. Under the infallible conviction—infallible, because the offspring of the Word of God—that he who walketh uprightly walketh surely, we have endeavoured to carry out a plan which shall have the effect of rendering to our servants, in the most comprehensive sense, "that which is just and equal." If others feel called to seduce them into grievous crime, and to ply them with instigations to insurrection and tumult, our firmest precautions against the threatened danger shall be the faithful discharge of our duties, which, while it preserves a conscience void of offence toward God, conciliates the confidence and affections of man.

If God shall enable us to maintain the moderation and dignity which becomes us, and to set an example of faithfulness and diligence in the discharge of the duties which spring from the relation of master and servant, it will be an omen of good. It will be a signal proof that He has not condemned us, and a cheering token that in the vicissitudes of human affairs truth will ultimately prevail, and we shall stand acquitted at the bar of the world. The agitations which are convulsing the kingdoms of Europe, the mad speculations of philosophers, the excesses of unchecked democracy, are working out some of the most difficult problems of political and social science; and when the tumult shall have subsided and reason resumed her ascendency, it will be found that the very principles upon which we have been accustomed to justify Southern Slavery are the principles of regulated liberty; that in defending this institution we have really been upholding the civil interests of mankind, resisting alike the social anarchy of communism and the political anarchy of licentiousness, that we have been supporting representative, republican government against the despotism of the masses on the one hand, and the supremacy of a single will on the other.

God has not permitted such a remarkable phenomenon as the unanimity of the civilized world, in its execration of Slavery, to take place without design. This great battle with the Abolitionists has not been fought in vain. The muster of such immense forces, the fury and bitterness of the conflict, the disparity in resources of the parties in the war, the conspicuousness, the unexampled conspicuousness of the event, have all been ordered for wise and beneficent results; and when the smoke shall have rolled away, it will be seen that a real progress has been made in the practical solution of the problems which produced the collision.

What disasters it will be necessary to pass through before the nations can be taught the lessons of Providence, what lights shall be extinguished, and what horrors experienced, no human sagacity can foresee. But that the world is now the theatre of an extraordinary conflict of great principles, that the foundations of society are about to be explored to their depths, and the sources of social and political prosperity laid bare—that the questions in dispute involve all that is dear and precious to man on earth, the most superficial observer cannot fail to perceive. Experiment after experiment may be made, disaster succeed disaster, in carrying out the principles of an atheistic philosophy, until the nations, wearied and heart-sickened with changes without improvement, shall open their eyes to the real causes of their calamities, and learn the lessons which wisdom shall evolve from the events that have passed. Truth must triumph. God will vindicate the appointments of His Providence: and if our institutions are indeed consistent with righteousness and truth, we can calmly afford to bide our time; we can watch the storm which is beating furiously against us, without terror or dismay; we can receive the assault of the civilized world, trusting in Him who has all the elements at His command, and can save as easily by one as a thousand. If our principles are true, the world must come to them; and we can quietly appeal from the verdict of existing generations to the more impartial verdict of the men who shall have seen the issue of the struggle in which we are now involved. It is not the narrow question of Abolitionism or Slavery—not simply whether we shall emancipate our negroes or not; the real question is the relations of man to society, of States to the individual, and of the individual to States—a question as broad as the interests of the human race.

These are the mighty questions which are shaking thrones to the centres, upheaving the masses like an earthquake, and rocking the solid pillars of this Union. The parties in this conflict are not merely Abolitionists and Slaveholders; they are Atheists, Socialists, Communists, Red Republicans, Jacobins on the one side, and the friends of order and regulated freedom on the other. In one word, the world is the battleground, Christianity and Atheism the combatants, and the progress of humanity the stake. One party seems to regard society, with all its complicated interests, its divisions and subdivisions, as the machinery of man, which, as it has been invented and arranged by his ingenuity and skill, may be taken to pieces, reconstructed, altered or repaired, as expedience shall indicate defects of confusion in the original plan. The other party beholds in it the ordinance of God; and contemplates "this little scheme of human life" as placed in the middle of a scheme, whose beginnings must be traced to the unfathomable depths of the past, and whose development and completion must be sought in the still more unfathomable depths of the future . . . and with which it is as awful temerity to tamper as to sport with the name of God.

It is a great lesson, that, as the weakness of man can never make that straight which God hath made crooked, true wisdom consists in discharging the duties of every relation; and the true secret of progress is in the improvement and elevation which are gradually superinduced by this spirit.

The part, accordingly, which is assigned to us, in the tumult of the age, is the maintenance of the principles upon which the security of social order and the development of humanity depend, in their application to the distinctive institutions which have provoked upon us the malediction of the world. The Apostle briefly sums up all that is incumbent, at the present crisis, upon the slaveholders of the South in the words: Masters, give unto your servants that which is just and equal, knowing that Ye also have a Master in heaven. It would be an useless waste of time to spend many words in proving that the servants contemplated by the Apostles were slaves. Finding it impossible to deny that Slavery, as an existing element of society, is actually sanctioned by Christ and His Apostles, those who would preserve some show of consistence in their veneration of the Scriptures, and their condemnation of us, resolve the conduct of the founders of Christianity into motives of prudence and considerations of policy. While they admit that the letter of the Scriptures is distinctly and unambiguously in our favour, they maintain that their spirit is against us; and, that our Saviour was content to leave the destruction of whatsoever was morally wrong in the social fabric to the slow progress of changes in individual opinions, wrought by the silent influence of religion, rather than endanger the stability of governments by sudden and disastrous revolutions. "The Apostle does not," says a learned commentator, "interfere with any established relations, however, as in the case of Slavery, morally and politically wrong, but only enjoins the discharge of the duties which the very persons themselves recognize." It is not for me to explain how the imputation of a defective morality can be reconciled with the great Protestant dogma, that the Bible is an adequate rule of faith and practice; or upon what principles slaveholders should be rejected from the fellowship of the Christian church now, when Paul received them as brethren, and sanctioned the bondage in which they held their servants.

But it may be worth while to expose the confusion of ideas, from which this distinction betwixt the letter and the spirit of the Gospel has arisen, and which has been a source of serious perplexity both to the defenders and the enemies of Slavery. Many Christian men have been led, in reference to this subject, to lend their sanction to principles which, in all other applications, they would reject with abhorrence, because they have felt that the genius and temper of Christianity were inconsistent with the genius and temper of Slavery; while others, driven to the opposite extreme, from a faithful study of the letter, have been led to deny the principles which lie at the foundation of all human progress, and to assume an attitude in regard to human rights and liberty, which, in their abstract forms, can be characterized as little less than monstrous. That is a desperate cause which is either incompatible with the general tone and spirit of Christianity, or with the progress of true liberty, which is only another name for the social and political development of man. If it can be shown that Slavery contravenes the spirit of the Gospel, that as a social relation it is essentially unfavourable to the cultivation and growth of the graces of the Spirit, that it is unfriendly to the development of piety and to communion with God; or, that it retards the onward progress of man, that it hinders the march of society to its destined goal, and contradicts that supremacy of justice which is the soul of the State and the life-blood of freedom—if these propositions can be satisfactorily sustained, then it is self-condemned; religion and philanthropy alike require us to labour for its destruction, and every good man amongst us would feel bound to contribute to its removal; and even the voice of patriotism would demand that we should wipe from our country the foul reproach of standing in the way of the destined improvement of mankind.

The confusion upon this subject has arisen from a twofold misapprehension—one in relation to the nature of the slavery tolerated in the letter of the Scriptures, and the other in relation to the spirit of Christianity itself.

It is common to describe Slavery as the property of man in man—as the destruction of all human and personal rights, the absorption of the humanity of one individual into the will and power of another. . . .

If this be a just description of Slavery, the wonder is, not that the civilized world is now indignant at its outrages and wrongs, but that it has been so slow in detecting its enormities; that mankind, for so many centuries, acquiesced in a system which contradicted every impulse of nature, every whisper of conscience, every dictate of religion—a system as monstrously unnatural as a general effort to walk upon the head or think with the feet. I have, however, no hesitation in saying, that, whatever may be the technical language of the law in relation to certain aspects in which Slavery is contemplated, the ideas of personal rights and personal responsibility pervade the whole system. It is a relation of man to man—a form of civil society of which persons are the only elements—and not a relation of man to things. Under the Roman code, in which more offensive language than that employed by ourselves as used in reference to the subject, the Apostles did not regard the personality of the slave as lost or swallowed up in the propriety of the master. They treat him as a man, possessed of certain rights, which it was injustice to disregard; and, make it the office of Christianity to protect these rights by the solemn sanctions of religion—to enforce upon masters the necessity, the moral obligation, of rendering to their bondmen that which is just and equal. Paul treats the services of slaves as *duties*—not like the toil of the ox or the ass, a labour extracted by the stringency of discipline, but a moral debt, in the payment of which they were rendering a homage to God. "Servants," says he, "be obedient to them that are your masters, according to the flesh, with fear and trembling, in singleness of your heart, as unto Christ; not with eye-service, as men-pleasers, but as the servants of Christ, doing the will of God from the heart; with good-will doing service, as to the Lord, and not to men; knowing that whatever good thing any man doeth, the same shall he receive of the Lord, whether he be bond or free." I need not say to those who are acquainted with the very elements of moral philosophy, that obedience, except as a figured term, can never be applied to any but rational, intelligent, responsible agents. It is a voluntary homage to law—implies moral obligation, and a sense of duty, and can only, in the way of analogy, be affirmed of the instinctive submission of brutes, or the mechanical employment of instruments and things.

The Apostle not merely recognizes the moral agency of slaves, in the phraseology which he uses, but treats them as possessed of conscience, reason and will, by the motives which he presses. He says to them, in effect, that their services to their masters are duties which they owe to God—that a moral character attaches to their works, and that they are the subjects of praise or blame according to the principles upon which their obedience is rendered. . . . He considered Slavery as a social and political economy, in which relations subsisted betwixt moral, intelligent, responsible beings, involving reciprocal rights and reciprocal obligations. There was a right to command on the one hand, an obligation to obey on the other. Both parties might be guilty of injustice and of wrong; the master might prostitute his power by tyranny, cruelty, and iniquitous exactions; the servant might evade his duty from indolence, treachery, or obstinate self-will. Religion held the scales of justice between them, and enforced fidelity upon each by the awful sanctions of eternity. This was clearly the aspect in which the Apostle contemplated the subject. . . .

If, then, Slavery is not inconsistent with the existence of personal rights and of moral obligation, it may be asked, In what does its peculiarity consist? What is it that makes a man a slave? We answer, The obligation to labour for another, determined by the Providence of God, independently of the provisions of a contract. The right which the master has is a right, not to the *man*, but to his *labour*; the duty which the slave owes is the service which, in conformity with this right, the master exacts. The essential difference betwixt free labour and slave labour is, that one is rendered in consequence of a contract; the other is rendered in consequence of a command. The labourers in each case are equally moral, equally responsible, equally men. But they work upon different principles. . . .

Whatever control the master has over the person of the slave is subsidiary to this right to his labour; what he sells is not the man, but the property in his services. True he chastises the man, but the punishments inflicted for disobedience are no more inconsistent with personal responsibilities than the punishments inflicted by the law for breaches of contract. On the contrary, punishment in contradistinction from suffering always implies responsibility, and a right which cannot be enforced is a right, which society, as an organized community, has not yet acknowledged. The chastisements of slaves are accordingly no more entitled to awaken the indignation of loyal and faithful citizens—however pretended philanthropists may describe the horrors of the scourge and the lash—than the penalties of disgrace, imprisonment, or death, which all nations have inflicted upon crimes against the State. All that is necessary, in any case, is that the punishment be *just*. Pain unrighteously inflicted is cruelty, whether that cruelty springs from the tyranny of a single master, or the tyranny of that greater master, the State. Whether adequate provisions shall be made to protect the slave from inhumanity and oppression, whether he shall be exempt from suffering except for disobedience and for crime, are questions to be decided by the law of the land; and in this matter the codes of different nations, and of the same nation at different times, have been various. Justice and religion require that such provisions should be made. It is no part of the essence of Slavery, however, that the rights of the slave should be left to the caprice or to the interest of the master; and in the Southern States provisions are actually made—whether adequate or inadequate it is useless here to discuss—to protect him from want, cruelty, and unlawful domination. Provisions are made which recognize the doctrine of the Apostle, that he is a subject of rights, and that justice must be rendered to his claims. When Slavery is pronounced to be essentially sinful, the argument cannot turn upon incidental circumstances of the system, upon the defective arrangement of the details, the inadequate securities which the law awards against the infringement of acknowledged rights; it must turn upon the nature of the relation itself, and must boldly attempt to prove that he ceases to be a man, who is under obligation, without the formalities of a contract, to labour under the direction and for the benefit of another. If such a position is inconsistent with the essential elements of humanity, then Slavery is inhuman; if society, on the other hand, has distinctly recognized the contrary as essential to good order, as in the case of children, apprentices and criminals, then Slavery is consistent with the rights of man, and the pathetic declamation of Abolitionists falls to the ground.

This view of the subject exposes the confusion—which obtains in most popular treatises of morals—of Slavery with *involuntary servitude*. The service, in so far as it consists in the motions of the limbs or organs of the body, must be voluntary, or it could not exist at all. If by *voluntary* be meant, however, that which results from hearty consent, and is accordingly rendered with cheerfulness, it is precisely the service which the law of God enjoins. Servants are exhorted to obey from considerations of duty; to make conscience of their tasks, with good-will doing service, as to the Lord, and not to men. Whether, in point of fact, their service, in this sense, shall be voluntary will depend upon their moral character. But the same may be said of free labour. There are other motives beside the lash that may drive men to toil, when they are far from toiling with cheerfulness or good-will. Others groan under their burdens as well as slaves, and many a man who works by contract is doomed to an "involuntary servitude," which he as thoroughly detests as the most faithless slave who performs nothing but the painful drudgery of eye-service. . . .

So far was the Apostle, therefore, from regarding "involuntary servitude" as the characteristic of Slavery, that he condemns such servitude as a sin. He treats it as something that is abject, mean, despicable; but insists, on the other hand, that Slavery dignifies and ennobles the servant who obeys from the heart.

But while it may be admitted that Slavery is not absolutely inconsistent with moral responsibility, or the freedom of a moral agent, it may be asked whether the slave is not stripped of some of the rights which belong to him essentially as a man; and in this view, whether the relation is not incompatible with the spirit of the Gospel, which asserts and promotes the dignity and perfection of our race; in other words, whether there is not a limitation upon the moral freedom of the slave—whether his situation does not preclude him from discharging his whole duty as a man; and, therefore, whether the relation is not ultimately destructive of the full complement of human rights.

This question, it seems to me, comprises the whole moral difficulty of Slavery; and it is at this point of the discussion, that the friends and enemies of the system are equally tempted to run into extravagance and excess; the one party denying the inestimable value of freedom, the other exaggerating the nature and extent of human rights, and both overlooking the real scope and purpose of the Gospel, in its relation to the present interests of man.

That the design of Christianity is to secure the perfection of the race is obvious from all its arrangements; and that, when this end shall have been consummated, Slavery must cease to exist is equally clear. This is only asserting that there will be no bondage in heaven. Among beings of the same nature, each relatively perfect, there can be no other inequalities than those which spring from superior endowments; the outward advantages of all must be of the same kind, though they may vary in degrees proportioned to the capacities of the individuals to enjoy them. If Adam had never sinned and brought death into the world, with all our woe, the bondage of man to man would never have been instituted; and when the effects of transgression shall have been purged from the earth, and the new heavens and the new earth wherein dwelleth righteousness given to the saints, all bondage shall be abolished. In this sense Slavery is inconsistent with the spirit of the Gospel—that it contemplates a state of things, an existing economy, which it is the design of the Gospel to remove. Slavery is a part of the curse which sin has introduced into the world, and stands in the same general relations to Christianity as poverty, sickness, disease or death. In other words, it is a relation which can only be conceived as taking place among fallen beings, tainted with a curse. It springs not from the nature of man as man, nor from the nature of society as such, but from the nature of man as sinful, and the nature of society as disordered.

Upon an earth radiant with the smile of heaven, or in the Paradise of God, we can no more picture the figure of a slave than we can picture the figures of the maimed, the lame and the blind; we can no more fancy the existence of masters and tasks than we can dream of hospitals and beggars. These are the badges of a fallen world. . . . It is a natural evil which God has visited upon society, because man kept not his first estate, but fell, and, under the Gospel, is turned like all other natural evils into the means of an effective spiritual discipline. The Gospel does not propose to make our present state a *perfect* one—to make our earth a heaven. Here is where the philanthropists mistake. They picture to themselves imaginary models of a perfect Commonwealth; they judge of good and evil by the standard of such ideal schemes; they condemn whatever comes short of their conceptions, without reference to the circumstances, which, after all, may make it relatively good. The sterility of the earth is, no doubt, in itself considered an evil; but in its relations to man, who has lost his integrity, and to whom labour has become a burden, it is a needful stimulus of industry, and is so overruled into a blessing. The distinction of ranks in society, in the same way, is an evil; but in our fallen world, an absolute equality would be an absolute stagnation of all enterprise and industry. Good and evil, it should never be forgotten, are relative terms, and what may be good for one man may be an evil to another, or what is good at one time may be hurtful to the same individual at another. It can be affirmed of no form of government, and of no condition of society, that it is absolutely the best or the worst; and, in the inscrutable Providence of God, it is, no doubt, arranged that the circumstances of individuals, and the social and political institutions of communities, are, upon the whole, those which are best adapted to the degree of their moral progress. . . . When we consider the diversities in moral position, which sin has been the means of entailing upon the race, we may be justified in affirming, that, relatively to some persons and to some times, Slavery may be a good, or, to speak more accurately, a condition, from which, though founded in a curse, the Providence of God extracts a blessing. We are not to judge of the institutions of the present by the standard of the future life; we are not to confound the absolute and relative. For aught that we know Slavery may stand in somewhat the same relation to political society, in a world like ours, in which mortality stands to the human body; and it may be as vain to think of extirpating it, as to think of giving man immortality upon earth. . . .

The fundamental mistake of those who affirm Slavery to be essentially sinful is that the duties of all men are specifically the same. Though they do not state the proposition in so many words, and in its naked form would probably dissent from it, yet a little attention to their reasoning puts it beyond doubt, that this is the radical assumption upon which they proceed—all men are bound to do specifically the same things. As there are obviously duties of some men, in some relations, which cannot be practised by a slave, they infer that the institution strips him of his rights, and curtails the fair proportions of his humanity. The argument, fully and legitimately carried out, would condemn every arrangement of society, which did not secure to all its members an absolute equality of position; it is the very spirit of socialism and communism.

The doctrine of the Bible, on the other hand, is that the specific duties—the things actually required to be done—are as various as the circumstances in which men are placed. Moral perfection does not depend upon the number of variety of single acts, but upon the general habitudes of the soul. He is upright whose temper of mind is in conformity with the law, and whose prevailing disposition would always prompt him, in all the relations of life, to do what is right. There may be many right things which he will never be required to perform, but he is entitled to the praise of excellence if he cultivates a spirit which would lead him to perform them, if circumstances should ever make them his duty. . . . Hence those moralists are grievously in error, who have represented Slavery as inconsistent with the full complement of human duty and as a consequent limitation upon the spiritual freedom of man, because there are duties which God has not connected with this condition of society. To maintain that the same things are universally obligatory, without regard to circumstances or relations, that what is exacted of one must necessarily be exacted from another, however different or even incongruous their outward states, is to confound the obligations of rulers and subjects, of parents and children, of guardians and wards, and to plunge the community into irretrievable confusion. All that can be affirmed is, that the same temper of universal rectitude is equally incumbent upon all, while it must be admitted that the outward forms of its manifestations and expression must be determined by the relations which Providence has actually assigned to our state. The slave is to show his reverence for God, the freedom of his inward man, by a cheerful obedience to the lawful commands of his master; the master, his regard for one who is his Master in heaven by rendering to the slave that which is just and equal. The character of both is determined, in the sight of God, by the spirit which pervades their single acts, however the acts may differ in themselves. . . .

No proposition can be clearer than that the rights of man must be ultimately traced to his duties, and are nothing more than the obligations of his fellows to let him alone in the discharge of all the functions, and the enjoyment of all the blessings, of his lot. Whatever puts an obstruction or hinderance to the complement of his duties, is an encroachment upon the complement of his rights, as a *man*. Whatever is incompatible with the exercise of his moral nature is destructive of the fundamental law of his being. But as the moral discipline of man is consistent with the greatest variety of external condition, it is consistent with the greatest variety of contingent rights—of rights which spring from peculiar circumstances and peculiar relations, and in the absence of which a man may still be a man. These cannot be treated as a fixed and invariable quantity. Dependent as they are upon our duties, which, in turn, are dependent upon our circumstances, they fluctuate with the gradations and progress of society, being wider or narrower according to the spheres in which we move. . . .

As to the influence of Slavery upon the advancement of society, there can be no doubt, if the government of God be moral, that the true progress of communities and States, as well as the highest interests of individuals, depends upon the fidelity with which the duties are discharged in every condition of life. It is the great law of providential education, that "to every one that hath shall be given and he shall have abundance; but from him that hath not shall be taken away even that which he hath." In this way the reign of universal justice is promoted, and wherever that obtains, the development of the individual, which is the great end of all social and political institutions, must infallibly take place. The prosperity of the State at the same time is secured, and secured, too, without the necessity of sudden changes or violent revolutions. It will be like the vigour of a healthful body, in which all the limbs and organs perform their appropriate functions without collision or tumult, and its ascension to a high degree of moral elevation will be like the growth of such a body, silent and imperceptible, the natural result of the blessing of God upon the means He has appointed. Let masters and servants, each in their respective spheres, be impregnated with the principle of duty—let masters resolve to render unto their servants that which is just and equal, never transcending the legitimate bounds of their authority, and servants resolve to cherish sentiments of reverence for their masters according to the flesh, never falling short of the legitimate claims on their obedience, and the chief good of each, as individuals and as men, will be most surely promoted, while each will contribute an important share to the strength and stability of the Commonwealth. . . .

Our highest security in these States lies in the confidence and affection of our servants, and nothing will more effectually propitiate their regards than consistent efforts, upon our part, to promote their everlasting good. They will feel that those are not tyrants who are striving to bring them unto God; and they will be slow to cast off a system which has become associated in their minds with their dearest hopes and most precious consolations. Brutal ignorance is indeed to be dreaded; the only security against it is physical force; it is the parent of ferocity, of rashness, and of desperate enterprises. But Christian knowledge softens and subdues. Christ Jesus, in binding His subjects to God, binds them more closely to each other in the ties of confidence, fidelity and love. We would say, then, to you and to all our brethren of the South, go on in your present undertaking; and though our common enemies may continue to revile, you will be consolidating the elements of your social fabric so firmly and compactly that it shall defy the storms of fanaticism, while the spectacle you will exhibit of union, sympathy and confidence among the different orders of the community, will be a standing refutation of all their accusations against us. Go on in this noble enterprise, until every slave in our borders shall know of Jesus and the resurrection; and the blessing of God will attend you, and turn back the tide of indignation which the public opinion of the world is endeavouring to roll upon you. Go on in this career, and afford another illustration of what all experience has demonstrated—that Christianity is the [chief] defence of every institution which contributes to the progress of man.

—— 32 ——

Trance Lecturers in Antebellum America

Ann Braude

In 1857 Annie Denton Cridge lost her first child within months of his birth. "My darling is gone! the fond great hope of my life! . . . How bitter the separation!" mourned the twenty-three-year-old socialist and woman's rights advocate. She poured out her grief in the pages of the *Vanguard,* the newspaper she published with her husband in Dayton, Ohio. Three obituaries recounted the brief life and lamented death of little Denton Cridge. According to the longest tribute, authored by the grieving mother, the conditions that separated Cridge from her baby, however bitter, were short-lived. During Denton's final moments, she saw the spirits of her own dead parents above his couch, "waiting to bear his sweet spirit away." She watched her baby's spirit withdraw from his body and assume a spiritual body, with the help of his grandparents. Since then, Cridge told her readers, she held her child in her arms every day. He weighed but nothing and within a week had recovered from the illness that took his life. Her spirit mother held the baby while she dressed.

Cridge was a Spiritualist, a member of a popular and controversial movement that assumed a self-conscious identity in North America in the mid nineteenth century. Spiritualism was a new religious movement aimed at proving the immortality of the soul by establishing communication with the spirits of the dead. Whether reverenced or ridiculed, Spiritualism was ubiquitous on the American scene at midcentury. For some it provided solace in the face of bereavement, for some entertainment, for some a livelihood earned from the credulous. For many it provided evidence of the immortality of the soul that formed the basis of a sincere religious faith. For iconoclasts and nonconformists it provided an alternative to the established religious order. It held two attractions that proved irresistible to thousands of Americans: rebellion against death and rebellion against authority.

Spiritualism was a religious response to the crisis of faith experienced by many Americans at midcentury. Based on the view that contact with the spirits of the dead provided empirical proof of the immortality of the soul, Spiritualism appealed to people in search of new justification for a wavering faith. For those no longer convinced by the "evidences" of Christianity, Spiritualism provided "scientific" evidence of religious truth. Initially, it required people to believe nothing. Rather, it asked them to become "investigators," to observe "demonstrations" of the truth of Spiritualism produced under "test conditions" in the séance room. It provided a way to remain religious for those disaffected from Calvinism or evangelicalism in the antebellum years and for those disillusioned by Darwinism, biblical criticism, and the rise of science later in the century. Considering its own methods to be scientific, the movement participated in the optimistic equation of science and progress that bolstered the conviction of so many nineteenth-century reform groups.

Spiritualism's claim to be scientific may draw smiles from twentieth-century readers, but the contention was not unreasonable within the context of popular scientific knowledge at midcentury. Few Americans viewed science and religion as enemies before the Civil War. Rather, investigators of each understood themselves as pursuing related inquiries into the nature of reality. Antebellum churchmen and scientists alike viewed the physical world as "one volume of God's Bible" in which God's will might be discovered in the laws he established to govern his creation. All scientists saw God's hand in nature, although Spiritualists may have seen it more clearly.

Spiritualism held a special attraction for nineteenth-century activists who felt oppressed by the traditional roles assigned to men and women. Such reformers found the entire social order in need of revision, and condemned the churches as perpetuators of repressive conventions. "The only religious sect in the world . . . that has recognized the equality of woman is the Spiritualists," claimed the *History of Woman Suffrage*, edited by Elizabeth Cady Stanton and Susan B. Anthony. Written in the 1880s, the official history of the nineteenth-century woman's rights movement recorded the equality of women as speakers and leaders throughout Spiritualism's thirty-seven-year history and the movement's vocal support for woman suffrage. The *History of Woman Suffrage* described a religious group whose beliefs and practices committed it to fostering female leadership. "They have always assumed that woman may be a medium of communication from heaven to earth," the *History* observed, "that the spirits of the universe may breathe through her lips."

As with the woman's rights movement, Spiritualism dated its inception to 1848 in upstate New York. The two movements intertwined continually as they spread throughout the country. Not all feminists were Spiritualists, but all Spiritualists advocated woman's rights, and women were in fact equal to men within Spiritualist practice, polity, and ideology. Certainly, as the *History of Woman Suffrage* stated, Spiritualists were the only religious group of which this could be said. Quakers, as the *History* noted, did have women ministers but did not appoint women to select meetings that had authority over both men's and women's meetings and censured members who spoke out on any political or reform subject. Detractors concurred and linked woman's rights and Spiritualism as illustrative of the follies and delusions of the nineteenth century. At a time when no churches ordained women and many forbade them to speak aloud in church, Spiritualist women had equal authority, equal opportunities, and equal numbers in religious leadership. While most religious groups viewed the existing order of gender, race, and class relations as ordained by God, ardent Spiritualists appeared not only in the woman's rights movement but also throughout the most radical reform movements of the nineteenth century. They led so-called ultraist wings of the movements for the abolition of slavery, for the reform of marriage, for children's rights, and for religious freedom, and they actively supported socialism, labor reform, vegetarianism, dress reform, health reform, temperance, and anti-Sabbatarianism to name a few of their favorite causes.

Because Spiritualism asserted that divine truth was directly accessible to individual human beings through spirit communication, the new faith provided a religious alternative that supported the individualist social and political views of antebellum radicals. Spiritualists in turn adopted a radical social program based on the same individualist principles that supported its unconventional religious practice. Spiritualists believed that, if untrammeled by repressive social or religious strictures, individuals could serve as vehicles of truth because each embodied the laws of nature in his or her being. Such individualism laid the foundation for Spiritualism's rejection of male headship over women—or indeed of any individual over any other—whether in religion, politics, or society. Spiritualists believed that the advent of spirit communication heralded the arrival of a new era, one in which humanity, with guidance from spirits, would achieve hitherto impossible levels of development. The accomplishment of a broad program of progressive social reforms and a complete reformation of personal life would characterize the new era. While other radicals struggled to reconcile their commitment to individualism with their belief in the sovereignty of God, Spiritualists found in their faith direct divine sanction for advancing social change.

The prominence of women within Spiritualism resulted from a staunchly individualistic form of religious practice. Feminist scholars have found that women have been able to exercise leadership where religious authority derives from direct individual spiritual contact or experience rather than from office, position, or training. Spiritualism produced an extreme case of these conditions, offering a unique opportunity for women to assume leadership. The movement viewed the individual as the ultimate vehicle of truth. Spirit communication could occur only through human mediumship. Individuals served as mediums for communication with spirits who revealed information about the divine order and the ultimate fate of the soul.

Mediumship circumvented the structural barriers that excluded women from religious leadership. By communicating directly with spirits, mediums bypassed the need for the education, ordination, or organizational recognition that secured the monopoly of male religious leaders. While men might bar women from church councils or from theological education, human authority could not supersede that given to mediums by the spirits who spoke through them. Spirit communication carried its own authority. If one accepted the message, one had little choice but to accept the medium. With spirit guidance, nineteenth-century women spoke in public, wrote books, and went on lecture tours. Mary Dana Shindler, for example, visited a medium in New York and asked the spirits, "Do you wish me to write the work I am thinking of?" "Yes—go on; it will sell well," was the encouraging reply. She took the spirit's advice and wrote *A Southerner Among the Spirits*. As mediums, women became sources of religious truth and, as such, assumed the authority of religious leaders. Spirits, it seemed, encouraged women to do things that other forces militated against.

Spiritualism departed from accepted social norms by encouraging women to speak in public, but the manner in which they spoke had a cultural significance of its own. Equal numbers of men and women spoke from the Spiritualist platform, both on the lecture circuit and at conventions, picnics, and grove meetings. But speakers observed a rigorous sexual division of labor. Men called meetings to order, forcefully presiding over gatherings that could number in the thousands. They addressed audiences in a "normal" state, expressing their own views on Spiritualist subjects. In contrast, the women at the podium were unconscious. Trance mediums were understood to be passive vehicles whose physical faculties were used by spirits to express the sentiments of these unseen intelligences. Trance speakers made their appearance in the early 1850s and served as the primary public representatives of Spiritualism during that decade. They presented not their own views but those of the spirits who spoke through them. The juxtaposition of men officiating at large assemblies with unconscious women voicing extemporaneous visions of heaven in verse both satisfied existing sexual stereotypes and pushed them a step further. The essential passivity of women was asserted in a public arena, displayed before thousands of witnesses.

The right of women to speak in public was hotly contested during the antebellum period. Following the historic antislavery lectures of the Grimm sisters in 1837, a few fearless reform women ventured before the public during the 1840s, most notably Ernestine Rose, Abby Kelly Foster, Lucretia Mott, and, at the end of the decade, Lucy Stone. Novelist Elizabeth Oakes Smith became a popular literary Lyceum lecturer. In addition, a few women, such as the holiness preacher Phoebe Palmer and the black Methodist Jarena Lee, appeared in public as Christian evangelists. However, the right of women to address "promiscuous assemblies," composed of both men and women, was still generally denied. Clerical opponents cited Paul's injunction against women speaking in public. However, by the end of the end of the 1850s, female trance speakers had become so popular that a woman speaking in public no longer caused a sensation.

Sparse qualifications in a trance speaker reinforced the claim that the lecture originated not with the speaker but with spirits. While men qualified for the public platform by wisdom, education, and experience, trance speakers qualified by innocence, ignorance, and frequently youth. The fact that a woman stood up in public and gave a lecture in itself evidenced spirit agency since few believed a woman could do such a thing unaided. Trance lectures illustrated women's direct access to religious knowledge that was superior to male theological education.

In general, Spiritualists considered the trance to be an elevated state, providing access to spirits and therefore to knowledge of the world beyond inaccessible to conscious human beings. But some questioned the accuracy of revelations received in trance. Because the ability to give a trance lecture depended on one's susceptibility to outside influences, the moral accountability of trance speakers was sometimes questioned. If trance speakers were merely passive vehicles, could they be held responsible for their behavior while in trance or for the content of their messages? The unaccountability of mediums was sometimes urged as an excuse for questionable behavior or even for fraud. Because of the unaccountability of mediums controlled by unseen intelligences, an editorial in the *Spiritual Age* asserted that the trance was not the optimum condition for spirit communication. It viewed the trance as higher than the normal state but lower than "conscious state inspiration."

By questioning the trance state, critics questioned the values and assumptions that fostered female leadership. The assertion that the passivity that gave women access to spirits made them morally unaccountable undercut women's claim to spiritual authority. Trance speakers, however, were the missionaries of Spiritualism, and their far-reaching itinerancy aided the rapid spread of the movement. Their lectures, often free to the public, might attract hundreds of people, while the séances of test mediums could accommodate only as many people as could fit around a table. The Spiritualist public had faith in their mediums and was unconcerned by critics' doubts about the trance state. Although more serious challenges to their leadership would emerge following the Civil War, trance speakers enjoyed the support of the mass of believers during the 1850s.

While descriptions suggest that some mediums were able to enter a trance spontaneously, trance speakers never developed consistent modes of trance behavior. According to observers, it was Cora Hatch's practice to enter the hall already entranced. During the preliminaries to her lecture, she "sat gazing upwards, with her eyes intently fixed." At the close of her lecture, "she looked and stared about her like one just awakened." But other mediums who claimed to be in a trance provided little evidence of an abnormal state. Because audiences were accustomed to viewing the trance as proof of spirit inspiration, a reporter describing the appearance of a lecturer in Boston felt compelled to explain that, although "Mrs. Warner is a conscious trance speaker," she "is entirely subject to the control of spirit influence while delivering her discourses." Because the trance was viewed as enabling women to speak who were otherwise unqualified to do so, the claim of entrancement became a convention used to support women's right and ability to ascend the public platform.

Trance speakers emphasized what they said rather than what they did. While test mediums might curse and swagger when controlled by the spirits of drunkards or sailors, trance speakers viewed the content of their speeches, along with the act of speaking, as inspired. High-toned trance speakers such as Lizzie Doten and Achsa Sprague did not give private sittings and did not receive messages from individually identifiable spirits. Nor did they produce the common "physical manifestations" of raps or table tipping. Unlike the test medium, the trance speaker might hold herself above "the external phenomena" of Spiritualism and dwell on "the great principles underlying them."

Lizzie Doten was one of two hundred or so women who made a living as a trance speaker in the two decades before the Civil War. The lecture printed here was delivered to one of several groups of Spiritualists who held regular Sunday meetings in Boston. It uses the format of a Protestant sermon, taking a biblical text as its topic. It is not clear from the account whether the text was selected by the audience, by the medium, or was suggested by spirit inspiration. In any case, the female speaker must have made quite an impression by addressing the very portion of the Bible that is most often used to argue that women should not speak aloud in church. Rather than disagreeing with the text, she took it as an opportunity to criticize the Calvinist theology identified with orthodox Protestantism. "Could the doctrines of Calvin have found their origin in a loving woman's nature?" Doten asked rhetorically, answering with a resounding "No." By linking women's natural piety with a theological critique of Calvinism, the trance lecture affirms the Spiritualist view that women are better suited than men to interpret religious truth and therefore must be promoted as public speakers.

In addition to her role as a trance speaker, Lizzie Doten wrote several novels and books of poetry, all of which address various issues of woman's rights. Her novels, in particular, portray true-hearted young women seduced and abandoned by duplicitous men, and then victimized by the double standard of morality that blamed innocent women for men's vices. Doten was also a staunch advocate of economic equality and of property rights for women. Self-supporting from an early age, she was well aware of the few economic alternatives women had to marriage. As with many Spiritualists, she believed that marriages resulting from economic necessity debased both husband and wife and prohibited spiritual growth. Her story "Marrying for Money" asserted that fewer women would marry if they had wages equal to men's and therefore had the option of supporting themselves. She advocated legislation requiring employers to pay women equal wages for equal work—legislation that would wait over a century to become a reality. The trance lecture criticizes the inaccurate and unfair view of woman's nature derived from the biblical narrative that formed the basis of contemporary morality. "As woman is, in the past, reputed the source of man's ruin, so, in the future, shall she be his savior." As audiences watched a woman utter such sentiments from the public platform, they witnessed a new model both of woman's role and of religious leadership.

The text below is from "Miss Lizzie Doten," in *Banner of Light* [February 2, 1861?], as given at the New Melodeon, Boston, January 29, 1860.

Futher Reading

Ann Braude, *Radical Spirits: Spiritualism and Women's Rights in Nineteenth-Century America* (Boston: Beacon, 1989); Bret E. Carroll, *Spiritualism in Antebellum America* (Bloomington: Indiana University Press, 1996); Mary Bednarowski, "Outside the Mainstream: Women's Religion and Women Religious Leaders in Nineteenth-

Century America," *Journal of the American Academy of Religion* 48 (1980): 2–19; Howard Kerr, *Mediums, Spirit-Rappers, and Roaring Radicals: Spiritualism in American Literature, 1850–1900* (Urbana: University of Illinois Press, 1972); Laurence R. Moore, *In Search of White Crows: Spiritualism, Parapsychology, and American Culture* (New York: Oxford University Press, 1977).

Miss Lizzie Doten's Trance Lecture

The Spiritualist services at the Melodeon, Boston, on Sunday, Jan. 29th, were conducted by Miss Lizzie Doten.

Miss Doten was, for the first time in her life, controlled to speak with her eyes opened. In the afternoon, when the discourse was upon *"Sunday Theatricals,"* the control was quite imperfect, and the effects were perceptible in the lecture, the ideas of which did not appear to be clearly developed as is usual with the speaker. The most noticeable feature was the declaration that the entire merging of the individuality of the medium in that of the spirit or spirits in control, is neither possible, nor, even in the extent to which it is often carried, desirable.

In the evening, the new method of control had become perfected, and the discourse was one of unusual excellence. The text was from St. Paul's first epistle to the Corinthians, chap. 14, verse 35: *"It is a shame for women to speak in the church."*

In the churches, where males are the speakers, the majority of the audience are females. In Spiritualist assemblages, where woman is the teacher, the hearers are, generally, in great part, males. The reason of this, said the lecturer, is that, to the harsher nature of man, the kindly utterances of woman are more grateful than those of a spiritual organization similar to his own. Now, in considering the question which had been selected as the starting point of the evening's discourse, we need, first, to inquire what is religion? According to the dictionaries, it is a system of facts—the collection and analyzation of the great religious ideas. This is well as far as it goes. And is woman capable of criticising this general theology? Many are of opinion that her intellectual traits and her phrenological development are not such as to give her this power. But let us view this theology. What are its tenets? Eternal punishment, total depravity, the vengeance of a terrible God, infant damnation. Is a woman, with her predominating affectional nature, capable of teaching these doctrines of the popular theology of this day? Every woman revolts at the thought. Could the doctrines of Calvin have found their origin in a loving woman's nature? No woman can, in her heart, believe these doctrines, even though in her speech she may recognize them.

But to woman's nature specially belongs the theology of love. Love is *attractive.* It is the law of gravitation. It is that which holds the worlds in their harmonious courses. That attraction is but the love of the planets for one another. Now, woman speaks not so much from her intellect as from her convictions. The affections are spontaneous: a simple flower growing in the forest appeals to the soul more strongly than the finest work of art. There is a direct and indirect influence emanating from each other, the one that which goes out volitionally, the other that which comes not from the man himself only, but from the action of another power than his own. And this indirect power is the power of woman. In her children the mother acts upon the world. The mother of Christ, by her indirect influence, has established the theology of Christendom.

But it has been denied, in all the past, that woman has an adequate power of expression. It is, indeed, often sneeringly said that woman is a great talker. But they deny that she is capable of expressing the religious element of her nature. It is, indeed, true that the affectional nature is more developed in her than her intellect. It is, then, impossible that there should be a balance and harmony of her nature? Woman has always held an inferior position to man. In some particulars this has been an advantage to her, for in the school of patience it is that the higher spiritual virtues are learned. The Divine education is that which comes through experience. But woman does not need to cultivate her intellect in order to perceive spiritual truths. Let her live, only, true to her Divine nature and her spiritual perceptions. "Seek ye first the kingdom of God, and all" else "shall be added unto you." Make a home in your heart for God, and His angels shall come, and all that is needed for spiritual perception and development comes in with that inspiration. But to examine woman's intellectual capacity for expressing spiritual truths. Woman has not been properly educated. She has been forced into a narrow circle of life, a dull routine of duties; and that is declared to be woman's sphere. But the teachers of our public schools will tell us that the female mind is quicker than that of man. That woman is capable of such development as will enable her to express Divine truth, is established. But God does not wait for this. He has made woman a religious teacher. There is more of religion in the tender smile of a true woman's face than between the lids of the Bible. It is not the dead letter, it is the living word. This influence it is that in the hour of the highest danger has made man courageous, patriotic, merciful. The silent influence of woman goes out with man into the workshop and the field. When the secret of this feminine influence is understood, the secret of spiritual intercourse will be comprehended. It is connected with all the finest spiritual truths. It is, as yet, but partially developed. The woman and the man rise together. Even the intellectual development shall come. A finished education is an impossibility to the most of mankind. To woman, with her domestic cares, this is especially so. But, as generation after generation comes, there shall be women, as men, with these exceptional educations. But her strength is in the unconscious inspiration of her presence—the most Divine, as it is the most silent, in its action. Woman has thus been a religious teacher in the past; but in the future shall be seen the perfect work of this great principle. Woman must teach man her theology of love; he must teach her his theology of wisdom. The harmonious combination of the two will sweep from the land the creeds so repulsive to our better nature, and bring the true and perfect religion of purity and love. As woman is, in the past, reputed the source of man's ruin, so, in the future, shall she be his saviour. He shall not, then, need angel inspiration; she shall be an angel in herself.

It is, indeed, a shame for woman to speak in the *Church*; and woman ought to be ashamed of the theology of the church. Let woman come out from the church; and, when she comes out, the minister and all the congregation will go out with her. She is the Divine Shekinah, she is the true Holy of Holies; in her shall man recognize the image of his God, and kneel and adore.

The Cremation versus Burial Debate

Stephen Prothero

Cremation, the incineration of a corpse by heat or fire, is an ancient practice with an intriguing history in modern America. At the end of the twentieth century, most Jews, conservative Christians, and Muslims in the United States vigorously opposed cremation. Yet roughly one in every four deceased Americans was cremated at the millennium's end, and the practice was more common than burial in Hawaii and many western states. Although cremation had failed to achieve the sort of dominance in the United States that it enjoyed in Japan, Great Britain, and Australia, it had emerged as a legitimate alternative to burial. Things were far different earlier in United States history. In colonial times, many Native American tribes cremated their dead. And in the eighteenth century, at least one European American—Colonel Henry Laurens, a prominent gentleman from South Carolina and once the president of the Continental Congress—was cremated in the open air. The practice, however, did not gather significant support until the 1870s, when social reformers began to argue for cremation for reasons of sanitation.

It is difficult to determine with much precision exactly when any movement begins, but the cremation movement can be readily dated to 1874. In January of that year, Sir Henry Thompson, the personal physician to Queen Victoria, published in England and New York a pro-cremation essay which lent instant credibility to the movement. Soon intellectuals across the United States were debating "whether to bury or to burn," and before the year was out, the *New York Times* was reporting that support for cremation was growing "suddenly and spontaneously."

That support did not translate into an actual cremation, however, until 1876. In that year, Colonel Henry Steel Olcott, the president of the Theosophical Society (established 1875) and a leading cremationist, asked Dr. Francis Julius Le Moyne, who had built a private crematory on his estate in Washington, Pennsylvania, to lend his facility to the cause. Le Moyne agreed, and on December 6, 1876, the corpse of one Baron De Palm, a recent immigrant from Germany and an ardent Theosophist, became the first person to be incinerated in an American crematory. Newspaper reporters from across the nation covered the story, and for the most part they judged the event as revolting. An Episcopal bishop spoke for many when he denounced cremation as "the freak of a disordered brain." But by the end of the century, cremation was spreading. In 1899, there were twenty-four crematories in fifteen states, and the corpses of roughly ten thousand Americans had been cremated.

In Victorian America, the argument for cremation was made largely by two groups: physicians and liberal Protestants. Theosophists and Spiritualists were also cremation-friendly, as were many Reform Jews. In 1893, members of the Central Conference of American Rabbis, a Reform Jewish organization, debated the relative merits of cremation and burial and then voted not to refuse to officiate at the cremation of deceased Jews "on the plea that cremation is anti-Jewish or irreligious." Catholics, by contrast, widely condemned cremation. In 1886 the Roman Catholic Church issued a formal ban on the activity. Cremationists agitated for their reform in medical journals such as the *Journal of the American Medical Association,* sanitation publications such as *The Sanitarian,* and newspapers like the *New York World* (which one poetic critic dubbed "the apostle of cremation / To an unwilling generation"). As the century wore on, cremationists also published a series of periodicals of their own, including *Modern Cremationist, The Urn,* and *Columbarium.*

In the cremation versus burial debate, cremationists made their case largely on sanitary grounds. The United States had been hit during the nineteenth century by a series of epidemics. The prevailing wisdom asserted that infectious diseases such as cholera were spread by "miasma," or the noxious gas emanating from decaying organic matter. Most sanitarians pointed to trash in overcrowded urban neighborhoods as the main miasma source, but cremationists claimed that decaying corpses in overcrowded urban graveyards were also to blame. Cremation in their view would put an end to this pollution of the living. By contrast, burial partisans made their case largely on religious grounds, contending that cremation flew in the face of a long tradition of burial and constituted an affront to the doctrine of the resurrection of the body. Both sides also debated the aesthetic, economic, and social effects of burial and cremation.

This debate died down in the late 1890s, when newspaper publishers decided that the workaday cremation no longer merited either reporting or editorializing. From that point onward, cremationists devoted themselves to building a nationwide cremation infrastructure, which by the end of the twentieth century included well over 1,300 crematories operating in all fifty states. The cremation rate (the ratio of cremations to deaths) bypassed 1 percent in the 1920s and climbed to just under 4 percent on the eve of World War II. By that point, however, it had been clearly established that the public health was in no way endangered by burial, and revelations about Nazi death camp crematoria further soured the American public on the practice. In the early 1960s, the cremation rate again stood at just under 4 percent.

Beginning in 1963, however, cremation gained ground. In that year, Jessica Mitford's bestseller, *The American Way of Death,* blasted the high cost of funerals and cast cremation as an inexpensive alternative to the embalm-and-bury regime. Also in 1963, the Catholic Church lifted its cremation ban. Immigration from

Asia, opened up in 1965 by changes in immigration law, further buoyed the practice, since cremation was common in many East and South Asian countries. The cremationists received an additional boost in the 1970s when businesses like the Telophase Society (established 1971) and the Neptune Society (established 1977) began offering cut-rate cremations for as little as $250. During that same decade, "saving the land for the living" and returning to simplicity in death rites became two more reasons to prefer cremation over burial.

The following three selections present a number of arguments for and against cremation. Each is drawn from the period of public controversy begun in 1874 and concluded in 1896, when all the pioneering cremationist journals had stopped publishing and cremation had ceased to be a matter of major public controversy. Together they provide a fair summary of the sanitary, theological, social, economic, and aesthetic arguments marshaled on both sides of the cremation versus burial debate.

"The Disposal of Our Dead" was delivered by the Reverend Octavius B. Frothingham in Lyric Hall in New York City on May 3, 1874, only months after the cremation debate began in the United States. Earlier in his life, Frothingham had aligned himself with the liberal impulse in American religion, more specifically, with conservative Unitarianism and Christian Transcendentalism. Over time he had become progressively more radical, and by 1874 he was one of the nation's foremost advocates of "free religion." The first president of the Free Religious Association (established 1867) and the author of *The Religion of Humanity* (1872), Frothingham was also an eager cremationist. His sermon makes the case for cremation and speaks approvingly of the religions of the East. Like other early cremationists, Frothingham tries to unmask the notion of peaceful sleep in the grave as an illusion. Buried corpses decay, he argues, polluting the earth and poisoning the living. For practitioners of a "religion enlightened by knowledge and sweetened by humanity," Frothingham concludes, cremation is the progressive and purifying choice.

"Christian Burial and Cremation," the second selection, was written in 1885 by the Reverend H. A. Brann for the *American Catholic Quarterly Review*. This article outlines the Catholic position against cremation, a practice which Brann regards as a product of "unphilosophic Protestantism" and its "purely spiritual system of religion." Brann dissents from Frothingham's sermon not only in his view of cremation but also in his conception of the human person. While Frothingham regarded human beings as largely, perhaps entirely, spiritual, Brann affirms the traditional Catholic position that the person is an amalgamation of spirit and matter and so "is not complete without his body, either in this life or in the next." In life, Brann asserts, the "sacred flesh" receives sacraments such as baptism. At death, it deserves last rites and a proper burial (overseen, he insists, not by the state but by the church). Brann was in many respects the ideal writer for this assignment. Born in Ireland and ordained a Catholic priest in New York, he was a prolific author and a seasoned controversialist. A few years before he took on the cremationists, Brann blasted Robert Ingersoll and other rationalists in *Age of Unreason* (1880).

The third and last piece, "Ashes to Ashes," is a Protestant rejoinder to the Catholic cremation critique. It was delivered in 1895 at the annual meeting of the New England Cremation Society by the Reverend George Hodges, who had become dean of the Episcopal Theological School in Cambridge, Massachusetts, one year earlier. An accomplished preacher and writer, Hodges was a believer in the social gospel, which emphasized saving society as much as converting souls. He was also an ardent cremationist. Here Hodges recalls the ridicule cremationists received in the days of Dr. Le Moyne and takes solace in the fact that cremation is "no longer considered an altogether Pagan and mad thing." Unlike Frothingham, who emphasized the sanitary benefits of cremation, Hodges emphasizes the spiritual. He dissents from the Catholic conception of the person, arguing that personality resides in the soul. He commends cremation for deflecting attention away from the material to the spiritual. Hodges also looks forward to a time when cremation's popularity will make possible a revival of the ancient Christian tradition of "laying the dead away in the churches." Finally, he advances a novel social argument for cremation as an egalitarian antidote to the "aristocracy in the graveyard."

Opponents of cremation contended the practice was a thoroughly secular desecration of the body. While it is true that cremation brought on (even as it benefitted from) shifts in the American religious landscape, cremation did not amount to the secularization of death. Instead cremation represented a diversification of American religion—the introduction of an Asian death rite into what in the nineteenth century remained a thoroughly Christianized America. That trend toward religious diversity, however, should not be overemphasized. Like the slavery debate that preceded it, the cremation debate of the last three decades of the nineteenth century was conducted largely in Christian terms. Cremation's enemies and advocates alike made their points inside a world infused with Christian scripture, metaphors, and traditions. So while cremation's rise points to the ongoing pluralization of American religion, it also demonstrates the persistence of Christian authority in Victorian America.

The selections below are found in: O. B. Frothingham, *The Disposal of Our Dead* (New York: D. G. Francis, 1874); H. A. Brann, "Christian Burial and Cremation," *American Catholic Quarterly Review* 10 (October 1885): 678–95; Reverend George Hodges, *Ashes to Ashes*, published as a pamphlet by the New England Cremation Society shortly after Hodges delivered the talk in 1895.

O. B. Frothingham, *The Disposal of Our Dead*

Christendom borrowed, or rather inherited its custom of interring the dead, from the Hebrews, with whom it was universal. . . . The custom of interment did not rest solely in private or social feeling. There was an idea in it: the idea that the body contained, in some sense, the soul; and that its burial was somehow a guarantee of the soul's peace. . . . The Pharisaic belief in a resurrection involved, as one of its chief features, the revival, in some shape, of the form. . . .

Through Paul—who was a Pharisee, and who taught the resurrection of a spiritual form from the carnal body, which could not, itself, enter the kingdom of heaven—the doctrine passed over to the Christian Church, where it became domesticated, and has found an abiding-place ever since. . . .

How sweet, too, the sentiment of rest that was associated with the grave where the beloved one lay! It is wonderfully expressed in Job. "Why died I not on issuing from the womb? For now should I have lain still and been quiet; I should have slept; I should have been at rest with kings and counselors of the earth; with princes that had gold and filled their houses with silver. There the wicked cease from troubling, there the weary are at rest. There the prisoners repose together; they hear not the voice of the oppressor. The small and the great are there; the servant is free from his master." These pathetic words come to us now whenever we think of the still forms that lie so peacefully beneath the monument or the sod, sleeping their unbroken sleep "after life's fitful fever." We know, on reflection, that this is an illusion. We know that there is no stillness in the grave; that Nature, which never rests, and allows no rest to organized or unorganized thing—Nature, which abhors rest, respecting not even the dread repose of death, seizes at once the cast-off body, and with occult chemistry and slow burning decomposes and consumes it. But the ancients did not know this as we do. That the body, left above ground, decayed, they perceived; and, to prevent the effect of it, would even resort to burning on occasion; but of all that went on beneath the ground they were not aware. They could not, therefore, be sensible, as we are, of the serious perils that were involved in the practice. . . .

But all this we see, and cannot be blind to. The eager science of our century, exploring the secret places of the earth and air, analyzing all substances and resolving the elements into finer elements, detecting the trail of the imponderable gases; and following the windings of invisible currents of movement, has brought to noon-day light the astounding fact that the dead are persecutors of the living, not as haunting specters, but as moldering forms. Yes, there is no room to doubt that men and women who have been healers and comforters during life, may be destroyers and saddeners after death; that they who were living benedictions may be dead curses; that they whose presence sweetened the air, whose breath was an aroma, became poisoners on leaving the earth; the grave, which their friends think of so tenderly, visit so piously, mourn over so sincerely, ponder upon so tranquilly, being, in fact, a laboratory where are manufactured the poisons that waste the fair places of existence, and very likely smite to the heart their own lovers. It is now demonstrated, the fact is attested by scientific observers and corroborated by medical testimony of unquestionable value, that the common practice of interring the dead is positively pernicious to the living. Were this the place to detail the evidence or give the testimonies at length, it would be easy to quote authorities from works within reach of all who can read. But now there is time only to say, in general terms, that the revelations made on this subject are of a nature to awaken serious reflection on the practice which, from old association, has become so dear to us, and to suggest a duty, on the part of true religion, to desist from a custom which the old religions sanctioned. . . .

There is but one method of disposing of the dead that is not open to similar objections, or to others almost equally weighty, peculiar to itself: that is the removal of them by fire. The practice of burning the dead does not, as I have said, yield in antiquity or in honorableness to the one we adopt. It is found among people in all respects as intelligent, refined, and worshipful as any. It is associated with feelings of the noblest kind, with veneration and tenderness, and regard to moral obligations. This practice, too, has an idea at the center of it; a religious idea, and, curiously, an idea intimately connected with that of immortality. It is the fashion to call cremation a pagan custom; and so it is; but it must be remembered that the whole ancient world was pagan, in the usual sense of the word; and that, in their day, the pagans were the greatest people on earth. If pagans burned, pagans buried too: the worst of pagans buried; so that if there is any reproach in the paganism it must be shared by the custom of interment.

The practice of burning the dead was sacred with people who, in the sun, the central fire, the glowing source of life, the visible lord of creation, saw the emblem of the Supreme Being. Fire was the holy element, spiritual, pure at once and purifying. These people kept the sacred fire always burning in their temples and their houses. It was divine; they worshiped it; they ascribed power to it—power to bestow health and happiness. They prayed to it, the eternal, the ever young, the ever beautiful, the universal nourisher and bestower of good. We find this worship throughout the East—in India, Greece, Italy. . . .

Christians object to cremation that it destroys the soul's tabernacle, and thwarts the hope of personal resurrection. How can the form revive after such a process? A moment's reflection suggests that, as nothing less than a miracle of Almighty power will avail to restore the form that has been dissipated into vapors by the chemistry of the soil, the same exertion of power will avail to restore it when it has been dissipated by the action of flame. To recover a shape from a heap of ashes can be no more difficult than to recover it from a mound of dust. The slow burning in the earth is as fatal to identity as the swift burning in the fire. The final result is as imponderable. If there be somewhere within the frame a spiritual form which disengages itself at death, or if, in some deep recess of it, there be an infinitesimal germ of life from which the spiritual man shall spring, fire could no more injure it than earth. It must, from its nature, be imperishable. Religiously viewed, the idea that animates the believer in cremation is nobler than the idea that animates the believer in interment; for, taking literally the statement that flesh and blood cannot inherit the kingdom of God, it makes haste to put them away, that the incorruptible portion may ascend by its proper motion to its celestial abode. They to whom the practice of cremation is native regard with compassion such as practice interment.

But to us the practice of cremation is recommended on the same ground that the other practice is condemned: namely the ground of human welfare, the comfort and safety of the living. It is recommended on other grounds also. On the score of economy it has the advantage. It dispenses with several conditions of expense, and with the conditions that bear hardest on poor people— the necessity of buying land, of constructing sepulchres, of transporting the dead long distances to their final home. . . .

On the aesthetic side, the side of beauty and grace, the practice of burning has clearly the advantage. It presents a sweeter field of contemplation to those who look beyond the moment of disappearance, into the day after death, and follow even a little way the destiny of the vanished form. The substitution of a swift and silent process of transmutation for the slow and distressing one of decay is, when fairly considered, a relief to the mind. The substitution of a pile of white ashes which the eye may look at without offence, for the mass of corruption which the eye cannot look at, or the mind contemplate at all; the substitution of a skillfully-contrived and well-arranged receptacle for the unsightly grave; of the graceful urn for the shapeless mound is, of itself, a recommendation. . . .

But in the discussion of a subject like this such considerations, however interesting, are of secondary moment. The burden of the argument rests on the ground of sanitary science. Which usage best consults the well-being of living men; is most favorable to health, usefulness and happiness; is most consonant with a civilization that makes the satisfaction of humanity on the globe its care? These are the questions, and these questions, it would seem, can be answered only in one day. All the danger attends the custom of interment; all the danger is avoided by the custom of cremation. . . .

Nobody expects that such a change will be effected in a day. It must come gradually, and by slow degrees. The proposition will be met by every species of objection; it will be laughed at, and it will be scoffed at. Some will argue, some will complain, some will denounce. Some will cry "nonsense," and some will cry "danger," and some will cry "blasphemy." The ignorant and superstitious will lift up their hands in horror; pious people will exclaim; sentimental people will grieve. To attempt an alteration in the shape of a religious creed, or in the shape of a religious ceremony, is arduous and audacious. But such difficulties, if they occur, should operate as stimulants—not as discouragements. This is precisely the task that rationalists contemplate. This is our task.

H. A. Brann, "Christian Burial and Cremation"

The fundamental reason for the discipline of the Catholic Church regarding the disposition of the dead is the dogma of the Apostles' Creed: "I believe in the resurrection of the body." Her philosophy is that the body is an essential part of the man, and that a religion which even partially ignores this fact is not universal, and, therefore, not true. Although she does not hold that there is nothing in the intellect which was not first in the senses, yet she recognizes the fact that they are necessary in the order of natural cognition as well as in the order of religious belief. Through the senses men's minds are corrupted, and through them they may be improved morally and elevated spiritually. Unphilosophic Protestantism began by ignoring the important role which the body and its senses play in the work of salvation. It made war on the religious pictures and statues through which spiritual ideas are conveyed to the mind, and attacked the old sacramental symbolism which, by the action of sensible signs and ceremonies on the body, conveys invisible grace to the invisible soul. To ignore the material and sensible in divine worship, to deny the sacramental system established by Christ, is indirectly to weaken faith in the mystery of the Word made flesh. To try to establish a purely spiritual system of religion for beings who have a mixed nature, a physical body as well as an immaterial soul connected with it, and dependent on it for reflex cognition as well as for outward expression of religious worship, is to attempt to build a steeple in the air without a church to put it on. Yet this is what Protestantism has tried to do in warring on the sensible devotions of the Catholic Church and abolishing her sacraments, in diminishing the number of religious ceremonies and the impressiveness of the Christian ritual. A Catholic has only to attend a Protestant funeral to feel the chill produced by the curtailing of the Catholic ritual. The Protestant dead is put away in a dark room; the corpse is shunned; it is carried in silence to the church, where pagan symbols in flowers, wreaths, and broken columns surround the coffin, where a few dry words of Scripture are read; and thence to a graveyard, beautifully laid out, indeed, with graveled walks, weeping willows, and evergreen trees, for there is a sentiment still even where faith has ceased to exist, but a graveyard, almost without a cross and without the figure of the kneeling widow, or father, or child—so often seen in the Catholic cemetery—praying at the tomb for the repose of the soul departed. There is no heart in the Protestant funeral. There is a hurry to put the offensive corpse out of sight, and then forget all about it. The old Church holds on to her dead with eternal affection. The dead body is the body of her child. It is sacred flesh. It has been the temple of a regenerated soul. She blessed it in baptism, poured the saving waters on its head, anointed it with holy oil on breast and back, put the blessed salt on its lips, and touched its nose and ears in benediction when it was only the flesh of a babe; and then, in growing youth, reconsecrated it by confirmation; and, before its dissolution in death, she again blessed and sanctified its organs, its hands and its feet, as well as its more important members. Even after death she blesses it with holy water, and incenses it before her altar, amid the solemnity of the great sacrifice of the New Law, and surrounded by mourners who rejoice even in their tears, for they believe in the communion of saints, and are united in prayer with the dead happy in heaven, as well as with those who are temporarily suffering in purgatory. The old Church, the kind old mother of regenerated humanity, follows the dead body of her child into the very grave. . . .

"The resurrection of the dead gives confidence to all Christians," wrote Tertullian in the third century. Two general councils—that of Constantinople and the fourth Lateran—have defined the resurrection of the body as an article of faith. The Christian belief on this point is inherited from the Hebrews, for Job says: "I know that my Redeemer liveth, and in the last day I shall rise out of the earth. And I shall be clothed again with my skin, and in my flesh I shall see my God.". . . .

This is not only the argument of Tertullian, but even of the pagan Seneca. And why should not the body live again, since the soul lives forever? Why should not the partner of the soul's toils, the instrument of its mortifications, of its abstinence and fasting, as well as of its sensuality, rise again to share its bliss or its misery? The whole man, not merely a part of him, is destined for eternity; and man is not complete without his body, either in this life or in the next. . . .

Therefore the Church claims the corpse. It has once been a holy tabernacle of the body and blood of Jesus Christ. She orders the civil power away from the bier and the graveyard. The funeral and requiem mass are hers. Her jurisdiction over them is supreme; and although it may not be always respected, it nevertheless exists, for the dead man was a Christian and has a right to Christian burial; and Christian burial is not a subject within the province of a civil magistrate. The Church, indeed, recognizes the right of the State to make sanitary regulations and order things of a purely civil character regarding funerals and cemeteries; but she considers interference with her ritual, or with property owned and consecrated by her, as intrusion and usurpation. . . .

But how stands the Catholic Church in regard to the revival of the pagan system of disposing of the dead—cremation? Can she tolerate it? Is there anything in it contrary to Catholic dogma or the essential discipline of the Church? The answer to these questions is, that the Church could tolerate cremation if she wished. She has the right of eminent domain over her own discipline. There is, indeed, a portion of that discipline of divine origin, and it she cannot change; but all things purely ecclesiastical, having been made by the Church, and those things in which our Lord has not forbidden alteration, can be by the Church modified or abrogated. . . .

But, having said so much as to the right or power of the Church to permit cremation, the moral question now arises whether, if a dying Catholic wished to be cremated instead of inhumed, and insisted upon *post-mortem* incineration, a priest could give him the sacraments? No! Such a man would not have the proper dispositions for receiving them. He would be in a condition of wilful insubordination to Church law and discipline. He would be asking what the Church refuses to grant. He would be disobeying or asking some one else to disobey the requirements of her sacred liturgy in a very important matter. In a word, although the Church may modify her burial service in certain extraordinary contingencies, it is certain that cremation is contrary to all her traditions and to all her legislation regarding Christian burial. . . .

Eusebius gives a reason for the Christian aversion to cremation, which still holds good, because "they (the Pagans) did this (cremated) to show that they could conquer God and destroy the resurrection of the bodies, saying, now let us see if they will arise." It is notorious that the modern revival of cremation as a mode of burial is due to pantheists, materialists, and other unbelievers in the resurrection of the flesh. . . .

The chief arguments in favor of cremation are from sanitary considerations. The cremationists say that inhumation poisons the air, and that cemeteries injure the healthfulness of the neighborhood in which they exist. But if proper precautions are taken, if the bodies are buried deep enough in the soil, as they must be, no danger can arise to the public health from the practice of inhuming the dead. The immense sewers which run through our populous cities do not injure health if they are properly built, although decaying refuse and poisonous vapors fill them. Neither can cemeteries properly managed, in which the graves are deep, and which are generally remote from the town or city. Would not the public health be far more endangered if the reeking stench of burning bodies, arising out of crematories on every side, were to pollute the atmosphere? On a moist summer's day, when the winds are still, how long would it take to get the smell of the crematory out of the nostrils of the community?

The Reverend George Hodges, *Ashes to Ashes*

When Dr. Le Moyne set up a crematory many years ago, not far from Pittsburgh, the whole neighborhood objected. I well remember riding by, along the country road, and seeing the building across the fields with ominous smoke ascending from its chimney. And I doubt not that my reflections were as foolish as the thoughts of most other people at that time. Cremation was considered to be a revival of old Paganism. And anyhow, Pagan or not, it was novel and eccentric and we resented it accordingly.

Human nature is amazingly conservative; the small boys who jeer in the street at the sight of an odd dress do but make evident a universal instinct. New fashions, if they depart very widely from the old, are to be shunned. Cremation has even yet to contend with this natural prejudice against novelty. Probably no other argument so weighs against it as the fact that it is unconventional. People who believe in it are accounted to be queer, and few persons are pleased to be called queer.

Time, however, and talk and public meetings and good examples remedy the defect of novelty. If we will but wait we shall find our heresies becoming orthodox. The fanatics, so-called, of a dozen years ago are held now in high esteem and adorned with laurel and halos. Even cremation is growing in favor and the crematory is to be found today in most large cities. It is no longer considered an altogether Pagan and mad thing to be burned rather than buried.

Thus people are more ready now-a-days than they were formerly to listen to arguments upon this subject.

The sanitary reasons for cremation are such as appeal forcibly to most intelligent people. At present, while there are, no doubt, many who would not consent to cremation for themselves or for their families, there are but few who do not consider it an admirable act, even a necessary procedure, in the case of some parts of the community. Our cities are growing so tremendously fast, presenting problems such as no other generation has ever had to meet, that the question of the disposal of the dead becomes a very serious and perplexing and imperative problem indeed, and the old-fashioned graveyard does not meet it.

That quiet, consecrated garden with the hedge about it and the old church in the middle of it, with its pleasant trees, like the Paradise of Eden, and its grassy walks between the graves, was quite a different place from the modern city cemetery, where hideous and pagan monuments mark the burial places of the rich, while the poor are thrust into the earth in long lines, crowded closely together as they were in life. Aristocracy in the graveyard! Slums in the cemetery! The devout associations of burial are lost in these great fields amongst the vulgar tombs, where the dead encroach upon the living and poison the wells.

A house of the departed, a shrine of our own saints, built in the midst of the city, adorned like the Pantheon at Paris, with golden frescoes, the walls recalling old stories of sanctity and heroism, with words of comfort from the sacred scriptures and the ashes of the dead reverently laid away without distinction of rank or money—this would be better. Flowers could grow there, sweet music could be played there, prayers could be said there, and the living could commune there with the spirits of the dead.

Or, better still, there might be a revival of the good old custom of laying the dead away in the churches. Cremation would make that possible. Heaven and earth would thus seem close together. There would be no more removal of the relics of the dead miles away out of our sight. And that devotion to the dead which at present prompts the erection of great piles of carved stone beside a grave, effecting no good purpose whatever, would lead to the enriching and beautifying of the House of God, so that all worshippers would be uplifted.

I am especially interested, however, in the spiritual significance of the practice of cremation. I believe that it is in accordance with true religion, especially in these two particulars—it agrees with the right idea of the resurrection of the body and it symbolizes the supremacy of the soul.

The body which is put in the grave will never come out again. "They that are in their graves shall come forth." Yes—but that is not to be understood as a literal and scientific statement of the resurrection. The dead are not in their graves. The dead will rise, but not in the body which is buried. That buried body vanishes away. Day by day, and year by year, through processes unspeakably dreadful to imagine, the physical body returns to its original elements, earth to earth, and dust to dust. The mediaeval pictures are not to be believed which show the dead crawling painfully like worms out of their graves. The body is laid away in the earth and that is the end of it.

Between burial and burning there is no difference in the final result. The difference is in the process. The inevitable change is wrought in the one case slowly, in the other quickly; in one by the action of clean flame, in the other by the action of damp earth. When the soul leaves the body it leaves it forever.

The resurrection body is not the physical body, not the natural body, but that strange thing, the "spiritual body." St. Paul says that the relation of this present body to that which shall be hereafter is like the relation of the seed to the flower, or of the grain to the stalk and fruit. It is the same and yet not the same. There is individual identity. On goes the human being into the other life just the same human being. That is the heart of the doctrine of the resurrection of the body.

The notion that our future state depends in any way upon the disposition which is made of our dead body has no place in the Christian religion. It may be found in Homer, who pictures the soul of the unburied wandering disconsolate along the bank of the black river, unable to rest until earth is cast upon the body. It is altogether Pagan. Jesus Christ taught no such thing. We believe no such thing.

Here is a hero hurrying into a burning house, taking his life in his hand that he may give it for the life of another, and he never comes out again. The ashes of his body mingle with the ashes of the fallen roof. Now what has happened? Is that brave man blotted out? Was his soul burned with his body? That heroic soul, will God punish it in any way because it happened that the body which it wore as a garment chanced to be burned instead of buried? One must have a strange idea of God to believe that. If that be true, if the burning of the body has any malign spiritual meaning, what shall be said, then, of the choicest of the saints, of the holy men and women who have died for love of God at martyrs' stakes?

The burning of the body is a symbol of the supremacy of the soul. In burial, attention is directed towards the body. It is carried to the cemetery, followed by friends, and in their presence is lowered into the ground. They stand about with tears in their eyes looking down into the black earth; and the little children who are in the company draw their natural inferences. The dead, they think, are in their graves. Even their elders do not wholly escape the influence of the sight. They go back, time and again, to the graveyard, vaguely imagining that they somehow get nearer to the dear departed.

But personality is not in the body, it is in the soul. To be absent from the body was St. Paul's idea of death. Burn the body, get rid of this subtle materialistic temptation. The sweet, pure flame, the symbol of the Holy Spirit, mounts up towards heaven, and our thoughts and hearts ascend with it. Henceforth, not the body but the soul, not death but life, not earth but the blessed Paradise beyond, is what we think of.

Cremation used to be called Pagan; but what can be more Christian?

INDEX

This index contains select proper names, terms, and titles of books and other publications. The names of individual American Indian tribes may be found as subentries under the general heading "Native Americans."